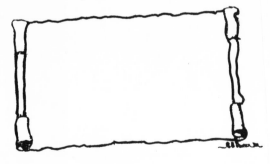

Recent Work in Philosophy

APQ LIBRARY OF
PHILOSOPHY

APQ LIBRARY OF PHILOSOPHY
Nicholas Rescher, Editor

Recent Work in Philosophy

Edited by
Kenneth G. Lucey
and
Tibor R. Machan

ROWMAN & ALLANHELD
Totowa, New Jersey

Dedicated to
Nicholas Rescher
Founder of the Recent Work Series

Copyright © 1983 in this collection by Rowman & Allanheld

First published in the United States 1983 by Rowman & Allanheld,
81 Adams Drive, Totowa, New Jersey 07512.

Library of Congress Cataloging in Publication Data
Main entry under title:

Recent work in philosophy.

  (APQ library of philosophy)
  Includes index.
  1. Philosophy, Modern — 20th century — Addresses,
essays, lectures. I. Lucey, Kenneth G., 1942–
II. Machan, Tibor R. III. Series.
B804.R35   1983   190'.9'04   82-3741
ISBN 0-8476-7103-9

Printed in the United States of America

Contents

Preface

Since 1967 there has been no comprehensive volume on work in contemporary philosophy. *Recent Work in Philosophy* is the anthology to fill this void.

The eleven articles contained in this book are thorough introductory essays to some of the most central areas of contemporary philosophy. The works originally appeared in the *American Philosophical Quarterly,* one of the leading philosophy journals in the English-speaking world. The articles were subjected to severe editorial evaluation in their original form and have been scrupulously updated or entirely rewritten for publication in the present volume. They have been prepared with an eye to serving the needs of both specialists and those who are not experts on the topics they cover. They are thus designed as generally accessible introductions for the reader with a serious interest in the progress of philosophy in our time.

All of our authors have structured their surveys in terms of their own view of what has been the most important literature of their areas. These are all conscientiously prepared surveys that keep in clear focus the need for a unified overview of a body of recent scholarship.

This volume begins with an essay by Michael J. Loux on key issues in ontology. Professor Loux has added an entirely new section on Possible Worlds, which is certainly the premier metaphysical issue of our day. Harald Ofstad weaves a rich tapestry of the multitude of different contemporary perspectives upon the Free Will Problem. In the third selection Henry E. Kyburg, Jr., provides an invaluable conceptual map of the convoluted labyrinth which is called Inductive Logic. Dr. Kyburg's bibliography is also a definitive one in his burgeoning area.

On the Philosophy of Mind, Daniel C. Dennett and Jerome Shaffer have written two neatly meshing essays that succinctly bracket the contemporary debates on issues of philosophical psychology. As both attest, the liveliest topic in this area is the issue of functionalism as a philosophy of mind.

In his survey of work on ethical egoism Tibor Machan has systematically reviewed a number of challenges to egoism as a viable ethical theory, and the critical responses thereto. Professors Rex Martin and James W. Nickel provide an incisive review of work on the concept of human rights. Thereafter Tibor Machan shifts the focus to an inventory of the plethora of distinct theories of human rights. The section on social and political philosophy concludes with William A. Parent's survey of the myriad senses of human liberty.

Professor Lilly-Marlene Russow chronicles the recent upsurge of interest in the topic of imagination. Her essay provides valuable links to the previous discussion of the Philosophy of Mind, and sets the stage for the final selection of the book. Dr. Joseph Margolis caps our tour by canvassing the last thirty years of Anglo-American analytic aesthetics.

The editors believe this volume fills an important gap and provides a synthesis unequalled elsewhere in the extant philosophical literature.

PART I

Metaphysics

chapter 1

Recent Work in Ontology

MICHAEL J. LOUX

In this chapter, I will examine recent work (1959 to the present) on two central problem-areas in ontology: (a) problems about the existence and nature of universals and (b) problems about the structure and individuation of particulars. A survey of this sort can emphasize either breadth or detail; one can deal with a large number of papers and books in a general way, or he can single out certain important writings and discuss them at greater length. Both approaches have their advantages and disadvantages. In the present survey, I have tended to stress detail. To compensate for lack of breadth, I have supplemented the survey with a fairly complete set of footnotes where I cite writings I do not discuss in the body of the essay. Doubtless, some would have preferred a comprehensive bibliography; but while helpful, bibliographies frequently have the effect of confusing the reader. The difficulty is that titles, by themselves, often fail to give sufficient information about the content of a paper or book.[1] By relating them to the points made in the survey itself, I have tried to place unexamined materials in a definite context. I hope this will provide the reader with a principle of selection, should he wish to pursue the issues discussed here.

I. The Problem of Universals

Recent literature on the problem of universals does not exhibit the unity which frequently characterizes work on philosophical problems. While there is a certain minimal give and take among philosophers working in this area, there are no on-going debates dominating the journals and, consequently, no common starting-points for investigation. The general picture is rather one of individual philosophers working in relative isolation from one another, each starting from scratch, rethinking the very context in which the problem is to be approached.

All of this makes it impossible to provide a unified picture of recent work on universals; however, something less ambitious and less tidy is possible. One can talk about individual papers and books and point, in a general way, to similarities and differences of approach. This I shall try to do. I shall first examine the work of philosophers who can reasonably be construed as defending some version of metaphysical realism; then, under the slightly misleading heading "Nominalism," I shall deal with the writings of philosophers who defend some other solution to the problem of universals.[2]

A. METAPHYSICAL REALISM

Throughout the history of philosophy, the analysis of predication has played a prominent role in the theories of metaphysical realists; nor is this surprising, as realists have often contended that it is in predication that universals are introduced into discourse. During the past decade or so, a number of philosophers have echoed this traditional theme. Very generally, their claim has been that predicates, along with subjects, must be construed as having referential force.[3]

Probably the most persistent exponent of this line of thought has been Gustav Bergmann. For more than two decades, Bergmann has defended the view that predicates are, in a fairly straight-forward way, names of universals.[4] Utilizing the machinery of his Ideal Language approach to philosophy, he has argued that subject-predicate sentences such as "This is red" involve entities of distinct logical types: the individual named by the subject-term and the common character named by the predicate-term. According to Bergmann, the point of such a sentence is to indicate that the named entities stand in the nexus of exemplification. This nexus is asymetrical. Individuals can exemplify characters, but they cannot themselves be exemplified. While he grants that exemplification is asymetrical, Bergmann contends that it cannot be a relation in any ordinary sense. Relations are themselves universals which objects can exemplify. Were exemplification a relation, one thing could exemplify another only in virtue of some higher level form of exemplification; and this new form of exemplification would require a still higher level form of exemplification, and so on ad infinitum.[5]

While Bergmann has remained constant on these points, his more recent writings have tended in the direction of an even more extreme Platonism. In his early writings, notions like "individual," "character," and "exemplification" are treated as meta-linguistic concepts; but in "Ineffability, Ontology, and Method" and subsequent papers, Bergmann contends that these concepts have an ontological status.[6] In this paper, he reiterates the claim that in being presented with a phenomenological object, like a red spot, I am presented with two things, an individual (a) and the simple character it exemplifies, (F). Bergmann makes the further claim, however, that in being presented with the red spot, I am presented with three additional entities (not "things") — the individuality of a, the universality of F, and the nexus of exemplification tying a and F together. In supporting this claim, he appeals to the Principle of Acquaintance. In knowing that the spot is red (that a is F), Bergmann claims to know that a is an individual, that F is a universal, and that a and F stand in the exemplification nexus; but he claims to be unable to account for his knowledge of these facts unless he grants that he is presentationally acquainted with the respective entities — individuality, universality, and exemplification.

Still, Bergmann denies that the ontological status of these notions is on a par with the status of individuals and the simple characters they exemplify. The latter are things; they exist. The former, however, are merely entities; they can only be said to subsist. Bergmann gives substance to these rather cryptic remarks by telling us that individuality, universality, and exemplification are ineffable; they cannot be named without (1) disaster and (2) futility. Apropos of (1), Bergmann argues that the attempt to name these entities generates a vicious infinite regress. If one is to name individuality, universality, and exemplification, he must construe these as the nominata of predicative expressions. Call these expressions *"I"*, *"U"*, and *"E"*. Now, Bergmann challenges us to use these expressions to state the facts at issue, i.e., that a is an individual, that F is a universal, and that a exemplifies F. Focusing on the first point, we write (in the symbolism of the Ideal Language), *"I(a)."* We may think that in this sentence the individuality of a is named, but is it really? No, Bergmann argues; it presents itself once again unnamed in the fact that *"a,"* an individual descriptive sign, is coupled with a predicative expression. By introducing a new predicate into the Ideal Language, we might try to label the individuality of a as it appears in this sentence. Unfortunately, this will not remove the difficulty; for we can couple this new predicate with *"a"* to form a sentence in which the individuality of a once again emerges unnamed. No matter how we increase our stock of names, we are never able to exclude this possibility. The individuality of a is systematically elusive, and the same is true of the universality of F and the exemplification tying a and F together.

As regards (2), the futility of naming these subsistents, Bergmann points to the fact that we can understand a language only when we know how the symbols of the language may be concatenated with each other, how symbols of different styles range over things of different types, etc. But to know these things is just to know the truths expressed by Ideal Language sentences like *"U(F)"* and *"I(a)."* It is to know, for example, that a symbol like *"F"* names an entity that is a universal and that a sign like *"a"* names an entity that is an individual. Thus, nothing would be accomplished by pinning names on subsistents like individuality and universality; in order that a person understand the sentences in which these names would appear, he would have to know in advance that the sentences are true.

It is difficult to assess Bergmann's work. This is especially true of his recent remarks about subsistence and ineffability. They are so deeply embedded in his Ideal Language approach that they appear immune to external criticism; nor do they invite internal criticism; for such criticism would seem to presuppose more agreement with Bergmann on methodological issues than one is likely to find among most philosophers. Nonetheless, it seems that one can quarrel (from a methodologically neutral stand-point) with the guiding principle of Bergmann's account, his view that predicates function as names. Bergmann's choice of example makes this view appear plausible. He takes sentences like "This is red" and "This is green" as paradigms of the subject-predicate form; in the case of these sentences, the view that predicates are names is not obviously untenable. If we turn to other sentences, however, the view is less appealing. In the case of "John is courageous," there is no temptation whatever to construe "courageous" as naming courage. The noun-form "courage" plays that role. Thus, with "courage" and "courageous," we distinguish between name and predicate. Color words, however, are misleading. As Wilfrid Sellars points out in "Naming and Saying," an expression like "red" is three grammatically distinct words wrapped into one—a singular noun, a general noun, and an adjective.[7] Qua singular noun (and possibly qua general noun), "red" can plausibly be construed as a name; but qua adjectival form, it cannot. Unfortunately for Bergmann, it is precisely qua adjectival form that "red" appears in "This is red."

In "Universals and Metaphysical Realism," Alan Donagan presents what appears to be a different version of the view that predicates are referential in function.[8] He wants to claim that all primitive predicates occurring nonredundantly in true propositions denote universals. Donagan calls this claim the Realist Principle, and he attributes it to Russell and Moore. He never defends the principle in any detail; but he claims that a defense would involve showing (a) that predicative expressions cannot be analyzed into nonpredicative expressions and (b) that the truth-value of propositions depends upon their relation to the world rather than upon their relation to the thinking of any individual.

Donagan's paper is extremely valuable in that he attempts to dispose of a large number of classical and contemporary criticisms of metaphysical realism. Nonetheless, the force of his own version of realism remains unclear; for he fails to explicate the notion of denotation that is operative in this formulation of the Realist Principle. Presumably, he means to use the term in the way that Russell and Moore did; unfortunately, neither of these philosophers was ever very clear about the notion. Donagan tells us that subject-expressions also denote "real things"; and he seems to hold that "denotes real things" is univocal over subjects and predicates. But, then, is Donagan's notion of denotation so very general that while "denotes" means the same thing for subjects and predicates, terms functioning as subject and terms functioning as predicate can, nonetheless, differ in style or mode of denotation? Or is Donagan committed to the view (held by Bergmann) that denotation is simply denotation, that subjects and predicates denote in precisely the same way? Donagan's paper raises, but does not answer, these questions.

P. F. Strawson's discussion in *Individuals* is much clearer on these points.[9]

Strawson holds that, strictly speaking, predicates have no referential force. It is by means of subjects that we refer to things; by means of predicates, we predicate other items of these things. Thus, both subject and predicate introduce nonlinguistic items (terms, in Strawson's terminology), but the style of introduction differs in the two cases. Semantically, we mark this difference by distinguishing between reference and predication; but even at the grammatical level, the difference comes through. Subjects introduce their terms in the substantival or noun-like style — in the style appropriate to lists; whereas predicates introduce their terms in the assertive or verbal style. Inasmuch as predicates incorporate some form of the verb in the indicative mood, they carry the mark of propositional assertion.

Strawson defends a traditional view when he argues that the particular-universal distinction is intimately related to the subject-predicate distinction. It is not that universals can never be introduced by subjects; clearly, they can. The point of the traditional doctrine, Strawson contends, is rather that particulars are the paradigmatic referents of subjects. While they are the subjects of the most basic kind of subject-predicate propositions, particulars can never be predicated of things of other kinds. Thus, in the basic kind of subject-predicate proposition, we couple a particular, as introduced in the substantival style, with a universal, as introduced in the assertive style. The predicated universal, however, can be of either of two types. It can be a sortal universal like *man* or *dog* or a characterizing universal like *green* or *courage*. In both cases, the universal collects all of those particulars of which it can be truly predicated, but the principle of collection differs. Roughly, a sortal universal collects all of those particulars which are instances of it; a characterizing universal collects all and only those particulars which are characterized by it.

An interesting feature of Strawson's account is his adaptation of Frege's views about saturated and unsaturated elements. Strawson's particulars, like Frege's objects, are saturated or complete; they unfold, he tells us, into facts. His universals, on the other hand, are like Frege's concepts in being incomplete. The point is that a particular can be introduced into discourse by a speaker only if he knows an individuating fact about that particular — only if he knows the truth of some empirical proposition that uniquely identifies the particular in question. In the case of universals, however, no such empirical knowledge is presupposed. All that is presupposed is the speaker's ability to use certain words correctly.

In a paper originally published in 1954 ("Form and Existence"), P. T. Geach expresses a view similar, in certain respects, to Strawson's. Although he is now less confident of the conclusions reached in that paper, Geach incorporates a revised version of "Form and Existence" in *God and the Soul*.[10] Like Strawson, Geach contends that subjects and predicates differ in mode of signification. Geach expresses this difference by saying that a predicate is true or false of what a subject stands for. While he finds this difference important, Geach thinks it legitimate to speak of the referents of predicates. He is never very clear about the nature of these entities, but he seems to construe them along the lines of Aquinas's forms and Frege's concepts.

Geach's account departs from Strawson's, however, on the subject of abstract singular terms. His view is that we cannot refer to the referents of predicates by using simple expressions like "wisdom" and "courage." Expressions of this sort purport to signify a "one over many"; but following the perplexing terminology of Aquinas and Frege, Geach claims that, in themselves, the referents of predicates are neither one nor many, although they can be "indifferently one or many."

As regards the use of abstract singular terms, Geach is avowedly nominalistic. He maintains that simple expressions like "wisdom" and "courage" are useful in that they provide handy abbreviations for longer, more complicated expressions; but he claims that philosophers have the right to use such terms only to the extent that they can eliminate them in favor of concrete forms like "wise" and "courageous." In this context, Geach goes so far as to say that a sentence containing an unanalyzable abstract singular term is unintelligible.

Geach is willing to grant, however, that we can refer to the referents of predicates by means of subjects. Such reference occurs when we speak of a form as individualized, when we use a complex expression like "wisdom of Socrates." Using an expression of this sort, we avoid the Platonistic mistake of construing a predicate-referent as a "one over many." We speak instead of a form as present in this or that individual. All of this is fairly straightforward. Geach goes on, however, to make some puzzling remarks. He says that in the complex expression "wisdom of Socrates," it is not "wisdom," but "wisdom of" that stands for the form itself (the form as not individualized). "Wisdom of Socrates," he argues, does not break up into "wisdom" and "of Socrates." This would be to grant too much to Platonism. Presumably, Geach is attempting to defend the Fregean view that predicate-referents are incomplete, while maintaining, against Frege, that such things can be the referents of subjects. The difficulty here is that "wisdom of" is not a referring expression, but a fragment of a referring expression. Geach, I think, wants to have it both ways.

Of the philosophers we have so far considered, only Strawson talks of nonpredicable universals. For Bergmann, Donagan, and Geach, the notion of a nonpredicable universal would seem to be incoherent. According to each of these philosophers, universals just *are* the sorts of things named, denoted, or referred to by predicative expressions. Strawson does make a few remarks about nonpredicable universals, but nothing like a general account of such entities emerges from his discussion. In "On the Nature of Universals," Nicholas Wolterstorff provides a more extensive treatment of this notion.[11] For Wolterstorff, nonpredicable universals are things like literary works, films, musical works, and art prints. His claim is that things of this sort exhibit a one-many relation that is analogous to the one-many relation exhibited by predicable universals (things like properties and actions) and their instances. Thus, a literary piece can have several copies, several recitations; a film, several showings; a musical work, several performances; and an art print, several impressions. According to Wolterstorff, the analogy rests on the fact that nonpredicable universals, like predicable universals, are kinds; qua kinds, they can have instances. All universals then, are kinds of things; but, Wolterstorff contends, kinds are not to be identified with the classes of the logician or the mathematician. Identity-conditions for classes can be specified in purely extensional terms; not so for kinds: a particular kind could have had other members than those it does, in fact, have, and two kinds with precisely the same members are not necessarily one and the same kind.

In both Strawson and Wolterstorff, then, some universals cannot be introduced by predicates. In *Modes of Referring and the Problem of Universals,* David Shwayder defends the more extreme view that predicates never introduce universals.[12] According to Shwayder, the case for metaphysical realism rests not on the subject-predicate distinction, but on the fact that language incorporates abstract singular terms with genuine referring uses. Shwayder's defense of realism is, by his own admission, very restricted. He considers only properties; and as he defines the concept, properties are limited to things like colors and shapes. Shwayder argues that property-words have their primary use in predication; but their use in predication, he contents, carries no ontic commitment. Functioning as predicates, property-words are not used to refer to or denote properties, but rather to distinguish or characterize the objects referred to by subjects. Nonetheless, the use of property-words in predication provides a basis for secondary uses of these words. In their secondary uses, property-words function as abstract singular terms and carry referential force. Their referents, of course, are properties; but, according to Shwayder, a property just is the primary use of a property-word — its use in distinguishing and characterizing objects.[13]

At first glance, it is difficult to see how this constitutes a defense of what has traditionally been called realism. On Shwayder's view, properties or universals turn out to be mere uses of words. They are hardly the sorts of things traditional realists have so vigorously defended against the attacks of nominalists. Indeed, it would be difficult to find a nominalist who would quarrel with the claim that properties, in Shwayder's sense, exist.

In fairness to Shwayder, there are contexts where his view is presented in more metaphysically charged terms. Thus, he sometimes claims that in their secondary uses, property-words take as their referents not the distinguishing uses of predicate-terms, but rather the theoretically possible distinctions we could draw by the primary uses of property-words. Further, Shwayder contends that the introduction of secondary uses of property-words involves the introduction of a whole new department of language, including new kinds of criteria for individuation, identity, etc.

A rather different approach characterizes Panayot Butchvarov's *Resemblance and Identity*.[14] According to Butchvarov, the analysis of abstract terms, as well as the analysis of predication, is irrelevant to the traditional problem of universals. What is relevant is the "recurrence of qualities." It is, Butchvarov contends, a fact of common-sense that individuals can agree in their qualities; the problem of universals has as its focus the appropriate philosophical description of this theoretically neutral fact. Most of Butchvarov's book is concerned with an examination of the forms of description provided by what he calls the Resemblance Theory and the Identity Theory. On the Resemblance theory, to say that a quality, F, recurs in individuals $a \ldots n$ is to say that $a \ldots n$ possess resembling, yet distinct, particular qualities. The Identity-Theory, on the other hand, speaks of a single quality as numerically identical in different individuals.

Butchvarov presents an extremely complex argument against the Resemblance Theory. Roughly, his contention is that since resemblance between qualities lacks the formal properties it would have to exhibit to constitute a relation between numerically different individuals, it must be construed as a form of identity. In support of this claim, he argues that propositions of the form "x resembles y" are necessarily incomplete. It is not that a proposition of this sort fails to specify how the relevant objects are alike, but rather that it fails to specify the degree to which they are alike. Butchvarov contends that resemblance, if a relation at all, is a relation that "admits of extremely wide variation of degrees." Consequently to make the claim "x resembles y" intelligible, one must indicate the extent of the resemblance. The only way of doing this, he claims, is to compare the resemblance holding between our original objects with the resemblance holding between other objects. Thus, "x resembles y," if intelligible at all, is short for "x resembles y more than w resembles z." In this respect, "x resembles y" is like "x is far from y"; in both cases, the claim is without sense unless construed as implicitly involving a comparison.

However, a consequence of this argument is that resemblance cannot be a relation. In the claim "x resembles y," resemblance does not function as a dyadic relation. The claim really involves four, not two, entities, but neither is resemblance a tetradic relation. Our claim is not that x, y, w, and z all resemble each other; it is rather that x and y (taken as a pair) are related to w and z (taken as a pair) by the relation not of resemblance, but of degree of resemblance. All relations, however, "have a definite, clear and unequivocal number of terms"; therefore, Butchvarov concludes, resemblance cannot be a relation.

But how does this constitute a refutation of the Resemblance Theory? Could not the proponent of that view agree that resemblance is not a relation and hold, nevertheless, that the recurrence of a quality is merely the resemblance holding between numerically different particular qualities? Butchvarov thinks not. In this context, he discusses the parallel claim "x is far from y." This claim really means, "The distance between x and y is greater than the distance between w and z." Similarly, he argues, "x resembles y," where x and y are qualities, means "The universal of least generality instantiated in x and y is of lower generality than the universal of least generality instantiated in w and z." The Identity Theory, in short, is correct in its account of the recurrence of qualities.

Despite its originality, Butchvarov's argument is somewhat less than convincing. His claim is that propositions of the form "*x* resembles *y*" are necessarily incomplete, but his only argument for this claim consists of a few remarks about the wide variation of degrees possible in resemblance. The same remarks would seem to apply to notions far less problematic than resemblance. Love, for example, is a relation that "admits of extremely wide variation of degrees", but it does not follow that claims of the form "*x* loves *y*" are incomplete. Butchvarov does speak of a distinction between necessarily comparative relations and relations where comparison is always possible but never necessary, but his sketchy remarks about variation in degree hardly serve to make clear the required distinction.

But even if we grant that propositions of the form "*x* resembles *y*" are incomplete in the way Butchvarov suggests, it is not obvious that the introduction of another case of resemblance will enable us to complete the sense of these propositions. If "*x* resembles *y*" is incomplete, so also is "*w* resembles *z*"; but, then, one might argue, we would only add to the incompleteness of "*x* resembles *y*" by introducing the sort of comparison Butchvarov says we must introduce.

Probably the most celebrated version of realism to appear in recent years is found in W. V. Quine's *Word and Object*.[15] Quine argues that unless we admit classes into our ontology, we impoverish mathematics to the point of leaving only "some trivial portions such as elementary arithmetic." More advanced mathematics requires quantification over classes; and by Quine's criterion of ontological commitment ("To be is to be the value of a bound variable") this commits anyone who does not wish to "accommodate his natural sciences unaided by mathematics" to the existence of classes.[16]

In the light of Quine's earlier aspirations for a language compatible with the most austere nominalism, his admission of classes does appear radical. Nevertheless, too much can be made of this "conversion." Classes are the only abstract entities Quine is willing to recognize; and surely among abstract objects, classes are the least obnoxious to the "lover of desert landscapes." Unlike the abstracta of traditional realists (attributes, propositions, etc.), classes have a "crystal-clear identity concept"; classes are the same if and only if they have the same members. The account of *Word and Object* can be called realistic, but a less exciting version of realism is hardly imaginable.

B. NOMINALISM

During the past decade or so, few philosophers have been willing to defend a thorough-going nominalism. The most severe critics of metaphysical realism have, more often than not, been equally severe in their criticism of nominalism. Thus, Renford Bambrough, in his well-known paper "Universals and Family Resemblances," utilizes Wittgenstein's remarks about family resemblances to undermine the claims of both the realist and the nominalist.[17] According to Bambrough, Wittgenstein showed (a) that the realist is wrong to suppose than an invariant set of properties is associated with every general term and (b) that the nominalist is wrong in claiming that things called by a general term have in common only that general term. Bambrough thinks, however, that Wittgenstein meant to do more than merely criticize traditional views. Supposedly, Wittgenstein provided a positive solution to the problem of universals. As Bambrough expresses it, Wittgenstein's solution consists in his insight that things called by a general term "*F*" have in common the fact that they are all *F*s.

Manley Thompson's discussion (in "Abstract Entities and Universals") goes a step further.[18] Thompson rejects realism and nominalism not because they are the wrong solutions to a genuine philosophical problem, but because they both make a show of resolving something that cannot be a problem at all. As Thompson interprets it, the problem of universals concerns what he calls Platonic entities, patterns or recipes accounting for the sameness among things.[19] The fact is that we make generalizations; we say that all the things of a kind are, in relevant respects, the same. These generalizations, however, go beyond any evidential base experience can provide.

Thus, the question arises: how can we know that the generalizations are true? According to Thompson, the realist answers the question by claiming that we have knowledge of Platonic entities, after the image of which all the things of a kind are patterned; the nominalist, on the other hand, rejects Platonic entities and seeks to account for our ability to make these generalizations in other ways.

Thus, the realist and the nominalist agree that while there are certain things we can know on the basis of observation, the relevant generalizations are not among them. Thompson finds this view incoherent; he argues that all knowledge, whether observational or not, presupposes the generalizations at issue. The attempt, then, to justify our knowledge of such generalizations is really the attempt to justify knowledge in general. But, according to Thompson, that is a hopeless task; it involves seeking "evidence for what we presuppose when we offer evidence."

Almost the reverse of the Bambrough-Thompson line is defended in one of Wolterstorff's early papers, "Qualities."[20] Wolterstorff argues that realism and nominalism are both complete, internally consistent positions and that, consequently, there is no basis for choosing between them. The paper is interesting because, in attempting to establish his thesis, Wolterstorff provides one of the few defenses of nominalism to be found in recent philosophical literature. Like Shwayder, Wolterstorff construes the analysis of abstract singular terms as central to the realism-nominalism debate; however, unlike Shwayder, he thinks that the nominalist can offer a cogent account of the referring uses of these expressions: the nominalist can construe abstract singular terms as referring to what Wolterstorff calls quality-classes. A quality-class is a class of particulars such that (a) every member of the class is similar to every other and (b) no non-member is similar to all of the members.

Wolterstorff notes, however, that this definition will prove unsatisfactory if we limit membership in quality-class to physical objects. To take one example, it could happen that all green things are round and vice versa; but if only physical objects are to be included in quality-classes, the definition would force us to construe greenness and roundness as one and the same thing. According to Wolterstorff, such difficulties disappear when we recognize that the category of particulars includes not only physical objects, but also what he calls aspects or abstract particulars. Roughly, Wolterstorff's aspects are Aristotle's first accidents, things like the roundness of this particular ball and the redness of that particular shirt. If we admit entities like these into our quality-classes, the original defintion works. For every quality of the realist, we have a distinct quality-class which we can take to be the possible referent of some abstract singular term.

One might want to challenge Wolterstorff's claim that he is presenting us with a form of nominalism. We generally think of the nominalist as the philosopher whose ontology does not incorporate abstract entities of any sort. Such theoretical parsimony, however, is surely lacking in Wolterstorff's account. Admittedly, his nominalist eschews common qualities, but that's about all. He is committed at once to classes and abstract particulars. Quine, in admitting only classes, construes himself as having abandoned the nominalist cause; compared with Quine, Wolterstorff's nominalist is a full-blown Platonist.

But, labels aside, there is a genuine difficulty in the view Wolterstorff defends. He wants to claim that abstract particulars enter into quality-classes with the physical objects that possess them; and on his account, things belonging to a single quality-class are similar. But does it even make sense to say, for example, that the redness of my shirt and the shirt itself are similar? The difficulty lies in specifying how they are similar; there would appear to be nothing we could say about the two things that would justify the claim that they are similar. Possibly, Wolterstorff would want to say that they are both red; but surely this is wrong; for *pace* Plato, the redness of my shirt is not itself red.

The only fully developed nominalistic account to appear in recent years is found in the writings of Wilfrid Sellars. In "Grammar and Existence: A Preface to Ontology," Sellars argues that logic and mathematics do not commit us to the existence of abstract entities.[21] The fact that both involve quantification over variables of higher levels than individual variables is not decisive. According to Sellars, Quine's dictum "To be is to be the value of a bound variable" rests on a misinterpretation of the logic of quantification. The existential quantifier is existence-involving only in a narrow range of cases; and, Sellars argues, the relevant quantifications in logic and mathematics are not among these.[22]

In the same paper, Sellars argues that ordinary talk about meaning is ontologically neutral. The Platonist claims that talk about meaning commits us to the existence of abstract entities; but according to Sellars, this is to misconstrue what we do when we state the meaning of a word. Talk about meaning generally conforms to the translation rubric, expressed by the schema

"———" (in L) means . . .

Thus, "'Dreieckig' (in German) means triangular." Using the translation rubric, we do not refer to abstract entities of any kind; we merely exhibit the use of a word (here, "Dreieckig") by using, not mentioning, another word (here, "triangular") with presumably the same use.[23]

Sellars would agree with philosophers like Shwayder and Wolterstorff that the major obstacle to nominalism is presented by abstract singular terms. He feels, however, that in many contexts the use of abstract singular terms is nonproblematic. Frequently we use abstract terms merely by the way of abbreviation. In such contexts, what we say by using abstract singular terms could just as well be said by using only concrete forms. Thus, "triangularity" in "Triangularity implies having three sides" presents no real problem for the nominalist; according to Sellars, the sentence in which it appears is simply another way of saying that if anything is a triangle, it has three sides.

Sometimes abstract singular terms enter into talk about exemplification. Thus, we might say that some object exemplifies triangularity. Sellars is one of the few nominalists (possibly the only one) to grant the truth of such remarks; but as he argues in "Naming and Saying," talk about exemplification is merely another way of talking about the truth of sentences. Thus, "x exemplifies triangularity" is analyzed as "Triangularity is true of x"; and this, in turn, becomes "That x is triangular is true."[24]

In some of their uses, however, abstract singular terms cannot be disposed of so easily. We say, for example, that triangularity is a quality and that mankind is a class. In such cases, we have what might be called essential occurrences of abstract singular terms. In an essential occurrence, an abstract singular term functions as subject; but it seems impossible to construe the expression as a stand-in for one or more concrete terms. What we say about the thing designated by the subject is something that can be correctly said only about an object that is, in a quite straightforward sense, an abstract entity.

In "Abstract Entities" Sellars attempts to deal with essential occurrences of abstract singulars.[25] He wants to claim that, in essential occurrences, abstract singular terms signify what he calls linguistic types. A linguistic type is a word "construed as a kind or sort which is capable of realization or embodiment in different linguistic materials." Qua kind or sort, it exhibits the linguistic role that expressions from historically different languages can have in common. Thus, "dreieckig" and "triangular" are different realizations of one and the same linguistic type. Sellars uses a dotting device for referring to linguistic types. "Dreieckig" and "triangular," he tells us, are both ·triangular·s; they both realize the linguistic type, the ·triangular·. It is this linguistic type that the abstract singular term "triangularity" signifies, so that in an essential occurrence, "triangularity" is synonymous with "the ·triangular·."

One might object that Sellars has merely replaced one kind of abstract object for another; for if linguistic types have different realizations, different embodiments, then surely they are to be reckoned universals. Sellars's contention, however, is that "the ·triangular·" does not signify a universal; it is rather what he calls a distributive singular term. It functions in the way "the lion" functions in "The lion is tawny." Here, we are not referring to the universal, the lion; for while "The lion is tawny" is true, "The universal, the lion is tawny," if intelligible at all, is false.

But what is a distributive singular term? According to Sellars, to use an expression of the form "the K" as a distributive singular term is not to refer to something over and above the things that are K's; it is rather to make a logically necessary statement about all Ks. Thus, all sentences of the form "The K is F" (where "the K" functions as a distributive singular term) are reducible to sentences of the form "All Ks are necessarily F."[26] Thus, to speak of the ·triangular· is not to speak of something over and above expressions that are ·triangular·s; it is simply to make a necessary claim about all those expressions in historically different languages which play the role that "triangular" plays in our language.

This analysis, however, disposes of only half of our original difficulty. We were concerned with sentences like "Triangularity is a quality" and "Mankind is a class." The terms "triangularity" and "mankind" are, on Sellars account, ways of referring to ·triangular·s and ·man·s; but what of the expressions "quality" and "class" as they appear in these sentences? Here Sellars appropriates Carnap's talk of quasi-syntactical sentences. Our examples are sentences in the material mode; but actually, they are remarks about the syntax of ·triangular·s and ·man·s; this is brought out, Sellars contends, when we translate them into the formal mode. "Triangularity is a quality" becomes "The ·triangular· is an adjective" and this, in turn, becomes "All ·triangular·s are necessarily adjectives." In similar fashion, "Mankind is a class" becomes "The ·man· is a common noun" and, finally, "All ·man·s are necessarily common nouns."

Unfortunately, Sellars is never clear about the force of his nominalism. Sometimes it appears that his analyses are meant to capture existing synonymies; but in other contexts Sellars seems to find the notion of strict translation too confining and speaks instead of reconstructing language along nominalist lines. Clearly, these are two quite different things; unless we know which of these aims is, in the final analysis, operative, we can hardly assess the particular moves in Sellars's account.

Aside from this difficulty, Sellars's notion of a linguistic type is troublesome. For one thing, Sellars appears to have Quine's remarks about the indeterminancy of translation to contend with; for certainly, one consequence of Quine's arguments is that it is impossible to identify linguistic roles across languages in the way Sellars claims we can.[27] More important, however, is the fact that when we eliminate a linguistic type in favor, for example, of materially different ·triangular·s, we seem to be left with a universal, the linguistic role that all ·triangular·s have in common. It will not do, of course, to suggest that the linguistic role that ·triangular·s share is itself susceptible to elimination via distributive singular terms; for this presupposes the introduction of what is also, *prima facie,* a universal, the linguistic role underlying the linguistic type, the ·linguistic role·.

Sellars, I suspect, would argue that linguistic roles need not be eliminated in this way. He would doubtless claim that we can explain all that is involved in a particular linguistic role by specifying what he calls the prescriptive criteria for the use of the word in question, by specifying, that is, all the moves that can be made in the language-game with that word. The difficulty here is that we have no guarantee that a specification of prescriptive criteria will not involve new universals and that in eliminating these, still others will not emerge.

II. Particulars, Substances, and Individuation

In this section I want to examine the cluster of problems surrounding the notion of a particular.[28] I shall first deal with the appeal to bare particulars found in the writings of Gustav Bergmann and his followers; then, I shall examine the work of philosophers who want to construe particulars as complexes of properties or qualities. In the third section I shall discuss the essentialist interpretations of particulars found in writers like Plantinga, Geach, and Wiggins; and finally, in the fourth section, I shall deal with the account of particulars provided by Strawson in *Individuals*.

A. BERGMANN ON INDIVIDUATION

In all of his writings, Bergmann is critical of substance ontologies. According to Bergmann a substance ontologist is committed to the view that objects can change while remaining numerically identical; identity through change, Bergmann argues, is *prima facie* contradictory.[29] The substance ontologist is committed to the view that a substance, *a*, both has and has not a certain character, *F*. To eliminate this contradiction, the substance ontologist must introduce temporal moments and say that *a* has *F* at *t* and *a* does not have *F* at *t* + *n*. Unfortunately, Bergmann claims, the introduction of temporal moments violates the Principle of Acquaintance. According to that principle an ontology must meet the demands of a strict empiricism; it may posit only such entities as are objects of possible acquaintance; but surely, Bergmann contends, we are never acquainted with nonrelational temporal moments.

Bergmann concludes that a sound ontology must construe the items out of which our common-sense world is constituted as changeless. In his earlier writings, Bergmann found in this claim support for phenomenalism, the view that our world is a construction of changeless sense-data. He has since rejected phenomenalism; but he still maintains that whatever we take to be the building-blocks of reality, we must construe them as changeless.[30]

When we reach the level of sense-data or their nonphenomenological counterparts, we have not yet, in Bergmann's view, reached the level of ontological simples. As our discussion of Bergmann on universals indicates, the level of simples incorporates talk about individuals and their characters. The relevant individuals, of course, are what Bergmann calls bare particulars. In his most recent book, *Realism,* Bergmann again presents the case for bare particulars; and here, as in his earlier writings, the notion of a bare particular is tied to considerations about numerical diversity.[31] It is logically possible, Bergmann contends, that two objects have all their nonrelational characters in common. This implies, he argues, that objects are not constituted exclusively by their characters. We cannot account for the individuation of objects by reference to their relational characters. Admittedly, qualitatively identical objects will differ relationally; but according to Bergmann, relations presuppose, rather than explain, numerical diversity. To account for the possibility of objects agreeing in all their nonrelational characters, we must grant that each object is constituted not only by a set of characters, but also by some nonrepeatable entity (a bare particular) to which we can attribute the identity of that object.

One might wonder whether bare particulars, any more than pure temporal moments, are compatible with the Principle of Acquaintance; for surely we are never acquainted with entities lacking all characters. Bergmann agrees that we never perceive bare particulars by themselves, we only meet with particulars as exemplifying characters; and this is connected with what he calls the Principle of Exemplification, the claim that particulars are never uncharacterized, nor characters unexemplified. Nevertheless, Bergmann contends that we can point to something in perception we can call bare particulars. Bergmann's view is clearly expressed in Edwin Allaire's "Bare Particulars."[32] According to Allaire, a bare particular just *is* the thing responsible for the individuation of objects alike in all their nonrelational characters; it just *is* the carrier of numerical difference; but then, in being acquainted with numerically different objects exemplifying the same non-relational characters, Allaire argues, we are *eo ipso* acquainted with bare particulars.

But there is a difficulty here. As the Principle of Exemplification makes clear, bare particulars are not merely the carriers of numerical diversity; they are also the items which, in the final analysis, exemplify characters. Considered in this light, Bergmann's notion of bare particulars seems less compatible with his empiricist criterion of ontology. The proponent of the Principle of Acquaintance may agree with Bergmann and Allaire that we are acquainted with bare particulars as carriers of numerical identity, but he will likely challenge the claim that we are acquainted with bare particulars qua possessors of characters; here he will merely be echoing Bergmann's contention that perception has as its object a *quale,* never a *quid.* What is needed is an argument to support the claim that the items responsible for the individuation of objects are also the items exemplifying the characters we associate with those objects; but as far as I can tell, Bergmann never presents such an argument.

The difficulty goes beyond the Principle of Acquaintance. It is not simply that experience does not reveal bare substrata to be the carriers of characters. The further question is whether we can even make sense of the notion of an unqualified possessor of qualities. In "Particulars," Wilfrid Sellars argues that Bergmann's view is contradictory;[33] Sellars invites us to translate into the symbolism of *Principia Mathematica* the claim that whatever exemplifies a character is itself bare. The result, he contends, is an out-and-out contradication:

$$(\forall x) \{[(\exists \phi) (\phi x)] \supset [-(\exists \phi) (\phi x)]\}.$$

Similarly, Bergmann's attack on substance ontologies is problematic. Bergmann's remarks on change and time are deeply rooted in his Ideal Language method. Why, for example, must the substance ontologist construe time as a series of nonrelational moments? Bergmann's answer is that this is the only account of time which, in conformity with the syntax of the Ideal Language, enables the substance ontologist to eliminate the contradiction inherent in change; and it is the syntax of the Ideal Language that proves central in the argument. Assuming that Bergmann is right on this point, the philosopher operating from outside Bergmann's system is likely to be impressed less with the inadequacies of substance ontologies than with the inadequacies of Bergmann's Ideal Language. If the syntax of a language is such that it permits us to say what we mean about change only if we assume an untenable view about time, then, we want to say, that language is hardly one that is "ideal" for all philosophical purposes.

B. "CLUSTERS" AND "BUNDLES"

Probably the most persistent critic of Bergmann's account of individuation is Herbert Hochberg. According to Hochberg, the bare particular analysis cannot, in any way, be reconciled with the Principle of Acquaintance.[34] On the contrary, the strict empiricist must claim that objects are merely complexes of universals, "bundles" or "clusters" of characters. Hochberg's main contention is that a view of this sort can handle difficulties about individuation at least as well as the bare particular analysis. In "Things and Qualities," Hochberg argues that complexes of universals are individuated of and by themselves.[35] He claims that bare particulars are posited merely to provide the ontologist with entities whose numerical diversity requires no further explanation. Supposedly, they do not differ "in anything; they simply differ." But why not hold, Hochberg asks, that complexes of characters are the sorts of things that do not differ "in anything," but "simply differ"?

In "Things and Descriptions," Hochberg presents a rather different account.[36] There he contends that relations individuate. Numerical difference among objects alike in all their nonrelational features has its source in the various relations obtaining among such objects. Hochberg agrees with Bergmann that relations presuppose numerical diversity, but he claims that the dependence may operate in both directions. Admittedly, relations can hold only between numerically distinct objects; but it may also be that numerical diversity in turn presupposes the existence of one or more relations.

Although critical of the appeal to bare particulars, Hochberg finds certain features of Bergmann's ontology indispensable. Thus, he denies that particulars are mere heaps of universals. One must postulate, he argues, a structural tie or connection (analogous to Bergmann's nexus of exemplification) among the various characters constituting an object. This tie accounts for the unity or connexity we find in objects and enables us to explain why some logically consistent sets of characters actually constitute objects, while others do not.[37] Further, Hochberg's objects, like Bergmann's, are changeless. Change involves an alteration in the characters associated with an object; but since objects just are these characters, change necessarily yields a numerically different object.

An interesting feature of Hochberg's account is his analysis of reference. It is frequently claimed that a "bundle" theorist is forced to construe most of our ordinary talk about objects as analytic. If an object just is a complex of characters, then to know which object is being referred to, a person must know in advance all of the characters that can be truly predicated of that object. But if this is true, no character could ever be truly, yet nontautologously, applied to an object. Hochberg denies that this is a real consequence of his view. In "Things and Qualities" he focuses on proper names. Proper names, he contends, are not mere labels for lists of characters. Indeed, they have no meaning at all, only a reference; nor is the referential connection between name and object effected by means of an object's characters; the connection is immediate. Thus, a true subject-predicate proposition in which a proper name functions as subject is not analytic; a person can understand the proposition and know which object it is about, without knowing in advance that it is true.

In "Things and Descriptions," Hochberg deals with propositions in which we refer to objects by means of definite descriptions. In a proposition of this sort, we pick out an object as the thing which has F, G, H, etc.; we focus on such characters as are jointly sufficient for uniquely identifying the object. Since relations individuate, the relevant characters will be only some of the many characters exemplifed by an object. Thus, we can go on and ascribe to an object so described other characters, and the resulting propositions will be synthetic. But, Hochberg argues, propositions in which we identify an object by a definite description and then ascribe to it one or more of the characters introduced in that description will also be synthetic. Certainly, propositions of this sort will be redundant; but since they incorporate a definite description in the role of grammatical subject, they are really only disguised existential propositions and, therefore, cannot be analytic.

Like Hochberg, Neil Wilson ("Substances without Substrata") is critical of the notion of a bare particular.[38] As Wilson interprets the doctrine, the proponent of substrata is committed to the view that objects are what they are regardless of the properties they possess. In refutation of this claim, Wilson asks us to imagine a world like ours in all respects except that all the properties of Marc Antony belong to Julius Caesar and vice versa. If the doctrine of substrata were correct, the resulting world would be different from ours; but, according to Wilson, the imagined world would, in no way, differ from our own world; it would not represent a new possibility—the substrata theory must be wrong.

Wilson is more sympathetic with the view that objects are merely "bundles" of properties. The "bundle" theorist, he contends, is right in construing the identity of objects as dependent upon the properties they possess; and in this connection, Wilson defends Leibniz's Identity of Indiscernibles, the principle that no two objects can exhibit the same set of properties. But, in the final analysis, Wilson finds the bundle analysis unsatisfactory. For one thing, the "bundle" theorist is committed to the view that objects cannot remain numerically identical through change; and Wilson, unlike Hochberg, thinks that this is too great a price to pay. Further, the "bundle" theorist wants to construe properties as concrete, as independent existents having an identity all their own;

but according to Wilson, neither objects nor their qualities are concrete in this sense. It is only facts that are what they are independently of other things. But is each individual fact concrete? Wilson thinks not; atomism, he contends, must give way to some form of Absolute Idealism. In the end, only a very large number of facts, possibly the totality of facts, constitutes a concrete existent.

Wilson's position, then, is not a version of the "bundle" theory; but, apart from the account presented by Hochberg, it is about the closest approximation to the "bundle" theory to be found in recent literature. Historically (although not logically), the "bundle" theory has been associated with Phenomenalism; and the decline, in recent years, of the latter view has left the former position with almost no proponents. Indeed, even A. J. Ayer, who earlier construed the "bundle" theory as obviously correct ("The Identity of Indiscernibles"), has become more cautious.[39] In "Names and Descriptions," Ayer argues that our language, as it stands, implies an ontology of Lockean substrata.[40] He seems to think that it is possible to construct a language free of this commitment; but even this, he argues, would not warrant adherence to the view that objects are simply "bundles" of properties. The "bundle" analysis commits one to the Identity of Indiscernibles, and Ayer is now willing to question (as he earlier was not) the truth of that principle.

Technical difficulties aside, it is not surprising that philosophers have been reluctant to adopt some version of the "bundle" theory. On that theory, ordinary objects are constructions out of qualities; the difficulty with this claim is that many of the qualities involved in the proposed construction would appear to be object-laden themselves. G.E.M. Anscombe argues persuasively for this point in "Substance."[41] She grants that some of the qualities associated with a substance are not substance-involving; i.e., they do not presuppose the concept of substance. According to Miss Anscombe, most of Locke's secondary qualities are of this sort. Thus, there could be a patch of color which did not constitute the surface of any physical object. However, secondary qualities are not, by themselves, sufficient for the construction of our substance-concepts. We need other qualities; and these, Miss Anscombe argues, are not logically independent of the notion of substance. Thus, qualities like malleability and *melts at 44°C* are substance-involving. These qualities can be instantiated only as the qualities of this or that physical substance. But surely, she concludes, it would be absurd to construe qualities like these as items out of which our substance-concepts are constructed; they already presuppose those concepts.

C. ESSENTIALISM AND IDENTITY

Some philosophers have wanted to distinguish between properties that are essential and properties that are only accidental to a particular. Very generally, the distinction is as follows: while an object can change with respect to its accidental properties, its essential properties are inseparable from the object; to lose one of them is to become numerically a different object. Essentialists (as proponents of this distinction are called) have, almost without exception, been critical of the two sorts of accounts of particulars we have so far examined. Against proponents of bare particulars, essentialists have argued that bare substrata can never function as logical subjects; the ultimate subjects of predication, they argue, are particulars essentially characterized. In opposition to the "bundle" theorist's radical denial of identity through change, essentialists have argued that where only accidental properties are involved, particulars can and do change while remaining numerically the same.

Essentialists, however, have disagreed among themselves about the nature of essential properties. Some (Leibniz, for example and probably Scotus) have spoken of individual essences, essences peculiar to particular objects; whereas others (most notably, philosphers in the Aristotelian tradition) have argued that essences are always general, common to all the members of a kind or sort.

In recent philosophy, the Leibnizian tradition is represented by Alvin Plantinga. In "World and Essence," he defends a notion of individual essence that is equally as rich as Leibniz's notion of haecceity or complete individual concept.[42] Before examining that paper, however, I want to look at the defense of essentialism presented in *God and Other Minds.*[43] Here, Plantinga does not defend any particular version of essentialism; he is concerned with the more general task of clarifying the distinction between essential and accidental properties. His claim is that we can explicate the notion of a necessary or essential property (*de re* necessity) in terms of the less problematic notion of necessity at work in talk about propositions (*de dicto* necessity). We can say that a property, *P*, is essential to an individual, *x*, if and only if *x* has *P* and the proposition *x lacks P* is necessarily false.[44]

Plantinga argues, however, that this characterization is adequate only if we place certain restrictions on the substituend sets of the variables "*x*" and "*P*". In its unrestricted form, the characterization forces us to construe properties as both accidental and essential to one and the same object.[45] Thus, "Seven lacks the property of being prime" is necessarily false; *being prime* is a property essential to seven. Now, suppose that seven is Quine's favorite number. Applying the criterion, *being prime* turns out to be accidental to seven; for while "Quine's favorite number lacks the property of being prime" is false, it is not necessarily false. The difficulty here lies in our ability to refer to the number seven in a variety of ways. The same difficulty can arise in the case of the property *being prime.* Thus, suppose *being prime* is the property that Quine is now thinking of. Again, the criterion forces us to construe *being prime* as accidental to seven; for "Seven lacks the property Quine is now thinking of" does not express a necessary falsehood.

According to Plantinga, the renegade labels are all definite descriptions; if we limit the substituend sets of the variables "*x*" and "*P*" appearing in the original characterization to proper names, the characterization works.[46] But, then, taking the criterion, as restricted in this way, we can accommodate cases where properties and/or the objects possessing them are identifed by definite descriptions. We can say: a property, *P*, is essential to an object, *x*, if and only if (a) *x* has *P* and the propositon *x* lacks *P* (where the substituend sets of "*x*" and "*P*" contain only proper names) is necessarily false or (b) *x* has *P* and there is an object, *y*, and a Property, *P'*, such that *x* is identical with *y* and *P* is identical with *P'* and *P'* is an essential property of *y* in the sense of (a).

In "World and Essence," Plantinga's approach is quite different. Appropriating the modal logician's talk about possible worlds, he claims that a property is essential to an object just in case that object has the property in every possible world in which it exists. Some properties, Plantinga claims, are trivially essential; thus, every object in every possible world has the property of *being colored if red.* Other properties are essential to some objects while accidental to others; *being Socrates or Greek,* for example, is essential to Socrates, but accidental to Plato and Aristotle. Still other properties—*being Socrates or Plato,* for example—are essential to all the objects possessing them.

In addition to these kinds of essential properties, there is for each object, Plantinga argues, an haecceity or individual essence, a property which (a) is essential to the object in question, (b) is possessed only by that object, and (c) entails all of the other properties essential to that object. Thus, Socrates has *Socrates-identity.* (a) This property is essential to Socrates—there is no possible world in which Socrates both exists and lacks this property; (b) no object distinct from Socrates has, in any possible world, *Socrates-identity;* (c) the property entails all of Socrates's other essential properties—there is no possible world in which Socrates has *Socrates-identity* but lacks one or more of his other essential properties.

Plantinga, however, wants to go much further than this. He wants to say, with Leibniz, that an Omniscient Being could, by reflecting on Socrates's essence, "read off" all of Socrates's properties, both accidental and essential. Suppose, for example, that

Socrates actually was snub-nosed in the real world. *Being snub-nosed* will doubtless be accidental to Socrates; but, Plantinga argues, *being snub-nosed in the actual world* is not accidental to him. There is no world in which Socrates both exists and lacks this second-level property; and qua essential to him, the property of being snub-nosed in the actual world is entailed by Socrates's individual essence. But we could take any property of Socrates and, in the same way, derive from it a property that is essential to Socrates and, therefore, entailed by his essence. Consequently, for any property, *P,* and any world, *W,* God could infer from Socrates's essence that Socrates has or has not *P* in *W.* However, God also knows which world is the actual world, so that, Plantinga concludes, He is able to "read off" all of the properties Socrates possesses in the actual world — accidental as well as essential.[47]

In the writings of P. T. Geach, we find a version of essentialism that falls within the Aristotelian tradition of common or general essences. Very roughly, Geach's view is that nothing can function as an object of reference unless it is possible to specify in general terms (i.e., terms appropriate to other things as well) the kind of thing the object is. More often than not, Geach presents his version of essentialism in the linguistic mode. In *Reference and Generality* and *Mental Acts,* he argues that a necessary condition for the correct use of a proper name is the ability to specify some count-noun true of the object bearing the name.[48] Geach's count-nouns are expressions like "man" and "dog"; essentially, they are Strawson's sortal terms. Besides furnishing us with principles for enumerating objects, they provide a classification of objects by indicating the kinds or sorts to which objects can belong. Count-nouns, Geach wants to say, tie proper names to their referents. Proper names are meant to be used repeatedly; but if I am to use a proper name correctly on different occasions, I must know whether or not the object I am referring to is the object bearing the relevant proper name. To know this is to know that a statement of numerical identity (a statement of the form "*x* is the same as *y*") is true. But, Geach argues, the claim that two things are the same is incomplete. To fill in the claim, one must answer the question, "Same what?"; and, according to Geach, it is only by means of count-nouns that one can do this.

The talk about proper names, then, is really subsidiary. The key issue is Geach's claim that statements of the form "*x* is the same as *y*" are incomplete. But why are they incomplete? The reason, Geach argues, is that identity is relative, relative to the count-noun one specifies. It is possible, he claims, for an object, *x,* and an object, *y,* to be the same *F,* but different *G.*[49] Thus, the mayor of Loogootie is the same man as the president of the Chickasaw County Board, but a different official personage. Similarly, what I bathed in today and what I bathed in yesterday are the same river, but not the same water. But since identity is relative in this way, I can hardly know what is being asserted by the bare claim that *x* is the same as *y.* I need to know the count-noun under which *x* and *y* are being judged identical.

It should be clear that Geach's account is incompatible with traditional accounts of identity. If, as Geach argues, identity is relative to the count-noun specified, then we must, among other things, reject the principle known as Leibniz's Law. Suppose that some object, *x,* and some object, *y,* are the same *F*; their identity under "*F*" does not guarantee that whatever is true of one is true of the other. They might, despite their identity as *F*s, be different *G*s; and, then, it will be false, for example, to say of *y* what can be truly said of *x* — that it is the same *G* as *x.*

In his review of *Reference and Generality,* Quine roundly criticizes Geach on this point.[50] Logic, he argues, requires an absolute notion of identity, one conforming to Leibniz's Law. In a similar vein, David Wiggins (*Identity and Spatio-Temporal Continuity*) complains that if we follow Geach in rejecting Leibniz's Law, we no longer have a justification for the substitution of identicals in deductive contexts, nor do we leave ourselves with anything more than the bare notions of reflexivity, transitivity, and symmetry to define the concept of identity.[51]

Wiggins distinguishes two claims: (a) the claim that statements of the form "x is the same as y" requires a count-noun to complete their sense and (b) the claim that identity is relative to the count-noun specified. Wiggins rejects (b), but defends (a), thereby accepting a form of essentialism while preserving Leibniz's Law. His attack on (b) involves a painstaking analysis of cases where we seem to have an x and a y identical under one count-noun, but different under another. In all cases but one, Wiggins claims to show that examples purporting to conform to Geachian identity actually fail to do so. The only real counter-example to Leibniz's Law is provided by the doctrine of the Trinity. According to that doctrine, three individuals are one and the same God, but numerically different Persons. Wiggins argues, however, that since in all other contexts identity conforms to the Leibnizian model, we have no option but to reject the doctrine of the Trinity.

Nonetheless, Wiggins maintains that an essentialist interpretation of identity-statements is correct. His own defense of that interpretation is limited to identity-statements involving material bodies. According to Wiggins, to say that two material objects, x and y, are identical is to say that if one traces them through space and time, he finds them to coincide. Spatio-temporal coincidence, however, is a "purely formal notion": there can be no such thing as a general account of what it is for two material objects to coincide in space and time. Consequently, Wiggins argues, claims to the effect that a material object, x, and a material object, y, are the same require completion, completion by means of terms which make it possible for us to know what spatio-temporal coincidence is for x and y. Such terms, Wiggins argues, are count-nouns or sortal terms.[52]

In a paper entitled "Identity," Geach attempts to answer his critics.[53] His main contention is that the account of identity provided by Leibniz's Law and its converse, the Identity of Indiscernibles, is untenable. He begins by arguing that the proponent of Leibnizian identity cannot accept the traditional formulation of the two principles. As it is often expressed, the conjunction of the two principles reads as follows: an object, x, and an object, y, are numerically identical if and only if whatever is true of x is true of y and vice versa. But Geach contends that to accept this formulation and use the locution "whatever is true of . . . " is to land oneself in "such notorious paradoxes as Grelling's and Richard's." To avoid the semantical paradoxes, one must rather say that objects are numerically identical if and only if they are indiscernible with respect to their predicates. But even amended in this way, Leibnizian or absolute identity encounters difficulties. Geach asks us to consider a set of objects like the following:

(1) a
(2) a

Now, Geach asks us to suppose that there exists a language so weak in predicates that it does not enable us to distinguish between types of expressions and their tokens. In that language it will be correct to say (provided we accept the amended account of Leibnizian identity) that (1) and (2) are identical. But let us further suppose that the language is supplemented in such a way that we can make the distinction between types and their tokens. When the original language is enriched in this way, (1) and (2) turn out to be numerically different objects. Thus, the proponent of Leibnizian identity is forced to grant that merely by expanding the ideology of a language (its descriptive resources), objects previously identical become diverse; and no Leibnizian, Geach contends, would welcome this consequence.

The proponent of absolute identity might respond by saying that when, in the weaker language, we make the true claim that (1) and (2) are identical, we aren't speaking of the same objects as when we say, in the enriched language, that (1) and (2) are different. Geach, however, finds this response unsatisfactory. To make this move, he claims, is to expose oneself to "indecently burgeoning existential commitments;" it is to multiply entities to the point where "the universe . . . shows itself as a baroque Meinongian structure." According to Geach, our only option is to reject the concept of absolute identity. We must admit instead that numerical identity and discernibility with respect to predicates are compatible; but this is to grant, among other things, Geach's point that it is possible for an object, x, and an object, y, to be the same F, but different Gs.

In "Geach and Relative Identity" Fred Feldman argues that even if sound, Geach's argument does not establish the view that identity is relative to the count-noun one specifies. The nub of Geach's argument is contined in his remarks about expanding ideology. As we expand the ideology of a language, statements of identity formerly true turn out to be false; but, according to Feldman, this only commits us to the view that identity is, in some way relative; it does not commit us to any particular account of the relatively. Thus, one could handle Geach's example without rejecting Leibnizian identity. One could say that statements of identity are relative, not to a count-noun, but rather to a language as a whole. On this view, statements of the form "x is the same as y" would be, as Geach suggests, incomplete; but to fill them in, one would indicate, not the count-noun governing the identity-statement, but the language, against the ideology of which the objects are being judged identical. Construed in this way, judgments of identity would still conform to the model provided by Leibniz's Law and its converse; for objects would be numerically identical in a language if and only if they were indiscernible with respect to the ideology of the language.

It is interesting how the relativism Feldman points to parallels the account of identity found in Quine's "Ontological Relativity."[54] Here, Quine argues that questions of identity and difference make sense only relative to some background language. The account of identity presented here is connected with Quine's thesis of ontological relatively. Essentially, that thesis is the claim that there is no such thing as specifying in an absolute way the items comprising the ontology of a language. The best we can do, Quine claims, is to identify those items relative to the referential base of a background language. But, according to Quine, "Identity is of a piece with ontology." If we can specify the ontology of a theory only relative to some background language, then it is impossible to speak of the identity of objects, except as relative to some chosen coordinate system. Quine illustrates the relativity of identity with an example that is, in some respects, like Geach's. If a branch of economic theory, which does not distinguish between people of the same income, is taken as our background language, then, Quine claims, we must construe persons who are (in terms of a background language with a richer ideology) numerically different as identical. Like Feldman, Quine finds in this sort of example no reason for rejecting Leibnizian identity. Indeed, Quine defends both Leibniz's Law and the Identity of Indiscernibles (in the sort of amended form Geach presents). Although judgments of identity are always relative to some background language, they are always made in conformity with the concept of Leibnizian identity; for according to Quine, to say that an object, x, and an object, y, are identical, is just to say that x and y are indiscernible with respect to the descriptive resources of that language.

D. STRAWSON ON PARTICULARS

Unquestionably the most influential treatment of particulars to appear in recent years is found in the first half of Strawson's *Individuals*. For Strawson, the notion of a particular is extremely broad; it includes not only material bodies and persons, but also things as diverse as states of consciousness and physical processes. His analysis of particulars focuses on what he calls particular-identification. He is concerned with the machinery our conceptual scheme affords us for making uniquely identifying references to particulars.[55]

In the most basic kind of case, Strawson claims, we refer to a particular environment. Since the particular is within the range of sensible discrimination, it can be identified demonstratively, by the use, that is, of pointing and the demonstratives "this" and "that." More problematic is the identification of particulars outside this range. According to the Identity of Indiscernibles (or one version of it), the nondemonstrative identification of particulars proceeds by way of purely general descriptions.[56] Strawson rejects this sort of account. No description of a particular in terms of purely general predicates (predicates involving no essential reference to particulars) carries with it any logical guarantee that it applies to just one individual. No matter how detailed the list of purely general predicates, it is always possible, Strawson argues, that the description formed out of those predicates will apply to several different particulars.

Like Kant, Strawson wants to claim that space and time together constitute a system of relations adequate for the purposes of particular-identification. We operate, he tells us, with a unified conceptual scheme in which every particualr is related to every other by means of space and time; but a consequence of this is that nondemonstrative identification can always be tied to demonstrative identification. We can always uniquely identify a particular outside our immediate perceptual environment by specifying its spatio-temporal relations to particulars within that environment.

Particulars can also be reidentified; we can, that is, identify a particular as numerically identical with a particular encountered earlier. In discussing reidentification, Strawson is concerned to undermine Humean scepticism about numerical identity through time. We speak of reidentifying particulars even where there is a break in our observation of them; but the fact that our observation of particulars is discontinuous, Strawson argues, provides no support for Humean scepticism. Indeed, it is a condition of our possessing the unified conceptual scheme we do possess that we ascribe numerical identity to objects discontinuously observed. If we never did this, there would be no question of a single unified scheme; we would have instead the notion of many fragmentary, discontinuous schemes, one for each stretch of uninterrupted observation. But if our experience were of this sort, the sceptic's doubts about numerical identity could never arise. For those doubts to be possible, we must have the very sort of unified framework the sceptic's doubts about reidentification call into question. Those doubts, Strawson concludes, cannot be other than incoherent.

Strawson agrees with Aristotle in holding that, among particulars, substances (material bodies and persons) have ontological primacy. In Strawson's account, this primacy exhibits itself in the role substances play in particular-identification. Substances, we are told, are the basic particulars of our conceptual scheme: the identification of substances need not depend upon the identification of nonsubstantial particulars; but were we unable to identify substances we could not make all of the identifying references we do make to particulars of other categories. In support of the claim that material bodies and persons are basic particulars, Strawson argues as follows:

It seems that we can construct an argument from the premise that identification rests ultimately on location in a unitary spatio-temporal framework of four dimensions, to the conclusion that a certain class of particulars is basic in the sense I have explained. For that framework is not something extraneous to the objects in reality of which we speak. If we ask what constitutes the framework, we must look to those objects themselves, or some among them. But not every category of particular objects we recognize is competent to constitute such a framework. The only objects which can constitute it are those which can confer upon it its own, fundamental characteristics. That is to say, they must be three-dimensional objects that endure through time. They must also be accessible to such means of observation as we have; and since those means are strictly limited in power, they must collectively have enough diversity, richness, stability, and endurance to make possible and natural just that conception of a single unitary framework which we possess. Of the categories of objects which we recognize, only those satisfy these criteria which are, or possess, material bodies—in a broad sense of the expression [pp. 28–29].

Although Strawson thinks that this argument is sound, he finds it "too vague and general." To supplement the argument, he works out a detailed account of the ways in which the identification of substances is involved in the identification of particulars of other sorts. There is, he contends, no general schema exhibiting the relevant identifiability-dependence. In some cases, the dependence is very direct. Thus, we can identify an individual sensation or mental event only by referring to the person whose sensation or mental event it is. In other cases, the dependence is much weaker. We can, for example, refer to a strike or a lock-out without referring to any material bodies or persons; nevertheless, Strawson argues, our ability, in general, to identify things like strikes and lock-outs presupposes our ability to make identifying references to things like persons, tools, and factories. In the case of still other nonsubstantial particulars, there is no dependence at all. Thus, Strawson is willing to grant the possibility of constructing a series of flashes and bangs such that the identification of the members of the series would, in no way, presuppose the ability to identify substances. What he is concerned to deny, however, is that particulars of this sort could function as the basic particulars of a conceptual scheme, in relevant respects, like ours.[57]

Strawson claims that his account is a case of descriptive rather than revisionary metaphysics; it is an attempt "to describe the actual structure of our thought about the world" rather than an attempt "to produce a better structure."[58] While I tend to be sympathetic with many of Strawson's substantive claims, I find this distinction puzzling. Strawson suggests that a large number of historical metaphysicians have been revisionists. Admittedly, some philosophers (Parmenides, for example) would want to label their work revisionary in Strawson's sense, but these philosophers have doubtless been in the minority. Philosophers like Descartes, Leibniz, and Berkeley (all of whom Strawson classifies as revisionists) would probably object to the label. How could one show them wrong here? Is it that their systems are bizarre? But what is to count as bizarre in a philosophical system? Possibly Strawson would say that their accounts are incompatible with the layman's picture of the world; but this is to imply that the layman has a properly philosophical picture, a picture that is at the same level as and can, therefore, compete with the philosopher's account. Surely, this is a dubious claim.

The difficulty here is that, by almost any reasonable criterion, one man's descriptivist will turn out to be another man's revisionist. The use of these labels presupposes and is relative to what we construe to be the correct account of the "actual structure of our thought about the world." But, then, of course, Strawson's distinction has, at most, polemical value; and Strawson does, in fact, use it as a polemical tool. There are contexts (luckily, few) where Strawson gives the impression that to refute a view, it is sufficient to show it revisionary in this or that detail.

Suppose, however, that we can make some minimal sense of the distinction. Why is it that a system of revisionary metaphysics is prima facie objectionable? In *Individuals* Strawson claims to be providing an account of the most general features of our thought about the world, an account of that "massive central core of our thinking which knows no history." But is it not at least conceivable that a revisionary account would be appropriate here? Is it not, at least in principle, possible that there be sound philosophical reasons for supposing that the "massive central core of our thinking" is inadequate, confused, or even inconsistent? Strawson evidently thinks not. As it turns out, these methodological claims do not play a central role in Strawson's arguments; and that, I think, is fortunate.

III. Possible Worlds

A. NEO-EXTENSIONALISM

Although the past decade has seen a number of books and articles exhibiting themes and approaches continuous with the works discussed in the earlier sections of this chapter, the mainstream of work in ontology in the seventies focused on the topic of possible worlds. To understand the recent fascination of that topic, one has to recall the strong extensionalist bias that dominated Anglo-American philosophy in the first half of the century. Intensional idioms, including attributions of modality (whether *de dicto* or *de re*), meaning talk, counterfactual conditionals, talk about intensional entities like attributes and propositions, and attributions of the propositional attitudes, presented special problems for the extensionalist; his task was to show these idioms to be derived forms of discourse. Typically, he took the contents of the actual world as his primitive ontology; insisting that that ontology could be exhaustively characterized in nonintensional terms, he tried to show how the application of the machinery of extensional logic to that primitive ontology was sufficient to generate the full range of intensional notions.

This was a difficult project; and the history of early analytic philosophy is, in large part, the history of the failure of the extensionalist's reductive program. The development of a semantics for modal logic in the late fifties and sixties,[59] however, gave philosophers grounds for thinking that the reduction of the intensional to the extensional was perhaps a real possibility. The intuitive core of the semantics was the Leibnizian idea that ours is just one of infinitely many possible worlds and that it is the totality of possible worlds that constitutes the subject-matter of intensional discourse. Invoking this idea, many philosophers insisted that the classical extensionalist's reductive program failed, not because of the irreducibility of intensional notions, but because of the classical extensionalist's preoccupation with the actual world and its contents. They suggested that by taking the full range of possible worlds, all of them characterized in strictly nonintensional terms, as antecedently given, the ontologist can affect precisely the kind of reduction of the intensional to the extensional that the classical extensionalist was after.

Thus, these neo-extensionalists suggested that we take attributions of *de dicto* modality to involve nothing more problematic than quantification over worlds.[60] To say that a proposition is necessary, they suggested, is just to say that it is true in *every* possible world; whereas, to say that a proposition is possible is to say it is true in *some* world. In a similar fashion, they took attributions of *de re* modality to involve the application of first-order theory to the domain of possible worlds.[61] The claim that an object necessarily exemplifies an attribute, they proposed, can be understood as the claim that it exemplifies that attribute in the actual world and in every world in which it exists; whereas, the claim that an object exemplifies an attribute only contingently can be analyzed as the claim that, while it exemplifies that attribute in the actual world, there is at least one world where it exists and fails to exemplify that attribute.

Furthermore, they suggested that the framework of possible worlds enables us to provide extensional interpretations of the intensional abstract entities (propositions and attributes) that attributions of *de dicto* and *de re* modality bring upon the scene.[62] Classical extensionalists had tried to provide set theoretical interpretations of these abstract entities in terms of their actual extensions, but the fact that numerically distinct attributes and numerically distinct propositions can have the same extensions in the actual world signaled the inadequacy of their approach. Neo-extensionalists insisted that these problems of coextensionality could be overcome if we were to treat intensional abstract entities as set theoretical constructions of their extensions across possible worlds. Thus, they proposed that we treat a proposition as a set of worlds (intuitively as the set of worlds where it is true) or as a function assigning truth values to worlds; and they proposed an analogous interpretation of attributes, holding that a property is a function which assigns to each world a set of objects (intuitively the set of all and only those objects that possess the property in the world) and that an n-place relation is a function from worlds to sets of ordered n-tuples.

These neo-extensionalists also contended that the framework of possible worlds provides us with the resources for explaining what meanings are. Like classical extensionalists, they took the insight that to know the meaning of a nonlogical expression is to have the ability to fix its extension as the warrant for reducing talk of meaning to talk of reference; but appealing to the vastly enriched stock of extensions provided by the framework of possible worlds, they claimed to have the resources for avoiding the notorious problems of traditional referential theories of meaning. Some of these neo-extensionalists combined their set-theoretical interpretation of intensional abstract entities with the long-standing idea that things like propositions, relations, and properties are meanings, and proposed that we identify the meaning of a one-place predicate with a property, the meaning of a two-, three-, or generally n-place predicate with a relation, and the meaning of a declarative sentence with a proposition.[63] Others, convinced that an adequate theory of meaning must confront the fact that the reference of indexical expressions varies systematically with the context, insisted on a more complicated recipe for reducing talk of meaning to talk of extensions, telling us that the meaning of a declarative, for example, is a function that takes us from a bundle of contextual indices (incorporating not just worlds but such additional features as times, places, speakers, and audiences) to truth values or a function that takes us from such a bundle to the proposition that would be expressed by the utterance of the sentence on that bundle.[64]

Neo-extensionalists further saw in the framework of possible worlds the resources for illuminating counterfactual discourse. Classical extensionalists had labored long and hard on counterfactuals, but the results were less than completely satisfactory. Possible worlds theorists suggests that the failures of classical extensionalists here were the result once again of their preoccupation with the actual. Counterfactuals, they claimed, are claims about how things would have gone had circumstances been different and, hence, must be construed as claims about possible worlds other than the actual. Not just any possible worlds, though. The truth of a counterfactual of the form {if it were the case that p, it would be the case that q} hinges only on features of worlds that bear certain relationships of overall resemblance to our world. Initially, it was proposed that for any given counterfactual, there is only one such world, that a counterfactual of the above form is to be understood as the claim that q is true is that p-world that most closely resembles the actual world;[65] subsequently, however, neo-extensionalists became unwilling to embrace the idea that for any given counterfactual, there is a single closest world, and they took counterfactuals to be claims about sets of resembling worlds.[66]

B. THE ONTOLOGY OF WORLDS

Partisans of possible worlds frequently went further, claiming that recalcitrant notions like knowledge and belief are likewise susceptible of extensional analyses;[67] but my remarks about modality, attributes, propositions, meaning, and counterfactuals are sufficient to show how the framework of possible worlds was taken to provide the materials for a reduction of the intensional to the extensional. Pretty clearly, though, the success of all these reductions hinges on the possibility of characterizing that framework in extensional terms; and when we look to the work of neo-extensionalists, we find two approaches to the ontology of possible worlds.

One is suggested in the writings of Richard Montague and Jaakko Hintikka and defended at length by David Lewis.[68] This approach takes the framework of worlds to require a possibilist ontology, one recognizing the existence of things over and above those found in the actual world. In claiming that there are things (possible worlds and their contents) not reducible to the contents of the actual world, proponents of this strategy might seem committed to a contradiction, one formally represented as follows:

$$(\exists x) \sim (\exists y) (x = y)$$

but possibilists like Lewis want to insist that the distinction between the merely possible and the actual has its counterpart in a distinction between two quantifiers, an unrestricted or possibilist quantifier (which we might symbolize as $(\exists_p \ldots)$) ranging over all possible objects, and a restricted or actualist quantifier (we might symbolize it as $(\exists_a \ldots)$) ranging only over the contents of the actual world. Invoking this distinction, Lewis insists that his contention that there are things not found in the actual world can be represented in terms of the following consistent formula:

$$(\exists_p x) \sim (\exists_a y) (x = y)^{69}$$

Lewis, of course, owes us an account of these two quantifiers; if we consider the matter from a theoretically neutral perspective, it should be clear that either of two accounts is possible, for the two quantifiers are *formally* interdefinable. Thus, taking the unrestricted quantifier as primitive, we could introduce the actualist quantifier by way of the following schema:

$$(\exists_a x)(\phi x) = df. \ (\exists_p x)(\phi x \& x \text{ is actual});$$

alternatively, we could take the restricted quantifier as primitive and introduce the possibilist quantifier by saying

$$(\exists_p x)(\phi x) = df \ \Diamond \ (\exists_a x)(\phi x).$$

But while these two schemata are formally on a par, neo-extensionalists like Lewis could not consistently endorse the strategy operative in the second schema, since it takes as given the notion of *de dicto* modality. Lewis seems to recognize this and takes the possibilist quantifier as primitive.

That strategy has as its intuitive core the idea that in the basic sense of "exists" all possibilia exist; but confronted with this idea, we want to ask for an account of the distinction between the merely possible and the actual. Lewis's answer is that there is no ontologically significant difference here. He denies that the predicate "actual" expresses any nonrelational property that our world has and other possible worlds lack. "Actual," he tells us, is an indexical expression, one whose reference depends upon "circumstances of utterance, to wit the world where the utterance is located."[70] Thus, when I identify the world as actual, I am not singling it out as that world among all worlds which has some special ontic status; I am merely picking it out as that world in which my utterance occurs. And, as Lewis tells us, inhabitants of other worlds have as much right as we do to call their respective worlds actual. But, then, the notion of existence expressed by the possibilist quantifier is not just the basic notion of existence; it is the only notion. Talk about the actual is just more possibilist talk supplemented by token reflexive reference, so that for Lewis, all worlds and their inhabitants are equally real, equally existent.

This democratic attitude toward worlds is reinforced by a refusal to reduce talk about worlds to anything more basic. According to Lewis, possible worlds other than the actual world are just more things of the same kind as the actual world, "differing from the actual world only in what goes on at them."[71] Such an approach might seem bizarre or counterintuitive; but Lewis insists that his possibilism is just common sense dressed up in philosophical jargon. He tells us that we all believe that *there are* ways things could have gone but didn't, and he insists that the possibilist's account is just a way of codifying this common-sense belief.[72]

Commonsensical or not, Lewis's possibilism represents one attempt to provide an extensionalist interpretation of possible worlds, for essentially what he has done is to take each of the possible worlds as primitive. Since he believes that alternative worlds are ontologically on a par with the total ontology of the classical extensionalist, he can be confident that embracing the framework of possible worlds commits one to nothing intensional among his primitives.

A quite different attempt to provide an extensionalist account of possible worlds is found in the work of Max Cresswell.[73] Cresswell is an actualist, in that he holds that there are no objects distinct from those making up the actual world; nonetheless, he insists that the complete framework of possible worlds can be constructed from materials found in the actual world. Cresswell's approach is atomistic: he insists that our world is made up of certain "atoms" and that their being arranged in a certain way is what gives the actual world its unique character. Other possible worlds are simply different arrangements of some or all of the "atoms" making up our world; according to Cresswell, the notion of an arrangement can be represented in the straightforwardly extensionalist terms of set theory. Thus, suppose we take certain physical particles to be the "atoms" making up our world; then, possible worlds can be represented as very complex sets of ordered n-tuples, which have the effect of assigning spatio-temporal location to the relevant physical particles. Following Cresswell, I have used a materialist example; but as Cresswell points out, his atomistic or combinatorialist strategy does not commit us to materialism. One might, for example, be a phenomenalist and insist that the "atoms" making up the actual world are sense-data, or one might be a Cartesian insisting upon a mixed ontology of spiritual and physical "atoms."

But however he decides on these grand-scale issues, the proponent of Cresswell's strategy will insist that the framework of worlds can be characterized in extensional terms. He will hold that each of his "atoms" can be identified in nonintensional terms and that the arrangement of "atoms" that gives us the actual world can be represented within the extensional framework of set theory; and since he holds that alternative possible worlds have the same kind of structure as the actual world, he will insist that the combinatorialist strategy gives the neo-extensionalist the requisite nonintensional interpretation of the framework of possible worlds.

C. PROBLEMS WITH NEO-EXTENSIONALISM

Neo-extensionalists have occasionally suggested other ways of interpreting that framework;[74] but their suggestions have tended to be sketchy, and the interpretations they have outlined, far less promising than Lewis's possibilism and Cresswell's combinatorialism. Consequently, where their criticisms have meant to show the poverty of an extensionalist treatment of possible worlds, opponents of neo-extensionalism have focused their critical efforts on the two accounts I have just outlined.

The central criticism of the combinatorialist strategy is that it fails to provide us with enough possible worlds, that it makes far too much metaphysically necessary.[75] According to the combinatorialist, a specification of the "atoms" making up our world provides us with the limits of metaphysical possibility, but then he has to deny the possibility of things or states of affairs that cannot be constructed out of those "atoms." Thus, whatever objects he identifies as atomic, the combinatorialist must hold that it is metaphysically impossible that there be even one more of those objects than there actually are;[76] and once he makes a choice as to the qualitative character of those "atoms," he has to deny the possibility of things of kinds not reducible to things with the chosen qualitative character. Thus, the combinatorialist who opts for a physicalist interpretation of atoms must deny the possibility of things like sense data and immaterial substances; whereas, the philosopher who endorses a phenomenalistic version of combinatorialism is forced to hold to the impossibility of irreducibly physical objects. Critics have pointed out, however, that it is counterintuitive to suppose that there couldn't have been more elementary physical entities, more sense data, or more Cartesian egos that there actually are and that it is hazardous to stipulate the impossibility of things qualitatively irreducible to anything actual.

Lewis's possibilism, on the other hand, typically evokes incredulous stares; but where they have invoked criticism rather than rhetoric, Lewis's opponents have focused on his treatment of transworld identity. Lewis denies that a single object can inhabit more than one possible world. His reasoning seems to be as follows: since no two worlds are qualitatively indiscernible, were an object, x, to exist in two different worlds, there would be at least one property, ϕ, such that x as existing in one of the worlds would have ϕ and x as existing in the other would lack ϕ; but since all worlds are equally real, the propositions true in the various worlds all have an equal claim to truth simpliciter; hence the suggestion that a single object exists in distinct possible worlds involves a contradiction.[77]

Transworld identity is not, however, a mere luxury for the neo-extensionalist. Since he wants to analyze modal truths about individuals in terms of nonmodal truths about those individuals as they exist in worlds other than the actual, the neo-extensionalist's strategy appears to require something like the notion of transworld identity. Lewis agrees, but insists that the neo-extensionalist can get by with what he calls the counterpart relation. While denying that an object can exist in two or more worlds, Lewis claims that an object existing in one world can have counterparts in other worlds, where a thing's counterpart is an object resembling it closely in content and context, more closely than do other objects in its world; and he insists that modal claims about objects can be analyzed in terms of nonmodal claims about their counterparts.[78]

Critics have agreed that Lewis's democratic realism about worlds precludes any relationship tighter than the counterpart relation, but they have denied that that relation is strong enough to carry out the neo-extensionalist program. Saul Kripke, for example, argues that the strategy of counterparts is counterintuitive.[79] According to Kripke, we believe that modal discourse about an individual is discourse about *that* individual and no other. He asks us to consider a certain counterfactual about Nixon: the proposition that had Nixon bribed a certain senator, he would have succeeded in having Carswell confirmed for the Supreme Court. Now, Kripke tells us that were Nixon, after the fact, to have supposed this counterfactual true, he might have regretted not offering the bribe. Kripke insists that such regrets are perfectly intelligible; he points out, however, that on the counterpart theorist's reading of the counterfactual (as a noncounterfactual claim about a man distinct from but closely resembling Nixon), those regrets would make no sense.

Fred Feldman and Alvin Plantinga raise a related but different objection to the strategy of counterparts.[80] Both ask us to consider a pair of actual objects, x and y, belonging to some single kind, K. They point out that both x and y could have been quite different, that it is possible that x resembles y as it actually is more closely than x as it actually is and, likewise, that y resembles x as it actually is more closely than y as it actually is. Both Feldman and Plantinga point out, however, that this possibility cannot be captured on the counterpart theorist's analysis of modal discourse; for the counterpart theorist insists that the truth of a modal claim about an individual hinges on the truth of a nonmodal claim about one of its counterparts; but since an object's counterpart is always an object resembling it "closely in content and context," no such nonmodal truths are forthcoming in the case of x and y.

Critics have, however, pointed to another kind of difficulty for the neo-extensionalist; it is not simply that the neo-extensionalist fails to provide us with an adequate account of possible worlds. Even if he were to succeed in this, his overall project would fail, since the required reductions of the intensional to the extensional do not succeed. Here, critics have raised difficulties with almost every one of the proposed reductions set out earlier, but the most frequent charge has been the inadequacy of the neo-extensionalist's treatment of propositions.[81] As we have seen, he takes propositions to be sets of worlds or functions from worlds to truth values. The objection is that this strategy fails to provide sufficiently fine-grained identity-conditions for propositions. Given the extensionality of sets, this strategy commits us to the idea that where a proposition, *p,* and a proposition, *q* are necessarily equivalent, *p* is identical with *q*; and this forces us to say that there is just one necessarily true proposition and just one necessary falsehood. Critics point out that such a consequence runs counter to our intuitions about propositional identity, which tell us that the proposition that two plus two equal four is distinct from the proposition that all bachelors are unmarried and, likewise, that the proposition that two plus six equals seventy-nine and the proposition that every object is self-diverse are two distinct propositions.

Now, it is tempting to construe this as an isolated problem for the neo-extensionalist, to see it as a single case where his reductive program fails. In fact, the difficulty has a generality outstripping that of an isolated counterexample; for if the neo-extensionalist treatment of proposition fails, it is difficult to see how much of his program can be salvaged. The notion of a proposition is crucial, and an extensionalist analysis of propositions would appear to be a requirement for the successful reduction of most intensional phenomena. The analysis of *de dicto* modality presupposes an analysis of propositions, since the *de dicto* modalities have to be seen as predicates of or operators on propositions. Likewise, the various attitudes (under at least one reading) take propositions as objects; propositions are generally construed as the meanings of at least some sentences; and counterfactuals represent one kind of proposition. Any difficulties in the neo-extensionalist's treatment of propositions is likely, then, to have serious consequences for his overall project.

Neo-extensionalists have been sensitive to the significance of this objection and have offered a number of strategies for responding to it. One such strategy is outlined in Robert Stalnaker's "Propositions."[82] For reasons that will become clear later, Stalnaker is not properly classified as a neo-extensionalist; but he does want to defend a possible worlds analysis of propositions as functions from worlds to truth values. He admits that the approach appears counterintuitive, but bites the bullet, insisting that there is just one necessary truth and one necessary falsehood; and he argues that what appear to be intuitions suggesting a diversity of necessarily equivalent propositions are really intuitions about something else. Stalnaker's focus is mathematics, where opposing epistemic attitudes toward different mathematical assertions and our practice of providing different proofs for diverse mathematical claims suggest that there is more than one mathematical truth. His response is to claim that where an individual assents to one true mathematical assertion but dissents from another, he is not expressing different beliefs about a single proposition; his beliefs are about sentences, beliefs about whether different sentences express the single mathematical truth. Likewise, Stalnaker tells us, the need for fresh proofs in mathematics derives from the need to demonstrate, in the case of different sentences, their expression of the one true proposition of mathematics.

This is a courageous strategy, but it is not one Stalnaker is still willing to defend.[83] It is not difficult to see why he should have doubts about it. Since it interprets much of our thinking about necessary truth/falsehood in terms of thought about sentences, the approach has difficulty in dealing with the fact that individuals using different languages can have the same beliefs about the necessary and the impossible. Thus, when a child whose only language is English comes to have a belief he expresses by assertively uttering, "Two plus two equals four," he comes to have precisely the same belief that a French child might express by saying, "Deux et deux font quatre." Likewise, when a Japanese mathematician offers a proof for his professional peers, he can be proving the *same* thing proved by a German mathematician, in spite of the fact that the two offer their proofs and theorems in different languages.

Most neo-extensionalists would agree, and most have tried to show that a possible worlds analysis can succeed in representing the distinction among necessarily equivalent propositions. One strategy here is to invoke impossible worlds. The idea is that while necessarily equivalent propositions share the same truth value across all possible worlds, their truth values diverge across impossible worlds, so that the neo-extensionalist can succeed in providing a set theoretical representation of the diversity of necessarily equivalent propositions. There is, however, a technical difficulty with this approach. The neo-extensionalist obviously needs many impossible worlds, as many as are required to distinguish all necessary truths and all necessary falsehoods. Unfortunately, it is plausible to suppose that there is just *one* impossible world. Worlds have a maximality property; they are *total* ways things might (or might not) have gone; but for every world, w, and every proposition, p, it must be the case that w's obtaining entails p or entails the negation of p. It is, however, impossible for an impossible world to obtain; hence, on any standard notion of entailment, an impossible world's obtaining entails every proposition; and given an inescapable assumption about the qualitative diversity of different worlds, that means that there is only one impossible world.

One might try to handle this difficulty by joining the relevant logicians and appealing to some tighter notion of entailment; but this move is hazardous, since it is notoriously difficult to identify a notion of relevant entailment that makes all the discriminations we want to make while preserving all the logical relations we want to preserve. Alternatively, one might follow Hintikka and deny that all worlds have a maximality property.[84] Hintikka insists on what he calls "small worlds," situations in which a given proposition might be true or false without prejudice to the truth value of other propositions. Such a strategy will work technically, since the neo-extensionalist can simply postulate a small world for every single necessary truth and every single necessary falsehood; but while conceding this, I doubt that Hintikka's strategy does much to vindicate the neo-extensionalist's overall reductive project. What is that small world, for example, which distinguishes the proposition that two plus two equals four from all the other necessary truths? It is that world in which two plus two equals four and nothing else obtains; and such a world begins to look disconcertingly like the intensional entity we were trying to eliminate. The small world in question just is that proposition, so that talk of reduction here is at best misleading.

Yet another strategy for dealing with necessarily equivalent propositions is outlined in Max Cresswell's *Logic and Language*.[85] Cresswell begins with sets of worlds, calling them propropositions, and he tells us that propropositions can enter into sets which he calls heavens. Propositions, he concludes, are sets of heavens. To see how this approach works, consider a mini-universe with just two worlds, W_1 and W_2; our task is to represent the distinction between two necessary truths, p and q, in this universe. Our mini-universe has only four propropositions: $\{W_1\}$, $\{W_2\}$, $\{W_1, W_2\}$, and the null set, which can be disregarded since our concern is with necessary truths. The three remaining propropositions yield the following heavens: $\{\{W_1\}\}$, $\{\{W_2\}\}$, $\{\{W_1 W_2\}\}$, $\{\{W_1\}\{W_1, W_2\}\}$, $\{\{W_2\}\{W_1, W_2\}\}$, $\{\{W_1\}\{W_2\}\}$, and $\{\{W_1\}\{W_2\}\{W_1, W_2\}\}$. What we want is sets of heavens that accommodate the root intuition of the possible worlds account, yet discriminate between p and q. Since p and q are necessary truths, the heaven $\{\{W_1\}\{W_2\}\{W_1 W_2\}\}$ will enter into their representation; but with the remaining heavens before us, we have the materials for representing the difference between p and q. We can say, for example, that $p = \{\{\{W_1\}\{W_2\}\{W_1, W_2\}\}\{\{W_1\}\}\}$ and that $q = \{\{\{W_1\}\{W_2\}\{W_1, W_2\}\}\{\{W_2\}\}\}$.

Our mini-universe, then, provides us with the materials for discriminating between p and q; but since it is plausible to assume that there is an infinity of possible worlds, it is reasonable to assume that the pool of heavens is sufficiently large to yield a set theoretical treatment of all propositions. But while Cresswell's strategy succeeds on this score, it is difficult to overlook the artificiality of its success. Reverting to the example provided by our mini-universe, we note that the heaven $\{\{W_1\}\{W_2\}\{W_1, W_2\}$

gives us what, from the neo-extensionalist's perspective, is a natural representation of the content of p and q; but we need more, so we select the additional heavens $\{\{W_1\}\}$ and $\{\{W_2\}\}$. Notice, however, that there was no intuitive reason for choosing just these heavens; $\{\{W_1\}\{W_1, W_2\}\}$ and $\{\{W_2\}\{W_1, W_2\}\}$ would have enabled us to represent the difference between p and q just as well, and with just as much intuitive foundation. Indeed, when we reflect on the matter, there is no reason why we had to select heavens to give the discrimination we were after; any two distinct things would have worked. We chose heavens only because we were claiming to provide possible worlds analysis of propositions; but the fact is that the intuitions behind a possible worlds account were exhausted by the appeal to the heaven $\{\{W_1\}\{W_2\}\{W_1, W_2\}\}$; the choice of the additional heavens was both arbitrary and artificial.

The last strategy I want to discuss is less artificial; it is the approach outlined by David Lewis in his impressive paper "General Semantics."[86] As Lewis admits, the approach has its roots in Carnap's notion of intensional isomorphism.[87] Lewis's concern is with a theory of meaning. He tells us provisionally that the meaning of a declarative sentence is a function from a bundle of indices (including worlds, times, places, speakers, etc.) to truth values and, then, notes that this account has the disadvantage of making sentences like "Two plus two equals four" and "All bachelors are unmarried" synonymous. Toward refining the theory, Lewis distinguishes between semantically simple and complex expressions, telling us that whereas the meaning of a simple expression is a function from indices to extensions, the meaning of a complex is an ordered n-tuple of the meanings of its semantic constituents. But, then, since sentences with the same truth value on all index-bundles are constructed out of semantically nonequivalent simples arranged in some unique order, necessarily coextensional sentences have different meanings or express different propositions.

Lewis's approach is not unattractive. It is rooted in the intuitively appealing idea that the meaning of a declarative sentence has an intensional structure, and it succeeds in capturing that insight within the extensional framework of set theory. But despite its appeal, the approach has its drawbacks. First, it forces us to endorse a distinction between semantical simples and complexes that many philosophers would find problematic. Second, it commits us to the assumption that no two semantically simple terms are coextensive across worlds; and even defenders of the notion of semantic simplicity have been willing to call that view into question.[88] Finally, in its attempt to provide a sufficiently fine-grained analysis of sentential meanings or propositions, Lewis's account goes overboard; for as Lewis himself points out, his approach forces us to discriminate meanings/propositions even in cases where, intuitively at least, we are not antecedently disposed to do so.[89] Thus, since he identifies the meaning/proposition associated with a sentence with an ordered n-tuple of the meanings of its parts, Lewis has to claim that the proposition expressed by a sentence of the form p or q is numerically different from that expressed by a corresponding sentence of the form q or p and that a sentence of the form p is heteronymous with a corresponding sentence of the form $\sim \sim p$. Lewis does not find these results problematic. He sees in them a kind of embarrassment of riches, as though his account had isolated a concept of meaning/proposition even more subtle than that at work in the tradition. One might wonder, though, whether this response is overly sanguine; for if the neo-extensionalist's aim is to provide an analysis of *our* notions of sentential meaning and proposition, these counterintuitive results suggest that, as attractive as it is, Lewis's approach has failed to do this.

D. INTENSIONALISM AND POSSIBLE WORLDS

The difficulties I have been discussing in the past two sections are thorny enough to have convinced some that the framework of possible worlds is a philosophical dead-end; but a number of philosophers, while repudiating the attempts of Montague, Hintikka, Lewis, Cresswell and others to reduce the intensional to the extensional, have wanted to hold onto the framework of possible worlds. They continue to find talk of possible worlds congenial, in part because they want to take a realistic interpretation of the semantics of modal logic, and in part because they agree with Lewis that the notion of a possible world has its roots in noncontroversial prephilosophical intuitions. Nonetheless, they want to deny that the framework of worlds can be characterized independently of an appeal to intensional notions. They insist that whatever theoretical role it plays, appeal to the framework presupposes that one or more intensional notion be taken as primitive.

Robert Stalnaker's defense of the framework in "Possible Worlds" provides one example of this approach.[90] Stalnaker's concern is Lewis's possibilism; and while he agrees that the notion of a possible world is rooted in prephilosophical intuitions about total ways things might have been, he insists that they can be captured within the context of an actualist ontology. As he sees it, the expression "the actual world" is a device for referring to everything there is, and he concludes that the totality of possible worlds is to be found within the actual world. What is needed, then, is some concept that allows us to interpret worlds in this way; according to Stalnaker, the concept of a property does the job. Properties are instantiable entities, but they exist independently of their being instantiated. Hence, if we construe worlds as certain properties, their possibility as the instantiability of those properties, and actuality as the instantiation of just one of them, we succeed in providing an actualist interpretation of worlds. Stalnaker insists that such an account conforms to the intuitive roots of talk about worlds, since possible worlds are the nonphilosopher's *ways* things might have gone, and talk about *ways* is most naturally construed in terms of the correlative concepts of property and instantiation.

For Stalnaker, then, possible worlds are certain instantiable properties, properties with a maximality condition built into them; and according to Stalnaker, the proper course for the ontologist is to take worlds understood in this way as primitive. The resulting approach is, of course, intensionalist, since the modal notions of a property and instantiability are taken as basic; but while Stalnaker's approach to the framework of worlds is not extensional, he is willing to use the framework as a tool for the analysis of intensional notions other than those primitives. Thus, we find Stalnaker using possible worlds to analyze the notion of counterfactuality, the notion of a proposition, and other critical semantical concepts.[91]

The idea that the concepts of property and instantiation are presupposed by the appeal to possible worlds can be found in other writers. Hector Neri-Castañeda, for example, wants to provide a bundle-theoretic interpretation of ordinary objects as "clusters" of properties. His view is that what Aristotelians have called substances are sets of properties, whose members enter into an empirical/contingent relation called consubstantiation. Like Stalnaker, Castañeda believes that the existence of properties is not tied to their instantiation; but, then, there are sets of properties that yield a complete conception of an individual but are such that their members are not consubstantiated. Merely possible objects can be identified with such sets; and since those sets can, by a diversity of operations, be partitioned off in various ways, they provide us with the materials required for an actualist interpretation of possible worlds.[92]

Castañeda's approach differs from Stalnaker's in being constructivist. Stalnaker postulates macro-properties with a maximality property, takes them as primitive, and identifies them with worlds; whereas, Castañeda takes ordinary, run-of-the-mill properties as primitive and sees worlds as complex constructs of those primitives. An approach with some similarities to Castañeda's is outlined in Nicholas Rescher's *A Theory of Possibility*.[93] While not a bundle theorist, Rescher agrees that the ordinary notion of a property provides us with the foundation for the framework of possible worlds. What is unique in Rescher's account, however, is his emphasis on *our* role in the constitution of the framework. Castañeda is a Platonist about properties; consequently, he holds that merely possible individuals and the worlds they constitute exist independently of our conceptual activities. Rescher, on the other hand, sees the framework of worlds as bound up with our conceptual acts of hypothesizing, supposing, projecting, and the like. As he sees it, we begin with qualitatively complete specifications of actually existing objects and, by hypothetical alterations in the properties making up those specifications, we generate descriptions of objects that are conceptual variants on actual individuals. By further hypothetical alterations of these new descriptions, we arrive at characterizations of objects that are so far removed from the actual as to constitute characterizations of merely possible objects. Then, taking these characterizations of variants on actual objects and of mere possibilia, we perform projective acts of combination and collection that give rise to the conception of alternative possible worlds. For Rescher, then, possible worlds are bult out of the objects and properties constituting the world as we know it, but their existence is tied to conceptual acts of hypothesis, projection, and combination.

A conceptualist approach to worlds is also suggested by some of Kripke's remarks about the ontology of possible worlds.[94] In dealing with identity across worlds, Kripke tells us that there can be nothing problematic in an actual object's existing in some other possible world, since possible worlds are counterfactual situations that have just those features we stipulate them to have. Hence, if our concern is with a possible world in which Nixon refuses to resign the presidency, there can be no question of Nixon's existing in that world; by our stipulation, the world just is one in which Nixon exists. Now, these contentions are subject to a variety of interpretations; but on one interpretation, they amount to the claim that possible worlds exist only as conceptual products of our stipulative, counterfactual thinking.

Alvin Plantinga's influential writings on possible worlds take us back to the Platonism of Stalnaker and Castañeda.[95] I discussed his ideas on this topic earlier in this chapter, so I shall make only such remarks as are required to relate his work to the debate over the past decade. Like Stalnaker, Plantinga takes possible worlds to be primitive entities, irreducible to anything more basic. They are maximally obtainable states of affairs; but unlike Stalnaker, Plantinga provides us with an account of the maximality property of those states of affairs that enables us to understand what worlds are in terms of the more familiar notion of a nonmaximal state of affairs.

In any case, worlds are abstract entities — states of affairs; their possibility consists in their obtainability; and the actuality of our world consists in its being the single maximally determinate state of affairs that obtains. The account is actualist, since states of affairs actually exist whether or not they obtain. Furthermore, it is intensionalist, since it refuses to provide any further account of the notions of a state of affairs or obtainability; but in fact its intensionalism goes much deeper, for Plantinga refuses to use the framework of possible worlds as a tool in the reduction of any intensional phenomena. Thus, he eschews possible worlds analyses of things like properties and propositions; he takes haecceities or individual essences as basic; and he expresses doubts about the possibility of a noncircular elimination of counterfactual discourse by reference to possible worlds.[96]

Plantinga's suggestion that possible worlds constitute a species of states of affairs suggests a slightly different approach. As Plantinga himself points out, talk about states of affairs and their obtaining is closely related to talk about propositions and their truth. Indeed, some philosophers have insisted that the two forms of discourse constitute discourse about one and the same thing. This suggests that we construe possible worlds as certain propositions, maximally possible propositions. Such an approach is suggested by Arthur Prior and elaborated by Kit Fine.[97] Prior refuses to see talk about worlds as more basic than modal discourse; but he agrees that such talk makes sense if it is seen as resting on the prior notions of a proposition and *de dicto* modality. Thus, Prior tells us that if we take these two notions as given, we can define a possible world as a proposition, q, such that it is possible (a) that q is true and (b) that, for any proposition, p, if p is true, q entails p.

If we leave aside the contentions about conceptual priority, Prior's account appears much like Plantinga's. One significant difference, however, consists in what Plantinga calls Prior's existentialism, his belief that the existence of a genuinely singular proposition requires the existence of the individual/s it is directly about.[98] Singular propositions about contingent individuals, then, turn out to be contingent themselves on Prior's account; whereas, on Plantinga's view, all propositions, general as well as singular, are necessary beings. Prior, on the other hand, wants to say that in those worlds where an individual does not exist, singular propositions about that individual do not exist either and, hence, are neither true or false. Such a proposal requires significant changes in the standard rules for modal inference; and Prior attempted to construct a modal logic, called Q, that systematizes those changes.[99]

But despite this difference, the accounts of both Plantinga and Prior give a holistic view of worlds, identifying them with irreducible wholes—states of affairs (in Plantinga's case) and propositions (in Prior's case). Robert Adams agrees with Prior in seeing talk about worlds as talk about propositions;[100] but his account is constructivist, taking worlds to be sets of ordinary, nonmaximal propositions. For Adams, a possible world is a set such that (a) for every proposition, p, either p or its contradictory belongs to the set and (b) it is possible that all the members of the set be jointly true; the actual world, for Adams, is that possible world all of whose members are true. This view appears familiar; it seems to identify worlds with abstract objects–sets of propositions and, hence, appears to make worlds sets of Platonic objects. In fact, what is unique in Adams's account is the suggestion that his interpretation of possible worlds is, subject to certain theological assumptions, amenable to a nominalistic interpretation: Adams wants to deny that propositions are irreducible ontic points, insisting that talk of propositions can be construed as talk about Divine Conceptual Acitivity. As Adams admits, there are problems with this interpretation of propositions; but rather than focus on those problems, I want, in closing, to point out how Adams's apparently intensionalist account of possible worlds has brought us back full-circle to the neo-exensionalist interpretation of possible worlds. If talk of propositions and their possible truth can be interpreted as talk about God's thought, then Adams's interpretation of the framework of worlds makes it the straightforwardly extensionalist framework that philosophers such as Montague, Hintikka, Lewis, and Cresswell claim it to be; nor does the intrusion of talk about God's thought compromise this extensionality; for what makes the propositional attitudes intensional is precisely the finitude of human thinkers. The thought of an omniscient, necessarily consistent being is, to use Quine's distinction, transparent and not opaque.

Notes

1. For bibliographies on the issues covered by this survey, see Guido Küng, *Ontology and the Logistic Analysis of Language*, tr. by E. Mays (Dordrecht, Holland, 1967) and Michael Loux, ed., *Universals and Particulars* (New York, 1970).

2. A general account of the problem of universals is presented in Loux's "The Problem of Universals" in *Universals and Particulars,* op. cit. Kung's *Ontology and the Logistic Analysis of Language,* op. cit., provides an excellent account of 20th-century work on the problem. For accounts of classical positions on the problem, see Richard Aaron, *The Theory of Universals,* 2nd ed. (London 1967); A. D. Woozley, "Universals," *Encyclopedia of Philosophy,* vol. 8, pp. 194–206; G.E.M. Anscombe and P. T. Geach, *Three Philosophers* (Oxford, 1963); and Farhang Zabeeh, *Universals* (The Hague, 1966).

3. For a discussion of issues central to this sort of approach see Rolf Eberle, "Universals as Designata of Predicates," *American Philosophical Quarterly* 6 (1969), pp. 151–57.

4. See, for example, ch. IV, X, XI, XII, and XIII of *Meaning and Existence* (Madison,

1960). Also see ch. II, VI, VII, VIII, and IX of *Logic and Reality* (Madison, 1964) and Pt. I of *Realism: A Critique of Brentano and Meinong* (Madison, 1967). For attempts to clarify and defend Bergmann's position on the problem of universals, see Edwin Allaire, "Existence, Independence, and Universals," *The Review of Metaphysics* 14 (1960), pp. 485–96 and Reinhardt Grossman, "Conceptualism," *The Review of Metaphysics* 14 (1960), pp. 243–54. These and other papers having a Bergmannian flavor are collected in *Essays in Ontology* (The Hague, 1963).

5. For a critical examination of this kind of argument, see Nicholas Wolterstorff, "Objections to Predicative Relations," *American Philosophical Quarterly* 7 (1970), pp. 238–45.

6. 'Ineffability, Ontology, and Method," *The Philosophical Review* 69 (1960), pp. 18–40; the paper reappeared as ch. II of *Logic and Reality,* op. cit. In this paper Bergmann wants to make the further claim that certain logical notions, such as the truth-functional connectives, have an ontological status. In "Existence and Generality," *Theoria,* vol. 28 (1962), pp. 1–26 later ch. III of *Logic and Reality,* op. cit., he argues that what is expressed by the universal quanitifier, as well as what is expressed by the existential quantifier, subsists. An interesting discussion of Bergmann's views on subsistence and ineffability is found in John Peterson, "Bergmann's Hidden Essences," *The Review of Metaphysics* 22 (1969), pp. 640–57.

7. "Naming and Saying," ch. VIII of Sellars' *Science, Perception, and Reality* (London, 1963).

8. "Universals and Metaphysical Realism," *Monist* 47 (1963), pp. 211–46.

9. See Part II of *Individuals* (London, 1959). For a criticism of Strawson's account, see ch. V of John Searle, *Speech Acts* (London, 1969). In this same chapter Searle briefly argues that realism is true, but he contends that the truth of the view is essentially tautological. For a criticism of Searle's own version of realism, see Gerald Vision, "Searle on The Nature of Universals," *Analysis* 20 (1970), pp. 155–60.

10. "Form and Existence" originally appeared in *Proceedings of the Aristotelian Society* 55 (1954), pp. 251–72. The revised version appears in *God and the Soul* (London, 1969). A similar account is presented in "Aquinas" in *Three Philosophers,* op. cit. For a statement of Geach's recent doubts about the position, see "What Actually Exists," *Proceedings of the Aristotelian Society,* Suppl. 42 (1968), pp. 7–16, reprinted in *God and the Soul.* For a response to this paper, see R. H. Stoothoff, "What Actually Exists," *Proceedings of the Aristotelian Society,* Suppl. 42 (1968), pp. 17–30.

11. Wolterstorff's paper originally appeared in Loux's *Universals and Particulars,* op. cit. It is part of a book, *On Universals* (The University of Chicago Press, 1970).

12. *Modes of Referring and the Problem of Universals* (Berkeley, 1961).

13. In the interests of space, I oversimplify a bit here. Shwayder does not claim that for every primary use and its corresponding secondary use, there is a single word playing both roles. This does happen with words like "red"; but Shwayder realizes that in the case of expressions like "wise" and "wisdom," we distinguish between word playing predicative role and word playing referential role. What Shwayder is anxious to show is that even in these cases, the predicative use is primary and lays the foundation for the referential use.

14. *Resemblance and Identity* (Bloomington, 1966).

15. *Word and Object* (Cambridge, Mass., 1960). For a discussion of Quine's views here, see C. S. Chihara, "Our Ontological Commitment to Universals," *Nous* 2 (1968), pp. 25–46.

16. The criterion was originally presented in the classic paper "On What There Is," *From A Logical Point of View* (Cambridge, Mass., 1953). Most recently, Quine defends the criterion (in a modified version) in "Existence and Quantification" (originally published in Joseph Margolis, *Fact and Existence* [Toronto, 1966] and later reprinted as ch. IV of *Ontological Relativity* [New York, 1969]). As he points out in that paper, his criterion of ontological commitment presupposes a referential or objectual, as opposed to a substitutional, interpretation of quantification. Very roughly, the referentialist wants to construe objects in the world as the values of bound variables. He wants to say, for example, that an existential quantification is true if and only if there is at least one object satisfying the predicates embedded in the quantification. The substitutionalist, on the other hand, takes linguistic expressions (names of objects) as the values of bound variables; he says that an existential quantification is true if and only if there is a name which, when substituted for the variable bound by the existential quantifier, makes the open sentence following that quantifier true. Quine claims that "where substitutional quantification serves, ontology lacks point"; he has, however, reasons which are independent of the question of ontological commitment for rejecting a substitutionalist interpretation of quantification.

17. *Proceedings of the Aristotelian Society* 61 (1960–1961), pp. 207–22. A great deal of

material has appeared on this topic in recent years. Some papers include K. Campbell, "Family Resemblance Predicates," *American Philosophical Quarterly* 2 (1965), pp. 238–44; Haig Khatchadourian, "Common Names and Family Resemblances," *Philosophy and Phenomenological Research* 18 (1957-1958), pp. 341–58; L. Pompa, "Family Resemblances," *The Philosophical Quarterly* 17 (1967), pp. 63–69; Robert Richman, "Something Common," *The Journal of Philosophy* 59 (1962), pp. 821–30.

18. *Mind* 76 (1967), pp. 365–81.

19. Thompson distinguishes between Platonic entities and abstract entities (things like numbers, colors, etc.). In an earlier paper, "Abstract Entities," *The Philosophical Review* 69 (1960), pp. 331–54, he argues that as regards abstract entities, to be is to be an element in a system. In the present paper, he alludes to this criterion and construes it as establishing that abstract entities present no real problem for the nominalist. Commitment to the existence of an abstract entity need not involve more than commitment to the existence of a certain system (e.g., elementary arithmetic or color theory).

20. *The Philosophical Review* 69 (1960), pp. 183–200.

21. *Mind* 69 (1960), pp. 499–533; also found in *Science, Perception, and Reality,* op. cit., ch. VIII.

22. Very generally, Sellars's rejection of Quine's criterion of ontological commitment has its source in Sellars's unwillingness to accept a referential interpretation of quantification. It is not altogether clear whether Sellars is a substitutionalist, but he does think it a mistake to read the existential quanitifier in the traditional ways as "There exists. . . ." He suggests instead that we read the quantifier as "Some . . ."; and he contends that this is the proper reading regardless of the style of variable bound by the quantifier. Nevertheless, he wants to say that the existential quanifier does play the role of ascribing existence in those cases where the variables it binds take as their values singular terms. Sellars's inclination to call linguistic expressions the values of variables leads one to believe that he is an out-and-out substitutionalist. My doubts about the label are due to some negative remarks I have heard Sellars make about the appropriateness of the term.

23. For further discussion of this and other topics central to the realism-nominalism debate, see Sellars's *Science and Metaphysics* (London, 1968). Although this book provides a synthesis of Sellars's views on a wide variety of topics, it tends to be very difficult reading and is best approached only after one has an acquaintance with some of Sellars's earlier papers.

24. The proposed translation might be contested on the grounds that it makes reference to a position and is not, therefore, completely nominalistic. Sellars would argue, I think, that propositions can be handled by the method of linguistic types, described in the following paragraphs.

25. *The Review of Metaphysics* 16 (1963), pp. 627–71; also reprinted as ch. IX of Sellars's *Philosophical Perspectives* (Illinois, 1967).

26. For a criticism of Sellars's reduction-schema for distributive singular terms, see Wolterstorff's "On the Nature of Universals," discussed earlier in this survey.

27. Quine's views on this topic are expressed in ch. II of *Word and Object,* op. cit., and ch. I–III of *Ontological Relativity,* op. cit.

28. For a general account of the problems considered in this section, see Michael Loux, "Particulars and Their Individuation," in *Universals and Particulars,* op. cit. See also Douglas Long, "Particulars and Their Qualities," *The Philosophical Quarterly* 18 (1968), pp. 193–206.

29. See ch. XI and XIV of *Meaning and Existence,* op. cit., ch. V of *Logic and Reality,* op. cit., and ch. VI of *Realism,* op. cit. For discussions of Bergmann's views here, see Reinhardt Grossman, "Particulars and Time," *Essays in Ontology* and John Kearns, "Substance and Time," *The Journal of Philosophy* 67 (1970), pp. 277–89.

30. For Bergmann's account of his rejection of phenomenalism, see "Realistic Postscript" in *Logic and Reality,* op. cit.

31. See especially ch. IV of *Realism,* op. cit.

32. *Philosophical Studies,* vol. 14 (1963), pp. 1–8. This paper spawned an interesting controversy. V. C. Chappel ("Particulars Re-Clothed," ibid., vol. 15 [1964], pp. 60–64), criticized Allaire's account and suggested that bare particulars are unnecessary as individuators since space and time suffice to individuate qualitiatively indistinguishable objects. Allaire responded ("Another Look at Bare Particulars," ibid., vol. 16 (1965), pp. 16–21) with the claim that differences in spatio-temporal location themselves presuppose numerical diversity and, therefore, bare particulars, a claim which J. W. Meiland criticized in "Do Relatives Individuate?" ibid., vol. 17 (1966), pp. 65–69. The controversy closed with Allaire's brief response, "Relations and the Problem of Individuation," ibid., vol. 19 (1068), pp. 61–63.

33. *Philosophy and Phenomenological Research* 13 (1952), pp. 184–99; reprinted as ch. IX of *Science, Perception, and Reality,* op. cit. A similar argument is found in Jonathan Bennett, "Substance, Reality, and Primary Qualities," *American Philosophical Quarterly* 2 (1965), pp. 1–17.

34. See Herbert Hochberg's "Ontology and Acquaintance," *Philosophical Studies* 17 (1966), pp. 49–55.

35. Herbert Hochberg, "Things and Qualities" appeared in W. H. Capitan and D. D. Merrill, *Metaphysics and Explanation* (Pittsburgh, 1964).

36. "Things and Descriptions," *American Philosophical Quarterly* 3 (1966), pp. 39–47.

37. The question of the relations holding among the qualities of an object is considered by Haig Khatchadourian in "Objects and Qualities," *American Philosophical Quarterly* 6 (1969), pp. 103–15. He contends that it is incorrect to speak of relations here. The consequences for the "bundle" theorist should be obvious.

38. *The Review of Metaphysics* 12 (1959), pp. 521–39. For a discussion of Wilson's "test-case," see A. N. Prior, "Identifiable Individuals," *The Review of Metaphysics* 13 (1960), pp. 684–96.

39. Included in Ayer's *Philosophical Essays* (London, 1953).

40. Found in Ayer's *The Concept of a Person* (London, 1964).

41. *Proceedings of the Aristotelian Society* Suppl. 38 (1964), pp. 69–78. For a discussion of Miss Anscombe's paper see Stephan Körner, "Substance," *Proceedings of the Aristotelian Society* Suppl. 38 (1964), pp. 79–90.

42. *The Philosophical Review* 79 (1970), pp. 461–92.

43. *God and Other Minds* (Ithaca, 1967).

44. An expanded version of this account is found in Plantinga's *"De Re et De Dicto,"* *Nous* 3 (1969), pp. 235–58.

45. This difficulty is doubtless familiar to most readers. It is raised by Quine in a variety of places. See, for example, *Word and Object,* op. cit., Sect. 41. See Hugh Chandler, "Essence and Accident," *Analysis* 26 (1966), pp. 185–88 for a rather different treatment of the difficulty.

46. In the interests of space, I oversimplify here. Plantinga does not hold that properties have proper names in the way persons, for example, do. There are, however, labels for properties (e.g., "courage") that are neither definite descriptions nor equivalent to such. It is these labels that are to be included in the relevant substituted sets. Further, Plantinga realizes that many objects lack proper names and many properties, uniquely referring labels of a nondescriptive sort. In *God and Other Minds,* op. cit., he does not make much of this point; but in *"De Re et De Dicto,"* op. cit., his characterization of essential properties is explicitly formulated to handle unnamed objects and label-less properties.

47. For further discussion of topics central to Plantinga's account, see Roderick Chisholm, "Identity Through Possible Worlds," *Nous* 1 (1967), pp. 1–8; Jaakko Hintikka, "Individuals, Possible Worlds, and Epistemic Logic," *Nous* 1 (1967), pp. 33–63; Leonard Linsky, "Reference, Essentialism, and Modality," *The Journal of Philosophy* 66 (1969), pp. 687–700; R. Purtill, "About Identity Through Possible Worlds," *Nous* 2 (1968), pp. 87–89.

48. See ch. II of *Reference and Generality* (Ithaca, 1962) and ch. XVI of *Mental Acts* (London, 1957). This theme is also developed in *Three Philosophers,* op. cit.; indeed, in almost all of Geach's writings and in many of Miss Anscombe's, one finds the view operative.

49. Again, I oversimplify here. It is not simply that an object, x, and an object, y, might be the same F and different Gs; they might be the same F, with one of them being a G and the other, not only not the same G, but not a G at all.

50. *The Philosophical Review* 73 (1964), pp. 100–104.

51. (Oxford, 1967). For a detailed discussion of Wiggins's book, see Sidney Shoemaker, "Wiggins on Identity," *The Philosophical Review* 79 (1970), pp. 529–44. Also see Gerald Vision, "Essentialism and the Sense of Proper Names," *American Philosophical Quarterly* 7 (1970), pp. 321–33, where both Wiggins's and Geach's views are examined.

52. For a development and defense of Wiggins's view, see M. Loux, "Identity-Statements and Essentialism," *The New Scholasticism* 44 (1970), pp. 430–39.

53. *The Review of Metaphysics* 21 (1967), pp. 3–12. For a critical discussion of this paper, see Fred Feldman, "Geach and Relative Identity," *Review of Metaphysics* 22 (1969), pp. 547–55. See also Geach's response to Feldman (ibid., pp. 556–59) and Feldman's rejoinder (ibid., pp. 560–61). Other discussions of Geach's argument in "Identity" include Jack Nelson, "Relative Identity," *Nous* 4 (1970), pp. 241–60 and John Perry, "The Same F," *The Philosophical Review* 79 (1970), pp. 181–200.

54. First appeared in *The Journal of Philosophy* 65 (1968), pp. 185-212. It is the second chapter of *Ontological Relativity,* op. cit.

55. For discussions of topics central to Strawson's account, see D. Pears, "A Critical Study of P. F. Strawson's *Individuals,*" *The Philosophical Quarterly* 11 (1961), pp. 172-85 and pp. 262-77; Julius Moravscik, "Strawson on Ontological Priority," *Analytical Philosophy,* ed. R. Butler (Oxford, 1965); Michael Woods, "Identity and Individuation," *Analytical Philosophy* (ibid.); David Wiggins, "The Individuation of Things and Places," *Proceedings of the Aristotelian Society* Suppl. 37 (1963), pp. 171-202; Michael Woods, "The Individuation of Things and Places," *Proceedings of the Aristotelian Society* Suppl. 37 (1963), pp. 203-16; B.A.O. Williams, "Mr. Strawson on Individuals," *Philosophy* 36 (1961), pp. 309-32.

56. The Identity of Indiscernibles is a many-faceted principle; or better, there are a number of related principles that go by that name. For a discussion of the various formulations and uses of the principle, see Loux's "Particulars and Their Individuation," op. cit. For further discussion of the Identity of Indiscernibles and related issues, see V. C. Chappell, "Sameness and Change," *The Philosophical Review* 69 (1960), pp. 351-62; Fred Feldman, "Leibniz and Leibniz's Law," *The Philosophical Review* 79 (1970), pp. 510-22; Robert Muehlmann, "Russell and Wittgenstein on Identity," *The Philosophical Quarterly* 19 (1969), pp. 221-30; Douglas Odegard, "Indiscernibles," *The Philosophical Quarterly* 14 (1964), pp. 204-13.

57. For an attempt to develop, somewhat along Strawsonian lines, the primacy of material bodies, see W. D. Joske, *Material Objects* (London, 1967).

58. For further discussions of this and other topics central to *Individuals,* see Strawson's book on Kant, *The Bounds of Sense* (London, 1967).

59. See, e.g., Saul Kripke's "Semantical Considerations on Modal Logic," *Acta Philosophica Fennica* 16 (1963), pp. 83-94. For a complete bibliography on this and other issues discussed in this supplement, see my *The Possible and the Actual* (Ithaca, 1979).

60. See, e.g., Chapter III of David Lewis's *Counterfactuals* (Cambridge, Mass., 1973).

61. See, e.g., Lewis's "Counterpart Theory and Quantified Modal Logic," *Journal of Philosophy* 65 (1968), pp. 113-26.

62. See, e.g., Max Cresswell's "The World Is Everything That Is the Case," *Australian Journal of Philosophy* 50 (1972), 1-13 and *Logics and Languages* (London, 1973).

63. See, e.g., Richard Montague's *Formal Philosophy,* edited by Richmond Thomason (New Haven, 1974).

64. See David Lewis's "General Semantics," pp. 169-218 in *Semantics of Natural Language,* edited by Gilbert Harmon and Donald Davidson (Dordrecht, 1973) and Robert Stalnaker's "Pragmatics," ibid., pp. 380-97.

65. See Stalnaker's "A Theory of Conditionals," pp. 98-112 in *Studies in Logical Theory,* edited by Nicholas Rescher (Oxford, 1968).

66. See, e.g., Lewis's *Counterfactuals* and John Pollock's *Subjunctive Reasoning* (Dordrecht, 1976).

67. For the possible worlds analysis of epistemic notions, see Jaakko Hintikka's *The Intensions of Intentionality* (Dordrecht, 1975).

68. See Montague's *Formal Philosophy,* and Hintikka's *Intensions of Intentionality* and *Models for Modalities* (Dordrecht, 1969). Lewis's possibilism is developed in Chapter III of *Counterfactuals.*

69. Lewis, *Counterfactuals.*

70. Ibid.

71. Ibid. See also Lewis's "Anselm and Actuality," *Nous* 4 (1970), pp. 175-88.

72. *Counterfactuals,* pp. 84-85.

73. See "The World Is Everything That Is the Case," and Chapters III and V of *Logics and Languages.*

74. See Carnap's attempt to interpret worlds as sets of sentences in *The Logical Foundations of Probability* (Chicago, 1950).

75. See Chapter III of Lewis's *Counterfactuals,* William Lycan's "The Trouble with Possible Worlds," pp. 274-316 in my *The Possible and the Actual,* and my "Modality and Metaphysics," ibid., pp. 15-64.

76. Actually, Cresswell's example of a materialist version of combinatorialism is not subject to this objection, since he does not take physical particles as atomic; his strategy is to take space-time points and the notion of being filled with matter as atomic.

77. For additional difficulties with transworld identity, see David Kaplan's "Transworld Heir Lines," pp. 88-109 in *The Possible and the Actual,* and Roderick Chisholm's "Identity Through

Possible Worlds: Some Questions,"*Nous* 1 (1967), pp. 1-8.

78. See "Counterpart Theory and Quantified Modal Logic."

79. "Identity and Necessity," p. 135-64 in Milton Munitz's *Identity and Individuation* (New York, 1971), and "Naming and Necessity," pp. 235-355 in *Semantics of Natural Language.*

80. See Feldman's "Counterparts," *Journal of Philosophy* 65 (1971), pp. 406-9, and Chapter VI of Plantinga's *Nature of Necessity* (Oxford, 1974).

81. See, e.g., Fred Katz and Jerrold Katz, "Is Necessity the Mother of Intension?" *Philosophical Review* 86 (1976), pp. 70-96, and Plantinga, "Actualism and Possible Worlds," *Theoria* 42 (1976), 139-60 for two nice statements of this difficulty.

82. "Propositions," pp. 79-91 in *Issues in the Philosophy of Language,* edited by A. F. McKay and D. D. Merrill (New Haven, 1976).

83. As revealed in conversation.

84. See, e.g., Chapter X of *The Intensions of Intentionality.*

85. *Logics and Languages,* pp. 38-46.

86. "General Semantics," pp. 182-86.

87. *Meaning and Necessity* (Chicago, 1947).

88. Gustav Bergmann, for example, takes this to be an empirical matter.

89. "General Semantics," pp. 182-83.

90. "Possible Worlds," *Nous* 10 (1976), pp. 65-75.

91. See Stalnaker's "Propositions," "Pragmatics," and "A Theory of Conditionals" for the reductive side of his work.

92. "Thinking and the Structure of the World." *Philosophia* 4 (1974), pp. 3-40.

93. *A Theory of Possibility* (Pittsburgh, 1975).

94. See, e.g., "Naming and Necessity," pp. 266-73.

95. For Plantinga's more recent work, see *Nature of Necessity* and "Actualism and Possible Worlds."

96. See, e.g., p. 178 of *Nature of Necessity.*

97. See *Worlds, Times, and Selves* by Prior and Fine (London, 1977).

98. See "De Essentia," pp. 101-2 in *Essays on the Philosophy of Roderick M. Chisholm* (Dordrecht, 1980), where Plantinga raises serious difficulties for Prior's view.

99. See *Worlds, Times, and Selves.*

100. "Theories of Actuality," *Nous* 8 (1974), pp. 211-31.

chapter 2

Recent Work on the Free-Will Problem

HARALD OFSTAD

"Men at some time are masters of their fates.
The fault, dear Brutus, is not in our stars,
But in ourselves."
Shakespeare, *Julius Caesar*

The free-will issue can be (and in fact is) discussed from quite different perspectives. Some discuss it because they want to find out whether there is a sense in which human beings are free, whereas animals are not. Their discussion is conducted from the perspective of drawing a distinction, or justifying a ranking, between humans and animals. Others take up the issue because they want to find a sense of "free will" in which free will becomes an ideal toward which we can aspire. And there are other perspectives.

In this study I shall be concerned with the recent free-will debate from the point of view of moral responsibility.

Solving the free-will problem from the point of view of moral responsibility requires solving three different kinds of problems: (*a*) In what sense (or senses) of "moral responsibility," if any, is it correct to assert that we may be morally responsible? (*b*) In what sense (or senses) of "free will," if any, is free will a condition of moral responsibility as clarified in (*a*)? (*c*) Under what conditions, if any, are we free in the senses clarified in (*b*)?

The issue cannot be solved by investigating whether or not our decisions and actions are caused, nor by studying our use of such sentences as "He could have decided (acted) otherwise," for it is not at all certain that "uncaused" is the correct answer to question (*b*), and it is not at all certain that the responsibility-relevant sense (or senses) of "free" happens to be expressed by our actual use of "could have decided or acted otherwise" sentences. The solution involves the clarification not only of scientific and analytic problems, but of moral problems as well.

Some Major Trends

Although the problems formulated and the answers given by contributors to the free-will discussion during the last twenty-five years vary immensely,[1] there are nevertheless certain noticeable trends. For instance, very few of the authors take it as *a priori* or empirically certain that the so-called principle of causality can be applied to human decisions and actions.[2] It is mostly considered as a working hypothesis.[3]

Moreover, due to the obvious difficulties of discussing the question of causation as an ontological issue, many tend to concentrate on the question whether or not our decisions and actions can be predicted or explained. In this connection the Bergsonian point, that a chooser cannot predict his future decision without making it,[4] has been taken up again by several authors. Some of them also stress the difference between things and human beings, denying the program of the unity of science movement, and advocating some variation of the old distinction between *verstehende* and *erklärende* explanations,[5] emphasizing the methodological dissimilarity between explanations of actions (in terms of reasons) and explanations of events (in terms of causes). Such concepts as reason, choice, decision, intention, and action have been subjected to numerous analyses, some of which indirectly may be of value to the free-will discussion.

We also find that some of the so-called indeterminists and libertarians accept that freedom in an indeterministic sense is not a sufficient, but only a necessary condition of freedom in the sense required by moral responsibility.

Moreover, some of the determinists have become interested in the analysis of such expressions as "tried," "was able to," "had the ability to," "could have acted (decided) otherwise," and "had it in one's power to act (decide) otherwise," rather than following their more traditional line, defining "freedom" as absence of compulsion or constraint. Thereby they have come closer to the libertarian position insofar as this stresses "the ability to make efforts of will."

This newly won interest, both of some determinists and indeterminists in the analysis of the sense in which we have it in our power to decide and act otherwise than we do, and the extent to which we have such power, is one of the most promising features of the recent discussion. My main reason for this evaluation is that this line of thinking seems to me to focus on the sense of "free" that is most relevant from the point of view of moral responsibility.

One of the great weaknesses of the recent discussion is the insufficient clarification of the moral context in relation to which the authors maintain that we are (or are not) free. Although quite a few are aware of the necessity of clarifying such expressions as "moral responsibility" in connection with the free-will dispute, the analysis is still at a preliminary level, and for some strange reason the overwhelming majority of writers consider moral responsibility equivalent with moral blameworthiness.[6] But, obviously, we may hold a person morally responsible without holding him blameworthy, e.g., may consider him morally guilty without considering him blameworthy. Moreover, too few have seen the moral relativity of the free-will issue. But given that we are interested in discovering whether or not we are free in the sense required by moral responsibility, we must admit that this sense may vary with the nature of the moral system within which the concept of responsibility is defined. Within the moral system E_1, for example, "moral responsibility" is defined in terms of moral guilt and an agent is considered guilty of a certain wrongdoing only if he acted freely in sense x; in contrast, according to E_2 and defining "responsibility" in terms of modifiability, an agent is responsible only if he acted freely in sense y. And if we now suppose that we are free in sense y, but not in sense x, do we then have a free will?[7] That depends upon whether the system E_2 is "more correct than" the system E_1. Hence, there is an important sense in which a solution of the free-will issue presupposes a clarification and solution of certain basic problems within ethics.

Freedom and Moral Responsibility

To simplify the comparisons of different positions, let us—whenever it is convenient—concentrate on an example of an action which we shall assume to be morally wrong: on May 1, 1980, Mr. Smith shot his aunt Olga to death. He admits whatever can be shown by a film of the happenings, but he maintains that he is not responsible because his will was not free. How would the recent contributors to the free-will debate deal with this contention?

Most would consider it impossible to take any standpoint until it had been clarified what Smith meant by saying "My will was not free." By the term "will" he may have referred, among other things, to his so-called volitional capacity, his choice, his decision or action. Let us suppose that he meant that his action was not free. But what did he mean by "not free"? Perhaps he meant that his action was compelled in some way, or that it was caused by certain special factors, e.g., neuro-physiological events or the so-called irrational part of himself, or perhaps he meant that he did not have it in his power to act otherwise that he did.

Let us suppose that Smith meant that his action was caused (T). We can then raise the questions (a) Is T sufficiently precise and (b) Is T true? But, as indicated above, a more fundamental question is (c) Is the lack of freedom in this sense of "freedom" sufficient to exclude moral responsibility? Or, formulated in more general terms, in what sense of "freedom" is absence of freedom a sufficient reason for accepting that Smith is not morally responsible? The answer will depend upon our concept of responsibility and the way in which we justify statements ascribing responsibility to agents. It is impossible in this essay to deal with these problems in any thorough way, but certain basic distinctions must be made.

When someone says that Smith is responsible for the death of Olga, one may mean (a) that her death was due to something Smith did, where "doing something" at least implies that Smith was sufficiently conscious to understand that his behavior was dangerous.[8] In relation to this sense it is appropriate to ask whether freedom in any sense is a condition of responsibility. Furthermore, one may mean (b) that Smith is morally guilty. The concept of moral guilt is somewhat neglected in recent literature, and insofar as it is taken up at all, the authors tend to conceive of it as identical with blameworthiness. But this is not correct, for a person who is against moral blame as a matter of principle—and therefore considers nobody blameworthy—may nevertheless consider someone guilty. If he finds that the utterance of the sentence "You are guilty" will be experienced as moral blame, he may stop saying such things but still think them.

To say that Smith is morally guilty of the death of Olga is to give a negative moral evaluation of Smith as the producer of this result in view of all the factors in favor and disfavor of him. And, analogously to criminal guilt, moral guilt can vary in degrees. To analyze the sense, if any, in which freedom is a condition of moral guilt is a crucial task within the free-will debate.

To say that Smith is morally responsible may also mean (c) that he is morally blameworthy. By "blameworthy" one often means that the agent—in my terminology—is morally guilty, and that we consequently have a reason for blaming him. I have already mentioned the relation between freedom and guilt, and the only new question raised by (c) is therefore concerned with the relation between freedom and blame. This problem, however, can be more adequately dealt with by turning to our fourth interpretation of saying that Smith is responsible: someone (but not necessarily *you* or *I*) ought to express moral disapproval of him (d). And the final question is: In what sense, if any, of the term "freedom" is freedom a condition of moral blame?

My exposition must be limited to some of these senses of "responsible," and by concentrating on sense (b), moral guilt, and (d), moral blame, we seem to have the best chance of getting at the most important issues.

Our problems can now be formulated thus: How do the contributors to the recent free-will debate deal with the question whether freedom in any sense is a condition of moral guilt and/or moral blame? What do they mean by "moral guilt," "moral blame," and "freedom"? How do they defend that freedom is—or is not—a condition of guilt or blame? And how do they defend that this condition is—or is not—fulfilled?

Connected with the debate concerning the correct analysis of "free" is another concerning the object of freedom.⁹ Some maintain that the important question is whether or not our actions can be free, others that the relevant issue is whether or not the self, the acting agent, or our decisions are free.

In view of the concepts used by the majority of the participants in the recent debate, it seems preferable to choose "decision" and "action" as our key terms. But if we take "freedom" in the sense of power to decide or act otherwise, talking about the freedom of decisions or actions is really to talk about the *agent's* power to decide or act otherwise.

Types of Positions

Before dealing with some representative contributors, it may be useful to present a short survey of the major types of positions.

1. *Indeterminism (volitional indeterminism).* Let us distinguish two variations:

   1.1. *Ontological indeterminism.* Decisions are not caused, or, at least, some of their characteristics are not caused.

   1.2. *Epistemic indeterminism.* It is impossible to predict decisions, or at least some of their characteristics cannot be predicted, at least not by the chooser when he is deliberating.

2. *Two-domainism:* The causal principle does not apply to decisions or actions, which are neither caused nor uncaused, but it applies to bodily movements, which are either caused or uncaused.

3. *Libertarianism and agency.* Let us distinguish two types:

   3.1. *Moral libertarianism.* The self, which decides between following our interests or doing what we consider our duty, is not completely causally determined, and we are always able (unless we are mentally sick) to put forth the effort required in order to decide in favor of the latter.

   3.2. *Neutral libertarianism.* The self, which decides between different courses of actions, is not completely causally determined, and we are always able (unless we are mentally sick) to put forth the effort required in order to decide in favor of any one of them.

4. *Fatalism.* I distinguish between:

   4.1. *Logical fatalism.* It is logically necessary that the future must be what it is going to be, and logically impossible that it can be anything other than what it is going to be.

   4.2. *Empirical fatalism.* Our deliberations do not influence our decisions and actions.¹⁰

5. *Hard determinism.* Moral responsibility presupposes that we, in a categorical sense of "could," could have decided or acted otherwise; but since our decisions and actions are caused, it follows that we are not free in this sense. Two variations may be distinguished, depending upon the moral consequences drawn:

   5.1. *Hard determinism of the anti-moral-blame type* implies that we are never justified in *morally* blaming anyone, but we may be justified in making use of nonmoral blame.

   5.2. *Hard determinism of the anti-merit-blame type* implies that we are never justified in maintaining that anyone *deserves* or *merits* blame, but that blame, moral as well as non-moral, may be justified, e.g., in terms of utility.

   Some authors have defended the position that the moral consequences mentioned in 5.1. and 5.2. follow, not from the principle of causality, but from the principle that we are products of hereditary and environmental factors. We may refer to this position as:

6. *Hard evolutionism.*

7. *Mild determinism.* Common to the positions characterized by this label is the contention that moral responsibility does not require that we are free in any sense that is incompatible with the assumption that our decisions and actions are caused. Some mild determinists even hold that responsibility presupposes that our decisions *are* caused.

Three variations may be distinguished, depending upon the sense of "freedom" considered crucial.

7.1. *Freedom as modifiability.* According to this position, the only requirement is that the agent is free in the sense that the use of blame will modify his behavior in the future. Knowledge about his past, e.g., about whether or not he could have decided otherwise, is of interest only insofar as it helps us to judge his present modifiability.

7.2. *Freedom as hypothetical behavior.* Moral responsibility requires that the wrongdoer would have decided or acted otherwise if this or that condition had been fulfilled, e.g., if he had chosen otherwise.

7.3. *Freedom as categorical power.* According to this view, moral responsibility (e.g., moral guilt) presupposes that the agent had it in his power (in a nonhypothetical sense) to have decided or acted otherwise. Moreover, it is contended that power in this sense is compatible with the principle of causality.

Ontological or Epistemic Indeterminism

The main arguments presented by recent authors accepting ontological or epistemic indeterminism are not based on empirical research or introspective reports about what we find ourselves believing when we choose, but on some kind of philosophical analysis of such concepts as intention, decision, and voluntary action. By the use of such analyses, they have tried to discover a logical proof for indeterminacy or unpredictability.

C. GINET

In their article "Decision, Intention and Certainty" (1958), Hampshire and Hart tried to show, among other things, that an agent cannot both know what he is going to do and deliberate about what to do. A similar line of thinking was later presented by Ginet (1962). He wanted to prove that (*a*) It is conceptually impossible that a decision should be caused.

Ginet maintains that (*a*) follows from the following two propositions: (*b*) If it were conceptually possible for a decision to be caused, then it would be conceptually possible for a person to know his own decision before he had made it, and (*c*) it is conceptually impossible for a person to know his own decision before he has made it.

Since (*c*) seems to be his most important thesis, I shall here assume, for the sake of argument, that (*b*) is true (but see below).

According to Ginet, the possibility of knowing one's own decision in advance involves an absurdity, because the statement "I already know that I shall later decide to do . . . , but I have not yet decided what I shall do . . . that is, I do not yet know what I shall do" (p. 51) makes two logically inconsistent claims.

The main weakness of this argument is Ginet's conception of a decision. He seems to conceive of a decision to do something as some kind of knowledge of something. Once this position is taken, it is rather easy to prove (*c*), because a person cannot claim both that he has and does not have the knowledge in question. However, we must distinguish between deciding and knowing. To decide to kill Olga on May 1 is not to know anything about the future, not even that one will try to kill her. To make a decision is to take a normative standpoint of a certain kind; it is to commit oneself to a certain alternative. Roxbee-Cox (1963), one of the critics of Ginet's position, says, aptly, "It is in fact rather misleading to emphasize that making up one's mind is a way of gaining knowledge, for this implies that discovering on empirical grounds that a certain decision will be made and actually making that decision are competing methods of gaining the same knowledge" (p. 90).[11]

We may, however, interpret Ginet's article in a different way, viz., as making the point that it is psychologically impossible to deliberate about what to do when one is convinced about what one actually will do.[12] This may be acceptable, although "impossible" is a very strong term. But this psychological difficulty is not a function of the agent's knowledge, but of his beliefs. And even knowledge is all right, as pointed out by Roxbee-Cox, if the agent forgets what he knows when he deliberates. Moreover, the difficulty has nothing to do with whether our decisions are caused or not.

Suppose Ginet had succeeded in proving that it is "conceptually impossible that a decision should be caused." This would not imply that Smith's decision was not caused, only that *if* it was a decision in Ginet's sense, then it was not caused (Ginet is quite aware of this point). Moreover, he gives no reasons to show that freedom in his sense is relevant to the moral questions of guilt and blame, and this, I think, was a wise omission.

S. HAMPSHIRE

Although Hampshire (1959) stresses, as does Ginet, that a decision involves knowledge of the future, his argument against the possibility of self-prediction does not seem to be based on a cognitive theory of decisions, but is valid, if valid at all, even if a decision is conceived as a normative standpoint of a certain kind. His main thesis, as far as the present problem is concerned, is that we cannot predict our own decisions without making them. But he admits that "involuntary" decisions, wherein he probably includes decisions based on habits, may be predicted without making them. So what his thesis really amounts to is that we cannot predict the decisions we have in our power to make or not to make—without actually making them. The argument we are about to consider presupposes that we have some decisions in our power.

He formulates his main argument in this way. "Either I take into consideration the reasons that will influence me, in which case I am already engaged in forming a plan; or I somehow contrive to ignore the factors that will influence me, in which case I cannot honestly profess any confidence in my own prediction" (p. 130). His point, in other words, seems to be that the detailed knowledge of our reasons for and against the different alternatives necessary in order to predict the forthcoming decision presupposes that the reasons are compared and considered in such a way that the decision actually is being made.

Does his argument prove his thesis? I think we can accept that in order to predict my own decision, I must study some "factors that will influence me." But this neither implies that it is necessary to take into consideration my reasons for and against the different alternatives, perhaps it will suffice to study certain neuro-physiological or psychological factors, nor that it is sufficient to do so: perhaps other factors also will influence me.

KNOWING ABOUT THE PREDICTION

Implicit in the line of reasoning so far considered is the view that the self-predicting agent is not confronted with an outcome that is independent of his own predictive activity, in the sense in which the occurrence of an eclipse of the sun is independent of the activity of the predicting astronomer. This view—the view of interaction—is acceptable and forms the basis for a different argument against the possibility of self-prediction, as follows: P's prediction at time t_1 of his decision at time t_2 may influence his actual decision at t_2 and thereby the possibility of predicting it. Also, another person's prediction may influence him if he gets to know about it, but this other person may have a second prediction in reserve, whereas the chooser necessarily will know his own last prediction.[13]

A short presentation of this difficulty is given in Oldenquist (1963-64). He wants to show that it is impossible to know one's decision in advance. He presents his argument as follows:

i. In order to know at t_1 that I at t_2 will make the decision D, I must, at t_1, know the conditions, say A, B, C, which are causally sufficient for D.

In order to know that A, B, C are causally sufficient for D, I must know that those factors, which might lead to *not-D*, will not do so. But my own activity in studying the conditions and predicting my decision may influence the outcome. Hence, I must at t_1 know that it is false that

ii. A, B, C plus my predictive activity, p_1, are sufficient for *not-D,* and, for the same reason, I must know that it is false that

iii. A, B, C plus p_1 plus my knowledge that *ii* is false are sufficient for *not-D.* Hence, we get into an infinite regress.

This point, also made by many other authors, seems to me correct, but I do not consider Oldenquist's conclusion well formulated. He says that his argument has shown that "I cannot possibly know that all circumstances besides A, B, C are causally irrelevant to my decision" (p. 56). This formulation does not take us to the heart of the matter, because it refers to a type of uncertainty that we encounter even in experimental science. The crucial thing is that as self-predictors we are always one step behind the mastering of the factors that may be relevant, or as it has been said by Bernard Mayo (1958b): "no . . . record can . . . include a record of the act of recording" (p. 229).

To assert that our predictions may influence our future decisions does not imply that they always will do so. I see no reason to accept the latter view. The motivations favoring the predicted decision may be so strong that they check whatever counter-influence the prediction might elicit. It is even possible that whereas prediction 1 influences the predicted decision so that a prediction 2 is needed, 2 does not modify the predicted result. Whether a decision will be influenced by one's own final prediction is an empirical question,[14] but if such influence takes place, the prediction will be falsified.

CONCLUSION

The authors presented have focused their attention on the possibility of self-prediction. With this as a starting-point, Ginet tried to prove that our concept of a decision implies that a decision is uncaused; Hampshire, that we cannot know our decisions in advance; and Oldenquist, that predictive knowledge is impossible because of the effect of knowing about the prediction. I have been more or less critical toward their whole approach. It may be of value from the point of view of obtaining a better understanding of some of our concepts or of the agent and his situation, but it is wasted from the point of view of solving the question of free will, given that we are interested in this question from the point of view of moral responsibility. This is easily seen if we assume that they had succeeded in proving that self-predictions are impossible, and that this discovery was communicated to Mr. Smith's judge, who then replied to Smith's excuse by saying "I am sorry, Smith, but you are to hang, for it has been discovered that your will was free in the sense that it was impossible for you to predict in advance that you would decide to kill Olga"—a reply which is either nonsensical or cruel, or both.

D. M. MacKAY

MacKay's position is related to, but also different from, the positions of the above authors. For the sake of argument he invites us to suppose that human "brains were as mechanical as clockwork, and as accessible to deterministic analysis," and that "what a man believes, sees, feels, or thinks is rigorously represented by the state of his brain, so that someone who 'knew the code' could 'read off' what goes on in his mind from the state of his brain." But now he says:

> It follows that even if the brain were as mechanical as clockwork, no completely detailed present or future description of a man's brain can be equally accurate whether the man believes it or not. (a) It may be accurate *before* he believes it, and then it would automatically be rendered out of date by the brain-changes produced by believing it; or (b) it might be possible to arrange that the brain-changes produced by his believing it would bring his brain into the state it describes, in which case it must be inaccurate *unless* he believes it, so he would not be in error to *disbelieve* it [1967, pp. 11–12].[15]

Hence, even if we assume that we have a completely detailed prediction of the future decision of a certain agent, this prediction does not apply to the agent from the moment he believes it. Consequently, it is false that there exists "an unalterably fixed specification of the future which is *already true,* in the sense that anyone would be correct to believe it, and in error to disbelieve it, if only he know it" (MacKay, 1973, p. 405). The prediction is "self-disqualified" from any unconditional claim to the agent's assent (MacKay, 1971, p. 276).

I accept MacKay's reasoning with the reservation that two kinds of brain state, which differ only with respect to the modifying effects corresponding to the agent's believing or not believing a statement regarding the physical state of his brain, may each be causally connected to one and the same decision.[16] Moreover, freedom in MacKay's sense is neither a necessary nor sufficient condition of having it in one's power to decide and act otherwise. (See Ayers, 1968, p. 33.)

Two-Domainism

According to Kant, our decisions and actions are causally determined *qua* appearances, but neither caused nor uncaused *qua* things in themselves. The logic of this attempt to solve the alleged dilemma between determinism and free will (splitting the world into two domains, one subjected to causality, another beyond it) has also some modern followers, of which Melden (1961) perhaps is the most emphatic.[17]

Applied to our example, Melden's view may be expressed thus: Smith's bodily movements, e.g., his pressing the trigger, can be described in behavioral or neurophysiological terms and are causally determined (he takes the term "cause" in what he calls a "Humean sense"); but Smith's action—his killing his aunt—although involving bodily movements, is not identical with a bodily movement, and neither caused nor uncaused.

I shall limit my discussion to three questions: (*a*) What is, according to Melden, an action "more than" a bodily movement? (*b*) Why is the causal model inapplicable to actions? (*c*) Does his line of thinking have any significance for the question of responsibility and freedom?

Melden tries to answer (*a*) by analyzing the example of a driver signaling at a crossroad. The driver moves his arm in a certain way, but "because of our familiarity with the rules of the road, we recognize . . . that he is signaling" (Melden, 1961, p. 191). The report that the driver is signaling is based on the same sense-impressions we receive when observing his bodily movements; no telescope is needed to see that the driver is signaling and not simply moving his arm. Melden says, quite explicitly, that although "moving the arm" and "signaling" are different descriptions, the former is, in appropriate circumstances, the "very same thing" as the latter. So what is the difference? His point seems to be that the observer seeing the movement of the arm as a case of signaling has been trained through certain social rules. He meets the stimuli with an acquired ability to understand what he observes, just as he meets certain geometrical figures on paper with an ability to perceive them as letters. Melden's idea, in other words, seems to be that P's bodily movement M in the situation S in society X at time t is an instance of the action A if and only if there is within X, at t, a rule according to which movements such as M, should, in S, be recognized as actions of type A.

But how shall we understand the term "action" here? What do the social rules help us to recognize the bodily movement as, an action? That is, as a bodily movement recognized as . . . ? The concept of an action remains unexplained. Moreover, social rules are not even infallible instruments for the identification of actions, for whereas the driver according to the rules of the road was signaling, actually he may have been pointing to a church, or his arm may have been made to move by an electric impulse transmitted to his brain by an evil spirit. Furthermore, a person may act, even if unconventionally, and do something we have not been trained to understand. He may have to explain the nature of his action. I find Melden's view unacceptable, because he puts the rules of society where he should have put the intention of the individual.[18]

Melden tries to establish (*b*), not by proving it, but by trying to show that our usual explanations of actions are of noncausal nature. For instance, to explain Smith's killing by saying that he had decided to kill is not a causal statement, for his decision is intelligible only as a decision to kill.

Very seldom do we explain actions with reference to decisions; moreover, Melden's argument is fallacious. Even if Smith's decision is described as a decision to kill Olga, his decision may or may not be followed by action. Perhaps he died just after his decision, or someone held his hand; even if he acted, he may not have done what he decided to do. And even if he did what he decided to do, the empirical relation between his decision and action may exemplify a universal relation between decisions of a certain type and actions of a certain type. Finally, even if Melden had been right on this point, it would have revealed only some features of our common ways of explaining actions. It would not have shown that a causal model is inapplicable to actions.

Let us assume, for the sake of argument, that Melden had succeeded in proving that actions are beyond causality. Would this have any significance for the free-will issue? Melden does not deny that Smith's bodily movements are causally determined. Hence, if the judge says (basing himself on Melden), "I hold you morally responsible because your action was neither caused nor uncaused," Smith can answer (basing himself on Melden), "Yes, that is true, but my killing involved a set of bodily movements and they were causally determined. They could not have been different from what they were. Hence, your condemnation is unjustified."

Melden, I am happy to say, has not tried to show that the statement that an action is neither caused nor uncaused implies that the agent had it in his power to act otherwise. So even if the thesis of his book were true, he would not have shown that we are free in the sense required by moral guilt or blame.

G. H. von WRIGHT

In his work (1975) von Wright gives a sophisticated defense of the view that the "outer" aspect of an action can be causally explained, whereas its "inner" aspect is beyond causality. The agent's muscular activity, his behavior, belongs to the "outer" aspect. The "inner" aspect is what von Wright calls "the intentionality of the action." According to the author, actions are conceptually intentional and, consequently, cannot be caused by the agent's intention. A certain sequence of behavior, e.g., pressing a button, may have a "Humean cause," but this sequence of behavior *meant as* the ringing of a bell (which exemplifies an action) cannot have a "Humean cause" (see, e.g., p. 129.

Von Wright (1975) mentions "events in the brain" (p. 129) and events operating in one's "nervous system" (p. 130) as possible causes of an agent's behavior. But why not his beliefs and ends? Can't we explain an agent's button-pressing movements by saying that they were caused by his pursuing the end to make the bell ring and his belief that unless he presses the button, the bell would not ring? Can't the brain events von Wright talks about correspond to such psychological phenomena as beliefs and the pursuing of ends?

Although actions, according to von Wright, cannot have "Humean causes," they can be explained in terms of a practical inference. An example: an agent's pressing-the-button movements constitute an action only if it can be explained in terms of an inference that the agent intended to make the bell ring and thought that unless he pressed the button, the bell would not ring. Therefore he pressed the button.

But even if we accept this, as well as that an action is conceptually, not causally, connected with its intention, it does not follow that actions cannot have "Humean causes." In order to show that they cannot, von Wright perhaps might reason in the following way: as I have defined "action," it includes not only the agent's acceptance of a certain intention (which might be described as a series of events), but also the cognitive contents of this intention (von Wright, p. 103), and this cognitive content is not a series of events which can have a "Humean cause."

Von Wright does not maintain that his concept of action delimits that area of activity and forbearance for which a person may be morally responsible, and he does not seem to imply that his sense of "uncaused action" gives us the sense of "free" in which a person must have acted freely in order to be responsible.

REASON VERSUS CAUSE

Hampshire's, Melden's, and von Wright's studies of intention, choice, action, voluntary action, reason for an action, etc., are parts of a general revival of so-called philosophical psychology. Let us look at two of the points often made by recent writers within this tradition, and let us formulate them so vaguely that we can use them as starting-points for different interpretations: (*a*) a decision or action is not a definite entity, and (*b*) we decide and act on the basis of reasons.

Let us limit our discussion to two questions: (*i*) Does (*a*) or (*b*) have any consequences for the question whether or not our decisions or actions are caused? (*ii*) Does (*a*) or (*b*) have any consequences for the question whether or not we have it in our power to decide or act otherwise? I start with (*a*) and distinguish three interpretations, formulating them in terms of our example.

(a_1): even the most minute observation of Smith's behavior is compatible with different hypotheses about what he was doing. His action may have been killing Olga, but it may also have been trying-to-find-out-whether-the-gun-is-loaded, or trying-to-find-out-whether-the-bullet-would-go-through-her-heart, or getting-rid-of-an-obstacle-in-order-to-get-hold-of-Olga's-cat. Interpretation (a_1) seems acceptable, although observations of a larger segment of Smith's behavior may certainly limit the class of plausible hypotheses. But since I cannot see that (a_1) has any consequences of the type indicated in (*i*) and (*ii*), I shall say no more about it.

(a_2): the statement that Smith killed Olga is not an empirical statement. Interpretation (a_2) is false. Whether Smith killed Olga or not depends, among other things, upon his behavior and intentions, and to decide what he intended is an empirical task.[19] But even if (a_2) were true, it would be irrelevant to the question of Smith's power to have acted otherwise. On the other hand, if we take the term "caused" in such a way that only empirical events can be caused, and interpret (a_2) to imply that an action is not an empirical event, then it follows that actions are not caused.

(a_3): Smith's action can be described in different ways. We can say "Smith killed Olga" or "Smith shot Olga" or "Smith shot Olga with his red gun," etc. Interpretation (a_3) is acceptable but has no implications for the question whether or not his action was caused. But could we say that the possibility of alternative descriptions gives a wonderful solution of the question whether or not Smith had it in his power to act otherwise? He did shoot her, but he could have acted otherwise, for he did have it in his power to do the action describable by the sentence "Smith shot Olga with his red gun." But this must be a joke.

Let us turn to (b). Does the statement "Smith had a reason for killing Olga" imply or exclude that "Smith's killing Olga was caused"? That depends, first of all, upon what we mean by "reason." If by Smith's "reason" we refer, *inter alia,* to his pro-attitude toward killing Olga (cf. Davidson, 1963, p. 687), it is rather obvious that to explain Smith's action in terms of his reasons may be an example of a causal explanation. On the other hand, if by Smith's "reason" we refer to Olga's death, saying that the fact that she would die if he pulled the trigger was the reason why he pulled the trigger (cf. Shwayder, 1965, p. 86), then a reason is not a cause, although Smith's anticipation of the fact in question may have been a causal factor. Similarly, if by Smith's "reason" we refer to what he thinks justifies his action ("She always was so angry with her cat"), his reason is not a cause, although his acceptance of this as a reason as well as his desire to improve the cat's condition may have been causal factors. Finally, if "reason" refers to the goal toward which his action was a means (e.g., to become a cat-owner), then, again, a reason is not necessarily a causal factor, but Smith's belief that shooting would help him to realize his goal might be. Hence, we sometimes use "reason" in such a way that a reason is a causal factor, but even when we do not use it that way, the statement that an action was done for a reason does not imply that it was not caused.[20]

Does the fact that we act on the basis of reasons have any consequences for the question whether we have it in our power to act otherwise than we in fact do? A plausible answer seems to be that we do have a certain degree of power both over the amount of positive or negative value that we attribute to a certain anticipated consequence and over the weight we give this value as compared with other values. By modifying our evaluations, or by trying to see our decision or action within a wider perspective of norms and values, we may increase our power to decide and act in different ways.[21]

Do we know of any actions which are caused? Has science been able to establish any universal law of behavior? So far neither psychological nor physiological research has succeeded in establishing any universal law of relevance to the present discussion. Moreover, it seems likely that at least some characteristics of some decisions and actions will remain statistically rather than universally related to other factors in the universe. One reason for this: the interaction between the predictor and the phenomena to be predicted has already been mentioned. Another reason is the limited intersubjective accessibility of the required data. In some cases it may be the morally most important characteristics that are only statistically related to other factors; in other cases these characteristics may perhaps be universally related to other factors.

Let us suppose that we know that those characteristics of Smith's decision that made it morally wrong had a low degree of statistical relation to other factors in the universe. Would this give us a basis for an answer to his excuse? We could say, "Smith, you are responsible, for your will was free in the sense that those characteristics of your decision that made it morally wrong had a low degree of statistical relation to other factors in the universe." But the answer is ridiculous because it is just as irrelevant as if we said, "Smith, you are responsible because your hair is green."

A relevant answer must show that Smith had it in his power to decide or act otherwise than he did; and it is highly controversial, and in my opinion false, to assert that indeterminacy is even a necessary condition for our power to decide or act otherwise.[22]

Libertarianism and Agency

C. A. CAMPBELL

Campbell is one of the most energetic defenders of the so-called libertarian position both before and within the period selected for this essay. His position can be summarized as follows:

i. The crucial question is whether we are free in the sense required in order that we shall "deem it proper to attribute moral praise or blame to agents" (Campbell, 1957, p. 159).

ii. In order to find this sense, we must analyze what Campbell calls the "moral consciousness."

iii. Such analysis shows (a) that the crucial question is whether our choices and decisions (our "inner acts") are free or not, because even if external circumstances prevent a morally wrong act, we may be responsible for having decided to do this act. On the other hand, we are not responsible for an action unless it is rooted in an "inner act," for we do not consider robots responsible. It also shows (b) that in order that we shall be proper objects of moral praise or blame, our decisions must be free in the sense that the two following conditions are fulfilled: (1) the sole cause (author) of the decision is the agent himself, and not his character as formed by heredity and environment (Campbell, 1957, p. 160), and (2) the agent could have decided otherwise than he in fact did, in a contra-causal sense of "could" (p. 164).

Campbell does not maintain that every decision is free in this sense. Our decisions to follow this or that desire are caused and hence not free in the sense indicated. Only the choice between following one's strongest desire and doing what one believes one ought to do is causally undetermined and has the self as sole author. In his own words: "In the act of deciding whether to put forth or withhold the moral effort required to resist temptation and rise to duty [which he calls on p. 173 "doing what one believes we ought to do"] is to be found an act which is free in the sense required for moral responsibility" (p. 168). Campbell's main reason for maintaining that we are free in the sense indicated is that an analysis of our "moral consciousness" shows that it is impossible for us to disbelieve that we are free in that sense.

I find it hard to take this line of argument seriously, but since its weaknesses have been pointed out by many authors,[23] I shall instead consider two other questions: Does freedom in the sense indicated suffice for moral responsibility? Has Campbell formulated the sense of "free" which he himself seems to consider crucial?

First, his position seems to imply that a wrong-doer who did not think about how he ought to act cannot be morally responsible (p. 221) — a very strange consequence. Second, Campbell seems to postulate a very odd principle of causality, for it withdraws in the moment the agent thinks about his duty and reappears as soon as he forgets about it. Third, even a person who thought about what he ought to do is not responsible if he did not decide to put forth or withhold effort. For if he did not, then he did not do the act that Campbell considers free. Fourth, let us suppose that Eichmann deliberated about whether to have the Jews shot, A_1 (which, we assume, was the solution he desired), or killed by gas, A_2 (which, we assume, he considered his duty), and that he decided to do what he believed to be his duty. Let us also assume that his decision was free in Campbell's sense. Does this imply that it was free in the sense required in order that he should be morally responsible for the killing? It does not, because it does not imply that Eichmann had it in his power to do something that would have been less evil than both A_1 and A_2 (taken separately). Let us suppose that if Eichmann had decided to save the Jews, they would have been saved. Even this does not show that he was morally responsible, for perhaps he did not have it in his power to believe that it could be right to act contrary to Hitler's order; even if he did have this in his power, perhaps he did not have it in his power to act on the basis of this belief. Finally, even if "Eichmann himself" was the "sole cause" of his decision, how can we avoid the consequence that that part of Eichmann formed by heredity and environment will experience our reactions?[24]

Campbell's philosophy of freedom seems to have been formulated by a person living within an unproblematic moral universe where the paradigm case of potential wrongdoing is: Shall I steal a little bit of mother's jam, or shall I "rise to duty"?

Let us turn to the second question. I do not think Campbell really means that a decision to put forth or withhold effort is free only in the sense he indicates, for this sense does not exclude that it is a matter of luck whether the effort will turn out to be of sufficient strength. He probably also means that the agent is free to mobilize the amount of effort required in order to resist any temptations (Campbell, 1957, p. 221). But if this is what he means, then he should have argued that we have it in our power to put forth this amount of effort, and not that we have contra-causal freedom. Freedom in the latter sense (no matter its exact meaning) does not exclude that the agent was powerless. Moreover, it is hard to reconcile his contra-causal sense of "could" with his belief that it may be more or less difficult to "rise to duty" (p. 220). This belief suggests that he has in mind a comparative concept of power to decide. My guess, therefore, is that a definition of "freedom" in terms of power to decide would have been a more adequate expression of his intentions.[25]

R. M. CHISHOLM

Like Campbell, Chisholm maintains that moral responsibility presupposes that the agent is the cause of the action, not the sole cause (Campbell) but the cause of "one of the events that are involved in that act" (Chisholm, 1966, p. 17).

Chisholm seems to have arrived at his position through the following reasoning (applied to my example): if Smith shall be responsible for killing Olga, it must have been in Smith's power not to perform that act. If it shall be true that Smith had it in his power not to kill Olga, Smith's action must not have been brought about, e.g., by his beliefs and desires. For if such factors caused the action, "*he* was unable to do anything other than just what he did do" (Chisholm, 1966, p. 13). On the other hand, if the killing was not caused at all, then no one was responsible for the act. Hence, the remaining possibility is that the agent is a prime mover unmoved (Chisholm, 1977, p. 17).[26]

An act of an agent of this kind is not caused by the agent's beliefs and desires. But neither is it caused by any other psychological phenomena, e.g., the agent's critical deliberation, his norms, evaluations, or morality. It is not even caused by some of the factors constituting the identity of the agent. For even in that case, Chisholm's conclusion would be the same: *they* caused the act, not the *agent*. This is strange: whatever the agent's self may contain of thoughts, values, efforts, and feelings of love and sympathy is taken out of it and referred to as ego-alien causal factors. Through this way of thinking the agent's self becomes an empty shell, devoid of all life.

How can Chisholm arrive at this position? He wants to believe that an agent can "rise above his desires" and that no set of statements about a man's desires, beliefs, and stimulus situation at any time implies a statement telling us what the man will try to do at that time. Agreed, but this cannot be obtained by castrating the agent, by postulating that he is an unmoved mover. It *can* be obtained only through hard labor—learning to discover and make use of our inner resources; getting into contact with what we *actually* feel in this or that situation, not only what we think we *ought* to feel; becoming aware of the factors influencing our decision processes and subjecting these factors to critical reflection and confrontation with those norms, values and mature feelings on which we try to base our identity. We need a vital and dynamic self to obtain it.

Let us, for the sake of argument, accept Chisholm's idea of the unmoved mover. Does such a Smith have it in his power to act otherwise than he in fact does? That Smith is "unmoved," i.e., not caused by any factors, does not in itself provide him with power to act otherwise. That his self is uncaused is *one* thing; whether he has the inner strength required for resisting the temptation to kill Olga is another. Does the fact that "one of the events that are involved in the act" is caused by Smith's uncaused self provide him with the power in question? It does not. Even if one such event were caused by Smith's uncaused self, he might lack the inner resources required for resisting the temptation to kill.

Chisholm seems to view human beings as baby gods. We cannot make light by uttering words, but we can freely produce any decision. For instance, at 10 o'clock we make a well-integrated decision to become a Catholic and at 10:15 a well-integrated decision to become a Moslem. We could give a nice performance in a circus.[27]

Indeterminism, Libertarianism, and the Belief in Transempirical Entities

One possible hypothesis when dealing with an author who maintains that moral responsibility presupposes freedom in the sense that the agent's decision or action was uncaused or unpredictable is that his thinking is confused. He may have failed to see the difference between the following two interpretations of "P, in S, could have decided D_2 instead of D_1": (a) it was equally probable that P, in S, should make the decision D_2 as D_1, and (b) P, in S, had it in his power to decide D_2 instead of D_1. The latter statement tells us something about the agent; the former tells us something about D_1 and D_2's relations to other events in the universe. Failing to distinguish between them, the author may try to prove (a), intending to prove (b).

There is also another and deeper reason why a philosopher may defend indeterminism: he may be dissatisfied with our empirical self or our limited power and postulate the existence of a transempirical self or power-center, defending some degree of indeterminism in order to exclude the applicability of Occam's razor.

Campbell does not use the expression "transempirical power-center," but his unwillingness to accept empirical disconfirmation of the statement "P had it in his power to decide D_2 instead of D_1" suggests that he postulates something like such a power-center. Taylor does not use the expression "transempirical self," but it is clear that he refers to a transempirical entity. Given this situation, libertarians may come to defend indeterminism to meet the following objection of the scientist: "I don't know whether we have a transempirical self or power-center or not. I don't even understand what these expressions mean. I know only that I don't have to worry about such things. I can predict the characteristics of our decisions without paying any attention to the operation of any such entities. And I must be permitted to say, therefore, that this self or power-center seems to live a rather quiet life." My hypothesis is that the libertarian will try to meet this objection by denying that the scientist can give perfect predictions. Such predictions are impossible, he may maintain, because the transempirical entity manifests itself in the empirical domain in a way that for the scientist must appear as partly random. In other words, my hypothesis is that the libertarian's indeterminism is intended as a wall of defense around his belief in certain transempirical entities.

Hard Determinism and Hard Evolutionism

The position of the hard determinist consists of three standpoints: (a) he asserts that our actions and decisions are parts of causal sequences (ancestorially caused), (b) he has a certain view on the morally correct or "proper" sense of "moral responsibility," and (c) he maintains that moral responsibility in this sense requires freedom in a sense which is incompatible with (a).

I have earlier distinguished two variations of hard determinism. According to the first, determinism is incompatible with moral guilt and blame, but we may be justified in holding people guilty and blaming them in a nonmoral sense. According to the second, determinism is incompatible with the notions of merit and deserts, but we may be justified in making use of moral as well as nonmoral blame on utilitarian grounds.

Recently hard determinism of the first kind has been defended, among others, by Paul Edwards in his contribution to *Determinism and Freedom in the Age of Modern Science,* S. Hook, ed. (1958).[28] He does not deny that determinism is compatible with freedom of action, if by calling an action "free" we mean only that it may be influenced through the use of blame (limiting ourselves to wrongdoings). He does not even deny that we use the expression "moral responsibility" in such a way that it requires freedom in this sense only. But he maintains that this is an improper sense, and that if we take "moral responsibility" in its "proper" sense, then determinism implies that we are not morally responsible. The crucial questions, then, are what Edwards means by "moral responsibility in the proper sense," why he holds this to be the proper sense, and why determinism excludes responsibility in this sense.

Edwards gives no explicit answers to the first and second questions, but he seems to mean that a judgment about guilt or blame, to be moral in the proper sense, must be independent of violent emotions and based on general principles.[29] Let us accept this and turn to the most relevant problem from the point of view of this essay: Why does the principle of causality exclude that we can be morally responsible in the "proper" sense?

Edwards's answer, applied to our example, can perhaps be expressed thus: in order that we shall be justified in morally blaming Smith for killing Olga, he must have had it in his power to act otherwise. To have had such power, he must have chosen his own character (Hook, ed., 1958, p. 123). But the principle of causality implies that our character is formed by heredity and environment. Since this principle must be accepted, it follows that we are not justified in morally blaming Smith.

This reasoning seems to me confused. First of all, the principle of causality implies at most that Smith's character is caused, not that it is caused by heredity and environment. Second, even if it did imply this, it does not follow that Smith was unable to abstain from killing. Third, even if it followed that Smith was powerless in this respect, it does not follow that he would be less powerless if he had chosen his own character. For the fact that Smith in the year 1900 chose his character does not guarantee that he on May 1, 1980, had it in his power to abstain from killing. Moreover, what does it mean to "choose one's own character"?[30] And who chose the character of that Mr. Smith who in 1900 chose the character of Mr. Smith?

Let us make the plausible assumption that Edwards requires that Smith in 1900 not only chose his character, but that he also had it in his power to choose another character than the one he actually chose. Then this gives us a sense of "having something in one's power," and if we apply this sense to the situation where Smith killed Olga, it is conceivable that in this sense he had it in his power not to have killed her. We have thereby reached the crucial question, whether Smith on May 1, 1980, had it in his power to act otherwise. No power over his character or over anything else could have helped if he lacked the required amount of power in that situation.

Hence, the critical thing for the hard determinist is to prove that there is a moral-responsibility–relevant sense of "having something in one's power," which is such that the agent's power to have abstained from that for which he is held responsible (a decision, an action, etc.) is reduced or annihilated if we assume that his decision or action was part of a causal sequence. Edwards's attempt to show that we have not chosen our own character — even forgetting about what this really can mean — misses the point.

While Edwards tried to reach his conclusions by arguing from so-called deterministic premises, other philosophers, like Hospers, have tried to reach similar conclusions from premises referring to hereditary and psychological factors (cf. J. Hospers, 1961, and his contribution to Hook, ed., 1958).[31]

Hospers distinguishes between what he calls an "upper" and a "deeper" level of moral discourse. If we conduct our discussion on the upper level, we are justified in considering people free insofar as they would have acted otherwise if they had wanted to, and we can make use of moral blame insofar as this helps to make them do what they ought to do. But if we talk about *deserving* moral blame, we must move on to a "deeper" level of discourse. Hospers's position seems to be that we would deserve blame for our wrongdoings only if we had caused our own character. But neither Smith nor anyone else is free in this sense, for, according to Hospers, our characters are formed by hereditary and environmental factors.

The arguments which showed that Edwards's view is untenable show also that Hospers's view is untenable.

Mild Determinism

If "mild determinism" refers to the view that the principle of causality is compatible with freedom in the sense required by moral responsibility, then an indeterminist can be a mild determinist, and this is a confusing terminology. Hence, I shall require that a philosopher, in order to be called a "mild determinist," accepts that our decisions and actions are caused.

In what sense of "morally responsible" do mild determinists maintain that we can be morally responsible? Some of them take this expression in the same sense as most hard determinists seem to do, viz., that we can be morally guilty or blameworthy. Others interpret it to mean that behavior is modifiable through the use of praise or blame. Those advocating the latter interpretation may agree with the hard determinists that determinism is incompatible with freedom in the sense required by moral guilt and blameworthiness. But instead of concluding, as the hard determinists do, that consequently we are not morally responsible, they conclude that the notions of guilt and blameworthiness are unacceptable and that the correct notion is modifiability of behavior through the use of praise or blame.

In the following I shall limit my discussion to the reasoning of those who at least appear to maintain that the principle of causality is compatible with freedom in the sense required in order to be morally guilty or blameworthy.

P. H. NOWELL-SMITH

Nowell-Smith, one of the ablest defenders of mild determinism,[32] does not define a notion of moral guilt, but from the list of sentences whose presuppositions he intends to discuss (1954, p. 270), we seem justified in interpreting his view in the following way:

i. Smith may be morally responsible for killing Olga both in the sense that he was morally bad in doing what he did (compare my sense of "moral guilt"), and in the sense that he was blameworthy.

That someone shall be justified in holding Smith responsible in these two senses, two other conditions must be fulfilled:

ii. In killing Olga, Smith did something morally wrong.

iii. Smith does not have an acceptable excuse for what he did.

Smith may excuse himself in different ways, but I shall limit myself to Nowell-Smith's discussion of the excuse that Smith did not act freely. The morally relevant sense of "free" is, according to Nowell-Smith, that the agent could have acted otherwise. If Smith could not have acted otherwise, then he is not guilty and not blameworthy. If he could have acted otherwise, then he is guilty and blameworthy, unless he has another acceptable excuse. The questions are then: How does Nowell-Smith interpret "Smith could have acted otherwise" (T)? Is it true that freedom in this sense is compatible with the principle of causality? Does freedom in this sense suffice for guaranteeing that Smith was free in the sense required by guilt and blameworthiness? According to Nowell-Smith,

iv. T is equivalent to "Smith would have acted otherwise, if this or that condition had been fulfilled" (T_1).

But it is always possible to find a substitution which will make T_1 true. Hence, we need some criterion to distinguish between permitted and forbidden substitutions, otherwise Smith can never excuse himself by saying that he was not free. Before looking at Nowell-Smith's criterion, let us, however, present his view as regards what kind of statement T is and how it can be verified and falsified.

His view seems to be that T cannot be directly verified or falsified by observing what Smith did, for the fact that he killed Olga neither proves nor disproves that he could have acted otherwise. To establish T we must show that Smith had the capacity to abstain from killing and that nothing in the situation prevented him from making use of his capacity. To disprove T it suffices to show that he either lacked the capacity or that something prevented him from making use of it.

How can we prove that Smith had the capacity and that nothing prevented him? Nowell-Smith's view seems to be that positive as well as negative evidence for this statement must be based upon observations of Smith's behavior in other situations. For instance, we must try to establish that Smith in earlier situations has been able to overcome impulses to kill. Positive evidence of this kind is always open to the objection "How can we be certain that this shows that he could have abstained on May 1, 1980?" and negative evidence is open to a similar objection: "How can we exclude the possibility that he might have been able to abstain on May 1?" But, according to the author, it would be absurd to base responsibility, as well as the absence of responsibility, on the logical possibility of such contingencies.

Let us now return to the question of how Nowell-Smith distinguishes between those if-substitutions that exclude guilt and blameworthiness and those that do not. His view on this point may be interpreted in different ways. The most plausible interpretation seems to me to be:

v. If T_1 is true for one if-substitution that presupposes conditions which the moral rules accept as an excuse, then Smith can excuse himself.[33]

For instance, moral rules accept unconsciousness as an excuse, and if Smith were unconscious when he killed Olga (so that T_1 is true for "if he had not been unconscious") then he had an acceptable excuse. But if he would have acted otherwise if he had tried to, then he is responsible, for the moral rules do not accept not-trying as an excuse. Nowell-Smith mentions "acted under physical compulsion" and "acted under ignorance of fact" as examples of excuses which the moral rules accept, and "not wanting to do what is right" or "being too dishonest" as typical examples of causes the rules do not accept as excuses. He tries to explain why moral rules accept only certain special conditions as excuses. His explanations seem to be that:

vi. Moral rules accept as excuses only conditions of such a kind that if wrongdoers acted under such conditions, then, as a general rule, it will be pointless to blame them.

If Smith would have acted otherwise only if he had not been unconscious or subjected to physical compulsion, then he has an acceptable excuse because it is, as a general rule, pointless to blame persons who acted wrongly for such reasons. And it is pointless because the purpose of blaming is to strengthen or weaken certain traits of character. Simplifying his view as much as I can, it seems to me to boil down to this:

vii. Smith's act in S is morally wrong and free if and only if Smith's act is in conflict with a moral rule and it is, in general, possible to discourage people from acting in the way Smith did by blaming them. (Let us express this by saying that the act is *modifiable in general.*)

If (*vii*) is fulfilled, then Smith acted freely and is guilty and blameworthy, and he is guilty and blameworthy even if blaming him will increase the likelihood that *he* will kill again. On the other hand, if Smith's act is not modifiable in general, then he was not free and is neither guilty nor blameworthy, even if blaming Smith would have had good effects on his character.

I find these consequences unacceptable. The emphasis on general modifiability may be convenient within legal systems, but in moral contexts we tend to hold that a person is not guilty unless he had it in his power to act otherwise. Nowell-Smith thinks about moral problems in a too legalistic way.[34] He talks about moral rules as if they constituted a definite group of rules roughly as legal rules. And he does not clearly distinguish between the conditions which certain rules recognize as valid excuses, and the conditions which ought to be accepted as valid excuses.

At this point it may be clarifying to distinguish between a general and a particular use of "could" and "power"-sentences. If we take "could" or "power" in a particular sense, to say that a person could or had it in his power to do A_2 instead of A_1, in S, means that he in that particular situation had it in his power to do A_2. The fact that he never before had been able to do so is not logically incompatible with the assertion. The fact that he always had been able to do so does not logically imply it. We are considering one isolated moment.

If we take "could" or "power" in a general sense, to say that a person could or had it in his power to do A_2 instead of A_1 in S, means that he generally has it in his power to do such actions as A_2. In this sense the agent could have acted otherwise in S even if he were unable to act otherwise in the particular sense. Using this terminology, my view can be expressed by saying that it is the particular and not the general use of "power" that is relevant to questions of moral guilt and blame. The general use of "power" is of significance only indirectly, as evidence for or against the possession of power in the particular sense.

In his answer (1960) to J. L. Austin's criticism of his view (1956), Nowell-Smith seems more aware of the distinction between the particular and the general use of "could" than in *Ethics,* and he raises the question whether we can exclude the possibility that a person who usually is able to do something may lack the ability "just then and there" (Nowell-Smith, 1960, p. 97), but he does not discuss the modifications that would have to be made in his earlier view if we accept the particular use of "could" as the morally relevant one.

This brings me to another point. Both in *Ethics* and in his answer to Austin, Nowell-Smith is too much influenced by the idea that the wrongdoer must have had an *ability* to act otherwise. But to say that he must have been able to act otherwise is not the same as to say that he must have had an ability to do so.[35] Smith may have had all the abilities pertaining to A_1 and A_2 that a person can have but nevertheless have been powerless, because it was a question of resisting a temptation, and to resist a temptation is not an ability.

Smith's situation is very different from the situation of a golfer. It makes good sense to say, "I am taking a course in how to hole six-foot putts. I am doing quite well. Very soon I shall usually succeed when I try, and then I shall obtain my diploma for having acquired an ability"; but it would be strange to say, "I am taking a course in how to resist temptations to kill aunts. I am doing quite well. Last week I resisted six out of ten temptations. As soon as I can resist eight out of ten (if there are any aunts left at that time!), I shall get my diploma for having acquired an ability."

It is misleading to say that moral guilt or blame presupposes the *ability* to act otherwise. This is one of the reasons why I prefer to say that guilt presupposes that the agent had it in his power to act otherwise.

As indicated above, Nowell-Smith points out that T can be proved or disproved only through inductive evidence, which, of course, is true. But when he classifies persons emphasizing the uncertainty of such evidence as ordinary sceptics of induction, he misses an important point, viz., that the uncertainty of the evidence primarily is due to the difficulty of getting hold of relevant evidence.

The answer to the second question I raised in the beginning of my discussion of Nowell-Smith's view, whether freedom in his sense is compatible with the principle of causality, is obviously in the affirmative. Let us turn to the third and more interesting question: whether freedom in Nowell-Smith's sense gives the agent the freedom required by moral guilt and blame.

He does not give a clear answer to this question. He begins his discussion by distinguishing between guilt, blameworthiness, and blame, but he does not discuss the presuppositions of guilt and blame separately, and in the end the concept of individual moral guilt disappears completely. His view seems to be that a person is guilty if and only if he has disobeyed a moral rule and if none of the excuses admitted by the rule applies to him. This means that a person is guilty if and only if he has acted contrary to the moral rules. And this view shows a remarkable confidence in the wisdom of moral rules.

What about free will as a condition of blame? In several of his publications Nowell-Smith has charged philosophers for introducing concepts of freedom whose moral relevance is not clear. As opposed to them, he maintains that his own sense; "P would have acted otherwise, if this or that condition had been fulfilled," can be justified as morally relevant, because it is pointless to blame unless the agent was free in some such sense. But as shown above, his requirement boils down to a requirement about general modifiability. And blaming Smith may discourage him from future wrongdoings even if the act in question is not modifiable in general, and even if it is, blame may have no effects on Smith. Let us interpret his requirement in such a way that it suffices that *Smith's* future behavior will be modified. To say that freedom in this sense can distinguish between exculpatory and nonexculpatory cases is, however, not very interesting, since it becomes analytically true. On the other hand, if we interpret his requirement to be that the agent would have acted otherwise if he had tried to act otherwise, his theory of justification for blaming people breaks down; for it may be useful, both in general and in the particular case, to blame a person even if he would not have acted otherwise if he had tried to, and it may be useless even if he would have acted otherwise if he had tried to.[36]

The requirement that Smith had it in his power to act otherwise may, however, come in as an empirical requirement: the likelihood of producing good effects through the use of blame may be higher if we blame only persons who in some sense had it in their power to act otherwise. But once we have raised this empirical question, we see that additional senses of "free" may be relevant, for the attitudes of the wrongdoer may be such that he is more likely to be modified if he experiences the blame as justified than if he experiences it as unjustified, and perhaps he will not experience it as justified unless he acted freely in the following sense. . . . Hence, in the same sense in which it, on Nowell-Smith's view, may be an empirical requirement that a wrongdoer would have acted otherwise, if he had tried to, it may also be an empirical requirement that he acted freely in other senses.

J. L. AUSTIN

A lively debate over the correctness, especially the linguistic but to some extent also the moral adequacy, of interpreting "P could have acted otherwise" as "P would have acted otherwise, if he had chosen or decided or tried to" (T_2), has taken place, especially as a result of Austin's paper (1956).[37] Mild determinists have been attacked by a united front of indeterminists, libertarians, and hard determinists. The main lines of attack may be summarized as follows:

(i). T_2 does not express what we in ordinary language mean when we say that someone could have acted otherwise.

(ii). Freedom in the sense formulated in T_2 is not equivalent to freedom in the sense of having it in one's power to act otherwise.

(iii). Freedom in sense T_2 is not equivalent to freedom in the sense required by moral guilt and blame.

One of Austin's central contentions is that we use such sentences as "Smith could have acted otherwise" with indeterministic implications, and that if-analyses therefore are inconsistent with actual usage.

I see no reason to deny that so-called ordinary usage is flexible enough to include a usage of the kind indicated by Austin. But the question is whether this observation has any consequences for the free-will problem. It seems to me that it has no such implications. Even if everyone always were to use such sentences as "Smith could have acted otherwise" in an indeterministic sense, this would not imply that it is freedom in this sense which is required by moral responsibility. To find the morally relevant senses of "freedom," we must raise the question of freedom in relation to different types of moral systems, e.g., teleological and deontological systems. If we, e.g., presupposes act-utilitarianism, it certainly is not freedom in an indeterministic sense that is relevant.

The most fruitful part of Austin's paper is his attempt to show that such sentences as "Smith could have acted otherwise" express categorical statements about the past and say that Smith was able to do something, and not that he would have been able to do something, if this or that condition had been fulfilled. Such sentences, at least sometimes, are probably used in this categorical way. But Austin's mistake is to believe that this categorical sense must be indeterministic.

Let us look at his example. A golfer faces a short putt. He attempts to knock the ball into the cup, but fails. He remains firmly convinced that he had the ability, then and there, to hole it. This is quite acceptable but does not imply that his failure was uncaused, only that the cause was not of such a kind that it took away his ability.

Nevertheless, Austin's linguistic analysis is irrelevant to the free-will issue, given that our perspective is moral responsibility. For even if we assume that "could"-sentences always express categorical statements about our power to decide and act, this would neither imply that we have such power nor that this sense of "freedom" is morally relevant. An act-utilitarian, e.g., will say that this sense is of no crucial importance to him, since all he wants to know is whether human beings are modifiable through the use of praise or blame. On the other hand, a philosopher accepting that human beings can be morally guilty may maintain that guilt presupposes that the agent had it in his power, in a categorical sense, to have acted otherwise; and would have to stand for his requirement even if no one actually used "could"-sentences so as to correspond with it.

Finally, even if it were completely misleading, from a linguistic point of view, to interpret "could"-sentences by the use of "would-have-if" sentences, it might nevertheless be freedom in the sense that Smith would have acted otherwise if he had tried to, which is relevant from the point of view of moral guilt and blame. Many of the articles about how to analyze "can"- and "could"-sentences are uninteresting from the point of view of the free-will debate because the authors fail to see that the free-will problem partly is of moral nature.

The Role of the Self

To declare Smith morally guilty, we require that the wrong act, A_1, in some sense can be attributed to him.[38] Furthermore, he must have had it in his power to act otherwise, i.e., to do A_2 instead of A_1, and if A_2 had occurred, we require that it was *his* action. How shall we conceive of the relation between an action and the self?

Taylor (1963), and in his article in Hook, ed. (1958), Campbell (1957) and Chisholm (1964), among others, seem to postulate the existence of a transempirical or substantial self. Forgetting about the difficulties of interpreting the meaning of this "self" or what kind of evidence would be relevant for and against it, it is hard to understand the nature of the relation between the substantial or transempirical self and such empirical things as deciding and acting. As long as this problem has not been clarified, it seems reasonable to remain sceptical toward the idea that attributing an action to an agent is to attribute it, not to him, but to his so-called transempirical self.

R. B. Edwards and D. H. Whittier, defending an empirical notion of the self, have argued that "the self *is* its activities as well as its experiences" (see Edwards, 1965, p. 274). If we accept this line of thinking, Smith's trying, deliberating, choosing, and deciding are activities of his self, and it may be empirically possible to connect his act to some of these activities and thereby to his self. But perhaps the relation between such activities and the self here becomes too intimate. It may be useful to distinguish between "trying to do A occurs in Smith" and "Smith tries to do A." In order that the trying shall be an activity of his self, we must require, it seems to me, that it is related to his identity as based on his norm- and value-system.

From the point of view of moral responsibility, however, the decisive thing is that the agent had control over those activities which led to his action, not that he considered them as parts of his self. An example: suppose we had asked Eichmann whether or not he had it in his power to refrain from sending the Jews to the gas-chambers, and that he had answered: "Yes, if I had tried to stop the transportations, I would have succeeded, but such a trying would not have been a trying of the good and obedient, but of the bad and disobedient Eichmann, and hence it would not really have been my trying at all."

If we assume that what he says is true, then the fact that his trying would not have been *his* activity in the sense indicated cannot be accepted as an excuse, given that he had it in his power to try.

Let us distinguish between being free, as a person, and deciding or acting freely. If the personality with which Eichmann identified himself was the result of an uncritically accepted process of upbringing and ideological indoctrination, then Eichmann, as a person, was not free, or his freedom was at least severely limited. But this lack of freedom reduced his moral responsibility at the action level only to the degree that it reduced his power to act in a better way.

The crucial point, of course, is that the answer we have attributed to Eichmann would not be true. Actually, his lack of freedom as a person made it extremely difficult for him to be disobedient to Hitler, and this limitation of his power to act otherwise reduced his moral responsibility. Nonetheless, the degree to which it was reduced would depend also upon the degree to which he was responsible for his uncritical acceptance of the personality structure and ideological convictions with which he happened to be provided.

Suppose Smith's deliberation, conceived as mental activity, did not influence his decisions and actions. Suppose his mental activity was an epiphenomenon only. Then, one might say, Smith has no self, and any power to act otherwise, located in his body, cannot be referred to as *his* power and give a basis for moral responsibility. But let us note that even if we assume that Smith's deliberation, conceived as mental activity, was caused by certain neuro-physiological processes, which were caused by some previous neuro-physiological processes and related by a law of nature to his action, this does not imply that his mental activity did not influence his action. In order to prove that his mental activity was superfluous, one would have to prove that the correlations between the act and the neuro-physiological processes in question would remain the same regardless of the characteristics of Smith's mental activity.

H. FRANKFURT AND G. WATSON

In his 1971 article, Frankfurt tries to relate the free-will issue to the concept of a person. To say that a person has free will "means that he is free to will what he wants to will" (p. 15). And wanting a certain desire to be one's will is, according to Frankfurt, essential to being a person, which ranks above "subhuman species." Frankfurt does not clarify what he means by "free" in "free to will," but perhaps he means that it is "up to" the agent (it is in his power) to select any one of the desires he happens to have in a certain situation, as his will (Frankfurt, 1971, p. 18). Nor does he try to prove that we have such power. Whether we do depends, first of all, upon what he means by "will." If "willing x" means making a well-integrated decision to bring about x, then perhaps some volitional athletes have such power. But some of us, thank God, do not. Given that our norm- and value-system is rooted in our personality, it is difficult (to say the least) to select as one's will a desire conflicting with one's fundamental values.

Let us assume that Smith's will was free in Frankfurt's sense, and that he had three desires concerning Olga: (*a*) to shoot her, (*b*) to boil her in oil, and (*c*) to see her go to Hell. He selected desire (*a*) as his will. Does he fulfill the requirement of freedom as far as responsibility is concerned? Frankfurt perhaps thinks so. But before we can hold Smith responsible for killing Olga, we must find out whether he also had it in his power to create within himself a desire to let her live. Frankfurt does not seem to be aware of this question.

Let us assume that Smith was not free in Frankfurt's sense. Does it follow that he is not responsible? According to the author, it does not, for responsibility does not presuppose that one's will is free. Smith is responsible for killing Olga even if he was not "in a position to have whatever will he wanted." Given that he did what he wanted to do and because he wanted it, he is morally responsible, and it is "quite irrelevant to the evaluation of his moral responsibility to inquire whether the alternatives that he opted against were actually available to him" (Frankfurt, 1971, p. 19). Hence, even if he were as powerless as Mercurius to behave in any other way than he did, he may be fully responsible. I hope Frankfurt applies this philosophy only to himself.

Watson (1975) argues that a person acts freely only insofar as the act is "his own," and it is his own only if it is in accordance with what he "most values." The actions of kleptomaniacs, dipsomaniacs, and the like are unfree because "the desires and emotions in question are more or less radically independent of the evaluational systems of these agents" (Watson, 1975, p. 220). They desire what they desire "in spite of themselves."

According to Watson, it is desirable to be able to form practical judgments concerning what one ought to do in this or that situation and to follow them in practice, even when so doing encounters strong inner resistance. Freedom in Watson's sense seems to be some kind of ideal; and only God is, according to the author, free, *sans phrase,* since in his case there can be "no disparity between valuational and motivational systems" (p. 220).

Does Watson hold that freedom in his sense is a condition of moral responsibility? If he does, we will be responsible only for those actions that are in accordance with what we "most value." Hence, Smith is not responsible, assuming that he followed a desire that was "radically independent" of his value system. But isn't this to be too merciful, assuming that Smith really had it in his power not to kill Olga?

Some important relations between freedom and self have been neglected in the recent discussion. Examples: (*a*) What does it mean that so and so is "up to the agent," or that one is one's own master? (*b*) Which conditions must be fulfilled in order to be a person in such a sense that it may be justified to hold him responsible? (*c*) In what sense must the Smith we hold responsible be "the same person" as the killer? (*d*) If Smith changed personality after the murder, why is it then more justified to punish him rather than someone else? Because he still occupies the same body?

DOES RESPONSIBILITY PRESUPPOSE THAT WE COULD HAVE ACTED OTHERWISE?

Above I distinguished between "responsible" in the sense of moral guilt and in the sense of "moral blame." It is commonly accepted that to be guilty of a certain action, the agent must have had it in his power to act otherwise, although it would not suffice, in Smith's case, that he had it in his power to kill Olga with his black gun instead of with his red gun. To say so would be like saying to a man whose body has been trapped under a tree: "Why do you complain about lack of freedom? You can still move your ears" (O'Shaughnessy, 1956). If boiling Olga in oil was Smith's only alternative, he merits praise for shooting her. In order to be responsible, the agent must have had it in his power to act in an ethically better way than he did. Moral blame (for an action) presupposes not only that the agent had it in his power to act in an ethically better way, but also that his behavior is modifiable by the use of blame.

Before turning to the discussion concerning the ethically relevant meaning of saying that an agent had it in his power to decide or act otherwise, let us look at a counter-example to the thesis that moral responsibility presupposes that the agent could have acted otherwsie. The example has been put forward by Frankfurt (1969) and runs as follows. Suppose that someone — call him Black — wants Jones to perform a certain action and that he is in a position to take steps that will guarantee that Jones will perform the action. Black prefers not to take these steps unless necessary, and so does nothing unless it becomes clear that Jones is going to decide to do something *other* than what he wants him to do. Finally, we are asked to suppose that Black finds it un-necessary to take the steps in question, since he infers, correctly, that Jones will decide to do and actually will do the thing Black wants him to do, on his own. But since Black is an excellent judge of such things, we can be sure that Jones would have acted as he did even if his initial preferences had been different, for then Black would have taken the necessary steps. So, whichever way we have it, Jones will behave as Black wants him to. Frankfurt's conclusion is that since Jones acted as he did for reasons of his own, he is responsible, although he could not have acted otherwise than he did.

It should be clear from the previous discussion that the position that an agent may be responsible even if he could not have acted otherwise is well known. But usually it is based on defining "moral responsibility" in terms of modifiability. Frankfurt, however, does not follow this line. He does not use the expression "moral guilt," but it seems plausible to interpret him to mean that we may give a negative moral evaluation of Jones as an agent, even if he could not have acted otherwise. Is this view correct?[39]

Going back to my example: if Smith made a serious effort to overcome his passion to kill Olga, but failed, his guilt is at least reduced. Frankfurt would probably agree on this. Moreover, if Smith had good reasons to believe that he was powerless so that it was useless to try to overcome his passion, then Smith is either not guilty or his guilt is reduced. But Frankfurt is wrong in maintaining that if Smith killed Olga "because it was what he really wanted to do," then he fulfills the requirement of "alternative possibilities" as far as responsibility is concerned. He does not. For instance, if Smith's passion is the product of a Brave-New-World indoctrination, he is not morally guilty. It may be useful to blame him, just as it may be useful to blame a dog, but he is not *morally* responsible. In general: if Smith's personality had been conditioned in such a way that he was powerless even to conceive of the possibility that it would be wrong to kill Olga or that he ought to put up an effort in order to overcome his desire to kill her, he is not responsible.

P. van Inwagen (1978) defends the thesis that "A person is morally responsible for failing to perform a given act only if he could have performed that act." He gives an example: X sees a person being robbed and decides that he ought to call the police. After further consideration that the robbers might hear of it and wreak their vengeance on him, he decides "not to get involved." But suppose now that the telephone was out of order. Is X morally responsible for failing to call the police? I accept van Inwagen's answer: "Of course not. I (or X) may be responsible for failing to *try* to call the police . . . or for refraining from calling the police, or for having let myself, over the years, become the sort of man who doesn't (try to) call the police under such circumstances. But I am simply not responsible for failing to call the police" (1978, pp. 204–205).

POWER TO DECIDE AND ACT OTHERWISE

Suppose Smith says that he thought it was wrong to kill Olga, that he tried not to kill her, that he made an effort not to kill her, decided not to kill her, and so on (and let us grant that what he says is true), then we would begin to wonder whether he really had it in his power not to kill her. On the other hand, if he did nothing of this sort, and we knew that if he had, he would not have killed her, we seem to have evidence for saying that he had it in his power to refrain from killing her. This suggests that "Smith, in S, had it in his power to do A_2 instead of A_1," in contexts of moral responsibility, implies: "If Smith, in S, had made an effort to do A_2 instead of A_1, then he would have done A_2 instead of A_1."

This suggestion seems acceptable from the point of view of moral responsibility insofar as it involves that Smith can excuse himself as being powerless if he did not succeed in doing A_2 although he made a serious effort to do so. On the other hand, the truth of "If Smith had made an effort to do A_2 instead of A_1, then he would have done A_2 instead of A_1" does not imply that he had it in his power to do A_2 instead of A_1, for we cannot *a priori* assume that Smith had it in his power to make an effort to do A_2. And if he did not have it in his power to make an effort, then he did not have it in his power to do A_2 instead of A_1, even if he would have done A_2 instead of A_1, if he had made an effort to do so.[40] We must admit this, just as we must admit that a person who did not have his head on did not have it in his power to nod at us in the morning, even if it is true that he would have nodded if he had had his head on.

Hence, it is necessary to improve the suggestion above by adding that Smith had it in his power to make an effort to do A_2. This seems better. On the other hand, now the term "power" reappears, and the question is how to interpret it. Different possibilities have been suggested:

i. It is misleading or meaningless to ask such questions as "Does P have it in his power to make an effort? Does he have it in his power to choose?"

ii. "P had it in his power to make an effort to do A_2" must be analyzed indeterministically, viz., as "P's making an effort, as well as his not making an effort, to do A_2 are (or would be) uncaused."

iii. "P had it in his power to make an effort" must itself be analyzed by the use of an if-analysis, e.g., as "P would have made an effort to do A_2, if he had made an effort to make an effort to do A_2."

iv. "P had it in his power to make an effort" must be analyzed as a categorical statement, implying that we can always make an effort.

Thalberg (1964) argues that concepts such as capacity, being able to and, probably also — although he does not say so explicitly — having something in one's power, have no application to normal cases of deciding and the making of efforts. Such concepts apply to actions, not to the will.[41] He tries to show this by an example: "If we take a high school graduate who is faced with a choice of two or three universities, it would be puzzling to ask, 'Can he make up his mind — has he the patience, the skill, the means for reaching a decision?'" (Thalberg, 1964, p. 413). I do not find the question puzzling.

Possibility *ii* does not work, because saying that P's not making an effort was not caused does not imply that he had it in his power to make an effort.

THE CONDITIONAL ANALYSIS DEFENDED:
K. LEHRER AND D. DAVIDSON

Possibility *iii,* it is maintained, leads to an endless regress. But in a recent paper Lehrer (1980) argued that a certain conjunction of conditionals may entail a "could have" statement (using the phrase "could have acted otherwise" rather than "having it in one's power to act otherwise"). I shall summarize his main point by the use of an example. Suppose a person has a preference for smoking over not smoking, and a second-order preference to have the first-order preference, and perhaps also a third-order preference to be a person with this kind of second-order preference. In other words, he has a hierarchy of preferences, and they are not in conflict with each other. If offered a cigarette, the person would probably accept it wholeheartedly.

Could he have acted otherwise? Lehrer seems to mean that whereas it *does not* make good psychological sense to analyze "P could have done A_2 instead of A_1," as "P would have done A_2 instead of A_1, if he had made an effort to do so, and he could have made an effort to do so in the sense that he would have made an effort to do so, if he had made an effort to make an effort to do so," it *does* make good psychological sense to analyze it in the following way: "P would have done A_2 instead of A_1, if he had preferred to do A_2 instead of A_1, and he could have preferred to do A_2 instead of A_1 in the sense that he would have preferred A_2 to A_1, if he had preferred to prefer A_2 to A_1." (According to Lehrer, there is no definite limit to the levels of preferences.)

Lehrer makes the further (and very dubious) assumption that if P had preferred, e.g., at level 3, not to have the second-order preference he actually had, then he would not have had it and, assuming that his preferences are not in conflict, his first-order preference would then change as a result of the change of his second-order preference. (See Lehrer, 1980, p. 201, note 3.)

Several questions must be raised: (*a*) Is it psychologically likely that we can change a hierarchy of preferences by making a change at the top? (*b*) In what way does Lehrer's idea solve the "but could he have had his head on?" problem? A hierarchy of hypothetical preferences does not guarantee that P has "the control he requires." (*c*) Suppose P started Lehrer's the cat-on-the-rat-and-the-rat-on-the-mouse game because he was manipulated to do so. Did he then have all the control he needed? (*d*) A hierarchy of hypothetical preferences is not less hypothetical than one preference, and does not solve the "But could you have had your head on?" problem better than one.

I guess Lehrer brought in the idea of a hierarchy because it sometimes may be very hard to obtain a change at the first-order level (e.g., to change from preferring smoking to nonsmoking to preferring nonsmoking to smoking). In order to obtain the change, we may have to make use of a more indirect approach, starting with something not directly connected with the strong habits and desires at the first level, e.g., reflecting on what sort of person one would like to be. From a therapeutic point of view, this may be a wise idea, but the question in what sense of "power" we have it in our power to engage in such a process is still unanswered.

Davidson (1972) defends a conditional analysis of "could" statements. He agrees that such statements as "P would have done A_2 instead of A_1, if he had tried to" does not imply that P could have done A_2, but he thinks the difficulty can be met if "the antecedent of a causal conditional that attempts to analyze . . . could" does not contain "any verb which makes sense of the question, Can someone do it?"

His own proposal may be roughly summarized as follows: an agent's beliefs and desires explain why he acted as he did (they rationalize the action) but are not themselves "actions or events about which the question whether the agent can perform them can intelligibly be raised." Hence, "P can do A_2 intentionally" may be taken to mean that if P has desires and beliefs that rationalize A_2, then P does A_2.

Davidson is not satisfied with this analysis, among other things, because it does not exclude the possibility that A_2 is brought about by "lunatic internal causal chains" (Davidson, 1972, p. 153). According to Davidson, the analysis does not work unless the beliefs and desires in question cause A_2 "in the right way—through a course of practical reasoning,"[42] and Davidson does not see how to define "the right way."

I shall not go into this difficulty but emphasize only that even if it were solved, his analysis could not give us that meaning of "freedom" in which freedom is a condition of responsibility, for even if Smith would have done A_2 (i.e., not killed Olga) if he had the beliefs and desires that rationalize his doing A_2, actually he did not have them and perhaps didn't know how to get them. And then he did not have it in his power to do A_2.

R. M. CHISHOLM

Chisholm (1968) also defends an analysis of "could have done otherwise" sentences which is partly conditional. In terms of my example, he seems to mean that "Smith could have done A_2 [not killing Olga] instead of A_1 [killing her]" implies that if Smith, e.g., at 10 o'clock, April 30, 1980, had seen a psychiatrist in order to overcome his desire to kill Olga, and if some other conditions were fulfilled also, then he would not have killed her. The thrilling question, then, is in what sense of "power" Chisholm maintains that Smith had it in his power to fulfill the if-clause. Chisholm's answer seems to be that we must assume that at 10 o'clock April 30, 1980, and at no time prior to that, was there sufficient causal condition for Smith's not then seeing a psychiatrist (Chisholm, 1968, p. 244). This point is not quite clear, however, for Chisholm maintains that any action is caused by events with the exception that "at least one of the events that is involved in any act is caused, not by any other event or set of events, but by the agent" (who is uncaused) (1968, pp. 242–43).

Suppose the events involved in Smith's choosing to see a psychiatrist would have been caused by the agent (Smith). Then even these events would have been caused and hence had sufficient conditions (unless Chisholm maintains that agent causality cannot be described in terms of sufficient conditions). But let us, for the sake of argument, assume that at 10 o'clock April 30 there were no sufficient causal conditions for Smith's not choosing to see a psychiatrist.

This does not imply that Smith had it in his power to choose to see a psychiatrist (and Chisholm, of course, is aware of this). The absence of causes is not the same as the presence of inner resources. Smith may have been completely empty inside at the given time or so filled with his desire to kill that he was powerless even to conceive of the possibility that it might be wrong to do so. Smith's having it in his power to choose seeing a psychiatrist in order to overcome his desire to kill Olga presupposes, first, that Smith had it in his power to feel or understand that it might be questioned whether killing was the right thing to do. Next, he must have been able to call forth, and come in contact with, psychological forces, e.g., feelings or reasons, opposed to killing. Having reached this stage, he might have been able to think about the consequences of what he planned to do.

Given that Smith had the inner resources required for starting a process of this kind, he might not have found it too difficult to decide to see a psychiatrist. But the absence of causes in Chisholm's sense does not guarantee the presence of such resources, and if Smith has them, nothing is gained by the absence of causes.

Chisholm talks about having something "directly" or "indirectly" within one's power. Smith may have had it directly within his power at 10 o'clock April 30 to make an effort to consider the possibility that it might be wrong to kill Olga, but he may then have had it only indirectly in his power to arrange things so that he would not kill her. Although Chisholm does not say so, perhaps he has in mind the idea of an indirect approach, according to which one starts out with a step that does not encounter too strong an inner resistance at the same time as it makes the next step somewhat less difficult than it otherwise would have been. Chisholm thinks that an agent "may have been so situated that, if he *had* taken the first step, then he *would* have had it directly within his power to take the second, and if he had then taken the second, then he would have had it directly within his power to take the third, and so on" (Chisholm, 1968, p. 245). Chisholm's way of expressing himself does not quite fit with the idea of an indirect approach, since he says that if the person takes the first step "then he would have had it directly within his power to take the second." An indirect approach is based on the idea of gradually increasing one's power to take further steps, and there is no given series. Nevertheless, I think he must have had an insight of this kind rather than the trivial idea that (following his example) taking one step toward Boston brings the next step directly within one's power.

THE CATEGORICAL ANALYSIS DEFENDED

Let us turn to the fourth suggestion mentioned above. According to Hampshire, Smith can excuse himself by saying that he tried with all his power and failed; or that he abstained from trying because he knew that he would fail (Hampshire, 1959, p. 183); but he cannot excuse himself by saying that he did not have it in his power to try, for "there is no sense in which it is impossible for him to intend to do something, provided that he knows what would be involved in doing it. He can always set out on the course of action, even if he knows that he will encounter difficulties at the very first stage of effective action, and even if he believes that he will in fact fail before any effective action has been taken" (Hampshire, 1959, pp. 182–83).

Whether we shall accept the thesis that in normal situations one can always intend to do something (or, as I prefer to say, make an effort to do something) depends upon what we mean by "making an effort." If we are willing to say that Smith made an effort not to kill Olga when he whispered certain sounds to himself, then we may probably assert, on empirical grounds, that we always have in our power to make an effort, for those who cannot whisper certain sounds to themselves are not rational animals, but vegetables. But if we take "making an effort" in such a weak sense, we at the same time reduce the likelihood that the statement "If the agent had made an effort to do A_2 instead of A_1, then he would have done A_2" will be true, except in very unimportant cases. On the other hand, if we take "making an effort" in a stronger sense, referring to an energetic effort like thinking about the consequences, studying the case closely, etc., then it probably is false that we can always make an effort.

Suppose Smith had it in his power to make an effort not to kill Olga, but that he did not think about the possibility of doing so. Let us even suppose that given his intelligence, upbringing, and imagination, he could not even be expected to think about this. Hampshire maintains that a person, in such a situation, can excuse himself (1959, p. 186), and I agree with him, if "could not be expected to" implies that the person was powerless. It is a virtue of Hampshire's exposition that he discusses such cases and tries to combine limitations of will with limitations of intellect. But if he really wanted to develop a philosophy of the freedom of the mind, not only of the will, he should also have discussed the influence of a person's moral convictions. Suppose Smith would have done A_2 if he had made an effort to do so. Suppose further that he had it in his power to make an effort and thought about doing so, but was firmly convinced that it would be morally wrong. Did he then have freedom of the mind? A person's moral convictions may be one of the most important limitations of his power to act, for bad or for good.

Making a serious effort not to kill Olga involves that Smith reconsiders the issue, thinks about the consequences of killing her and of the misery and suffering he will produce, thinks about the fact that he will break moral rules that he may be interested in having others obey toward him, and so on. And he must not only be able to think about these things, but to react emotionally to his cognitive expectations. He must be able to react toward Olga, and other persons involved, not as dead things, but as living creatures whose suffering would be analogous to what his own suffering would be.

Locke (1962) interprets "*P* could have tried" in a categorical way: nothing prevented *P* from trying (p. 253). But a person who is empty inside is not prevented from trying, but does not for that reason have it in his power to try.

According to Danto (1965), trying is "a basic action": it is not something we bring about by first doing something else. Unless we have something in our power in a direct sense, we have nothing in our power; for having everything in our power only in the sense that we can bring it about by first doing something else would lead to an endless regress. But cannot even trying be a nonbasic action? One *may* try by deciding to try.

Danto tries to define a normal person in terms of a certain repertoire of basic actions, saying that persons who are unable to do these actions are abnormal. If we assume that making an effort is a basic action, this gives a simple solution of the "But could he have had his head on?" problem: unless a person is abnormal, he is always able to make an effort. The difficult task of finding out whether or not Smith had it in his power to make a serious effort is reduced to the simpler task of finding out whether or not he was crazy. (I admit however, that a person who does not have it in his power to have his head on must be either crazy, abnormal, or, more likely, dead as a doornail.)

Kenny (1978) seems to imply that Smith had it in his power not to kill Olga only if he had what Kenny calls the "opportunity" and "ability" not to do so. Glover (1970) takes a similar view: "Someone can do something in the 'all-in' sense when he has the opportunity to do it, and the ability both to decide to do it and to put his decision into effect" (p. 77). And Ayers (1966) says " 'John could have won' is not to hint . . . that an antecedent condition is not fulfilled." The statement is not conditional. It is rather to imply that "the power, ability, possibility, capacity or potentiality in question is not, or was not, or will not be exercised" (Ayers, 1966, p. 119. See also Ayers, 1968, pp. 102f.)

I interpret the above authors to mean that "*P* in *S* had it in his power to do A_2 instead of A_1" is an empirical statement about the agent and his situation. I agree on this, but the term "ability" is misleading. Smith may have it in his power to resist his temptation to kill Olga, even if he does not have an ability to resist such temptations (see above, p. 56).

A so-called hard determinist has no reason to deny that we may have something in our power in the sense indicated above. Let us take an example: Mr. *X* is born in Oslo and talks Norwegian fluently. Mr. *Y* is born in Nairobi and does not talk Norwegian. At 10 o'clock April 30 neither of them talked Norwegian. A determinist will maintain that in both cases this can be explained in terms of sufficient conditions. Let us, for the sake of argument, accept this. Nevertheless, the determinist must accept that there is an important difference between them: whereas *X* in the given situation had the resources required for talking Norwegian, *Y* did not. Hence, in this sense of "power" *X* had it in his power to talk Norwegian (we assume that there were no external obstacles) at the given time, whereas *Y* did not. But, the hard determinist will maintain that there is another (and more important!) sense of "power" in which determinism implies that both were equally powerless to talk Norwegian at 10 o'clock that day. It remains to clarify what this sense is, and to discuss whether it is in this or in the previous sense of "power" that the lack of power ought to be accepted as a moral excuse.

Keeping to the first sense of "power," society expects that we have it in our power to follow its moral rules. The expectation is not ungrounded, for our power to do so is correlated with our power to function normally in other respects: to be able to buy milk and bread, to look after our house and fire. But the important thing, from the point of view of moral responsibility, is that we cannot exclude the possibility that a person functioning normally, in a specific situation, did not have it in his power to act otherwise. Perhaps he was mentally disturbed at the crucial moment. He was unable to think about the consequences of killing his wife and hold this cognitive image before his mind for the amount of time required to react emotionally to it, or he was unable to experience her as a living creature in analogy with himself. Hence, we can never be certain that a person who did not do A_2 really had it in his power to do A_2.

If we could have a sort of psychological X-ray giving us a picture of all the forces operating within the agent during his deliberation, and if we knew how to interpret it, we could, in principle, decide whether or not Smith had it in his power to refrain from killing Olga.

POWER VERSUS BELIEFS ABOUT POWER

If God went mad, he might start to believe that he was a powerless sparrow, forgetting that he could create universes by his bare words. If an ordinary mortal went mad, he might start to believe that he could create solar systems by a smile or a pointed finger. Thus, a discrepancy may exist between the power we actually have and the power we believe we have.[43] To return to our example: suppose Smith has been taught, from his childhood on, that there is no point in his trying to resist evil impulses, because he is a powerless creature. Then, even if Smith had it in his power to refrain from killing Olga in the sense indicated above, he may not have been fully responsible, or perhaps not responsible at all, because he believed what he had been taught. In some cases we could perhaps maintain that he had it in his power to understand that he accepted a false belief about himself. But in other cases we could not, and even when we could, this would not change the fact that this agent, ethically speaking, is different from a person who knew about his own power, for a person who believes he is powerless in a sense is powerless. Hence, in order to be morally responsible for a certain wrongdoing, the agent must not only have it in his power to do something that would have been ethically better; he must also have no good reasons for believing that he lacked this power.

DEGREES OF POWER

Some of the above ideas may suggest that it is more fruitful to talk about power in comparative than in dichotomous terms. Let us try to indicate some of the factors determining our degree of power, limiting ourselves to our power to *decide* otherwise.

It seems a plausible hypothesis that the power of a certain person, P, in a certain situation S, to decide D_2 instead of D_1 (his actual decision) was greater the less effort he would have had to make in order to decide D_2 instead of D_1, and this effort would be less

1. the less the value distance between D_2 and D_1 as interpreted by P in view of his ethical system. For example: between deciding to give a child a Norwegian or a Swedish crown, equally strongly desired, there is, for P, no difference in value. The situation is an indifference situation. On the other hand, there is great difference in value between giving him a crown or taking a crown away from him,

2. the stronger his motivation toward D_2 as compared with his motivation toward D_1,

3. the stronger his conviction that he ought to decide D_2 as compared with his conviction that he ought to decide D_1,

4. the stronger the cognitive support of his belief that he ought to decide D_2 as compared with the support of his belief that he ought to decide D_1,

5. the more conscious he was of the possibility of deciding D_2,

6. the more he knew about how to proceed in order to make himself prefer D_2 to D_1.

This list, which is not meant to be exhaustive, indicates some of the difficulties involved in determining to what degree a certain agent had it in his power to decide otherwise than he in fact did, and thereby also some of the difficulties involved in ascribing a certain degree of moral responsibility to an agent. (O'Connor is one of the few who has commented on the idea that freedom is a matter of degree [1971], p. 122. See also Naess's discussion of Spinoza's concept of freedom [1975], pp. 55f.)

POWER AND CAUSALITY

Let us turn to the question whether power to decide and act otherwise is compatible with the principle of causality. Let us formulate the problem in the following way:

Given the two statements, (a) Smith's killing Olga (A_1), in S, was caused, and (b) Smith, in S, had it in his power to do A_2 instead of A_1, does (a) imply that (b) is false?

I have argued that (b) implies "If Smith, in S, had made an effort to do A_2 instead of A_1, then he would have done A_2" and "Smith, in S, had it in his power to make an effort to do A_2."

Obviously, (a) does not imply that the first implication is false. The crucial question, therefore, is whether (a) implies that it is false that Smith in S had it in his power to make an effort to do A_2. In order to make the problem as simple as possible, let us assume that Smith did not make an effort to do A_2, and that his not-making-an-effort (NoE) was caused. Therefore, (c) Smith's NoE in S was caused, and (d) Smith, in S, had it in his power to make an effort to do A_2.

The standard argument for showing that (c) implies that (d) is false, is this: if NoE was caused, then certain conditions, C, were causally sufficient for NoE. If C were causally sufficient for NoE, then it was causally impossible for Smith, in S, to make an effort to do A_2. If it was causally impossible for Smith to make an effort to do A_2, then he could not make an effort to do A_2. And if he could not make an effort to do A_2, then he did not have it in his power to make an effort to do A_2.

Let us grant that if NoE was caused, then C was causally sufficient for NoE. The crucial question is whether this admission implies that it was causally impossible for Smith, in S, to make an effort to do A_2 in such a sense of "causally impossible" that it follows that Smith did not have it in his power to make an effort to do A_2 in that sense of "power" in which the lack of power is a moral excuse.

If we interpret "It was causally impossible for Smith, in S, to make an effort to do A_2" in such a way that what is asserted follows from what we have admitted, viz., that C was causally sufficient for NoE, then it may be formulated in the following way: (c.1) C was the case in S, and it would be inconsistent with certain laws of nature to assert that C was the case in S, and that NoE did not occur in S.

Does (c.1) imply that (d) is false? The answer, it seems to me, is in the negative. (c.1) does not assert that given C and the laws of nature, it nevertheless was empirically possible or probable to this or that degree that Smith, in S, would make an effort to do A_2. (d) talks about Smith's *power* to make an effort, not of his exercise of this power. (c.1), on the other hand, implies that C and Smith's making an effort to do A_2 in S add up to an empirically impossible totality, but does not say a word about Smith's power. For instance, it does not assert that Smith would have had to overcome strong inner resistance in order to make an effort to do A_2 in S. In relation to (c.1) it might have been just as easy for Smith to make an effort to do A_2 as to utter his name. Hence, since (c.1) and (d) talk about different things in this sense, (c.1) can neither imply that (d) is false, nor that it is true.

The view that causality is compatible with power to act otherwise (compatibilism) is defended by Canfield (1962), Aune (1962–63), Hampshire (1965), MacKay (1967), Ayers (1968), Saunders (1968), Glover (1970), Kenny (1978), and Ofstad (1961 and 1981). Disregarding minor differences, the compatibilists agree that we must distinguish between *power* to act otherwise and the *exercise* of this power. If determinism is true, then the fact that Smith in S did not exercise his power to do A_2 and actually did A_1 has causally sufficient conditions. But this does not imply that Smith in S did not have the capacity and opportunity to act otherwise.

P. van INWAGEN

P. van Inwagen (1974) pretends to give a disproof of compatibilism.[44] He does not deny that free will may be compatible with the principle that every event has a cause, but maintains that it is incompatible with determinism, which he defines as the conjunction of the following two theses:

(*a*) For every instant of time, there is a proposition that expresses the state of the world at that instant.

(*b*) If A and B are any propositions that express states of the world at some instants, the conjunction of A with the laws of physics entails B (van Inwagen, 1974, p. 186).

By a "law of physics" he understands a law of nature (e.g., a law about chemical valences) that is not about the voluntaristic behavior of rational agents. According to van Inwagen, it is a conceptual truth that we do not have it in our power to render a law of physics false (1974, p. 193).

His disproof is related to an example: a certain judge, J, had only to raise his right hand at a certain time, t, to prevent the execution of a sentence of death upon a certain criminal, but he did not do it. If determinism is true, J did not at t have it in his power to raise his arm.

Before presenting his argument, we note that t_0 denotes some instant of time earlier than J's birth, P_0 denotes the proposition that expresses the state of the world at t_0, P denotes the proposition that expresses the state of the world at t, and L denotes the conjunction into a single proposition of all laws of physics.

Here is the argument:

1. If determinism is true, then the conjunction of P_0 and L entails P.
2. If J had raised his arm at t, then P would be false.
3. If (2) is true, then if J could have raised his arm at t, J could have rendered P false.
4. If J could have rendered P false, and if the conjunction of P_0 and L entails P, then J could have rendered the conjunction of P_0 and L false.
5. If J could have rendered the conjunction of P_0 and L false, then J could have rendered L false.
6. J could not have rendered L false.
7. If determinism is true, J could not have raised his arm at t.

If we accept van Inwagen's definition of "determinism," his conception of a physical law, his idea that statements saying that we have something in our power can "easily be translated" into statements saying that we could have rendered this or that statement false (3 above) and, finally, that we cannot change the past, then it follows that determinism is incompatible with asserting that J, and t, could have raised his arm. (For a somewhat similar argument, see Kant, *Kritik der praktischen Vernunft*, herausg. von Hartenstein [Leipzig, 1838], vol. IV, pp. 210–11.) The crucial question is in what sense of "could not" it has been shown that the judge could not have raised his arm.

Let us assume that the law of gravitation is an example of a law we cannot falsify. One day, in bad humor, we jump from the Empire State Building. Refreshed by the trip, we change our mind and make an effort to stop, but in vain. Remembering that religious conversion may be sufficient to stop addiction to heroin, we try to stop the fall by starting to believe in God. But in this situation religion is of no help. Down we go to asphalt and final judgment.

If all laws were of this kind, we would be powerless in a simple and conspicuous sense. But the judge was not necessarily powerless in this sense, for his not raising his arm may have been caused by his herculean effort to keep his arm down, in spite of his strong compassion for the condemned. If we make this assumption, then the judge, at t, exercised his power. On the other hand, if the judge, at t, knowing that the verdict was wrong, made a strenuous effort to raise his arm but was unable to do so because he was afraid of public criticism, then he was powerless. From the point of view of morality there is an important difference between these two versions of the judge. Let us call the state of the world at t given the first version , P_1, and the state of the world given the second version, P_2. Following van Inwagen, we also distinguish between P_{01} and P_{02}. We would then still have that P_{01} and L entails P_1, and P_{02} and L entails P_2. But the one judge had it in his power to act as he thought he ought to, the other did not.

We may have a third version, too: the judge may be rather indifferent to the verdict. He held his arm down but could easily have raised it as far as his inner capacities were concerned.

Van Inwagen does not have to disagree with the above reasoning. But the question remains: In what sense of "could not" does he mean that the judge could not have raised his arm? Does he mean that the judge could not have raised his arm in such a sense of "could not" that the judge, in version one, is equally powerless as the judge in version two? And, consequently, are they on the same footing as far as that kind of powerlessness is concerned which is of moral interest? The weak point of his article is that van Inwagen does not clarify his meaning of "could not".[45]

THE FAULT, DEAR BRUTUS

Let us grant that even if any event has a cause, yes, even if determinism is true, the agent may have it in his power to act otherwise in the sense mentioned earlier, viz., that he may have the opportunity, resources, and capacities, e.g., the sensitivity and perceptiveness for acting otherwise. Then the question is: Does having it in one's power to do A_2 instead of A_1 in this sense, and believing that one does, suffice to fulfill the requirement of power to act otherwise as far as moral responsibility is concerned? Going back to our example: If Smith, in S, had it in his power to let Olga live in the above sense, does he then fulfill the requirement of power, or must we assume something else or something more in order that our judgment about his moral guilt shall be justified?[46]

Some require what they believe to be something more. They require that Smith had it in his power to act otherwise in exactly that situation in which he killed Olga, or, as others would say, that he some time earlier, when he was doing so and so, had it in his power in *that* situation (exactly as it was) to start a process that might prevent the killing, e.g., visiting a psychiatrist. The contention is that unless he could have done so, he was powerless even if he were free in the above capacity-opportunity sense.

I find it hard to understand this point of view. First, if we say that Smith, in S, had the capacity and opportunity for acting otherwise, this is a categorical statement about Smith and the situation in which he acted. It is not a statement to the effect that if Smith's situation had been different in this or that respect, he would then have had the required capacity and opportunity. Second, Smith is not a powerless object to the forces operating in the situation. He would have been so if his situation had been like the jumping-from-the-Empire-State-Building. In that situation, his knowledge of the law of gravitation and the forces operating did not help him a bit. But a decision situation is not of that kind. In a decision situation it is, in principle, up to the agent to get knowledge of the forces operating and to use his knowledge in order to change the situation and himself. Suppose he understands that he is dominated by a passion to kill Olga. This knowledge makes it possible for him to take steps preventing his fall. And the same holds for any force or causal factor we can conceive of, even for a report about the neuro-physiological state of his brain.

Of course, Smith's power to act otherwise may turn out to be very limited. But this is not a consequence of causality or determinism. His power wouldn't increase if he suddenly became an unmoved mover or the universe became nondeterministic. His power can increase only through deeper insight, better reasoning, closer contact with his own feelings, more well-founded evaluations, stronger identity — in short, through whatever helps to make one master of oneself. "The fault, dear Brutus, is not in our stars. But in ourselves."

Power and Empirical Conditions

The fact that the principle of causality does not annihilate or reduce our power to decide or act otherwise does not imply that we have such power.

Our power may be limited by empirical conditions, such as our lack of imagination and knowledge, or by our inner conflicts and ethical convictions. Hence, we must raise the following question: To what degree do we, from an empirical point of view, have it in our power to decide and act? My comments below will be limited to our power to decide, since I consider this the most fundamental question.

The answer depends, *inter alia,* on the conditions we require in order to say that a decision has been made. If by "decision'" we refer to low-integrated decisions, our power is rather unlimited.[47] Even the most-aggressive person can say, "I ought to be friendly toward all people"; even the most-benevolent person can say, "All people ought to be tortured to death." Hence, if by "decision" we mean just forming the words "I ought to do so and so," then all who can think have the power to make any decision whatsoever. The statement "Every person has it in his power to make any decision" may even become analytically true, if "person" is so defined that the ability to form sentences is one of the conceptual characteristics. This interpretation, though seldom made explicit, may be one source of the strength of the conviction that we have a completely free will. We believe that we can do anything because we can say anything.

Let us turn to the question of our power to make stable decisions that are high-integrated. Even such decisions can easily be made if they encounter no inner resistance. The crucial question, therefore, concerns our power to make decisions that are stable even though they meet with strong inner resistance. We may formulate the questions thus: To what degree does a person, who in a certain situation decided in an ethically wrong way and felt a strong resistance against deciding as he ought to, have it in his power to make a stable and ethically right decision? And, conversely, to what extent does a person have it in his power to decide in an ethically wrong instead of in an ethically right way?

I cannot here and now create within myself a stable decision to exterminate humanity. The conditions of such a decision do not exist. The decision would presuppose a change in my personality. And I cannot here and now form my own personality just as I form a piece of clay. I have it in my power — as unconditionally as I have anything in my power — to say the words "I ought to exterminate humanity"; I may even envisage some good consequences of this action, but there is nothing I can do, no instructions I can give myself, no process of reasoning I can carry out, by the use of which I can get myself to make a stable decision to this effect. It is like my decision to become an angel. It is easy to say the words "I ought to become an angel." It is more difficult to be able to make the feathers grow.[48]

"WHAT WOUND DID EVER HEAL, BUT BY DEGREES"?

Even decisions over which we have no immediate power may be brought about eventually, for our power is neither an innate ability nor a product finished once and for all. Just as we acquire the ability to make use of symbols, we acquire the ability to use symbols for building and strengthening motivational and cognitive orientations toward certain goals.

Suppose that a man engaged to Miss C is considering breaking the engagement, but is unable to make a high-integrated and stable decision to break it. Seeking advice from his philosophical friend, he is told that he should not force himself to make the decision, but rather should find a more indirect approach: instead of aiming at the break directly, he should try to find out what is holding him back. Although he has great trouble in making a stable decision to break the engagement, he may have less trouble in trying to find out *why* this is so, and still less in noticing changes in his behavior in certain situations. By a procedure of this kind the man may find a point from which he can direct his attacks toward the further goal. As a first step he may try to keep some records of his verbal and nonverbal responses to a number of cues related to his problem and note his "marginal thoughts."[49] When responding to this flow of information, he may be able to label some of his suppressed action-tendencies and to develop, on the symbolic level, more adequate forms of discrimination and generalization. Furthermore, he may try to notice what kind of verbal and nonverbal responses are most strongly associated with anxiety. Through this the person gradually changes. His perceptions, cognitions, and valuations of his environment and self become different. A person who, after an interval of this kind, returns to a more-direct consideration of arguments for and against his planned decision may find that he does not have to *make* a decision at all; it may have developed as a by-product of his thinking and analysis.

I do not believe that an approach of the kind indicated always will be successful. But some decisions that could not have been made by a direct attempt may develop as the result of a more-indirect procedure.

Ethics and Free Will

A philosopher who holds an optimistic opinion concerning our power to decide and act otherwise may nevertheless maintain that our will is not free, because he holds that moral guilt does not presuppose freedom in this sense but in the sense that we can create our own character, something he denies. On the other hand, a philosopher who maintains that we do not have it in our power to decide and act otherwise may hold that we have a free will, because he believes that the notion of moral guilt is metaphysical nonsense and that the question of freedom concerns our modifiability through the use of blame.

Hence, a solution of the free-will issue presupposes that we have clarified (a) in what sense of "moral responsibility" it is correct to assert that we may be responsible, and (b) in what sense of "free will," if any, free will is a condition of responsibility.

MORAL GUILT AND POWER

Power to act otherwise is not the only condition of moral guilt; knowledge of facts and the acceptance of moral norms are necessary, too. Moral guilt, like criminal guilt, should be conceived of in such a way that it can vary in degree. An agent may be guilty to a high degree if he intentionally did evil and had a high degree of power to act otherwise. He may be guilty to a low degree if he either did not expect any harmful consequences of his behavior or had a very low degree of power to act otherwise. A maximum of guilt presupposes power to act otherwise in its highest degree, yet we seldom, if ever, have this amount of power, especially in situations where we acted wrongly. It may be emotionally convenient to believe that the great evildoers are maximally guilty, but usually they are closer to evil things than evil agents, petrified by their limited power to act otherwise as well as by their limited knowledge and moral understanding.

Power to act otherwise is a condition of moral guilt because a wrongdoer who is unable to act rightly is not a morally bad man. If he acted wrongly in spite of the fact that he tried with all his energy to act rightly, he may be a morally good person. The same holds for a wrongdoer who on sufficiently good grounds held the false opinion that he was so completely powerless to act rightly that he had no reason to try. But what should we say about a wrongdoer who did not have it in his power to act rightly but believed that he did, and nevertheless refrained from even trying to do so? It seems to me that such a person may be just as morally bad as one who actually had the power in question. Nevertheless, it would be misleading to say that he is guilty of the wrongdoing, although he may be guilty of not having tried to act rightly.

MORAL BLAME, POWER AND MODIFIABILITY

Just as we may have to catch a tiger and lock it up, we may have to catch a man running wild. And just as we may blame a dog, we may blame a man simply because it is useful. But in such cases we should talk about nonmoral, rather than moral, blame.

According to my own ethical position (which I cannot try to formulate and defend in this essay), moral blame presupposes moral guilt, but guilt is not a sufficient condition. To blame a person is to act toward him in a certain way, and an act is unjustified if it makes the world worse than if one had acted otherwise. Hence, moral blame presupposes utility as well as guilt.[50] And we must ask: Is blame a more-useful means of reformation, prevention, deterrence, or moral education than other means we could use? We do not know, but a large number of studies on the effects of punishment suggest that the use of blame is an ineffective way of modifying people's behavior.[51] Perhaps use of blame fulfills a function for the moral judge, whereas argumentation, knowledge, or a nicer wife (or husband) are more effective instruments of change. Hence, although it is not logically contradictory to assert that a wrongdoer ought to be morally blamed, it is seldom that our imperfect world satisfies those conditions of guilt and utility that give us the right to engage in this noble practice.

Power and Uncertainty

The crucial question within the free-will debate concerns our power to decide and act otherwise than we in fact do. These powers vary in degrees, and the degree depends upon the agent's personality and the situation. What one man can do is not necessarily what another can do, and what we can accomplish in one situation may be different from what we can accomplish in another.

In order to know to what degree a certain person had it in his power to act otherwise, we would have to have a correct picture of all the forces—positive and negative—operating within him during his deliberation. But our evidence on such matters is indirect and inconclusive, to say the least. Hence, in most cases we cannot know to what degree a person had it in his power to decide or act otherwise. We can only have a more or less well-grounded opinion. Consequently, since moral blame and guilt presupposes power, we can neither be certain that our wrongdoer is morally guilty, nor that he ought to be blamed. And this is not a bad reason for moderation in attributing guilt and blame.

Notes

1. This, of course, is quite an arbitrary delimitation of a period of debate.
2. Blanshard is one of the few exceptions. See his "The Case for Determinism" in Hook, ed. (1958). (Complete references can be found by consulting the bibliography.) Different definitions of "the principle of causality" are discussed in the literature referred to.
3. See, e.g., Nagel (1961), pp. 316 ff.
4. Bergson, *Time and Free Will* (London, 1910), pp. 184 ff.

5. Cf. W. Dilthey, "Ideen über eine beschreibende und zergliedernde Psychologie," published 1894, reprinted in *Gesammelte Schriften* (Leipzig und Berlin, 1924), Book V, pp. 139–240; and H. Rickert, *Kulturwissenschaft und Naturwissenschaft* (Tübingen, 1915). Recently von Wright (1975) has given a penetrating discussion of "explanation" and "understanding."

6. Taylor is one of the exceptions. See his "Determinism and the Theory of Agency" in Hook, ed. (1958), p. 226.

7. The thesis — that moral systems determine the sense of "free" required by moral responsibility — I first developed in *Freedom of Decision*, I–IV, Institute for Social Research, Oslo, 1953, and later in Ofstad (1961). Austin's "A Plea for Excuses" (1956–57) stimulated interest in the moral context of the free-will problem, but judging from his "Ifs and Cans" he did not always clearly understand the implications of his own approach. The relativity of the interpretation of "free will" to moral systems is discussed in Beardsley (1960–61), Kaufman (1962), Whiteley (1962–63), Bronaugh (1964), Kaufman (1967), Aune (1969–70), White (1973), and Ross (1975).

8. Somewhat similar distinctions are made by Feinberg (1965). See also Brandt (1958), Friedrich (1960), and Hospers (1961). A useful discussion of the concept of criminal responsibility can be found in Wootton (1959).

9. See Thalberg (1964).

10. I regard the dispute over fatalism and free will as a "How-do-you-handle-this-argument?" game rather than as serious philosophy. (Indirectly it may have a certain philosophical value in pressing forward more precise analyses of "having something in one's power.") I shall pay no attention to the dispute in this essay. A bibliography including some of the articles can be found in Steven Cahn's "Fatalistic Arguments," *The Journal of Philosophy* 61 (1964), p. 295.

11. The discussion elicited by Ginet's article includes contributions by, among others, Canfield (1961–62), Swiggart (1962–63), Lehrer (1963), Thalberg (1963–64), Berofsky (1964), and Taylor (1964a).

12. Some of the psychological problems rooted in the distinction between agent and spectator are discussed by Hampshire (1959) and O'Shaughnessy (1963), and by several authors in *The Monist* 49 (1965).

13. As regards the implications of knowing about the prediction, see also Lyon (1959), MacKay (1960), C.J.F. Williams (1960–61), Canfield (1961), Beck (1965), and Perry (1965).

14. Compare Stenner (1964). See also Popper (1950).

15. Cf. my discussion of "observation-sensitive phenomena" (Ofstad, 1961, pp. 71–82).

16. Cf. Grünbaum (1971), p. 317, and Ofstad (1961), p. 133. For a discussion of MacKay's view, see Evans and Landsberg (1972) and Watkins (1971). See also Popper's classical paper (1950) in which he states that "there exist finite specified classical mechanical prediction tasks which no classical mechanical predictor can perform" (p. 128).

17. Critical comments on Melden will be found in Ewing (1963–64) and Hamlyn (1964). Also see Davidson (1963) and G. J. Warnock's "Actions and Events" in Pears, ed. (1963).

18. Cf. Yolton (1962).

19. Cf. Geach (1960).

20. Cf. Ayer (1963), pp. 266 ff. See also Smart (1963) and Feigl and Meehl's discussion of Popper's "Of Clouds and Clocks" in Schilpp, ed. (1974).

21. Cf. Hampshire (1959), p. 129; and Ofstad (1961), pp. 196–203.

22. For a different point of view, see Popper (1972), p. 226 and Margenau (1967). For a discussion of causality and determinism, see Farrer (1958), Ofstad (1961), Berofsky (1971) and von Wright (1974). A discussion of different interpretations of "determinism" and different arguments pertaining to this issue will be found in Hook (1958), Pts. I & II. See also Brandt (1959); Hospers (1961); Pears (1963), Ch. 4; and Taylor, "Determinism" in P. Edwards, ed., *The Encyclopedia of Philosophy*, vol. 1 (New York, 1967), pp. 359–73. The use of causal explanations in science is discussed in Bohm (1957), Grünbaum (1957), Scriven (1957), Bunge (1959), Waismann (1959), Munn (1960), Nagel (1961), and Boring (1963).

23. Campbell's way of thinking was defended by Lehrer (1960). Criticism can be found in R. D. Bradley (1958), Franklin (1962), and Nowell-Smith (1954). Campbell's answers will be found in (1958), (1962), and, to Nowell-Smith, in (1957), pp. 214–28.

24. Obviously, my use of this example does not pretend to correspond to the historical facts.

25. In his book (1968) Franklin defends a libertarian view based on the assertion that "we can always control the movement of our attention" (p. 73). Says Franklin: "In a clash between what is believed to be our duty and temptation, what actually happens at the moment of decision? Is it not that we either direct our attention to the fact that this is our duty, and refuse to think about

the attractiveness of the other course, and simply try to put our duty out of our mind as best we can?" (p. 77). According to the author, this selective directing of attention implies that "there must be a crucial lack of determinism in the phenomena of the brain" (p. 143).

26. A somewhat similar view has been formulated by Taylor. See his contribution to Hook, ed. (1958) and his books (1963) and (1966), pp. 55 and 111f.

27. The notion of agent causality is criticized by Davidson (1971) and by Thalberg (1972), pp. 35-47. The former maintains that "a man is the agent of an act if what he does can be described under an aspect that makes it intentional" (p. 7). Davidson thinks causality central to the concept of agency, "but it is ordinary causality between events that is relevant" (p. 16). For criticism of Chisholm's view on responsibility, see Ranken (1967).

28. Baylis (1958), pp. 37-38, seems to take the second position, but I shall not go into his reasoning here.

29. He seems to mean that theories stressing modifiability must be based on emotions – not reasons – but he gives no reasons for this.

30. Hook, in his contribution "Necessity, Indeterminism, and Sentimentalism" to Hook, ed. (1958), points to this unclarity on pp. 187-88. And A. Pap maintains that it is just as meaningless to talk about "choosing my own character" as "eating my own character." See his "Determinism, Freedom, Moral Responsibility, and Causal Talk" in Hook, ed. (1958), p. 215.

31. A somewhat similar point of view has been developed by Matson (1956).

32. Arguments in favor of this view can also be found in Blanshard, op. cit.; Ducasse, "Determinism, Freedom, and Responsibility" in Hook (1958); Hook, op. cit.; Pap, op. cit.; Brandt (1959); Mandelbaum (1959-60), Ofstad (1961), ch. 6, sect, 18; Zink (1962); and Vivian (1964). Cf. also Hampshire (1965).

33. Suppose the moral rules of a certain society accept being subjected to threat as an excuse, but not being too inattentive or too cowardly. Suppose now that Smith would not have killed if he had not been threatened to do so. According to the rules in question, he can then excuse himself. But even if threatened, perhaps he would not have killed if he had been more courageous or more alert. In order to decide whether or not Smith can excuse himself under such conditions, we must make an evaluation of all the morally relevant factors in the situation: How frightening was the threat? How frightening did Smith perceive it to be? How courageous would he have had to be in order to disregard the threat? How attentive would he have had to be in order to discover the threat in time?, and so on. Only when all such factors have been considered, can we decide whether or not Smith has an acceptable excuse.

34. As does Audi (1974), who maintains that "we surely should not accept a claim that x could not have done otherwise if we believe a morally sound person in the relevant circumstances could reasonably have been expected to do otherwise" (p. 11). See also Watson (1977).

35. Cf. Locke (1962) and Thalberg (1961-62).

36. Cf. Hart (1962), p. 25; Richman (1969), p. 196. Dore (1966) even goes so far as maintaining that P was able to do A_2 instead of A_1 if A_2 "can be brought about by persuasion, punishment or blame" (p. 140). He seems to believe that free will = manipulability.

37. The discussion elicited by Austin's paper includes contributions by Lehrer (1959-60), Nowell-Smith (1960), O'Connor (1960), Taylor (1960), Goldberg and Heidelberger (1960-61), Lehrer (1961-62), Thalberg (1961-62), R. D. Bradley (1962), Kaufman (1962), Locke (1962), Dore (1962-63, 1963-64), Scarrow (1962-63), Whiteley (1962-63), Aune (1962-63), Baier (1961), Henschen-Dahlquist (1963), Ewing (1963-64), Honoré (1964), Chisholm (1964), Ayers (1966), and Davidson (1973).

38. Cf. in this connection Wilson (1958). See also Ralls's discussion of the relation between responsibility and personal identity (1963). Philippa Foot defends the tough line that "The argument that it will be a different *me* who will be beaten tomorrow carries no weight, for 'different' or not, the back which will be beaten is the one about which I am concerned today" (1962, p. 78).

39. Blumenfeld (1971) seems to think so (see p. 341).

40. Taylor (1966) gives a clarifying analysis of this point. See pp. 47f.

41. Cf. also Pap in Hook, ed. (1958).

42. Cf. Baier (1961), p. 25.

43. Chisholm (1968) is one of the few who has seen the importance of this distinction.

44. See also Ginet (1966), Berlin (1969), Honderich (1973), and Lamb (1977).

45. In note 7 (1974, p. 198), van Inwagen says that he does not take "J could have raised his arm at t" in the sense that "J possessed, at t, the ability to raise his arm," but in the sense "J possessed the ability to bring it about that his arm rose at t." If J was unparalyzed at t but

paralyzed at all earlier instants, then he could have raised his arm in the first, but not in the second sense.

I don't understand this. Isn't van Inwagen's point that even if J was unparalyzed at t and able to raise his arm, he could not—if determinism is true?

46. Cf. Slote (1969), pp. 334–35.

47. I distinguish between low- and high-integrated decisions, and between more or less well-integrated decisions. A decision D_1, made by P_1, is more well integrated than D_2, made by P_2, if, and only if, D_1 more than D_2 is supported by the agent's motivational, ethical, and cognitive orientations. A high-integrated decision is deeply rooted in the agent's ethical system, supported by arguments and deep-lying traits of his personality, whereas a low-integrated decision has a minimum of such support. See Ofstad (1961), pp. 17–18. See also *The Confessions of St. Augustine,* Cardinal edition (New York, 1952), pp. 141–42.

48. Some of the scholastic philosophers seem to have seen, more clearly than we do today, that our power to choose and decide depends, not on the absence of causes, but on the relative strength of the forces operating in the situation. They distinguished between *libertas specificationis* (the power to choose between different alternatives within a certain narrow class of alternatives, such as an alcoholic who has it in his power to choose one type of liquor rather than another); *libertas contradictionis* (the power to choose A or not to choose A); and *libertas contrarietatis* (the power to choose either of two contrary things, e.g., to do something good instead of something evil). Cf. C. Baeumker and G. von Hertling, eds., *Beiträge zur Geschichte der Philosophie des Mittelalters,* vol. 10 (Münster, 1891–1927), pp. 12–13.

49. Cf. H. S. Sullivan, *Conceptions of Modern Psychiatry* (Washington, 1947), pp. 99f, and K. Horney, *Self-Analysis* (London, 1950).

50. For a similar point of view applied to legal responsibility, see Hart (1962), p. 30.

51. See W. K. Estes, "An Experimental Study of Punishment," *Psychological Monographs* 57 (1944).

Bibliography

This bibliography covers works written in English and printed 1954 to 1980. Articles have been included from the following periodicals: *American Philosophical Quarterly, Analysis, The Australasian Journal of Philosophy, The British Journal for the Philosophy of Science, Ethics, The Journal of Philosophy, Mind, The Monist, Proceedings of the British Academy, The Philosophical Quarterly, The Philosophical Review, Philosophy, Philosophy and Phenomenological Research, Proceedings of the Aristotelian Society* (including supplementary volumes), *Theoria,* and *Inquiry.* Some minor articles and notes have been left out.

Useful bibliographies will be found in Adler (1958–61) and Ofstad (1961). See also the short bibliography by Roland Hall in *The Philosophical Quarterly* 15 (1965): 179–81, and especially the annotated bibliography in P. Edwards and A. Pap, eds., *A Modern Introduction to Philosophy,* rev. ed. (New York, 1973). I am indebted to Hans Mathlein (University of Stockholm) for commenting on an earlier draft of this essay, and to Lena Gemzöe (University of Stockholm) for helping me with the bibliography.

Adler, M. J., ed. 1958, 1961. *The Idea of Freedom.* 2 vols. New York.

Anscombe, G.E.M. 1957. *Intention.* Oxford.

_____ . 1963. "The Two Kinds of Error in Action." *The Journal of Philosophy* 60: 393–401.

_____ . 1971. *Causality and Determinism.* Cambridge: Cambridge University Press.

Audi, R. 1974. "Moral Responsibility, Freedom and Compulsion." *American Philosophical Quarterly* 11: 1–14.

Aune, B. 1962–1963. "Abilities, Modalities, and Free Will." *Philosophy and Phenomenological Research* 23: 397–413.

_____ . 1966. "Hypotheticals and 'Can': Another Look." *Analysis* 27: 191–95.

_____ . 1969–1970. "Free Will, 'Can' and Ethics: A Reply to Lehrer." *Analysis* 30: 77–83.

_____ . 1967. "Can." In P. Edwards, ed., *The Encyclopedia of Philosophy,* vol. 2. New York and London. Pp. 18–20.

Austin, J. L. 1956. "Ifs and Cans." *Proceedings of the British Academy* 42: 109–32. Reprinted 1961 in *Philosophical Papers.* Oxford.

_____ . 1956–1957. "A Plea for Excuses." *Proceedings of the Aristotelian Society* 57: 1–30. Reprinted 1961 in *Philosophical Papers.* Oxford.

Ayer, A. J. 1963. "Fatalism." *The Concept of a Person.* New York: St. Martin's Press.

Ayers, M. R. 1966. "Austin on 'Could' and 'Could Have.'" *The Philosophical Quarterly* 16: 113-20.

———. 1968. *The Refutation of Determinism*. London.

Baier, K. 1961. "Could and Would." *Analysis* Suppl. 23: 20-29.

———. 1965. "Action and Agent." *The Monist* 49: 183-95.

———. 1970. "Responsibility." In M. Brand, ed., *The Nature of Human Action*. Glenview, Ill.: Scott, Foresman.

Baylis, C. A. 1958. *Ethics*. New York. Chapter 2.

Beardsley, E. L. 1960-1961. "Determinism and Moral Perspectives." *Philosophy and Phenomenological Research* 21: 1-20.

Beck, L. 1965. "Agent, Actor, Spectator, and Critic." *The Monist* 49: 167-82.

Bennett, J. 1963-1964. "The Status of Determinism." *The British Journal for the Philosophy of Science* 14: 106-19.

Bergmann, F. 1971. *On Being Free*. London.

Berlin, I. 1963-1964. "From Hope and Fear Set Free." *Proceedings of the Aristotelian Society* 64: 1-30.

———. 1969. *Four Essays on Liberty*. Oxford.

Berofsky, B. 1964. "Determinism and the Concept of a Person." *The Journal of Philosophy* 61: 461-75.

———. 1971. *Determinism*. Princeton, N.J.: Princeton University Press.

Binkley, R.; Bronaugh, R.; and Marras, A., eds. 1971. *Agent, Action, and Reason*. Oxford.

Blumenfeld, D. 1971. "The Principle of Alternate Possibilities." *The Journal of Philosophy* 68: 339-45.

———. 1972. "Free Action and Unconscious Motivation." *The Monist* 56: 426-43.

Bohm, D. 1957. *Causality and Chance in Modern Physics*. London.

Boring, E. G. 1963. "When Is Human Behavior Predetermined?" In D. E. Dulany, ed., *Contributions to Modern Psychology*. Oxford.

Bradley, M. C. 1959. "A Note on Mr. MacIntyre's *Determinism*." *Mind* 68: 521-26.

Bradley, R. D. 1958. "Free Will: Problem or Pseudo-problem?" *The Australasian Journal of Philosophy* 36: 33-45.

———. 1962. "'Ifs,' 'Cans,' and Determinism." *The Australasian Journal of Philosophy* 40: 146-58.

———. 1962-1963. "Determinism or Indeterminism in Microphysics." *The British Journal for the Philosophy of Science* 13: 193-215.

———. 1963. "Causality, Fatalism, and Morality." *Mind* 72: 591-94.

Braithwaite, R. B., ed. 1955. "Analysis Problem No. 7." *Analysis* 16: 1-5. Contributions by Brian Ellis, "Candidus," and Nicholas Rescher.

Brand, M., ed. 1970. *The Nature of Human Action*. Glenview, Calif.

Brandt, R. 1958. "Blameworthiness and Obligation." In A. I. Melden, ed., *Essays in Moral Philosophy*. Seattle, Wash.

———. 1959. *Ethical Theory*. Englewood Cliffs, N.J.: Prentice-Hall. Chapter 20.

———, and Kim, J. 1963. "Wants as Explanations of Action." *The Journal of Philosophy* 60: 425-35.

Bretherton, D. 1962-1963. "'Ought' Implies 'Can Say.'" *Proceedings of the Aristotelian Society* 63: 145-66

Broadie, F. 1965-1966. "Trying and Doing." *Proceedings of the Aristotelian Society* 66: 27-40.

Bronaugh, R. 1964. "Freedom as the Absence of an Excuse." *Ethics* 74: 161-73.

———. 1968. "The Logic of Ability Judgments." *The Philosophical Quarterly* 18: 122-30.

Bunge, M. 1959. *Causality: The Place of the Causal Principle in Modern Science*. Cambridge.

Campbell, C. A. 1957. *On Selfhood and Godhood*. London.

———. 1958. "Free Will: A Reply to Mr. R. D. Bradley." *The Australasian Journal of Philosophy* 36: 46-56.

———. 1962. "Moral Libertarianism: A Reply to Mr. Franklin." *The Philosophical Quarterly* 12: 337-47.

———. 1967. *In Defence of Free Will*. New York.

Candlish, S. I., and Nesbitt, W. 1973. "On Not Being Able to Do Otherwise." *Mind* 82: 321-30.

Canfield, J. 1961. "Determinism, Free-Will and the Ace Predictor." *Mind* 70: 412-26.

———. 1961-1962. "Knowing about Future Decisions." *Analysis* 22: 127-29.

———. 1962. "The Compatibility of Free Will and Determinism." *The Philosophical Review* 71: 352-68.

_____ . 1963. "Free Will and Determinism: A Reply." *The Philosophical Review* 72: 502–4.

Chisholm, R. M. 1964a. "The Descriptive Element in the Concept of Action." *The Journal of Philosophy* 61: 613–25.

_____ . 1964b. *Human Freedom and the Self.* The Lindley Lecture of the University of Kansas.

_____ . 1964. "J. L. Austin's Philosophical Papers." *Mind* 73: 1–26.

_____ . 1966. "Freedom and Action." In K. Lehrer, ed., *Freedom and Determinism.*

_____ . 1968. "He Could Have Done Otherwise." In J. H. Gill, ed., *Philosophy Today.* New York. Pp. 236–49.

_____ . 1969. "Some Puzzles about Agency." In K. Lambert, ed., *The Logical Way of Doing Things.* New Haven, Conn.: Yale University Press. Pp. 199–217.

_____ . 1971. "Reflections on Human Agency." *Idealistic Studies,* vol 1. Pp. 33–46.

Cohen, M. F. 1964. "Motives, Causal Necessity and Moral Accountability." *The Australasian Journal of Philosophy* 42: 322–34.

Cowan, J. L. 1969. "Deliberation and Determinism." *American Philosophical Quarterly* 6: 53–60.

D'Alessio, J. 1972. "Austin on Nowell-Smith's Conditional Analyses of 'Could-have' and 'Can.'" *Mind* 81: 260–64.

D'Angelo E. 1968. *The Problem of Freedom and Determinism.* University of Missouri Studies, vol. 48.

Danto, A. C. 1958–1959. "The Paradigm Case Argument and the Free-Will Problem." *Ethics* 69: 120–24.

_____ . 1963. "What We Can Do." *The Journal of Philosophy* 60: 435–45.

_____ . 1965. "Basic Actions." *American Philosophical Quarterly* 2: 144–48.

Danto, C., and Morgenbesser, S. 1957. "Character and Free Will." *The Journal of Philosophy* 54: 493–505.

_____ . 1970. "Causation and Basic Actions." *Inquiry* 13: 108–25.

D'Arcy, E. 1963. *Human Acts.* Oxford. Chapter 3.

Daveney, T. F. 1964. "Choosing." *Mind* 73: 515–26.

Davidson, D. 1963. "Actions, Reasons, and Causes." *The Journal of Philosophy* 60: 685–700.

_____ . 1971. "Agency." In R. Binkley, R. Bronaugh, and A. Marras, eds., *Agent, Action, and Reason.*

_____ . 1973. "Freedom to Act." In T. Honderich, ed., *Essays on Freedom of Action.*

Dilman, I. 1961–1962. "The Freedom of Man." *Proceedings of the Aristotelian Society* 62: 39–62.

Diodorus, Cronus. 1965–1966. "Time, Truth, and Ability." *Analysis* 26: 137–47.

Donnellan, K. S. 1963. "Knowing What I Am Doing." *The Journal of Philosophy* 60: 401–9.

Dore, C. 1962–1963. "On the Meaning of 'Could Have.'" *Analysis* 23: 179–81.

_____ . 1963. "Is Free Will Compatible with Determinism?" *The Philosophical Review* 72: 500–501.

_____ . 1963–1964. "More on the Meaning of 'Could Have.'" *Analysis* 24: 41–43.

_____ . 1966. "On Being Able to do Otherwise." *The Philosophical Quarterly* 16: 137–45.

Dworkin, G. 1970. "Acting Freely." *Nous* 4: 367–83.

Edwards, R. 1965. "Agency Without a Substantive Self." *The Monist* 49: 273–89.

Ehman, R. R. 1967. "Causality and Agency." *Ratio* 9: 140–54.

Evans, D. A., and Landsberg, P. T. 1972. "Free Will in a Mechanistic Universe? An Extension." *The British Journal for the Philosophy of Science* 23: 336–42.

Evans, J. L. 1955. "Choice." *The Philosophical Quarterly* 5: 303–15.

Ewing, A. C. 1959. *Second Thoughts in Moral Philosophy.* London.

_____ . 1963–1964. "May Can-Statements Be Analysed Deterministically?" *Proceedings of the Aristotelian Society* 64: 157–76.

Fain, H. 1958. "Prediction and Constraint." *Mind* 67: 366–78.

Falk, W. D. 1963. "Action-guiding Reasons." *The Journal of Philosophy* 60: 702–18.

Farrer, A. 1958. *The Freedom of the Will.* London.

Feigl, H., and Meehl, P. E. 1974. "The Determinism-Freedom and Body-Mind Problems." In P. A. Schilpp, ed., *The Philosophy of Karl Popper,* vol. 1. La Salle, Ill. Pp. 520–59.

Feinberg, J. 1964. "On Being 'Morally Speaking' a Murderer." *The Journal of Philosophy* 61: 158–71.

_____ . 1965. "Action and Responsibility." In Max Black, ed., *Philosophy in America.* Ithaca, N.Y.

_____ . 1970. *Doing and Deserving.* Princeton, N.J.: Princeton University Press.

Ferré, F. 1973. "Self-determinism." *American Philosophical Quarterly* 10: 165–76.
Fingarette, H. 1955–1956. "Psychoanalytic Perspectives on Moral Guilt and Responsibility: A Re-evaluation." *Philosophy and Phenomenological Research* 16: 18–36.
Flew, A. 1955. "Divine Omnipotence and Human Freedom." In A. Flew and A. MacIntyre, eds., *New Essays in Philosophical Theology.* London.
———. 1959. "Determinism and Rational Behaviour." *Mind* 68: 377–82.
Foley, R. 1979. "Compatibilism and Control over the Past." *Analysis* 39: 70–74.
———. 1980. "Reply to van Inwagen." *Analysis* 40: 101–103.
Foot, P. 1957. "Free Will as Involving Determinism." *The Philosophical Review* 66: 439–50. Reprinted 1962 in Morgenbesser and Walsh, *Free Will.*
Frankfurt, H. 1969. "Alternative Possibilities and Moral Responsibility." *The Journal of Philosophy* 66: 829–39.
———. 1971. "Freedom of the Will and the Concept of a Person." *The Journal of Philosophy* 68: 5–20.
Franklin, R. L. 1961. "Dissolving the Problem of Free-will." *The Australasian Journal of Philosophy* 39: 111–24.
———. 1962. "Moral Libertarianism." *The Philosophical Quarterly* 12: 24–35.
———. 1968. *Free Will and Determinism.* London.
Friedrich, C. J., ed. 1960. "Responsibility." In *Nomos* III. New York.
Gale, R. M. 1961. "Endorsing Predictions." *The Philosophical Review* 70: 376–85.
Gallagher, K. T. 1964. "On Choosing to Choose." *Mind* 73: 480–95.
Gallie, W. B. 1957. *Free Will and Determinism Yet Again.* An inaugural lecture, The Queens University of Belfast.
Gallois, A. 1977. "van Inwagen on Free Will and Determinism." *Philosophical Studies* 32: 99–105.
Gallop, D. 1962. "On Being Determined." *Mind* 71: 181–96.
Gasking, E. 1955. "Causation and Recipes." *Mind* 64: 479–87.
Gauthier, D. P. 1967. "How Decisions Are Caused." *The Journal of Philosophy* 64: 147–51.
Geach, P. T. 1960. "Ascriptivism." *The Philosophical Review* 69: 221–225.
Gibbs, B. 1970. "Real Possibility." *American Philosophical Quarterly* 7: 340–48.
Ginet, C. 1962. "Can the Will Be Caused?" *The Philosophical Review* 71: 49–55.
———. 1966. "Might We Have No Choice?" In K. Lehrer, ed., *Freedom and Determinism.*
Glasgow, W. D. 1956–1957. "On Choosing." *Analysis* 17: 135–39.
———. 1959–1960. "The Concept of Choosing." *Analysis* 20: 63–67.
Glass, B. 1963. "The Relation of the Physical Sciences to Biology-Indeterminacy and Causality." In B. Baumrin, ed., *Philosophy of Science,* the Delaware Seminar. New York.
Glover, J. 1970. *Responsibility.* London.
Goldberg, B., and Heidelberger, H. 1960–1961. "Mr. Lehrer on the Constitution of Cans." *Analysis* 21: 96.
Goldman, A. I. 1970. *A Theory of Human Action.* Englewood Cliffs, N.J.: Prentice-Hall.
Gomberg, P. 1978. "Free Will as Ultimate Responsibility." *American Philosophical Quarterly* 15: 205–11.
Grünbaum, A. 1957. "Complementarity in Quantum Physics and Its Philosophical Generalization." *The Journal of Philosophy* 54: 713–27.
———. 1971. "Free Will and Laws of Human Behaviour." *American Philosophical Quarterly* 8: 299–317.
Gustafson, D. F. 1963–1964. "Voluntary and Involuntary." *Philosophy and Phenomenological Research* 24: 493–501.
Haines, N. 1955. "Responsibility and Accountability." *Philosophy* 30: 141–63.
Haksar, V. 1964. "Aristotle and the Punishment of Psychopaths." *Philosophy* 39: 323–40.
Halverson, W. H. 1964. "The Bogy of Chance." *Mind* 73: 567–70.
Hamlyn, D. W. 1964. "Causality and Human Behaviour." *Proceedings of the Aristotelian Society* Suppl. Vol 38: 125–42.
Hampshire, S. 1959. *Thought and Action.* London.
———. 1963. "Reply to Walsh on Thought and Action." *The Journal of Philosophy* 60: 410–24.
———. 1965. *Freedom of the Individual.* London.
Hampshire, S., and Hart, H.L.A. 1958. "Decision, Intention, and Certainty." *Mind* 67: 1–12.
Handy, R. 1959–1960. "Determinism, Responsibility, and the Social Setting." *Philosophy and Phenomenological Research* 20: 469–76.
Hanson, N. R. 1955. "Causal Chains." *Mind* 64: 289–311.

Hardie, W.F.R. 1957. "My Own Free Will." *Philosophy* 32: 21-38.

Hare, R. M. 1963. *Freedom and Reason*. Oxford. Chapter 4.

Harré, R. 1970. "Powers." *The British Journal for the Philosophy of Science* 21: 81-101.

Hart, H.L.A. 1959-1960. "Prolegomenon to the Principles of Punishment." *Proceedings of the Aristotelian Society* 60: 1-26.

———. 1961. "Negligence, *Mens Rea,* and Criminal Responsibility." In A. G. Guest, ed., *Oxford Essays in Jurisprudence*. Oxford University Press.

———. 1962. *Punishment and the Elimination of Responsibility*. L. T. Hobhouse Memorial Trust Lecture, University of London.

———. 1968. *Punishment and Responsibility*. Oxford.

Hartshorne, C. 1958. "Freedom Requires Indeterminism and Universal Causality." *The Journal of Philosophy* 55: 793-811.

Hedenius, I. 1959. "Broad's Treatment of Determinism and Free Will." In P. A. Schlipp, ed., *The Philosophy of C. D. Broad*. New York

Henschen-Dahlquist, Ann-Mari. 1963. "Remarks to Austin's Criticism of Moore's Analysis of 'Can.'" *Theoria* 29: 305-15.

Herbst, P. 1957. "Freedom and Prediction." *Mind* 66: 1-27.

Honderich, T., ed. 1973. *Essays on Freedom of Action*. London. Contributions by D. Davidson, D. C. Dennett, H. G. Frankfurt, T. Honderich, A. Kenny, D. Pear, J. Watling, M. Warnock, and D. Wiggins.

Honoré, A. M. 1964. "Can and Can't." *Mind* 73: 463-79.

Hook, S., ed. 1958. *Determinism and Freedom in the Age of Modern Science*. New York. Contributions by W. Barrett, E. L. Beardsley, M. Black, B. Blanshard, R. Brandt, P. W. Bridgman, R. M. Chisholm, C. J. Ducasse, P. Edwards, H.L.A. Hart, C. G. Hempel, H. W. Hintz, S. Hook, J. Hospers, A. Landé, A. Lerner, M. K. Munitz, E. Nagel, F.S.C. Northrop, A. Pap, A. Schultz, D. W. Sciama, R. Taylor, P. Weiss, and H. Wilson.

Hospers, J. 1961. *Human Conduct*. New York. Chapter 10.

Kaufman, A. S. 1962. "Moral Responsibility and the Use of 'Could Have.'" *The Philosophical Quarterly* 12: 120-28.

———. 1963. "Ability." *The Journal of Philosophy* 60: 537-51.

———. 1967. "Responsibility, Moral and Legal." In P. Edwards, ed., *The Encyclopedia of Philosophy,* vol. 7. New York and London. Pp. 183-88.

Kenner, L. 1964. "Causality, Determinism and Freedom of the Will." *Philosophy* 39: 233-48.

Kenny, A. 1963. *Action, Emotion, and Will*. London.

———. 1975. *Will, Freedom, and Power*. Oxford.

———. 1978. *Free Will and Responsibility*. London.

Körner, S. 1964. "Science and Moral Responsibility." *Mind* 73: 161-72.

Lacey, A. R. 1957-1958. "Free Will and Responsibility." *Proceedings of the Aristotelian Society* 58: 15-32.

Lamb, J. W. 1977. "On a Proof of Incompatibilism." *The Philosophical Review* 86: 20-35.

Lehrer, K. 1959-1960. "Ifs, Cans, and Causes." *Analysis* 20: 122-24.

———. 1960. "Can We Know That We Have Free Will by Introspection?" *The Journal of Philosophy* 57: 145-57.

———. 1961-1962. "Cans and Conditionals: A Rejoinder." *Analysis* 22: 23-24.

———. 1963. "Decisions and Causes." *The Philosophical Review* 72: 224-27.

———. 1963-1964. "'Could' and Determinism." *Analysis* 24: 159-60.

———. 1964a. "Doing the Impossible." *The Australasian Journal of Philosophy* 42: 86-97.

———. 1964b. "Doing the Impossible; A Second Try." *The Australasian Journal of Philosophy* 42: 249-51.

———, ed. 1966. *Freedom and Determinism*. New York. Contributions by R. M. Chisholm, A. Danto, C. Ginet, K. Lehrer, R. Taylor, and W. Sellars.

———. 1968. "Cans Without Ifs." *Analysis* 29: 29-32.

———. 1980. "Preferences, Conditionals, and Freedom." In P. van Inwagen, ed., *Essays Presented to Richard Taylor*. Boston, London.

Lehrer, K., and Taylor, R. 1965. "Time, Truth, and Modalities." *Mind* 74: 390-98.

Lewis, H. D. 1962. "Freedom and Responsibility." In Lewis, *Freedom and History*. London.

Locke, D. 1962. "Ifs and Cans Revisited." *Philosophy* 37: 245-56.

Locke, D., and Frankfurt, H. 1975. "Three Concepts of a Free Action." *Proceedings of the Aristotelian Society* Suppl. Vol 49: 95-112.

———. 1980. "Digging Deeper into Determinism." *Mind* 89: 87-89.

Lucas, J. R. 1970. *The Freedom of Will.* Oxford.

Lyons, A. 1959. "The Prediction Paradox." *Mind* 68: 510-17.

Mabbott, J. D. 1956. "Freewill and Punishment. In H. D. Lewis, ed. *Contemporary British Philosophy.* London.

McGill, V. J. 1959-1960. "Conflicting Theories of Freedom." *Philosophy and Phenomenological Research* 20: 437-52.

MacIntyre, A. C. 1957. "Determinism." *Mind* 66: 28-41.

MacKay, D. M. 1960. "On the Logical Indeterminacy of a Free Choice." *Mind* 69: 31-40.

_____ . 1967. "Freedom of Action in a Mechanistic Universe." Eddington Memorial Lecture, Cambridge University.

_____ . 1971. "Choice in a Mechanistic Universe: A Reply to Some Critics." *The British Journal for the Philosophy of Science* 22: 275-85.

_____ . 1973. "The Logical Indeterminateness of Human Choices." *The British Journal for the Philosophy of Science* 24: 405-8.

Mackie, J. L. 1965. "Responsibility and Language." *The Australasian Journal of Philosophy* 33: 143-59.

_____ . 1955. "Evil and Omnipotence." *Mind* 64: 200-212.

_____ . 1971. *Ethics.* Penguin Books.

MacKinnon, D. M. 1962. *A Study in Ethical Theory.* New York: Collier. Books. Chapter 4.

Macklin, R. 1969. "Action, Causality, and Teleology." *The British Journal for the Philosophy of Science* 19: 201-16.

MacMurray, J. 1957. *The Self as Agent.* London.

Madden, E. H. 1957-1958. "Psychoanalysis and Moral Judgeability." *Philosophy and Phenomenological Research* 18: 68-79.

Mandelbaum, M. 1959-1960. "Determinism and Moral Responsibility." *Ethics* 70: 204-19.

Margenau, H. 1967. "Quantum Mechanics, Free Will, and Determinism." *The Journal of Philosophy* 64: 714-25.

Margolis, J. 1970. "Danto on Basic Actions." *Inquiry* 13: 105-8.

Matson, W. I. 1956. "On the Irrelevance of Free-Will to Moral Responsibility, and the Vacuity of the Latter." *Mind* 65: 489-97.

Mayo, B. A. 1958a. "A Logical Limitation on Determinism." *Philosophy* 33: 50-55.

_____ . 1958b. *Ethics and the Moral Life.* London. Chapter 12.

_____ . 1962. "The Open Future." *Mind* 71: 1-14.

_____ . 1968. "On the Lehrer-Taylor Analysis of 'Can-statements.'" *Mind* 77: 271-78.

Melden, A. I. 1961. *Free Action.* London.

Miller, G. 1964. "An Examination of Ofstad's Radical Contextualism." *Inquiry* 7: 209-18.

Montefiore, A. 1957-58. "Determinism and Causal Order." *Proceedings of the Aristotelian Society* 58: 125-42.

_____ . 1958. "'Ought' and 'Can.'" *The Philosophical Quarterly* 8: 24-40.

Morgenbesser, S., and Walsh, J., eds. 1962. *Free Will.* Englewood Cliffs, N.J.: Prentice-Hall.

Morris, H., ed. 1961. *Freedom and Responsibility.* Stanford, Calif.

Munk, A. 1965. "The Self as Agent and Spectator." *The Monist* 49: 262-72.

Munn, A. M. 1960. *Free-Will and Determinism.* London.

Murphy, A. 1959. "Jonathan Edwards on Free Will and Moral Agency." *The Philosophical Review* 68: 181-202.

Naess, A. 1975. *Freedom, Emotion, and Self-subsistence: The Structure of a Central Part of Spinoza's Ethics.* Oslo.

Nagel, E. 1961. *The Structure of Science.* New York. Chapter 10.

Narveson, J. 1972. "Compatibilism Defended." *Philosophical Studies* 32: 83-87.

Neely, W. 1974. "Freedom and Desire." *The Philosophical Review* 83: 32-54.

Nesbitt, W., and Candlish, S. I. 1978. "Determinism and the Ability to Do Otherwise." *Mind* 87: 415-20.

Nowell-Smith, P. H. 1954a. "Determinists and Libertarians." *Mind* 63: 317-37.

_____ . 1954b. *Ethics.* New York and London. Chapters 19 and 20.

_____ . 1957-58. "Choosing, Deciding, and Doing." *Analysis* 18: 63-69.

_____ . 1960. "Ifs and Cans." *Theoria* 26: 85-101.

O'Connor, D. J. 1956-1957. "Determinism and Predictability." *The British Journal for the Philosophy of Science* 7: 310-15.

_____ . 1960. "Possibility and Choice." *Proceedings of the Aristotelian Society* Suppl. Vol. 34: 1-24.

_____. 1971. *Free Will*. New York.

Ofstad, H. 1955. "Broad on Ought and Can." *Theoria* 21: 105–16.

_____. 1959a. "Can We Produce Decisions?" *The Journal of Philosophy* 56: 89–94.

_____. 1959b. "Frankena on Ought and Can." *Mind* 68: 73–79.

_____. 1961. *An Inquiry into the Freedom of Decision*. Oslo-Stockholm-London.

_____. 1963. "Libertarianism and the Belief in Transempirical Entities, L. J. Rusell on Causation and Agency." In *Philosophical Essays Dedicated to Gunnar Aspelin*. Lund.

_____. 1967. "Recent Work on the Free-Will Problem." *American Philosophical Quarterly* 4: 179–207.

_____. 1972. "Responsibility and Freedom." In R. E. Olson and A. M. Paul, eds., *Contemporary Philosophy in Scandinavia*. Baltimore and London. Pp. 285–305.

_____. 1981. "Are We Free in the Sense Required by Moral Responsibility?" In *Proceedings of the Fifth International Wittgenstein Symposium*. Vienna.

Oldenquist, A. 1963–1964. "Causes, Predictions, and Decisions." *Analysis* 24: 55–58.

Oppenheim, F. 1961. *Dimensions of Freedom*. New York.

O'Shaughnessy, B. 1956. "The Limits of the Will." *The Philosophical Review* 65: 443–90.

_____. 1963. "Observation and the Will." *The Journal of Philosophy* 60: 367–92.

Papanoutsos, E. P. 1959. "Freedom and Causality." *Philosophy* 34: 193–203.

Pears, D. F., ed. 1963. *Freedom and the Will*. London. Contributions by P. L. Gardiner, S. Hampshire, H.L.A. Hart, I. Murdoch, D. F. Pears, P. F. Strawson, J. F. Thomson, G. J. Warnock, M. Warnock, and B. Williams.

Perry, D. 1965. "Prediction, Explanation and Freedom." *The Monist* 49: 234–47.

Peters, R. S. 1958. *The Concept of Motivation*. London.

Pike, N. 1965. "Divine Omniscience and Voluntary Action." *The Philosophical Review* 74: 27–46.

_____. 1977. "Divine Foreknowledge, Human Freedom, and Possible Worlds." *The Philosophical Review* 86: 209–16.

Pitcher, G. 1960. "Hart on Action and Responsibility." *The Philosophical Review* 69: 226–35.

_____. 1961. "Necessitarianism." *The Philosophical Quarterly* 11: 201–12.

Plantinga, A. 1965. "The Free Will Defence." In Max Black, ed., *Philosophy in America*. Ithaca, N.Y.

Plaut, H. C. 1960–1961. "Condition, Cause, Free Will, and the Direction of Time." *The British Journal for the Philosophy of Science* 11: 212–21.

Popper, K. R. 1950. "Indeterminism in Quantum Physics and in Classical Physics." *The British Journal for the Philosophy of Science* 1: 117–33.

_____. 1972. *Objective Knowledge*. Oxford.

Powell, B. 1959. "Uncharacteristic Actions." *Mind* 68: 492–509.

Raab, F. V. 1955. "Free Will and the Ambiguity of 'Could.'" *The Philosophical Review* 64: 60–77

_____. 1963. "The Relevance of Morals to Our Denials of Responsibility." In H. Castañeda and C. Nakhnikian, eds., *Morality and the Language of Conduct*. Detroit.

Ralls, A. 1963. "The Ascription of Personal Responsibility and Identity." *The Australasian Journal of Philosophy* 61: 346–58.

Ranken, N. 1967. "The Unmoved Agent and the Ground of Responsibility." *The Journal of Philosophy* 64: 403–8.

Rankin, K. W. 1960. "Doer and Doing." *Mind* 69: 361–71.

_____. 1961. *Choice and Chance*. Oxford.

_____. 1963. "A Deterministic Windmill." *The Australasian Journal of Philosophy* 41: 233–45.

Raphael, D. D. 1955. *Moral Judgment*. London. Chapter 10.

Richman, R. J. 1969. "Responsibility and the Causation of Actions." *American Philosophical Quarterly* 6: 186–97.

Roberts, M. 1965. *Responsibility and Practical Freedom*. Cambridge.

Ross, A. 1975. *On Guilt, Responsibility and Punishment*. London.

Roxbee-Cox, J. W. 1963. "Can I Know Beforehand What I Am Going To Decide?" *The Philosophical Review* 72: 88–92.

Ryan, A. 1965. "Freedom." *Philosophy* 40: 93–112.

Sankowski, E. 1980. "Freedom, Determinism, and Character." *Mind* 89: 106–13.

Saunders, J. T. 1968. "The Temptations of Powerlessness." *American Philosophical Quarterly* 5: 100–108.

Scarrow, D. S. 1962-1963. "On an Analysis of 'Could Have.'" *Analysis* 23: 118-20.

Schlesinger, G. 1974. "The Unpredictability of Free Choices." *The British Journal for the Philosophy of Science* 25: 209-21.

Shwayder, D. S. 1965. *The Stratification of Behaviour.* London.

Scriven, M. 1957. "The Present Status of Determinism in Physics." *The Journal of Philosophy* 54: 727-41.

Sellars, R. W. 1957. "Guided Causality, Using Reason, and 'Free-will.'" *The Journal of Philosophy* 54: 485-93.

Sellars, W. 1966. "Thought and Action." In K. Lehrer, ed., *Freedom and Determinism.* New York.

Shute, C. 1961. "The Dilemma of Determinism after Seventy-five Years." *Mind* 70: 331-50.

Silber, J. 1963-1964. "Human Action and the Language of Volitions." *Proceedings of the Aristotelian Society* 64: 199-220.

Skinner, R. C. 1963. "Freedom of Choice." *Mind* 72: 463-80.

Slote, M. A. 1969. "Free Will, Determinism and the Theory of Important Criteria." *Inquiry* 12: 317-38.

———. 1980. "Understanding Free Will." *The Journal of Philosophy* 77: 136-51.

Smart, J.J.C. 1961. "Free-Will, Praise, and Blame." *Mind* 70: 291-306.

———. 1963. *Philosophy and Scientific Realism.* London.

———. 1964. "Causality, and Human Behaviour." *Proceedings of the Aristotelian Society* Suppl. Vol. 38: 143-48.

Smith, J. W. 1961. "Impossibility and Morals." *Mind* 70: 362-75.

Spakovsky von Anatol. 1963. *Freedom, Determinism, Indeterminism.* The Hague.

Stenner, A. J. 1964. "On Predicting Our Future." *The Journal of Philosophy* 61: 415-28.

Stoutland, F. 1968. "Basic Actions and Causality." *The Journal of Philosophy* 65: 467-75.

Strawson, P. F. 1962. "Freedom and Resentment." *Proceedings of the British Academy* 48: 187-211.

Swiggart, P. 1962-1963. "Doing and Deciding To Do." *Analysis* 23: 17-19.

Taylor, R. 1960. "I Can." *The Philosophical Review* 69: 78-89.

———. 1963. *Metaphysics.* Englewood Cliffs, N.J.: Prentice-Hall.

———. 1964a. "Deliberation and Foreknowledge." *American Philosophical Quarterly* 1: 73-80.

———. 1964b. "Not Trying To Do the Impossible." *The Australasian Journal of Philosophy* 42: 98-100.

———. 1966. *Action and Purpose.* Englewood Cliffs, N.J.: Prentice-Hall.

———. 1967. "Determinism." In P. Edwards, ed., *The Encyclopedia of Philosophy,* vol. 1. New York and London. Pp. 359-73.

Thalberg, I. 1961-1962. "Abilities and Ifs." *Analysis* 22: 121-26.

———. 1963-1964. "Foreknowledge and Decisions in Advance." *An   4.

———. 1964. "Freedom of Action and Freedom of Will." *The J(   )f Philosophy* 61: 405-15.

———. 1972. *Enigmas of Agency.* London.

Thomas, G. 1964. "Comments: Abilities and Physiology." *The Journal of Philosophy* 61: 321-28.

Thornton, J. 1968-1969. "Determinism and Moral Reactive Attitudes." *Ethics* 79: 283-97.

van Inwagen, P. 1974. "A Formal Approach to the Problem of Free Will and Determinism." *Theoria* 40: 9-22.

———. 1975. "The Incompatibility of Free Will and Determinism." *Philosophical Studies* 27: 185-99.

———. 1977a. "Reply to Narveson." *Philosophical Studies* 32: 90-98.

———. 1977b. "Reply to Gallois." *Philosophical Studies* 32: 107-11.

———. 1978. "Ability and Responsibility." *The Philosophical Review* 88: 201-24.

———. 1980. "Compatibilism and the Burden of Proof." *Analysis* 40: 98-100.

Vesey, G.N.A. 1961. "Volition." *Philosophy* 36: 352-65.

Vivian, F. 1964. *Human Freedom and Responsibility.* London.

von Wright, G. H. 1974. *Causality and Determinism.* New York.

———. 1975. *Explanation and Understanding.* London.

Waismann, F. 1959. "The Decline and Fall of Causality." In A. Crombie, ed., *Turning Points in Physics.* Amsterdam.

Walter, E. 1977-1978. "Is Libertarianism Logically Coherent?" *Philosophy and Phenom-*

enological Research 38: 505-13.

Warnock, M. 1973. "Freedom in the Early Philosophy of J. P. Sartre." In T. Honderich, ed., *Essays on Freedom of Action*. London.

Watson, G. 1975. "Free Agency." *The Journal of Philosophy* 72: 205-20.

_____ . 1977. "Scepticism About Weakness of Will." *The Philosophical Review* 86: 316-39.

Watkins, J.W.N. 1971. "Freedom and Predictability: An Amendment to MacKay." *The British Journal for the Philosophy of Science* 22: 263-74.

Weil, V. 1980. "Neurophysiological Determinism and Human Action." *Mind* 89: 90-95.

Weissmann, H. A. 1958-1959. "Freedom in Ethics—A Transcausal Concept." *Philosophy and Phenomenological Research* 19: 341-53.

White, M. 1973. "Positive Freedom, Negative Freedom, and Possibility." *The Journal of Philosophy* 70: 309-17.

Whiteley, C. H. 1962-1963. "Can." *Analysis* 23: 91-93.

Whittier, D. 1965. "Causality and the Self." *The Monist* 49: 290-303.

Wild, J. 1963. *Existence and the World of Freedom*. Englewood Cliffs, N.J.: Prentice-Hall. Part III.

Will, F. L. 1964. "Intention, Error, and Responsibility." *The Journal of Philosophy* 61: 171-79.

Williams, C.J.F. 1960-1961. "Logical Indeterminacy and Free-Will." *Analysis* 21: 12-13.

Williams, G. 1958-1959. "The Natural Causation of Human Freedom." *Philosophy and Phenomenological Research* 19: 529-31.

Wilson, J. 1958. "Freedom and Compulsion." *Mind* 67: 60-69.

Wolf, S. 1980. "Assymetrical Freedom." *The Journal of Philosophy* 77: 151-66.

Wootton, B. 1959. *Social Science and Social Pathology*. London. Chapter 8.

Yolton, J. W. 1962. "Act and Circumstance." *The Journal of Philosophy* 59: 337-50.

Zink, S. 1962. *The Concepts of Ethics*. London. Chapters 6-8.

PART II

Logic

chapter 3

Recent Work in Inductive Logic

HENRY E. KYBURG, JR.

Since this essay first appeared, in 1964, a great many changes have taken place in the study of inductive logic. Problems that were once taken as central are no longer discussed; entirely new questions and problems have come to the fore. These changes represent not mere changes in fashion—although there is of course an element of that—but also genuine philosophical progress. Certain ways of approaching scientific inference—for example by formulating a few very general "postulates," from which, with the addition of some observational statements, scientific generalizations follow with deductive certainty or with high probability—no longer seem viable and have, I believe, disappeared from the philosophical scene once and for all. Other ways of approaching scientific inference (for example, in terms of subjective probability, or in terms of the social power of groups of scientists) are quite new and still the subject of controversies which will in due course distill whatever truth lies hidden in them.

If one were to try to characterize a trend in the study of inductive logic over the past two decades, one would say that it is a trend toward an empirical approach to the topic; this entails an effort to take more seriously both what scientists do and what they say they do, in making inferences from data, but it also often involves a tendency to suppose that there is no objective standard to which scientific inference ought to conform. One may see this as part of a quite general cultural revolt against authority. But of course one philosopher's empirical truth is another philosopher's *a priori* bias, and if the cogency of a scientific inference is a matter of opinion, some opinions are more worthy of respect than others. And despite these changes, most frequently evidenced in the current enthusiasm for "subjective probability," most writers on inductive logic still impute a normative dimension to the subject of their discipline.

These many changes, together with the requirement of keeping the length of the essay essentially unchanged, have made the revision of the original very difficult. My solution has been to follow the format of the original essay as far as possible, deleting large parts of some sections and adding to others. Since the bibliography has been regarded by many as the most useful part of the original essay, I at first hoped to retain the old entries and to add items that have appeared since 1964. When I broke through the thousand-item barrier, I decided that this was not feasible. I have therefore kept those items of the original bibliography that I refer to in the text, and incorporated as many new items as I have been able to track down. A relatively complete bibliography thus consists of the union of the current bibliography and the bibliography of 1964. A serious scholar should not mind having to go to two places. He should also consult the bibliography compiled by Ralph Slaght (Slaght, 1970).

There has been a great deal written about inductive logic in recent years. For the purposes of this chapter I have taken the year 1951 as a benchmark; what transpired before that I take to have been largely assimilated by the philosophical world. Thus, on the early side of the benchmark we find Carnap's monumental *Logical Foundations of Probability,* Russell's *Human Knowledge,* Kneale's *Probability and Induction,* Williams's *The Ground of Induction,* and von Wright's *Treatise on Induction and Probability.* Taking for granted that the reader has some familiarity with these materials (at the least of the most general sort), I propose to deal with the developments of 1951 and later.

It is difficult to know what should be regarded as inductive logic. There are writers (Popper, for example) for whom there is no such thing as inductive logic, and writers (Toulmin, for example) for whom all interesting logic is more or less inductive. There are writers who feel that it makes sense to talk about inductive *logic* only after induction has been justified or vindicated in general (Burks), there are writers who feel that inductive logic is nothing but a theory of probability (Carnap), and there are those who think that probability has nothing to do with the matter (Popper). There are those who think the question of causality is fundamental (Ewing) and those who think that the fundamental questions concern decision in the face of uncertainty (Churchman). I have felt that I had to deal with all of these issues, to some degree; but I have tried to stray no further from the central topic of this essay, inductive logic, than forced by my conscience.

Despite the faint pull of conscience, I have made no attempt to survey the rapidly increasing body of literature in computer science on inductive inference, and I have referred only peripherally to the psychological literature concerning the dynamics of belief and intuitive statistical inference.

I

One question about inductive logic concerns whether or not inductive conclusions are certain.

There are two ways in which necessity may be attributed to inductive conclusions: the conclusions themselves may be regarded as certain, i.e., as following necessarily and incorrigibly from the evidence for them, and the conclusions themselves may be taken to express some sort of necessity, such as causal necessity. Ideally, Mill's methods were to reveal necessary connections in a necessary manner, and thus to involve necessity in both senses.

There are few philosophers left who are still willing to maintain that scientific method yields certainties. One way of achieving certainty for inductive conclusions is provided by ordinary language analysts. Thus J. O. Nelson writes, "scientists all the time conclusively establish . . . hypotheses." For example, we may speculate about the existence of life on Mars; when scientists have amassed enough evidence of the right sort, they do not say that it is "highly probable" that there is life on Mars, but that it is now certain, it has now been conclusively established, that there is life on Mars, because "It has been conclusively established by spectrographs that the green spots are lichen" (Nelson, 1958). To talk in any other way, according to Nelson, is to abuse language. But it is clear that the issue here can no more be settled by taking a poll of common usage than can the issue of whether a whale is to be regarded as a fish or a mammal. As L. Resnick points out in his comments on Nelson's article, "probability" is used in philosophy, as in science, as a technical term (Resnick, 1959).

W. Kneale, it will be recalled, presented a doctrine according to which general synthetic propositions of a certain sort could be considered certain, although they could not be known *a priori* (Kneale, 1949, 1951). J. P. Day, who follows Kneale's lead in other ways, follows him in this as well; he argues that not all ampliative induction is probable, "For we do often call generalizations true or certain" (Day, 1961, p. 256).

I think it can more plausibly be maintained that certainty in this sense is a liability to scientific conclusions than that it is an asset. As long as we can regard a counter-instance as possible, the conclusion is not certain; and to regard a counter-instance as *impossible* is just to commit oneself to explaining it away, come what may—i.e., it is to regard the conclusion as analytic and uninformative.

It is possible to maintain that at least *some* scientific hypotheses are without empirical content in this sense—that they serve as standards by means of which we can derive quantitative theories of errors of observation (Kyburg, 1977c, 1979c). This is particularly clear in the theory of measurement where a series of judgments of the form *a* is the same length as *b* may easily conflict with the transitivity of equality of length, but this conflict leads us to impute error to the judgments, not to the transitivity principle (Kyburg, 1979b).

It is also true that many of the arguments that are used in science—arguments that for the moment I am lumping together as inductive, perhaps in defiance of etymology—are conclusive, or at least give the appearance of being conclusive, in the sense that the conclusion follows *deductively* from premises—general as well as particular—that we *accept* in a given inquiry. The analysis of these arguments is the analysis of *demonstrative induction*. The most extensive general work on demonstrative induction is that of G. H. von Wright (1951). In his book he is mainly concerned with the logical problem of analyzing the inferential mechanism of induction rather than either the psychological problem of discovery or the specifically philosophical problem of justification. Chapters Four, Five, and Six are on the logic of *necessary, sufficient,* and *necessary and sufficient* conditions. (The other chapters are concerned with nondemonstrative induction, but that is considered from the same point of view as consisting essentially in the *probable* elimination of causal laws.) We have here an elaborated version of Mill's canons of induction.

In each case considered by von Wright, we begin with the knowledge that the necessary, or sufficient, or necessary and sufficient, condition is to be found among a list of candidates that is constructed in a mechanical way from a finite list of potential conditioning properties. It is easy to see that given a list of possible conditions, one could construct a list of all the possible causal laws relating these conditioning properties to a given conditional property. Even if all the possible combinations of causal factors in this list are allowed, von Wright shows, it is still possible for inductive elimination to lead to certainty: when all the possible sufficient conditions but one are eliminated, the one that remains will be the conjunction of all the possible conditioning properties; and when all the possible necessary conditions but one are eliminated, it turns out to be the disjunction of all the conditioning properties.

It is obvious that this is not a very interesting result. By imposing special conditions on the form of the properties in which we are interested we can get more interesting results, but in any event we can get no results that we could not get by composing a list of possible causal laws and attempting to eliminate all but one. Indeed, if the interest of constructing an inductive logic is to throw light on the sort of thing scientists actually do, the latter procedure is far more realistic than the former. It is far more sensible to suppose that in a determinate inquiry we have narrowed the plausible possibilities down to three or four specific laws, and that we then proceed to eliminate them as best we can (consider, e.g., the well-known procedure of Pasteur), than it is to suppose that we write down a list of properties that *might,* in some combination or other, be conditioning properties, and that we then try to eliminate all but one of the much larger list of *possible* laws that we can construct on the basis of this list of possibly conditioning properties.

In principle, and at a certain level, at any rate, there is nothing problematic about the logic of elimination: the law is a general statement, and the observation report can be a singular statement that contradicts the law. But something might well be written about the construction of the sets of laws of which we are to eliminate all but one; this might be a contribution to the actual practice of science as well as to the logic of induction. Where does a useful set of possible laws come from? On what grounds can we accept the hypothesis that one of these laws will be found to hold? Do such sets of hypotheses exhibit an internal structure? They clearly do not exhibit the exhaustive structure that Mill and von Wright suppose they do. But as far as I know, nothing has been done along these lines.

A way of handling the elimination of an infinite number of hypotheses, where the inference concerns natural kinds, is developed in Kyburg (1960). Here is an example of a common form of scientific argument that can be explicated by the techniques of this paper: a species S falls under a certain genus; a property P belongs to a certain class of properties. We know that all species of that genus are such that if one member of the species has a given property belonging to that class, then all members of that species have that property. The inductive argument then proceeds from this generalization and the observation of a particular instance of one of the species in question, to a general conclusion: all members of this species have that property. As a typical example, a pure chemical compound will have (under standard pressure) exactly one melting point. If one sample of compound X melts at T degrees centigrade, then all samples of that compound will melt at T degrees centigrade. We do not achieve certainty, of course, for our inductive conclusion that all samples of compound X will melt at T degrees under standard pressure. There are two sources of doubt: (1) the generalization concerning natural kinds is only probable—although there could be argument concerning where the element of uncertainty entered and how, and (2) the particular statement that serves as a premise may be subject to doubt: we can only have *good grounds* for believing that the sample we tested actually did melt at T degrees, because we must allow for experimental error. The same two comments apply to von Wright's reconstruction, of course. In any real situation the hypothesis that one of a set of possible hypotheses holds is only probable, and in any interesting case the relevant "observations," like the observation of the melting point of a substance, will only be probable.

A more general approach along these lines, interesting both because it avoids the excess generality of von Wright's approach and because it deals with genuine numerical laws and theories, is pursued by Clark Glymour (1980). Glymour notes that many of our scientific laws invoke constants that can be evaluated only by computations involving the very theory of which the law forms a part. On his view, we may *confirm* a theory by performing experiments that lead to computations that provide instantiations of the theory. Confirmation of this sort is not quantitative, but the structure of such arguments suggested by Glymour is more detailed and more plausible than that provided by the mere claim that generalizations are confirmed by their instances.

S. Nowak (1960) carries the analysis of necessary and sufficient conditions into the field of statistics and derives some interesting results. As an example, suppose that A and S are necessary and sufficient for B; if S_1 is an essential component of S (i.e., if S is composed of S_1 and S_2), then the probability of B given A, $P(B/A)$ will be the product of the probability of S_1 given A, $P(S_1/A)$, and the probability of B given A and S_1, $P(B/AS_1)$. If these probabilities are interpreted as relative frequencies, this relationship is empirically testable and may throw light on the possible causal relationship between B and S_1. Results like this, Nowak shows, may be of considerable practical and theoretical importance in actual statistical work in the constructing and testing of statistical hypotheses. They enable us, for example, to discuss such things as spurious correlation and spurious independence more carefully and rigorously than we could without the analysis into necessary and sufficient conditions.

II

There are many writers of many persuasions who feel that inductive conclusions often express some kind of necessary connection, but there are few who make this necessity bear much of the burden of inductive logic. Most of those who do feel that the concept of necessary connection enters into the canons of inductive logic simply formulate postulates, as did Russell in *Human Knowledge* (1948), which are alleged to be sufficient to establish (with the help of empirical evidence) the cogency of inductive conclusions. Few writers still seek an explicit list of general metaphysical postulates that will serve to found the cogency of inductive arguments.

But there are writers who propose to found induction on general empirical premises construed as "assumptions" or "presuppositions," rather than as "postulates." In this form, the premises cry out for justification only softly. The best known attempt to found both inductive logic and inductive justification on broad factual assumptions is that of Arthur Burks (1953, 1977). Burks argues that we must turn to presuppositions because there are three inductive methods which conflict with each other, and yet which meet all the requirements of coherence. (But see Salmon's refutation of this claim, discussed below.) The three methods, informally, are these: the more often you see *p*, the more often it will recur (standard method); the more often you find *p*, the less often it will recur (inverse method); and past and future occurrences of *p* are stochastically independent (random method). Burks argues that we can have no *inductive* ground for choosing among these three methods; to choose one is clearly to adopt a presupposition, an assumption.

In another article Burks (1954) goes on to show that the standard presupposition does not suffice for the justification of induction. There he adds two new presuppositions: (1) a presupposition concerning limited variety—that there are a finite number of irreducible, first-order, extensional, monadic, symbolic properties; and (2) a presupposition concerning uniformity—i.e., causality. This latter principle has two parts: (a) if one substitution instance of a causal universal is true, then the causal universal is true, and (b) there is a region in which some causal connections hold. It is not hard to see that the generality of these presuppositions precludes their use in the justification of any particular inductive inferences (as usual for presuppositions); even for the general justification of induction they are too weak. "If we could justify the claim that, relative to the presuppositions, each causal universal under consideration is as likely to be in the group of true ones as any other causal universal, we would have the result we are looking for. It is clear that our three presuppositions do not suffice to justify this claim, or any similar claim that leads to the result we are looking for, and we must confess that we have not yet found a presuppositional statement which will do this" (Burks, 1954, p. 597). There is no point, on Burks's view, in trying to pretend that these presuppositions, if and when they are properly formulated, are anything but presuppositions, that is to say, bare-faced assumptions. To say that they are probable only, as Keynes said of his principle of the Limitation of Natural Variety, is just as synthetic an assertion as to say that they are true.

In his most recent book Burks (1977) feels that he has succeeded in characterizing the presuppositions of induction. They are the same three presuppositions already mentioned, but they are formulated differently, and developed in conjunction with a "double-aspect" (propensity and inductive) notion of probability.

John Kemeny, too, professes to find factual assumptions underlying science. "In short, induction cannot be justified. We can only base it on a more or less plausible sounding assumption. . . . We may not be able to justify the assumption, but we must have faith in some such assumption if life is to be possible" (Kemeny, 1959, p. 121). W. Donald Oliver also claims that "we need to invoke certain general assumptions about the nature of the subject matter of science" (Oliver, 1952, p. 778). H. G. Alexander arrives at much the same conclusion (Alexander, 1960).

None of these writers attempts to justify his assumptions. Such a justification would be a justification of induction, and that, as Hume showed, is not to be had in the sense that these writers desire it. For in none of them is the truth of their postulates more than a pious wish. As Goodman says, the "course of accepting an unsubstantiated and even dubious assumption much more sweeping than any actual predictions we make seems an odd and expensive way of justifying [inductions]" (Goodman, 1955, p. 65). Furthermore, the assertion that these postulates will actually help us to reconstruct a specific piece of scientific argument on a sound basis is highly suspect. The arguments offered by the authors of such postulates are invariably of a highly abstract character, and the more plausible a postulate is made to seem, the further into abstraction it appears to be removed from living science.

III

The principles and postulates that have been offered for the justification of induction have been criticized on two grounds: the difficulty of accepting them, and their impotence in providing grounds for actual scientific arguments. One of these two criticisms is met by another approach to inductive logic, that which takes the principle of induction itself (or something presumably equivalent to it) as analytic. (A special and elaborate case of this is the taking of a logical theory of probability as the foundation of inductive logic. I shall return to this approach later.)

It has been maintained that the uniformity of nature is a tautology, on the grounds that if things started acting very oddly, we would not decide that nature was no longer uniform, but simply that we were dreaming and no longer observing nature (Brown, 1957, p. 19). This gambit, like that of K. Campbell (1962), who calls our attention to the fact that continuing concommitances are *presupposed* in our language and thought, simply won't do what is expected of it. Even if the existence of uniformities were enough to enable us to justify induction – which it is not, since we can justify induction through uniformity only when we have some further indication as to where the uniformities are and how far they extend – the analyticity of the uniformity principle would prevent us from using it to justify extrapolations into the future. If the uniformity of nature is made analytic, the continuing existence of nature cannot be regarded as analytic, but becomes contingent, and is precisely what inductive justification would have to depend on.

It is more plausible to maintain that the principle of induction itself is analytic, and at the same stroke to justify the belief that past uniformities will continue, and that nature, as we know it, will continue to exist. The first explicit statement that I know of the thesis that the principle of induction is analytic is by Asher Moore (1952a). The principle of induction that he formulates is "It is more probable than not that uniformities, either universal or statistical, which have been observed to hold uniformly in the past experience, will continue to hold uniformly in the future" (Moore, 1952a, p. 741). This principle, he says, is analytic; it is analytic of what we mean by "probable" or "reasonable." (It goes without saying that the word "probable" here does not carry any commitment concerning future frequencies.) Against this view, May Brodbeck (1952) argues that by making the principle of induction analytic, we find ourselves with no basis on which to construct an inductive logic. What is the basis for preferring large samples to small ones? Highly varied ones to homogeneous ones? According to her, all such knowledge is based on induction. Furthermore, the real problem of justification is untouched: to say that we have observed uniformity in the past and that this *analytically* implies that it is reasonable to expect uniformity in the future is to say no more than that we have observed uniformity in the past. "Yet if there is any problem of induction, it is about the relationship between the observed and unobserved" (Brodbeck, 1952, p. 750), which is not touched at all by an analytical principle of induction. Moore answers that "The rules of induction, concerning mixing, large samples, varied data, and so on, constitute the full expansion of the Principle of Induction itself" (Moore, 1952b, p. 752). He neither develops an inductive logic nor discusses in any detail Brodbeck's most serious contention, that the problem of induction concerns the relationship between the observed and the unobserved, and that an analytic principle can have nothing to contribute to the elucidation of this relationship.

Grover Maxwell does attack that problem, maintaining that "It is necessarily true that the future will to some extent resemble the past" (Maxwell, 1961, p. 43). His argument for this is that we can ask questions only within a conceptual framework; to doubt that crows will be black in the future, as they have been in the past, presupposes that crows will remain an identifiable species, and that there will be this much uniformity in the future at least; "unless it is presupposed that the future will to some extent resemble the past, we cannot meaningfully ask questions about the future at all" (Maxwell, 1961, p. 44). It does not seem to me that this follows. We are, after all, asking the questions now; that the questions will not be meaningless in the future is still open to question; and what is even more serious from the point of view of this essay is the fact that even an answer to that question would not lead us to any principles of inductive logic for the justification of particular inductions on the basis of particular evidence. The important question is, "In *what respects* will the future resemble the past?" Observe that in this respect Maxwell's thesis is only a slightly attenuated form of Campbell's.

H. A. Nielsen (1959) develops a similar principle for statistical inference, arguing that arguments proceed not from a *subclass* to a population, but from a sample to a population. The latter inference is sound, because *fairness* is a logical requirement of a sample. Thus, according to Nielsen, a sample *must* be like the population from which it was drawn. (Nielsen is wrong in supposing this—a certain proportion of fair samples *must* be *unlike* the population from which they are drawn.) The problem remains, of course, that it is difficult to tell when a particular subclass is a *sample* in Nielsen's technical sense.

Some writers have maintained the analyticity of the principle of induction in a less sweeping (and more plausible) form. Thus N. R. Hanson (1961) maintains that nothing but reflection is needed to discover the goodness of reasons. G. Buchdahl says, "There is a logic built into our language . . . such that we view testing procedures [sic] as evidence for universal laws, naturally described as inferring techniques" (Buchdahl, 1960). Hanson, too, wants to think of the results of induction as "inference tickets"—Ryle's term—rather than as universal propositions. I shall have comments to make on this thesis when I deal with the pragmatic approach to induction.

Max Black and Nelson Goodman adopt a similar point of view with respect to induction. Black, although he states flatly that he rejects "the view that induction needs any 'justification' or 'vindication' in the sense which philosophers have usually attached to these words" (Black, 1962, p. 262), is perfectly willing to talk of the "unsolved problem of a satisfactory formulation of the canons of inductive inference" (1962, p. 211).

Goodman writes, "An argument that [conforms to the general rules of deductive inference] is justified or valid, even if its conclusion happens to be false. . . . Analogously, the basic task in justifying an inductive inference is to show that it conforms to the general rules of induction" (Goodman, 1955b, p. 66). Goodman argues that the solution of the problem of spelling out these rules depends on the prior solution of the problem of projectibility, to which I shall return in due course; this is a problem that plagues nearly all the formalistic approaches to the construction of an inductive logic.

Another writer in this vein is Jerrold Katz, who claims that the traditional search for an *a priori* inductive logic is misconceived and should be replaced by a factual examination of the reasons for which scientists do accept those hypotheses they accept (Katz, 1962).

Although Toulmin (1958) denies that significant arguments of any sort are "analytic," he really has a theory of induction that places him in the same category as the writers we have been considering. Arguments may use either deductive or inductive warrants to get from their premises to their conclusions; there is no real difference, for neither type of warrant yields a conclusive argument, and neither type of warrant (with the exception of the type of warrant used in mathematics) is strictly analytic. Some inductive arguments are warrant establishing, as well as warrant using, while deductive arguments are not warrant establishing. To find out what forms of argument are acceptable in physics, we must look at the ways physicists argue. "There is no explanation of the fact that one sort of argument works in physics, for instance, except a deeper argument also within physics. Practical logic has no escape route . . . into the *a priori*" (Toulmin, 1958, p. 258). No analysis of the strength of arguments is possible for Toulmin, because he regards "probably" simply as a modal term, which indicates the speaker's *attitude* toward the proposition in question. To say that it will probably rain is simply to say that it will rain, but to say it guardedly.

P. F. Strawson takes a position much like Toulmin's. He argues explicitly against the existence of a formal inductive logic: "In fact, we can never describe the strength of the evidence more exactly than by the use of such words as 'slender,' 'good,' 'conclusive'" (Strawson, 1952, p. 247). It is possible to answer the question "Will induction continue to be successful?" in the affirmative, because we have good evidence for this; but that induction is *reasonable* is simply analytic. Like Toulmin, he feels that the way to find out how inferences *should* be made in a particular field is to look at the way in which inferences *are* made in that field. Strawson argues that there is no way of justifying induction in general, although there are ways of justifying particular inductions (Strawson, 1958). Further, he regards the problem of finding a general justification unreal. It is sufficient that inductive beliefs, as Hume pointed out, are natural. Strawson challenges his critics to *try* to choose a counterinductive policy. "If it is said that there is a problem of induction and that Hume posed it, it must be added that he solved it" (Strawson, 1958, p. 21).

J.J.C. Smart agrees: "There are countless general truths which we just find that we know; we never went through a process of arriving at them. . . . Science never began with the programme of establishing such truths inductively from observation of particular instances" (Smart, 1950, p. 198).

R. Harré follows the trail blazed by Strawson and Toulmin. Like Strawson, he regards sensible questions about induction to be of the form "How is this particular procedure justified?" and the request for a general justification of inductive standards to be misconceived. "There are no general standards of reasonableness everywhere appealed to" (Harré, 1957). Like Toulmin, he takes many of the statements of science to formulate principles of inference, which do not, according to him, require inductive justification. (This is surely a curious doctrine; it suggests that if we call something a principle of inference, we don't care whether or not it will lead us astray, while if we consider the corresponding statement, we take seriously the possibility that it might be in error.)

Hanson also writes in this vein: "'That *F* obtains a good reason for *G*' is necessarily true, if it is true at all. Nothing but reflection is needed to discover the goodness of reasons" (Hanson, 1961, p. 123). Hanson, too, distinguishes between the problem (he admits that it *is* a problem) of justifying inference permits and the problem of justifying general statements. "'All *F*'s are *G*'s' does not, by itself, disclose whether it is up for scrutiny *qua* inference-permit or *qua* the factual support for that permit" (Hanson, 1961, p. 127).

The temptation to disregard completely the normative element that can be discerned in the appraisal of inductive arguments has been succumbed to by a number of writers. Strawson, Toulmin, and Harré — and to some extent Hanson — have all said that to evaluate inductive arguments we must look at inductive arguments that are actually regarded as valid in certain fields; Strawson even refers to Hume's observation that induction is a natural instinct. But far more extreme views of this sort are held by D.G.C. McNabb, who claims that since induction is founded on instincts that we share with higher animals, the way to understand it is to look to biology rather than to logic (McNabb, 1952); and by E. Gross, who writes, "science is the culture of a society of scientists." Since "All cultures have (are) a set of behavioral prescriptions for satisfying needs" (Gross, 1957, p. 838), what we must do is to apply sociological methods to the culture in question in order to uncover the rules of inductive logic.

Toulmin's claim that it is profitable to look at certain classes of general statements as rules of inference has been examined carefully by H. G. Alexander (1958a). He concludes that nothing is added to the traditional account in terms of enthymemes by talking instead of "material rules of inference" or "inference tickets." Further discussion of the logical aspects of the curious doctrine of inference tickets (originally proposed, I believe, by Gilbert Ryle [Ryle, 1950, 1957]) may be found in Casteñeda (1957, 1960) and Cooley (1959).

If we are going to take what scientists *do* as the raw material from which we are to derive our understanding of scientific inference, then we had better take a more serious look than usual at the history of science. In the period since the first publication of this essay, research along these lines has become a major industry. The most influential book in this area is Thomas Kuhn's *Structure of Scientific Revolutions* (Kuhn, 1962a). The thesis presented there is that two kinds of scientific development may be distinguished: normal scientific inquiry, in which there is in a certain body of science an accepted set of standards for inference and evidence, and revolutionary development, in which not only specific law and theories come to be discarded or modified, but in which old standards of evidence and inference are overthrown, and even the *language* in which empirical facts are reported becomes altered. What scientists *do,* he argues, depends on where they are in the historical development of their discipline.

The most extreme version of this approach is that of Feyerabend (1961, 1964, 1970a), who argues that different scientific theories, even those having the same subject matter, such as Copernican and Ptolomaic astronomy, are strictly incommensurable. They cannot even be said to contradict each other, since they have no common language and logic. Feyerabend's view goes as far as anyone's in eliminating both the possibility and the need for inductive logic. There is nothing to be said about even the *comparative* support for different scientific hypotheses and theories. Kuhn himself sees a structure and a role for rationality in the process of theoretical change (Kuhn, 1970a and b). A large number of philosophers whose views have been influenced by Kuhn still believe that the demand for systematization and analysis in scientific inference is legitimate. One of the most influential of these is Imre Lakatos, whose theory of progressive and regressive research programs derives both from the falsificationism of Popper and the emphasis on historical reality inculcated by Kuhn (Lakatos, 1968b). A more recent effort along similar lines is that of Larry Laudan (1977). In a similar vein, Stephen Toulmin (1972) has changed the emphasis of his approach from the ordinary language analysis of general and schematic arguments to the more detailed assessments of real scientific arguments in their social and historical settings.

IV

One of the defects of all the "ordinary language" approaches is that they do not make the logical structure of "good inductive reasons" explicit. In a brief paper Nicholas Rescher (1960) tries to formalize the concept of plausible implication. This formalization he regards as "a step towards the formulation of a logical theory of inductive modes of reasoning." In an earlier paper, Rescher (1958) attempted to formulate a theory of evidential support. In both of these papers, Rescher presupposes the availability of a logical measure function L defined for sentences p and q in a definite formalized language. He defines the *degree of evidential support* that q gives to p, *des(p,q)* as

$$des(p,q) \; = \; \frac{L(p,q) - L(p)}{1 - L(p)} \, L(q)$$

where $L(p,q)$ is the conditional measure of p *given* q, i.e., $L(p \cdot q)/L(q)$. A statement q is confirming evidence for p if (1) q renders p more likely than not, and also if (2) q renders p more likely than before. Like the authors mentioned above, he feels that the inductive problem is to "analyze and codify the rules of evidence in various domains" (Rescher, 1958). He uses his definitions to lay down some general rules of evidence, applicable to all domains. For example, he shows that a statement that entails another is evidence for it, and that a component of a conjunction is evidence for it. He also points out "illicit rules" — for example, that it is not the case that if p is evidence for q, and r entails p, then r is evidence for q.

Another proposal along similar lines has been made by Kemeny and Oppenheim (1952). Again, a logical measure function m, giving each state description in a definite language a weight, is presumed to be on hand. The technique is analytic, where Rescher's technique was synthetic. Kemeny and Oppenheim lay down ten conditions which an adequate theory of factual support should, on their view, satisfy. The fourth condition, for example, concerns equivalent hypotheses and equivalent evidence: If $\vdash H \equiv H'$ and $\vdash E \equiv E'$, then $F(H,E) = F(H',E')$, i.e., the degree of factual support given H by E will be the same as that given H' by E'. The sixth condition stipulates that F is to be a function of the following measures only: $m(H,E)$, $M(H,\overline{E})$, $m(\overline{H},\overline{E})$ and $m(\overline{H},E)$. Having laid down the conditions of adequacy, they look for the simplest function of the measures mentioned in the sixth condition that will satisfy all the other conditions as well. The result is surprising and interesting. The function p, which assigns to each state description the same probability (the "Wittgensteinian" measure function), is introduced as an auxiliary function; it is related to the general function m by a certain number q. In the final formula, if the m-functions are expressed in terms of q and the p-functions, all the qs cancel out, and we are left with

$$F(H,E) \;=\; \frac{p(E,H) - p(E,\overline{H})}{p(E,H) + \text{-}(E,\overline{H})}$$

for the degree of factual support lent H by the evidence E.

Popper, whose general theory of scientific logic we shall consider later, also offers a number of formulas, expressed in terms of logical probabilities, for *degree of corroboration*. They are presented in a series of three notes in the *British Journal for the Philosophy of Science* (Popper 1954, 1956, 1957a).* In the first of these articles he defines the degree of explanatory power of x, with respect to y, $E(x,y)$ as:

$$E(x,y) = \frac{P(y,x) - P(y)}{P(y,x) + P(y)}$$

This definition is very nearly the same as that used by Kemeny and Oppenheim for degree of factual support. For Popper it is only a starting point; he then defines the degree of corroboration of x, given by y, $C(x,y)$, as

$$C(x,y) = E(x,y)\,(1 + P(x)\,P(x,y))$$

and shows that this function satisfies all of *his* conditions of adequacy for degree of corroboration.

Both the concept of explanatory power and the concept of degree of corroboration may be relativized to a statement (of background knowledge, for example) z.

These papers are reprinted as Appendix IX in Popper (1959). Page references are to the reprinted versions.

$E(x,y,z)$, the explanatory power of x with respect to y in the presence of z, is defined as

$$\frac{P(y,xz) - P(y,z)}{P(y,xz) + P(y,z)}$$

and $C(x,y,z)$, the degree of corroboration of x, with respect to y, in the presence of z is defined as

$$C(x,y,z) = E(x,y,z)\,(1 + P(x,z)\,P(x,yz)$$

Popper later discovered that his desiderata could be satisfied by a simpler formula:*

$$C(x,y) = \frac{P(y,x) - P(y)}{P(y,x) - P(xy) + P(y)}$$

In the second article, Popper considers the possibility of using a logarithmic measure of content, as had been suggested by both Kemeny (1953, p. 297) and C. L. Hamblin.† The third article is concerned primarily with the use in statistical inference of the concepts defined in the first article.

Isaac Levi argues (1962) that considerations of epistemic utility (in particular, the principle that the utility of accepting a statement when it is true be independent of the evidence for the statement) are violated by Popper's notion of degree of corroboration, if that is taken as a guide to acceptance of scientific hypotheses. Instead, Levi offers the very simple utility assignments $P(\sim x)$ and $- P(x)$, where P is the logical probability measure. Our epistemic expectation in accepting x on the evidence is thus $U(x,y) = P(x,y)\,P(\sim x) - P(\sim x,y)\,P(x)$.

H. A. Finch has also dealt with the problem of the relation between the confirming power of observations among hypotheses (Finch, 1960). He works from the point of view of modern decision theory (J. Neyman, R. A. Fisher), and from the point of view of information theory, and comes to the conclusion that the crucial quantity in confirming power is

$$\frac{P_r(o/h) - P_r(o)}{P_r(o)}$$

this is the measure of the power of o to confirm or disconfirm h.

Just to make the picture complete, I should also mention Carnap's measure of *increase of confirmation* of h, by e, as against the *a priori* probability of h; he regards $c(h,e) - c(h)$ as the suitable measure.

Table 3.1 shows the extent to which the intuitions of these writers coincide. All of the proposed measures turn out to be directly proportional to either the difference between the probability of the evidence e on the hypothesis h and the prior probability of e, or the difference between the probability of the evidence e on the evidence h and the probability of e on the denial of h; and almost all the measures are inversely proportional to the prior probability of e.

Interest in providing formal measures for inductive support has fallen away sharply since this table first appeared. Two relatively recent works constitute exceptions of a

---

*This was announced in a note appearing on p. 33 of *The British Journal for the Philosophy of Science*, not p. 359, as stated on p. 400 of Popper (1959); observe also that the formula is given there incorrectly with $P(y,z)$ being written for $P(y,x)$.

†Unpublished thesis referred to by Popper.

TABLE 3.1

Author	Proposed Measure of Corroboration or Evidential Power	Notation Rendered Uniform Simple Substitutions Made
Carnap	$c(h,c) - c(h)$	$P(h)\left[\dfrac{P(e,h) - P(e)}{P(e)}\right]$
Rescher	$des(p,q) = \dfrac{L(p,q) - L(p)}{1 - L(q)}\,L(q)$	$\dfrac{P(h)}{P(\bar h)}\,[P(e,h) - P(e)]$
Kemeny-Oppenheim[a]	$F(H,E) = \dfrac{P(E,H) - P(E,\bar H)}{P(E,H) + P(E,\bar H)}$	$\dfrac{[P(e,h) - P(e,h)]}{P(e,h) + P(e,\bar h)}$
Popper 1	$C(x,y) = \dfrac{P(y,x) - P(y)}{P(y,x) + P(y)}\,(1 + P(x)P(x,y))$	$1 + P(h)(P(h,e))\left[\dfrac{P(e,h) - P(e)}{P(e,h) + P(e)}\right]$
Popper 2	$C(x,y) = \dfrac{P(y,x) - P(y)}{P(y,x) - P(x,y) + P(y)}$	$\dfrac{P(e,h) - P(e)}{P(\bar h)\,P(e,h) + P(e)}$
Levi	$U(x,y) = P(x,y)\,P(\sim x) - P(\sim x,y)\,P(x)$	$P(h)\,P(\bar h)\,\dfrac{P(e,h) - P(e,\bar h)}{P(e)}$
Finch	$\dfrac{Pr(o|h)}{Pr(o)} - 1$	$\dfrac{P(e,h) - P(e)}{P(e)}$
Törnebohm taking content $(H) = $ $C(H) = -\log P(H)$	$Dc(H|E) = \dfrac{C(H) - C(H|E)}{C(H)}$	$\dfrac{-\log P(h) + \log P(h,e)}{-\log P(h)}$
Törnebohm taking content $(H) = $ $C(H) = P(\sim H)$	$Dc(H|E) = \dfrac{C(H) - C(H|E)}{C(H)}$	$\dfrac{P(h)}{P(\bar h)} \cdot \dfrac{P(e,h) - P(e)}{P(e)}$

[a]Notice here that $P(e)=P(h)P(e,h)+P(h)P(e,h)$, so that the denominator is just the sum of the unweighted probabilities of e on h and $\bar h$.

sort. L. J. Cohen (1966a and b, 1970b) proposes a measure of evidential support that depends on the field a hypothesis belongs to, and within that field, on the number and nature of the experimental tests to which the hypothesis has been subjected. A.W.F. Edwards argues (1972) that *all* the information provided by data bearing on the relative merits of two hypotheses is embodied in their likelihood ratio. Neither the likelihood ratio, nor Cohen's inductive probability, satisfies the axioms of the probability calculus. On the other hand, they do admit of quantification, and they are free from what has been seen by many to be the chief drawback of the proposals discussed above, viz., their dependence on a prior logical measure defined over the whole language of science.

V

Some writers, convinced of the dishonesty of simply postulating certain material principles that will justify induction (as Russell says, such postulation has the same advantages as theft) and yet profoundly dissatisfied with an analytic principle of induction that does not give what they want — namely, some assurance that induction will often, if not always, lead to success — have seriously tried to show that the principle of induction can be justified without circularity on an inductive basis. One such attempt, that of R. B. Braithwaite (1953) has been commented on by both A. Shimony (1953) and me (Kyburg, 1963) and found wanting. Braithwaite does not avoid circularity, according to Shimony; and that he certainly provides no persuasive inductive argument for the inductive principle is indicated by my counterexamples. But Braithwaite's argument was brief and incidental to the main line of argument in his book; it would be unwise and unfair to regard it as the last word in the inductive justification of inductive arguments.

Max Black has been one of the staunchest supporters of the noncircularity of the inductive justification of induction (Black, 1954). The possibility of constructing an inductive argument supporting a principle of induction that avoids circularity depends on the distinction between a *premise* of an inference, and a *rule* in accordance with which one infers. The most important argument Black examines is this one (1954, p. 197):

> In most instances the use of R_2 in arguments with true premises examined in a wide variety of conditions, R_2 has been successful.

Hence (probably),

> In the next instance to be encountered of the use of R_2 in an argument with a true premise, R_2 will be successful.

where R_2 is: "To argue from "Most instances of A's examined in a wide variety of conditions have been B' to (probably) 'The next A to be encountered will be B' "(Black, 1954, p. 196).

Black argues that this argument cannot possibly be circular, since its conclusion is not one of its premises, or even hidden in one of its premises. Indeed, the conclusion does not even follow *deductively* from the premises: the premises could perfectly well be true and the conclusion false. Although this would be bad for a deductive argument, it saves our inductive argument from circularity. Furthermore, such an argument may perfectly well be legitimate (Black, 1954, p. 203), if we have gone to great lengths to satisfy ourselves of the propriety of using the rule we are using; and indeed the argument may also be "correct without triviality" (Black, 1954, p. 204), for there is nothing to prevent us from taking as the evidential premise in such an argument, material that we did not refer to in the examination of the legitimacy of the rule of inference in accordance with which we make the inference.

Peter Achinstein (1961) offers two objections to the cogency of Black's argument.

The first is a counterexample. Consider the rule of inference: Argue from "No *F* is *G*" and "Some *G* is *H*," to the conclusion "All *F* is *H*." Call this rule of inference *D*. Now look at the self-supporting nature of the following argument:

> *premise:* No argument using *D* as its rule of inference is an argument which contains a premise beginning with the term "all"; some arguments containing premises beginning with the term "all" are valid.
> *conclusion:* All arguments using *D* as their rule of inference are valid.

Black would maintain, of course, that there is no parallel here. There is a similarity of structure, to be sure, but while in the inductive case we know that the rule of inference is good—that is, we have "subjected it to scrutiny" and so on—in this case we know that the rule of inference is *not* good.

Achinstein's other argument is more telling; it is that "to claim that a nondeductive rule of inference is correct or valid is to imply, . . . that it will probably be successful in the next instance of its use" (Achinstein, 1961, p. 139). If we call the self-supporting inductive argument (*a*), "the assumption that (*a*) is valid . . . does involve the claim that (*a*)'s conclusion is probable" (Achinstein, 1961, p. 140). In a later note, Black agrees with this portion of Achinstein's argument (Black, 1962). According to Achinstein this makes (*a*) circular, since (*a*) is designed to show its conclusion probable. Now, Black maintains that the conclusion of (*a*) is that *R* will be successful in its next application, and this is quite different from the assumption that *R* will probably be successful. Achinstein isn't satisfied by this gambit, and neither am I. I find myself asking what possible ground there can be for accepting the conclusion of the argument. The only ground that I can imagine being given is that *R* is probably a generally successful rule. Although, as Black points out, that *R* will probably be successful does not entail that it will be successful on its next application, it still seems to me that *R's* probable success provides the *ground* for accepting the conclusion of the argument (*a*). There is a form of circularity here: we cannot get to know the adequacy, the correctness, of the *rule of inference*, in accordance with which we construct the argument, without "simultaneously or antecedently" (Black, 1954, p. 198) getting to know the *ground* of the conclusion. A more careful analysis of "ground" would be required before we could spell out the type and degree of circularity involved in the simple inductive justification of induction. For our purposes here it really suffices that the inductive argument for the inductive principle has not been presented in such a way that all (or even most) philosophers find it cogent and are willing to found their inductive logic on its basis.

What alternative ways are there of establishing the foundations of an inductive logic? One way, not unrelated to the foregoing attempt to achieve self-support, is to seek to justify the canons of inductive logic pragmatically. It is possible to argue, as Gilbert Ryle does (1960) that there is no inductive inference (and hence no inductive logic) and that the matter is settled as simply as this: we simply *see* that induction works. We do not, on Ryle's view, establish the general statement "All *A* are *B*" by observing *A*'s and *B*'s. We adopt the rule of inference: from the fact that something is an *A*, infer that it is a *B*; then we see from the success of the inferences made in accordance with this rule of inference that the rule *works*. This is not satisfactory. As already stated, there is no advantage, and there is considerable danger, in the attempt made by Strawson and Ryle, as well as by others, to deal with *material* rules of inference. In the second place, as Achinstein has argued, the problem is not to show that the rule (if that is how you wish to reconstruct the inference) has worked in the *past;* the problem is to show that it will continue to work. "The scientist not only points to the past successes of his theory, but he infers to its future successes as well" (Achinstein, 1960, p. 8). He charges that Ryle is playing on the ambiguity of "it works." Ryle denies (1960) that he is playing on the ambiguity of "works"; a general law or theory, he says, is like a design or a recipe: it is tenseless. There is no inference from successful inference to the truth of the *basis* of that inference any more than there is an *inference* from a successful soufflé to the validity of the recipe in accordance with which it was made. We *learn* the merits and demerits of a design or recipe by testing it — but to learn is not to infer.

The dispute is, I think, settled by Harry V. Stopes-Roe (1960), who says "the fact is that, when one shows the goodness of a recipe or a theory by means of successful instances, there is a gap between what is literally shown — namely the successes to date — and the goodness of the recipe or theory." Whatever be the nature of this gap (and many would be happy to withhold the term "inference" from the process that leads us across it), it is that gap which an inductive logic or an examination of scientific method is called upon to fill.

VI

In 1950 Herbert Feigl published an article, "De Principiis non Disputandum . . .?" (Feigl, 1950) that has become one of the most mentioned pieces on the inductive problem; in it he distinguishes between *justification* and *vindication*. To ask for a general justification of inductive procedures is to ask the impossible, he argues. We can justify particular inductions by reference to general principles of induction, but we cannot justify the principles in the same way. What we can do, however, is to ask for a vindication of the adoption of the rule of induction. Such a vindication consists precisely in showing that *if* the goal of predicting the future can be achieved, the rule of induction is a way to achieve it. (It is not necessarily the only way, or even the best way.) This was the kind of "justification" provided by H. Reichenbach for his "straight rule" of induction (Reichenbach, 1940). It is the kind of justification sought by many other writers — most notably in recent years by W. Salmon.

D. Kading argues that no pragmatic vindication succeeds, since, given the aim of predicting the future correctly, "we have no proof that inductive procedure would be the best method of fulfilling this aim" (Kading, 1960). This argument misses the point: Feigl never claimed that induction was the *best* method. But both Black (1959) and E. Madden (1958) observe that in any *finite* run, we *can't* even be sure that if anything will work induction will. This is the problem of the "short run." Reichenbach felt that it could not be solved directly.

John Lenz also mentions the "short-run problem" as a problem for the pragmatic vindication of induction (Lenz, 1958). He also points to the fact that any asymptotic rule (e.g., estimate the relative frequency of As among Bs to be $m/n + f(n)$, where $f(n)$ approaches 0 as n increases) allows the same justification as the conventional "straight rule"; and finally he argues that we have "no assurance that any of the predictions that science actually makes are correct or even probably correct."

Starting in 1956, Salmon has launched a heroic one-man attack on the opponents of the pragmatic vindication. Black argued (1949) that the pragmatic justification could apply as well to the counterinductive policy (if m of n As have been B, predict a future ration of $n - m/n$) as to the conventional one (recall that Burks offered the same argument as one of the grounds for accepting his presupposition theory). This policy is self-corrective (that is, it reflects changes in our background knowledge), it may lead to success, and so on. Salmon shows (1956) that this is not the case. Indeed, predictions made in accordance with Black's rule are contradictory: if 1/8 of the As are B_3, 5/8 of them B_1, and 2/8 of them B_2, then Black's rule would lead to the prediction that 7/8 of the As are B_3, 6/8 B_2, and 3/8 B_1, or (supposing that B_1, B_2, and B_3 are mutually exclusive) that 16/8 of the As have one or another of these properties. Salmon formulates the following two conditions that preclude such nonsensical results; the rules still allowed by them he calls *regular* rules, since their formal properties are those possessed by Carnap's regular c-functions.

Condition I: Given (1) a sequence S_i of events defined by the attribute A, (2) a set of properties $B_1 \ldots B_k$ which are mutually exclusive and exhaustive within S_i and (3) a sample of members of S_i, m_j of which have the property $B_j (1 \leqslant j \leqslant k)$; then, any rule R for making estimates E_j of the probability $P(A,B_j)$ or of the relative frequency $F(A,B_j)$ of B_j, within the total sequence S_i must be such that

$$\sum_{j=1}^{k} E_j = 1$$

Condition II: Under the circumstances detailed in Condition I, E_j must never be negative (Salmon, 1956, pp. 386–87).

Such irregular rules as Black and Burks have considered are thus shown to lead to contradiction.

Salmon attempted to deal with the short-run problem about the same time (Salmon, 1955) by suggesting that we make an estimate of the relative frequency and then apply that estimate to the short run. As he realized soon afterwards (Salmon, 1957) there are completely arbitrary rules — just as there are for inductive estimation generally — that admit the same justification that he offers for the natural rule.

Salmon provided a further development along these lines in 1961. He suggested two criteria — the criterion of convergence, and the criterion of linguistic invariance — that were offered in the hope that they would lead to plausible solutions both for the "short-run" problem and for the problem of selecting a *unique* member of the family of asymptotic rules (Salmon, 1961). The criterion of linguistic invariance states that "no inductive rule is acceptable if the results it yields are functions of the arbitrary features of the choice of language" (Salmon, 1961, p. 246). On this ground he rejects, for example, Carnap's theory of induction, since the degrees of confirmation reflect the richness of the language for which they are defined. In fact Salmon shows that every methodological rule of estimation, with the possible exception of the straight rule, will ultimately violate these two criteria. This is a large step toward a vindication of induction; it is much more than one would have believed it possible to prove. In the same paper he offers a solution to the short-run problem — again, the natural one of making the short-run estimate as close as possible to the estimate of the limiting frequency. Only this short-run rule, of all possible asymptotic short-run rules, appears not to violate the criterion of linguistic invariance.

Stephen Barker's comments (1961a) put this conclusion in a rather depressing light, for Barker shows, with no trouble at all, that the straight rule also violates the criterion of linguistic invariance. Consider Nelson Goodman's curious predicates "Grue" and "Bleen," with "Grue" meaning green and occurring before 2000 A.D. or blue and later than that; "Bleen" is defined correspondingly. Clearly the straight rule, as applied to a sequence of emeralds, will lead us to make the estimate that the proportion of emeralds that are green is 1, and also that the proportion of emeralds that are grue is 1; but nothing can be both grue and green, if it lasts long enough, so that we are led again to an inconsistency.

Salmon attempts to answer Barker's problem by stipulating that the straight rule of estimation be applied only to purely ostensive predicates (Salmon, 1963a). He argues that Goodman-type predicates are not "purely ostensive" because they must be defined — grue things don't *look* alike, while green ones do. A purely ostensive predicate is one with these characteristics: "(1) it *can* be defined ostensively, (2) its positive and negative instances for ostensive definition *can* be indicated nonverbally, (3) the respect in which the positive instances resemble each other and differ from the negative instances is open to direct inspection" (Salmon, 1963a, p. 38).

This solution is not altogether satisfactory. As the discussion following Salmon's paper showed, not all philosophers find the criterion of linguistic invariance as natural as Salmon does (Kyburg, 1963a). Furthermore, even if we accept Salmon's solution, it involves abandoning a large part of what one took to be the program of inductive vindication. There remains the problem of the short run. Black's main argument against Salmon is that the whole approach is wrong, because "Anything we observe in the short run is compatible with any value of the limiting frequency" (Black, 1963).

Finally, this new result makes the second part of Barker's criticism of the earlier paper even more telling: "It remains to show how other types of inductive rules can be vindicated. It seems to me especially important to vindicate a rule for inferring from the limit of a relative frequency to short run relative frequencies and to introduce more complex rules of inductive inference to deal with the relation between scientific hypotheses and their evidence" (Barker, 1961b, p. 54). Here, for the moment, this approach to inductive logic rests. There have been few contributions to it since 1964.

VII

Salmon and Barker were among the few inductive logicians to take the "short-run" problem seriously and see that short-run predictions in the case of complete statistical knowledge are just as problematic as the inductive inference itself. The predictive inference forms the cornerstone of my own system of inductive logic (Kyburg 1961a, 1974a). In this system the notion of randomness is fundamental. It is not taken as a primitive notion but is defined as a syntactical relation, and the statistical syllogism is preserved from inconsistency by a randomness requirement that has built in a requirement of total evidence. The result is a *logical* concept of probability, but one that does not require or depend on a logical measure function defined over the statements of a fixed language.

The object language of the system developed in 1961 was Quine's ML, and formal definitions of probability and randomness were developed in Quine's protosyntax. A number of changes were made in the system in response to criticism, and a new development was provided in 1974 in which the object language was a general first-order language that included set theory; an ordinary set-theoretical metalanguage was employed in the syntactical characterization of probability.

In both developments, the statistical syllogism is central. The probability of a statement of the form $a \in A$ is the interval $[p,q]$ relative to a body of knowledge or rational corpus K, just in case there is a term B such that a is known in K to belong to B (i.e., "$a \in B$" $\in K$), it is known in K that the proportion of Bs that are As lies in the interval $[p,q]$, and a is, relative to K, a *random* member of B. By adopting the principle that if S is known in K to be equivalent to T, the probability of S should be the same as the probability of T, relative to K, we can ensure through the resources of set theory that since every statement is equivalent to one of the form "$a \in A$", every statement has a probability.

Induction may begin in the highest-level corpus, where we have such analytically true statistical statements as: the proportion of 1000-member samples of A that have a relative frequency of B that is almost the same as the relative frequency of B in all of A lies between .9 and 1. Relative to this highest-level corpus, then, we can get such probability statements as: the probability is [.9,1] that the proportion of all As that are Bs lies between .74 and .76.

The construction of lower-level rational corpora proceeds by means of a rule of detachment: a statement is an ingredient of a rational corpus of level r_i if and only if the probability of that statement relative to a rational corpus of higher level is at least r_i. Thus, we would be entitled, on the basis of the probability statement above, to include the statement "The proportion of As that are Bs lies between .74 and .76" in the rational corpus of level .9.

In the first version of my system (Kyburg, 1961a), I suggested that we might consider a finite sequence of rational corpora of various levels. Fred Schick showed (1963a) that in my system this led to deductive closure in all corpora but the highest two, and I showed (reluctantly) that this led to the result that all but the highest two levels were empty (Kyburg, 1963c). In the later version of the system (Kyburg, 1974a) I abandoned the attempt to consider a whole sequence of rational corpora and settled for three: an Ur-corpus consisting of incorrigible statements, mathematical and logical statements, and the like; a corpus of moral certainties; and a corpus of practical certainties. The latter two corpora are characterized by indices of acceptance that may be taken to have values depending on the context of a discussion of decision.

One of the most crucial problems for any system that contains a rule of detachment for inductive conclusions is that of avoiding inconsistency. The problem, now known as the lottery paradox, was first discussed in Kyburg (1961a, p. 197) and has since been the source of considerable controversy in the shadowy area between inductive logic and epistemology. It is discussed in Kyburg (1970c) and also by a number of other authors (Hintikka, 1966b; Hilpinen, 1968).

The problem is this: it is easy enough to think of a large set of statements each of which is practically certain in as strict a sense as you wish, but which is also such that their conjunction is certainly (or almost certainly) false. Consider, for example, the set of statements "ticket i will not win the Irish Sweepstakes." It is clear that we must either abandon complete logical closure for rational corpora—that S_1 and S_2 are so practically certain as to belong to a rational corpus should not entail that their conjunction will be that certain—or else we must abandon the possibility of a "high probability" rule of acceptance.

The principle of direct inference embodied in my definition of randomness, which validates the statistical syllogism, has been criticized by Levi (1977b, 1978a) and Seidenfeld (1978) on the grounds that it violates the principle of conditionalization that is central to the subjectivistic and logical measure approaches to inductive logic to be discussed below. I have acknowledged this, but claimed that the price is not too high to pay (Kyburg, 1977d, 1980d).

Another problem arises in my system as it did in Salmon's, and which appears to come up in every attempt to formalize induction: the problem of artificial Goodman-type predicates, such as grue and bleen. The problem cannot be solved by considering only ostensive predicates, because it also arises in the need to distinguish between arguments based on such logically true statistical premises as "Practically all 1000-member subclasses of A exhibit a proportion of Bs which lie between $r - \delta_1$ and $r - \delta_2$ or between $r + \delta_3$ and $r + \delta_4$, where r is the proportion of Bs in A." In my book I solved the problem by the high-handed and ad hoc procedure of stipulating that only a certain set of expressions, constructed by certain techniques from the primitive predicates and operations, was to be considered in the probability system. As between the two statistical statements just mentioned, for example, I chose to follow Neyman in basing my inference on a shortest confidence interval, as is obviously sensible. The logical basis of this preference, however, remains arbitrary.

So far the peculiar predicates have resisted any general characterization. Goodman offered (1955) a relative solution in terms of "entrenchment"—the degree to which a predicate is entrenched in our language. But might it not be that we could be speaking a different language? S. Barker and P. Achinstein (1960) attempt to show that we could not. Goodman (1960) rejects their attempt to establish a logical asymmetry between "grue" and "green," and so does his student J. Ullian (1961). K. Small also tries to exhibit a significant asymmetry between "grue" and "green" (Small, 1961). Salmon's solution (green things look alike, while grue things do not) (Salmon, 1963a) is like Goodman's (predicates that are well entrenched may be projected) in presupposing a principle of induction of the very sort they are designed to elucidate. Salmon's solution presupposes that things that look alike will continue to look alike, while Goodman admits that entrenchment in the past must be *assumed* a good guide to usefulness in the future.

Both H. Leblanc (1963a and b) and C. Hempel (1960) have dealt recently with the problem created by Goodman's peculiar predicates. Leblanc carefully exhibits the inconsistencies into which one is led by the usual rules of inductive extrapolation, when one considers Goodman's peculiar predicates. He offers no solution to the problems that he raises. Hempel points out that the problem is not one of being able to determine which statements are lawlike and which are not (as Goodman claimed), for the same problem arises in connection with the extrapolation of numerical relations as quantitative laws: there are an infinite number of laws of the form $y = f_1(x)$, $y = f_2(x)$, . . . which are mutually inconsistent, which are equally supported by the evidence, and which are equally lawlike. He too has no solution to offer, although both he and Leblanc point out that in formal theories of confirmation no *inconsistencies* are generated by the peculiar predicates. They nevertheless have unwelcome consequences.

It has been suggested (by Barker, 1961b) that this is a problem peculiar to the view that enumerative induction is basic to scientific inference. But it is clearly just as much a matter of concern to those who claim that scientific inference is a matter of selecting the simplest from a class of acceptable hypotheses, for, if we spoke in a grue-bleen language, the hypothesis that all emeralds are grue would be much simpler (it would involve no reference to time, for example) than the hypothesis that they are green—i.e., grue until the year 2000, and bleen thereafter. The problem of finding some way of distinguishing between sensible predicates, like "blue" and "green," and the outlandish ones, suggested by Goodman, Barker, and others, is thus surely one of the most important problems to come out of recent discussions of inductive logic. It is also one of the most pressing, since only 17 years are left in which to solve it.

VIII

One of the most popular approaches to inductive logic is that followed, with variations, by Popper (1959), Barker (1957), Wisdom (1952), and others. It consists, first of all, in the denial that "induction" is fundamental to scientific inference. In its most extreme form, this denial is strengthened into a denial that there is any form of inference from experimental results to general scientific hypotheses, and that the contrary assertion is to be regarded as a regression into authoritarianism (Agassi, 1958). On this view of scientific method, what is fundamental is the free, unhindered construction of imaginative scientific hypotheses, on the one hand, and on the other, the subjection of these free creations to the most conscientious, rigorous, and severe tests we can devise. One of the most attractive features of this view is its simplicity. There is no need to worry about the relation between a scientific hypothesis and the data that suggested it, because the source of a hypothesis is utterly irrelevant. Whether I arrive at H by observing nature, by observing a crystal ball, or by a combination of deep breathing and free association, doesn't matter once the hypothesis is there; what matters is how well it stands up to tests. But the *logical* relationship between a hypothesis and the tests devised to test it is straight-forwardly *deductive:* from H and boundary conditions and perhaps auxiliary hypotheses, a statement is deduced that can be directly tested. The relationship between a hypothesis and the tests we apply to it is *more* than logical, of course: the tests, to be significant, must be our sincere attempts to refute the hypothesis. This is a psychological matter and offers nothing to the logician.

There are still problems for the logician to consider, however. For one thing, it is obvious that there will be, in any stage of knowledge, an infinite number of hypotheses that are not refuted by experience. It is true that we may not have thought of them all explicitly, but this seems to be accidental, and at any rate there is no doubt but that there are occasions when we consider a large number of hypotheses. (We can say that in considering functional generalization – when we seek the function that will relate pressure to temperature of a gas kept under constant volume, for example – there are an infinite number of possible laws that we are considering.) Two criteria have been suggested for making this choice: simplicity and content According to some writers we should choose the simplest hypothesis (perhaps on the ground that it is most probable), while according to others we should choose the hypothesis that says the most (perhaps on the ground that it is most falsifiable, i.e., least probable!).

The most common view is that when we have to make a choice among unfalsified laws, we properly choose the simplest. For the inductive logician, however, this merely raises the question as to what simplicity is and how it should be measured. A number of proposals have been made in recent years, ranging from the elegant proposal made by Svenonius (1955) to the rather simple-minded suggestion made by me (Kyburg, 1961b). Some of these proposals concern the logical simplicity of "primitive extra-logical vocabularies" (Goodman, 1958) and thus seem to have relatively little to do with the problems of inductive logic. The work of L. Svenonius (1955), Goodman (1952), Kemeny (1955a), and P. Suppes (1956) falls into this category. My theory of simplicity takes it to be characteristic of a whole system of knowledge and takes as its basic measure the fewness of the number of quantifiers needed in the axioms and laws of the system. H. Jeffreys offers a definition of simplicity for functional laws (not for basic vocabularies) that depends on the number and type of parameters in the algebraic form of the law (Jeffreys, 1931, p. 38). Barker proposes a measure of simplicity that uses Kemeny's logical measure functions (Kemeny, 1953) and that applies to theories: theory S is simpler than theory T if its logical measure is less than that of T, i.e., if for large enough n, T can be true of n things in more ways than S can (Barker, 1957, pp. 180–82). Barker argues (1957, p. 94; 1961c, p. 273) as does Jeffreys (1931) that we choose the simpler law not just because it is simpler but also because it is "most probably true." This issue, and others relating to the use of the criterion of simplicity in induction, are discussed by R. Harrod (1956), P. G. Frank (1954a), and Kemeny (1959). M. Scriven reminds us that simplicity is only one desideratum among others (Scriven, 1955). Harré introduces a distinction that might help to explain some of the conflicts about simplicity, the distinction between *formal* and *conceptual* simplicity (Harré, 1959). Goodman and his followers have mainly been concerned with conceptual simplicity – the simplicity of the extra-logical basis of a language for science; Jeffreys and most other writers have been concerned with the simplicity of various laws written within a *given* language. But as Harré also argues, the two kinds of simplicity are not logically independent.

The whole discussion of simplicity has been curiously inconclusive. Not only has there been no growing body of agreement concerning the measurement of simplicity, but there has been no agreement concerning the concept of simplicity for which we should seek a measure, or concerning the precise role that simplicity should play in the acceptance of scientific hypotheses.

Popper prefers to base the selection of a hypothesis from among those possible on a principle of falsifiability rather than on a principle of simplicity. We should accept that hypothesis which will be most quickly eliminated by tests if it is false, i.e., the most falsifiable hypothesis, the hypothesis with the greatest content. But he also shows (Popper, 1959c, Ch. vii) that falsifiability in this sense corresponds closely to our intuitive notion of simplicity. This correspondence leads to one of those curiously paradoxical-sounding conflicts that seem more prone to rise in inductive logic than in any other field. The conflict is this: Barker and Jeffreys claim that, given a choice, we should select the most probable hypothesis, "most probable" corresponding with "simplest" (Jeffreys, 1931, p. 36). Popper, using a perfectly analogous concept of logical probability, claims the opposite, that we select the *least* probable (the most daring, the most falsifiable) hypothesis (Popper, 1959c, p. 141). This conflict has been discussed by J. L. Harsanyi (1960), who tends to side with Jeffreys in saying that we should prefer the hypothesis with the highest posterior probability. This misses the point for two reasons: first, Popper does not regard the notion of posterior probability (Carnap's "degree of confirmation") as a useful one; and second, the hypothesis with the highest posterior probability is simply that which describes what *has happened* (i.e., just describes the evidence) and leaves the whole future course of events undetermined. But this hypothesis would be selected by no one.

Indeed, the most interesting thing about this entire conflict is that neither Barker, Popper, Jeffreys, nor any other inductive logician would have any difficulty in deciding what hypothesis to accept in an ordinary experimental situation. This suggests that the very hypothesis "most probable" for Jeffreys is precisely that which is "least probable" for Popper. A part of the explanation is suggested by Harsanyi: a law which is most probable *a posteriori* may not have been most probable *a priori*. But it *is* true that if two hypotheses each imply evidence *e*, the law most probable *a priori* will also be the most probable *a posteriori* relative to *e*. Other factors are these: Jeffreys is supposing that we have a list of possible *general* laws that might possibly govern occurrences of a certain sort. (Thus he does not even consider the laws Popper regards as "most probable" – i.e., laws going only slightly beyond our observations.) Furthermore, Jeffreys is using Bayes's theorem, according to which the probability of the hypothesis on the given evidence is equal to the probability of the evidence on the hypothesis (generally taken to be one), multiplied by the ratio of the *a priori* probability of the hypothesis to the *a priori* probability of the evidence. Disregarding the *a priori* probability of the hypothesis, we obtain a reconciliation of the two views by observing that to say that the hypothesis is highly falsifiable is to say that the *a priori* probability of the evidence is very small. But this is just what Jeffreys says: the posterior probability of the hypothesis is proportional to the reciprocal of the probability of the evidence. Even the ranking of laws in order of simplicity is roughly the same on the two views: a straight-line relationship is highly falsifiable (and highly improbable) on Popper's view, and in general a theory involving a small number of parameters (by ruling out a large number of sets of possibilities) will be less probable than one involving a great number of parameters (Popper, 1959, pp. 380–81). For Jeffreys, the theory with fewer adjustable parameters is both more probable and simpler. Other things being equal, then, the simplest law on both views is the one with the least number of parameters.

The major, and the only serious, conflict between the two views is that expressed in Popper's refusal to identify corroboration with posterior probability. This refusal is based on his denial that we choose the most probable hypothesis and his assertion that we accept the hypothesis that has the greatest content, and which has stood up to severe tests and sincere attempts to refute it. Of course, this conception of scientific acceptability raises certain problems, as Popper's critics have been quick to point out. D. C. Stove argues (1960) that these psychological characterizations of what constitutes a test (it must be "sincere," an "attempt to falsify," etc.) are quite irrelevant to the matter of evidential import: "To suppose otherwise would be to let differences of intention between two persons who subjected the same theory to the same test affect the question of the support, if any, which passing the test gives to the theory." Then there is the question of whether "test" is to be understood in a generic sense. If so, we may ask, as G. J. Warnock does (1960), why passing one application of a test should convince us that a theory will pass subsequent applications of the same test; and if not, we may ask why we should believe that it will pass different tests. P. C. Gibbons (1962) rejects the notion that there is any useful ordering of tests into more and less severe. Popper himself admits that "the requirement of sincerity cannot be formalized." If is possible to go one step further (for, as Buchdahl has remarked, [1960] the notion of a "test" is ambiguous) and to assert that what it is for an observation to *be* a test of a theory cannot be formalized. This will become clear in the discussion of the paradoxes of confirmation; even J.W.N. Watkins (1959a) admits that there are circumstances in which the observation of a white shoe constitutes a "test" of a theory that all crows are black. And R. H. Vincent (1962a) has shown that Popper's criteria, like everyone else's, founder on Goodman's reef.

All this psychologism is distasteful to the logician who is looking for the timeless quality of evidential power. Furthermore, everyone recognizes differences in the degree to which hypotheses have been tested and stood up to tests. Not all advocates of the hypothetico-deductive method agree that the problem of distinguishing between well-supported hypotheses and highly speculative ones is a serious one, but Popper, for example, has taken it seriously enough to offer a definition of "degree of corroboration" to explicate the distinction.

IX

There is an approach to inductive logic that takes the distinction between well-confirmed and not-so-well confirmed as fundamental. The central proponent of this approach is Carnap, whose continuing researches into logical probability as the framework of an inductive logic have inspired considerable admiration and emulation in the past thirty years. His original treatise (Carnap, 1950) exhibited certain shortcomings of which he himself was quite aware. Many of these shortcomings have been overcome by himself and his followers. The original system of logical probability was limited to first-order functional calculi consisting of a finite number of individual signs and a finite number of one-place predicates that were assumed to be logically independent (this would exclude color predicates, for example, which could be assumed to be logically exclusive) and logically complete in the sense that anything to be said about the world could be said in terms of the predicates. These restrictions were quickly eliminated. Kemeny eliminated the requirement of logical independence (Kemeny, 1951a) simply by stipulating (in the metalanguage) that the measure function m is to assign real numbers to all noncontradictory state descriptions so that the sum of the values is 1. At the same time, Y. Bar-Hillel pointed out that a problem is created for Carnap's system by the fact that relations generally have a logical structure (Bar-Hillel, 1951), i.e., a relation may be transitive, irreflexive, etc.; but this problem, though a real one for Carnap (1951), was soon dealt with by Kemeny for languages consisting of a first-order functional calculus with properties, relations, and an identity sign. Later he published a more general system (Kemeny, 1953) applicable to functional calculi of all finite orders, in which there was no restriction on the interdependence of the atomic sentences of the calculus, but only the following mild restrictions on the language itself:

1. The object language must be consistent.
2. It must not contain an axiom of infinity.
3. The number of types of individuals must be finite.
4. There must be a finite number of constants.
5. Each constant must be of finite order.

The measure function m', reflecting the facts of logical interdependence, is obtained from a measure function m defined for all state descriptions by the following relation:

$$m'(W) = \frac{m(A \cdot W)}{m(A)}$$

where W is an arbitrary statement and A is the conjunction of all the axioms reflecting logical structure in the language.

There have been a number of other workers in the same vineyard. R. M. Martin claimed to provide a simplification of the semantic basis of Carnap's theory (Martin,

1958). Hilary Putnam has provided a definition for languages free of even Kemeny's restrictions (Putnam, 1956). Hugues Leblanc has provided a number of studies of various aspects of Carnapian logical probability (Leblanc, 1962).

Several writers (Kemeny, 1955b; Lehman, 1955; Shimony, 1955) have found a justification for Carnap's criteria of adequacy in the consideration of bets as reflecting degrees of belief. Thus if $P(A)$ is the probability of A, I should be willing to bet on A at the odds of $P(A):(1 - P(A))$, and if $P(\overline{A})$ is the probability of the negation of A, I should be willing to bet on $\overline{A}$ at odds of $P(\overline{A}):(1 - P(\overline{A}))$. But these are simply the opposite sides of the same bet, so we must have

$$\frac{P(A)}{1 - P(A)} = \frac{1 - P(A)}{P(\overline{A})} \text{ or } P(A) = 1 - P(\overline{A}).$$

Relations sufficient to develop the whole of the probability calculus can be developed in this way. Recently, Carnap has adopted this approach to the axioms of the calculus (Carnap, 1962). He has also been working with Kemeny and Jeffrey on the development of a theory of confirmation applicable to *families* of predicates (e.g., color words).

One objection that has been raised against Carnap's theory is the arbitrariness of the values of degree of confirmation. In the first place, the value may reflect the number of primitive predicates in the language; by adding a primitive predicate that does not appear in either h or e, we may change the value of $c(h, e)$. And $c(h, e)$ is also arbitrary in the sense that its value depends on the logical measure function with which we start, and the selection of one particular measure function from among the infinite number possible seems arbitrary. Kemeny suggested (1952) making the arbitrariness explicit. Let e_0 be the statement that s individuals all have each of t properties; h_0 be the hypothesis that some other individual will have them too; and take

$$c(h_0, e_0) = \frac{s + k(1/2)^t}{s + k}.$$

Taking $k = 2^P$, where P is the number of primitive predicates, yields Carnap's function c^*. This proposal is close to that made subsequently by Carnap himself (1952, 1952a).

This arbitrariness is unsettling. Carnap (1952, pp. 75-77) suggests that we can take the success of our inductive method in our actual universe as a guide to its suitability; but J. W. Lenz has argued (1956) that in choosing a particular c-function we must be either basing our decision on the hypothesis that c-functions that have been most adequate in the past will continue to be most adequate in the future (a synthetic hypothesis demanding justification), or we are basing our decision on some synthetic principle of induction. We do not need the principle of induction to justify probability statements, but we do need to make an assumption in choosing a c-function. "And where the principle needs to be assumed seems to me less important than that it has to be assumed" (Lenz, 1956, p. 235).

Carnap gave up the attempt to find a confirmation function that will compel universal acceptance. "At the present time, I do not assert that there is only one rational Cr_0-function," Shimony has promised to look for an analytic principle of indifference which will provide the basis for an inductive logic (Shimony, 1955, p. 28). Jeffreys, who also adopts a logical conception of probability, does not even regard the problem as serious; in the case of conflict among our intuitions, he says, we can always refer the problem of deciding on the *a priori* probabilities of laws to an international body of scientists (Jeffreys, 1931, p. 39).

Carnap's approach to inductive logic has generated a literature concerning logical measures. Hintikka (1965a and c, 1966a, 1968) has been prominent in this field, and a sizeable number of other writers have contributed (Hilpinen, 1966; Tuomela, 1966;

Pietarinen, 1970; Batens, 1971; Kuipers, 1973, 1978; Niiniluoto, 1973, 1977b). Two volumes (Carnap and Jeffrey, eds., 1971; Jeffrey, ed., 1980) devoted to the exploration of this approach have appeared.

Carnap's original vision has been altered over the years in two ways. One group of authors (those mentioned above) have taken Carnapian measure functions to be a way of *representing* inductive logic, rather than as characterizing a unique *a priori* inductive logic. They do not regard these logics as a route to the justification of induction, but rather as a way of providing a formal reconstruction of what goes on in science. But it is hard to find anything in the actual conduct of scientific inference that these formal reconstructions justly reconstruct. The other variation on Carnap's original vision — one to which Carnap himself seemed to incline in his later years — was the substitution of subjective measures for logical measures. We shall deal with this variation later.

X

I shall return to the question of arbitrariness shortly. Of more immediate concern are the arguments that have been presented purporting to show that any logical theory of probability, interpreted as explicating confirmation, is inherently paradoxical, or even contradictory.

To begin with, there is the classical paradox of confirmation. Consider the statement "All crows are black." Anyone who believes in a logic of confirmation at all would regard the observation of a black crow as a (slight) confirmation of this statement. One of the most natural properties of confirmation is that if a sentence S confirms a sentence T, and T' is logicaly equivalent to T, then S confirms T' as well. "All crows are black" is logically equivalent to "All nonblack things are non-crows," so the observation of a white shoe (which confirms the latter just as the observation of a black crow confirms the former) will confirm "All crows are black." Finally, the original hypothesis can be expressed: "Everything is either not a crow or else it is black"; and it is not hard to show that this hypothesis is confirmed by any object that is black (whether or not it is a crow) and any object that is not a crow (whether or not it is black). Thus, as confirming instances for the law we have: a black crow, a white shoe, and a black cat.

Watkins recently offered this paradox as an argument against an inductivist view of the distinction between analytic and empirical statements (Watkins, 1957). In answer, Hempel (1958b) admitted that these consequences of confirmation theory are "intuitively paradoxical," but insisted that they are "systematically unobjectionable." He also pointed out that perfectly analogous consequences arise on the Popper-Watkins theory of falsification. A white shoe can perfectly well be regarded as the outcome of an attempt to falsify the theory that all crows are black: when I first looked I thought it was a crow, even though it was white, but then when I examined it, I saw that it was a shoe (Hempel, 1958b). The argument was carried on by I. Scheffler (1960, 1961), who attacked Watkins's arguments (Watkins, 1957, 1961) and finally pointed out that the disagreement may have stemmed from the fact that Hempel is not offering methodological prescriptions, while Popper is. Another exchange was instigated by D. C. Stove (1959), who tried to throw some light on the argument by distinguishing between the pragmatic notion of a *test* and the logical notion of *evidence*. The "attempt" to falsify the hypothesis that all crows are black by examining white shoes is obviously futile on anybody's theory, but "the *attempts* that might be made to falsify or instantially confirm a hypothesis are quite irrelevant to the weight of the evidence, if any, resulting from such attempts" (Stove, 1959). A discussion ensued between Stove and the indefatigable Watkins (Watkins, 1959a; Stove, 1960a; Watkins, 1960).

H. G. Alexander (1958b) also observed that the Watkins-Popper theory of falsification was subject to the same paradoxes as the theory of confirmation, but he pointed out that if we take account of our background knowledge we can save confirmation theory by looking at the matter quantitatively. Following J. Hosiasson-Lindenbaum (1940), Alexander pointed out that since we know that most things in the world aren't ravens, the observation of a white shoe is not going to confirm "all ravens are black" as much as the observation of a black raven. J. Agassi jumped into the fray to save Popper and Watkins against Alexander and observed (after a few polemical remarks about authoritarianism) that while a white shoe might be relevant on Popper's theory, as on Hempel's, it could be so only if it were observed as a result of a *test* of the generalization about ravens (Agassi, 1958). Watkins also contributed to the discussion of background knowledge (Watkins, 1959b), and I. J. Good clarified some of the quantitative aspects of the "paradox" (Good, 1960, 1961, 1966b).

The discussion was admirably summed up by J. L. Mackie (1962), who traced the whole argument (overlooking only the Scheffler-Watkins exchange) and came to much the same conclusions that are apparent above. Given a complete lack of background knowledge, Hempel is perfectly correct, and a white shoe, a black cat, and a black raven will all confirm the generalization. Given some knowledge about the relative numbers of black objects and ravens and nonblack objects and non-ravens, the bite may be taken out of the paradox by quantitative considerations, as Good, Hosiasson-Lindenbaum, and Alexander show. And if we allow unlimited background knowledge to give meaning to the notion of a *test*, the observations of black ravens and nonblack, non-ravens confirm the generalization to a worthwhile degree only if they are made in genuine *tests* of the generalization, and observations of black non-ravens never confirm it to a worthwhile degree, in view of the fact that such an observation can never result from a genuine test.

Three other paradoxes are cited as arguments against confirmation theory. The first I shall consider is the paradox of ideal evidence, discussed both by Popper (1959, p. 407) and by R. H. Vincent (1962b). Let *a* be the assertion that a particular toss of a given coin yields heads. It is clear that in the absence of any knowledge at all the *a priori* probability of *a* may plausibly be supposed to be 1/2. Now let us subject the coin to extensive tests, and suppose that (say on the basis of a million tosses) we become very sure that the relative frequency of heads is $1/2 \pm \varepsilon$. Let the body of evidence for this assertion be *e*. Then the probability of *a*, given *e*, is also 1/2. Therefore the examination of a million tosses of the coin is utterly irrelevant to *a*. This is clearly paradoxical. The problem here is that of finding a way of taking account of the "weight of evidence," but according to Popper this cannot be done in view of the fact that "The fundamental postulate of the subjective theory [confirmational theory] is the postulate that degrees of the rationality of beliefs in the light of evidence exhibit a linear order" (Popper, 1959, p. 408).

Although I myself regard this as a serious difficulty for most theories of degrees of confirmation, it is not as decisive as Popper makes it sound. These theories always contain, as an extra-formal requirement, a principle of total evidence, which demands that if we have information about the behavior (or structure) of the coin, we use it; this may be taken as a principle demanding that we maximize the weight of evidence. It could also be maintained that there is no behavioristic way of distinguishing between the two situations Popper describes: I shall, in either case, be willing to wager on the truth of *a* at even money. I think, however, that a difference does arise when we consider *A*, the conjunction a set of five hundred statements like *a*. Given the evidence *e*, I will be very sure that very nearly half of the statements in *A* will turn out to be true. Without the evidence *e*, I will not be nearly so sure that nearly half the statements in *A* will turn out to be true. This difference in sureness will be reflected in my betting behavior.

The next paradox arises, like the classical one, from a conflict between our intuitive assessments of probability and our lightning calculations of related quantities. Vincent uses it to attempt to show that no plausible theory of confirmation can accept the multiplication axiom (Vincent, 1961). Let q consist of a hypothesis (such as Newton's laws) together with boundary conditions sufficient to entail p, where p is the statement "A freely falling body near the earth will fall 144 feet in three seconds." Since $q \rightarrow p$, we have $(q \cdot p) \leftrightarrow q$, and (writing $c(x,y)$ for the degree of confirmation of x given y), $c(p \cdot q, r) = c(q,r)$. According to the multiplication axiom,

$$c(p \cdot q \cdot r) = c(p,r) \times c(q,p \cdot r)$$

or

$$c(p,r) = \frac{c(q,r)}{c(q,p \cdot r)}$$

Since p cannot contribute much to the confirmation of q, $c(q,p \cdot r) \approx c(q,r)$ and $c(p,r) \approx 1$.

A numerical example shows that the conclusion is not valid and that its paradoxical air results from thinking loosely about numbers. I borrow the example from Vincent, making it only slightly more specific. He says that if q is "All balls in urn U are red," and p is "The first three balls drawn are red," then by the above argument, p will be practically certain relative to our background knowledge. But assuming the equi-probability of structure descriptions and that we have five balls in the urn, we have

$$
\begin{aligned}
c(p,r) &= 3/10 \text{ (drawing with replacement)} \\
c(p,q \cdot r) &= 1 \qquad c(q,r) = 1/16 \\
c(q,p \cdot r) &= 5/9
\end{aligned}
$$

so that

$$c(p,r) = \frac{3}{10} = \frac{c(q,r)}{c(q,p \cdot r)} = \frac{1/6}{5/9}$$

To say that if the number of balls were larger, so that $c(q,p \cdot r)$ were closer to $c(q,r)$ we would find a paradox is false: $c(q,r)$ and $c(q,p \cdot r)$ will both decrease, but their ratio need not at all approach unity—indeed it may well *decrease*.

The last paradox is that regarded by Popper as a straight-forward contradiction in Carnap's system. The paradox is that "There are cases in which x is strongly supported by z and y is strongly undermined by z, while at the same time x is confirmed by z to a lesser degree than is y" (Popper, 1959, p. 390). For example, if x is the statement that a six will turn up on the next throw of a die, and y is the statement that some other number than six will turn up, and z is the statement that an even number turned up, then z increases the probability of x, decreases that of y, while at the same time con-firming x less than it confirms y:

$$
\begin{aligned}
c(x) &= 1/6; \; c(x,z) = 1/3 \\
c(y) &= 5/6; \; c(y,z) = 2/3
\end{aligned}
$$

while $\qquad c(x,z) < c(y,z).$

Popper claims that this is a self-contradictory state of affairs, for he claims that it is always self-contradictory to say that "x has the property P . . . and y has not the property P and y has the property P in a higher degree than x" (Popper, 1959, p. 391).

This is a valid objection to Carnap's way of talking, for Carnap himself claimed that the statement "a is warm and b is not warm and b is warmer than a" was self-contradictory, and the statement about confirmation sounds the same. In fact, however, it is not the same, and the similarity stems from a confusion in the *informal* characterization of the classificatory concept of confirmation. This confusion is cleared up in the preface to the new edition of his book (Carnap, 1962, p. xvi), where

Carnap distinguishes two distinct triples of concepts, neither of which allows Popper's paradox:

Firmness	Increase in firmness
1. h is firm on e	h is made firmer by i
2. h on e is firmer than h' on e'	h is made firmer by i than h' is by i'
3. the degree of firmness of h on e is u.	the increase in firmness of h by i is u.

Each of these concepts admits of a simple and obvious explication in terms of confirmation functions. The paradox observed by Popper arose only through Carnap's mistaken selection of (1) under Increase in firmness and (2) and (3) under Firmness as a triple of concepts analogous to "warm," "warmer," and "of such and such a temperature." It is not the case, of course, that x can be firm on z, and y not firm on z, and y firmer on z than is x on z. One of the most serious objections to the basic idea of confirmation theory thus turns out to be (as Bar-Hillel observed, 1955) a matter of terminological confusion.

XI

Confirmation theory does not provide an inductive logic, however, until the problem of establishing a choice among the infinite number of confirmation functions available has been solved. In principle (and winking at some classical curiosities, such as that the degree of confirmation of a universal law will generally by 0), all the problems of inductive logic will be solved by the use of Bayes's theorem — once the required *a priori* probabilities are available. (To choose a confirmation function is of course to accept a set of *a priori* probabilities.) I mentioned that Jeffreys, being of a practical turn of mind, suggested that the problem of *a priori* probabilities could be settled by an international board of scientists. This solution does seem extreme, and a bit authoritarian. But there is one school of thought that avoids the authoritarian overtones of this proposal by going even further in the same direction: it is the subjectivistic or personalistic school of statistical inference.

Although one of the founders of this approach to inductive logic was a philosopher, F. P. Ramsey (1931), it was given its greatest impetus by mathematical statisticians, such as L. J. Savage (1954) and B. de Finetti (1964). Perhaps this school more than any other has dominated decision theory and inductive logic in the past few years. These strides may have been made across thin philosophical ice, but they have nonetheless opened up a whole new approach to inductive logic. According to this theory, probability statements are regarded as being essentially subjective, in the sense that any statement may be legitimately assigned any degree of probability by any person. There is also, it must quickly be added, a logical element: the probability statements that express a given person's beliefs must be *coherent* — they must satisfy the axioms of the probability calculus. Thus, while any particular statement may be assigned any degree of probability, one assignment will impose restrictions on the freedom with which other assignments may be made. If I assign the value p to the probability of a statement S, I am in rationality bound to assign the value $1 - p$ to its negation, and I cannot assign a value greater than p to the conjunction of S with another statement.

The most important things to come out of the study of subjective or personalistic probability concern the invariance of posterior probabilities for wide variations in prior probabilities. The earliest of these results were established by de Finetti some time ago. He showed, for example, that though two people may start with widely different degrees of belief concerning the likelihood that an A kind of thing will be a B kind of thing, it will nevertheless generally be the case that after the observation of a large number of A things by both of them, the principles of coherence will force them to have nearly the same degrees of belief concerning the likelihood of a subsequent A being a B (de Finetti, 1964).

W. Edwards, H. Lindeman, and L. J. Savage published a long article (1963) on (subjectivistic) Bayesian inference in which they discuss in detail some of the circumstances under which posterior distributions of belief are almost entirely determined by the evidence, and are very nearly independent of the initial subjective opinions with which one starts. This important article does not require more mathematical background than most philosophers have who are concerned with inductive logic and confirmation theory. There is also an accessible discussion of the subjectivistic approach by Savage and holders of frequency or classical views of probability (Barnard and Cox, eds., 1962), and there is a book of readings that includes the contribution of Savage (just mentioned) and the paper by de Finetti as well as papers by other writers (Kyburg and Smokler, eds., 1964, 1980).

The fundamental theorem, on this view, is of course Bayes's theorem; there is no problem in finding prior probabilities to feed into it, because these prior probabilities merely reflect our initial opinions made coherent. But the theory has been criticized on the following grounds (Kyburg, 1961a, 1970a). There is perfect logical symmetry between premises and conclusions of the inductive argument with respect to the assignment of probabilities. There is thus no logical reason why I cannot decide in advance what conclusions I wish to believe (and to what degree), and then, in the light of the evidence, adjust my so-called initial probabilities so that, given the evidence that I am in fact given, I shall be "required" by conditions of coherence to attribute just that degree of probability to the conclusions that I began by stipulating that I *would* attribute to them. The only answer to this objection is that, in point of fact, people do not adjust their "initial" probabilities in the light of experience in order to arrive at the posterior probabilities they want to arrive at. Although this is possible *logically,* the subjectivist might ask, why should the inductive logician go that far out of his way looking for trouble? This attitude amounts to a denial that the relation between evidence and inductive conclusion is *logical* at all; it is reminiscent of the extreme sociological-anthropological views mentioned earlier: inductive inference proceeds in such and such a way because what we call inductive inferences are inferences that proceed that way. This denial *may* be cogent; it may be that it is impossible on strictly logical grounds to set any limitations to people's degrees of belief. But so far the only *evidence* that this is the case is the fact that as yet no general theory which would impose such logical restrictions has gained anything like universal acceptance.

Just as subjective probability itself represented a step away from what one might call logical authoritarianism and toward a realistic representation of the ways in which people actually make inferences and deicisions and change their beliefs in the face of evidence, so the subjective theory itself is now coming under criticism from philosophers and psychologists, who note that the theory does not provide an accurate reflection of these sociological and personal phenomena (Edwards, 1960, 1962; Hacking, 1967a, 1968; Kahneman and Tversky, 1974). At the same time, however, it is not at all trivial to decide what rationality, even viewed from a subjectivist perspective, amounts to. Some of the experiments that are alleged to reveal the irrationality of ordinary people instead reveal that the experimenters themselves have curious ideas of rationality (Cohen, 1981).

Meanwhile, since the first publication of this essay, the theory of subjective probability has flourished in philosophy. Philosophers of many epistemological and metaphysical persuasions have become convinced that this is the theory from which to start their philosophical investigations. Although the theory has not been without critics (Baillie, 1973; Kyburg, 1978d; Chihara and Kennedy, 1979) it has provided an irresistible playground for the philosophical imagination. In part this is due to the very flexibility that its critics have frowned upon. In part it is due to the fact that the subjectivist theory leads to technical problems that people feel they can eventually solve. And in part it is due to the fact that it has proved possible to embed subjective probability in a modal logic and in fashionable possible-world semantics (Stalnaker, 1970; Harper, 1975b, 1976b; Lewis, 1976; Skyrms, 1979).

This philosophical enthusiasm for subjective probability has its beginnings in Richard Jeffrey's book *The Logic of Decision* (1965b), which appeared in the mid-sixties. The subjective theory has now become almost standard in many discussions of decision theory and of social choice. No discussion of modal conditionals is now complete without a consideration of Stalnaker's thesis: that the probability of a conditional is a conditional subjective probability (Stalnaker, 1970).

While many people take the formalism of subjective probability for granted, yet there are a number who suppose that there is more to be said about probability than is provided for by that theory. A number of writers (Skyrms, 1979, 1973; Lewis, 1980) seek to incorporate some form of principle of direct inference into a system of subjective probability. It is not clear that this attempt has met with success, nor even that it *can* meet with success.

XII

A fairly recent development in inductive logic has been the introduction of *values* into the evaluation of the evidence bearing on a hypothesis. This approach has been stimulated by developments in statistical decision theory and game theory. These disciplines have studied the characteristics of policies for the "acceptance" or "rejection" of hypotheses. For example, let us consider the choice between two hypotheses: H_1, which asserts that the proportion of As that are Bs is p_1, and H_2, which asserts that the proportion is p_2. Let us draw a sample of six As to serve as evidence. (Decision theory is generally concerned with small samples.) Taking only the statistical make-up of the sample as relevant (disregarding the order of Bs and non-Bs), there are seven possible ratios of Bs to As in the sample, ranging from 0/6 to 6/6. A *decision rule* tells us when to accept H_1 and when to accept H_2. One rule would tell us, for example, to accept H_1 if the proportion of Bs in the sample is 3/6, 5/6, or 6/6, and to accept H_2 otherwise. Obviously, some rules are more sensible than others. Since, it must be remembered, we are using "accept" in an uncritically Pickwickian sense here, we cannot evaluate rules without knowing something about the costs of various possible mistakes and the benefits of the various ways of being right. Suppose that we gain r_1 units if we correctly accept H_1, and r_2 units if we correctly accept H_2, and that the losses entailed by choosing H_1 when H_2 is true are l_2, and those resulting from the erroneous acceptance of H_2 are l_1.

If we have *a priori* probabilities for H_1 and H_2 — whether these are subjective, objective and logical, or objective and derived from some general acceptable theory — then we can compute the best rule to follow by means of the classical theory of mathematical expectation. Let s stand for the experimental evidence. Then the computation of $c(s, H_1)$ and of $c(s, H_2)$ offers no problems in principle, whether or not we have *a priori* probabilities for H_1 and H_2. Given these *a priori* probabilities, we can compute:

$$c(s) = c(s \cdot H_1) + c(s \cdot H_2) = c(H_1)c(s, H_1) + c(H_2)c(s, H_2)$$

and thus

$$c(H_1, s) = \frac{c(H_1)c(s, H_1)}{c(s)} \quad c(H_2, s) = \frac{c(H_2)c(s, H_2)}{c(s)}.$$

To maximize our expectations, we need merely compare

$$r_1 c(H_1, s) - l_2 c(H_2, s) \text{ and } r_2 c(H_2, s) - l_1 c(H_1, s).$$

This is the way subjectivists and confirmation theorists would handle the problem. Nothing is added by the decision-theorist's framework except the curious terminology of "accepting" and "rejecting" hypotheses where a terminology concerning actions would seem more natural.

But if we do *not* have the *a priori* probabilities $c(H_1)$ and $c(H_2)$, the situation is different. We can no longer compare mathematical expectations. We must look instead at a $2 \times n$ table, where n is the number of possible rules (here $n = 128$, the number of ways of dividing the seven possible samples in two groups).

	H_1	H_2
rule 1	a_{11}	a_{12}
rule 2	a_{21}	a_{22}
. . . .		
rule n	a_{n1}	a_{n2}

The entries in the table represent conditional mathematical expectations under the alternative hypotheses. Thus, $a_{11} = r_1 \times$ (the probability of correctly choosing H_1, under rule 1, when H_1 is true) $- l_1 \times$ (the probability of incorrectly choosing H_2 when H_1 is true). The classical minimax policy directs us to choose among the rules by first picking out the minimum entry in each row (the *value* of the rule under the least favorable hypothesis) and then choosing the rule (of the n rules) that maximizes this minimum value.

Braithwaite (1953, 1963), on whose lucid presentation I have modeled mine, has pointed out, following D. V. Lindley (1953), that if we regard the entries a_{ij} as containing a factor representing the *a priori* probability of the hypothesis j, then the non-minimax policy of choosing the rule k for which the sum $a_{k1} + a_{k2}$ is a maximum will correspond precisely to the Bayesian solution of the decision problem. We may thus use the same matrix whether we are Bayesians or game theorists, and confine our discussions to the choice of a general overall policy for choosing among rules.

As I have pointed out before (Kyburg, 1963a), this does not achieve a reconciliation between the two approaches, but it does focus our attention on the fact that *if* we do regard the numbers a_{ij} as containing factors representing the *a priori* probabilities of the hypotheses, *then* there is no doubt about the fact that *we* should use a Bayesian (least sum) policy. On the other hand, a perfectly coherent and intelligible inductive logic can be based on the assumption that there is no such thing as the *a priori* probability of a hypothesis.

It should also be mentioned that there is considerable ambiguity involved in the notion of the *acceptance* of a scientific hypothesis. Although it is possible to maintain, as Churchman does (1956), that to accept a hypothesis H and to perform the corresponding action mean exactly the same thing, most philosphers I think would argue against this strong identification of belief and action; there is no self-contradiction in saying that I shall act on hypothesis H, even though I *believe* that it is false, provided that there is a chance that it is true, and provided the possible gains outweigh the probable losses. On the other hand, it is clear that there is some connection, in most cases, between accepting a hypothesis and acting as if it were true.

The richest and most successful attempt to construct a general theory of scientific inference along these lines is that of Isaac Levi (1980c). His earlier book, *Gambling with Truth* (Levi, 1967a) presented an outline of a general theory of scientific inference based on decision theory, but it was incomplete in a number of respects. The new work (1980c) employs a more realistic treatment of probability, and deals not only with truth, but with a number of other values people are inclined (or forced) to gamble on.

XIII

A number of problems have come to the fore in the past few decades of work in inductive logic. Although the assessment of these problems as important reflects a personal bias, I think it is safe to say that those to whom any problems in inductive logic and scientific method are important will find that the following problems — or some of them — are worthy of serious study.

Central to most theories of inductive logic is the notion of probability. Is it possible to provide a logical reconstruction of probability statements that will gain universal acceptance and restrict the freedom of probability assessments allowed by subjectivistic theories? Does the relatively new propensity theory of probability provide any sort of bridge? (See Popper, 1957b; Mellor, 1971; Giere, 1973b; Gillies, 1973; and Fetzer, 1974b.) Or is it possible (which seems very unlikely) to show that no such reconstruction can be provided, or perhaps even that probability, as it is used by philosophers, is a modal term that does not even obey the rules of the probability calculus? Or, finally, should we regard even the term "probability" as irrelevant to issues in the problem of inductive confirmation and speak instead of "degree of factual support," "degree of corroboration," and so on?

There is a relation, of course, between our point of view regarding probability and our point of view regarding statistical inference and statistical decisions. If there exist logical, *a priori,* probabilities, then the only sensible policy is Bayesian. But if these probabilities don't exist, the question as to whether we should introduce subjective probabilities into our statistical reasoning and follow Bayesian procedures, or instead refrain from introducing them and follow minimax procedures, may turn out to be a deep philosophical question. A number of recent approaches to inductive probability have involved upper and lower probabilities, or intervals (Kyburg, 1961a, 1974a; Smith, 1961; Good, 1962; Dempster, 1967a; Fine, 1973; Levi, 1974; Shafer, 1976). But it turns out that the statistical decision theory is profoundly altered by the use of interval probabilities, regardless of how they are construed (Runnalls, 1978). Isaac Levi's recent work (1980c) provides a framework in which both Bayesian procedures and minimax procedures are represented. My system (Kyburg, 1974a) also attempts to provide a place for each.

Nearly all the more or less formal theories of scientific inference I have discussed above have, at one point or another, run into the grue-bleen problem. This problem has many ramifications that haven't yet been explored, and no solution to even the simple cases has gained anything like universal acceptance. Salmon's solution (1971) applies only to ostensive predicates, and even then depends on the fact that "looks alike" has a conventional meaning. (I find it easy to imagine creatures to whom all grue things look alike, and who would be horribly surprised if in the year 2000 all grue things suddenly turned bleen.) But the problem is perhaps not most happily discussed in the form of simple predicates. The issue does not concern the specific predicates *grue* and *bleen,* but the characterization of the regularities we project in the process of accepting scientific theories. Another way to put the problem is to ask how the linguistic changes that so often accompany scientific changes can be judged or justified.

There is the continuing problem of elucidating the structure of inductive arguments as they are actually found to be used in scientific inquiries. This can often be done by formalizing the arguments within an ordinary logical symbolism. Although some work has been done along these lines in connection with the big theories of our scientific history (Newtonian Mechanics, Special Relativity, the Copernican theory, Quantum Mechanics), there is still a lot to be learned. Often the reconstructions are not really formal, and the background knowledge on which so much depends is left implicit, instead of being at least partially spelled out explicitly. One particular type of argument that begs for careful analysis and formalization to exhibit its logical structure is statistical inference. Only a handful of writers have focused their attention on statistical inference in the abstract, and almost none has considered the problem of attempting to elucidate particular historically important statistical arguments.

The justification of induction no longer seems to be the problem it used to be, because the justification, if any, is now regarded as subsidiary to and dependent on the logic of induction, rather than vice versa. In the same way, the search for postulates that, if true, could serve to establish the cogency of scientific reasoning (if only we had grounds for believing them) no longer seems terribly relevant.

I find myself unimpressed by the ordinary language analysis of inductive arguments, but for those who enjoy this sort of activity the world is full of arguments that have yet to receive this philosophical treatment. I only hope that such analysis removes or takes account of the ambiguities of ordinary language, rather than (as we have observed *can* happen) taking advantage of them.

Another problem that has not received the attention it deserves is the vexing problem of acceptance — the question of whether or not inductive conclusions (or anything else) are ever accepted. What is at issue here is not merely the question of whether we should speak of accepting hypotheses, for hypotheses are evaluated relative to data that is itself subject to error and no more than probable. The Bayesian view of induction typically supposes that there is a set of propositions that are taken as *evidence* by the agent. But Bayesianism neither allows hypotheses to become accepted (to be given probability 1) nor allows evidence, once accepted, to be reconsidered and rejected.

The more carefully one attends to the arguments between proponents of the hypothetico-deductive method and inductivists (falsification theorists and confirmation theorists), the more important does this problem appear. Popper regards Carnap as going beyond the pale of true Humean skepticism in saying that hypotheses might become probable; Popper will accept a hypothesis (tentatively, of course) but will never make the assertion that it is probable. But Carnap looks askance at Popper for nearly the same reason: it would on his view be altogether unwarranted, and flying in the face of sound Humean skeptical arguments, to accept a hypothesis, tentatively or any other way. All we can hope for is to be able to assign some degree of probability to the hypothesis.

Inductive logic meets epistemology here, and one of the most exciting problems for the future is to explore their relations. Such casually used terms as "incorrigible," "infallible," "evident," "tentative," "acceptable," and the like need to be characterized more crisply, both with regard to induction and with regard to epistemology. Questions such as those raised by the lottery paradox and by deductive argument as well as inductive argument, need to be considered in a broad epistemological context.

Finally, there is the very general question — relevant to deductive logic as well as to inductive logic — of the relation between the normative and descriptive elements of logic. Obviously, a normative inductive logic cannot simply be a counsel of perfection, appropriate only to angels. Equally obviously, if the object of philosophy is to improve, and not merely to record, human understanding, inductive logic should not amount to an historical, sociological, or psychological record. What we seek is a normative theory that we can aspire to approach in our own epistemic behavioral, though it need not present a goal we can altogether satisfy. We want an ideal that we can approach and that will serve as a standard for resolving, or helping to resolve, actual disputes about scientific evidence and inference.

There has been real progress in inductive logic in recent decades — more real progress, perhaps, than one might expect to find in a branch of philosophy. But of course there has been more activity than progress, fads and fashions come and go, and much time is still spent on artificial and parochial problems (the paradoxes of confirmation, for example, or Goodman's problem in its grue and bleen form). And we have more complex and thorny problems facing us than were conceived of by the writers of even twenty-five years ago. I hope that the foregoing review of events of the past few decades will make it easier for those who wish to work on these new problems to find their bearings in a foggy field.

Bibliography: Unedited Works

Achinstein, Peter. 1960. "From Success to Truth." *Analysis* 21: 6–9.
———. 1961. "The Circularity of Self-Supporting Inductive Argument." *Analysis* 22: 138–41.

_____ . 1963. "Variety and Analogy in Confirmation Theory." *Philosophy of Science* 30: 207–21.

_____ . 1964. "Models, Analogies, and Theories." *Philosophy of Science* 31: 328–50.

_____ . 1965. "The Problem of Theoretical Terms." *American Philosophical Quarterly* 2: 193–203.

_____ . 1966a. "Rudolf Carnap I." *Review of Metaphysics* 19: 517–49.

_____ . 1966b. "Rudolf Carnap II." *Review of Metaphysics* 19: 758–79.

_____ . 1968. *Concepts of Science*. Baltimore: The Johns Hopkins University Press.

_____ . 1970. "Inference to Scientific Laws." In R. H. Stuewer, ed., *Minnesota Studies in the Philosophy of Science, V.* Pp. 87–103.

_____ . 1980. "Discovery and Rule-Books." In T. Nickles, ed., *Scientific Discovery, Logic, and Rationality.* Pp. 117–32.

Ackerman, Robert. 1962. "Some Remarks on Kyburg's Modest Proposal." *Philosophical Review* 71: 236–40.

_____ . 1963. "Inductive Simplicity in Special Cases." *Synthese* 15: 436–44.

_____ . 1966a. *Nondeductive Inference*. London: Routledge & Keegan Paul.

_____ . 1966b. "Discussion: Projecting Unprojectibles." *Philosophy of Science* 33: 70–75.

_____ . 1967. "Conflict and Decision." *Philosophy of Science* 34: 188–93.

_____ . 1969. "Some Problems of Inductive Logic." In Davis, Hockney, and Wilson, eds., *Philosophical Logic.* Pp. 135–51.

Adams, Ernest. 1976. "Prior Probabilities and Counterfactual Conditionals." In Harper and Hooker, eds., *Foundations of Probability Theory, Statistical Inference, and Statistical Theories of Science*, vol. I. Pp. 1–21.

Adler, Jonathan E. 1976. "Evaluating Global and Local Theories of Induction." In Suppe and Asquith, eds., *PSA 1976*, vol. I. Pp. 212–23.

_____ . 1980. "Criteria for Good Inductive Logic." In Cohen and Hesse, eds., *Applications of Inductive Logic.* Pp. 379–405.

Agassi, Joseph. 1958. "Corroboration Versus Induction." *British Journal for the Philosophy of Science* 9: 311–17.

_____ . 1963. "Empiricism and Inductivism." *Philosophical Studies* 14: 85–86.

_____ . 1964. "Analogies and Generalizations." *Philosophy of Science* 31: 351–56.

_____ . 1966. "The Mystery of the Ravens." *Philosophy of Science* 33: 395–402.

_____ . 1973. "The Logic of Scientific Inquiry." *Synthese* 26: 498–514.

Ajdukiewicz, K. 1977. "The Problem of the Rationality of Fallible Methods of Inference." In Przelecki and Wojcicki, eds., *Twenty-Five Years of Logical Methodology in Poland.* Pp. 13–30.

Alexander, H. Gavin. 1958a. "General Statements as Rules of Inference." In Feigl, Scriven, and Maxwell, eds., *Minnesota Studies in the Philosophy of Science II.* Pp. 309–29.

_____ . 1958b. "The Paradoxes of Confirmation." *British Journal for the Philosophy of Science* 9: 227–33.

_____ . 1959. "The Paradoxes of Confirmation—A Reply to Dr. Agassi." *British Journal for the Philosophy of Science* 10: 229–34.

_____ . 1960. "Convention, Falsification, and Induction." *Proceedings of the Aristotelian Society,* Suppl. Vol. 34: 131–44.

Alexander, Peter. 1964. "Speculations and Theories." In Gregg and Harris, eds., *Form and Strategy in Science.* Pp. 30–46.

Allen, Edward H. 1976. "Uses of Signed Probability Theory." *Philosophy of Science* 43: 53–70.

Anscombe, F. J. 1961. "Bayesian Statistics." *American Statistician* 15: 21–24.

Anscombe, F. J., and Aumann, R. J. 1963. "A Definition of Subjective Probability." *Annals of Mathematical Statistics* 34: 199–205.

Arrow, Kenneth J. 1966. "Exposition of the Theory of Choice Under Uncertainty." *Synthese* 16: 253–69.

Axinn, Sidney. 1966. "Fallacy of the Single Risk." *Philosophy of Science* 33: 154–62,

Baillie, Patricia. 1969. "That Confirmation May Yet Be a Probability." *British Journal for the Philosophy of Science* 20: 41–51.

_____ . 1970. "Falsifiability and Probability." *Australasian Journal of Philosophy* 48: 288–89.

_____ . 1971. "Confirmation and Probability: A Reply to Settle." *British Journal for the Philosophy of Science* 22: 285–86.

_____ . 1973. "Confirmation and the Dutch Book Argument." *British Journal for the Philosophy of Science* 24: 393–97.

Bar-Hillel, Yehoshua. 1951. "A Note on State Descriptions." *Philosoophical Studies* 2: 72–75.

_____ . 1955. "Comments on 'Degree of Confirmation' by Professor K. R. Popper." *British Journal for the Philosophy of Science* 6: 155-57.

_____ . 1956. "Further Comments on Probability and Confirmation." *British Journal for the Philosophy of Science* 7: 245-48.

_____ . 1964. "On An Alleged Contradiction in Carnap's Theory of Inductive Logic." *Mind* 73: 265-67.

_____ . 1968. "On Alleged Rules of Detachment in Inductive Logic." In I. Lakatos, ed., *The Problem of Inductive Logic*. Pp. 120-28.

Barker, Stephen F. 1957. *Induction and Hypothesis*. Ithaca: Cornell University Press.

_____ . 1961a. "Comments on Salmon's 'Vindication of Induction.'" In Feigl and Maxwell, eds., *Current Issues in the Philosophy of Science*. Pp. 257-60.

_____ . 1961b. "Rejoinder to Salmon." In Feigl and Maxwell, eds., *Current Issues in the Philosophy of Science*. Pp. 276-78.

_____ . 1961c. "The Roleof Simplicity in Explanation." In Feigl and Maxwell, eds., *Current Issues in the Philosophy of Science*. Pp. 265-73.

_____ . 1961d. "On Simplicity in Empirical Hypotheses." *Philosophy of Science* 28: 162-71.

Barker, Stephen F., and Achinstein, Peter. 1960. "On the New Riddle of Induction." *Philosophical Review* 69: 511-12.

Barnard, George A. 1962. "Comments on Savage." In Barnard and Cox, eds., *The Foundations of Statistical Inference*. Pp. 39-49.

_____ . 1964. "Logical Aspects of the Fiducial Argument." *Bulletin of the International Statistical Institute,* Ottawa. Pp. 870-83.

_____ . 1972a. "The Logic of Statistical Inference." *British Journal for the Philosophy of Science* 23: 123-32.

_____ . 1972b. "Two Points in the Theory of Statistical Inference." *British Journal for the Philosophy of Science* 23: 329-31.

Bartlett, M. S. 1962. "Comments on Savage." In Barnard and Cox, eds., *Foundations of Statistical Inference*. Pp. 36-39.

Bartley, W. W., III. 1968. "Goodman's Paradox: A Simple-minded Solution." *Philosophical Studies* 19: 85-88.

Basu, D. 1971. "An Essay on the Logical Foundations of Survey Sampling." In Godambe and Sprott, eds., *Foundations of Statistical Inference*. Pp. 203-34.

Batens, Diderick. 1971. "Some Objections to Keith Lehrer's Rule I.R." *British Journal of the Philosophy of Science* 22: 357-62.

_____ . 1975. *Studies in the Logic of Induction and in the Logic of Explanation*. Brussels: De Tempel.

Baumer, William H. 1963. "Evidence and Ideal Evidence." *Philosophy and Phenomenological Research* 24: 567-72.

_____ . 1964. "Confirmation Without Paradoxes." *British Journal for the Philosophy of Science* 15: 177-95.

_____ . 1965. "Invalidly Invalidating a Paradox." *Philosophical Quarterly* 15: 350-52.

_____ . 1967. "The One *Systematically Ambiguous* Concept of Probability." *Philosophy and Phenomenological Research* 28: 264-68.

_____ . 1969. "In Defense of a Principle Theorem." *Synthese* 20: 121-42.

Binkley, Robert W. 1973. "Change of Belief or Change of Meaning." In Pearce and Maynard, eds., *Conceptual Change*. Pp. 55-76.

Birnbaum, Allan. 1961. "On the Foundations of Statistical Inference: Binary Experiments." *Annals of Mathematical Statistics* 32: 414-35.

_____ . 1962a. "Another View on the Foundations of Statistics." *American Statistician* 16: 17-21.

_____ . 1962b. "On the Foundations of Statistical Inference." *Journal of the American Statistical Association* 57: 269-306.

_____ . 1969. "Concepts of Statistical Evidence." In Morgenbesser, Suppes, and White, eds., *Philosophy, Science, and Method*. Pp. 112-43.

_____ . 1977. "The Neyman-Pearson Theory as Decision Theory and as Inference Theory, with a Criticism of the Lindley-Savage Argument for Bayesian Theory." *Synthese* 36: 19-49.

Black, Max. 1949. "The Justification of Induction." In M. Black, ed., *Language and Philosophy*. Pp. 59-88.

_____ . 1954. "Inductive Support of Inductive Rules." In M. Black, ed., *Problems of Analysis*. Pp. 191-208.

_____ . 1959. "Can Induction be Vindicated?" *Philosophical Studies* 10: 5-16.

_____. 1962. "Self-Support and Circularity: A Reply to Mr. Achinstein." *Analysis* 23: 43–44.

_____. 1966a. "Notes on the 'Paradoxes of Confirmation.'" In Hintikka and Suppes, eds., *Aspects of Inductive Logic*. Pp. 175–97.

_____. 1966b. "The *Raison D'Etre* of Inductive Argument." *British Journal for the Philosophy of Science* 17: 177–204.

_____. 1969. "Some Half-Baked Thoughts about Induction." In Morgenbesser, Suppes, and White, eds., *Philosophy, Science, and Method*. Pp. 144–51.

_____. 1970. "Induction and Experience." In Foster and Swanson, eds., *Experience and Theory*. Pp. 135–60.

Blair, David G. 1975. "On Purely Probabilistic Theories of Scientific Inference." *Philosophy of Science* 42, 1: 242–49.

Bloxham, M. 1976. "A Note on Publication and the Value of Significance Tests." *Theory and Decision* 7: 135–39.

Boden, Margaret. 1980. "Real-World Reasoning." In Cohen and Hesse, eds., *Applications of Inductive Logic*. Pp. 359–75.

Bogdan, Radu. 1976. "Hume and the Problem of Local Induction." In R. Bogdan, ed., *Local Induction*. Pp. 217–34.

_____. 1980. "Two Turns in Induction." In Cohen and Hesse, eds., *Applications of Inductive Logic*. Pp. 406–15.

Bolker, Ethan. 1967. "A Simultaneous Axiomatization of Utility and Subjective Probability." *Philosophy of Science* 34: 333–40.

Borch, Karl. 1975. "Probabilities of Probabilities: A Comment on Jacob Marschak." *Theory and Decision* 6: 155–59.

Boudot, Maurice. 1972. *Logique Inductive et Probabilité*. Paris: Librarie Armand Colin.

Bradie, Michael P. 1977. "The Development of Russell's Structural Postulates." *Philosophy of Science* 44: 441–63.

Braithwaite, Richard B. 1953. *Scientific Explanation*. Cambridge: Cambridge University Press.

_____. 1963. "The Role of Values in Scientific Inference." In Kyburg and Nagel, eds., *Induction: Some Current Issues*. Pp. 180–93.

Brodbeck, May. 1952. "An Analytic Principle of Induction?" *Journal of Philosophy* 49: 747–50.

Brody, B. A. 1968. "Confirmation and Explanation." *Journal of Philosophy* 65: 282–99.

Brown, G. Spencer. 1957. *Probability and Scientific Inference*. New York: Longmans Green & Co.

Brown, Peter M. 1976. "Discussion: Conditionalization and Expected Utility." *Philosophy of Science* 43: 414–19.

Bub, Jeffrey, and Radner, Michael. 1968. "Miller's Paradox of Information." *British Journal for the Philosophy of Science* 19: 63–67.

Buchdahl, G. 1960. "Convention, Falsification, and Induction." *Proceedings of the Aristotelian Society* Suppl. Vol. 34: 113–30.

Buehler, R. J. 1959. "Some Validity Criteria for Statistical Inference." *Annals of Mathematical Statistics* 30: 845–63.

Buehler, R. J., and Fedderson, A. P. 1963. "Note on a Conditional Property of Student's *t*." *Annals of Mathematical Statistics* 34: 1098–1100.

Bunge, Mario. 1962. "The Complexity of Simplicity." *Journal of Philosophy* 59: 113–35.

Burks, Arthur W. 1953. "The Presupposition Theory of Induction." *Philosophy of Science* 20: 177–97.

_____. 1954. "On the Presuppositions of Induction." *Review of Metaphysics* 8: 574–611.

_____. 1963. "On the Significance of Carnap's System of Inductive Logic for the Philosophy of Induction." In P. A. Schilpp, ed., *The Philosophy of Rudolf Carnap*. Pp. 739–60.

_____. 1977. *Chance, Cause, Reason*. Chicago: University of Chicago Press.

_____. 1980. "Enumerative Induction versus Eliminative Induction." In Cohen and Hesse, eds., *Applications of Inductive Logic*. Pp. 172–89.

Buxton, Richard. 1978. "The Interpretation and Justification of the Subjective Bayesian Approach to Statistical Inference." *British Journal for the Philosophy of Science* 29: 25–38.

Campbell, Keith. 1962. "One Form of Scepticism about Induction." *Analysis* 23: 80–83.

Canfield, J. 1962. "On the Paradox of Confirmation." *Metrika* 5: 105–18.

Cannavo, Salvator. 1974. *Nomic Inference: An Introduction to the Logic of Scientific Inquiry*. The Hague: Nijhoff.

Cardwell, Charles E. 1971. "Gambling and Content." *Journal of Philosophy* 68: 860–64.

Carlson, Roger. 1976. "Discussion: The Logic of Tests of Significance." *Philosophy of Science* 43: 116–28.

Carnap, Rudolf. 1950. *The Logical Foundations of Probability*. Chicago: University of Chicago Press.

_____. 1952. *The Continuum of Inductive Methods*. Chicago: University of Chicago Press.

_____. 1962. *The Logical Foundations of Probability*. 2nd ed., Chicago: University of Chicago Press.

_____. 1963a. "Discussion: Variety, Analogy, and Periodicity Inductive Logic." *Philosophy of Science* 30: 220–27.

_____. 1963b. "Remarks on Probability." *Philosophical Studies* 14: 65–75. Reprint of preface of Carnap, 1962.

_____. 1963c. "Replies and Systematic Exposition." In P. A. Schilpp, ed., *The Philosophy of Rudolf Carnap*. Pp. 966–98.

_____. 1963d. "The Aim of Inductive Logic." In Nagel, Suppes, and Tarski, eds., *Logic, Methodology, and Philosophy of Science*. Pp. 303–18. Reprinted in S. A. Luckenbach, *Probabilities, Problems, and Paradoxes*.

_____. 1966. "Probability and Content Measure." In Feyerabend and Maxwell, eds., *Mind, Matter, and Method*. Pp. 248–60.

_____. 1968. "Inductive Logic and Inductive Intuition." In I. Lakatos, ed., *The Problem of Inductive Logic*. Pp. 258–67.

_____. 1971a. "A Basic System of Inductive Logic, Part I." In Carnap and Jeffrey, eds., *Studies in Inductive Logic and Probability I*. Pp. 33–165.

_____. 1971b. "Inductive Logic and Rational Decisions." In Carnap and Jeffrey, eds., *Studies in Inductive Logic and Probability I*. Pp. 5–31.

_____. 1973. "Notes on Probability and Induction." *Synthese* 25: 269–90. Also in J. Hintikka, ed., *Rudolf Carnap*. 1975. Pp. 293–324.

_____. 1980. "A Basic System for Inductive Logic, Part II." In R. C. Jeffrey, ed., *Studies in Inductive Logic and Probability II*. Pp. 7–155.

Carnap, Rudolf, and Stegmuller, Wölfgang. 1959. *Induktive Logik und Wahrscheinlichkeit*. Vienna: Springer.

Casteñeda, Hector Neri. 1957. "Are Conditionals Principles of Inference?" *Analysis* 18: 77–82.

_____. 1960. "On a Proposed Revolution in Logic." *Philosophy of Science* 27: 279–92.

Chao-tien, Lin. 1978. "Discussion: Solutions to the Paradoxes of Confirmation, Goodman's Paradox, and Two New Theories of Confirmation." *Philosophy of Science* 45: 415–19.

Chatalian, George. 1952. "Probability: Inductive versus Deductive." *Philosophical Studies* 3: 49–56.

Cheng, Chung Ying. 1966. "Peirce's Probabilistic Theory of Inductive Validity." *Transactions of the Peirce Society* 2: 86–112.

_____. 1968. "Requirements for the Validity of Induction: An Examination of Charles Peirce's Theory." *Philosophy and Phenomenological Research* 28: 392–402.

Chihara, Charles, and Kennedy, Ralph. 1979. "The Dutch Book Argument: Its Logical Flaws, Its Subjective Sources." *Philosophical Studies* 36: 19–33.

Chuaqui, Rolando. 1977. "A Semantical Definition of Probability." In Arruda, da Costa, and Chauqui, eds., *Non-Classical Logics, Model Theory, and Computability*. Pp. 135–67.

Churchman, C. West. 1956. "Science and Decision Making." *Philosophy of Science* 23: 247–49.

_____. 1961. *Prediction and Optimal Decision*. Englewood Cliffs, N.J.: Prentice-Hall.

Clendinnen, F. John. 1965. "Katz on the Vindication of Induction." *Philosophy of Science* 32, 19: 370–76.

_____. 1966. "Induction and Objectivity." *Philosophy of Science* 33: 215–29.

_____. "Discussion: A Response to Jackson." *Philosophy of Science* 37: 444–48.

_____. 1979. "Inference, Practise and Theory." In W. C. Salmon, ed., *Hans Reichenbach: Logical Empiricist*. Pp. 85–128.

Coffa, Alberto. 1974. "Hempel's Ambiguity." *Synthese* 28: 141–64.

Cohen, B., and Madden, E. H. 1973. "Harré and Non-Logical Necessity." *British Journal for the Philosophy of Science* 29: 176–82.

Cohen, L. Jonathan. 1966a. "A Logic for Evidential Support I." *British Journal for the Philosophy of Science* 17: 21–43.

_____. 1966b. "A Logic for Evidential Support II." *British Journal for the Philosophy of Science* 17: 105–26.

_____. 1966c. "What Has Confirmation To Do With Probabilities?" *Mind* 75: 463–81.

_____. 1968. "Discussion: Confirmation Still Without Paradoxes." *British Journal for the*

Philosophy of Science 19: 57–71.

———. 1970a. "Some Applications of Inductive Logic to the Theory of Language?" *American Philosophical Quarterly* 7: 299–310.

———. 1970b. *The Implications of Induction.* London: Methuen & Co.

———. 1970c. "The Role of Inductive Reasoning in the Interpretation of Metaphor." *Synthese* 21: 469–87.

———. 1971. "The Inductive Logic of Progressive Problem-shifts." *Revue Internationale de Philosophie* 25: 62–67.

———. 1972. "A Reply to Swinburne." *Mind* 8: 249–50.

———. 1973. "A Note on Inductive Logic." *Journal of Philosophy,* 70: 27–40.

———. 1975. *Probability—the One and the Many.* Oxford: Oxford University Press.

———. 1976. "A Conspectus of the Neo-Classical Theory of Induction." In R. Bogdan, ed., *Local Induction.* Pp. 235–62.

———. 1977. *The Probable and the Provable.* Oxford: Oxford University Press.

———. 1980. "What Has Inductive Logic to Do with Causality?" In Cohen and Hesse, eds., *Applications of Inductive Logic.* Pp. 156–71.

———. 1981. "Can Human Irrationality be Experimentally Demonstrated?" *The Behavioral and Brain Sciences* 4.

Collins, Arthur W. 1966. "The Use of Statistics in Explanation." *British Journal for the Philosophy of Science* 17: 127–40.

Cooley, John C. 1959. "Toulmin's Revolution in Logic." *Journal of Philosophy* 56: 297–319.

Cooper, Neil. 1965. "The Concept of Probability." *British Journal for the Philosophy of Science* 16: 226–38.

Copeland, Arthur H., Sr. 1966. "Mathematical Proof and Experimental Proof." *Philosophy of Science* 33: 303–16.

Cornman, James W. 1972. "Craig's Theorem, Ramsey Sentences, and Scientific Instrumentalism." *Synthese* 25: 82–126.

———. 1977. "On Acceptability Without Certainty." *Journal of Philosophy* 74: 29–47.

Crow, C. 1963. "Some Remarks on Induction." *Synthese* 15: 379–87.

Cunningham, R. L. 1963. "Inducive Ascent the Same as Inductive Descent?" *Mind* 72: 598.

Curd, Martin. 1980. "The Logic of Discovery: An Analysis of Three Approaches." In T. Nickles, ed., *Scientific Discovery, Logic, and Rationality.* Pp. 201–19.

Czerwinski, T. 1958. "On the Relation of Statistical Inference to Traditional Induction and Deduction." *Studia Logica* 7: 245–64.

———. 1960. "Enumerative Induction and the Theory of Games." *Studia Logica* 10: 29–36. Reprinted 1977 in Przelecki and Wojcicki, eds., *Twenty-Five Years of Logical Methodology in Poland.* Pp. 81–91.

———. 1977. "The Problem of Probabilistic Justification of Enumerative Induction." In Przelecki and Wojcicki, eds., *Twenty-Five Years of Logical Methodology in Poland.* Pp. 65–80.

Dacey, Raymond. 1978. "A Theory of Conclusions." *Philosophy of Science* 45: 563–74.

Dale, A. I. 1976. "Probability and Coherence." *Philosophy of Science* 43: 254–65.

———. 1980. "Probability, Vague Statements, and Fuzzy Sets." *Philosophy of Science* 47: 38–55.

Danielsson, Sven. 1967. "Modal Logic Based on Probability Theory." *Theoria* 33: 189–97.

Darmstadter, Howard. 1975. "Better Theories." *Philosophy of Science* 42: 20–27.

Davidson, Donald. 1966. "Emeroses by Other Names." *Journal of Philosophy* 63: 778–80.

Davidson, Donald, and Suppes, Patrick. 1956. "A Finitistic Axiomatization of Subjective Probability and Utility." *Econometrica* 24: 264–75.

Davidson, Donald; Suppes, Patrick; and Siegel, Sidney. 1957. *Decision Making: An Experimental Approach.* Stanford, Calif.: Stanford University Press.

Dauer, F. W. 1980. "Epistemic Probabilities." *Mind* 89: 27–48.

Day, John P. 1961. *Inductive Probability.* New York: Humanities Press.

De Finetti, Bruno. 1964. "Foresight: Its Logical Laws, Its Subjective Sources." In Kyburg and Smokler, eds., *Studies in Subjective Probability.* 1st ed., pp. 93–158. 2nd ed., 1976, pp. 53–118.

———. 1969. "Initial Probabilities: A Prerequisite for any Valid Induction." *Synthese* 20: 2–15.

———. 1972. *Probability, Induction, and Statistics.* New York: John Wiley & Sons.

_____ . 1973. "Bayesianism: Its Unifying Role for Both the Foundations and the Applications of Statistics." *Proceedings of the 39th Session of the International Statistical Institute,* Vienna. Pp. 349-68.

_____ . 1976. "Probability: Beware of Falsifications." *Scientia* 111: 283-303. Reprinted in Kyburg and Smokler, eds., *Studies in Subjective Probability,* 2nd ed. Pp. 193-224.

_____ . 1980. "On the Condition of Partial Exchangeability." In R. Jeffrey, ed., *Studies in Inductive Logic and Probability II.* Pp. 193-205.

De Mare, Jacques. 1972. "A Comment on Gillies's Falsifying Rule for Probability Statements." *British Journal for the Philosophy of Science* 23: 335.

Dempster, Arthur P. 1967a. "Upper and Lower Probabilities Induced by a Multi-Valued Mapping." *Annals of Mathematical Statistics* 38: 325-39.

_____ . 1967b. "Upper and Lower Probability Inferences Based on a Sample from a Finite Univariate Population." *Biometrika* 54: 515-28.

_____ . 1968. "A Generalization of Bayesian Inference." *Journal of the Royal Statistical Society,* Series B, 30: 205-47.

Derksen, A. A. 1978. "The Alleged Lottery Paradox Resolved." *American Philosophical Quarterly* 15: 67-73.

Diaconis, Percy, and Freedman, David. 1980. "De Finetti's Generalizations of Exchangeability." In R. Jeffrey, ed., *Studies in Inductive Logic and Probability II.* Pp. 233-49.

Dorling, John. 1972. "Bayesianism and the Rationality of Scientific Inference." *British Journal for the Philosophy of Science* 23: 181-90.

_____ . 1973. "Demonstrative Induction: Its Significant Role in the History of Physics." *Philosophy of Science* 40: 360-72.

_____ . 1975. "The Structure of Scientific Inference." *British Journal for the Philosophy of Science* 26: 61-71.

_____ . 1976. "The Applicability of Bayesian Convergence-of-Opinion Theorems." *British Journal for the Philosophy of Science* 27: 160-61.

_____ . 1980. "A Personalist's Analysis of Statistical Hypotheses and Some Other Rejoinders to Giere's Anti-Positivist Metaphysics." In Cohen and Hesse, eds., *Applications of Inductive Logic.* Pp. 271-81.

Durbin, Paul R. 1968. *Logic and Scientific Inquiry.* Milwaukee, Wisc.: Bruce.

Dusek, Val. 1969. "Ampliative Inference, Abduction, and Philosophical Dialectics." *Telos* 4: 181-87.

Edwards, A.W.F. 1972. *Likelihood.* Cambridge: Cambridge University Press.

Edwards, Ward. 1960. "Measurement of Utility and Subjective Probability." In Gulliksen and Messick, eds., *Psychological Scaling.* Pp. 109-28.

_____ . 1962. "Subjective Probabilities Inferred from Decisions." *Psychological Review* 69: 109-35.

Edwards, W.; Lindeman, Harold; and Savage, L. J. 1963. "Bayesian Statistical Inference for Psychological Research." *Psychological Review* 70: 193-242.

Ellis, Brian. 1965. "A Vindication of Scientific Inductive Practises." *American Philosophical Quarterly* 2: 296-304.

_____ . 1973. "The Logic of Subjective Probability." *British Journal for the Philosophy of Science* 24: 125-52.

_____ . 1979. *Rational Belief Systems.* Totowa, N.J.: Rowman and Littlefield.

Emmerich, David, and Greeno, James. 1966. "Some Decision Factors in Scientific Investigation." *Philosophy of Science* 33: 262-70.

Enc, Berent. 1976. "Reference of Theoretical Terms." *Nous* 10: 261-82.

Ennis, Robert H. 1968. "Enumerative Induction and Best Explanation." *Journal of Philosophy* 65: 523-29.

Essler, Wilhelm K. 1975. "Hintikka versus Carnap." *Erkenntnis* 9: 229-33. Also in J. Hintikka, ed., *Rudolf Carnap: Logical Empiricist.* Pp. 365-70.

Evans, J. St.B.T.. 1972. "On the Problems of Interpreting Reasoning Data: Logical and Psychological Approaches." *Cognition* 1: 373-82.

Ezorsky, Gertrude. 1965. "On Verifying Universal Empirical Propositions." *Analysis* 26: 110-12.

Faber, Roger J. 1976. "Discussion: Re-Encountering a Counter-Intuitive Probability." *Philosophy of Science* 43: 283-85.

Fain, Haskell. 1967. "The Very Thought of Grue." *Philosophical Review* 76: 61-73.

Fann, K. T. 1970. *Peirce's Theory of Abduction.* The Hague: Nijhoff.

Feigl, Herbert. 1950. "De Principiis Non Disputandum . . .?" In M. Black, ed., *Philosophical Analysis*. Pp. 113-47. Also reprinted in 1972 in S. A. Luckenbach, *Probabilities, Problems, and Paradoxes*.

_____ . 1970. "The 'Orthodox' View of Theories: Remarks in Defense as Well as Critique." In Radner and Winokur, eds., *Minnesota Studies in the Philosophy of Science IV*. Pp. 3-16.

Fensted, J. E. 1967a. "Representations of Probabilities Defined on First Order Languages." In J. N. Crossley, ed., *Sets, Models and Recursion Theory*. Pp. 156-72.

_____ . 1967b. "Review: *Aspects of Inductive Logic*, edited by Hintikka and Suppes." *Synthese* 17: 449-60.

_____ . 1968. "The Structure of Logical Probabilities." *Synthese* 18: 1-23.

_____ . 1980. "The Structure of Probabilities Defined on First Order Languages." In R. Jeffrey, ed., *Studies in Inductive Logic and Probability II*. Pp. 251-62.

Fetzer, James H. 1970. "Dispositional Probabilities." In Buck and Cohen, eds., *Boston Studies in the Philosophy of Science*. Pp. 473-82.

_____ . 1974a. "A Single Case Propensity Theory of Explanations." *Synthese* 28: 171-98.

_____ . 1974b. "Statistical Probabilities: Single Case Propensities vs. Long Run Frequencies." In Leinfellner and Köhler, eds., *Developments in the Methodology of Social Science*. Pp. 387-97.

_____ . 1976. "Elements of Induction." In R. Bogdan, ed., *Local Induction*. Pp. 145-70.

_____ . 1977. "Reichenbach, Reference Classes, and Single Case 'Probabilities.'" *Synthese* 34: 185-217. Reprinted 1979 in W. C. Salmon, ed., *Hans Reichenbach: Logical Empiricist*. Pp. 187-219.

Feyerabend, Paul K. 1961. *Knowledge without Foundations*. Oberlin, Ohio: Oberlin College.

_____ . 1962. "Explanation, Reduction, and Empiricism." In Feigl and Maxwell, eds., *Minnesota Studies in the Philosophy of Science III*. Pp. 28-97.

_____ . 1963a. "Scientific Explanation, Prediction, and Theories." In B. Baumrin, ed., *Philosophy of Science*. Pp. 3-39.

_____ . 1963b. "How To Be a Good Empiricist." In B. Baumrin, ed., *Philosophy of Science*.

_____ . 1964. "A Note on the Problem of Induction." *Journal of Philosophy* 61: 349-53.

_____ . 1965. "Problems of Empiricism." In R. G. Colodny, ed., *Beyond the Edge of Certainty*. Pp. 145-260.

_____ . 1969. "A Note on Two 'Problems' of Induction." *British Journal for the Philosophy of Science* 19: 251-53.

_____ . 1970a. "Against Method: Outline of an Anarchistic Theory of Knowledge." In Radner and Winokur, eds., *Minnesota Studies in the Philosophy of Science IV*. Pp. 17-130.

_____ . 1970b. "Problems of Empiricism, Part II." In R. G. Colodny, ed., *The Nature and Function of Scientific Theories*. Pp. 275-353.

Field, Hartry. 1973. "Theory Change and Indeterminacy of Reference." *Journal of Philosophy* 70: 462-81.

_____ . 1978. "A Note on Jeffrey Conditionalization." *Philosophy of Science* 45: 361-67.

Finch, Henry A. 1957. "Validity Rules for Proportionally Quantified Syllogisms." *Philosophy of Science* 24: 1-18.

_____ . 1960. "Confirming Power of Observations Metricized for Decisions Among Hypotheses." *Philosophy of Science* 27: 293-307.

Fine, Authur I. 1967. "Consistency, Derivability, and Scientific Change." *Journal of Philosophy* 64: 231-40.

Fine, Terrence. 1971. "A Note on the Existence of Quantitative Probability." *Annals of Mathematical Statistics* 42: 1182-86.

_____ . 1973. *Theories of Probability*. New York: Academic Press.

_____ . 1977a. "An Argument for Comparative Probability." In Butts and Hintikka, eds., *Basic Problems in Methodology and Linguistics*. Pp. 105-19.

_____ . 1977b. "*A Mathematical Theory of Evidence*, by Glenn Shafer." *Bulletin of the American Mathematical Society* 83: 667-72.

_____ . 1978. "*The Emergence of Probability*, by Ian Hacking." *Philosophical Review* 87: 116-23.

Firth, Roderick. 1964. "Coherence, Certainty, and Epistemic Priority." *Journal of Philosophy* 61: 547-57.

Fishburn, P. C. 1967. "Preference-Based Definitions of Subjective Probability." *Annals of Mathematical Statistics* 38: 1605-19.

Fisher, Ronald A. 1956. *Statistical Methods and Scientific Inference*. New York: Haffner.

Fisk, Milton. 1970. "Are There Necessary Connections in Nature?" *Philosophy of Science* 37: 385–404.

Fogelin, Robert. 1967. "Inferential Constructions." *American Philosophical Quarterly* 4: 15–27.

Frank, Philipp G. 1954a. "The Variety of Reasons for the Acceptance of Scientific Theories." In P. G. Frank, ed., *The Validation of Scientific Theories.* Pp. 3–18.

Freudenthal, Hans. 1968. "Realistic Models in Probability." In I. Lakatos, ed., *The Problem of Inductive Logic.* Pp. 1–14.

_____. 1977. "Henry E. Kyburg, Jr.: *The Logical Foundations of Statistical Inference.*" *Synthese* 36: 479–92.

Frey, Gerhard. 1977. "Wissenshaftliche Begrundung Bei Carnap und Popper." *Conceptus* 11: 243–48.

Friedman, K., and Shimony, A. 1971. "Jaynes's Maximum Entropy Prescription and Probability Theory." *Journal of Statistical Physics* 3: 381.

Friedman, Michael. 1979. "Truth and Confirmation." *Journal of Philosophy* 76: 361–82.

Gaifman, H. 1964. "Concerning Measures on First Order Calculi." *Israel Journal of Mathematics* 2: 1–18.

_____. 1971. "Applications of de Finetti's Theorem to Inductive Logic." In Carnap and Jeffrey, eds., *Studies in Inductive Logic and Probability I.* Pp. 235–51.

Garber, Daniel. 1980. "Field and Jeffrey Conditionalization." *Philosophy of Science* 47: 142–45.

Gärdenfors, P. 1978. "Conditionals and Changes of Belief." In Niiniluoto and Tuomela, eds., *The Logic and Epistemology of Scientific Change.* Pp. 381–404.

Gibbard, Alan, and Harper, William. 1978. "Counterfactuals and Two Kinds of Expected Utility." In Hooker, Leach, and McClennen, eds., *Foundations and Applications of Decision Theory I.* Pp. 125–62.

Gibbons, P. C. 1962. "On the Severity of Tests." *Australasian Journal of Philosophy* 40: 79–82.

Gibson, L. 1969. "On 'Ravens and Relevance' and a Likelihood Solution of the Paradox of Confirmation." *British Journal for the Philosophy of Science* 20: 75–80.

Giere, Ronald N. 1969. "Bayesian Statistics and Biased Procedures." *Synthese* 20: 371–87.

_____. 1970. "An Orthodox Statistical Resolution of the Paradox of Confirmation." *Philosophy of Science* 37: 345–62.

_____. 1972. "The Significance Test Controversy." *British Journal for the Philosophy of Science* 23: 170–81.

_____. 1973a. "*The Matter of Chance,* by D. H. Mellor." *Ratio* 15: 149–55.

_____. 1973b. "Objective Single-Case Probabilities and the Foundations of Statistics." In P. Suppes et al., eds., *Logic, Methodology, and Philosophy of Science IV.* Pp. 467–84.

_____. 1975a. "The Epistemological Roots of Scientific Knowledge." In Maxwell and Anderson, eds., *Minnesota Studies in the Philosophy of Science VI.* Pp. 212–61.

_____. 1975b. "Popper and the Non-Bayesian Tradition: Comments on Richard Jeffrey." *Synthese* 30: 119–32.

_____. 1976a. "Empirical Probability, Objective Statistical Methods, and Scientific Inquiry." In Harper and Hooker, eds., *Foundations of Probability Theory, Statistical Inference, and Statistical Theories of Science II.* Pp. 63–93.

_____. 1976b. "A Laplacean Formal Semantics for Single-Case Propensities." *Journal of Philosophical Logic* 5: 321–54.

_____. 1977a. "Alan Birnbaum's Conception of Statistical Evidence." *Synthese* 36: 5–13.

_____. 1977b. "Testing Versus Information Models of Statistical Inference. "In R. G. Colodny, ed., *Logic, Laws, and Life.* Pp. 19–70.

_____. 1979a. *Understanding Scientific Reasoning.* New York: Holt, Rinehart, & Winston.

_____. 1979b. "Foundations of Probability and Statistical Inference." In Asquith and Kyburg, eds., *Current Research in Philosophy of Science.* Pp. 503–33.

_____. 1980. "Causal Systems and Statistical Hypotheses. "In Cohen and Hesse, eds., *Applications of Inductive Logic.* Pp. 251–70.

Gillies, D. A. 1972. "Reply to De Mare." *British Journal for the Philosophy of Science* 23: 335–36.

_____. 1973. *An Objective Theory of Probability.* London: Methuen and Co.

Glymour, Clark. 1975. "Relevant Evidence." *Journal of Philosophy* 72: 403–26.

_____. 1979. "Reichenbach's Entanglements." In W. C. Salmon, ed., *Hans Reichenbach: Logical Empiricist.* Pp. 221–37.

_____. 1980. *Theory and Evidence.* Princeton, N.J.: Princeton University Press.

Godambe, V. P., and Thompson, M. E. 1976. "Survey of Survey-Sampling Practice." In Harper and Hooker, eds., *Foundations of Probability Theory, Statistical Inference, and Statistical Theories of Science* II. Pp. 103–22.

Good, I. J. 1962. "Subjective Probability as a Measure of a Non-Measurable Set." In Nagel, Suppes, and Tarski, eds., *Logic, Methodology and Philosophy of Science.* Pp. 319–29.

_____. 1965. *The Estimation of Probabilities.* Cambridge, Mass.: MIT Press.

_____. 1966a. "On the Principle of Total Evidence." *British Journal for the Philosophy of Science* 17: 319–21.

_____. 1966b. "The White Shoe is a Red Herring." *British Journal for the Philosophy of Science* 17: 322.

_____. 1968. "Corroboration, Explanation, Evolving Probability, and a Sharpened Razor." *British Journal for the Philosophy of Science* 19: 123–43.

_____. 1969. "Discussion: Bruno De Finetti's Paper 'Initial Probabilities: A Prerequisite for any Valid Induction.'" *Synthese* 20: 17–24.

_____. 1970. "A Suggested Resolution of Miller's Paradox." *British Journal for the Philosophy of Science* 21: 288–89.

_____. 1971. "The Probabilistic Explication." In Godambe and Sprott, eds., *Foundations of Statistical Inference.* Pp. 108–41.

_____. 1974. "A Little Learning Can Be Dangerous." *British Journal for the Philosophy of Science* 25: 340–42.

_____. 1975a. "Explicativity, Corroboration, and the Relative Odds of Hypotheses." *Synthese* 30: 39–73.

_____. 1975b. "Replies to Comments on 'Explicativity, Corroboration, and the Relative Odds of Hypotheses.'" *Synthese* 30: 83–93.

_____. 1975c. "Comments on Ronald Giere's 'Popper and the Non-Bayesian Tradition.'" *Synthese* 30: 133.

_____. 1976. "The Bayesian Influence, or How to Sweep Subjectivism Under the Carpet." In Harper and Hooker, eds., *Foundations of Probability Theory, Statistical Inference, and Statistical Theories of Science* II. Pp. 125–74.

_____. 1977. "Rationality, Evidence, and Induction in Scientific Inference." In D. Michie, ed., *On Machine Intelligence.* Pp. 171–74.

Goodman, Nelson. 1952. "New Notes on Simplicity." *Journal of Symbolic Logic* 17: 189–91.

_____. 1955a. "Axiomatic Measurement of Simplicity." *Journal of Philosophy* 52: 709–22.

_____. 1955b. *Fact, Fiction, and Forecast.* Cambridge: Harvard University Press.

_____. 1958. "Recent Developments in the Theory of Simplicity." *Philosophy and Phenomenological Research* 19: 429–46.

_____. 1960. "Positionality and Pictures." *Philosophical Review* 69: 523–25.

_____. 1966a. "The New Riddle of Induction." *Journal of Philosophy* 63: 281.

_____. 1966b. "Comments on 'The New Riddle of Induction.'" *Journal of Philosophy* 63: 328–31.

_____. 1967. "Two Replies." *Journal of Philosophy* 64: 286–87.

Goosens, William K. 1975. "Duhem's Thesis, Observationality, and Justification." *Philosophy of Science* 42: 286–98.

_____. 1976. "A Critique of Epistemic Utilities." In R. Bogdan, ed., *Local Induction.* Pp. 93–114.

Gottinger, H. W. 1974. "Review of Concepts and Theories of Probability." *Scientia* 109: 83–110.

Grandy, Richard E. 1967. "Some Comments of Confirmation and Selective Confirmation." *Philosophical Studies* 18: 19–24.

Grant, John. 1978. "Confirmation of Empirical Theories by Observation Sets." *Philosophia* 8: 367–80.

Greeno, James G. 1970. "Evaluation of Statistical Hypotheses Using Information Transmitted." *Philosophy of Science* 32: 279–94.

Grofman, Bernard, and Hyman, Gerald. 1973. "Probability and Logic in Belief Systems." *Theory and Decision* 4: 175–99.

Gross, Edward. 1957. "Toward a Rationale for Science." *Journal of Philosophy* 54: 829–38.

Grunbaum, Adolf. 1979. *Falsifiability and Rationality.* Pittsburgh: Pittsburgh University Press.

Gruner, Rolf. 1968. "Historical Facts and the Testing of Hypotheses." *American Philosophical Quarterly* 5: 124–29.

Grunstra, Bernard. 1969. "The Plausibility of the Entrenchment Concept." *American Philosophical Quarterly Monograph Series* 3: 100–127. Reprinted 1972 in S. A. Luckenbach, *Probabilities, Problems, and Paradoxes.*

Gutting, Gary. 1977. "Metaphysics and Induction." *Process Studies* 1: 171–78.

Hacking, Ian. 1963. "Guessing by Frequency." *Proceedings of the Aristotelian Society* 64: 55–70.

———. 1964a. "*Statistical and Inductive Probabilities* by Leblanc." *Philosophical Quarterly* 14: 281.

———. 1964b. "On the Foundations of Statistics." *British Journal for the Philosophy of Science* 15: 1–26.

———. 1965a. *The Logic of Statistical Inference.* Cambridge: Cambridge University Press.

———. 1965b. Salmon's Vindication of Induction." *Journal of Philosophy* 62: 260–66.

———. 1965c. "Salmon's Vindication." *Philosophy of Science* 32: 269–71.

———. 1965d. "*Studies in Subjective Probability,* Kyburg and Smokler, eds." *British Journal for the Philosophy of Science* 16: 334–39.

———. 1967a. "Slightly More Realistic Personal Probability." *Philosophy of Science* 34: 311–25.

———. 1967b. "*Gambling With Truth,* by Isaac Levi." *Synthese* 17: 444–48.

———. 1968. "On Falling Short of Strict Coherence." *Philosophy of Science* 35: 284–86.

———. 1969. "Linguistically Invariant Inductive Logic." *Synthese* 20: 25–47.

———. 1971a. "Equipossibility Theories of Probability." *British Journal for the Philosophy of Science* 22: 339–55.

———. 1971b. "Jacques Bernoulli's Art of Conjecturing." *British Journal for the Philosophy of Science* 22: 209–29.

———. 1972. "Likelihood." *British Journal for the Philosophy of Science* 23: 132–37.

———. 1973. "Propensities, Statistics, and Inductive Logic." In Suppes et al., eds., *Logic, Methodology, and Philosophy of Science IV.* Pp. 485–500.

———. 1975. *The Emergence of Probability.* Cambridge: Cambridge University Press.

———. 1980. "The Theory of Probable Inference: Neyman, Peirce, and Braithwaite." In D. H. Mellor, ed., *Science, Belief, and Behavior.* Cambridge: Cambridge University Press. Pp. 141–60.

Hall, R. J. 1970. "Kuhn and the Copernican Revolution." *British Journal for the Philosophy of Science* 21: 196–97.

Hallden, Soren. 1966. "On Preferences, Probability, and Learning." *Synthese* 19: 307–20.

Hamburg, Jurgen. 1971. "The Principle of Insubstantial Relevance." In Carnap and Jeffrey, eds., *Studies in Inductive Logic and Probability I.* Pp. 225–33.

Hammerton, M. 1968. "Bayesian Statistics and Popper's Epistemology." *Mind* 77: 109–12.

Hanen, Marsha. 1966. "Goodman, Wallace, and the Equivalence Condition." *Journal of Philosophy* 58: 271–80.

———. 1971. "Confirmation and Adequacy Conditions." *Philosophy of Science* 38: 361–68.

Hanson, Norwood Russell. 1958. *Patterns of Discovery.* Cambridge: Cambridge University Press.

———. 1961. "Good Inductive Reasons." *Philosophical Quarterly* 11: 123–34.

———. 1965. "The Idea of a Logic of Discovery." *Dialectica* 4: 48–61.

———. 1967. "An Anatomy of Discovery." *Journal of Philosophy* 64: 321–52.

———. 1969. *Perception and Discovery.* San Francisco: Freeman, Cooper.

Hanson, William H. 1975. "Names, Random Samples, and Carnap." In Maxwell and Anderson, eds., *Minnesota Studies in the Philosophy of Science VI.* Pp. 367–87.

Harman, Gilbert. 1964. "How Belief is Based on Inference." *Journal of Philosophy* 61: 353–59.

———. 1965. "The Inference to the Best Explanation." *Philosophical Review* 74: 88–95.

———. 1967. "Detachment, Probability, and Maximum Likelihood." *Nous* 1: 401–11.

———. 1968. "Knowledge, Inference, and Explanation." *American Philosophical Quarterly* 5: 164–73.

———. 1970. "Induction: A Discussion of the Relevance of the Theory of Induction (with a Digression to the Effect That Neither Deductive Logic Nor the Probability Calculus Has Anything To Do With Inference)." In M. Swain, ed., *Induction, Acceptance, and Rational Belief.* Pp. 83–99.

———. 1980. "Reasoning and Explanatory Coherence." *American Philosophical Quarterly* 17: 151–57.

Harper, William L. 1975a. "Comments on I. J. Good's 'Explicativity, Corroboration and the Relative Odds of Hypotheses.'" *Synthese* 30: 75–78.

———. 1975b. "Rational Belief Change, Popper Functions, and Counterfactuals." *Synthese* 30: 221–62.

———. 1976a. "Ramsey Test Conditionals and Iterated Belief Change." In Harper and Hooker, eds., *Foundations of Probability Theory, Statistical Inference, and Statistical*

Theories of Science. Pp. 117–35.

———. 1976b. "Rational Belief Change, Popper Functions, and Counterfactuals." In Harper and Hooker, eds., *Foundations of Probability Theory, Statistical Inference, and Statistical Theories of Science.* Pp. 73–115.

———. 1977. "Rational Conceptual Change." In Suppe and Asquith, eds., *PSA 1976* II. Pp. 462–94.

Harper, William, and Kyburg, Henry E., Jr. 1968. "The Jones Case." *British Journal for the Philosophy of Science* 19: 247–51.

Harré, Ron. 1957. "Dissolving the 'Problem' of Induction." *Philosophy* 32: 58–64.

———. 1959. "Simplicity as a Criterion of Induction." *Philosophy* 34: 229–34.

———. 1964. "*The Problem of Induction and Its Solution, by J. J. Katz.*" *Mind:* 457–58.

———. 1970. *The Principles of Scientific Thinking.* Chicago: University of Chicago Press.

Harré, Ron, and Moran, G. J. 1973. "The Necessity of Nature." *Dialogue* 12: 318–21.

Harris, John H. 1974. "Popper's Definition of Verisimilitude." *British Journal for the Philosophy of Science* 25: 166–77.

Harrod, Roy. 1956. *Foundations of Inductive Logic.* New York: Harcourt Brace & Co.

Harsanyi, John C. 1960. "Popper's Improbability Criterion for the Choice of Scientific Hypotheses." *Philosophy* 35: 332–40.

Heidelberger, Herbert. 1963a. "Knowledge, Certainty, and Probability." *Inquiry* 6: 242–50.

———. 1963b. "Probability and Knowledge: A Reply to Miss Weyland." *Inquiry* 6: 417–18.

Hempel, Carl G. 1958a. "The Theoretician's Dilemma: A Study in the Logic of Theory Confirmation." In Feigl, Scriven, and Maxwell, eds., *Minnesota Studies in the Philosophy of Science II.* Pp. 37–98. Reprinted 1965 in C. G. Hempel, *Aspects of Scientific Explanation.*

———. 1958b. "Empirical Statements and Falsifiability." *Philosophy* 33: 342–48.

———. 1960. "Inductive Inconsistencies." *Synthese* 12: 439–69. Reprinted 1962 in Anonymous, ed., *Logic and Language.* Pp. 128–58; 1965 in C. G. Hempel, *Aspects of Scientific Explanation.*

———. 1965. *Aspects of Scientific Explanation.* New York: The Free Press.

———. 1966. "Recent Problems of Induction." In R. G. Colodny, ed., *Mind and Cosmos.* Pp. 112–34. Reprinted 1972 in S. A. Luckenbach, ed., *Probabilities, Problems, and Paradoxes.*

———. 1967. "The White Shoe: No Red Herring." *British Journal for the Philosophy of Science* 18: 239–40.

———. 1968a. "On a Claim by Skyrms Concerning Lawlikeness and Confirmation." *Philosophy of Science* 35: 274–78.

———. 1968b. "Maximal Specificity and Lawlikeness in Probabilistic Explanation." *Philosophy of Science* 35: 116–33.

Hesse, Mary. 1964. "Analogy and Confirmation Theory." *Philosophy of Science:* 319–27.

———. 1968. "Consilience of Inductions." In I. Lakatos, ed., *The Problem of Inductive Logic.* Pp. 232–57.

———. 1969a. "Confirmation of Laws." In Morgenbesser, Suppes, and White, eds., *Philosophy, Science, and Method.* Pp. 74–91.

———. 1969b. "Ramifications of 'Grue.'" *British Journal for the Philosophy of Science* 20: 13–25.

———. 1970a. "Is There an Independent Observation Language?" In R. G. Colodny, ed., *The Nature and Function of Scientific Laws.* Pp 35–77.

———. 1970b. "Theories and the Transitivity of Confirmation." *Philosophy of Science* 37: 50–63.

———. 1970c. "An Inductive Logic of Theories." In Radner and Winokur, eds., *Minnesota Studies in the Philosophy of Science IV.* Pp. 164–80.

———. 1971. "Probability as the Logic of Science." *Proceedings of the Aristotelian Society* 72: 257–72.

———. 1973. "Models of Theory Change." In Patrick Suppes, et al., eds., *Logic Methodology, and Philosophy of Science IV.* Pp. 379–92.

———. 1975. "Bayesian Methods and the Initial Probabilities of Theories." In Maxwell and Anderson, eds., *Minnesota Studies in the Philosophy of Science VI.* Pp. 50–105.

———. 1977. "Truth and the Growth of Knowledge." In Suppe and Asquith, eds., *PSA 1976* II. Pp. 261–80.

———. 1980. "What is the Best Way to Assess Evidential Support for Scientific Theories?" In Cohen and Hesse, eds., *Applications of Inductive Logic.* Pp. 202–17.

Hillman, Donald. 1963. "The Probability of Induction." *Philosophical Studies* 14: 51–56.

Hilpinen, Risto. 1966. "On Inductive Generalization in Monadic First-Order Logic with Identity." In Hintikka and Suppes, eds., *Aspects of Inductive Logic*. Pp. 133–54.

_____. 1968. *Rules of Acceptance and Inductive Logic*. *Acta Philosophica Fennica* 21: Amsterdam: North-Holland.

_____. 1970. "On the Information Provided by Observations." In Hintikka and Suppes, eds., *Information and Inference*. Pp. 97–122.

_____. 1971a. "*Problems of the Logic of Scientific Knowledge*, P. V. Tavanec (ed)." *Synthese* 23: 342–46.

_____. 1971b. "Knowledge and Justification." *Ajatus* 33: 7–39.

_____. 1971c. "Relational Hypotheses and Inductive Inference." *Synthese* 23: 266–86.

_____. 1973. "Carnap's New System of Inductive Logic." *Synthese* 25: 307–33. Reprinted 1975 in J. Hintikka, ed., *Rudolf Carnap: Logical Empiricist*. Pp. 333–59.

_____. 1974. "Approximate Truth and Lawlikeness." In Przelecki and Wojcicki, eds., *Formal Methods in the Methodology of Empirical Sciences*. Pp. 19–42.

Hilpinen, Risto, and Hintikka, Jaakko. 1971. "Discussion: Rules of Acceptance, Indices of Lawlikeness, and Singular Inductive Inferences; Reply to a Critical Discussion." *Philosophy of Science* 38: 303–7.

Hintikka, Jaakko. 1965a. "Towards a Theory of Inductive Generalization." In Y. Bar-Hillel, ed., *Logic, Methodology, and Philosophy of Science II*. Pp. 274–88.

_____. 1965b. "Distributive Normal Forms in First-Order Logic." In Crossley and Dummett, eds., *Formal Systems and Recursive Functions*. Pp. 48–91.

_____. 1965c. "On a Combined System of Inductive Logic." *Acta Philosophica Fennica* 18: 21–30.

_____. 1966a. "A Two-Dimensional Continuum of Inductive Methods." In Hintikka and Suppes, eds., *Aspects of Inductive Logic*. Pp. 113–32.

_____. 1966b. "Knowledge, Acceptance, and Inductive Logic." In Hintikka and Suppes, eds., *Aspects of Inductive Logic*. Pp. 1–20.

_____. 1968. "Induction by Enumeration and Induction by Elimination." In I. Lakatos, ed., *The Problem of Inductive Logic*. Pp. 191–216.

_____. 1969. "Statistics, Induction, and Lawlikeness: Comments on Dr. Vetter's Paper." *Synthese* 20: 72–83.

_____. 1970. "On Semantic Information." In Hintikka and Suppes, eds., *Information and Inference*. Pp. 3–27.

_____. 1971a. "Unknown Probabilities, Bayesianism, and de Finetti's Representation Theorem." In Buck and Cohen, eds., *PSA 1970*. Pp. 325–41.

_____. 1971b. "Inductive Generalization and Its Problems: A Comment on Kronthaler's Comments." *Theory and Decision* 1: 393–98.

_____. 1975a. "Carnap and Essler Versus Inductive Generalization." *Erkenntnis* 9: 235–44. Also in J. Hintikka, ed., *Rudolf Carnap: Logical Empiricist*. Pp. 371–80.

Hintikka, Jaakko, and Niiniluoto, Ilkka. 1974. "An Axiomatic Foundation for the Logic of Inductive Generalization." In Przelecki and Wojcicki, eds., *Formal Methods in the Methodology of Empirical Science*. Pp. 57–81. Reprinted 1980 in R. C. Jeffrey, ed., *Studies in Inductive Logic and Probability II*. Pp. 157–81.

Hintikka, Jaakko, and Pietarinen, Juho. 1966. "Semantic Information and Inductive Logic." In Hintikka and Suppes, eds., *Aspects of Inductive Logic*. Pp. 96–112.

Hooker, C. A. "Goodman, 'Grue', and Hempel." *Philosophy of Science* 35: 232–47.

_____. 1968a. "Craigian Transcriptionism." *American Philosophical Quarterly* 5: 152–63.

_____. 1968b. "Five Arguments Against Craigian Transcriptionism." *Australasian Journal of Philosophy* 46: 265–76.

Hooker, C. A., and Stove, D. 1967. "Relevance and the Ravens." *British Journal for the Philosophy of Science* 18: 305–15.

Horwich, Paul. 1978a. "A Peculiar Consequence of Nicod's Criterion." *British Journal for the Philosophy of Science* 29: 262–63.

_____. 1978b. "An Appraisal of Glymour's Confirmation Theory." *Journal of Philosophy* 75: 98–113.

Hosiasson-Lindenbaum, Janina. 1940. "On Confirmation." *Journal of Symbolic Logic* 5: 133–48.

Howson, Colin. 1972. "The Plain Man's Guide to Probability." *British Journal for the Philosophy of Science* 23: 157–70.

_____. 1973. "Must the Logical Probability of Laws be Zero?" *British Journal for the Philosophy of Science* 24: 153–63.

_____. 1975. "The Rule of Succession, Inductive Logic, and Probability Logic." *British Journal for the Philosophy of Science* 26: 187–98.

_____. 1976. "The Development of Logical Probability." In Cohen, Feyerabend, and Wartofsky, eds., *Essays in Memory of Imre Lakatos.* Pp. 277–98.

Hullett, James, and Schwartz, Robert. 1966. "Grue: Some Remarks." *Journal of Philosophy* 58: 259–71.

Humphreys, Willard C. 1968. "Statistical Ambiguity and Maximal Specificity." *Philosophy of Science* 35: 112–15.

Hunt, G.M.K. 1970. "A Conditional Vindication of the Straight Rule." *British Journal for the Philosophy of Science* 21: 198–99.

Jackson, Frank. 1969. "On Entailment and Support." *Nous* 3: 345–49.

_____. 1970a. "Discussion: A Reply to 'Induction and Objectivity.' " *Philosophy of Science* 37: 440–43.

_____. 1970b. "Discussion: Reply to a Response." *Philosophy of Science* 37: 449–51.

Jackson, Frank, and Paragetter, Robert. 1973. "Indefinite Probability Statements." *Synthese* 26: 205–17.

_____. 1980. "Confirmation and the Nomological." *Canadian Journal of Philosophy* 10: 415–28.

Jamison, Dean. 1970. "Bayesian Information Usage." In Hintikka and Suppes, eds., *Information and Inference.* Pp. 28–57.

Jardine, R. 1965. "The Resolution of the Confirmation Paradox." *Australasian Journal of Philosophy* 43: 359–68.

Jarvie, I. C. 1976. "Toulmin and the Rationality of Science." In Cohen, Feyerabend, and Wartofsky, eds., *Essays in Memory of Imre Lakatos.* Pp. 311–34.

Jaynes, E. T. 1968. "Prior Probabilities." *IEEE Transactions on Systems Science and Cybernetics* (SSC) 4: 227–41.

_____. 1976. "Confidence Intervals vs. Bayesian Intervals." In Harper and Hooker, eds., *Foundations of Probability Theory, Statistical Inference, and Statistical Theories of Science* II. P. 175–213.

Jeffrey, Richard C. 1956. "Valuation and Acceptance of Scientific Hypotheses." *Philosophy of Science* 23: 237–46.

_____. 1964. "Popper on the Rule of Succession." *Mind* 73: 129.

_____. 1965a. "New Foundations for Bayesian Decision Theory." In Y. Bar-Hillel, ed., *Logic Methodology and Philosophy of Science II.* Pp. 289–300.

_____. 1965b. *The Logic of Decision.* New York: McGraw-Hill.

_____. 1966a. "Solving the Problem of Measurement." *Journal of Philosophy* 63: 400–401.

_____. 1966b. "Goodman's Query." *Journal of Philsophy* 63: 281–88.

_____. 1968a. "Probable Knowledge." In I. Lakatos, ed., *The Problem of Inductive Logic.* Pp. 166–80.

_____. 1968b. "Gambling With Truth, by Isaac Levi." *Journal of Philosophy* 65: 313–22.

_____. 1970a. "Statistical Explanation vs. Statistical Inference." In N. Rescher, ed., *Essays in Honor of Carl G. Hempel.* Pp. 104–13.

_____. 1970b. "Dracula Meets Wolfman: Acceptance vs. Partial Belief." In M. Swain, ed., *Induction, Acceptance, and Rational Belief.* Pp. 157–85.

_____. 1971. "Probability Measures and Integrals." In Carnap and Jeffrey, eds., *Studies in Inductive Logic and Probability.* Pp. 167–221.

_____. 1973. "Carnap's Inductive Logic." *Synthese* 25: 299–306. Reprinted 1975 in R. Hintikka, ed., *Rudolf Carnap: Logical Empiricist.* Pp. 325–32.

_____. 1975a. "Probability and Falsification: Critique of the Popper Program." *Synthese* 30: 95–117.

_____. 1975b. "Replies." *Synthese* 30: 149–57.

_____. 1975c. "Carnap's Empiricism." In Maxwell and Anderson, eds., *Minnesota Studies in the Philosophy of Science VI.* Pp. 37–49.

_____. 1977. "Savage's Omelet." In Suppe and Asquith, eds., *PSA 1976 II.* Pp. 361–71.

_____. 1978. "Axiomatizing the Logic of Decision." In Hooker, Leach, and McClennen, eds., *Foundations and Applications of Decision Theory.* Pp. 227–31.

_____. 1980a. "How is it Possible to Base Preferences on Estimates of Chance?" In D. H. Mellor, ed., *Science, Belief, and Behavior.* Pp. 179–88.

_____. 1980b. "Choice, Chance, and Credence." In von Wright and Floistad, eds., *Philosophy of Logic,* The Hague: Nijhoff.

Jeffreys, Harold. 1931. *Scientific Inference.* Cambridge: Cambridge University Press.

Jones, Gary. 1979. "Discussion: Clendinnen, Jackson, and Induction." *Philosophy of Science* 46: 466–69.

Jones, K. 1973. "Verisimilitude Versus Probable Verisimilitude." *British Journal for the Philosophy of Science* 24: 174–76.

Jones, Robert M. 1965. "The Non-Reducibility of Koopman's Theory of Probability in Carnap's System for M C." *Philosophy of Science* 32: 368–69.

Kading, Daniel. 1960. "Concerning Mr. Feigl's 'Vindication' of Induction." *Philosophy of Science* 27: 405–7.

Kahane, Howard, 1965. "Nelson Goodman's Entrenchment Theory." *Philosophy of Science* 32: 377–83.

_____ . 1967a. "Reply to Ackermann." *Philosophy of Science* 34: 184–87.

_____ . 1967b. "Baumer on the Confirmation Paradoxes." *British Journal for the Philosophy of Science* 18: 52–56.

Kahneman, Daniel. 1973. "On the Psychology of Prediction." *Psychological Review* 80: 237–51.

Kahneman, Daniel, and Tversky, Amos. 1974. "Subjective Probability: A Judgment of Representativeness." In C.-A. Staël von Holstein, ed., *The Concept of Probability in Psychological Experiments*. Pp. 25–48.

_____ . 1979. "Intuitive Prediction: Biases and Corrective Procedures." *Management Science* 12: 313–27.

Kalbfleisch, J. G., and Sprott, David A. 1976. "On Tests of Significance." In Harper and Hooker, eds., *Foundations of Probability Theory, Statistical Inference, and Statistical Theories of Science* II. Pp. 259–70.

Kantorovich, Aharon. 1977. "An Ideal Model for the Growth of Knowledge in Research Programs." *Philosophy of Science* 45: 351–59.

Katz, Jerrold J. 1962. *The Problem of Induction and Its Solution*. Chicago: Chicago University Press.

Kaufman, S. A. 1974. "The Preservation of Epistemic Systematization Within the Extended Craigian Program." *Synthese* 28: 215–21.

Keene, G. B. 1961. "Confirmation and Corroboration." *Mind* 70: 85–87.

Kemeny, John G. 1951a. "The Logical Foundations of Probability, by Rudolf Carnap." *Journal of Symbolic Logic* 16: 205–7.

_____ . 1951b. *"The Logical Foundations of Probability, by Rudolf Carnap." Review of Metaphysics* 5: 145–56.

_____ . 1952. "A Contribution to Inductive Logic." *Philosophy and Phenomenological Research* 13: 371–74.

_____ . 1953. "A Logical Measure Function." *Journal of Philosophy* 52: 722–33.

_____ . 1955a. "Two Measures of Complexity." *Journal of Philosophy* 52: 722–33.

_____ . 1955b. "Fair Bets and Inductive Probabilities." *Journal of Symbolic Logic* 20: 263–73.

_____ . 1959. *A Philosopher Looks at Science*. Princeton: Princeton University Press.

_____ . 1963. "Carnap's Theory of Probability and Induction." In P. A. Schilpp, ed., *The Philosophy of Rudolf Carnap*. Pp. 711–38.

Kemeny, John G., and Oppenheim, Paul. 1952. "Degree of Factual Support." *Philosophy of Science* 19: 307–24.

Kempthorne, Oscar. 1976. "Statistics and the Philosophers." In Harper and Hooker, eds., *Foundations of Probability Theory, Statistical Inference, and Statistical Theories of Science* II. Pp. 273–314.

Kiefer, J. 1977. "The Foundations of Statistics — Are There Any?" *Synthese* 30: 161–76.

Kirschenmann, Peter. 1972. "Concepts of Randomness." *Journal of Philosophical Logic* 1: 395–413.

Kitcher, Philip. 1978. "Theories, Theorists, and Theoretical Change." *Philosophical Review* 87: 519–47.

Kleiner, Scott A. 1971. "Ontological and Terminological Commitment and the Methodological Commensurability of Theories." In Buck and Cohen, eds., *PSA 1970*. Pp. 506–18.

Kneale, William. 1949. *Probability and Induction*. Oxford: Oxford University Press.

Koertge, Noretta. 1971. "Inter-Theoretic Criticism and the Growth of Science." In Buck and Cohen, eds., *PSA 1970*. Pp. 160–73.

_____ . 1979. "The Problem of Appraising Scientific Theories." In Asquith and Kyburg, eds., *Current Research in Philosophy of Science*.

Kolmogoroff, A. N. 1950. *Foundations of the Theory of Probability*. New York: Chelsea.

Kordig, Carl R. 1971a. "Objectivity, Scientific Change, and Self-Reference." In Buck and Cohen, eds., *PSA 1970*. Pp. 519–23.

_____. 1971b. *The Justification of Scientific Change.* Dordrecht: Reidel.

_____. 1978. "Discovery and Justification." *Philosophy of Science* 45: 110–17.

Kotarbinska, J. 1977. "The Controversy: Deductivism versus Inductivism." In Przelecki and Wojcicki, eds., *Twenty-Five Years.* Pp. 261–78.

Kraft, Victor. 1966. "The Problem of Induction." In Feyerabend and Maxwell, eds., *Mind, Matter and Method.* Pp. 306–18.

Krüger, Lorenz. 1973. "Falsification, Revolution, and Continuity in the Development of Science." In P. Suppes, et al., eds., *Logic Methodology and Philosophy of Science IV.* Pp. 333–44.

Kuhn, Thomas, 1962a. *The Structure of Scientific Revolutions.* Chicago: Chicago University Press.

_____. 1970a. "Reflections on My Critics." In Lakatos and Musgrave, eds., *Criticism and Growth of Knowledge.* Pp. 231–78.

_____. 1970b. "Logic of Discovery or Psychology of Research." In Lakatos and Musgrave, eds., *Criticism and the Growth of Knowledge.* Pp. 1–23.

_____. 1971. "Notes on Lakatos." In Buck and Cohen, eds., *PSA 1970:* 137–50.

_____. 1974. "Second Thoughts on Paradigms." In P. Suppe, ed., *The Structure of Scientific Theories.* Pp. 459–82.

_____. 1977a. *The Essential Tension.* Chicago: University of Chicago Press.

_____. 1977b. "Theory-Change as Structure-Change: Comments on the Sneed Formalism." In Butts and Hintikka, eds., *Historical and Philosophical Dimensions of Logic, Methodology and Philosophy of Science.* Pp. 289–309.

Kuipers, Theo A. 1973. "A Generalization of Carnap's Inductive Logic." *Synthese* 25: 334–36. Reprinted 1975 in J. Hintikka, ed., *Rudolf Carnap: Logical Empiricist.* Pp. 361–63.

_____. 1978a. *Studies in Inductive Logic and Rational Expectation.* Dordrecht: Reidel.

_____. 1978b. "On the Generalization of the Continuum of Inductive Methods to Universal Hypotheses." *Synthese* 37: 255–84.

_____. 1980. "A Survey of Inductive Systems." In R. Jeffrey, ed., *Studies in Inductive Logic and Probability.* Pp. 183–92.

Kutschera, F. von. 1973. "Induction and the Empiricist Model of Knowledge." In P. Suppes, et al., eds., *Logic Methodology, and Philosophy of Science IV.* Pp. 345–56.

Kyburg, Henry E., Jr. 1960. "Demonstrative Induction." *Philosophy and Phenomenological Research* 21: 80–92.

_____. 1961a. *Probability and the Logic of Rational Belief.* Middletown, Conn.: Wesleyan University Press.

_____. 1961b. "A Modest Proposal Concerning Simplicity." *Philosophical Review* 70: 390–95.

_____. 1963a. "Comments on Braithwaite's Paper." In Kyburg and Nagel, eds., *Induction: Some Current Issues.* Pp. 196–99.

_____. 1963b. "A Further Note on Rationality and Consistency." *Journal of Philosophy* 60: 463–65.

_____. 1964a. "Recent Work in Inductive Logic." *American Philosophical Quarterly* 1: 1–39.

_____. 1964b. "Probability, Rationality, and a Rule of Detachment." In Y. Bar-Hillel, ed., *Logic, Methodology, and Philosophy of Science II.* Pp. 301–10.

_____. 1965a. "Comments on Salmon's 'Inductive Evidence.'" *American Philosophical Quarterly* 2: 10–12.

_____. 1965b. "Salmon's Paper." *Philosophy of Science* 32: 147–51.

_____. 1966. "Probability and Decision." *Philosophy of Science* 33: 250–61.

_____. 1968a. "*The Logic of Decision,* by Richard Jeffrey." *Philosophical Review* 77: 250–53.

_____. 1968b. "Bets and Beliefs." *American Philosophical Quarterly* 5: 54–63.

_____. 1968c. "The Rule of Detachment in Deductive Logic." In I. Lakatos, ed., *The Problem of Inductive Logic.* Pp. 98–119.

_____. 1968d. "*The Philosophy of Rudolf Carnap,* Schilpp (ed)." *The Journal of Philosophy* 65: 503–15.

_____. 1968e. "*Aspects of Inductive Logic,* Hintikka and Suppes eds." *Philosophical Review* 77: 526–28.

_____. 1970a. *Probability and Inductive Logic.* New York: The Macmillan Co.

_____. 1970b. "Discussion: More on Maximal Specificity." *Philosophy of Science* 37: 295–300.

_____. 1970c. "Conjunctivitis." In M. Swain, ed., *Induction, Acceptance and Rational Belief*. Pp. 55-82.

_____. 1971a. "Probability and Informative Inference." In Godambe and Sprott, eds., *Foundations of Statistical Inference*. Pp. 82-107.

_____. 1971b. *"Induction, Probability, and Causation: Selected Papers by C. D. Broad."* *Philosophical Review* 80: 244-51.

_____. 1971c. *"Rules of Acceptance and Inductive Logic*, by Risto Hilpinen." *Synthese* 22: 482-87.

_____. 1974a. *The Logical Foundations of Statistical Inference*. Dordrecht: Reidel.

_____. 1974b. "Propensities and Probabilities." *British Journal for the Philosophy of Science* 25: 358-75.

_____. 1974c. "Randomness." In Shaffner and Cohen, eds., *PSA 1972*. Pp. 137-49.

_____. 1975a. "Hintikka: 'Induction by Enumeration and Induction by Elimination.'" *Journal of Symbolic Logic* 40: 449-50.

_____. 1975b. "Niiniluoto and Tuomela: *Theoretical Concepts and Hypothetico Inductive Inference*, and Tuomela: *Theoretical Concepts*." *Journal of Philosophy:* 491-98.

_____. 1975c. "The Uses of Probability and the Choice of a Reference Class." In Maxwell and Anderson, eds., *Minnesota Studies in the Philosophy of Science VI*. Pp. 262-94.

_____. 1976a. "Local and Global Induction." In R. Bogdan, ed., *Local Induction*. Pp. 191-215.

_____. 1976b. "Chance." *Journal of Philosophical Logic* 5: 355-93.

_____. 1976c. "Statistical Knowledge and Statistical Inference." In Harper and Hooker, eds., *Foundations of Probability Theory, Statistical Inference, and Statistical Theories of Science II*. Pp. 315-36.

_____. 1977a. "Reply to Professor Freudenthal." *Synthese* 36: 493-98.

_____. 1977b. "Decisions, Conclusions, and Utilities." *Synthese* 36: 87-96.

_____. 1977c. "All Acceptable Generalizations are Analytic." *American Philosophical Quarterly* 14: 201-10.

_____. 1977d. "Randomness and the Right Reference Class." *Journal of Philosophy* 74: 501-20.

_____. 1978a. "How to Make Up a Theory." *Philosophical Review* 87: 84-87.

_____. 1978b. "An Interpolation Theorem for Inductive Logic." *Journal of Philosophy* 75: 93-98.

_____. 1978c. "Ian Hacking: The Emergence of Probability." *Theory and Decision* 9: 205-19.

_____. 1978d. "Subjective Probability: Considerations, Reflections, and Problems." *Journal of Philosophical Logic* 7: 157-80.

_____. 1979a. "L. Jonathan Cohen's *The Probable and the Provable*." *Nous* 14: 623-30.

_____. 1979b. "Direct Measurement." *American Philosophical Quarterly* 16: 259-72.

_____. 1980a. "Acts and Conditional Probabilities." *Theory and Decision* 12: 149-71.

_____. 1980b. "Conditionalization." *Journal of Philosophy* 77: 98-114.

_____. 1980c. "Statistical Statements: Their Meaning, Acceptance, and Use." In D. H. Mellor, ed., *Science, Belief, and Behaviour*. Pp. 161-77.

_____. 1980d. "Inductive Logic and Experimental Design." In Cohen and Hesse, eds., *Applications of Inductive Logic*. Pp. 90-101.

Kyburg, Henry E., Jr., and Harper, William. 1968. "Discussion: The Jones Case." *British Journal for the Philosophy of Science* 19: 247-58.

Lakatos, Imre. 1968a. "Changes in the Problem of Inductive Logic." In I. Lakatos, ed., *The Problem of Inductive Logic*. Pp. 315-417.

_____. 1968b. "Criticism and the Methodology of Scientific Research Programmes." *Proceedings of the Aristotelian Society* 69: 149-86.

_____. 1970. "Falsification and the Methodology of Scientific Research Programmes." In Lakatos and Musgrave, eds., *Criticism and the Growth of Knowledge*. Pp. 91-195.

Langtry, Bruce. 1977. "Popper on Induction and Independence." *Philosophy of Science* 44: 326-31.

Largeault, J. 1978a. "Hasards et Probabilités." *Dialogue* 17: 634-58.

_____. 1978b. "Henry Kyburg: *The Logical Foundations of Statistical Inference*." *Archives de Philosophie* 41: 687-88.

_____. 1979. "Sur des Notions du Hasard." *Revue Philosophique Français* 169: 33-65.

Laudan, Larry. 1977. *Progress and Its Problems*. Berkeley: University of California Press.

_____. 1980. "Views of Progress: Separating the Pilgrims From the Rakes." *Philosophy of the Social Sciences* 80: 273-86.

Laymon, Ronald. 1976. "Newton's Advertised Precision and His Refutation of the Received Laws of Refraction." In Machamer and Turnbull, eds., *Studies in Perception*. Pp. 231–58.

———. 1977. "Feyerabend, Brownian Motion, and the Hiddenness of Refuting Facts." *Philosophy of Science* 44: 225–47.

Leblanc, Hugues. 1962. *Statistical and Inductive Probabilities*. Englewood Cliffs, N.J.: Prentice-Hall.

———. 1963a. "A Revised Version of Goodman's Confirmation Paradox." *Philosophical Studies* 14: 49–51.

———. 1963b. "That Positive Instances Are No Help." *Journal of Philosophy* 60: 453–62.

———. 1966. "On Requirements for Conditional Probability Functions." *Journal of Symbolic Logic* 25: 238–42.

Leclerq, René. 1974. *The Logic of the Plausible and Some of Its Applications*. London: Plenum Press.

Lehman, Hugh. 1972. "Statistical Explanation." *Philosophy of Science* 39: 500–506.

Lehman, R. Sherman. 1955. "On Confirmation and Rational Betting." *Journal of Symbolic Logic* 20: 251–62.

Lehrer, Keith. 1963. "Descriptive Completeness and Inductive Methods." *Journal of Symbolic Logic* 28: 157–60.

———. 1964. "Knowledge and Probability." *Journal of Philosophy* 61: 368–72.

———. 1965. "Letter: On Knowledge and Probability." *Journal of Philosophy* 62: 67–68.

———. 1969. "Induction: A Consistent Gamble." *Nous* 3: 285–97.

———. 1970a. "Theoretical Terms and Inductive Inference." *American Philosophical Quarterly*, Mon. Ser. 3: 30–41.

———. 1970b. "Induction, Reason, and Consistency." *British Journal for the Philosophy of Science* 21: 103–14.

———. 1970c. "Justification, Explanation, and Induction." In M. Swain, ed., *Induction, Acceptance, and Rational Belief*. Pp. 100–133.

———. 1971. "Induction and Conceptual Change." *Synthese* 23: 206–25.

———. 1973a. "Evidence, Meaning, and Conceptual Change." In Pearce and Maynard, eds., *Conceptual Change*. Pp. 94–122.

———. 1973b. "Evidence and Conceptual Change." In Bogdan and Niiniluoto, eds., *Logic, Language, and Probability*. Pp. 100–107.

———. 1975a. "Induction, Rational Acceptance, and Minimally Inconsistent Sets." In Maxwell and Anderson, eds., *Minnesota Studies in the Philosophy of Science VI*. Pp. 295–323.

———. 1975b. "Social Consensus and Rational Rational Agniology." *Synthese* 31: 141–60.

———. 1975c. "Reason and Consistency." In K. Lehrer, ed., *Analysis and Metaphysics*. Pp. 57–74.

———. 1976. "Induction, Consensus, and Catastrophe." In R. Bogdan, ed., *Local Induction*. Pp. 115–44.

———. 1978. "Consensus and Comparison." In Hooker, Leach, and McClennen, eds., *Foundations and Applications of Decision Theory*. Pp. 283–309.

———. 1980. "Truth, Evidence, and Error." In Cohen and Hesse, eds., *Applications of Inductive Logic*. Pp. 130–42.

Lenz, John W. 1956. "Carnap on Defining 'Degrees of Confirmation.'" *Philosophy of Science* 23: 230–36.

———. 1958. "Problems for the Practicalists' Justification of Induction." *Philosophical Studies* 9: 4–8.

Levi, Isaac. 1962. "Corroboration and Rules of Acceptance." *British Journal for the Philosophy of Science* 13: 307–13.

———. 1965a. "Deductive Cogency in Inductive Inference." *Journal of Philosophy* 62: 68–77.

———. 1965b. "Hacking Salmon on Induction." *Journal of Philosophy* 62: 481–87.

———. 1966. "On Potential Surprise." *Ratio* 8: 107–29.

———. 1967a. *Gambling with Truth*. New York: Alfred A. Knopf.

———. 1967b. "Utility and Acceptance of Hypotheses." In S. Morgenbesser, ed., *Philosophy of Science Today*. New York: Basic Books.

———. 1967c. "Probability Kinematics." *British Journal for the Philosophy of Science* 18: 197–209.

———. 1969a. "Confirmation, Linguistic Invariance, and Conceptual Innovation." *Synthese* 20: 48–55.

———. 1969b. "If Jones Only Knew More." *British Journal for the Philosophy of Science* 20: 153–59.

_____. 1969c. "Information and Inference." *Synthese* 17: 369–91.

_____. 1970. "Probability and Evidence." In M. Swain, ed., *Induction, Acceptance, and Rational Belief.* Pp. 134–56.

_____. 1971a. "Certainty, Probability, and the Correction of Evidence." *Nous* 5: 299–312.

_____. 1971b. "Truth, Content, and Ties." *Journal of Philosophy* 68: 865–76.

_____. 1973. "But Fair to Chance." *Journal of Philosophy* 70: 52–55.

_____. 1974. "On Indeterminate Probabilities." *Journal of Philosophy* 71: 391–418. Reprinted 1978 in Hooker, Leach, and McClennen, eds., *Foundations and Applications of Decision Theory I.* Pp. 233–61.

_____. 1976a. "A Paradox for the Birds." In Cohen, Feyerabend, and Wartofsky, eds., *Essays in Honor of Imre Lakatos.* Pp. 371–78.

_____. 1976b. "Acceptance Revisited." In R. Bogdan, ed., *Local Induction.* Pp. 1–72.

_____. 1977a. "Epistemic Utility and the Evaluation of Experiments." *Philosophy of Science* 44: 368–86.

_____. 1977b. "Direct Inference." *Journal of Philosophy* 74: 5–29.

_____. 1978a. "Confirmational Conditionalization." *Journal of Philosophy* 75: 730–37.

_____. 1978b. "Coherence, Regularity, and Conditional Probability." *Theory and Decision* 9: 1–15.

_____. 1978c. "Abduction and the Demands of Information." In Niiniluoto and Tuomela, eds., *The Logic and Epistemology of Scientific Change.* Pp. 405–29.

_____. 1978d. "Irrelevance." In Hooker, Leach, and McClennen, eds., *Foundations and Applications of Decision Theory* I. Pp. 263–75.

_____. 1978e. "Newcomb's Many Problems." In Hooker, Leach, and McClennen, eds., *Foundations and Applications of Decision Theory.* Pp. 369–83.

_____. 1979. "Inductive Appraisal." In Asquith and Kyburg, *Current Research in Philosophy of Science.* Pp. 339–51.

_____. 1980a. "Induction as Self-Correcting According to Peirce." In D. H. Mellor, ed., *Science, Belief, and Behaviour.* Pp. 127–40.

_____. 1980b. "Potential Surprise: Its Role in Inference and Decision-Making." In Cohen and Hesse, eds., *Applications of Inductive Logic.* Pp. 1–27.

_____. 1980c. *The Enterprise of Knowledge: An Essay on Knowledge, Credal Probability, and Chance.* Cambridge: M.I.T. Press.

Lewis, David. 1971. "Immodest Inductive Methods." *Philosophy of Science* 38: 54–63.

_____. 1976. "Probabilities of Conditionals and Conditional Probabilities." *Philosophical Review* 85: 297–315.

_____. 1980. "A Subjectivist's Guide to Objective Chance." In R. Jeffrey, ed., *Studies in Inductive Logic and Probability II.* Pp. 263–93.

Lindley, D. V. 1953. "Statistical Inference." *Journal of the Royal Statistical Society, Series B,* 15: 30–76.

_____. 1965. *Introduction to Probability and Statistics.* 2 vols. Cambridge: Cambridge University Press.

_____. 1972. *Bayesian Statistics: A Review.* Philadelphia: SIAM.

_____. 1975. "The Failure of Statistics — A Bayesian 21st Century." *Supplement to Advances in Applied Probability* 7: 106–15.

_____. 1976. "Bayesian Statistics." In Harper and Hooker, eds., *Foundations of Probability Theory, Statistical Inference, and Statistical Theories of Science II.* Pp. 353–63.

_____. 1977. "The Distinction Between Inference and Decision." *Synthese* 36: 51–58.

Link, Godehard. 1980. "Representation Theorems of the de Finetti Type for (partially) Symmetric Probability Measures." In R. Jeffrey, ed., *Studies in Inductive Logic and Probability II.* Pp. 208–31.

Loewer, B.; Laddaga, R.; and Rosenkrantz, R. 1978. "On the Likelihood Principle and an Alleged Antinomy." In Asquith and Hacking, eds., *PSA 1978.* Pp. 279–88.

Los, J. 1977. "The Foundations of a Methodological Analysis of Mill's Methods." In Przelecki and Wojcicki, eds., *Twenty-Five Years.* Pp. 291–325.

Lucas, J. R. 1965. "The One Concept of Probability." *Philosophy and Phenomenological Research* 26: 180–99.

_____. 1970. *The Concept of Probability.* Oxford: Clarendon Press.

Lungarzo, Carlos. 1975. "Characteristicas del Metodo Inductivo en Ciencia." *Dialogos* 25: 56.

Lykken, David. 1968. "Statistical Significance in Psychological Research." *Psychological Bulletin* 70: 151–59.

McEvoy, John G. 1975. "Discussion: A 'Revolutionary' Philosophy of Science: Feyerabend and the Degeneration of Critical Rationalism into Skeptical Fallibilism." *Philosophy of Science* 42: 49–66.

Machamer, Peter. 1973. "Feyerabend and Galileo: The Interaction of Theories and the Reinterpretation of Experience." *Studies in History and Philosophy of Science* 1: 1–46.

Mackie, J. L. 1962. "The Paradox of Confirmation." *British Journal for the Philosophy of Science* 13: 265–77.

_____. 1966. "Miller's So-Called Paradox of Confirmation." *British Journal for the Philosophy of Science* 17: 144–47.

_____. 1969. "The Relevance Criterion of Confirmation." *British Journal for the Philosophy of Science* 20: 27–40.

McNabb, D.G.C. 1952. "Hume on Induction." *Revue Internationale de Philosophie* 6: 184–98.

Madden, Edward H. 1958. "The Riddle of Induction." *Journal of Philosophy* 6: 705–18.

Malinovich, S. 1964. "The Verification of Universal Empirical Propositions." *Analysis* 25: 202–4.

Margolis, J. 1967. "'Entitled to Assert.'" *Synthese* 17: 292–98.

Marschak, Jacob. 1974. "Information, Decision, and the Scientist." In C. Cherry, ed., *Pragmatic Aspects of Human Communication.* Pp. 145–78.

_____. 1975. "Personal Probabilities of Probabilities." *Theory and Decision* 6: 121–53.

Martin, Richard M. 1958. "A Formalization of Inductive Logic." *Journal of Symbolic Logic* 23: 251–56.

Martin-Löf, Per. 1977. "Exact Tests, Confidence Regions, and Estimates." *Synthese* 36: 195–206.

Massey, Gerald J. 1968. "Hempel's Criterion of Maximal Specificity." *Philosophical Studies* 19: 43–47.

Masterman, Margaret. 1970. "The Nature of a Paradigm." In Lakatos and Musgrave, eds., *Criticism and the Growth of Knowledge.* Pp. 59–89.

Mathers, Ruth Anne. 1963. "A Note on R. H. Vincent's Cognitive Sensibilities." *Philosophical Studies* 14: 75–77.

May, Sherry, and Harper, William. 1976. "Toward an Optimization Procedure for Applying Minimum Change Principles in Probability Kinematics." In Harper and Hooker, eds., *Foundations of Probability Theory, Statistical Inference, and Statistical Theories of Science* I. Pp. 137–66.

Mays, W. 1963. "Probability Models and Thought and Learning Processes." *Synthese* 15: 204–21.

Maxwell, Grover. 1961. "An 'Analytic' Vindication of Induction." *Philosophical Studies* 12: 43–45.

_____. 1975. "Induction and Empiricism: A Bayesian-Frequentist Alternative." In Maxwell and Anderson, eds., *Minnesota Studies in the Philosophy of Science VI.* Pp. 106–65.

Meehl, Paul E. 1967. "Theory Testing in Psychology and Physics: A Methodological Paradox." *Philosophy of Science* 34: 103–15.

Mellor, D. H. 1965a. "Experimental Error and Deducibility." *Philosophy of Science* 32: 105–22.

_____. 1965b. "Connectivity, Chance, and Ignorance." *British Journal for the Philosophy of Science* 16: 209–25.

_____. 1966. "Inexactness and Explanation." *Philosophy of Science* 33: 345–59.

_____. 1967. "Imprecision and Explanation." *Philosophy of Science* 34: 1–9.

_____. 1969. "Chance." *Proceedings of the Aristotelian Society* 43: 11–46.

_____. 1971. *The Matter of Chance.* Cambridge: Cambridge University Press.

Menger, Gunter, and Kofler, E. 1976. "Cognitive Decisions under Partial Information." In R. Bogdan, ed., *Local Induction.* Pp. 183–90.

Merrill, Gary H. 1979. "Confirmation and Prediction." *Philosophy of Science* 46: 98–117.

Michalos, Alex. 1965a. "Two Theorems on Degree of Confirmation." *Ratio* 7: 196–98.

_____. 1965b. "Estimated Utility and Corroboration." *British Journal for the Philosophy of Science* 16: 327–31.

_____. 1966. "Hacking: *Logic of Statistical Inference.*" *Dialectica* 5: 647–49.

_____. 1967. "Descriptive Completeness and Linguistic Variance." *Dialogue* 6: 224–28.

_____. 1971a. "Cost Benefit vs. Expected Utility Acceptance Rules." In Buck and Cohen, eds., *PSA 1970.* Pp. 375–402.

_____. 1971b. *The Popper-Carnap Controversy.* The Hague: Nijhoff.

_____ . 1974. "Rationality Between the Maximizers and the Satisfiers." In Shaffner and Cohen, eds., *PSA 1972*. Pp. 423–45.

Miller, David. 1966a. "A Paradox of Information." *British Journal for the Philosophy of Science* 17: 59–61.

_____ . 1966b. "On the So-Called So-Called Paradox: A Reply to Professor J. L. Mackie." *British Journal for the Philosophy of Science* 17: 147–49.

_____ . 1968. "The Straight and Narrow Rule of Induction: A Reply to Dr. Bub and Mr. Radner." *British Journal for the Philosophy of Science* 19: 145–62.

_____ . 1974. "Popper's Qualitative Theory of Verisimilitude." *British Journal for the Philosophy of Science* 25: 166–77.

_____ . 1975. "The Measure of All Things." In Maxwell and Anderson, eds., *Minnesota Studies in the Philosophy of Science VI*. Pp. 350–66.

_____ . 1980. "Can Science Do Without Induction?" In Cohen and Hesse, eds., *Applications of Inductive Logic*. Pp. 109–29.

Miller, Richard W. 1975. "Propensity: Popper or Peirce?" *British Journal for the Philosophy of Science* 26: 123–32.

Minas, J. Sayer. 1965. "Comment on Richard C. Jeffrey's 'Ethics and the Logic of Decision.'" *Journal of Philosophy* 62: 542–44.

Mirabelli, André. 1978. "Belief and Incremental Confirmation of One Hypothesis Relative to Another." In Asquith and Hacking, eds., *PSA 1978*: 287–301.

Moore, Asher. 1952a. "The Principle of Induction." *Journal of Philosophy* 49: 741–47.

_____ . 1952b. "The Principle of Induction (II): A Rejoinder to Miss Brodbeck." *Journal of Philosophy* 49: 750–58.

Morgenbesser, Sidney. 1962. "Goodman and the Ravens." *Journal of Philosophy* 59: 493–95.

Mortimer, Halina. 1973. "A Rule of Acceptance Based on Logical Probability." *Synthese* 26: 259–63.

Mortimore, G. W., and Maund, J. B. 1976. "Rationality in Belief." In Benn and Mortimore, eds., *Rationality and the Social Sciences*. Pp. 11–33.

Musgrave, Alan. 1971. "Kuhn's Second Thoughts." *British Journal for the Philosophy of Science* 22: 287–97.

_____ . 1973. "Falsification and Its Critics." In P. Suppes, et al., eds., *Logic, Methodology and Philosophy of Science IV*. Pp. 393–406.

Mustonen, Seppo. 1973. "A Note on Dean Jamison's Paper 'Bayesian Information Usage.'" *Synthese* 26: 322–23.

Nagel, Ernest. 1963. "Carnap's Theory of Induction." In P. A. Schilpp, ed., *The Philosophy of Rudolf Carnap*. Pp. 785–826.

Nalimov, Bassili V. 1977. "The Receptivity of Hypotheses." *Diogenes*. Pp. 179–97.

Nelson, E. J. 1963. "Causal Necessity and Induction." *Proceedings of the Aristotelian Society* 64: 289–300.

Nelson, John O. 1958. "The Confirmation of Hypotheses." *Philosophical Review* 67: 95–100.

_____ . 1961. "Are Inductive Generalizations Quantifiable?" *Analysis* 22: 59–65.

_____ . 1968. "Logical Notation and Indoor Ornithology." *Ratio* 10: 169–72.

Nielsen, Harry A. 1959. "Sampling and the Problem of Induction." *Mind* 68: 474–481.

Niiniluoto, Ilkka. 1972. "Inductive Systematization: Definition and a Critical Survey." *Synthese* 25: 25–81.

_____ . 1973. "Empirically Trivial Theories and Inductive Systematization." In Bogdan and Niiniluoto, eds., *Logic, Language, and Probability*. Pp. 108–14.

_____ . 1974a. "Inducibility and Epistemic Systematization: Rejoinder to Kaufman." *Synthese* 28: 223–32.

_____ . 1974b. "Inductive Logic and Theoretical Concepts." In Przelecki and Wojcicki, eds., *Formal Methods in the Methodology of Empirical Sciences*. Pp. 93–112.

_____ . 1976. "Inquiries, Problems, and Questions: Remarks on Local Induction." In R. Bogdan, ed., *Local Induction*. Pp. 263–96.

_____ . 1977a. "On the Truthlikeness of Generalizations." In Butts and Hintikka, eds., *Basic Problems in Methodology and Linguistics*. Pp. 121–47.

_____ . 1977b. "On a *k*-Dimensional System of Inductive Logic." In Suppe and Asquith, eds., *PSA 1976 II*. Pp. 245–47.

_____ . 1980. "Analogy, Transitivity, and the Confirmation of Theories." In Cohen and Hesse, eds., *Applications of Inductive Logic*. Pp. 218–34.

Niiniluoto, Ilkka, and Tuomela, Raimo. 1973. *Theoretical Concepts and Hypothetico-Inductive Inference*. Dordrecht, Reidel.

Nowak, Stefan. 1960. "Some Problems of Causal Interpretation of Statistical Relationships." *Philosophy of Science* 27: 23–38.

_____. 1972. "Inductive Inconsistencies and Conditional Laws of Science." *Synthese* 23: 357–73.

O'Connor, John. 1967. "Differential Properties and Goodman's Riddle." *Analysis* 28: 59.

Öfsti, Audin. 1962. "Some Problems of Counter-Inductive Policy as Opposed to Inductive." *Inquiry* 5: 267–83.

Oliver, W. Donald. 1952. "A Re-Examination of the Problem of Induction." *Journal of Philosophy* 49: 769–80.

Onicescu, Octav. 1973. "Extension of the Theory of Probability." In P. Suppes, et al., eds., *Logic, Methodology and Philosophy of Science IV.* Pp. 439–50.

Pietarinen, Juhani. 1970. "Quantitative Tools for Evaluating Scientific Systematizations." In Hintikka and Suppes, eds., *Information and Inference.* Pp. 123–47.

_____. 1972. *Lawlikeness, Analogy and Inductive Logic.* Amsterdam: North-Holland.

Pole, Nelson. 1971. "'Self-Supporting' Inductive Arguments." In Buck and Cohen, eds., *PSA 1970.* Pp. 496–503.

Pollock, John L. 1962. "Counter-Induction." *Inquiry* 5: 284–94.

_____. 1972. "The Logic of Projectibility." *Philosophy of Science* 39: 302–14.

_____. 1973. "Laying the Raven to Rest." *Journal of Philosophy* 70: 747–54.

Popper, Karl R. 1954. "Degree of Confirmation." *British Journal for the Philosophy of Science* 5: 143–49.

_____. 1956. "A Second Note on Degree of Confirmation." *British Journal for the Philosophy of Science* 7: 350–55.

_____. 1957a. "A Third Note on Degree of Corroboration or Confirmation." *British Journal for the Philosophy of Science* 8: 294–302.

_____. 1957b. "The Propensity Interpretation of the Calculus of Probability and the Quantum Theory." In S. Körner, ed., *Observation and Interpretation.* Pp. 65–70.

_____. 1959. The Logic of Scientific Discovery. London: Hutchinson and Co.

_____. 1966a. "A Comment on Miller's New Paradox of Information." *British Journal for the Philosophy of Science* 17: 61–69.

_____. 1966b. "A Paradox of Zero Information." *British Journal for the Philosophy of Science* 17: 141–43.

_____. 1967. "The Mysteries of Udolpho: A Reply to Professors Jeffrey and Bar-Hillel." *Mind* 76: 103–10.

_____. 1970. "Normal Science and Its Dangers." In Lakatos and Musgrave, eds., *Criticism and the Growth of Knowledge.* Pp. 51–58.

Pratt, John W. 1962. "Comments on A. Birnbaum's 'On the Foundations of Statistical Inference.'" *Journal of the American Statistical Association* 57: 314–15.

_____. 1977. "'Decisions' as Statistical Evidence and Birnbaum's 'Confidence Concept.'" *Synthese* 36: 59–69.

Price, John. 1976. "On the Probability of Laws Being Zero." *British Journal for the Philosophy of Science* 27: 392–95.

Putnam, Hilary. 1956. "A Definition of Degree of Confirmation for Very Rich Languages." *Philosophy of Science* 23:58–62.

_____. 1963. "'Degree of Confirmation' and Inductive Logic." In P. A. Schilpp, ed., *The Philosophy of Rudolf Carnap.* Pp. 761–84.

Quine, W.V.O., and Ullian J. S. 1970. *The Web of Belief.* New York: Random House.

Rabinowica, Wlodzimerz. 1979. "Reasonable Belief." *Theory and Decision* 10: 61–81.

Rakitov, A. N. 1970. "The Statistical Interpretation of Fact and the Role of Statistical Methods in the Structure of Empirical Knowledge." In P. V. Tavanec, ed., *Problems in the Logic of Scientific Knowledge.* Pp. 394–425.

Ramsey, Frank P. 1931. *The Foundations of Mathematics.* London: Routledge and Kegan Paul.

Redhead, M.L.G. 1974. "On Neyman's Paradox and the Theory of Statistical Tests." *British Journal for the Philosophy of Science* 25: 265–71.

Reichenbach, Hans. 1940. "On the Justification of Induction." *Journal of Philosophy* 37: 97–103.

Renyi, Alfred. 1970. *Foundations of Probability.* San Francisco: Holden-Day.

Rescher, Nicholas. 1958. "Theory of Evidence." *Philosophy of Science* 25: 83–94.

_____. 1960. "Plausible Implication." *Analysis* 21: 128–35.

_____. 1976. "Peirce and the Economy of Research." *Philosophy of Science* 43: 71–98.

Resnick, Lawrence. 1959. "Confirmation and Hypothesis." *Philosophy of Science* 26: 25–30.

Robinson, Richard E. 1965. "Measurement and Statistics: Towards a Clarification of the Theory of 'Permissible Statistics.'" *Philosophy of Science* 32: 229–43.

Rogers, B. 1971. "Material Conditions on Tests of Statistical Hypotheses." In Buck and Cohen, eds., *PSA 1970*. Pp. 403–12.

———. 1979. "The Probabilities of Theories as Frequencies." In W. C. Salmon, ed., *Hans Reichenbach: Logical Empiricist*. Pp. 169–85.

Rosenkrantz, Roger. 1970. "Experimentation as Communication with Nature." In Hintikka and Suppes, eds., *Information and Inference*. Pp. 169–85.

———. 1971. "Induction and Probabilism." *Synthese* 23: 167–205.

———. 1973a. "Probability Magic Unmasked." *Philosophy of Science* 40: 227–33.

———. 1973b. "Probabilistic Confirmation Theory and the Goodman Paradox." *American Philosophical Quarterly* 10: 157–62.

———. 1973c. "The Significance Test Controversy." *Synthese* 26: 304–21.

———. 1976a. "Simplicity." In Harper and Hooker, eds., *Foundations of Probability Theory, Statistical Inference, and Statistical Theories of Science* I. Pp. 167–203.

———. 1976b. "Cognitive Decision Theory." In R. Bogdan, ed., *Local Induction*. Pp. 73–92.

———. 1977a. *Inference, Method, and Decision*. Dordrecht: Reidel.

———. 1977b. "Support." *Synthese* 36: 181–93.

———. 1978. "The Copernican Revelation." In Hooker, Leach, and McClennen, eds., *Foundations and Applications of Decision Theory I*. Pp. 399–426.

———. 1979. "Bayesian Theory Appraisal: A Reply to Seidenfeld." *Theory and Decision* 11: 441–51.

———. 1980. "Rational Information Acquisition." In Cohen and Hesse, eds., *Applications of Inductive Logic*. Pp. 68–89.

Rozeboom, William W. 1968. "New Dimensions of Confirmation." *Philosophy of Science* 35: 134–55.

———. 1969. "New Mysteries for Old, the Transfiguration of Miller's Paradox." *British Journal for the Philosophy of Science* 19: 345–53.

———. 1970. "New Dimensions of Confirmation Theory II: The Structure of Uncertainty." In Buck and Cohen, eds., *PSA 1970*. Pp. 342–74.

Runnalls, A. R. 1978. "Difficulties of the Lindley-Savage Argument." *Synthese* 37: 369–85.

Russell, Bertrand. 1948. *Human Knowledge*. New York: Simon & Schuster.

Russo, F. 1978. "La Connaissance Scientifique selon Karl Popper." *Études* 348: 385–401.

Ruzvin, G. I. 1970. "Probability Logic and Its Role in Scientific Research." In P. V. Tavanec, ed., *Problems of the Logic of Scientific Knowledge*. Pp. 212–65.

Ryle, Gilbert. 1950. "'If', 'So', and 'Because'." In Max Black, ed., *Philosophical Analysis* Englewood Cliffs, N.J.: Prentice-Hall, Inc., 302–18.

———. 1957. "Predicting and Inferring." In S. Körner, ed., *Observation and Interpretation*. Pp. 165–70.

———. 1960. "Comment on Mr. Achinstein's Paper." *Analysis* 21: 9–11.

Salmon, Wesley. 1955. "The Short Run." *Philosophy of Science* 22: 214–21.

———. 1956. "Regular Rules of Induction." *Philosophical Review* 65: 385–88.

———. 1957. "The Predictive Inference." *Philosophy of Science* 24: 180–90.

———. 1961. "Vindication of Induction." In Feigl and Maxwell, eds., *Current Issues in the Philosophy of Science*. Pp. 245–57.

———. 1963a. "On Vindicating Induction." In Kyburg and Nagel, eds., *Induction: Some Current Issues*. Pp. 27–41.

———. 1963b. "Inductive Inference." In B. Baumrin, *Philosophy of Science*. Pp. 341–70.

———. 1965a. "Consistency, Transitivity, and Inductive Support." *Ratio* 7: 164–69.

———. 1965b. "The Concept of Inductive Evidence." *American Philosophical Quarterly* 2: 1–6.

———. 1965c. "Rejoinder to Barker and Kyburg." *American Philosophical Quarterly* 2: 13–16.

———. 1965d. "The Status of Prior Probabilities in Statistical Explanation." *Philosophy of Science* 32: 137–46.

———. 1965e. "Reply to Kyburg." *Philosophy of Science* 32: 152–54.

———. 1966a. "Use, Mention and Linguistic Invariance." *Philosophical Studies* 17: 13–18.

———. 1966b. "The Foundations of Scientific Inference." In R. G. Colodny, ed., *Mind and Cosmos*. Pp. 135–275.

———. 1967a. *The Foundations of Scientific Inference*. Pittsburgh: University of Pittsburgh Press. (Reprint of Salmon, 1966b, with the addition of a short addendum.)

_____ . 1967b. "Carnap's Inductive Logic." *Journal of Philosophy* 64: 725–39.
_____ . 1968a. "The Justification of Inductive Rules of Inference." In I. Lakatos, ed., *The Problem of Inductive Logic*. Pp. 24–43.
_____ . 1968b. "Inquiries into the Foundations of Science." In D. L. Arm, ed., *Vistas in Science*. Pp. 1–24. Reprint 1972 in S. A. Luckenbach, ed., *Probabilities, Problems, and Paradoxes*. Pp. 139–58.
_____ . 1968c. "Who Needs Acceptance Rules?" In I. Lakatos, ed., *The Problem of Inductive Logic*. Pp. 139–44.
_____ . 1969. "Induction and Intuition." In Davis, Hockney, and Wilson, eds., *Philosophical Logic*. Pp. 158–63.
_____ . 1970a. "Partial Entailment as a Basis for Inductive Logic." In N. Rescher, ed., *Essays in Honor of Carl G. Hempel*. Pp. 47–82.
_____ . 1970b. "Bayes's Theorem and the History of Science." In R. H. Stuewer, ed., *Minnesota Studies in the Philosophy of Science V*. Pp. 68–86.
_____ . 1970c. "Explanation and Relevance." In Buck and Cohen, eds., *PSA 1970*. Pp. 27–39.
_____ . 1973. "Reply to Lehman." *Philosophy of Science* 40: 397–402.
_____ . 1974. "Russell on Scientific Inference, or Will the Real Deductivist Please Stand Up?" In G. Nakhnikian, ed., *Bertrand Russell's Philosophy*. Pp. 183–208.
_____ . 1975. "Confirmation and Relevance." In Maxwell and Anderson, eds., *Minnesota Studies in the Philosophy of Science IV*. Pp. 3–36.
_____ . 1977a. "A Third Dogma of Empiricism." In Butts and Hintikka, eds., *Basic Problems in Methodology and Linguistics*. Pp. 149–66.
_____ . 1977b. "Hempel's Conception of Inductive Inference in I-S Explanation." *Philosophy of Science* 44: 180–85.
_____ . 1977c. "Objectively Homogeneous Reference Classes." *Synthese* 36: 399–414.
Salmon, Wesley; Jeffrey, Richard; and Greeno, James. 1971. *Statistical Explanation and Statistical Relevance*. Pittsburgh: Pittsburgh University Press.
Sanford, David H. 1970. "Disjunctive Predicates." *American Philosophical Quarterly* 7: 162–70.
Savage, Leonard J. 1954. *Foundations of Statistics*. New York: John Wiley.
_____ . 1962. "Subjective Probability and Statistical Practise." In Barnard and Cox, eds., *Foundations of Statistical Inference*. Pp. 9–35.
_____ . 1966. "Implications of Personal Probability for Induction." *Journal of Philosophy* 58: 593–607.
_____ . 1967. "Difficulties in the Theory of Personal Probability." *Philosophy of Science* 34: 305–10.
_____ . 1973. "Probability in Science: A Personalistic Account." In P. Suppes, et al., eds., *Logic, Methodology and Philosophy of Science IV*. Pp. 417–528.
Schaffner, Kenneth. 1974. "Logic of Discovery and Logic of Justification in Regulatory Genetics." *Studies in History and Philosophy of Science* 4: 349–85.
Scheffler, Israel. 1960. "A Note on Confirmation." *Philosophical Studies* 11: 21–23.
_____ . 1961. "A Rejoinder on Confirmation." *Philosophical Studies* 12: 19–20.
_____ . 1963. *The Anatomy of Inquiry*. New York: Alfred A. Knopf.
_____ . 1968. "Reflections on the Ramsey Method." *Journal of Philosophy* 65: 269–74.
Schick, Frederick. 1963a. "Rationality and Consistency." *Journal of Philosophy* 60: 5–19.
_____ . 1963b. "Katz: *The Problem of Induction and Its Solution.*" *Journal of Philosophy* 60: 435–62.
_____ . 1966a. "Jeffrey: *The Logic of Decision.*" *Journal of Philosophy* 63: 396–400.
_____ . 1966b. "Consistency." *Philosophical Review* 75: 467–95.
_____ . 1970. "Three Logics of Belief," Swain (ed)." *Induction, Acceptance, and Rational Belief:* 6–26.
Schlesinger, George. 1967. "The Probability of the Simple Hypothesis." *American Philosophical Quarterly* 4: 152–58.
_____ . 1970. "On Irrelevant Criteria of Confirmation." *British Journal for the Philosophy of Science* 21: 288–89.
_____ . 1971. "Induction and Parsimony." *American Philosophical Quarterly* 8: 179–85.
_____ . 1975a. "Confirmation and Parsimony." In Maxwell and Anderson, eds., *Minnesota Studies in the Philosophy of Science VI*. Pp. 324–42.
_____ . 1975b. "Rejoinder to Professor Teller." In Maxwell and Anderson, eds., *Minnesota Studies in the Philosophy of Science VI*. Pp. 347–49.
Schoenberg, Judith. 1964. "Confirmation by Observation and the Paradox of the Ravens." *British Journal for the Philosophy of Science* 15: 200–12.

Scott, Dana, and Krauss, Peter. 1966. "Assigning Probabilities to Logical Formulas." In Hintikka and Suppes, eds., *Aspects of Inductive Logic*. Pp. 219–64.

Scriven, Michael. 1955. "The Principle of Inductive Simplicity." *Philosophical Studies* 6: 26–30.

Seidenfeld, Teddy. 1977. "A Review of Kyburg's *Logical Foundations of Statistical Inference*." *Journal of Philosophy* 74: 47–61.

———. 1978. "Direct Inference and Inverse Inference." *Journal of Philosophy* 75: 709–30.

———. 1979a. *Philosophical Problems of Statistical Inference*. Dordrecht: Reidel.

———. 1979b. "Why I am not an Objective Bayesian." *Theory and Decision* 11: 413–40.

———. 1981. "Statistical Evidence and Belief Functions." In Asquith and Hacking, eds., *PSA 1978* II.

Sellars, Wilfrid. 1964. "Induction as Vindication." *Philosophy of Science* 31: 197–231.

———. 1970. "Are There non-Deductive Logics?" In N. Rescher, ed., *Essays in Honor of Carl G. Hempel*. Pp. 83–103.

———. 1973. "Conceptual Change." In Pearce and Maynard, eds., *Conceptual Change*. Pp. 77–93.

Settle, Tom W. 1970a. "Confirmation as a Probability: Dead But It Won't Lie Down." *British Journal for the Philosophy of Science* 21: 200–201.

———. 1970b. "Is Corroboration a Non-Demonstrative Form of Inference?" *Ratio* 12: 151–54.

———. 1972. "Propensity Theories of Probability Unscathed: A Reply to White." *British Journal for the Philosophy of Science* 23: 331–35.

———. 1973. "Are Some Propensities Probabilities?" In Bogdan and Niiniluoto, eds., *Logic, Language, and Probability*. Pp. 115–20.

———. 1975. "Presuppostions of Propensity Theories of Probability." In Maxwell and Anderson, eds., *Minnesota Studies in the Philosophy of Science VI*. Pp. 388–415.

———. 1977. "Popper Versus Peirce on the Probability of Single Cases." *British Journal for the Philosophy of Science* 28: 177–80.

Shafer, Glenn. 1976. *A Mathematical Theory of Evidence*. Princeton: Princeton University Press.

———. 1976. "A Theory of Statistical Evidence." In Harper and Hooker, eds., *Foundation of Probability Theory, Statistical Inference, and Statistical Theories of Science* II. Pp. 365–434.

Shapere, Dudley. 1974. "Discovery, Rationality, and Progress in Science: A Perspective in the Philosophy of Science." In Schaffner and Cohen, eds., *PSA 1972*. Pp. 407–19.

———. 1977. "The Influence of Knowledge on the Description of Facts." In Suppe and Asquith, eds., *PSA 1976 II*. Pp. 281–98.

Shimony, Abner. 1953. "Braithwaite on Scientific Method." *Review of Metaphysics* 7: 644–60.

———. 1955. "Coherence and the Axioms of Confirmation." *Journal of Symbolic Logic* 20: 1–28.

———. 1967. "Amplifying Personal Probability Theory: Comments on L. J. Savage's 'Difficulties in the Theory of Personal Probability.'" *Philosophy of Science* 34: 326–32.

———. 1970. "Scientific Inference." In R. G. Colodny, ed., *The Nature and Function of Scientific Theories*. Pp. 79–172.

———. 1973. "Comment on the Interpretation of Inductive Probabilities." *Journal of Statistical Physics* 9: 187.

———. 1975. "Vindication: A Reply to Paul Teller." In Maxwell and Anderson, eds., *Minnesota Studies in the Philosophy of Science VI*. Pp. 204–11.

———. 1976. "Comments on Two Epistemological Theses of Thomas Kuhn." In Cohen, Feyerabend, and Wartofsky, eds., *Essays in Memory of Imre Lakatos*. Pp. 569–88.

Shoemaker, Sydney. 1980. "Properties, Causation, and Projectivility." In Cohen and Hesse, eds., *Applications of Inductive Logic*. Pp. 291–312.

Short, T. L. 1980. "An Analysis of Conceptual Change." *American Philosophical Quarterly* 17: 301–9.

Siemens, Warren D. 1971. "A Logical Empiricist Theory of Scientific Change." In Buck and Cohen, eds., *PSA 1970*. Pp. 524–35.

Sklar, Lawrence. 1970. "Is Probability a Dispositional Property?" *Journal of Philosophy* 67: 355–66.

———. 1973. "Statistical Explanation and Ergodic Theory." *Philosophy of Science* 40: 194–212.

Skyrms, Brian. 1965. "On Failing to Vindicate Induction." *Philosophy of Science* 32: 253–68.
_____ . 1966a. "Nomological Necessity and the Paradoxes of Confirmation." *Philosophy of Science* 33: 230–49.
_____ . 1966b. *Choice and Chance: An Introduction to Inductive Logic.* Belmont, Calif.: Dickenson.
_____ . 1973. "Unfair to Frequencies." *Journal of Philosophy* 70: 41–52.
_____ . 1981. "Statistical Laws and Personal Propensities." In Asquith and Hacking, eds., *PSA 1978* II.
Slaght, Ralph L. 1970. "Induction, Acceptance, and Rational Belief: A Selected Bibliography." In M. Swain, ed., *Induction, Acceptance, and Rational Belief.* Pp. 186–227.
Sleigh, Robert C. 1964. "A Note on Knowledge and Probability." *Journal of Philosophy* 61: 478.
Sloman, A. 1964. "Rules of Inference, or Suppressed Premises?" *Mind* 73: 84–96.
Slote, Michael A. 1966. "Some Thoughts on Goodman's Riddle." *Analysis* 27: 128–32.
Slovic, P.; Fischoff, B.; and Lichtenstein, S. 1977. "Behavioral Decision Theory." *Annual Review of Psychology* 28: 1–39.
Small, Kenneth. 1961. "Professor Goodman's Puzzle." *Philosophical Review* 70: 544–52.
Smart, J.J.C. 1950. "Excogitation and Induction." *Australasian Journal of Philosophy* 28: 191–99.
_____ . 1972. "Science, History, and Methodology." *British Journal for the Philosophy of Science* 23: 266–74.
Smith, C.A.B. 1961. "Consistency in Statistical Inference and Decision." *Journal of the Royal Statistical Society,* Series B, 23: 1–37.
_____ . 1962. "Comments on Savage." In Barnard and Cox, eds., *Foundations of Statistical Inference.* Pp. 58–62.
_____ . 1965. "Personal Probability and Statistical Analysis." *Journal of the Royal Statistical Society,* Series A., 128: 469–99.
_____ . 1977. "The Analogy between Decision and Inference." *Synthese* 36: 71–85.
Smokler, Howard. 1965. "Consistency and Rationality: A Comment." *Journal of Philosophy* 62: 77–80.
_____ . 1966a. "Goodman's Paradox and the Problem of Rules of Acceptance." *American Philosophical Quarterly* 3: 71–76.
_____ . 1966b. "Hempel: *Aspects of Scientific Explanation.*" *Synthese* 16: 110–22.
_____ . 1967. "The Equivalence Condition." *American Philosophical Quarterly* 4: 300–307.
_____ . 1968. "Conflicting Conceptions of Confirmation." *Journal of Philosophy* 65: 300–312.
_____ . 1977. "Semantical Questions in Carnap's Inductive Logic." *British Journal for the Philosophy of Science* 28: 129–35.
Smokler, Howard, and Rohr, Michael. 1969. "Confirmation and Translation." In Davis, Hockney, and Wilson, eds., *Philosophical Logic.* Pp. 172–80.
Sneed, Joseph D. 1966. "Strategy and the Logic of Decision." *Synthese* 16: 270–83.
_____ . 1967. "Entropy, Information, and Decision." *Synthese* 17: 329–407.
_____ . 1971. *The Logical Structure of Mathematical Physics.* Dordrecht: Reidel.
_____ . 1977. "Describing Revolutionary Scientific Change: A Formal Approach." In Butts and Hintikka, eds., *Historical and Philosophical Dimensions of Logic, Methodology and Philosophy of Science.* Pp. 245–68.
Sober, Elliott. 1975. *Simplicity.* Oxford: Oxford University Press.
Solomonoff, R. 1957. "An Inductive Inference Machine." *IRE National Convention Record* 2: 56–62.
Spector, M. 1966. "Theory and Observation." *British Journal for the Philosophy of Science* 17: 1–20.
Spielman, Stephen. 1972. "Lewis on Immodest Inductive Models." *Philosophy of Science* 39: 375–77.
_____ . 1973. "A Refutation of the Neyman-Pearson Theory of Testing," *British Journal for the Philosophy of Science* 24: 202–22.
_____ . 1974a. "On the Infirmities of Gillies's Rule." *British Journal for the Philosophy of Science* 25: 261–65.
_____ . 1974b. "The Logic of Tests of Significance." *Philosophy of Science* 41: 211–26.
_____ . 1976. "Bayesian Inference with Indeterminate Probabilities." In Suppe and Asquith, eds., *PSA 1976 I.* Pp. 185–96.

_____ . 1977. "Physical Probability and Bayesian Statistics." *Synthese* 36: 235–69.

_____ . 1978a. "Statistical Dogma and the Logic of Statistical Testing." *Philosophy of Science* 45: 120–35.

_____ . 1980. "Seidenfeld's Critique of Kyburgian Statistics." *Journal of Philosophy* 77: 791–97.

Staël von Holstein, C. 1973. "The Concept of Probability in Psychological Experiments." In P. Suppes, et al., eds., *Logic, Methodology and Philosophy of Science IV.* Pp. 451–66.

Stalnaker, Robert. 1968. "A Theory of Conditionals." In N. Rescher, ed., *Studies in Logical Theory.* Pp. 98–112.

_____ . 1970. "Probability and Conditionals." *Philosophy of Science* 37: 64–80.

Stegmuller, W. 1966. "Explanation, Scientific Systematization, and Non-Explanatory Information." *Ratio* 8: 1–24.

_____ . 1971. "Das Problem der Induktion: Humes Herausforderung und Moderne Antworten." In H. Lenk, ed., *Neue Aspekte der Wissenshaftstheorie.* Vieweg: Braunschweig. P. 104.

_____ . 1973a. *Personelle und Statistische Wahrseheinlichkeit.* 2 vol. Berlin and Heidelberg: Springer.

_____ . 1973b. "Carnap's Normative Theory of Inductive Probability." In P. Suppes, et al., eds., *Logic, Methodology and Philosophy of Science IV.* Pp. 501–14.

_____ . 1976a. "Accidental ('non-substantial') Theory Change and Theory Dislodgement: To What Extent Logic Can Contribute to a Better Understanding of Certain Phenomena in the Dynamics of Theories." *Erkenntis* 10: 147–78.

_____ . 1976b. *The Structure and Dynamics of Theories.* New York: Springer-Verlag.

_____ . 1978. "A Combined Approach to the Dynamics of Theories." *Theory and Decision* 9: 39–75.

Stemmer, Nathan. 1971. "Three Problems in Induction." *Synthese* 23: 287–308.

_____ . 1975a. "A Relative Notion of Natural Generalization." *Philosophy of Science* 42: 46–48.

_____ . 1975b. "The Goodman Paradox." *Zeitschrift fur Algemeine Wissenschaftstheorie* 6: 340–54.

_____ . 1978. "The Reliability of Inductive Inferences and Our Innate Capacities." *Zeitschrift fur Allgemeine Wissenshaftslehre* 9: 93–105.

Stenner, Alfred J. 1967. "A Note on 'Grue.'" *Philosophical Studies* 18: 76–78.

Stoothoff, R. H. 1963. "Day: *Inductive Probability.*" *Philosophical Quarterly* 13: 87–88.

_____ . 1965. "Katz: *The Problem of Induction and Its Solution.*" *Philosophical Quarterly* 15: 85–86.

Stopes-Roe, Harry V. 1960. "Recipes and Induction: Ryle v. Achinstein." *Analysis* 21: 115–20.

Stove, D. C. 1959. "Popperian Confirmation and the Paradox of the Ravens." *Australasian Journal of Philosophy* 37: 149–55.

_____ . 1960a. "A Reply to Mr. Watkins." *Australasian Journal of Philosophy* 38: 51–54.

_____ . 1965a. "Hempel and Goodman on the Ravens." *Australasian Journal of Philosophy* 43: 300–310.

_____ . 1965b. "Hume, Probability, and Induction." *Philosophical Review* 74: 160–77.

_____ . 1965c. "Hempel's Paradox." *Dialectica* 4: 444–55.

_____ . 1965d. "On Logical Definitions of Confirmation." *British Journal for the Philosophy of Science* 16: 265–72.

_____ . 1966. "Hempel's Paradox." *Dialogue* 4: 446.

Strawson, Peter. 1952. *Introduction to Logical Theory.* New York: John Wiley.

_____ . 1958. "On Justifying Induction." *Philosophical Studies* 9: 20–21.

Strong, John V. 1976. "The Infinite Ballot Box of Nature: DeMorgan, Boole, and Jevons on Probability and the Logic of Induction." In Suppe and Asquith, eds., *PSA 1976 I.* Pp. 197–211.

Suppes, Patrick. 1956. "Nelson Goodman on the Concept of Logical Simplicity." *Philosophy of Science* 23: 153–59.

_____ . 1960. "Some Open Problems in the Foundations of Subjective Probability." In Machol and Gray, eds., *Recent Developments in Information and Decision Processes.* Pp. 162–69.

_____ . 1966a. "A Bayesian Approach to the Paradoxes of Confirmation." In Suppes and Hintikka, eds., *Aspects of Inductive Logic.* Pp. 199–207.

_____ . 1966b. "Probabilistic Inference and the Concept of Total Evidence." In Hintikka and Suppes, eds., *Aspects of Inductive Logic.* Pp. 50–65.

_____ . 1966c. "Concept Formation and Bayesian Decisions." In Hintikka and Suppes, eds.,

Aspects of Inductive Logic. Pp. 21–48.

———. 1974a. "The Structure of Theories and the Analysis of Data." In P. Suppes, ed., *The Structure of Scientific Theories.* Pp. 266–83.

———. 1974b. "The Measurement of Belief." *Journal of the Royal Statistical Society,* Series B, 36: 160–91.

———. 1976. "Testing Theories and the Foundations of Statistics." In Harper and Hooker, eds., *Foundations of Probability Theory, Statistical Inference, and Statistical Theories of Science* II. Pp. 437–55.

Svenonius, Lars. 1955. "Definability and Simplicity." *Journal of Symbolic Logic* 20: 235–50.

Swain, Marshal. 1970. "The Consistency of Rational Belief." In M. Swain, ed., *Induction, Acceptance, and Rational Belief.* Pp. 27–54.

Sweigart, John S., and Stewart, John P. 1959. "Another Look at Fact, Fiction, and Forecast." *Philosophical Studies* 10: 81–89.

Swinburne, R. G. 1967. "Grue." *Analysis* 28: 123–28.

———. 1970. "Choosing Between Confirmation Theories." *Philosophy of Science* 37: 602–13.

———. 1971a. "The Probability of Particular Events." *Philosophy of Science* 38: 327–43.

———. 1971b. "The Paradoxes of Confirmation—a Survey." *American Philosophical Quarterly* 8: 318–30.

———. 1971c. "Probability, Credibility, and Acceptability." *American Philosophical Quarterly* 8: 275–83.

———. 1973. *An Introduction to Confirmation Theory* London: Methuen.

———. 1974. "Meaningfulness without Confirmability: A Reply." *Analysis* 35: 22–27.

———. 1980. "Properties, Causation, and Projectability." In Cohen and Hesse, eds., *Applications of Inductive Logic.* Pp. 313–20.

Szaniawski, Klemens. 1967. "The Value of Perfect Information." *Synthese* 17: 408–24.

———. 1976. "On Sequential Inference." In R. Bogdan, ed., *Local Induction.* Pp. 171–82.

———. 1977a. "A Method of Deciding between *N* Statistical Hypotheses." In Przelecki and Wojcicki, eds., *Twenty-Five Years of Logical Methodology in Poland.* Pp. 615–23.

———. 1977b. Interpretations of the Maximum Likelihood Principle." In Przelecki and Wojcicki, eds., *Twenty-Five Years of Logical Methodology in Poland.* Pp. 625–34.

Teller, Paul. 1969. "Goodman's Theory of Projection." *British Journal for the Philosophy of Science* 20: 219–38.

———. 1973. "Conditionalization and Observation." *Synthese* 26: 218–58.

———. 1975a. "Shimony's *a priori* Arguments for Tempered Personalism." In Maxwell and Anderson, eds., *Minnesota Studies in the Philosophy of Science VI.* Pp. 166–203.

———. 1975b. "Comments on 'Confirmation and Parsimony.'" In Maxwell and Anderson, eds., *Minnesota Studies in the Philosophy of Science VI.* Pp. 343–46.

———. 1976. "Conditionalization, Observation and Change of Preference." In Harper and Hooker, eds., *Foundations of Probability Theory, Statistical Inferences and Statistical Scientific Theories* I. Pp. 205–59.

———. 1980. "Zealous Acceptance." In Cohen and Hesse, eds., *Applications of Inductive Logic.* Pp. 28–53.

Teller, Paul, and Fine, Arthur. 1975. "A Characterization of Conditional Probability." *Mathematics Magazine* 48: 267–70.

Thompson, Judith Jarvis. 1966a. "Grue." *Journal of Philosophy* 62: 529–34.

———. 1966b. "More Grue." *Journal of Philosophy* 62: 529–34.

Tibbetts, Paul E. 1980. "The Weighted Coherence Theory of Rationality and Justification: A Critique and Alternative." *Philosophy of Social Science* 10: 259–72.

Tichy, Pavel. 1974. "On Popper's Definition of Verisimilitude." *British Journal for the Philosophy of Science* 25: 155–60.

Todd, William. 1964. "Counterfactual Conditions and the Presuppositions of Induction." *Philosophy of Science* 31: 101–10.

———. 1967. "Probability and the Theory of Confirmation." *Mind* 76: 260–63.

Törnebohn, Haken. 1964. *Information and Confirmation.* Göteborg: University of Göteborg.

———. 1966. "Two Measures of Evidential Strength." In Hintikka and Suppes, eds., *Aspects of Inductive Logic.* Pp. 81–95.

———. 1976. "On Piecemeal Knowledge-Formation." In R. Bogdan, ed., *Local Induction.* Pp. 297–318.

Torretti, Roberto. 1972. "Remarks on Salmon's Paradox of Primes." *Philosophy of Science* 39: 260–62.

Toulmin, Stephen. 1956. "On Probability." In A. Flew, ed., *Essays in Conceptual Analysis*. Pp. 157–91.

_____. 1958. *The Uses of Argument*. Cambridge: Cambridge University Press.

_____. 1970. "Does the Distinction between Normal and Revolutionary Science Hold Water?" In Lakatos and Musgrave, eds., *Criticism and the Growth of Knowledge*. Pp. 39–47.

_____. 1972. *Human Knowledge*. Princeton: Princeton University Press.

_____. 1974. "Rationality and Scientific Discovery." In Schaffner and Cohen, eds., *PSA 1972*. Pp. 387–406.

Tricker, Ronald A. R. 1965. *The Assessment of Scientific Speculation: A Survey of Certain Current Views*. London: Miles and Boon.

Tukey, John W. 1960. "Conclusions versus Decision." *Technometrics* 2: 423–33.

Tuomela, Raimo. 1966. "Inductive Generalization in an Ordered Universe." In Hintikka and Suppes, eds., *Aspects of Inductive Logic*. Pp. 155–74.

_____. 1973. *Theoretical Concepts*. New York and Vienna: Springer-Verlag.

_____. 1976. "Confirmation, Explanation, and the Paradoxes of Transitivity." In R. Bogdan, ed., *Local Induction*. Pp. 319–28.

Uchii, Soshichi. 1972. "Inductive Logic with Causal Modalities: A Probabilistic Approach." *Philosophy of Science* 39: 162–78.

_____. 1973a. "Inductive Logic with Causal Modalities: A Deterministic Approach." *Synthese* 26: 264–303.

_____. 1973b. "Higher Order Probabilities and Coherence." *Philosophy of Science* 40: 373–81.

_____. 1977. "Induction and Causality in a Cellular Space." In Suppe and Asquith, eds., *PSA 1976 II*. Pp. 448–61.

Uemov, A. I. 1970. "The Basic Forms and Rules of Inference by Analogy." In P. V. Tavanec, ed., *Problems of the Logic of Scientific Knowledge*. Pp. 266–331.

Ullian, J. S. 1961. "More on 'Grue' and Grue." *Philosophical Review* 70: 386–89.

van Fraassen, Bas C. 1972. "Probabilities and the Problem of Individuation." In S. Luckenbach, ed., *Probabilities, Problems, and Paradoxes*. Pp. 121–38.

_____. 1976. "Probabilities of Conditionals." In Harper and Hooker, eds., *Foundations of Probability Theory, Statistical Inference, and Statistical Theories of Science* I. Pp. 261–308.

_____. 1979. "Relative Frequencies." In W. C. Salmon, ed., *Hans Reichenbach: Logical Empiricist*. Pp. 129–67.

_____. 1980a. "Rational Belief and Probability Kinematics." *Philosophy of Science* 47: 165–87.

_____. 1980b. *The Scientific Image*. Cambridge: Cambridge University Press.

Vetter, Herman. 1969. "Logical Probability, Mathemtical Statistics, and the Problem of Induction." *Synthese* 20: 56–71.

_____. 1971. "Inductivism and Falsificationism Reconcilable." *Synthese* 23: 226–33.

Vickers, John M. 1965. "Some Remarks on Coherence and Subjective Probability." *Philosophy of Science* 32: 32–38.

_____. 1966. "Some Features of Theories of Belief." *Journal of Philosophy* 63: 197–201.

_____. 1967. Characteristics of Projectible Predicates." *Journal of Philosophy* 64: 280–86.

_____. 1969. "Judgement and Belief." In K. Lambert, ed., *The Logical Way of Doing Things*. Pp. 39–64.

_____. 1970. "Probability and Non-Standard Logics." In K. Lambert, ed., *Philosophical Problems in Logic*. Pp. 102–20.

_____. 1973. "Rules for Reasonable Belief Change." In Bogdan and Niiniluoto, eds., *Logic, Language, and Probability*. Pp. 129–42.

_____. 1976. *Belief and Probability*. Dordrecht: Reidel.

Vincent, R. H. 1961. "A Note on Some Quantitative Theories of Confirmation." *Philosophical Studies* 12: 91–92.

_____. 1962a. "Popper on Qualitative Confirmation and Disconfirmation." *Australasian Journal of Philosophy* 40: 159–66.

_____. 1962b. "The Paradox of Ideal Evidence." *Philosophical Review* 71: 497–503.

_____. 1963a. "Discussion Concerning an Alleged Contradiction." *Philosophy of Science* 30: 189–94.

_____. 1963b. "On My Cognitive Sensibility." *Philosophical Studies* 14: 77–79.

_____. 1963c. "Corroboration and Probability." *Dialectica* 2: 194–205.

_____. 1963d. "Leblanc: *Statistical and Inductive Probabilities*." *Dialectica* 2: 475–80.

_____. 1964a. "The Problem of the Unexamined Individual." *Mind* 73: 550–56.

_____. 1964b. "The Paradoxes of Confirmation." *Mind* 73: 273–79.

Walk, Kurt. 1966. "Simplicity, Entropy, and Inductive Logic." In Hintikka and Suppes, eds., *Aspects of Inductive Logic.* Pp. 66–80.

Wallace, John R. 1965. "Goodman, Logic, Induction." *Journal of Philosophy* 63: 310–28.

Warnock, G. J. 1960. "Popper: *The Logic of Scientific Discovery.*" *Mind* 69: 99–101.

Watkins, J.W.N. 1957. "Between Analytic and Empirical." *Philosophy* 32: 112–31.

———. 1959a. "Mr. Stove's Blunders." *Australasian Journal of Philosophy* 37: 240–41.

———. 1959b. "Confirmation Without Background Knowledge." *British Journal for the Philosophy of Science* 10: 318–20.

———. 1960. "A Reply to Mr. Stove's Reply." *Australasian Journal of Philosophy* 38: 54–58.

———. 1961. "Professor Scheffler's Note." *Philosophical Studies* 12: 16–19.

———. 1970. "Against 'Normal Science.'" In Lakatos and Musgrave, eds., *Criticism and the Growth of Knowledge.* Pp. 25–37.

Wetterstein, John R. 1975. "Good's Compromise: Comments on I. J. Good." *Synthese* 30: 79–82.

Weyland, F. 1964. "A Note on 'Knowledge, Certainty, and Probability.'" *Inquiry* 7: 417.

Wheatley, Jon. 1966. "Entrenchment and Engagement." *Analysis* 27: 119–27.

White, Alan R. 1972. "The Propensity Theory of Probability." *British Journal for the Philosophy of Science* 23: 35–43.

Will, Frederick L. 1965. "The Preferability of Probable Beliefs." *Journal of Philosophy* 62: 57–67.

———. 1966. "Consequences and Confirmation." *Philosophical Review* 75: 34–58.

———. 1974. *Induction and Justification.* Ithaca, N.Y.: Cornell University Press.

Williams, Donald C. 1947. *The Ground of Induction.* Cambridge, Mass.: Harvard University Press.

———. 1953. "On the Direct Probability of Induction." *Mind* 62: 465–83.

Williams, J. S. 1966. "The Role of Probability in Fiducial Inference." *Sankhyā,* Series A, 28: 271–96.

Williams, L. Pearce. 1970. "Normal Science, Scientific Revolutions, and the History of Science." In Lakatos and Musgrave, eds., *Criticism and the Growth of Knowledge.* Pp. 49–50.

Williams, P. M. 1968. "The Structure of Acceptance and its Evidential Base." *Philosophy of Science* 19: 325–44.

———. 1974. "Indeterminate Probabilities." In Przelecki and Wojcicki, eds., *Formal Methods in the Methodology of Empirical Sciences.* Pp. 229–46.

Wilson, P. R. 1964a. "A New Approach to the Confirmation Paradox." *Australasian Journal of Philosophy* 42: 393–401.

———. 1964b. "On the Argument by Analogy." *Philosophy of Science* 31: 34–39.

———. 1964c. "On the Confirmation Paradox." *British Journal for the Philosophy of Science* 15: 196–99.

Winograd, Terry. 1980. "Extended Inference Modes in Reasoning by Computer Systems." In Cohen and Hesse, eds., *Applications of Inductive Logic.* Pp. 333–58.

Wisdom, John Oulton. 1952. *Foundations of Inference in Natural Science.* London: Methuen.

Workman, Rollin W. 1962. "Two Extralogical Uses of the Principle of Induction." *Philosophical Studies* 13: 27–32.

Wright, G. H. von. 1951. *A Treatise on Induction and Probability.* New York: Harcourt Brace.

———. 1966. "The Paradoxes of Confirmation." In Hintikka and Suppes, eds., *Aspects of Inductive Logic.* Pp. 208–19.

———. 1970. "A Note on Confirmation Theory and the Concept of Evidence." *Scientia:* 1–21.

Yates, F. 1964. "Fiducial Probability, Recognizable Subsets, and Behren's Test." *Biometrics* 20: 343–60.

Ziemba, Z. 1977. "Rational Belief, Probability, and the Justification of Inductive Inference." In Przelecki and Wojcicki, eds., *Twenty-Five Years of Logical Methodology in Poland.* Pp. 709–35.

Ziff, Paul. 1972. "Something About Conceptual Schemes." In Pearce and Maynard, eds., *Conceptual Change.* Pp. 31–41.

Bibliography: Edited Volumes

Anonymous, ed. 1962. *Logic and Language.* Dordrecht: Reidel.

Arm, David L., ed. 1968. *Vistas in Science.* Albuquerque: University of New Mexico Press.

Arruda, da Costa, and Chuaqui, eds. 1977. *Non-Classical Logics, Model Theory, and Comput-*

ability. Amsterdam: North-Holland.

Asquith, Peter D., and Hacking, Ian, eds. 1978. *PSA 1978 I*. East Lansing, Mich.: Philosophy of Science Association.

Asquith, Peter, and Kyburg, Henry E. Jr., eds. 1979. *Current Research in Philosophy of Science*. East Lansing, Mich.: Philosophy of Science Association.

Bar-Hillel, Y., ed. 1965. *Logic, Methodology, and Philosophy of Science II*. Amsterdam: North-Holland.

Barnard, George A., and Cox, D. R., eds. 1962. *The Foundations of Statistical Inference*. New York: John Wiley & Sons.

Baumrin, Bernard, ed. 1963. *Philosophy of Science*. New York: John Wiley & Sons.

Benn, S. I., and Mortimore, G. W., eds. 1976. *Rationality in the Social Sciences*. London: Routledge and Kegan Paul.

Black, Max, ed. 1949. *Language and Philosophy*. Ithaca, N.Y.: Cornell University Press.

———, ed. 1950. *Philosophical Analysis*. Englewood Cliffs, N.J.: Prentice-Hall. Reprint 1963.

———, ed. 1954. *Problems of Analysis*. Ithaca, N.Y.: Cornell University Press.

Bogdan, Radu, ed. 1976. *Local Induction*. Dordrecht: Reidel.

Bogdan, Radu, and Niiniluoto, Ilkka, eds. 1974. *Logic, Language and Probability*. Dordrecht: Reidel.

Buck, Roger, and Cohen, Robert, eds. 1971. *PSA 1970*. Dordrecht: Reidel.

Butts, Robert E., and Hintikka, Jaakko, eds. 1977. *Basic Problems in Methodology and Linguistics*. Dordrecht: Reidel.

———, ed. 1977. *Historical and Philosophical Dimensions of Logic, Methodology, and Philosophy of Science*. Dordrecht: Reidel.

Carnap, Rudolf, and Jeffrey, Richard, eds. 1971. *Studies in Inductive Logic and Probability I*. Berkeley: University of California Press.

Cherry, Colin, ed. 1974. *Pragmatic Aspects of Human Communication*. Dordrecht: Reidel.

Cohen, Jonathan, and Hesse, Mary, eds. 1980. *Applications of Inductive Logic*. Oxford: Oxford University Press.

Cohen, Robert S., and Wartofsky, Marx W., eds. 1974. *Proceedings of the Boston Colloquium for the Philosophy of Science 1969/1972*. Dordrecht: Reidel.

Cohen, Robert S.; Feyerabend, Paul K.; and Wartofsky, Marx W., eds. 1976. *Essays in Memory of Imre Lakatos*. Dordrecht: Reidel.

Colodny, Robert G., ed. 1965. *Beyond the Edge of Certainty*. Englewood Cliffs, N.J.: Prentice-Hall.

———, ed. 1966. *Mind and Cosmos*. Pittsburgh: University of Pittsburgh Press.

———, ed. 1970. *The Nature and Function of Scientific Theories*. Pittsburgh: University of Pittsburgh Press.

———, ed. 1977. *Logic, Laws and Life*. Pittsburgh: University of Pittsburgh Press.

Crossley, J. N., ed. 1967. *Sets, Models and Recursion Theory*. Amsterdam: North-Holland.

Crossley, J. N., and Dummett, M.A.E., eds. 1965. *Formal Systems and Recursive Functions*. Amsterdam: North-Holland.

Davis, J. W.; Hockney, D. J.; and Wilson, W. K., eds. 1969. *Philosophical Logic*. Dordrecht: Reidel.

Feigl, Herbert, and Maxwell, Grover, eds. 1961. *Current Issues in the Philosophy of Science*. New York: Holt, Rinehart & Winston.

———, eds. 1962. *Minnesota Studies in the Philosophy of Science III*. Minneapolis: University of Minnesota Press.

Feigl, Herbert; Scriven, Michael; and Maxwell, Grover, eds. 1958. *Minnesota Studies in Philosophy of Science II*. Minneapolis: University of Minnesota Press.

Feyerabend, Paul, and Maxwell, Grover, eds. 1966. *Mind, Matter and Method*. Minneapolis: University of Minnesota Press.

Flew, Anthony, ed. 1956. *Essays in Conceptual Analysis*. London: Macmillan & Co.

Foster, Lawrence, and Swanson, J. W., eds. 1970. *Experience and Theory*. Amherst: University of Massachusetts Press.

Frank, Philipp, G., ed. 1954. *The Validation of Scientific Theories*. Boston: Beacon Press.

Godambe, V. P., and Sprott, D. A., eds. 1971. *Foundations of Statistical Inference*. Toronto: Holt, Rinehart & Winston of Canada.

Gregg, John R., and Harris, F.T.C., eds. 1964. *Form and Strategy in Science*. Dordrecht: Reidel.

Gulliksen, Harold, and Messick, Samuel, eds. 1960. *Psychological Scaling*. New York: John Wiley.

Harper, William, and Hooker, C. S., eds. 1976. *Foundations of Probability Theory, Statistical Inference, and Statistical Theories of Science.* 3 vols. Dordrecht: Reidel.

Hintikka, Jaakko, ed. 1975. *Rudolf Carnap: Logical Empiricist.* Dordrecht: Reidel.

Hintikka, Jaakko, and Suppes, Patrick, eds. 1966. *Aspects of Inductive Logic.* Amsterdam: North-Holland.

_____, eds. 1970. *Information and Inference.* Dordrecht: Reidel.

Hooker, C. A.; Leach, J.; and McClennen, E., eds. 1978. *Foundations and Applications of Decision Theory I.* Dordrecht: Reidel.

Jeffrey, Richard C., ed. 1980. *Studies in Inductive Logic and Probability II.* Berkeley: University of California Press.

Körner, Stefan, ed. 1957. *Observation and Interpretation.* New York: Academic Press.

Kyburg, Henry E., Jr., and Nagel, Ernest, eds. 1963. *Induction: Some Current Issues.* Middletown, Conn.: Wesleyan University Press.

Kyburg, Henry E., Jr., and Smokler, Howard, eds. 1964. *Studies in Subjective Probability.* 1st ed., New York: John Wiley & Sons.

_____, eds. 1980. *Studies in Subjective Probability.* 2nd ed., Huntington, N.Y.: Krieger.

Lakatos, Imre, ed. 1968. *The Problem of Inductive Logic.* Amsterdam: North-Holland.

Lakatos, Imre, and Musgrave, Alan, eds. 1970. *Criticism and the Growth of Knowledge.* Cambridge: Cambridge University Press.

Lambert, Karel, ed. 1969. *The Logical Way of Doing Things.* New Haven, Conn.: Yale University Press.

_____, ed. 1970. *Philosophical Problems in Logic.* Dordrecht: Reidel.

Lehrer, Keith, ed. 1975. *Analysis and Metaphysics.* Dordrecht: Reidel.

Leinfellner, Werner, and Kohler, Eckhard, eds. 1974. *Developments in Methodology of Social Science.* Dordrecht: Reidel.

Lenk, Hans, ed. 1971. *Neue Aspekte der Wissenshaftstheorie.* Braunschweig: F. Vieweg.

Luckenbach, Sidney A., ed. 1972. *Probabilities, Problems, and Paradoxes.* Encino and Belmont, Calif.: Dickenson.

Machamer, Peter, and Turnbull, Robert, eds. 1978. *Studies in Perception.* Columbus: Ohio State University Press.

Machol, Robert Engel, and Gray, Paul, eds. 1962. *Recent Developments in Information and Decision Processes.* New York: Macmillan.

Maxwell, Grover, and Anderson, Robert, eds. 1975. *Minnesota Studies in the Philosophy of Science VI.* Minneapolis: University of Minnesota Press.

Mellor, D. H., ed. 1980. *Science, Belief, and Behaviour.* Cambridge: Cambridge University Press.

Michie, Donald, ed. 1974. *On Machine Intelligence.* New York: John Wiley.

Morgenbesser, Sidney, ed. 1967. *Philosophy of Science Today.* New York: Basic Books.

Morgenbesser, Sidney; Suppes, Patrick; and White, Morton, eds. 1969. *Philosophy, Science, and Method.* New York: St. Martin's Press.

Nagel, Ernest; Suppes, Patrick; and Traski, Alfred, eds. 1962. *Logic Methodology and the Philosophy of Science.* Stanford, Calif.: Stanford University Press.

Nakhnikian, George, ed. 1974. *Bertrand Russell's Philosophy.* London: Duckworth.

Nickles, Thomas, ed. 1980. *Scientific Discovery, Logic, and Rationality.* Dordrecht: Reidel.

Niiniluoto, Ilkka, and Tuomela, Raimo, eds. 1978. *The Logic and Epistemology of Scientific Change, Acta Philosophica Fennica 30.* Amsterdam: North-Holland.

Olkin, Ingram, ed. 1960. *Contributions to Probability and Statistics.* Stanford, Calif.: Stanford University Press.

Pearce, Glenn, and Maynard, Patrick, eds. 1973. *Conceptual Change.* Dordrecht: Reidel.

Przelcki, Marian, and Wojcicki, R., eds. 1974. *Formal Methods in the Methodology of the Empirical Sciences.* Dordrecht: Reidel.

_____, eds. 1977. *Twenty-Five Years of Logical Methodology in Poland.* Dordrecht: Reidel.

Radner, Michael, and Winokur, Stephen, eds. 1970. *Minnesota Studies in the Philosophy of Science IV.* Minneapolis: University of Minnesota Press.

Rescher, Nicholas, ed. 1968. *Studies in Logical Theory, American Philosophical Quarterly Monograph Series Number 2.* Oxford: Basil Blackwell.

_____, ed. 1970. *Essays in Honor of Carl G. Hempel.* Dordrecht: Reidel.

Ringle, Martin, ed. 1979. *Philosophical Perspectives in Artificial Intelligence.* Atlantic Highlands, N.J.: Humanities Press.

Salmon, Wesley C., ed. 1979. *Hans Reichenbach: Logical Empiricist.* Dordrecht: Reidel.

Schaffner, Kenneth, and Cohen, Robert, eds. 1974. *PSA 1972.* Dordrecht: Reidel.

Schilpp, P. A., ed. 1963. *The Philosophy of Rudolf Carnap*. La Salle, Ill.: Open Court.

Staël von Holstein, Carl-Axel S., ed. 1974. *The Concept of Probability in Psychological Experiments*. Dordrecht: Reidel.

Stuewer, Roger H., ed. 1970. *Minnesota Studies in the Philosophy of Science V*. Minneapolis: University of Minnesota Press.

Suppe, Frederick, ed. 1974. *The Structure of Scientific Theories*. Urbana, Ill.: University of Illinois Press.

Suppe, Frederick, and Asquith, Peter, eds. 1977. *PSA 1976*. 2 vols. East Lansing, Mich.: Philosophy of Science Association.

Suppes, Patrick, et al., eds. 1971. *Logic Methodology and Philosophy of Science IV*. Amsterdam: North-Holland.

Swain, Marshall, ed. 1970. *Induction, Acceptance and Rational Belief*. Dordrecht: Reidel.

Swinburne, Richard, ed. 1974. *The Justification of Induction*. Oxford: Oxford University Press.

Tavanec, P. V., ed. 1970. *Problems of the Logic of Scientific Knowledge*. Dordrecht: Reidel.

von Wright, G. H., and Floistad, G., eds. 1980. *Philosophy of Logic*. The Hague: Nijhoff.

Weingartner, Paul, and Zecha, Gerhard, eds. 1970. *Induction, Physics, and Ethics*. Dordrecht: Reidel.

PART III

Philosophy of Mind

chapter 4

---◆---

Current Issues in the Philosophy of Mind

D. C. DENNETT

The philosophy of mind is one of the most active fields in philosophy today. It has changed so drastically in the last twenty years that many of the traditionally central topics and theories have been transformed almost beyond recognition, and new concerns now loom that have no clear ancestors in the old tradition. An assessment of current work requires an understanding of recently evolved assumptions about the burdens and goals of the field, which can best be provided by a brief history of the shifts of outlook in recent years.*

I. Investigating the Language of Mind

The new era in philosophy of mind can be dated from the publication in 1949 of Gilbert Ryle's *The Concept of Mind.* In that book Ryle argued that the philosophy of mind rested on a colossal error, a "category mistake" that had in effect given birth to a whole field of investigation—the philosophy of mind—where none ought to be; the questions composing the inquiry were so radically misconceived that straightforward attempts to answer them ineluctably led to nonsense. Before Ryle there had been *theories* of mind—such redoubtable "isms" as idealism, materialism, neutral monism, epiphenomenalism, interactionism—contending in an arena of shared assumptions about the nature of the problem defining the field: the mind-body problem. Ryle suggested there was no such problem at all but only a confusion bred in an injudicious and insensitive use—or abuse—of the ordinary language we use in everyday life to aver the familiar facts of mentality that comprise the data for any investigation or science of the mind.

A careful *analysis* of the ways of common talk about the mind would dissipate the confusions, dissolve the problems, and thus render otiose both dualism and its negation, monism, and among varieties of monism, both idealism and its opposite, materialism—in short, all the rival metaphysical views that had been the chief product

*This overview was originally commissioned by the American Journal of Psychiatry, which eventually declined it on the grounds of being "much beyond" its readership. The somewhat elementary tone of the paper is explained by its originally intended audience. I am indebted to Ned Block, Jeff Titon, Bo Dahlbom, and Sue Stafford for valuable criticisms of earlier drafts of this paper.

of the field. Ryle's work was the major entry of what came to be called *ordinary language philosophy* into the philosophy of mind, and its influence should be measured not by a census of converts (philosophies seldom display their influence by attracting proponents, but rather by remaining controversial for long periods of time), but by the fact that for more than a decade after the appearance of *The Concept of Mind, theories* of mind were unfashionable to the point of extinction. Theories were held to be the creations of those who had failed to see that the problems — at least the problems philosophers were equipped to address — arose from mistaken and naive assumptions about the way mind-words worked in the language. Theory-construction was replaced by the much more cautious and modest activity of "conceptual analysis": the delicate and persistent, if informal and unsystematic, canvasing of the idioms of ordinary language, the collective product of which is a broad and still largely unsystematized array of acutely observed distinctions and nuances, adduced in the course of making usually quite small points about various mental concepts. At its best, in the work of Ryle (1949), Wittgenstein (1953), Anscombe (1957) and Austin (1961, 1962), this method uncovered deep conceptual issues that still shape current thinking and will continue to do so. At its worst, like the worst in any field, it produced mountains of trivia; but in the middle there was a good deal of very clever and useful work, whose point was seldom to solve problems and almost never to advance general theories, but typically to alert the incautious to the existence of more problems and distinctions than one would have expected (see Wisdom, 1946; Urmson, 1952; Warnock, 1954; Peters, 1958; Ryle, 1958; White, 1959–60; Melden, 1961; and Gustafson, 1967). There seemed in those days to be very little in the way of a substantial generalization that could be defensibly advanced.

The basic tactic then was "semantic ascent" (Quine, 1960); when one runs into perplexities when talking about things (in this case, minds, sensations, thoughts and the like), it often helps to shift one's focus and talk about how to talk about those things, about "what one would ordinarily say" under various circumstances, or (if one is not enthralled by *ordinary* language) what one *ought* to say under various circumstances. There is no denying the value of the tactic, as the great work in the field amply demonstrates; but contrary to the creed of many at the time, it has not turned out that *all* the problems in philosophy of mind evaporate under linguistic analysis, and it is fair to say that a great deal of the researches into ordinary idiom failed to produce anything more important or enlightening than an intense appreciation for the subtlety of English expression. Moreover, although semantic ascent excuses one from expounding or defending an "ism," it does not permit one to operate innocent of assumptions, assumptions that ultimately implicate one in something rather like a theory. Typically (for Ryle, Malcolm, Anscombe and many others) the tacit theory was "logical behaviorism," the view that the truth of ascriptions of mental states and events implies and is implied by the truth of various statements purely about behavior. There were dissenters from this view: Strawson (1959), for instance, apparently committed himself to a cryptic revival of the *double-aspect theory* (a *person* is not to be analyzed into a body plus a mind, but is nevertheless a proper subject of both mental and physical attributes), and on Shaffer's analysis (1961), ordinary language was held to incorporate dualism.

This tendency to evince theory in the course of conceptual analysis had the effect, at least in its most virulent forms, of squandering the useful indirectness of semantic ascent altogether, and bodies of doctrine emerged that looked suspiciously like the old metaphysical theories about the *things* (minds, sensations, thoughts), though generated from considerations scrupulously restricted to *words* ("mind," "sensation," "thought"). This was not a happy development. Perhaps you can learn all about the *concept* of a horse by studying the way we ordinarily use the word "horse," and no doubt you can learn a great deal about horses from studying the concept of a horse (since much of what people *think* is true of horses is embodied somehow in our concept), but in the end there are some left-over facts about horses of nonnegligible interest and even puzzlement that can be discovered only by looking at a horse or two, or at least by reading the works of those who have taken the trouble to do this.

II. *Philosophy of Mind Naturalized*

Ordinary language philosophy of mind has now played itself out to the point where it can be comfortably viewed as a historical phenomenon. As an essentially critical and reactive discipline, it was bound to die of its own successes when it had run out of important errors and confusions to diagnose, while its infirmities became more apparent as it descended into trivia. Although its most characteristic doctrines and methods have been widely rejected or abandoned, its contributions to current thinking are positive and pervasive. Most important, the new way with words really did destroy the traditional way of composing a philosophical theory of mind. The traditional theorists were guilty, as charged, of making aprioristic generalizations, which were nothing if not the products of (ill-considered and unself-conscious) conceptual analysis, mixing these with a handful of casual introspections and observations about normal people's experiences and powers, and promoting the mixture to the status of metaphysical verities about the essences of things mental. If there were to be theories of mind at all, they were not to be produced by the old armchair methods, so the philosopher of mind had three choices: abandon philosophy and pursue empirical theories in the domain of psychology or brain science, abandon theory and settle for the modest illuminations and confusion-cures of purely linguistic analysis, or become a sort of meta-theorist, a conceptual critic of the empirical theories advanced by the relevant sciences. It is this last conception of the enterprise, where it is seen as a branch of philosophy of science, that dominates the best work in the field today. Its most salient difference from both the traditional theorizing and the ordinary language approach is its interest in the theories and data of psychology, the brain sciences, artificial intelligence, and linguistics.

In 1932, H. H. Price's classic work, *Perception* contained a succinct apology for the philosopher's ignorance of science: our grounds for believing the physiological accounts of perception "are derived from observation, and mainly if not entirely from visual observation." But the reliability of observation is just what is at issue for the epistemologist, and "since the premises of Physiology are among the propositions into whose validity we are inquiring, it is hardly likely that its conclusions will assist us." As long as one is engaged in a Cartesian attempt to justify all knowledge from scratch, from whatever minimal foundation can be protected from systematic skepticism, this familiar rationale can be maintained (though it provides no good reason not to *peek* at physiology). Such foundationalism in epistemology and philosophy generally is now on the wane, replaced by a "naturalistic" attitude (not a theory) that assumes from the outset that by and large our quotidian beliefs are true and warranted, that epistemology can learn from psychology, and that the best way to derive the canons of justification is to see how good science is done. (The attitude is well expressed by Quine, one if its most influential promoters, in "Epistemology Naturalized," 1969.)

The danger of this drift might seem to be that it leaves philosophy with no standpoint from which to launch truly radical critiques of current science, but this is probably a misconceived worry, for the history of science suggests that revolutions in scientific thought must be internally bred. Still, the claim that the new naturalism is a capitulation to the excessive prestige of modern science has something to be said for it, although it should not be forgotten that philosophy's current friendship with science is not a novelty. The great philosophy of the 17th century, for instance, was in intimate communication with the contemporaneous birth of modern science and contributed as much to that infancy as it gained in return. In any event, philosophers have discovered a vein that will be mined, very probably to the mutual enlightenment of science and philosophy.

While this emergence from the intellectual isolationism of the recent past is thus a logical development out of the best in the linguistic analysis tradition, it nevertheless required the rejection of a troika of doctrines central to that tradition: verificationism, logical behaviorism, and what might be called conceptual conservatism. In its most exigent form, verificationism is the doctrine that the method of verifying the application of a term just *is* its meaning; in its milder forms verificationism maintains that claims that cannot in principle be verified are senseless. This surviving brainchild of logical positivism is a plausible enough doctrine until one gets severe or doctrinaire about what is to count as verifiability, as typically happens. Consider, for instance, this simplified statement of the notorious "problem of other minds." How do I know that other people have minds? I cannot directly see or otherwise sense their minds (as I can introspect my own); all I have for data are observed facts about their behavior. Perhaps their behavior is good inductive *evidence* for the existence of their minds. But it could not be, for in order to establish that it was good evidence, we would have to have *confirmed* cases of the co-occurrence of such behavior with other minds, and this requires, *per impossibile*, an independent method of verifying the existence at those times of those other minds. As the slogan had it, something can be a *symptom* of *x* only if something else is the *criterion* of *x* (Albritton, 1959; Lycan, 1971). Criteria were thought to be not (merely) *empirically reliable* but rather *logically sufficient* or at least *decisive* or "certainty-providing" indicators of whatever they were criteria for. Then, since an appeal to ordinary language shows that the claim that there are other minds is not senseless (the man in the street knows full well there are other minds), it must be verifiable, and since the only evidence by which to verify it is behavioral, and since symptomatic evidence is logically dependent on criterial evidence, *there must be purely behavioral criteria for all (meaningful) claims about other minds.* Thus is logical behaviorism born of verificationism. But now suppose some mental item, say *pain*, does have purely behavioral criteria. That means that the assertion that someone is in pain is really (logically equivalent to) a statement about that person's behavior or dispositions to behave. But no statement about inner physiological happenings could be logically equivalent to a statement just about a person's overt behavior, so the truths of physiology, whatever they turn out to be, are *irrelevant*—except symptomatically—to the truth of claims about pain. Since the concept of pain has behavioral criteria, it cannot also have physiological criteria. Were scientists to propose physiological criteria for pain, they would be "proposing a new concept" of pain, and anything they told us about *their* sort of pain would not be about our *ordinary* concept of pain at all. Science cannot revise or improve on ordinary concepts, but is bound to abide by the criteria of use enshrined in ordinary language, on pain of either changing the topic or talking nonsense. Thus is conceptual conservatism born out of logical behaviorism.

The development of this line of thought in the literature was immeasurably more subtle, guarded, and attenuated by provisos and acknowledgments than the sketch of it given here (see, e.g., Lycan, 1971) and of course there was much in it that was true, but it lent support to a dubious claim; if psychologists and neurophysiologists thought they could study the mind, they were wrong; the study of mind was the study of (ordinary) mental *concepts,* and since these had ordinary behavioral criteria of application, once these criteria had been adumbrated by philosophers, there was nothing left to do. This message was intolerable even to many of the adherents of the method of ordinary language analysis that had led to this embarrassing result. It was the work of many hands to dismantle the edifice of argument and assumption that led to this impasse, but the whole process is graphically epitomized by Putnam's classic attack (1962) on Malcolm (1956, 1959), by Fodor's polemics against Ryle (1968, 1975) and by Chihara and Fodor (1965).

III. The Identity Theory and Its Descendants

The first proclaimed alternative to logical behaviorism to draw serious attention was the identity theory of mind: minds are brains, and the contents of minds—pains, thoughts, sensations, and the like—just *are* (identical with) various happenings, processes, and states of our brains. The early papers supporting the identity theory, by Place (1956), Feigl (1958, 1967), Smart (1959, 1963), and Armstrong (1968) had the flavor of manifestos; their point was to secure as directly as possible what was deemed to be the requisite conceptual foundation for a purely physicalistic or materialistic science of the mind, a bulwark against both the impertinent dismissals of the logical behaviorists and the metaphysical excesses of dualistic alternatives.

Since it is widely granted these days that dualism is not a serious view to contend with, but rather a cliff over which to push one's opponents, a capsule "refutation" of dualism, to alert if not convince the uninitiated, is perhaps in order. Suppose, with the dualists, that there are nonphysical effects (or accompaniments) of brain events. Then either the occurrence of these effects has itself *no effect whatsoever* on subsequent events in the brain (and hence behavior) of the person (epiphenomenalism), or it does (interactionistic or Cartesian dualism). In the former case the postulation of the nonphysical effects is utterly idle, for *ex hypothesi* were the effects to cease to occur (other things remaining the same), people would go right on making the same sorts of introspective claims, avowing their pains, and taking as much aspirin as ever. Even more vividly, were a person's epiphenomena to be gradually delayed until they ran, say, ten years behind her physical life, she and we could never discover this! In the latter case of interactionistic dualism, since the occurrence of *nonphysical* events (events having temporal location and presumably particular-person dependency but lacking spatial location and mass-energy) would be required to trigger unproblematically physical events in the brain, the conservation laws of physics would be violated. Either way, one pays an exorbitant price for dualism.

The identity theory was to be an empirical theory, conceptually outlined by philosophy but with the details filled in by science, and its ontology was typically presumed to include only scientifically well-credentialed entities—no *élan vital,* no psi forces, no ectoplasm, only brain cells and their biochemistry and physics. The identity theory's defining claim, the claim that mental events are not merely parallel to, coincident with, caused by, or accompaniments of brain events, but *are* (strictly identical with) brain events, divides people in a curious fashion. To some people it seems obviously true (though it may take a little fussing with details to get it properly expressed), and to others it seems just as obviously false. The former tend to view all attempts to resist the identity theory as motivated by an irrational fear of the advance of the physical sciences, a kind of humanistic hylephobia, while the latter tend to dismiss identity-theorists as blinded by misplaced science-worship to the manifest preposterousness of the identity claim.

This antagonism has created a very large literature over the last fifteen years—much of the best of it (Place, 1956; Feigl, 1958, 1967; Smart, 1959, 1963; Feyerabend, 1963; Nagel, 1965; Rorty, 1965; Taylor, 1967; Armstrong, 1968; Dennett, 1969; Davidson, 1970; Lewis, 1972), is anthologized in Borst (1970)—and out of it has emerged a panoply of sophistications that leaves the original bluff identity theory far behind while advancing basically unrevised its basic project of providing a conceptual pedigree for the physical sciences of the mind. The difficulties encountered by the identity theory can be divided without major loss and distortion into three basic areas: problems arising from Leibniz's law, problems about generalization, and abstract logical puzzles about the identity relation.

It is Leibniz's law that makes identity a stronger logical relation than mere similarity, co-occurrence, or equivalence. It states that "x is identical with y" entails that *whatever* is true of the thing denoted by "x" is true of the thing denoted by "y" and vice-versa. The principle is unassailable, since in the case of any true identity "x" and "y" will denote the very same thing, and whatever is true of that thing is true of it, whatever it is called. But now suppose some thought of mine is witty, or profound, or obscene; the identity theory must then claim that some brain process or event (the brain process or event identical with that thought) is witty, profound, or obscene, and at least at first glance brain processes don't seem to be the type of thing that could be witty or profound or obscene, any more than they could be the square root of 7 or loyal or capitalistic. One reply to this objection, variously expressed and defended, is: take another glance, and you will see that a brain process *can* be witty or profound or obscene in just those cases where it happens to be a thought. Not all events in the brain are thoughts—some are just metabolic events, for instance, and they cannot be witty, but they are not the only brain events. Of course the success of this position depends heavily on having an account of what it could be about a brain process or event that made it a thought (and one thought rather than another), and as we shall see, there are important problems in this area. (Another plausible reply to the objection distinguishes the thought as *event* from the thought as *content* or *proposition,* and claims that such features as wittiness properly apply to the content, not the event; but again, this position is no stronger than one's theory of the individuation of events by their content.)

There are in any case apparently harder problems raised by Leibniz's law (Lycan, 1972). Suppose I am subjected to visual stimulation that subsequently produces in me a round, orange after-image. There is no round, orange image on my retina, of course. Are we to suppose that there is a round, orange brain event or brain state that is identical with my after-image? Nothing that is not round and orange can be identical with something that is round and orange, so either my after-image is identical with some round, orange brain-state (which no one believes, I trust), or my after-image is not round and orange (could we claim it just seemed to be?), or my after-image is something (mental) other than—in addition to—any brain event and hence the identity theory is false, or there simply are no such things as round, orange after-images. It is no doubt tempting to anyone unfamiliar or unimpressed with the conceptual horrors of dualism to abandon the identity theory at this point, and admit after-images and their ilk to his ontology as extra nonphysical, epiphenomenal by-products of brain activity, but this is just what the identity theorist refuses to do (Cornman, 1971). The favored step instead is the last one: to deny that there are, strictly speaking, any such things as after-images at all. What there are, we are told, are havings-of-after-images, or experiences-of-after-images, and *these* are neither round nor orange. The difference between experiencing an orange after-image and experiencing a green after-image is not that the former experiencing is orange while the latter is green (Ryle, 1949; Smart, 1959, 1963, 1970; Dennett, 1969; Cornman, 1971). This move calls into question what might be called the normal semantics of ordinary mind-talk. We speak, casually and ordinarily, using words like "pain," "image," "belief," "brainstorm," "hunch," etc., as if these words were unproblematic referring expressions denoting perfectly real items in our minds (whatever they are). But perhaps our ordinary talk embodies a fossilized myth-theory, and once science teaches us what is really happening in our heads, we will abandon the search for referents for our ordinary mind-terms, just as we have abandoned our search for mermaids, witches, and demons. We talk as if there really were such things as after-images, and so there seem to be; we also talk as if the sun really rose in the east, and so it seems to, but science can render the former mode of expression, like the latter, metaphorical. This line of reasoning can lead in the extreme to a variety of positions often gathered under the rubric of the "disappearance form" of the identity theory: science will not *discover the identities* of the problematic mental items, but rather those items will disappear as candidates for identification as a more sophisticated scientific picture supercedes the old (Feyerabend, 1963; Rorty, 1965; Dennett, 1969; Taylor, 1973).

The second set of problems with the identity theory concerns generalization. These problems arise because the normal role of identity claims in theories is to permit generalization. (If this cloud is identical with a collection of water droplets, then so perhaps are the others; if this gene is a DNA molecule, the tempting hypothesis to test is that all genes are.) But it is far from clear that the identity theory could—or should—provide us with *any* generalization beyond its umbrella claim that every mental item is identical with some brain item or other. Suppose Mary thinks about *pi* at noon, and the identity theorist claims that Mary's thought is identical with her noontime brain process *p* (having defining physical features F, G, H). It is not remotely plausible to suppose that every *thought about pi* is a brain process with features F, G, H, if only because there is no reason to suppose intelligent creatures elsewhere in the universe would need to share our neurophysiology or even our biochemistry in order to think about *pi* (Putnam, 1967). It is not even plausible that every *human thought about pi,* or even every *thought of Mary's about pi,* is identical with a brain process falling into a class specifiable solely in terms of the physical features of the members. It would seem to be a burden of any theory of the mind that it tell us what it is about thoughts that makes them thoughts, and what it is about thoughts about *pi* that makes them thoughts about *pi,* and it does not appear that the general features we are looking for are physical features. The *weak* reply that the identity theorist can make is that all he needs to claim in order to avoid dualism is that each *particular* mental event (each "token") is some brain event or other (no mental event is a *non*physical *non*brain event). Thus we distinguish a "token" identity theory from a "type" identity theory and abandon the latter in philosophy of mind. Perhaps no one today supposes that *types* of mental items can be distinguished directly by purely physical features, but almost no one any longer supposes this was a reasonable goal of physicalism (Davidson, 1970). The *strong* reply goes beyond the avowal of a token identity theory and claims that the sought-for distinguishing marks of the types of mental items are definable in terms of *causal* roles filled (Armstrong, 1968; Lewis, 1972), or in terms of the *logical* states of the abstract Turing machine "realized" by a human being's nervous system (Putnam, 1960, 1964, 1967a,b, 1975), or in terms of the *functional* roles filled (Fodor, 1965, 1968, 1975). As the differences between these three views have been sorted out and deficiencies noted and corrected, a single widely shared view has emerged called *functionalism:* mental states are functional states, that is, states individuated by their functional role within the whole system. To say that a particular belief, or pain, for instance, is a particular functional state, is to say that anything, regardless of its composition, chemistry, shape, or other physical features, that fulfilled the same functional role in a functionally equivalent system would be the same belief, or pain, and nothing that fulfilled such a functional role could fail to be such a belief, or such a pain. Functionalism has become the dominant doctrine in philosophy of mind today (that is, it is the only theory being widely criticized and defended in the journals), and hence will receive more detailed discussion below. It should be already clear that this sort of functionalism has little to do with the brand of functionalism encountered in sociology or anthropology.

The third area of investigation initiated by the identity theory concerns the logic of the identity relation itself. It was initially supposed by Smart and other early defenders of the identity theory that the concept of identity was perfectly safe and well understood. It was a common tactic to elucidate the identity theory of mind by drawing analogies to presumably innocent and familiar identities encountered in less puzzling quarters, such as the identity of lightning bolts with electrical discharges in the air, the Morning Star with the Evening Star, genes with DNA molecules. These, however, turn out not to be unproblematic at all. One may even wonder if any identity claim is ever unproblematic. As the disanalogies, distinctions, and perplexities about identity itself began to multiply, the problem of identity took on a life of its own as a logical and metaphysical issue, and the researches no longer illuminated in any specific way the problems of mind. This was partly due to the diminishing reliance by physicalistically inclined philosophers of mind on any notion of identity at all. The disappearance form of the identity theory is after all misnamed; it is really not an identity theory but only a physicalistic alternative to the identity theory, and as Putnam observed in his earliest exposition of functionalism (1960), the question of whether to *identify* a logical state of a (realized) Turing machine with its concrete realization in hardware is a relatively idle metaphysical concern. When the two tactics, the disappearance view and functionalism, are put together—as there are strong reasons to do (Dennett, 1978)—whatever identities are still left to acknowledge concern rather curious and abstract entities. (For instance, one might be left claiming that the *state of affairs* of Tom's having a pain was identical with the *state of affairs* of his brain being in some particular functional situation.) At this point, the initial motivation for proclaiming *identities,* to save us from the ghostly items of dualism, has vanished.

So it was something of an anachronism when, in 1971, Saul Kripke included a startling "refutation" of the identity theory of mind as an illustrative by-product of his extraordinarily influential, even revolutionary, new account of necessity, designation, and identity (Kripke, 1971, 1972). Kripke's argument depends on some technical innovations. A "rigid designator" is an expression that designates the same entity "in all possible worlds." Thus "Benjamin Franklin" is a rigid designator, while "the inventor of bifocals" is not, though in *this* world they designate the same individual. Kripke argues convincingly that all proper identity claims are composed of terms that are rigid designators and hence when they are true, they are true not contingently, but necessarily. The application to philosophy of mind comes when he argues that expressions such as "my pain" and "my brain state" are both rigid designators, but identity claims composed of them could not be *necessarily* true, hence could not be true at all. (Cf. Matson, 1976.) Kripke's argument is subtle and ingenious and repays careful study, but it has not commanded assent. Even if one accepts Kripke's new theory of identity and necessity, his arguments to show that the relevant terms are rigid designators are not only vulnerable to straightforward exception, but seem to require assumptions that modern materialists (such as Armstrong) had already been at pains to deny (Feldman, 1974; Lycan, 1974). In retrospect, Kripke's argument can be seen not to have revitalized dualism, but only to have given materialists more and possibly better (deeper) reasons for shunning certain tempting identity claims they had already for the most part learned to avoid.

IV. Why Functionalism?

As befits a view that is the prevailing favorite, functionalism has much to be said for it. Not only does it seem satisfactorily to evade the philosophical objections to all the other forms of materialism, but it is particularly well suited to serve as the conceptual underpinning for current work in psychology, linguistics, and cybernetics or artificial intelligence. All of these disciplines operate somewhat self-consciously at a certain level of abstraction, and functionalism provides the rationale and justification for just such a strategy. In a way, there is nothing new about it. Psychologists as diverse as Freud and Skinner have shared the basic functionalist tactic: just as Freud eventually realized that any claims he might make about the physical location, composition, or operation of his functionally distinguished entities (the id, ego, and superego) were premature speculations, so Skinner, while granting that no doubt there were *some* internal, physiological mechanisms subserving reinforcement, has abjured speculation or commitment on that score, and settled, with Freud, for mapping the predicted consequences under a variety of circumstances of functionally characterized interactions.

Skinner, of course, has been less clear than Freud about the fact that he has been committed to a functionalistic model of internal processes. He thinks his peripheralism evades that "charge." That he should worry at all on this score is an embarrassment to philosophers, for had he and the other behaviorists not drunk so deeply at the well of logical positivism and the fashionable "operationalism" and "instrumentalism" of that era, they would not have been motivated to constrain their theorizing within such a paralyzing and misguided notion of rigor. Twenty years after logical positivism has been all but forgotten by philosophers, its dogmas are alive and healthy in the text-books of behaviorists. It is with some modesty and trepidation, then, that philoso-phers of mind currently urge their doctrines on their colleagues in other fields. It ap-pears, by the way, that history is about to repeat itself. Now that philosophers of mind have finally succeeded in banishing their fear of internal, "para-mechanical" theoreti-cal entities, a fear they learned from Ryle (Ryle, 1949; Fodor, 1975; Dennett, 1977), Roy Schafer (1975) has taken Ryle's strictures to heart and bids fair to initiate an era of Rylean logical behaviorism in psychoanalytic theory. The by now standard arguments against Ryle's behavior-dispositional analyses (they utterly fail to ramify or generalize; they are either obviously false or " saved" by *ceteris paribus* clauses that render them vacuous) seem at least at first glance to transfer intact as criticisms of Schafer.

More specifically, functionalism provides the conceptual under-pinnings for current work in cognitive psychology, psycholinguistics, and artificial intelligence modeling. In these disciplines one research strategy can be characterized in terms of (one version of) Chomsky's distinction between competence and performance: given a specifica-tion of a certain sort of competence, say a discriminative competence or a linguistic competence, the task is to devise a performance model — often a computer simulation program — that exhibits that competence (usually artificially isolated and hedged in various ways) and if possible has a claim to "psychological reality" as well (Fodor, 1975; Dennett, 1977). That is, getting the cat skinned at all can be a major accomplish-ment; getting it skinned in the way people seem to get it skinned is even better. This sort of research strategy permits highly abstract constraints and difficulties to be ex-plored (how could *anything* learn a natural language? how could *anything* achieve a general capacity for pattern recognition in an unstereotypic environment?) without worrying about the mechanics and the biochemistry of concrete "realizations" in the head, while at the same time not abandoning the fundamental physicalistic constraint that one's functionally described systems be *somehow* physically realizable (Dennett, 1975). At its most general and abstract, this sort of research merges with research in epistemology and philosophy of mind, and it is precisely at this meeting ground that the most promising and exciting work is being done today (e.g., Pylyshyn, 1973; Har-man, 1973; Minsky, 1973; Rosenberg, 1974; Fodor, 1975; Savage, 1978).

Of course functionalism has its skeptics and critics (Kalke, 1969; Block and Fodor, 1972; Block, 1978; Rorty, 1972; Lycan, 1973, Nagel, 1974; Shoemaker, 1975), and the most unsettling problems wear surprisingly traditional garb. First there are problems about the *qualia* of experience, the way it feels to be conscious, and second, there are problems — alluded to earlier — about how a functionally individuated state or event can have *meaning* or *content* in some presumably full-blooded sense required of men-tal entities. How could a functional state be a pain, and how could a functional state be a thought about *pi*?

V. *Qualia*

There is no satisfactory definition of *qualia,* which seems to have become the pet term in the discussions, but the requisite general sense of what qualia are supposed to be is easily captured by an example that figures centrally in the current discussion. Suppose that when you look at a clear "blue" sky you see what I see (insofar as color goes) when I look at a ripe apple, and vice versa, and so forth through all the colors of the spec-trum. Your perceived spectrum is, let us say, a systematic inversion of mine. But since you learned the use of color words just as I did (your parents pointed up at the sky and said "blue," etc.) our use of color words would be indistinguishable, and since we will both associate the color of glowing iron from the blacksmith's hearth with heat, and the color we perceive ice to be with cold, even our secondary descriptions of color (red is a warm color, blue is cool, etc.) might match. In fact, with regard to perceived colors and other qualia such as pains, tickles, sounds, aromas and tastes, do we have any evidence at all, or reason to believe, that any two people experience similar qualia under similar perceptual circumstances? This, the "inverted spectrum" thought experiment, is not new. It was a popular argument among the verificationists who took the "self-evident" unverifiability-in-principle of the hypothesis to mark the meaninglessness of the initial assumption that there are inner sensations or "raw feels" — to use a term philosophy took from the psychologist Tolman — of the requisite sort at all. As Wittgenstein said, "An 'inner process' stands in need of outward criteria" (Wittgenstein, 1953), and although the exegesis of this remark is controversial, it is easy and common to interpret this as an expression of logical behaviorism, an assertion of the incoherence of any doctrine that admits private sensations or experiences of qualia.

It has often been pointed out that today's functionalism is a spiritual descendent of logical behaviorism. Where the logical behaviorists said that being in pain was a matter of behaving or being disposed to behave in a particular way, the functionalists say that being in pain is a matter of being in a functional state of a certain sort — viz., a state that *inter alia* disposes one to certain behavior under certain conditions. From one vantage point, the only difference between the two doctrines appears to be the functionalist's willingness to abandon peripheralism (by countenancing explicitly internal functional states), and the concomitant willingness to define function not just in terms of dispositions to behave, but also in terms of dispositions to change functional state. If, as Skinner says, the skin is not that important a boundary, if internal state-switching counts as behavior, then functionalism is just logical behaviorism in new clothes. It is not surprising then that in the headlong rush away from the verificationism of the recent past, philosophers should attempt to turn the inverted spectrum argument on its head and show that functionalism commits the sin of verificationism by failing to grant sense to something that (clever argument reveals) does make sense: the hypothesis of spectrum inversion (Block and Fodor, 1972; Block, 1978; Lycan, 1973; Shoemaker, 1975). In a similar vein, Nagel has argued (1974) that there are certain undeniably meaningful hypotheses about our inner lives and the inner lives of others, about "what it is like to be" a person or a dog or a bat, of which functionalism can give no account.

The strategy of the debate is transparent. The lovers of qualia attempt to establish that functionalism unavoidably *leaves something out:* the wonderful tastes, tones, and colors that make life worth living. The functionalists attempt to show that they have not left anything *real* out, and that the alternative to functionalism can only be some insupportable variety of epiphenomenalism. The issue is not yet resolved, nor will it be resolved by the straight-forward victory of one side or the other in a purely conceptual debate. The burden for functionalism is inseparable from the burden of the variety of cognitivistic theories for which it provides the conceptual underpinnings. If an empirical psychological theory develops that is both strongly confirmed and predictive of the rich variety of phenomena of consciousness, we can inspect it for an answer to the question. If it contains a theoretical role for something like qualia, we shall "countenance" qualia in our ontology, but as theoretical entities, not epiphenomena; if no such role appears to be filled, then the very power of the theory will undermine the intuitions that now make the denial of qualia so counterintuitive (Dennett, 1976, 1978). If no functionalistically conceived theory proves up to handling the undisputed facts about consciousness, then that failure of empirical theory, and not any purely philosophical argument, will show that functionalism does in fact leave something out. The philosophical investigations of the issue are not entirely parasitic, however, on the advance of empirical research; they can illuminate the terrain, revealing blind alleys and pitfalls, without attempting to dictate the solution.

VI. Internal Representation and the Problem of Meaning

A similar supportive role can be seen for the philosophical contributions to the other main perplexity facing functionalistic theories in psychology: the problem of meaning or content. No problems of philosophy have received more, or more expert, attention in recent years than the problems of meaning, and an overview summarizing the work in that area would have to be book length. (There are several fine anthologies of recent work (Fodor, 1964; Steinberg and Jakobovitz, 1971; Davidson and Harman, 1972, 1975; Harman, 1974.) Almost all of it is at least indirectly relevant to the problems of mind, and some of it is of central importance.

In the late 19th century Franz Brentano claimed to have discovered the feature that sundered the mental from the physical: Intentionality. Mental phenomena, he said, differed from physical phenomena in always being directed upon an object (the object of thought or desire or perception) or related to a content (the content of a hope or thought or belief). This was a special sort of relatedness, for the objects of mental phenomena enjoyed a curious sort of "inexistence." I can want a sloop without there being a sloop I want; the object of my desire is "Intentionally inexistent" (which does *not* mean deliberately inexistent: Intentionality has nothing directly to do with what one intends to do). In the 1950's, Chisholm (1957) revived Brentano's notion of Intentionality and (using the tactic of semantic ascent to great effect) turned it into a feature of *language:* the sentences we typically use to talk about mental events have certain peculiarities of logic. Chisholm attempted to characterize those peculiarities of logic in such a way that his distinction between Intentional and non-Intentional *sentences* mirrored Brentano's distinction between Intentional and non-Intentional *phenomena.* In the ensuing years, Intentionality, viewed as a logical feature of certain classes of propositions, has been exhaustively and fruitfully studied, though it is fair to say that no very broad unanimity has been achieved about the precise definition, status, or role of Intentional discourse (Quine, 1960; Sellars, 1963, 1964; Chisholm, 1967; Kaplan, 1968; Lycan, 1969; Dennett, 1971). Interest in Intentionality has survived the disagreements and difficulties surrounding its definition not only because it represents an unresolved perplexity of logical theory, but because intuitively it does mark an important divide in our conceptual scheme, though not quite the divide Brentano supposed. The Intentional idioms of our language are roughly those Russell called the idioms of propositional attitude; these idioms typically take "that"-clauses and hence form complex, but not truth-functional, propositions out of others: e.g., "Tom believes that it is raining" contains the proposition "it is raining," but the truth value of the whole is independent of the truth value of the enclosed proposition. *Roughly,* again, the Intentional idioms are those idioms in our language that relate people, their parts, their acts, their artifacts to *propositions.* Rougher still, we use Intentional idioms to endow things — any sorts of things at all — with *meaning:* if we want to say what Tom believes, what the sentence means, what the frog's eye tells the frog's brain, what is innately and tacitly known by the infant language learner (Stich, 1975), what the ego is trying to keep from the superego, what information is stored on the tape, what Houston is signalling to Mariner IV, we use Intentional discourse. A theory of Intentionality, then, would be a theory that made explicit the conceptual ties between these various cognitivistic, information-theoretic, semantic approaches, and that set down the constraints and assumptions involved in the ascription of Intentionally characterized features to things. That there are very deep problems here can be brought out by considering cognitive psychology.

What unites cognitive psychologists and distinguishes them best from other theorizers in psychology is their willingness to view the individual not simply as a system of functionally individuated parts or subsystems, but of *Intentionally* individuated parts, parts whose functions are to "say that *p*," "remember the *q*," "figure out that r''—to encode, store, transmit or transform parcels of information. In fact it is their use of Intentional idioms in their science that best marks them off from the behaviorists, in particular Skinner, who has typically misconceived the difference as one between dualists ("mentalists") and materialists (Dennett, 1971, 1975, and 1978). Cognitive psychologists have generally thought that their use of information-talk is not only proper and well grounded in the mathematical rigor of information-theory and computer science, but positively a great step forward in the fruitful conceptualization of psychology; and so in the end it will be, I believe, but it is not unproblematic. To say that the function of some system is to carry certain information from *a* to *b* is not just like saying the function of the tube is to carry lubricant to the bearing, or the function of the teletype is to convey symbol strings from place to place. Moving information about is not so easily conceived, or if, for some special sense of information, it *is* thus easily conceived, one has purchased the simplicity at the cost of postponing solution to the central problem of Intentionality, as a little thought experiment will show.

Suppose you find yourself locked in a windowless room, with two walls covered with flashing lights, two walls covered with little buttons, and a note telling you that you are imprisoned in the control center of a giant robot on whose safety your own life now depends. Your task is simply to guide the robot through its somewhat perilous environment, learning to discriminate and cope with whatever comes along, finding "nourishment" and safe haven for the robot at night (so you can sleep), and avoiding dangers. All the *information* you need is conveyed by the flashing lights, and the robot's motor activity is controllable by pushing the buttons. To your dismay, however, you see that none of the lights or buttons is labeled. You can't tell whether the insistently flashing light in the upper left corner is warning danger, signaling a "full belly," informing you of the location of the sun, or requesting grease for a heel bearing. You don't know whether when you push a button and the light goes out, you've scratched an itch, occluded your view of something, or destroyed an attacker.

Clearly, if that is all you are given to go on, your task is impossible; if you succeeded in guiding your robot through the day it would be sheer luck. Yet in one sense (and a very familiar sense to cognitive psychologists) all the information you need is conveyed to you. For we needn't suppose the lights are mere repeaters of peripheral stimulation; their flashing can represent the products of perceptual analysis machinery as sophisticated as you wish, and similarly the output can be supposed to initiate devious actions guided by hierarchical subroutine systems informed by multi-layered feedback. In short, the entire array of systems devised by the cognitivist psychologists could be built into this robot, so that it conveyed to its control center highly mediated and refined information; and yet, though in one sense the information would be there, in another more important sense, it would not. Yet the task described is in a sense just the brain's task; it has no windows out of which it can look in order to correlate features of the world with its input.

The problem of the control room could be solved for you. of course, if all the lights and buttons were correctly labeled (in a language you knew), but this can hardly be the brain's solution. The job of getting the input information *interpreted* correctly is thus *not* a matter of getting the information translated or transcribed into a particular internal code, unless getting the information into that code is *ipso facto* getting it into functional position to govern the behavioral repertoire of the whole organism. This is the problem of meaning that must eventually be faced by any theorist who wishes to appeal to "internal representations" as explicative of psychological phenomena. Some recent work in philosophy directly addresses this issue (Pylyshyn, 1973; Dennett, 1969, 1977, 1978; Harman, 1973; Minsky, 1973; Rosenberg, 1974; Fodor, 1975; Savage, 1978); this literature depends to various degrees on the fundamental work on meaning that has developed in response to such central themes as Quine's thesis of the indeterminacy of radical translation (1960), Austin's work on speech acts (1962), and Grice's account of nonnatural meaning (1957, 1969). A particularly active controversy within the area of internal representation concerns the nature of the supposed vehicles of representation: are they propositional (like sentences) or imagistic or analogical (like pictures or maps) or are there other sorts of "data structures" with no familiar analogues among external vehicles of representation? Work by philosophers in this area merges quite smoothly with that of psychologists and cyberneticists (e.g., Pylyshyn, 1973; Minsky, 1973), and one can expect this unforced interdisciplinary exchange to produce some genuine advances in outlook in the next few years.

VII. Other Areas of Current Activity

This survey of current work is intended to capture the main lines of inquiry, but has left some work unmentioned that is not at all peripheral. For instance, the perplexing status of "introspection" has been carefully studied in a growing literature on "privileged access" and the presumed "incorrigibility" of introspective reports (Smart, 1962; Armstrong, 1968; Dennett, 1969, 1978; Margolis, 1970; Parsons, 1970; Rorty, 1970, 1972a; Alston, 1971, 1976; Arbib, 1972; Gunderson, 1972; Tormey, 1973; Klein, 1975), and philosophers have usefully turned their attention to specific issues arising in other fields, such as R. Sperry's split-brain cases and the various claims being advanced about the different roles of the cerebral hemispheres (e.g., Nagel, 1971) and the physiology of pain (Pitcher, 1970a,b; Dennett, 1978). There has also been a rediscovery of Freud (Wollheim, 1974), and in particular the problem of self-deception has provoked some excellent work (Fingarette, 1969; De Sousa, 1970; Hamlyn and Mounce, 1971; Rorty, 1972). The "minds and machines" literature has evolved from its early preoccupation with the question "can computers think?" (e.g., Anderson, 1964) into a much more detailed and informed examination of conceptual issues at the heart of current research in artificial intelligence and automata theory (e.g., Boden, 1974, 1977; Nelson, 1975a and b, 1976 a and b). An optimistic prognosis would be that these various strands of inquiry will coalesce into a fairly stable and broadly accepted understanding of the conceptual underpinnings of the functionalistic and physicalistic approach to the mind; but if one attends to the great diversity of opinion in the field, the deep difficulties that can already be seen to attend such a view, and the lesson of history, a more realistic prediction would be that this still fragmentary and tenuous consensus will prove as evanescent as its predecessors and be replaced by a currently unimagined set of doctrines and problems.

Bibliography

Albritton, Rogers. 1959. "On Wittgenstein's Use of the Term 'Criterion.'" *Journal of Philosophy* 56: 845–57. Reprinted 1968 in George Pitcher, ed., *Wittenstein: The Philosophical Investigations*. New York.
Alston, William P. 1971. "Varieties of Privileged Access." *American Philosophical Quarterly* 8: 223–51.
_____. 1976. "Self-Warrant: A Neglected Form of Privileged Access." *American Philosophical Quarterly* 13: 257–72.
Anderson, Alan R., ed. 1964. *Minds and Machines*. Englewood Cliffs, N.J.: Prentice-Hall.
Anscombe, G.E.M. 1957. *Intention*. Oxford.
Arbib, Michael A. 1972. "Consciousness: The Secondary Role of Language." *Journal of Philosophy* 69: 579–91.
Armstrong, David M. 1968. *A Materialist Theory of the Mind*. London.
Austin, John L. 1961. *Philosophical Papers*. In J. O. Urmson and G. J. Warnock, eds. Oxford.
_____. 1962a. *How To Do Things with Words.* Oxford.
_____. 1962b. *Sense and Sensibilia*. Oxford.
Block, Ned J. 1978. "Troubles with Functionalism." In C. Wade Savage, ed., *Minnesota Studies in the Philosophy of Science* 9. Minneapolis.

Block, Ned J., and Fodor, Jerry. 1972. "What Psychological States Are Not." *The Philosophical Review* 81: 159-81.

Boden, Margaret. 1974. "Freudian Mechanisms of Defense: A Programming Perspective." In Richard Wollheim, ed., *Freud: A Collection of Critical Essays.* Garden City, N.Y.: Doubleday.

_____ . 1977. *Artificial Intelligence and Natural Man.* Hassocks, England.

Borst, Clive V., ed. 1970. *The Mind/Brain Identity Theory.* New York.

Chihara, Charles, S., and Fodor, Jerry. 1965. "Operationalism and Ordinary Language: A Critique of Wittgenstein." *American Philosophical Quarterly* 2: 281-95. Reprinted 1968 in George Pitcher, ed., *Wittgenstein: The Philosophical Investigations.* New York.

Chisholm, Roderick. 1957. *Perceiving: A Philosophical Study.* Ithaca, N.Y.

_____ . 1967. "On Some Psychological Concepts and the 'Logic' of Intentionality." In Hector-Neri Castañeda, ed., *Intentionality, Minds, and Perception.* Detroit.

Cornman, James W. 1971. *Materialism and Sensations.* New Haven, Conn.

Davidson, Donald. 1970. "Mental Events." In Lawrence Foster and Joe W. Swanson, eds., *Experience and Theory.* Amherst, Mass.: University of Massachusetts Press.

Davidson, Donald, and Harman, Gilbert, eds. 1972. *Semantics of Natural Language.* Dordrecht: Reidel.

_____ . 1975. *The Logic of Grammar.* Encino, Calif.

Dennett, Daniel C. 1969. *Content and Consciousness.* London.

_____ . 1971. "Intentional Systems." *The Journal of Philosophy* 68: 87-106.

_____ . 1975. "Why the Law of Effect Will Not Go Away." *Journal of the Theory of Social Behaviour* 5: 169-87.

_____ . 1976. "Are Dreams Experiences?" *The Philosophical Review* 85: 151-71.

_____ . 1977. "Critical Notice of Jerry Fodor, *The Language of Thought* (New York, 1975)." *Mind* 86: 265-80.

_____ . 1978. *Brainstorms: Philosophical Essays on Mind and Psychology.* Montgomery, Vt.

De Sousa, Ronald. 1970. "Self-Deception." 1971. *Inquiry* 13: 308-34.

Feigl, Herbert. 1958. "The 'Mental' and the 'Physical.'" In Feigl, Michael Scriven, and Grover Maxwell, eds., *Concepts, Theories, and the Mind-Body Problem. Minnesota Studies in the Philosophy of Science* 2. Minneapolis.

_____ . 1967. *The "Mental" and the "Physical"—The Essay and a Postscript.* Minneapolis.

Feldman, Fred. 1974. "Kripke and the Identity Theory." *The Journal of Philosophy* 71: 665-67.

Feyerabend, Paul. 1963. "Materialism and the Mind-Body Problem." *Review of Metaphysics* 17: 49-66.

Fingarette, Herbert. 1969. *Self-Deception.* London.

Fodor, Jerry. 1965. "Explanation in Psychology." In Max Black, ed., *Philosophy in America.* Ithaca, N.Y.

_____ . 1968. *Psychological Explanation.* New York.

_____ . 1975. *The Language of Thought.* New York.

Fodor, Jerry, and Katz, Jerrold J., eds. 1964. *The Structure of Language.* Englewood Cliffs, N.J.: Prentice-Hall.

Grice, H. P. 1957. "Meaning." *The Philosophical Review* 66: 377-88.

_____ . 1969. "Utterer's Meaning and Intentions." *The Philosophical Review* 78: 147-77.

Gunderson, Keith. 1972. "Content and Consciousness and the Mind-Body Problem." *The Journal of Philosophy* 69: 591-604.

Gustafson, Donald, ed. 1967. *Essays in Philosophical Psychology.* London.

Hamlyn, D. W., and Mounce, H. O. 1971. "Self-Deception." *Aristotelian Society* Suppl. Vol. 45: 45-72.

Harman, Gilbert. 1973. *Thought.* Princeton, N.J.: Princeton University Press.

_____ . 1974. *On Noam Chomsky: Critical Essays.* Garden City, N.Y.: Doubleday.

Kalke, William. 1969. "What Is Wrong with Fodor and Putnam's Functionalism." *Nous* 3: 83-93.

Kaplan, David. 1968. "Quantifying In." *Synthese* 19: 178-214.

Klein, Barbara V. E. 1975. "Some Consequences of Knowing Everything (Essential) There Is To Know About One's Mental States." *Review of Metaphysics* 29: 3-18.

Kripke, Saul. 1971. "Identity and Necessity." In Milton Munitz, ed., *Identity and Individuation.* New York.

_____ . 1972. "Naming and Necessity." In Donald Davidson and Gilbert Harman, eds., *Semantics of Natural Language.* Dordrecht: Reidel.

Lewis, David. 1972. "Psychophysical and Theoretical Identifications." *Australasian Journal of Philosophy* 50: 249–58.

Lycan, William G. 1969. "On Intentionality and the Psychological." *American Philosophical Quarterly* 6: 305–12.

_____. 1971. "Noninductive Evidence: Recent Work on Wittgenstein's Criteria." *American Philosophical Quarterly* 8: 109–25.

_____. 1972. "Materialism and Leibniz' Law." *Monist* 56: 276–87.

_____. 1973. "Inverted Spectrum." *Ratio* 15: 315–19.

_____. 1974a. "Kripke and the Materialists." *The Journal of Philosophy* 71: 677–89.

_____. 1974b. "Mental States and Putnam's Functionalist Hypothesis." *Australasian Journal of Philosophy* 52: 48–62.

Malcolm, Norman. 1956. "Dreaming and Skepticism." *The Philosophical Review* 65: 14–37.

_____. 1959. *Dreaming*. London.

Margolis, Joseph. 1970. "Indubitability, Self-Intimating States and Logically Privileged Access." *The Journal of Philosophy* 67: 918–31.

Matson, Wallace. 1976. *Sentience*. Berkeley, Calif.

Melden, A. I. 1961. *Free Action*. London.

Minsky, Marvin. 1973. "Frame Systems: A Framework for Representing Knowledge." MIT Artificial Intelligence Lab Report.

Nagel, Thomas. 1965. "Physicalism." *The Philosophical Review* 74: 339–56.

_____. 1971. "Brain Bisection and the Unity of Consciousness." *Synthese* 22: 396–413.

_____. 1974. "What Is It Like To Be a Bat?" *The Philosophical Review* 83: 435–50.

Nelson, Raymond. 1975a. "Behaviorism, Finite Automata and Stimulus Response Theory." *Theory and Decision* 6: 249–67.

_____. 1975b. "On Machine Expectation." *Synthese* 31: 129–39.

_____. 1976a. "Mechanism, Functionalism and the Identity Theory." *The Journal of Philosophy* 73: 365–85.

_____. 1976b. "On Mechanical Recognition." *Philosophy of Science* 43: 24–52.

Parsons, Kathryn P. 1970. "Mistaking Sensations." *The Philosophical Review* 79: 201–13.

Peters, Richard. 1958. *The Concept of Motivation*. London.

Pitcher, George. 1970a. "The Awfulness of Pain." *The Journal of Philosophy* 67: 481–92.

_____. 1970b. "Pain Perception." *The Philosophical Review* 79: 368–93.

Place, U. T.. 1956. "Is Consciousness a Brain Process?" *British Journal of Psychology* 42: 44–50.

Price, H. H. 1932. *Perception*. London.

Putnam, Hilary. 1960. "Minds and Machines." In Sidney Hook, ed., *Dimensions of Mind*. New York. Reprinted 1975 in *Philosophical Papers vol. II*.

_____. 1962. "Dreaming and 'Depth Grammar.'" In R. J. Butler, ed., *Analytical Philosophy*. Oxford.

_____. 1964. "Robots: Machines or Artificially Created Life." *The Journal of Philosophy* 61: 668–91.

_____. 1967a. "Psychological Predicates." In *Art, Mind, and Religion*. Pittsburgh. Reprinted 1975 as "The Nature of Mental States" in Putnam, "Mind, Language and Reality." *Philosophical Papers vol. II*. Cambridge.

_____. 1967b. "The Mental Life of Some Machines." In Hector-Neri Castañeda, ed., *Intentionality, Minds and Perception*. Detroit. Reprinted 1975 in "Mind, Language and Reality." *Philosophical Papers vol. II*. Cambridge.

Pylyshyn, Zenon. 1973. "What the Mind's Eye Tells the Mind's Brain: A Critique of Mental Imagery." *Psychological Bulletin* 80: 1–24.

Quine, W.V.O. 1960. *Word and Object*. Cambridge, Mass.: Harvard University Press.

_____. 1969. "Epistemology Naturalized." In his *Ontological Relativity and Other Essays*. New York.

Rorty, Amelie O. 1972. "Belief and Self-Deception." *Inquiry* 15: 387–410.

Rorty, Richard. 1965. "Mind-Body Identity, Privacy and Categories." *Review of Metaphysics*. 19: 24–54.

_____. 1970. "Incorrigibility as the Mark of the Mental." *The Journal of Philosophy* 67: 399–424.

_____. 1972a. "Dennett on Awareness." *Philosophical Studies* 23: 153–62.

_____. 1972b. "Functionalism, Machines and Incorrigibility." *The Journal of Philosophy* 69: 203–20.

Rosenberg, Jay. 1974. *Linguistic Representation.* Dordrecht: Reidel.

Ryle, Gilbert. 1949. *The Concept of Mind.* London.

———. 1958. "A Puzzling Element in the Notion of Thinking." *Proceedings of the British Academy* 44: 129–44. Reprinted 1968 in Peter Strawson, ed., *Studies in Philosophy of Thought and Action.* Oxford.

Savage, C. Wade, ed. 1978. *Minnesota Studies in the Philosophy of Science* 9.

Schafer, Roy. 1975. *A New Language for Psychoanalysis.* New Haven, Conn.

Sellars, Wilfrid. 1963. *Science, Perception and Reality.* London.

———. 1964. "Notes on Intentionality." *The Journal of Philosophy* 61: 655–66.

Shaffer, Jerome. 1961. "Could Mental States Be Brain Processes?" *The Journal of Philosophy* 58: 813–22.

Shoemaker, Sidney. 1975. "Functionalism and Qualia." *Philosophical Studies* 27: 291–315.

Smart, J.J.C. 1959. "Sensations and Brain Processes." *The Philosophical Review* 68: 141–56.

———. 1962. "Brain Processes and Incorrigibility." *Australasian Journal of Philosophy* 40: 68–70.

———. 1963. *Philosophy and Scientific Realism.* London.

———. 1970. "Critical Notice of *Content and Consciousness* by D. C. Dennett." *Mind* 79: 616–23.

Steinberg, Danny D., and Jakobovitz, Leon A., eds. *Semantics.* Cambridge.

Stich, Steven, ed. 1975. *Innate Ideas.* Berkeley, Calif.

Strawson, Peter F. 1959. *Individuals.* London.

Taylor, Brandon. 1973. "Mental Events: Are There Any?" *Australasian Journal of Philosophy* 51: 189–200.

Taylor, Charles. 1967. "Mind-Body Identity, a Side Issue?" *The Philosophical Review* 76: 201–13.

Tormey, Alan. 1973. "Access, Incorrigibility and Identity." *The Journal of Philosophy* 70: 115–28.

Troyer, John G., and Wheeler, Samuel, eds. 1974 "Intentionality, Language and Translation." *Synthese* 23: 123–56.

Urmson, J. O. 1952. "Motives and Causes." *Aristotelian Society.* Suppl. Vol. 26: 179–94.

Warnock, G. J. 1954. "Seeing." *Proceedings of the Aristotelian Society* 55: 201–18.

White, Alan R. 1959–60. "Different Kinds of Need Concepts." *Analysis* 20: 112–16.

Wisdom, John. 1946. "Other Minds." *Aristotelian Society* Suppl. vol. 20: 122–47.

Wittgenstein, Ludwig. 1953. *Philosophical Investigations.* Oxford.

Wollheim, Richard, ed. 1974. *Freud: A Collection of Critical Essays.* Garden City, N.Y.

———◆———

chapter 5

Recent Work on the
Mind-Body Problem (II)

JEROME SHAFFER

Considering the wide spectrum of possible mind-body theories, it is a remarkable fact that most of the recent work on this topic has been in exploration, defense, and criticism of a rather extreme form of materialism, one which holds not only that all things in nature are physical, but that all of their properties are physical as well (by "physical" is meant those entities and properties postulated by the physics of today and the near future). Such time-honored views as idealism, mind-body interactionism, epiphenomenalism, double-aspect theories, and forms of neutral monism have few philosophers defending them these days (for three notable exceptions, see dualists Popper [1974, 1977], H. D. Lewis [1970, 1973], and Puccetti [1978]). Brave souls who defend such views meet disbelief and even disdain from the philosophical establishment. The anthologies that have brought together leading recent articles have reflected this trend in their very titles: *Modern Materialism: Readings on Mind-Body Identity* (O'Connor, 1969), *The Mind-Brain Identity Theory* (Borst, 1969), *The Philosophy of the Body: Rejections of Cartesian Dualism* (Spicker, 1970), and *Materialism and the Mind-Body Problem* (Rosenthal, 1971). The main fighting is about how radical or moderate a materialism to espouse. Not that the fighting is not intense — indeed, there is as much controversy as ever — but it is a limited war, occurring in a small area of the available logical space.

The mind-body problem is part of a wider collection of problems constituting the philosophy of mind, which examines the nature of particular mental phenomena and their interrelations, their common features and their differences, as well as their relation to the physical. In this chapter I shall leave open the question of characterizing the mind or the mental, and focus primarily on the narrow range of examples that have held center stage in much recent discussion: sensations like aches or pains and visual experiences of after-images or color patches, with occasional mention of other phenomena such as beliefs, desires, and intentions.

My earlier examination of the mind-body problem (Shaffer, 1965) reviewed work done from roughly 1945 to 1965. That article, which discussed theories about the nature of the mental, Smart's identity theory, issues raised by computer research, and dualistic theories, was somewhat broader in scope than this chapter, which was written especially for this volume.
I am indebted to John Taylor and Sally Winchester for their help.

The Identity Theory

If one wished to date the beginning of the current era, one might well point to 1959, when Smart's "Sensations and Brain Processes" was published. This view came to be known as the identity theory and also as central state materialism. Smart cites earlier papers by Place (1956) and Feigl (1958), but it was Smart's statement of the view that served as the focus for the considerable discussion that followed. Smart says:

> The thesis that sensations are brain processes . . . is not the thesis that, for example, "after-image" or "ache" means the same as "brain process of sort X" (where "X" is replaced by a description of a certain sort of brain process). It is that, insofar as "after-image" or "ache" is a report of a process, it is a report of a process that *happens to be* a brain process. It follows that the thesis does not claim that sensation statements can be *translated* into statements about brain processes. Nor does it claim that the logic of a sensation statement is the same as that of a brain-process statement. All it claims is that insofar as a sensation statement is a report of something, that something is in fact a brain process [Smart, 1959, pp. 144–45].

The idea here is that while expressions like "after-image" and "brain process of sort X" differ in meaning, they, as a matter of empirical fact (an hypothesis which Smart admits may be false), *refer* to the same thing.

Perhaps the most important consequence of Smart's approach was to show that there was a way of treating mental phenomena as *inner* phenomena, which could have causes and effects on physical phenomena and other mental phenomena, without falling into a dualism. Prior to Smart's formulation, many philosophers worried that talk of *inner* phenomena would commit them to a traditional dualism that postulates the existence of a nonphysical substance (the mind), which undergoes special nonphysical states, processes, and events possessing nonphysical properties. To avoid such commitments, philosophers tried to characterize the mental in terms of outward, observable behavior (Ryle, 1949) or at least demand that "an 'inner process' stands in need of outward criteria" (Wittgenstein, 1958, section 580). Now, on Smart's view, inner processes can be postulated as fully real, and we can drop the scare quotes which cast doubt on the propriety of talk about inner processes. The inner processes turn out to be brain processes, the existence and status of which no materialist need have any qualms.

Smart's theory presupposes a distinction going back to Mill, Frege, and Russell between meaning and reference. This distinction has been a matter of much discussion in recent years. (See Putnam, 1970, 1973a, 1975a; Kripke, 1971, 1972, 1977; and Donnellan, 1966.) But since Frege we know that *something* more than reference must be involved here. Statements asserting identities of reference, e.g., "Venus is the Morning Star," are informative (unlike "Venus is Venus"); and expressions that have no reference will differ more than typographically (e.g., "Pegasus" and "Olympus"). So some dimension in addition to reference is needed, be it meanings, concepts, rules, beliefs, causal origins, possible worlds, conventions, pictures, criteria, etc. In particular, even if we grant that "after-image" and "brain process of sort X" have the same referents, we still must give some account of how these expressions differ.

Smart, in the Frege tradition, held that the expressions differed in meaning, and he gave an account of the meaning of such expressions as "after-image" that he termed a "topic-neutral" account (1959, p. 149), i.e., one which would allow attributions of these expressions to be compatible with *any* mind-body theory about the nature of the entities, states, or events involved. The way Smart proposed was to take such expressions as "is an after-image" and "is a sensation" to attribute "likenesses and unlikenesses of certain internal processes" (Smart, 1962, p. 69). Thus, Smart suggests, "When a person says, 'I see a yellowish-orange after-image' he is saying something like this: '*There is something going on which is like what is going on when* I have my eyes open, am awake, and there is an orange illuminated in good light in front of me'" (Smart, 1959, p. 149). Given this rough definition, the way is open for it to turn out (as Identity theorists believe it will) that the something-going-on (that the description refers to) will be a brain-state or brain process or brain event. Thus, having an after-image is identical with undergoing a brain process.

There is an ambiguity here that yields a weaker and a stronger thesis. On the one hand there are what can be called "particular identities" (Taylor, 1967, fn. 5) or "token identities" (Block and Fodor, 1972, fn. 2), and what can be called "general identities" or "type identities" on the other hand. Thus we can claim that every having of an after-image is identical with a brain process of one type or another, or we can claim more strongly that every having of an after-image is identical with a brain process of some particular type. Smart held the stronger version, maintaining that "sensations (are) brain processes of a certain type" (1959, p. 144), since the weaker token-identity theory leaves us with mental types that are non-identical with any physical types and therefore cry out for further explanation. In what follows, we will take the identity theory to hold the stronger thesis.

Putting aside doubts about the meaning-reference distinction, there are two particular objections to Smart's account of the meaning of sensation expressions as what is going on when: first, it makes them too vague—after all, lots of things other than sensation are going on when; and second, in limiting itself to causes or stimuli, the theory omits what many believe to be equally or even more essential to referents of such expressions, namely their *effects*.

To rectify these shortcomings in the "topic neutral" account, theorists suggested a way of making them more precise, namely by specifying effects as well as causes. David Lewis, offering what he called an elaboration and generalization of Smart's theory, says of experience (such as seeing red or having pain):

> The definitive characteristic of any (sort of) experience as such is its causal role, its syndrome of most typical causes and effects. . . . These causal roles . . . belong by analytic necessity to experiences [D. Lewis, 1966, 17].

And Armstrong says:

> The concept of a mental state is primarily the concept of a state of the person apt for bringing about a certain sort of behavior. . . . In the case of some mental states only they are also states of the person apt for being brought about by a certain sort of stimulus [Armstrong, 1968, 82].

This causal approach is "topic neutral" with respect to whether the events picked out by the definitions are mental or physical. But it is not *theory* neutral. It is compatible with, for example, Cartesian interactionism, since it allows for nonphysical causes and effects. It is, however, incompatible with epiphenomenalism (which denies that experiences have physical effects) and with parallelism or double-aspect theories (which deny that experiences have physical causes either). By weakening causality to universal correlations (perhaps plus appropriate counterfactuals), we could accommodate these theories as well.

If we take the causal account to be providing *definitions* or *analytic truths* or *translations* of such expressions (Armstrong, 1968, p. 82, denies that they are translations but he is rather vague as to what they are), we run into not only all the general reservations originally raised by Quine (1953) concerning these notions, but the specific objection, put forcefully by Levin (1979, pp. 113–15), that pains, for example, might have had entirely different causes or effects from what in fact they have and also that those very causes and effects of pain might have been correlated with something quite different from pain. Such possibilities seem even more likely for such things as yellow after-images, where both their causes and effects seem quite remote, obscure, and variable, hardly the sorts of things that would provide a definition; it was, after all, an interesting discovery that violet objects cause yellow after-images.

Levin suggests we take the causal account as a way of, in Kripke's (1971, 1972) words, *fixing the reference* of such expressions. Levin calls his view "modified topic neutralism" (Levin, 1979, pp. 117–25). Pains and after-images in our world turn out to be identical with the effects of certain stimuli and the causes of certain subsequent responses, and therefore topic-neutral descriptions of the form "what intervenes between" can be used to fix the reference of "is in pain." But it is merely a contingent fact that such expressions pick out pains rather than, say, tickles.

The idea of "fixing the reference," as Levin himself asserts, is still not well worked out (Levin, 1979, p. 119). It is intended as weaker than providing a definition, but stronger than merely providing an expression with the same extension. Is it supposed to refer to some datable event, perhaps in the life of each language user, perhaps in the history of the linguistic community? In what is the event supposed to consist? Is it a theory about language learning, language use, semantics, pragmatics, or "the logic of language"? In particular, how is this idea supposed to apply to such ubiquitous and age-old terms as *pain*?

Assuming Levin's suggestions concerning "fixing the reference" work (1979, pp. 119–25), "modified topic neutralism" leaves open the possibility of an identity theory. However, we are still left with the question what the reference of "pain" is. On Levin's view, "pain" is a "connotationless name," but presumably it names a type. What is the status of this type? Is it a natural kind? Is it *identical* with some physical type or is it a nonphysical type? If the latter, what is its relation, if any, to physical types? Identity theorists have hoped that mental types would turn out to be identical to physical types. Is this plausible?

The problem that gave type-identity theorists the most difficulty emerged when it was pointed out, by Putnam (1967a,b) and Davidson (1970), that it is clearly possible, and very probably the case, that many types of characteristically mental processes could occur in things that differ very widely in physical composition and structure. They held that it is reasonable to suppose, for example, that pain or vision can occur in creatures with radically different sorts of brains—mammalian, reptilian, molluscan (e.g., octopuses)—not to mention the possibility of pain or vision in extraterrestrial beings or artificially created beings. So it is very unlikely that each type of mental state will be correlated with some type of brain state. It is possible that all share some common property that corresponds to pain, but there is at present no reason to think so. At best we can expect *token* identities, in which every token of a particular mental-state type will be identical with a token of any one of a number of different physical-state types. Even if we could produce a type consisting of the disjunction of all those physical-state types, there is no reason to think such a type would behave lawfully, have any interesting physical features in common, or include all the possibilities (we shall return to this objection below).

It has been suggested (Plantinga, 1967; Kim, 1972) that this objection can be met by specifying our types more narrowly. Let us distinguish mammalian pain from reptilian pain, perhaps even human pain from bovine pain. Then we may be more likely to get type identities. But as Lycan (1974) points out, this is really to abandon the idea that there is any such thing as pain (in general), which is not the Identity theory view but the view to be considered below called "eliminative materialism."

If we give up the idea that types of mental phenomena are identical with types of physical phenomena, we are left with the problem of explaining the existence and nature of these mental types. At present, the favored view of the nature of these types is known as functionalism.

Functionalism

Hearkening back to the biologist's distinction between structure and function, functionalist theories interpret mentalistic terms as signifying not structure but function, not how things are constituted but what things *do* or the *roles* things play. As Fodor puts it:

> In typical cases of functional analysis, . . . one asks about a part of a mechanism *what role it plays* in the activities that are characteristic of the mechanism as a whole [Fodor, 1968, p. 113].

The distinction entails that things composed or constituted in different ways can play the same role, and that things composed in the same way can play different roles. Constitution and role are logically distinct properties; neither is reducible to the other. Thus, if we take mentalistic properties to be functional properties, we have a dualism of properties. But it is a dualism that can exist in a wholly materialistic world view, which holds that the only entities that exist are physical entities, but that these physical entities have functional as well as structural properties. This view allows for token-identity without type-identity. Thus, to use Fodor's example, in a particular car the valve lifter (a functional characterization) will be token-identical with the camshaft (a characterization by physical structure), but in another car the mechanism for lifting valves may be token-identical with something of a quite different physical structure. Applying this to the mind-body problem, we have the view that mentalistic terms ascribe various functions to, in the case of human and animals, brain states to characterize the roles that those brain states play in conjunction with other brain states to determine overall behavior of the individual. This leaves open the possibility that the set of brain states characterized in any particular functional way may have no common nature other than functional equivalence. It also leaves open the possibility that nonneurological states and even nonphysical states should serve the same function, although the materialist will insist that the instantiations of these functions will always be *physical* structures. This is the token-identity hypothesis, at any rate, and it is entirely compatible with functionalism. The new materialism which superceded type-identity theory is token-identity functionalism.

As Fodor himself admits, the idea of function is "notoriously unclear" (Fodor, 1968, p. 113). The very distinction between structure and function is quite arbitrary in its application to actual systems (Kalke, 1969; Rorty, 1972), since what is thought of as structural at one level of abstraction can be thought of as functional at another; Lycan (1981, p. 47) claims that even "neuron" admits of a functional interpretation. Furthermore, since Fodor talks of the role things play "in the production of behavior," how are we to distinguish functionalism from a causal theory? Presumably, functionalism involves the idea of the effects that are *supposed* to obtain (the idea of *malfunction* is essentially connected to the idea of function), which leads us into the deep waters of normative concepts and/or teleology (on the latter, see Wimsatt, 1976). If what is meant by "function," as in the case of valve-lifters, is what the thing was *designed* by its builders to do, then it is not clear how it applies to natural systems like humans. If what is meant is the biological function, its contribution to the survival and propagation of the kind to which it belongs, then in the case of humans, at least, it will be a hopelessly crude, overly general account; even if pain does function as a device to alert the system to harm or the possibility of harm, what is the biological function of indignation or remorse, daydreaming or composing blank verse? If we could assign biological functions to these mental phenomena, we still would be far from giving either necessary or sufficient conditions for them. If what is meant by the function of the thing is the role it plays in contributing to the goals, ends, or purposes which the individual has, then we cannot provide a functional account of what it is for the individual to have a goal, end, or purpose which has no further goal, end, or purpose. If what is meant is its effect on behavior, then it would seem we are back to causal theories and their *structural* states. If what is meant is its intended effect, then we cannot provide a functional account of *intentions*. How are we to apply the idea of function to mental terms? To provide clarity and rigor, functionalists turned to the idea of a Turing machine.

Turing Machine Functionalism

Originally Putnam (1961) put forward an analogy between human beings and Turing machines and concluded that every alleged problem in the mind-body relation could be formulated and dissolved by seeing how a parallel problem could be formulated and dissolved in the case of Turing machines. In time, Putnam (1967b) began to claim that mental states are not merely analogous to Turing machine states but actually are (probabilistic) Turing machine states. The basic idea of a (probabilistic) Turing Machine, as Putnam (1961) presents it, is that for a given system there will be a set of instructions, called the machine table, which will specify for each possible state of the system and input what (the probability of) the succeeding state and output will be. The machine table will provide a complete description of all possible behavior of the system, both internal and external, relative to all possible stimulations of the system. Putnam's idea, as it developed, was that all mental states, e.g., being in pain, are definable in terms of the occurrence of a particular set of inputs, plus a machine table that contains the appropriate set of instructions for responding to such inputs. On this view, although at present we know very little about the machine tables for humans or any other organisms, at least we know what definitions of mental states would look like in principle.

At this point a difficulty arises for Turing machine functionalism (Block and Fodor, 1972, pp. 174–75) that is curiously reminiscent of the difficulty Putnam raised against the Identity theory. Just as it is likely that diverse types of physical structures will exemplify a particular mental type, so it is equally likely that diverse types of machine tables will exemplify a given mental type. Many different types of machine programs accomplish addition, color recognition, information storage, decision-making, etc. If we are to think of descriptions of mental processes as "functional" descriptions, they cannot be "functional" in the sense that they are identical to some one machine table, since quite diverse tables can accomplish the same function. Of course, it is *possible* that we can develop topologies of machine tables that will precisely correspond to topologies of mental processes, just as it is possible we will develop topologies of physical structures that will precisely correspond to topologies of mental processes. But in either case, at this time it seems unlikely.

For different reasons, Putnam (1975b, pp. xi–xiv, 298–99) himself has decided that the Turing machine approach is essentially wrong, explaining, "I was too much in the grip of the reductionist outlook." Since a Turing machine is characterized by a machine table, which defines the transitions from one discrete, total, momentary state to another, Putnam concludes that Turing machine states so defined cannot capture continuing psychological states, simultaneous diverse psychological states (e.g., being in pain, hearing a shrill whine, and being about to say "three" all at the same time), or states that entail prior or subsequent states (e.g., being jealous). (These points are set out in greater detail by Block and Fodor, 1972.) So, for various reasons it seems reasonable to conclude that mental states cannot be identified with states of a Turing machine.

Computational Functionalism

To free oneself from "the grip of the reductionist outlook" is to accept the irreducibility of the mental. Let us unashamedly use mental concepts, but confine ourselves to those that can be applied to unquestionably physical systems such as computers, making use of the developments that have occurred in the recently emerging fields of artificial intelligence (Winston, 1977) and cognitive psychology (Neisser, 1976). (For misgivings, see Dreyfus, 1979, and Haugeland, 1978, respectively.) Thus, Dennett envisages mental operations (e.g., recognizing a face) as broken down into subsystems of mental operations (e.g., feature detecting, memory searching, reporting, evaluating, decision-making, commanding) that are yet further broken down until we are left with very simple, specific tasks which a machine can accomplish. This is a functional approach because all the operations and suboperations are characterized in terms of rule-governed changes from certain inputs to outputs. But it is also a "functional" approach in the *role* sense, using unabashedly mentalistic terms to describe these simple, specific tasks, e.g., telling if a particular square is empty or not. Lycan (1981) calls this "homuncular functionalism" and agrees with Dennett that it is nontrivial, since we are not simply duplicating a function by postulating a little man inside who does the very same thing, but are breaking down the function into a group of different subfunctions.

Since these inner events and processes are characterized mentalistically, we are still left with a dualism of events or processes. Fodor is a token-identity theorist, holding that the events and processes are physical; but he accepts property dualism and the irreducibility of psychological laws, saying "not all the kinds (not all the classes of things and events about which there are important, counterfactual supporting generalizations to make) are, or correspond to physical kinds" (Fodor, 1975, p. 24). Fodor accepts as scientifically legitimate most of the psychological concepts of ordinary life—beliefs, inferences, preferences, representations, inductions, perceptions, hypothesizing, etc., although he does think there is no useful distinction between conscious and unconscious psychological states (Fodor, 1975, p. 52, fn 19). The job of psychology is to discover the internal subprocesses (basically, computational, according to Fodor) that account for our psychological responses.

Dennett is ambivalent on the issue of property dualism. On the one hand, he says that we finally get down to

> homunculi so stupid (all they have to do is remember whether to say yes or no when asked) that they can be, as one says, 'replaced by a machine'. One *discharges* fancy homunculi from one's scheme by organizing armies of such idiots to do the work [Dennett, 1978, p. 124].

On this view, we are left with psychological processes (answering questions, remembering) down to the very end. But on the same page Dennett also says, "all homunculi are ultimately discharged," as though, in the end, psychological processes are explained away. Dennett points approvingly to developments in Artificial Intelligence research to explain how physical systems can admit of psychological processes, saying, "if the (computer) program works then we can be certain that all homunculi have been discharged from the theory" (Dennett, 1978, p. 81). But in fact there is no way "all homunculi are ultimately discharged," since at the lowest level, e.g., the individual rod or cone in the retina, the homunculus is still either detecting light or not while the rod or cone is either discharging energy or not. Even allowing token-identity, and therefore only *one* process, we still have nonsynonomous descriptions, neurological descriptions vs. mentalistic descriptions, and therefore a dualism that still needs explaining.

Artificial Intelligence (A.I.) is alleged by Dennett to have explained human understanding in terms of data structures which are internal "self-understanding representations"; but if one questions whether these data structures are really "self-understanding representations," Dennett tells us that "internal pseudo-representations may do as well" (1978, p. 125). And indeed they may for the purposes of A.I., which could very well end up with pseudo-psychological processes when all is said and done. But this would mean that A.I. casts little light on the mind-body problem (unless we, too, have nothing but pseudo-psychological processes, in which case one wonders what the force of "pseudo" is and what "real" psychological processes would look like).

The Stonehenge Problem

The computer as model for a mind-body system appears to make it plausible how a purely physical system is describable in fancy mentalistic terms, such as "making deductions," "proving theorems," "solving differential equations." But suppose it turns out that these descriptions apply only because these systems are viewed, interpreted, or used in a particular deduction-deriving, theorem-proving, or equation-solving way by *people*? Suppose these mentalistic terms apply to those physical systems only by virtue of the relation of those systems to minds? Then we could not use those systems to cast light on the mind-body problem. It is precisely this situation which obtains, I shall argue.

Suppose it turns out that Stonehenge, that mysterious arrangement of stones and earthworks built over 3,000 years ago, was a computer, set up for the purpose of predicting astronomical phenomena. How could we find this out? Suppose we find that Stonehenge can be used that way. Suppose we find it can also be used to predict the stock market. That it admits of both functions does not settle which one its function was. It might even do *better* at predicting the stock market than astronomical phenomena, but it still would be ludicrous to assign that function to it. What its true functional description is can only be settled by finding out the purposes and uses of the ancient people that built and used it. Stonehenge has no mind of its own, no Turing machine table intrinsically connected to it. The same is true of any artifact. A machine is a chess-playing machine if it was designed to be used to play chess and can be so used. That a machine is a dishwasher as opposed to a water dirtier is a fact not about it alone, but about it and its purposeful designers and users. As MacKay puts it:

> Calling it a computer, then, is not attributing any mental properties whatsoever to the physical situation, but only specifying the function that it can serve for me or some other thinking agent. Only someone's readiness to place a mathematical interpretation on what is going on makes it a computing operation [MacKay, 1980, p. 52].

The fact that some artifact computes presupposes the existence of a mind that designed or used it to compute. So we cannot explain the existence and nature of a mind by the existence and nature of a computing artifact. (For a similar point, see Matson, 1976, chapter 4.) For this reason, in the end, computational functionalism fails to illuminate the mind-body problem.

The Qualia Problem

Some critics of functionalism and causal theories claim that neither approach can account for a central feature of mental life, namely "the subjective character of experience" (Nagel, 1979, chapters 12–14) — the raw feel or phenomenological character of mental events, how such events are for the subject who experiences them. When, for example, I am in pain or am experiencing a red after-image, I am having a recognizable experience that has its own special qualitative content for me. The term quale (plural, qualia) is currently often used to refer to this subjective content. It is claimed that functionalist and causal theories, in focusing on the role, typical causes and effects, and correlates of mental events, necessarily omit qualia. This is because it is possible that indefinitely many qualia might have had the same role or same causes and effects, and any given quale might have had a quite different role or quite different causes and effects. Thus, we cannot use roles or causes and effects to characterize qualia. This claim is given dramatic support by appeal to various thought experiments. It is claimed that it is conceivable that there be an experience qualitatively quite different from, say, pain, which played exactly the role that the experience of pain plays in our lives, e.g., arising under the same circumstances, serving to warn of damage, leading in the same circumstances to the same behavior, etc.; and it is claimed that it is conceivable that just that qualitative content, pain, should arise in quite different circumstances, serve different functions, lead to different behavior from how things are at present. Thus we are forced to distinguish the quale, pain, from what can be characterized functionally or causally. To turn to visual experience, it is claimed one can conceive undergoing "spectrum reversal," i.e., a sudden systematic change in the content of one's visual experience, that, given suitable new training (e.g., changing linguistic habits), would produce the same old behavior of, say, leading me to stop the car when the upper traffic light comes on (although it would now look the way the lower traffic light used to look). In time we might even forget how things used to look and come to think (falsely) that one's visual qualia were the same as they had always been. Again the result of the thought experiment is to show that the particular content of different visual experiences is different from the role they play in our lives.

There are many variants on the thought experiments just mentioned. Some argue for the possibility that, say, pain might have exactly the role it does with the quale entirely absent (Block and Fodor, 1972, p. 173; Block, 1978, pp. 277–304; Block, 1980). Some argue for the possibility that different people might have qualia of different sorts that still play the same role for each (Lycan, 1973). These variants raise special further problems, e.g., the possibility of verification. The simplest cases are quale changes within a single personal history, in particular in one's own case. Yet even here many have wished to deny the possibility of such an occurrence. The support for such a denial could come from the Private Language Argument (Wittgenstein, 1958, sections 258–70), about which many volumes have been written. Judith Jarvis Thomson's (1964) discussion remains the classic critique of this argument. (For further discussion and references, see Morick, 1967.)

The existence of qualia seems reasonable to many contemporary theorists. Of course, not all mental states or events have associated qualia. Coming to believe something, making an inference, remembering, noticing, forming an intention, or coming to want something often lack experiential content. But having sensations or sensory impressions do seem to be clear cases where the experiencing of qualia occurs.

Dennett (1979) tries to give a functionalist account of qualia by referring to "the deliverances of proprietary . . . and possibly idiosyncratic . . . sets of property detectors." While it is indeed plausible to think of, say, color qualia as personal detectors of kinds of light, it would seem that rather different qualia could serve the same function, thereby still leaving us with a difference that escapes functionalist characterization. Shoemaker concedes that "particular qualitative states cannot be functionally defined" (Shoemaker, 1975, p. 306), but he argues that "qualitative states can be accommodated within the framework of a functional, or causal, analysis of mental states" (p. 310). On the assumption that the presence or absence of qualitative states will make a difference to the subject, we can provide "a functionalist account of what it is for a state to be a qualitative state" (Shoemaker, 1975, p. 310). And on the assumption that similar qualitative states will have similar effects and changes in qualitative states (e.g., produced in spectrum reversal) will also have effects, "we can give a functional account of qualitative similarity and difference" (p. 306).

But why should we accept these assumptions? For example, why assume a change of qualia must have effects? To be sure, spectrum reversal, as it is usually explained, is indeed noticed by the subject. But it is easy enough to imagine a scenario in which the reversal (through extensive neural rewiring, for example) is eventually accommodated for, so that in the end behavior is just as it used to be despite the change in qualitative state. If that is possible, then spectrum reversal undetected by the subject (through immediate rewiring) is also possible. If so, there might be no functional differences resulting from a change of qualia. In the same way, qualitatively similar qualia might, because of other changes in the nervous system, come to function differently. As for the assumption that the presence or absence of qualia will make a difference, here again there seems to be no difficulty in conceiving of a nonqualitative state that would play the same role as that played by a qualitative state.

Qualia remain an anomaly for functional and causal theories. Of course, it is quite true that qualia have important *functional* roles to play in our mental life (Block, 1978, p. 309). It would be surprising if they did not. Color qualia do function as feature detectors; pain qualia do function to warn of danger or damage. But it is also the case that they have a nature or character over and above their functional properties. Thus, a proponent of the functional approach to much of our mental life, Fodor, maintains that "the problem of qualitative content poses a serious threat to the assertion that functionalism can provide a general theory of the mental" (Fodor, 1981, p. 122). But it is also true that much of our mental life does not involve qualia. Belief, desires, memory, deductive and inductive inference, motives, emotions, learning, and know-how do not have qualia typically associated with them, at least not always or essentially. For such phenomena, the quale objection to functional and causal theories is inapplicable. Furthermore, it is doubtful that expressions like "red" or "sweet," taken as terms in our ordinary language, designate qualia (as contrasted with "how red looks to S" or "how sweet tastes to S," which clearly do designate qualia). It might be claimed that even "pain," as the expression is ordinarily used, does not designate a quale (as contrasted with "how pain is for S," which would designate a quale), since we are inclined to attribute pain to quite different organisms (e.g., bats) while wondering whether pain is the same for them as it is for us. One might speculate that "pain" is equivocal, designating both a function and a quale (Block, 1978). But even if "pain" does designate a quale, it is an empirical fact that qualia are correlated in regular ways with their typical causes and effects and play stable roles in our mental life. So, if qualia are an anomaly for functional and causal theories, much of our mental life is still there for such theories to describe and explain, assuming they can overcome the objections raised above.

Qualia as Identical with Brain States

If qualitative states escape functionalist and causal accounts, it becomes reasonable to reconsider the view of them as structural or compositional states (Block, 1978, p. 323, fn. 22), and this leads us back to an identity theory for qualia. After all, Place (1956, p. 44) explicitly rules out the identity thesis for "cognitive concepts like 'knowing', 'believing', 'understanding', 'remembering', and volitional concepts like 'wanting' and 'intending'" (on the somewhat dubious ground that in these cases "an analysis in terms of dispositions to behave is fundamentally sound") and reserves the identity thesis for "concepts clustering around the notions of consciousness, experience, sensation, and mental imagery." Smart (1959) confines himself to "sensations," giving as his examples the having of after-images, how things look or feel to an individual, aches and pains. (Of course, as identity theorists always insist, we are to identify the physical state with *experiencing* the sensation, not with the sensation itself.)

As we saw, it was a major objection to the identity theory that it has the implausible implication that structurally different systems could not instantiate the same mental states; since mammalians and non-mammalians might still both have *vision*, vision cannot be identical with a certain anatomical structure. While it is plausible that mammals and non-mammals should both have vision, there is no reason to think that they should have similar visual qualia, but individuals with the same physical structures would presumably have the same visual qualia (Levin, 1979, p. 135). Type-type identity for qualia and physical states would be a reasonable empirical hypothesis. And it would fit in with the thought-experiments that associate qualia changes with changes in the brain that result from surgery that involves rewiring connections or inverting neural association areas (Lycan, 1973).

There is an argument against identifying qualia with physical states to be found in the writings of Saul Kripke (1971, 1972). (This argument is discussed by Feldman [1973, 1974], Lycan [1974], and Levin [1975, 1979].) Take the identity of Cicero and Tully. It is possible that Cicero, who is Tully, should appear to everyone to be other than Tully; after all, the identity is known by experience, and experience can mislead. Now if we assume the identity of some particular brain state with the quale pain, then it should be possible that that very brain state appear to everyone to be some other brain state and therefore appear to be other than a pain quale (for example, a tickle quale). But it is actually quite impossible that a pain quale should appear to everyone (including the subject) to be other than a pain quale, say a tickle quale. For a pain quale is just what *appears* to the subject to be a pain quale. Its appearance is its very nature, its essence, its defining characteristic; to be a pain quale is just to appear that characteristic way. Since identifying the pain quale with a brain state leads to an impossible situation, the identity theory cannot be true. (This argument applies to token-identity as well as type-identity.)

Notice that this argument does not work if we take pains, say, to be functional or causal states (Lewis, 1980). For there is no impossibility in a functional or causal state of a certain sort appearing to be other than the functional or causal state it is. It is only at the level of qualia, whose essences consist in their appearances, that the impossibility arises. Kripke himself speaks only of pain rather than pain qualia, and that could make a difference to the argument. For if we think of pains as occurring both in mammals and non-mammals, then it is plausible to think that we have in mind something other than pain as quale, and the distinction between pain and its appearance becomes more tenable, thereby vitiating the argument. Nevertheless, Kripke does argue in terms of pain's "immediate phenomenological quality" (Kripke, 1972, p. 340), which is what we have taken a pain quale to be.

If qualia remain the stubborn residue resisting materialist analysis, what are we to make of them? They seem truly ineffable, inhospitable to informative description, available only to be pointed to. Each of us in his or her own case knows "what it is like" to feel pain and how scarlet looks, but do we have any reason to believe there are similar qualia in the case of others or even in the case of our own past? To justify such beliefs we may appeal to the (reasonable) hypothesis that organisms with very similar structures will experience similar qualia. As the differences increase, the inference is weakened to the point that we would have very little idea, to use Nagel's example, of what it is like to be a bat and how such things are for it. Someone who could present an account of how qualia fit into the rest of our picture of the world will have provided a crucial part of the solution to the mind-body problem.

Eliminative Materialism

If we are right about qualia, at least some mentalistic terms have defied reduction. At best, we have been left with a dualism of properties, features, or types. One way out is to claim that troublesome mentalistic terms have no reference at all, that there are no pains or after-images, and even, perhaps, that there are no beliefs or desires. Thus, Feyerabend recommends "a purely physiological approach to human beings" (1963, p. 296). This, of course, is not for now but to be achieved in the future, assuming physiology continues to develop toward a complete explanation of human behavior.

There are two ways in which eliminative materialists can look at current mentalistic talk, although the distinction should not be taken as entirely sharp or clear. One is as an *empirically* false theory, like astrology, demonic possession, or phlogiston theory (Rorty, 1965; Churchland, 1980, sections 15 and 16). It might have been that people have aches and pains, beliefs and desires, but it turns out that no one does; there just are not, as a matter of fact, such kinds of states or events. The basic argument for this conclusion depends on the assumption that mentalistic explanation of behavior is incompatible with physiological explanation and the assumption that physiological explanation will prove to be a true explanation of behavior. But both of these assumptions are debatable. To put it very briefly, it can be argued that "behavior" is ambiguous; mentalistic concepts explain actions, whereas physiological concepts explain bodily movements. If actions are reducible to bodily movements plus other physical circumstances, both theories can be true accounts of the same subject-matter, perhaps like physics and chemistry; if not, each will be an autonomous science, perhaps like physics and economics, to use Fodor's example (1975, pp. 15-17). (For discussion of the relation of action to movement, see Davis, 1979; Care and Landesman, 1968; Brand, 1970; and Binkley, et al., 1971.)

The other defense of eliminative materialism consists in arguing that mentalistic terms are essentially confused, conceptually unclear, even incoherent (Dennett, 1978, p. xx and *passim*). Nothing *could* be a pain or a belief, because the very notions are riddled with unclarities and contradictions. In reply, it might be pointed out that there is a question of how high our standards of clarity should be. Philosophical examination of the concepts of *physics* expose conceptual difficulties there, too, yet the theory does serve. And surely, a similar conclusion is appropriate for at least the typical, working development of mentalistic concepts. In many cases, at least, they provide us with excellent explanations and predictions of human behavior. It is indeed most difficult to envisage any alternative. When Dennett admits it would not be easy "to convince someone that there are no pains or beliefs," (Dennett, 1978, p. xx), what could he have in mind by "convince" except "bring someone by argument to belief?" At any rate, it will be a long time indeed before we have anything better than our present mentalistic concepts and theories. But that is something the eliminative materialist will concede. On the other hand, if a theoretically adequate and practically manageable physiology develops, mentalistic language may wither away, taking with it the mind-body problem. Such a world would be simpler, but philosophically a lot duller.

Bibliography

Armstrong, David M. 1968. *A Materialist Theory of Mind*. London: Routledge & Kegan Paul.

Binkley, Robert; Bronaugh, Richard; and Marras, Ausonio, eds. 1971. *Agent, Action and Reason*. University of Toronto.

Block, Ned J. 1978. "Troubles with Functionalism." In C. Wade Savage, ed., *Perception and Cognition. Minnesota Studies in the Philosophy of Science* 9. Minneapolis: University of Minnesota Press.

———. 1980. "Are Absent Qualia Impossible?" *The Philosophical Review* 89: 257-74.

Block, Ned J., and Fodor, Jerry A. 1972. "What Psychological States Are Not." *The Philosophical Review* 81: 159-81,

Borst, C. V., ed. 1969. *The Mind-Brain Identity Theory*. New York: Macmillan.

Brand, Myles, ed. 1970. *The Nature of Human Action*. Glenview, Ill.: Scott, Foresman.

Care, Norman S, and Landesman, Charles, eds. 1968. *Readings in the Theory of Action*. Bloomington: University of Indiana Press.

Churchland, Paul. 1980. *Scientific Realism and the Plasticity of Mind*. Cambridge: Cambridge University Press.

Cornman, James W. 1971. "The Identity Theory of Mind and Body." In David M. Rosenthal, ed., *Materialism and the Mind-Body Problem*. Englewood Cliffs, N.J.: Prentice-Hall.

Davidson, Donald. 1970. "Mental Events." In Lawrence Foster and J. W. Swanson, eds., *Experience and Theory*. Amherst: University of Massachusetts Press.

Davis, Lawrence H. 1979. *Theory of Action*. Englewood Cliffs, N.J.: Prentice-Hall.

Dennett, Daniel C. 1978. *Brainstorms: Philosophical Essays on Mind and Psychology*. Montgomery, Vt.: Bradford.

———. 1979. "Quining Qualia." Unpublished.

Donnellan, Keith. 1966. "Reference and Definite Descriptions." *The Philosophical Review* 75: 281-304.

Dreyfus, Hubert L. 1979. *What Computers Can't Do*. Rev. ed. New York: Harper & Row.

Feigl, Herbert. 1958. "The 'Mental' and the 'Physical,'" *Concepts, Theories and the Mind-Body Problem. Minnesota Studies in the Philosophy of Science* 2. Minneapolis: University of Minnesota Press.

_____ . 1961. "Mind-Body, *Not* a Pseudo-Problem. In Sidney Hook, ed., *Dimensions of Mind*. Collier.

Feldman, Fred. 1973. "Kripke's Argument Against Materialism." *Philosophical Studies* 24: 416-19.

_____ . 1974. "Kripke on the Identity Theory." *Journal of Philosophy* 71: 665-76.

Feyerabend, Paul K. 1963. "Mental Events and the Brain," *The Journal of Philosophy* 60: 295-96.

Fodor, Jerry A. 1968. *Psychological Explanation*. New York: Random House.

_____ . 1975. *The Language of Thought*. Cambridge, Mass.: Harvard University Press.

_____ . 1981. "The Mind-Body Problem." *Scientific American* 244: 114-23.

Gunderson, Keith. 1971. *Mentality and Machines*. New York: Anchor Books, Doubleday.

Harman, Gilbert. 1973. *Thought*. Princeton, N.J.: Princeton University Press.

Haugeland, John. 1978. "The Nature and Plausibility of Cognitivism." *The Behavioral and Brain Sciences* 2: 215-60.

Kalke, William. 1969. "What is Wrong with Fodor and Putnam's Functionalism." *Nous* 3: 83-94.

Kim, Jaegwon. 1972. "Phenomenal Properties, Psychophysical Laws and the Identity Theory," *Monist* 56: 177-92.

_____ . 1978. "Supervenience and Nomological Incommensurables." *American Philosophical Quarterly* 15: 149-56.

Kripke, Saul. 1971. "Identity and Necessity." In Milton K. Muntz, ed., *Identity and Individuation*. New York University Press.

_____ . 1972. "Naming and Necessity." In Donald Davidson and Gilbert Harman, eds., *Semantics of Natural Language*. Dordrecht: Reidel.

_____ . 1977. "Speaker's Reference and Semantic Reference." *Midwest Studies in Philosophy* 2: 255-76. Reprinted 1979 in Peter French, Theodore F. Wehling, Jr., and Howard K. Wettstein, eds., *Contemporary Perspectives in the Philosophy of Language*. Minneapolis: University of Minnesota Press.

Levin, Michael E. 1975. "Kripke's Argument Against the Identity Thesis." *Journal of Philosophy* 72: 149-67.

_____ . 1979. *Metaphysics and the Mind-Body Problem*. Oxford: Oxford University Press.

Lewis, David. 1966. "An Argument for the Identity Theory." *Journal of Philosophy* 63: 17-25.

_____ . 1980. "Mad Pain and Martian Pain." In Ned Block, ed., *Readings in the Philosophy of Psychology* 1. Cambridge: Harvard University Press.

Lewis, Hywel D. 1970. *The Elusive Mind*. London: Allen and Unwin.

_____ . 1973. *The Self and Immortality*. New York: Seabury Press.

Lycan, William G. 1973. "Inverted Spectrum." *Ratio* 15: 315-19.

_____ . 1974a. "Kripke and the Materialists." *Journal of Philosophy* 71: 667-89.

_____ . 1974b. "Mental States and Putnam's Functionalist Hypothesis." *Australasian Journal of Philosophy* 52: 48-62.

_____ . 1981. "Form, Function, and Feel." *Journal of Philosophy* 78: 24-50.

MacKay, Donald M. 1980. *Brains, Machines and Persons*. Cleveland, Ohio: Wm. Collins and World.

Malcolm, Norman. 1968. "The Conceivability of Mechanism." *The Philosophical Review* 77: 45-72.

Matson, Wallace I. 1976. *Sentience*. Berkeley: University of California Press.

Morick, Harold. 1967. *Wittgenstein and the Problem of Other Minds,* New York: McGraw-Hill.

Nagel, Thomas. 1979. *Mortal Questions*. Cambridge: Cambridge University Press.

Neisser, Ulric. 1976. *Cognition and Reality*. San Francisco: W.H. Freeman.

Nelson, R. J. 1976. "Mechanism, Functionalism, and the Identity Theory." *The Journal of Philosophy* 73: 365-85.

O'Connor, John. 1969. *Modern Materialism: Readings on Mind-Body Identity*. New York: Harcourt, Brace & World.

Place, U. T. 1956. "Is Consciousness a Brain Process?" *British Journal of Psychology* 47: 44-50.

Plantinga, Alvin. 1967. "Comments on 'The Mental Life of Some Machines.'" In Hector-Neri Castañeda, ed., *Intentionality, Minds and Perception*. Detroit: Wayne State University.

Popper, Karl. 1974. "Replies to My Critics." In Paul Arthur Schilpp, ed., *The Philosophy of Karl Popper*. Vol. 2. La Salle, Ill.: Open Court. Pp. 1048-80.

Popper, Karl, and Eccles, John C. 1977. *The Self and Its Brain*. New York: Springer.

Puccetti, Roland, and Dykes, Robert W. 1978. "Sensory Cortex and the Mind-Brain Problem." *The Brain and Behavioral Sciences* 3: 337-75.

Putnam, Hilary. 1960. "Dreaming and Depth Grammar." In Ronald J. Butler, ed., *Analytic Philosophy.* New York: Barnes and Noble.

_____ . 1961. "Minds and Machines." In Sidney Hook, ed., *Dimensions of Mind.* Collier. Pp. 138–64.

_____ . 1964. "Robots: Machines or Artificially Created Life?" *Journal of Philosophy* 61: 668–91.

_____ . 1965. "Brains and Behavior." In Ronald J. Butler, ed., *Analytical Philosophy,* 2nd ser. Oxford University Press. Pp. 1–20.

_____ . 1967a. "The Mental Life of Some Machines." In Hector-Neri Castañeda, ed., *Intentionality, Minds, and Perception.* Detroit: Wayne State University.

_____ . 1967b. "Psychological Predicates." In William H. Capitan and Daniel D. Merrill, eds., *Art, Mind and Religion.* Pittsburgh.

_____ . 1970. "Is Semantics Possible?" *Metaphilosophy* 1: 187–201.

_____ . 1973a. "Meaning and Reference." *Journal of Philosophy* 70: 699–711.

_____ . 1973b. "Reductionism and the Nature of Psychology." *Cognition* 2: 131–46.

_____ . 1975a. "The Meaning of 'Meaning.'" In K. Gunderson, ed., *Minnesota Studies in the Philosophy of Science* 7. Minneapolis: University of Minnesota Press.

_____ . 1975b. "Philosophy and Our Mental Life." In *Mind, Language and Reality.* Cambridge: Cambridge University Press.

Quine, W.V.O. 1953. "Two Dogmas of Empiricism." In *From a Logical Point of View.* New York: Harper & Row.

Rorty, Richard. 1965. "Mind-Body Identity, Privacy, and Categories." *The Review of Metaphysics* 19: 24–54.

_____ . 1972. "Functionalism, Machines, and Incorrigibility." *The Journal of Philosophy* 69: 203–20.

Rosenthal, David M., ed. 1971. *Materialism and the Mind-Body Problem.* Englewood Cliffs, N.J.: Prentice-Hall.

Ryle, Gilbert. 1949. *The Concept of Mind.* New York: Barnes & Noble.

Shaffer, Jerome A. 1963. "Recent Work on the Mind-Body Problem." *American Philosophical Quarterly* 2: 1–24.

Shoemaker, Sidney. 1975. "Functionalism and Qualia." *Philosophical Studies* 27: 291–315.

Smart, J.J.C. 1959. "Sensations and Brain Processes." *The Philosophical Review* 68: 141–56.

_____ . 1962. "Brain Processes and Incorrigibility." *The Australasian Journal of Philosophy* 40: 68–70.

Spicker, Stuart F., ed. 1970. *The Philosophy of the Body: Rejections of Cartesian Dualism.* New York: Quadrangle/Times Books.

Taylor, Charles. 1967. "Mind-Body Identity, A Side Issue?" *The Philosophical Review* 76: 201–13.

Thomson, Judith Jarvis. 1964. "Private Languages." *American Philosophical Quarterly* 1: 20–31.

Wimsatt, William C. 1976. "Reductionism, Levels of Organisation, and the Mind-Body Problem." In Gordon G. Globus, Grover Maxwell, and Irwin Sarodnik, eds., *Consciousness and the Brain.* New York: Plenum Press.

Winston, Patrick H. 1977. *Artificial Intelligence.* Reading, Mass.: Addison-Wesley.

Wittgenstein, Ludwig. 1958. *Philosophical Investigations.* 2nd ed., Macmillan.

PART IV

Ethics

chapter 6

Recent Work in Ethical Egoism

TIBOR R. MACHAN

Crito: When you are gone, Socrates, how can we best act to please you?
Socrates: Just follow my old recipe, my friend: do yourselves concern yourselves with your own true self-interest; then you will oblige me, and mine, and
yourselves too.

Plato, *Phaedo* 115b

What is most important is that motives of this sort [civil disobedience] be
distinguished from the typical criminal motive: self-interest.

Jeffrie G. Murphy, *Civil Disobedience and Violence*

I

Critics of egoism usually charge that the doctrine cannot be a bona fide ethical or
moral theory, let alone the correct guide to how we should conduct our lives. While
earlier the prominent issue was whether psychological (or descriptive) egoism was true,
today ethical egoism occupies the attention of numerous moral philosophers. Ethical
egoism will also be the concern of this essay. Other than utilitarianism, egoism has
been the most widely discussed substantive ethical position (in academic philosophy)
in recent years. Altruism, perhaps the most widely voiced ethics in our culture, has
received scant attention by comparison.

Although difficult to achieve without preempting the discussion to follow, it will be
useful to start with a broad characterization of the two sides of the egoism/antiegoism
debate. To do so, we might consider how the debate would be understood in terms
familiar to anyone concerned with human affairs.

Sometimes people are said to be obligated to act in some ways unrelated to their
own benefit; this is regarded by some as their basic duty. Those who deny this view
and yet accept a place for morality are in effect advancing the ethical egoist position.
They maintain that basic principles of human conduct must always be related, in
however remote a fashion or complicated a manner, to some benefit for the agent. The
precise nature of this benefit would presuppose some version of ethical egoism. The
precise nature of the basic duty that is not related to such benefit, in contrast, would
presuppose some nonegoistic ethics. Nevertheless, broadly speaking, advocates of a
morality tied to benefiting the agent are egoists, while advocates of a morality without
such a tie are nonegoists.[1]

Among egoists, or rather, among the doctrines regarded as egoistic by either advocates or critics, are many varieties. In this essay I will keep in focus two distinctive
types: subjective ethical egoism, where a code is applicable to the unique individual

one happens to be, and what I call classical ethical egoism, in which the ego or self is regarded as an individual of a kind (namely, a human being). The distinction between these will become clearer as we proceed.

This chapter will review and comment briefly on works, beginning with the early 1950s, that discuss egoism and self-interest or self-enhancement ethics. I will stress the positive arguments and will not aim for strict chronological development, but will focus on cohesive groups of essays and books that have dealt with different versions of ethical egoism. In the end I will pull together strands of the various arguments and sketch a version of ethical egoism that could well be the answer to the central question that has prompted our substantive moral philosophizing.

In moral philosophy, the terms of the discussion of egoism have drawn abundantly from the contributions of all philosophers in the past, so to begin with the second half of the 20th century may appear to be arbitrary. Yet it is at this time that some Anglo-American philosophers began to show dissatisfaction with an earlier version of morality or ethics. The last is best exemplified in A. J. Ayer (1936) and in the more directly ethical works of C. L. Stevenson (1945) and John Mackie (1946). From the extreme positivist subjectivism espoused by these philosophers and their kindred spirits, moral philosophy began its recovery by way of the greater prominence of ordinary-language philosophical methodology.[2] This development occurred close enough to mid-20th century that we are entitled to take it as our starting point.

Before philosophers employing this new approach to ethics had produced any substantive ethical positions, a number of contributions to journals and books appeared aiming to show that egoism could not even be a candidate for the right morality. Although initially none defended egoism, a few philosophers argued that whether or not egoism is the correct moral theory, it at least might be. Only outside of academic philosophy were various versions of egoism proposed as good systems. Economists tended to embrace the neo-Hobbesian view that everyone necessarily promotes his own interest, a point still advocated by many. Ayn Rand (1964, 1967), whose works were eventually discussed within academic philosophy, advocated the view that given a clear understanding of what one is—a human being—each person should live so as to promote his or her self-interest.

For now, let us simply consider those early academic philosophers who wished to show that egoism can be a bona fide ethical theory. Their work was in the nature of replies to other moral theorists—e.g., R. M. Hare (1954–55) and Kurt Baier (1958)—who had argued that egoism fails to satisfy even the minimum criteria of being a candidate for an ethical theory. J. A. Brunton's attempt to defend egoism against this charge is our starting point.

II

Brunton (1956) takes up Hare's charge that egoism is not universalizable. Hare held that ultimate principles are open to choice—i.e., none can be discovered or identified as objectively binding on us all—but that, even so, to choose egoism is incoherent, something that cannot be an ultimate moral *principle*. Brunton answers this charge by noting that the egoist

> is just as sensitive to the distinction between oneself and others as other recognized moralists are. Since many moralists are commended because they advocate that one should care more about an equal pain suffered by someone else than about one's own, can the Egoist be condemned on *formal* grounds if he cares less?" [Brunton, 1956, p. 297].

Brunton defends against the universalizability charge by noting that

> the non-parallelism in the Egoist's attitude toward himself and others is not only shared, in a different direction, by altruistic moralists, but is also backed by the good sound reason that the logic of personal experience is in its favour. . . . [T]he

fight against Egoism and its extensions cannot, in the main, be waged by pointing out logical inconsistencies. Egoists and their fellow travellers (e.g., doting parents and uncritical patriots), and, indeed, the egoistic part in all of us, will always find rules, reasons, and justification [Brunton, 1956, pp. 298 ff.].

What Brunton has done is to argue that any practically viable morality must admit to some biases (e.g., altruism has a bias toward others, utilitarianism toward the well-being or pleasure of the majority), and egoism does likewise. To ask of a moral position that it be completely unbiased, impartial, and universalizable is to ask the improbable, perhaps even impossible, of human beings. So, Brunton's "defense" of egoism concludes, "[I]f . . . we do not like, want, or choose Egoism, we can best fight it by the psychological and persuasive process of trying to get ourselves and others actively to identify ourselves and imaginatively sympathise with other people of all kinds and races" (Brunton, 1956, p. 303).

To Brunton's defense of the possibility of egoism as (if not a moral theory) "one's own choice of a way of life," there have been objections. Carlson notes that even if all moralities are advocated and practiced with the expectation of inconsistencies, the point is that as ideals they must be consistently practicable—without prompting conduct and institutions that are impossible when the doctrine is fully and consistently adopted (Carlson, 1973, p. 32). If egoism could not be practiced (including advocated) as a (possible) fully consistent way of life for someone, then its failure as a moral or ethical position would have to be admitted in spite of what Brunton has argued.

Among those critics who hold that egoism cannot be even an ethics within non-cognitivism or emotivism, Kai Nielsen has been a prominent example. Although he has advanced numerous arguments aiming to prove this point, he has not criticized any defender of ethical egoism, and few have taken up his objections. (Stevenson [1945] and Dwyer [1975, 1976] are two who have. But their points are treated here as made by other critics.) In Nielsen's 1959 paper he argues that ethical egoism cannot succeed as a moral theory whether we regard it as "a doctrine of *ends*" or as "a doctrine of *means*" (p. 502). What Nielsen means by the first is the general doctrine to the effect that "The final test of the valuable is what I like in the way of experience" (Nielsen, 1959, p. 506). This is a doctrine of ends of a very narrow type, namely, where the ends are identified by reference to the arbitrary criterion of "what I like." As such, it is a clear example of subjectivist, personal egoism. And what some defenders of egoism, not mentioned by Nielsen, will point out, is that much of what one likes may not be in one's self-interest. One may like to eat lots of chili-pepper–flavored chips, but they add to one's already heavier-than-healthy body. And one may positively dislike physical exercise, but it does improve the strength of one's heart muscles, which is (by the best information that is reasonably available) going to keep a person healthier than not possessing a strong heart (all other things being equal).

When Nielsen turned to the doctrine of egoism as a means, he meant by this the view Adam Smith held, namely, that by pursuing one's own interest one will best serve the common good, which is admittedly the desired goal. But this view is not egoistic at all. Here the good to be sought by an individual may be his own, but it must be justified by reference to something other than the individual's own good (however this last is to be understood). The theory involved is, therefore, not egoistic, even if it makes room for egoistic motives in human conduct.

Nielsen has advanced other kinds of arguments against egoism and I will turn to some of these later. In all of them, however, Nielsen formulates his own version of egoism, thus leaving his readers in the dark as to whether anyone really holds the target position. And Nielsen is by no means the only antiegoist who proceeds along such lines.

Jesse Kalin is one of the few academic philosophers who has long defended egoism as both a plausible and a sound ethical doctrine. I will return to Kalin when I come to later works on egoism and mention here but a few of the points he makes in his "In Defense of Egoism" (Kalin, 1968).

Kalin's early piece, which has not received sufficient attention from critics of egoism, argues that while egoism may not be a "standard morality" (Kalin, 1968, p. 65), it is a plausible personal ethical doctrine. He allows that his type of egoism would lead to conflicts among egoists but thinks that this is neither crucial nor necessary. He holds that an egoist could take an interest in others but "the source of [any] obligation is his interest in them" (Kalin, 1968, p. 65). He formulates his egoism as the view that "A person ought to do a specific action, all things considered, if and only if that action is in that person's overall (enlightened) self-interest" (Kalin, p. 66). He rejects a formulation of egoism by Frankena on grounds that Frankena switches the agent and spectator positions in his own rendition of egoism, thus generating a contradiction in the basic egoistic principle. Kalin believes that as a spectator an egoist must accept that other persons should seek their own self-interest, contrary to what Frankena believes. And against Medlin, another critic of egoism, Kalin rejects that egoism leads to inconsistency. To aid his rebuttal to Medlin, Kalin invokes two important ideas. First, he tells us that his version of egoism "rests upon both teleological and deontological elements" (Kalin, p. 74) and, second, he introduces the distinction between a material and a formal conception of valuation (Kalin, p. 77). The former stresses the achievement of concrete, particular objectives – e.g., the winning of a particular game of chess, acquiring a given job – while the latter emphasizes the seeking of kinds of goals – e.g., aiming at successful participation in competitive or combative games, obtaining a suitable position.

Kalin has been attacked by George R. Carlson on grounds that his distinction will not save the egoist from having inconsistent wants: "Insofar as he sincerely believes . . . Kalin's universalized egoistic axiom . . . the egoist cannot avoid wanting X to do Y, when it is in X's overall self-interest to do Y [where Y is against or not in the egoist's self-interest and is a particular action]" (Carlson, 1973, p. 29). It is Kalin's reliance on the combative game analogy to illustrate some aspects of egoism that leads to Carlson's criticism, an analogy Kalin later abandons.

III

Different from Kalin's apparently subjectivist type of egoism are those theories closer to the sort Plato seems to advance in the *Republic* and Aristotle suggests (in the form of a certain kind of self-love) can motivate a good human being (*Nicomachean Ethics*, 119a12). Recently C. J. Wheeler (1976) has argued that crucial elements of ancient Greek morality were explicitly egoistic; indeed, Hardie (1965) has recently explained the sense in which Aristotle can be considered an egoist.

In our era, this sort of self-enhancing, even self-regarding morality has been given support by certain philosophers. Although he is not regarded an egoist, mainly because he does not advance a comprehensive moral position, W. D. Falk's work provides a good deal of support to the broader, classical egoism I have distinguished at the outset of this paper (and will come back to later).

Falk points out that for the Greeks the "right-living person was one who would keep himself in good shape as a sane and self-possessed being, and who would do whatever good and sufficient reasons directed him to do" (Falk, 1965). Such reasons could directly benefit oneself or others, and Falk chides those who would, following Kant, reject prudential conduct as morally irrelevant. As to the social dimensions of morality, he says

One incurs [social commitments], if through anyone's doing, through one's own: as someone willing to seek direction from the counsel of cogent reasons. The involvement of human beings in this practice [of incurring social commitments] is personal: it turns on their stake in the kind of self-preservation which requires that one should be able to bear before oneself the survey of one's own actions. [Falk, 1950, p. 88].

Falk's views have, to the detriment of related scholarly developments, received little attention from other moral philosophers. His careful analysis of prudence, for example, did not appear to impress later writers such as Thomas Nagel and David Gauthier, both of whom have made considerable critical reference to prudential conduct in connection with their ethical writings and criticism of egoism.

Since Falk has received little criticism for having given egoism some support, I need to mention what might be objectionable about taking his views as supportive of any sort of egoism.

First, the theory of value that underlies a classical self-enhancement ethics probably will not give support to egoism. In both Plato and Aristotle, the ultimate good toward which the self-actualizing, self-enhancement process would aim would have to be something outside oneself. The contemplative life is good, for example, because it is closest to the divine. The orderly soul of an individual is good in its relationship to the separate form of good. Even Aristotle's conception of virtue as the actualization of one's essential nature is tied to his view about the *intrinsic* value of the intellectual life.

Second, the numerous arguments about whether it is possible to make clear sense of the idea of *the nature* of man or *the essence* of human self would have to be adequately resolved to give full support to Falk's line of analysis. Falk might meet these sorts of objections, but he has not addressed them directly in his substantive moral discussions.

We need to consider a defender of ethical egoism, close to Falk in philosophical mode, who does address the second of these issues. Ayn Rand, a widely read, controversial novelist and philosophical essayist, has outlined a philosophical system, Objectivism, within which her ethical egoism occupies an integral part. In 1961 she placed on record a summary statement of her ethics (reprinted in her book on ethics), during a University of Wisconsin symposium, "Ethics in Our Time." Her approach to defending egoism can be gleaned from her view that first we need to know: "*Why* does man need a code of values?" (Rand, 1964, p. 13). Rand contends that "ethics is an objective, metaphysical necessity of man's survival" (p. 23) and defends this on grounds that (a) human beings do not possess instincts, as do other animals, directing them toward the attainment of natural goals; (b) our distinctive type of awareness is conceptual; (c) we must choose to engage in this awareness; and (d) life is (metaphysically) the ultimate value and what "makes the concept of 'Value' [epistemologically] possible" (Rand, 1964, p. 17). By Rand's analysis, the concept "good or evil" can ultimately apply "only to a living entity" (pp. 15-16); that is, the base of the chain of conceptual relations that leads to the valid concept of value is the concept (or phenomenon) of life.

Within the framework of morality—i.e., where choosing values is at issue—Rand holds that we must regard "man's life as the *standard* of value—and *his own life* as the ethical purpose of every individual" (Rand, 1964, p. 25). Here is where Rand's ethical egoism emerges, for to her the "achievement of his own [eudaimonistic] happiness is man's highest moral purpose" (p. 27). This morality of *rational selfishness,* Rand holds, consists of the pursuit of "the values required for man's survival *qua* man—which means: the values required for *human* survival—not the values produced by the desires, the emotions, the 'aspirations,' the feelings, the whims or the needs of irrational [people]" (Rand, 1964, p. 31). Contrary to the way many thinkers conceive of rational egoism, Rand holds, according to her version of the ethics of rational self-interest, that "*human* good does not require human sacrifices and cannot be achieved by the sacrifice of anyone to anyone" (Rand, 1964, p. 31).

Rand's egoism has been criticized by James Rachels, Robert Nozick, and Hazel Barnes, among others. It will be useful to take a brief look at the faults these philosophers have found in this version of egoism.

Rachels (1977) gives a skimpy rendition of what is, after all, an ambitious attempt to develop a systematic ethical theory. He calls Rand's position the "really quite radical doctrine" that "a person is under no obligation to do anything except what is in his own interest" and gives the following as a possible implication of this view:

> Suppose I have an urge to set fire to some public building (say, a department store) just for the fascination of watching the spectacular blaze: according to this view, the fact that several people might be burned to death provides no reason whatever why I should not do it. After all, this only concerns *their* welfare, not my own, and according to the ethical egoist the only person I need think of is myself [Rachels, 1977, p. 63].

Does this supposition accurately represent what Rand's position implies (or would render as morally permissible)? The plausibility of Rachel's case derives from his focusing on the egoist's primary regard for himself. But the case entirely omits from consideration the fact that Rand's ethical egoism sets the standard for a bona fide concern for oneself to be human nature, that is, conduct that is consistent with the essential nature of human beings. Thus, as may be expected, for Rand the highest virtue is rationality, which means "the recognition and acceptance of reason as one's only source of knowledge, one's only judge of values and one's only guide to action. . . . [I]t means a commitment to reason, not in sporadic fits or on selected issues or in special emergencies, but as a permanent way of life" (Rand, 1964, pp. 25–26). Implementing this virtue in one's own case would include the realization that others are, like oneself, committed to seeking their happiness, that it is their moral responsibility to do so, and that any urge to set fire to them does not override the implications of this realization. Ethical egoism, thus developed as a universalized, abstract principle, applies to all persons including those in the building. But that, in turn, implies that they have their own purposes that are not available for someone else to abridge or interfere with. (Precisely this thesis is defended by Mack in his "Egoism and Rights" (1973), namely that others have rights, which are derived from their being entities like oneself with their own well-being and purposes as their highest end.)

There are some gaps in Rand's argument, some beyond those made unavoidable in my very sketchy rendition. The connection between the prime human virtue of rationality and the respect others deserve from one who lives by the ethical egoist code needs to be developed in considerable detail. We will see that several ethical egoists have made the attempt to establish this connection, although not to the evident satisfaction of egoism's critics.

Others have criticized Rand's argument, among them Robert Nozick in his "On the Randian Argument" (1971). Although in this work Nozick undertakes a lengthy critique of Rand, he unfortunately provides a very confusing reconstruction of Rand's case, and his reconstruction does Rand's actual statement of her case less than full justice. In the final analysis, Nozick criticizes Rand on grounds that her argument is not deductively conclusive (Nozick, 1971, p. 282). He does not take into consideration Rand's elaborate efforts to develop the epistemological framework within which her argument should, she believes, be appraised. As a result of this omission, Nozick is led to level a crucial charge against Rand's theory, one not pertinent to her substantive ethics directly but to her theory of definitions, which Nozick does not take up. He remarks (parenthetically) that "if the essence mentioned in [her] argument is real essence, it's a dubious theory" (Nozick, 1971, p. 289), leaving untreated the critical reference Rand makes to man *qua* man (where essence is crucial).[3]

It should be noted, however, that Rand explicitly rejects the realist theory of essences and defends, instead, the view that "essence" is an epistemological concept, albeit (necessarily) with an objective foundation (Rand, 1964, p. 49).

It is in this same domain that Hazel Barnes criticizes Rand's views. Barnes, in her *An Existentialist Ethics,* devotes a chapter to Ayn Rand's "egoistic humanism" and advances fairly standard existentialist objections against the naturalist, or essentialist, ethics Rand defends. Following Sartre, Barnes holds that the sort of naturalism we find in Rand—one in terms of which a code of ethics requires a correct definition of the concept "human being," i.e., a correct identification of human nature—implies the existence of "an absolute judgment which stands outside the immediate involvement of the individual life"; or, as she elaborates, "her system needs Aristotle's Unmoved Mover" (Barnes, 1976, p. 131). Here again, the objection does not emerge from a critique of ethical egoism and would apply to any ethical system claiming to be rationally grounded, objective, universalizable, etc. Of course, this does not show that Rand's ethical egoism is sound, but it does indicate that criticisms of her position center on various metaethical or other philosophically preethical points.[4] Given her clear intent to build her ethics on such prior, controversial philosophical conclusions, such criticism is certainly not beside the point. It would not be possible to follow through the debate, however, when important elements of the position in question reach so far beyond substantive ethical theory. Suffice it to observe that the ethical egoism we discover in Rand is closer to the classical than to the personal or subjective varieties mentioned at the outset of this chapter. And it appears that such a position invites wide-ranging philosophical work. While the strength of a position such as Rand's lies in its elaborate, detailed, hierarchical foundation, which gains support from all branches of philosophy, its weakness is that if some of the links in the chain of argument are themselves undeveloped, the ethics involved remains inconclusive. Whether such a system could still turn out to be the best available depends upon just what criterion is appropriate for appraising the adequacy of ethical theories. Later in this chapter I shall briefly discuss that issue; here I will point to just one more feature of the egoist/antiegoist debate that is highlighted by the above discussion of Rand's views.

It is often noted by parties to the discussion of egoism that the doctrine gains much of its prominence from its close association with Thomas Hobbes's political theory. Rachels makes this clear in his paper in *Philosophia* (1974), for example, and Kalin, too, observes the point in several places.

One of the distinctive features of Hobbesian egoism is that it presupposes a view of the human self such that the motivation underlying human action consists of the combination of various passions and interests.[5] Hobbes's nominalism, in turn, does not permit the employment of the classical idea of the nature of man. The myriad passions motivate human conduct, tempered only by everyone's interest in self-preservation.

Critics of egoism tend to focus on the self as represented by the Hobbesian analysis. By this account, when we consider egoism or rational (as in economics) self-interest, we must mean the passion-driven, multidirectional, normatively unspecifiable self or ego (e.g., see Schmitt, 1973). And ordinary-language analysis does not enable us to go beyond this meaning, since much discourse, even in normative contexts, conforms to the Hobbesian view. Yet as Falk points out, analyses and definitions of normatively significant terms seem to require further treatment than is afforded by the ordinary-language approach; that approach biases inquiry toward a kind of moral democracy, and in evaluating ethical theories this would be a severe obstacle.

IV

Now I turn briefly to an exchange that once again pertains to the plausibility of egoism as a moral position. My task here is complicated somewhat by the critics' attention to egoism without taking up the relatively elaborate treatments of it, or of aspects of it, by Kalin, Falk, Rand, et al. Even Joseph Butler is only mentioned in one or two books on egoism, and he is flatly dismissed by Kalin as not an egoist at all, because for him "there is also in man conscience and 'a natural principle of benevolence'" (Kalin, 1968, p. 65). Surely Kalin is begging the question by so dismissing Butler's egoism.

Let us recall Medlin's and Baier's well-known objections to egoism. Medlin (1957) objects to what he claims to be the best version on grounds that the egoist's ultimate principle cannot provide the guidance to human conduct we must have from ethics. (He holds, incidentally, that altruism is similarly flawed.)

Baier introduces a slightly different problem, reiterated by many critics of egoism, namely, that as a general principle of human conduct egoism will necessarily yield contradictory judgments as to what someone should do. In case of B and K both vying for the presidency, for example, "It follows that if K prevents B from liquidating him, his act must be said to be both wrong and not wrong — wrong because it is the prevention of what B ought to do, his duty, and wrong for B not to do it; not wrong because it is what K ought to do, his duty, and wrong for K not to do it" (Baier, 1958, p. 190). Baier finds this intolerable because "morality is designed to apply in just such cases, namely those where interests conflict."

John Hospers replied to both these criticisms in 1961, urging that in Medlin's case the egoist was misunderstood to be having to give advice about what to achieve, whereas in fact all the egoist should be understood to be saying is, "Each of you should *try* to come out the victor"; and, says Hospers, "There is surely no inconsistency here" (Hospers, 1961, p. 16). To Baier's charge, Hospers replies by focusing on whether egoism *must* generate a contradiction when used as a code of conduct by all. Hospers notes of Baier's example that although it involves "two acts of the same *kind,* namely attempted murder (or the attempt to foil the murder-attempt of the other) . . . there is no contradiction in two such acts being attempted or in both being right" (Hospers, 1961, p. 11). Hospers believes that neither the personal nor the impersonal ethical egoist — roughly the two types I have called subjectivist and classical, respectively — is committed to advising both parties.

But can Hospers's version of egoism meet the "ought implies can" proviso of a bona fide ethical theory? This is the question Richmond Campbell asks of Kalin in the *Canadian Journal of Philosophy* (1972). Eric Mack tries to answer it by considering a case in which A ought to do *s* and B ought to prevent *s* when, of course, both *s* and the prevention of *s* cannot occur. Mack shows that (1) there is no perspective from which "*s* and the prevention of *s* ought to be done" is true. Hence, there is no *ought* such that, given it and "ought implies can," one is forced to the conclusion that *s and* the prevention of *s* can happen. (2) Clearly one cannot get to this absurd conclusion from the fact that (a) *s* is possible and (b) the prevention of *s* is possible.

The exchange between Hospers and the critics, followed by several papers, did not end with Mack's essay. But these follow-up works would take too much space to cover in sufficient detail. Since they were not path-breaking in any important respect, I will forego discussion of them.

V

In none of the papers discussed thus far, excepting Rand's, was the issue whether ethical egoism is the correct ethical theory. The problem focused upon was, and to a large degree remains, whether any version of egoism could be candidate for the right ethical system, that is, a bona fide ethical theory. This is why the critics tend to emphasize the un-universalizability, etc., of egoism, while defenders stress that the doctrine is not plagued by such shortcomings. A full, comparative appraisal of egoism has not been produced thus far, although the doctrine has been advocated as the correct ethics by some professional moral philosophers.

Robert G. Olson, for example, advances what he considers an egoistic or self-interest–oriented morality.

> I regard right conduct as conduct that simultaneously promotes public and private good. . . . And although I do not [hold] that there never is or can be an ultimate conflict between private and social good, I am *not* convinced that conflicts of this

kind ever do occur, and I *am* convinced that if they do they occur much more rarely than is generally supposed [Olson, 1965, p. 7].

Despite calling it the morality of self-interest, Olson tries very hard to show that the general welfare is promoted by self-interested conduct. As a result, he is open to the sort of objection Kai Nielsen has advanced against "ethical egoism as a doctrine of *means.*" If the good sought is really not one's own but that of the public or society, and if the merits of the theory are ascertained by reference to this feature, then it is basically incorrect to call this an egoistic or self-interest–oriented moral position. Instead, it would be more to the point to regard Olson's book as a discussion of how the welfare of society might be brought about by encouraging individuals to pursue their long-range, enlightened self-interests.

A more strictly egoistic ethical theory has been developed in the wake of several less substantial, critical, and positive discussions of egoism in the pages of *The Personalist.* In 1969 Donald Emmons rejected the attempts to undercut egoism by demonstrations that it involves inconsistencies or contradictions. Emmons recommended, instead, that the doctrine, if treated as a cognitivist metaethical theory, must be refuted "by citing *moral* facts" (Emmons, 1969, p. 318). The only form of cognitivism Emmons acknowledged as having some chance of philosophical success is intuitionism. But he did not consider the success likely, and so, if "the non-cognitivists are correct, we cannot really *refute* [the egoist] at all." He concluded that "In either case, the only appropriate stance is one of moral opposition" (Emmons, 1969, p. 318).

This essay started a long-lasting debate in the same journal, culminating (for awhile) with a comprehensive treatment by Eric Mack in his paper "How to Derive Ethical Egoism" (1971). Mack produced a neo-Aristotelian, functionalist, essentialist case for the objective status of morality and argued for the view that the content of the correct moral code amounts to a form of egoism. The argument is laid out systematically in propositions, glosses, and theorems. It will not be possible to reproduce the entire argument, but a brief (structurally incomplete) summary of it will be helpful here.

Mack proposes first that if there is some "need . . . which explains the existence of some thing, . . . then that thing functions well" *iff* its use satisfies that need. For living things, "it is the fact that remaining in existence as a living thing . . . requires the successful completion of numerous processes that explains the existence of valuation." From these two propositions (both accompanied by explanations), Mack derives his theorem that "Valuation functions well [*iff*] its use . . . satisfies the requirement of the valuing organism to complete processes successfully if it is to remain a living thing."

Theorem II, derived from the second proposition, states that "Valuation is a process that is carried on by living things; it is goal-directed action." After several additional (logically indispensable) theorems, Mack states in theorem VI that "Performing successfully the actions that sustain its life is that which is good with respect to any given organism." The following proposition brings in the moral element: "If a standard for goal-directed action is complied with as a result of choices made by the acting entity, then the (normally) resulting good is a moral good, and the actions (specifically choices) of the agent are morally good." After several more steps, Mack concludes with the ethical egoist position:

> The morally good, with respect to each human being, is the successful performance, and the results of the successful performance, of those actions that sustain his existence as a living thing [Mack, 1971, pp. 736–37].

Mack's argument draws on several philosophically troublesome concepts, and he goes on to defend it against two objections that focus on such concepts. First, he defends the existence of objective functions that are "independent of persons' actions, hopes, wants, etc." (Mack, 1971, p. 737). He also defends the view that there can be functions of things independently of and prior to the use to which the thing may be put. (This aspect of his argument concerns the derivation of "ought" from "is" propositions.) His argument for the prior availability of various essential functions in the life of an organism, such as a human being, counters Nozick's charge that such analysis involves question begging — that is, it does not accomplish the derivation of normative conclusions from nonnormative facts. (No doubt, Mack's discussion is incomplete in that numerous difficult philosophical issues — e.g., the analytic/synthetic dichotomy, the distinction between the intensional and extensional scope of definitions and concepts — require full treatment so as to secure his conclusion with sufficient firmness.)

Unfortunately, Mack's argument still awaits confrontation by the antiegoists, not to mention moral skeptics or non-cognitivists. Although numerous critics have since produced arguments against their own versions of egoism, Mack's case has not met with any criticism in the literature. Mack's argument is, to date, the most systematic and comprehensive case for a version of ethical egoism, and we will leave the position as it stands and turn to other discussions.

VI

James Rachels has advanced a detailed criticism of egoism in which he maintains that egoism is a threat to "the social-political ideal of human freedom" and that it "is simply a wicked view" (Rachels, 1974, p. 298). In support of the first point Rachels says,

> There are situations in which it would best promote the interest of one person, X, to do a certain act A, while it would best promote the interest of another person Y to stop X from doing A. [Rachels, 1974, p. 303].

Rachels's point is similar to that made earlier by Baier in the case of the two presidential contenders. What distinguishes his treatment is that he tried to address the reply that "such conflicts of interest cannot occur" (1974, p. 304).

Rachels refers to Hobbes as someone who tries to show that from an egoistic viewpoint it is in one's self-interest to abide by the rules that lead to social harmony. Rachels counters this view by noting that "While it surely is to the individual's own advantage to live in a society in which the ordinary moral rules are obeyed, he does not have to obey them himself all the time in order to live in such a society" (Rachels, 1974, p. 305). We have here a reply to a type of egoism of the subjectivist or personal variety, and Rachels does not consider ethical egoists of the classical type.

Eric Mack addresses himself exactly to this contention of the antiegoist (although not to Rachels directly). Mack says:

> Let us suppose that Smith is acting, pursuing certain goals. In the course of these actions, Jones is used. That is, as a result of the actions performed by Smith (not necessarily actions that are in Smith's interest) some portion of Jones's life is consumed. Smith acts in a way that would be justified only if that portion of Jones's life were at his disposal, in the same sense that an unclaimed natural resource might be at Smith's disposal. It is this sort of action, action wherein Jones is used, treated as a natural resource at the actor's disposal, that I claim are actions done as if it is not the case that Jones ought to act in his own interest. These are the actions that cannot be justified with the egoistic principle [Mack, 1973, p. 30].

Failing to see that ethical egoism is a principle of conduct for human beings, Rachels does not realize that it would be egoistically wrong to abridge the social-political ideal of human freedom. By taking as his adversary Hobbes (whom Rachels paraphrases throughout), the essentialist element of egoism escapes Rachels's attention.

Rachels's second criticism is based on the view that "we do not determine what is right *merely* by consulting theories of rightness. Such a theory may be helpful in difficult cases, when we are not sure what to think; but in *clear* cases, in which it is *plain* what is right and what is wrong, then the theory is tested by how well it corresponds to the moral 'facts,' and not the other way around" (Rachels, 1974, p. 313). Of course, objections may be raised against this intuitionist approach—e.g., that many people have very wicked ideas about what is *clearly* wrong, *plainly* right. But we can look at Rachels's argument and see whether it works even if his moral appraisals are accepted.

A friend told Rachels the story of a physician (in a small southern town where no other doctor was available) who took the last $12 from a destitute black woman for services rendered that did the black woman no benefit at all. Rachels advances the folowing argument relating the physician's conduct to egoism:

(1) If ethical egoism is correct, then the doctor did the right thing.
(2) The doctor did not do the right thing.
(3) Therefore, ethical egoism is not correct. [Rachels, 1974, p. 309].

Rachels accepts (1) as obviously true and proceeds to spend several pages on (2). In reply to this neglected portion of his argument, the ethical egoist can advance the following objections:

A. it is not at all obvious that (always or simply) enriching oneself is right as judged by ethical egoist standards. Quite apart from whether it is egoistically good for one to act in callous ways, it is possible that it is not egoistically good for the physician in question to pursue the course he did; he might be jeopardizing his reputation, for example. So (1) is by no means obviously true.

B. Ethical egoism includes versions that stress the rational nature of man. If the egoist holds that rationality is egoistically proper for us, and if reason shows (as it clearly might) that regarding the welfare of another is more rewarding than $12, (1) could again turn out to be far from obviously true.

C. The rational possibility of the feeling of empathy, as stressed by such egoists as Branden, Rand, et al., cannot be omitted from consideration as Rachels's case is scrutinized. One can hurt oneself by countering one's natural feelings.

Each of these reasons by itself shows that (1) is very dubious. Rachels's systematic neglect of the more sophisticated forms of egoism has led him to maintain an untenable position. He even fails to give Hobbes's actual arguments and chooses, instead, his own rendition of Hobbes's position.

In general, most critics of egoism fail to heed the arguments and statements advanced by egoists themselves—which has contributed, in part, to the difficulty of dealing with the discussion in a coherent fashion. Another critic who gives his own rendition of egoism is David Gauthier in his paper "The Impossibility of Rational Egoism." He tells us that "An egoist is a person who on every occasion and in every respect acts to bring about as much as possible of what he values." He then proceeds to argue, with ingenious hypothetical cases and carefully developed game-theoretical arguments, that "it is not possible to act, on every occasion and in every respect, to bring about as much as possible of what one values" (Gauthier, 1974, p. 442). He thus contends that "If to act in this way were rational, rationality would be incoherent." (Regarding Gauthier's paper, I merely want to point out that it is precisely to establish *what* is of value that ethical egoism would be invoked.)[6]

Another critic of egoism, Warren Quinn, advances antiegoist arguments without once citing a defender of ethical egoism in order to anchor the target position to a supportive argument. In his paper, "Egoism as an Ethical System" (1974), the author is more directly concerned than Gauthier with the issues earlier considered by Kalin, Baier, Medlin, Hospers, et al. Quinn himself notes that he is close to Medlin and Baier in several of his objections to egoism *qua* ethical theory, but only one novel argument is advanced as follows:

Moreover, the goodness involved in rightness is obviously a result of the good aspects of the right act, e.g., that the act is an instance of benefitting others, benefitting oneself, keeping a promise, etc. Thus, moral rightness must derive from a type of moral goodness which is intensional, i.e., which applies to acts *under descriptions*. In other words, the concept of moral rightness seems to presuppose some variety or other of the moral approbatives. But, as far as I can see, there are only two such varieties that actually function in moral thought: the impersonal and the quasi-personal. . . . But moral rightness cannot be a species of quasi-personal goodness for the simple reason that an action can be right without being "good of" its agent. By elimination, therefore, the type of goodness presupposed by moral rightness would seem to be impersonal [Quinn, 1974, p. 472].

Quinn believes, moreover, that an impersonal conception of goodness precludes the possibility of giving an account of right action in solely egoistic terms.

Certainly, Mack's argument would have provided Quinn with a suitable target; but in the absence of a joined debate, I will simply indicate what the ethical egoist of Mack's variety could say to Quinn's objection.

The impersonal goodness Quinn believes is required for an adequate account of right action seems to be necessitated because "an action can be right without being 'good of' its agent." But is this true? No argument is provided. It is possible that an ethical egoist account of the concept of goodness would show that each instance of right that is appropriately intensional falls under description by way of a broad conception of goodness that relates back to the good of the person involved *qua* the kind of being any person is, namely, a human being. The egoist could then argue that the good of human beings must be the good of an individual human being. So although no strictly *impersonal* (i.e., nonhuman) goodness would be invoked, a universal human goodness that *must* pertain is the goodness of particular *instances of* the universal (on metaphysical and related grounds).

In short, Quinn's case lacks adequate support. The "simple reason that an action can be right without being 'good of' its agent" is not simple at all. The ethical egoist appears to have an analysis of his own that requires direct refutation.

A somewhat different criticism from Quinn's is advanced by Steven A. Smith in his "Ethical Egoism and Value." Smith wants to reject egoism because "it entails an unsatisfactory theory of value" (Smith, 1974, p. 95). Smith regards ethical egoism as tied to a teleological theory of value and means by this that "the rightness of an action is simply its productivity of goodness." Since this theory of value "is implausible and apparently false," ethical egoism "is . . . unsatisfactory as a theory of right" (Smith, 1974, p. 95).

Smith considers Kalin's defense of egoism. Although he finds Kalin's distinction between material and formal valuation "helpful to the ethical egoist," he does not seem to appreciate its full force. Smith quotes Kalin's claim that

What the egoist is saying . . . is that his welfare has ultimate (or intrinsic) value *to* himself, though not *to* anyone else, and that Tom's welfare has ultimate (or intrinsic) value *to* Tom, but not *to* himself or others. [Smith's emphasis]

He then translates Kalin to mean that

The egoist holds that there are no person-neutral values; the only goods which exist are goods which are strictly personal and relative to the individual. When it comes to values, every man is an island; the ultimate good for each man is an ultimate good for no other man [Smith, 1974, p. 98].

It is uncertain whether this rendition is correct, and it is certain that it does not have to be. Kalin's introduction of formal valuation permits a different interpretation. The ultimate good for all men is the achievement of rational self-interest, but the concrete implication of this *abstract* principle, as Rand makes clear, requires that each person achieve his or her self-interest (*qua* human being). Person-neutrality has not been achieved, admittedly, in the sense that *no* one benefits, but person-impartiality has been achieved.

What Smith argues is that since more goods exist for each of us "than merely the satisfaction of the self-interest of the agent . . . the doctrine that the *only* good for each man is the satisfaction of his own self-interest" is wrong (discredited) (Smith, 1974, p. 99). The ethical egoist would argue that Smith is wrong to think ethical egoism says that "the *only* good for each man is the satisfaction of his own self-interest." Surely, for example, an egoist may acknowledge the good of another person's welfare or success or good fortune. An egoist can put himself in another's shoes and appreciate another's success (or failure), provided his egoism is of the ethical, *ergo* universalizable, variety. Moreover, egoists such as Branden, Rand, et al. have often argued that contrary to widespread belief—notably expressed by Rawls (1971, p. 488 ff.)—it is not altruism but egoism that engenders genuine benevolence and good will among human beings. Nevertheless, Smith's point deserves more extensive treatment by defenders of ethical egoism. Mentioning his views here might result in some fruitful exchange on this issue.

VII

I want to end my survey with a brief summary of Jessie Kalin's latest paper in support of ethical egoism, "Two Kinds of Moral Reasoning: Ethical Egoism as a Moral Theory." Kalin's paper is important not only for some original ideas concerning the character of egoism as a moral doctrine but also in view of Kalin's diligent discussion of some critics of ethical egoism mentioned in the present discussion.

Kalin's recent paper has, in my view, a more comprehensive approach to moral philosophy in general and to ethical egoism, specifically. He defends ethical egoism now as a system of personal ethics for all human beings and argues that "morality as a set of nontraditional principles and rules"—that is, as the "interpersonal" and "conventional" principles of social conduct so many critics of egoism take morality to be—"can be based on egoistic reasons" (Kalin, 1975, p. 328). The idea is that egoism is indeed the best ethical system in the sense of providing an objectively true set of principles for guiding human conduct and for selecting the most convenient or suitable social system (which is itself, however, deduced from changeable special purposes). The volatile nature of communities requires social morality to be conventional, instead of strictly deducible from more basic facts or (fixed) values.

Men such as Robinson Crusoe, living alone, need invoke only a system of traditional morality. Kalin believes that

> For the traditionalist, the point of moral reasoning is to discover the truth of a particular position. Moral reasoning is just 'reasoning about a case.' Crusoe can do this as well as anyone else.

So Kalin no longer holds that morality is necessarily social in character. Crusoe could, after all, be negligent, courageous, conscientious, temperate, etc.

> For the nontraditionalist, the point of moral reasoning, however, is the attainment of mutually satisfactory roles of interaction: it is to bring about agreement in the strong sense and thus settle (frequently in advance) conflicts of interest. Moral reasoning is 'reasoning *with* another about a case.' [Kalin, 1975, p. 326].

Since the principle "A person ought, all things considered, to do an action if and only if that action is in his overall self-interest" is more plausible than, e.g., "A person ought, all things considered, to do an action if and only if that action is in the general interest (where each person's welfare and interests are coordinate with every other person's welfare and interests, and each person is regarded as an 'end in himself') (Kalin, 1975, p. 328), Kalin finds it morally compelling.

As to what Baier, Medlin, et al. call the "moral point of view," Kalin thinks it arises in answer to the question "Ought I to enter into this activity (as conducted here) [e.g., social cooperation] or not?" He argues that "This is a personal question, hence such assessment must be made from the point of view of the first [i.e., egoistic] activity" and concludes that "the only traditional reasons one can have for engaging in the activity of mutually assessing actions are self-interested, egoistic reasons" (Kalin, 1975, p. 331).

Kalin believes that social morality is well founded when based on the "egoistic purpose" of utilizing social institutions and settings. It is up to the person whether he or she will engage in the activity of social moral reasoning, so the principles that are agreed to for purposes of carrying on with the social process will be binding only if one "has adopted those rules and principles as governing his, that is, their activity of moral reasoning" (Kalin, 1975, p. 334). In this discussion Kalin avoids his earlier analogy with combative games and relies, instead, on the analogy with choosing the rules for group activities (e.g., playing street baseball) grounded on the purpose agreed on and the particular circumstances the group faces. This points up the sense in which the rules of social interaction are conventional, that is, not a necessary feature of human life.

At the conclusion of this paper, Kalin claims that egoism could be a moral position just as much as other action-guiding codes. And it is interesting to note that some critics of egoism appear to have abandoned the idea that morality must necessarily be a system of guiding principles for social conduct. Rachels, for example, changes the form of criticism and charges egoism with the inability to sustain a just *political* system. That is, only because the consequences of being guided by egoism include rejection of certain political values is the system defective, not because it fails to meet the basic criterion of being a bona fide moral theory. The strategy of rejecting egoism because it does not appear to offer immediate help in solving our social moral problems leads to what Stanley Cavell calls the condition "in which morality has become politicalized." While it may well be that a sound moral theory should enable us to conceive of solutions of our social moral problems, such a theory need not take this task on as a primary objective. And Kalin argues precisely that, as long as we can approach our social situations based on egoistic reasoning, in view of the implausibility of other moral systems, egoism must be accepted not only as plausible but as the best moral theory.

Kalin is following the tradition of such political theorists as Hobbes and Locke who, in their different egoistic arguments, defended political theories that promote interpersonal harmony. Rand and Mack are also concerned to show egoism's compatibility with rights and justice. But in the case of the latter it seems that certain aspects of social (political) conduct are guided by nonconventional principles, based in part on the universalizability feature of a sound ethical system. In this respect they, more so than Kalin, belong within the classical egoist category of ethical egoists, while Kalin is still one of those who takes egoism to be primarily subjectivist, that is, a system or code of principles tailored to the unique individual who practices egoism.

VIII

In this concluding section I will consider a few recurring objections to ethical egoism and then offer a summary of a version of the position that I believe warrants close scrutiny.

First, is ethical egoism universalizable? Subjectivist egoism (e.g., Brunton's, Hospers's and Kalin's earlier views, etc.) does not satisfy this criterion of a bona fide ethical position — required because an ethical position must be action-guiding for all moral agents. If anything one wants, desires, or wishes counts as in one's interest, then an egoist would have neither personal nor public standards of conduct that could lead to consistent, mutually adoptable practice. The most forceful exponents of subjective egoism, James L. Walker and John Beverley Robinson, both followers of Max Stirner, admitted this and accepted the results. Robinson said that egoism "is the realization by the individual that he *is* an individual; that, as far as he is concerned, he is the *only* individual" (Robinson, 1915, p. 1). But ethical egoism, wherein the self is a self of a certain (human) kind, rationally requires and includes universalization, and there are such versions.

Second, must egoism engender social disharmony or conflict? Stirnerite or Hobbesian egoism would fall prey to this charge, making the view impracticable in society, but classical egoism does not. Here self-interest is (barring certain lifeboat cases Mack discusses in his "Egoism and Rights") socially compatible among all who pursue it. (Norton's *Personal Destinies,* 1976, chapter 5, shows the metaphysical support for this in his own individualist ethics.) But would egoistic conduct avoid all possible and logically possible conflict among (egoistically) good persons? I take this requirement to be unwarranted (see footnote 6). If it is true, as Kalin, Mack, and others have argued, that given available theories and knowledge egoism is the most coherent, socially appropriate (in its classical version), and advantageous action-guiding system, it is theoretically adequate. What is needed is for defenders of ethical egoism to provide more detailed illustrations of the concrete applicability of their position. (A study of general virtues compatible with egoism appears in the works of Rand, Butler, Falk, Norton, and Spencer.)

Third, does egoism accord with our natural or ordinary intuitions concerning morality? Rachels's point that sound moral insight and opinion do not necessarily presuppose a finished moral theory seems compelling. Yet someone with no theory, but merely firm convictions, would lose out (in debate, at least) to one with a well-developed theory. In particular cases, many moral judgments conflict. This may be less apparent at the level of general moral virtues, such as integrity, courage, honesty, justice, generosity, etc.; but it becomes evident even here when questions arise about the proper hierarchy of these virtues. At this point careful argument must take over. If, however, ethical egoism, as best formulated, does lead to obvious morally odious results when practiced even by consistent egoists, extreme caution is warranted. If hard cases do not make good ethics (as they may not make good law), they do point up areas of unpreparedness, even probable inadequacy. But even then we need to recall that appearances can mislead; what *seems* terrible (e.g., terrorism) *is* on rare occasions the proper course to take. If egoism provides the most consistent, least generally inadequate and impracticable ethical framework within which sense can be made of such difficult cases (even admitting absence of deductively necessary conclusions concerning some cases), the system would be correct despite the yield of what appear to be morally repugnant results. (It is important to note, also, that our intuitions are under the influence of our theories or preconceptions, so they cannot be, *pace* Rachels, treated as decisive.) This matter cannot be given full treatment here, but the foregoing will indicate an answer to the challenge to ethical egoism, one made frequently (see Rawls, 1971, p. 136).

We may now turn to the crucial question of whether ethical egoism is correct. Although this has not been the issue in the bulk of the discussions of egoism in recent decades, it seems appropriate to indicate, drawing on the previous overview, a case for egoism — partly to set the stage for future development or scrutiny by those interested in this position, pro or con.[7]

Essentially, we want an answer to "How should I conduct myself?" Egoism answers by saying that one should conduct one's life so as to achieve in one's particular case, excellence as the kind of being one is. This is because the conduct of one's life is really up to the individual's direction (choice, decision, deliberation) in crucial respects not shared by other living things (that pursue their best course automatically); and in this one might well succeed at what is, in the case of all life, a good thing — namely, its excellence or flourishing. Considered from the elaborate framework of philosophical ethics (including metaphysics, epistemology, philosophy of mind, etc.) this answer appears to be as right as answers in the domain of ethics can reasonably be expected to be.

Egoism stresses the equal significance of the concrete, particular, or individual, and the essence or nature of that being, that is, the abstract universal (see Norton, 1976, chapter 5, and Machan, 1975, chapter 3, respectively). As a rational being, one's excellence is best secured through the fullest use of one's mind within one's particular case. The classical egoism gleaned from various positions discussed above would emphasize the fundamental role of reason or rational thought in one's life, in whatever context, at whatever time of history. Rationality—not the narrow economic but the Aristotelian conception of this activity—would have to be seen as the prime egoistic virtue, from which others, such as honesty, integrity, justice, and other private and public normative principles, would be derivable in the context of any individual's (human) life.

Finally, ethical egoism is neither exclusively consequentialist (end-state-oriented) nor purely deontological (principled), but both. The doctrine may be said to stress the principled guidance of one's life toward its (process of) flourishing. The goal-directedness of ethical egoism is its teleological, while its relevance to rational (human) beings brings in its deontological, element. The two are distinguishable but not separable.

These few paragraphs bring together promising strands of the various egoistic positions discussed in this chapter and should serve as a reasonable sketch for purposes of generating further discussion. My aim here has been not only to inform and scrutinize, but to help toward the construction of a philosophically adequate and humanly practicable ethical theory. Those whom I have discussed have helped make this a reasonable prospect.

Notes

1. More or less formal ways of stating the same, general, essentially egoistic doctrine are possible, and various alternatives will be evident throughout this paper.

2. Perhaps the turning point was W. D. Falk's paper "Goading and Guiding," where Falk shows that ordinary language indicates that moral statements, e.g., moral advice, are often treated as either true or false, justified or unjustified, reasonable or unreasonable, etc. Reduction of guiding to goading seems, therefore, unwarranted from the point of view of ordinary language.

3. A thorough discussion of Nozick's paper occurs in Douglas Den Uyl and Douglas Rasmussen, "Nozick on the Randian Argument," *The Personalist* 59 (1978), pp. 184-205.

4. A very careful formulation of Rand's argument occurs in J. Roger Lee, "On a Putative Foundation for Natural Rights," a paper given at a meeting of the American Association for the Philosophic Study of Society, Milwaukee, October 8, 1977. In the end, Lee rejects Rand's case on grounds that "Rand's work on concept formation, on which so much of this argument depends, is hopeless."

5. For a clear treatment of these issues see Albert O. Hirschman, *The Passions and the Interests* (Princeton, 1977).

6. Gauthier says that "no complete principle of action meets the conditions of egoism. By [this] I mean a function whose domain includes every possible situation in which a person might find himself and whose values include every possible action he might perform" (Gauthier, 1974, p. 441). I ignore this (extended) point in Gauthier's paper because, by his criterion, not only would no ethical theory succeed, but it is doubtful that any theory in any domain could meet it. See Imre Lakatos, "Infinite Regress and the Foundations of Mathematics," *Aristotelian Society* Suppl. Vol. 36, pp. 155-84. (Only in metaphysics which must treat the past, present, future, and possible, does Gauthier's criterion apply.)

7. I omit the important issue of comparative assessment. Two views should be considered, both of which appear diametrically opposed to egoism. Thomas Nagel defends a version of altruism that appears to require, as do Mack's, Branden's, and Rand's version of egoism, only that others must be treated as ends, not means to one's own ends (primarily). This apparently antiegoist theory is compatible with a type of egoism. Nicholas Rescher's morality of unselfishness, which stresses the idea of the vicarious affects—roughly, emotions such as compassion, empathy, or an unselfish interest in others' lot—is opposed only to utilitarian or hedonistic egoisms (as in economic views of human action). Classical egoist positions are fully compatible

with this. Where Rescher clashes with the egoist is in his holistic (Platonic or Hegelian) theory of social good. The egoist would stress what Norton calls *consequent sociality*, an outgrowth of an essentially individualist ethical theory. Neither Nagel's nor Rescher's view can be evaluated here, but an attempt to discover what ethical theory is correct would need to provide such an evaluation.

Bibliography

Ashmore, R. D., Jr. 1977. "Friendship and the Problem of Egoism." *Thomist* 41: 105-30.

Ayer, A. J. 1936. *Language, Truth and Logic*. New York. Chapter 6.

Baier, Kurt. 1958. *The Moral Point of View*. Ithaca, N.Y. Chapter 8.

_____. 1973. "Ethical Egoism and Interpersonal Compatibility." *Philosophical Studies* 24: 357-68.

Barnes, H. E. 1967. *An Existentialist Ethics*. New York. Chapter 6.

Branden, Nathaniel. 1970. "Rational Egoism: A Reply to Professor Emmons." *The Personalist* 51: 196-211.

Brunton, J. A. 1956. "Egoism and Morality." *The Philosophical Quarterly* 6: 289-303.

Burrill, Donald. 1976. "The Role-egoism Principle." *The Personalist* 57: 408-10.

Campbell, Richmond. 1972. "A Short Refutation of Ethical Egoism." *Canadian Journal of Philosophy* 2: 249-54.

_____. 1979. *Self-Love and Self-Respect: A Philosophical Study of Egoism*. Ottawa.

Carlson, G. R. 1973. "Ethical Egoism Reconsidered." *American Philosophical Quarterly* 10: 25-33.

Den Uyl, D. J. 1975. "Ethical Egoism and Gewirth's PCC." *The Personalist* 56: 423-47.

Dwyer, William. 1975. "Criticism of Egoism." *The Personalist* 56: 214-27.

_____. 1976. "Egoism and Renewed Hostilities." *The Personalist* 57: 279-89.

Emmons, Donald. 1969. "Refuting the Egoist." *The Personalist* 50: 309-19.

_____. 1971. "Rational Egoism: Random Observations." *The Personalist* 52: 95-98.

Falk, W. D. 1950. "Morality and Nature." *Australasian Journal of Philosophy* 28: 69-92.

_____. 1953. "Goading and Guiding." *Mind* 62: 145-71.

_____. 1965. "Morality, Self, and Others." In Hector-Neri Castañeda and George Nakhnikian, eds., *Morality and the Language of Conduct*. Detroit. Pp. 25-67.

Foot, Philippa. 1972. "Morality as a System of Hypothetical Imperatives." *Philosophical Review* 81: 305-32.

Frankena, William. 1963. *Ethics*. Englewood Cliffs, N.J.: Prentice-Hall. Pp. 16-18.

Gauthier, David. 1967. "Morality and Advantage." *Philosophical Review* 76: 460-75. Reprinted 1970 in Gauthier, ed., *Morality and Rational Self-Interest*. Englewood Cliffs, N.J.: Prentice-Hall.

_____. 1974. "The Impossibility of Rational Egoism." *The Journal of Philosophy* 71: 439-56.

Hardie, W.F.R. 1965. "The Final Good in Aristotle's *Ethics*." *Philosophy* 40: 277-95.

Hare, R. M. 1954-55. "Universalizability." *Proceedings of the Aristotelian Society* 55: 295-312.

Hospers, John. 1961. "Baier and Medlin on Ethical Egoism." *Philosophical Studies* 12: 10-16.

_____. 1972. *Human Conduct*. 2nd rev. ed. New York. Chapter 4.

_____. 1973. "Rule Egoism." *The Personalist* 54: 391-95.

Kalin, Jesse. 1968. "In Defense of Egoism" (in Gauthier, above).

_____. 1969. "On Ethical Egoism." *American Philosophical Quarterly Monograph* 1: 26-41.

_____. 1975. "Two Kinds of Moral Reasoning." *Canadian Journal of Philosophy* 5: 323-56.

Machan, T. R. 1974. "Selfishness and Capitalism." *Inquiry* 17: 338-44.

_____. 1975. *Human Rights and Human Liberties*. Chicago. Chapter 3.

_____. 1978. "Was Rachels' Doctor Practicing Egoism?" *Philosophia* 8: 1-2.

Mack, Eric. 1971. "How to Derive Ethical Egoism." *The Personalist* 52: 735-43.

_____. 1973. "Egoism and Rights." *The Personalist* 54: 5-33.

_____. 1974. "Campbell's Refutation of Egoism." *Canadian Journal of Philosophy* 3: 659-63.

_____. 1977. "Egoism and Rights Revisited." *The Personalist* 58: 282-88.

Mackie, John. 1946. "A Refutation of Morals." *Australasian Journal of Philosophy* 24: 77–90.

Medlin, Brian. 1957. "Ultimate Principles and Ethical Egoism." *Australasian Journal of Philosophy* 35: 111–18.

Milo, R. D., ed. 1973. *Egoism and Altruism*. Belmont, Calif.

Nagel, Thomas. 1970. *The Possibility of Altruism*. Oxford.

Nielsen, Kai. 1959. "Egoism in Ethics.'" *Philosophy and Phenomenological Research* 29: 502–10.

_____. 1974. "On the Rationality of 'Rational Egoism.'" *The Personalist* 55: 398–400.

Norton, D. L. 1976. *Personal Destinies: A Philosophy of Ethical Individualism*. Princeton, N.J.: Princeton University Press.

Nozick, Robert. 1971. "On the Randian Argument."*The Personalist* 52: 282–304.

Oldenquist, Andrew. 1980. "The Possibility of Selfishness." *American Philosophical Quarterly* 17: 25–33.

Olson, R. G., 1965. *The Morality of Self-Interest*. New York.

Quinn, Warren. 1974. "Egoism as an Ethical System." *The Journal of Philosophy* 71: 456–72.

Rachels, James. 1974. "Two Arguments Against Ethical Egoism." *Philosophia* 4: 297–314.

_____. 1977. "The Psychological and Ethical Egoism." In A. K. Beirman and J. A. Gould, eds., *Philosophy for a New Generation*. New York.

Rand, Ayn. 1964. *The Virtue of Selfishness: A New Concept of Egoism*. New York. Chapter 1.

_____. 1967. *Introduction to Objectivist Epistemology*. New York.

Rawls, John. 1971. *A Theory of Justice*. Cambridge.

Regis, Edward, Jr. 1979. "Ethical Egoism and Moral Responsibility." *American Philosophical Quarterly* 16: 45–52.

_____. 1980. "What is Ethical Egoism?" *Ethics* 91: 50–62.

Rescher, Nicholas. 1975. *Unselfishness*. Pittsburgh.

Robinson, J. B. 1915. "Egoism." *Reedy's Mirror*.

Sanders, S. M. 1976. "A Credible Form of Egoism?" *The Personalist* 57: 272–78.

_____. 1977. "Egoism's Concept of the Self." *The Personalist* 58: 59–67.

Schmitt, Richard. 1973. "The Desire for Private Gain." *Inquiry* 16: 149–67.

Smith, S. A. 1974. "Ethical Egoism and Value." *The Southern Journal of Philosophy* 12: 95–102.

Stevenson, Charles. 1945. *Ethics and Language*. New Haven, Conn.: Yale University Press.

Thomas, Laurence. 1980. "Ethical Egoism and Psychological Dispositions." *American Philosophical Quarterly* 17: 73–78.

Trivus, Sidney. 1978. "On Playing the Game." *The Personalist* 59: 82–84.

Walker, J. L. 1972. *The Philosophy of Egoism*. Colorado Springs. Originally published 1907.

Williams, Granville. 1951. *Humanistic Ethics*. New York.

_____. 1955."Universal Hedonism vs. Hedonistic Individual Relativism." *The Journal of Philosophy* 52: 72–77.

Wheeler, C. J. 1976. "Ethical Egoism in Hellenic Thought." Ph. D. dissertation, University of Southern California.

PART V

Social and Political Philosophy

chapter 7

Recent Work on the Concept of Rights

REX MARTIN and JAMES W. NICKEL

This is a critical review of work on the concept of rights, including the concept of human rights, from 1963 to 1978. Our focus is mainly on issues of the analysis of rights and human rights. We do not deal with the closely related issues bearing on the normative foundations of moral and human rights. Section I surveys general characterizations of rights. In section II we discuss treatments of the defeasibility of rights, with special attention to the notion of a prima facie right. Section III takes up attempts to give an account of human rights. Section IV provides a brief conclusion. A bibliography listing what we take to be the most important works in this area, including everything cited in our essay, is appended.[1] For a more historical treatment of our topic, we refer the interested reader to helpful studies by Benn (1967), Golding (1978), Milne (1968, chapter 2), Roshwald (1958-59), and Wellman (1975a, chapter 10) and to essays in Raphael (1967b) and in Villey (1969, on Occam, Hobbes, Jhering).

I. Issues about the General Character of Rights

Our concern in this section is with attempts to answer the question "What is a right?" In reply, theorists have generally thought it desirable to give an account that explains what various specific rights—legal, moral, or human rights—have in common as rights.

Such a general characterization might focus on any one of three aspects of rights. The first is the normative element, or set of considerations, of which a right is typically constituted. Thus, one finds attempts to characterize rights in terms of second-party duties or other normative categories, such as liberties, claims, and immunities. The second aspect is the functions that rights serve. Here one could explain what rights are by indicating what one can do with them, e.g., protect interests or confer control of some state of affairs. A third aspect of rights concerns the kind of justification normally involved. Thus, one might characterize rights by referring to some distinctive justificatory theme or pattern which they require, such as appeal to fundamental interests (or basic needs)[2] or to the worth and dignity of persons.

This tripartite framework—of constituent normative elements, function(s), justification—provides, we believe, a helpful schema for identifying various ways in which rights may be understood. Since the usual approach has been to emphasize the first dimension, our survey begins with theses about the mutual entailment between rights and duties and then proceeds to discuss other analyses that focus on constitutive normative elements. After that we discuss functionalist theories. It should be noted, parenthetically, that some theorists appeal quite explicitly to more than one of the three aspects in their attempt to offer an adequate general characterization of rights; we think such multilevel theories afford a number of advantages.

RIGHTS AND DUTIES

Many rights are obviously connected with second-party duties, and hence many theorists have held that the normative elements that constitute rights are duties. The view that rights and duties are correlatives was advocated in several of the very influential early essays on the concept of rights, most notably by Bradley (1927, the second edition of the 1876 original) and W. D. Ross (1930), and has been supported more recently by Benn and Peters (1965). Brandt (1959) asserted the common view when he suggested that rights can be defined in terms of obligations, that the difference between A's right against B and B's duty to A is mainly the difference between the passive and the active voice, and therefore that "when one person has a moral right, some other person or persons have corresponding obligations" (Brandt, 1959, p. 436; see generally pp. 433–41).[3]

A salient feature of recent work on the concept of rights is that this simple approach to the characterization of a right has been heavily criticized and generally rejected. If a right is only a duty seen from another perspective, then every duty will entail a right and every right will entail a duty. But both of these alleged entailments seem to fall prey to counterexamples.

Feinberg makes out a case against entailments of the first sort by providing examples of "duties-without-correlative-rights" (Feinberg, 1966, 1970). One such example is duties of charity that "require us to contribute to one or another of a large number of eligible recipients, no one of whom can claim our contribution from us as his due" (Feinberg, 1970, p. 244). These are the duties that Kant and Mill called "imperfect." The person with such a duty has considerable discretion as to when he will discharge it, and the person who will benefit from the discharge of the duty is not assignable or determinate. The duty here has not been "individuated" and hence does not generate a corresponding right. Thus it seems clear that not all duties entail rights of other people—even though such a correlation does exist for *many* duties. (For a helpful statement on this see Feinberg, 1966, p. 142. See also Hart, 1973, p. 190.)

The other thesis involved in analyzing rights in terms of duties, namely that every right entails a closely related second-party duty, has not fared much better. It involves, however, more complex issues and will be the focus of our attention in this section.[4] The most interesting arguments against entailments of this sort derive from Wesley Hohfeld's classification of rights. On his view a legal right can be constituted by any one of four elements: by a claim, by a liberty, by a power, or by an immunity.[5] An ordinary liberty right to do A (say, to paint designs on the exterior walls of a house that one owns) consists in the mere absence of any duty not to do that particular thing. And since such rights exist in all areas where there is an absence of obligation, they are apt to be rather numerous. More important, there may be in most of these cases no duties that specifically protect the particular liberty right in question. Hence, we can dismiss a strong version of the rights-entail-duties thesis that asserts that every right has a specifically correlated duty.

Even so, there might still be standing duties that prohibit such things as trespass and violence against persons or property and that effectively restrain the neighbors, who detest the paintings, from stopping the owner or from removing the designs. These unspecialized, standing duties constitute a sort of "perimeter"—to use Hart's phrase (1973, pp. 180–81)—on which any number of liberty rights could rest. Where such general duties can be called into play, as supplements to a given liberty right, it becomes impossible to use the supplemented right (effectively *any* liberty right) as an example of a right without some corresponding obligations.

David Lyons (1970, p. 53) does not think that we can infer a logical entailment from the impossibility of counterexamples here. His point is that, although certain generally applicable obligations may support a person's right to do A, these obligations are not in fact logically entailed by that right. In opposition, Braybrooke (1972) and Singer (1972) argue that the prior existence of a standing duty does not always cast doubt on the entailment between a right and that duty; they hold that to think otherwise is to confuse logical implication with causal generation. But this criticism, though sound, does not dispose of Lyons's other arguments, which suggest that some rights are constituted by immunities and hence are to be correlated with second-party disabilities rather than with duties.

In one such argument, again deriving from Hohfeld's analysis, Lyons focuses on the constitutional right of Americans to free speech. This right does not create an area of free choice by imposing obligations on others; instead it does so by imposing a disability or lack of authority on Congress. The first amendment deprives Congress "of the authority . . . to enact laws requiring or prohibiting speech of certain kinds" (Lyons, 1970, p. 50). An attempt by Congress to legislate in this area presumably could be challenged successfully in court and declared null and void. Thus, although the right to freedom of speech has a conceptual correlative, "it is not an obligation; it is a legislative disability." (Lyons, 1970, p. 51).

Braybrooke, in an argument against Lyons, challenges us to imagine someone asserting the existence of a right, while allowing that no one is under any duty regarding the acts covered by the right. In such a case, Braybrooke says, "the alleged right has turned out to be a right that has no meaning. . . . The alleged right does not protect him; it does not even give him a ground for complaint. There is nothing for him to gain in invoking it before, during or after any attempts at interference" (Braybrooke, 1972, p. 361). But we can imagine such a right being useful if we imagine it to be correlated with a disability on the part of other persons. If someone purports to do what he lacks the legal authority to do (e.g., legislate away freedom of speech, or deprive someone of citizenship on grounds of race or religion), there is a ground for complaint—at least if this harms one's interests—and there may indeed be something to gain in invoking such a right, namely that the invalidity of the action will be officially declared and deprived of practical effect.

More generally, the most important means of institutionalizing some rights may be to create second-party disabilities or liabilities rather than duties. This will often be the solution in cases where a legal duty cannot be expected to be particularly effective (where, for example, it would prove difficult to enforce the duty against police and prosecutors or against a branch of government).

Of course, it may continue to be said that Congress has a duty not to make laws "abridging the freedom of speech"; but this particular duty cannot even be properly stated without bringing in the notion of a disability, nor is it enforceable along the lines of most duties, but it requires instead the "sanction" of nullity. There is considerable bite, then, to the contention that a disability or lack of authority rather than a duty may sometimes be the correlative of a right. Other duties will no doubt be lurking in the background, but these may be standing or "perimeter" duties and thus not specifically correlated with the right.

It seems, therefore, that arguments based on the existence of liberty or immunity or power rights of the sorts advanced by Lyons are telling against the view that every right entails a closely related second-party duty. The existence of rights other than claim rights is most obvious in the legal sphere, but it could be argued (as does Wellman, 1978b) that there are significant moral examples as well (*pace* Kleinig, 1978). And we can still accept Braybrooke's point that a right that doesn't guide anyone's behavior is no right at all; but to do this we should add that this guidance need not involve a duty—a disability or liability will do as well in some contexts. The truth, which the rights-entail-duties thesis skews, is that any genuine right must involve some normative direction of the behavior of persons other than the holder.

RIGHTS AS CLAIMS

Although the attempt to explain rights in terms of second-party duties is subject to serious criticisms, some philosophers within the period of our survey have utilized an approach of the same general sort, namely, one which attempts to explain what a right is by characterizing the normative elements it contains. Joel Feinberg analyzes rights as claims, typically as *valid* claims.[6] "To have a right is to have a claim *to* something and *against* someone, the recognition of which is called for by legal rules or, in the case of moral rights, by the principles of an enlightened conscience" (Feinberg, 1974, pp. 43–44).

For such a characterization to be illuminating, an account needs to be given of what a claim is and of what makes a claim valid. Feinberg thinks that much can be learned about the nature and value of claims by attending to the activity of claiming—an activity in which people demand things as their due, not as a matter of the giver's generosity (see Feinberg, 1970, especially pp. 249–52). But Feinberg does not accept the view that what makes a claim valid is some feature of the activity of claiming. Rather, he invokes, as the quotation above suggests, legal and moral principles to explicate the notion of a valid claim. When there is a set of reasons based on legal rules or moral principles which supports a person's being able to do or have A, then that person *has a claim*. To have a claim is to be in position to *make a claim*. But one can have a claim without that claim amounting to a right. Such a claim might, though given some support, not be conclusively established by the governing principles. To be a right, a claim must pass this and other relevant tests; it must be fully validated (Feinberg, 1970, pp. 253–55; 1973, pp. 64–67).[7]

Feinberg tries to explain what else is involved in such a validation by distinguishing between claims-to and claims-against (Feinberg, 1970, p. 256).[8] He suggests that we can speak meaningfully of someone having a claim-to without knowing whom that claim-to might be against. "Imagine," he says, "a hungry, sickly, fatherless infant . . . in a squalid Mexican slum. Doesn't this child have a *claim* to be fed, to be given medical care, to be taught to read? Can't we know this before we have any idea where correlative duties lie?" (Feinberg, 1966, p. 142). The distinction between claims-to and claims-against corresponds to different aspects of the validation of a complete claim. A valid claim-to calls for, but does not entail, an obligation on some party to act in such a way as would satisfy it. If it is practicable for a claim-to to be satisfied, then it can serve as a justifiable basis for calling on the duties of other persons. But a valid claim-to is only part of the justification for a claim-against, for the latter claim requires, by definition, that there be duties of assignable individuals. The recognition of a claim-against need not, however, involve creating new duties; it may instead involve hooking on to existing ones.

Thus, in Feinberg's theory a right always has two principal elements: a valid claim-to something and a valid claim-against someone. Although one of these elements may be more visible in particular contexts, both elements are always present in a full-fledged right (Feinberg, 1970, pp. 256–57). A claim-against involves duties of specific people, and thus it is part of Feinberg's theory that a full-fledged right entails duties of other people. He allows, however, that there is a weaker sense of "right"—which he calls the "manifesto sense"—that does not (yet) entail duties of other people, because the claim-to has not (yet) become practicable on a scale sufficient to generate a valid claim-against. "Natural needs," Feinberg suggests, "are real claims if only upon hypothetical future beings not yet in existence. . . . A natural need for some good as such . . . is always a reason in support of a claim to that good. A person in need, then, is always 'in a position' to make a claim, even when there is no one in the corresponding position to do anything about it" (Feinberg, 1970, p. 255). A manifesto right can be constituted by a partially validated claim-to alone, but a full-fledged right—that is, one that does not involve the use of "rhetorical license" (Feinberg, 1970, p. 255)—requires the union or merger of a valid claim-to with a valid claim-against.

Feinberg's idea that rights are valid claims allows him to treat a moral right and a legal right as parallel in character: both are rights in the same sense. What differentiates them is the kind of norm from which they derive validity. Moral principles figure in the case of moral rights; it is by reference to such principles that claims-to are adjudged to be morally valid; and it is moral duties that are involved in such claims-against. Correspondingly, for legal rights we consider legal rules and principles to determine the validity of claims-to, and it is legally created duties that are invoked in such claims-against. Human rights enter this picture as a special class of moral rights. Some human rights may be full-fledged moral rights; others—the ones called "manifesto" rights—are at best emerging or proto-rights. Thus, Feinberg's theory succeeds in relating legal and moral rights, while leaving a place for the latter, and allows for somewhat looser usages in connection with human rights while still measuring them ultimately against a standard of some rigor.

It is a consequence of Feinberg's theory—since a valid claim always consists of two elements, a claim-to *and* a claim-against—that every full-fledged right implies a second-party duty; thus the theory is vulnerable to Lyons's argument that the second-party correlate of some rights is a disability rather than a duty. Feinberg's theory has no explicit place for rights constituted in this way although, perhaps, his theory could be modified to allow claims-against to involve second-party disabilities and possibly liabilities as well as duties. Another alternative would be to restrict his analysis to claim rights alone, but this would severely limit its usefulness in dealing with the full range of legal and even moral rights. In any event, it seems likely that some claim rights will involve—as Feinberg himself suggests (1970, p. 249)—liberties, powers, and immunities (e.g., the liberty to exercise the right, the power to sue to have the right enforced, an immunity from having the right arbitrarily nullified). It is unclear how these elements can join a valid claim in constituting a right if a right is merely a valid claim. This suggests that a right may have to be viewed as a *group* of normative elements.

RIGHTS AS ENTITLEMENTS

In order to avoid the potential restrictiveness of the notion of claims, especially where these are interpreted in a strictly Hohfeldian way, some theorists have turned to a different kind of normative element in their characterization of rights. They are motivated here not only by what they want to avoid but also by what they hope to achieve: a nonreductive analysis of rights, an analysis able to bring out the distinctiveness and ultimacy of rights as a normative category. Thus, H. J. McCloskey takes entitlement rather than claim or duty to be the basic notion—at least as regards the moral rights that seem to be his primary concern. Rights, according to McCloskey, are best "explained positively as entitlements to do, have, enjoy, or have done, and not negatively as something against others, or as something one ought to have" (McCloskey, 1976b, p. 99). Unlike Feinberg, McCloskey holds that a full-fledged right need not specify who is obligated to provide what the right is *to*. The connection between rights and second-party duties becomes very loose.

Rights as entitlements are "intrinsic to their possessors" and are held "independently of other people and . . . of what else ought to be" (McCloskey, 1976b, p. 99, italics deleted). According to McCloskey, an entitlement need not depend on the will of anyone, including the rightholder. It rests, rather, on objective moral considerations—on a moral authority to act in a certain way (McCloskey, 1965, p. 120) and, more specifically, on what McCloskey calls "the nature of autonomous existence" (1975, p. 417; see also 1975, pp. 413–16, and 1965, pp. 124–25).[9]

McCloskey particularly wants to deny that a right can be equated with a particular set of duties or claims-against. Perhaps his strongest arguments for this view are that we do speak of rights in situations where it is far from clear who is to bear the burden of realizing them (McCloskey, 1965, p. 118), and that since "circumstances determine which claims arise from a right," one who tried to define or delimit a right by the particular claims-against that it had generated would have to allow that it was "in a continual state of flux" (McCloskey, 1976b, p. 100). Just as the "realist" refuses to characterize a chair as merely the set of appearances that it presents at various times, McCloskey refuses to characterize a right as merely the set of normative elements that it may generate at various times. An entitlement, on his view, seems to be that ill-defined something that generates the specific duties and liberties that we find in particular situations where entitlements apply. Of course, rights do normally "give rise to" duties (McCloskey, 1965, p. 116; 1976b, p. 103), but McCloskey wishes to deny that there is any entailment here and to emphasize the logical priority of entitlements to claims-against.

Although McCloskey's theory is an alternative to accounts employing a notion of claim itself definable in terms of duties, his notion of an entitlement is akin to Feinberg's notion of a valid claim-to. Both notions are separable from the duties of particular second parties, and both provide a major part of the grounds for the creation of such duties. McCloskey emphasizes, in a way that Feinberg does not, that an entitlement or claim-to is an independent element that is deeply rooted in the nature of human beings. For Feinberg, a mere claim-to can generate only a "manifesto" right rather than a full-fledged right. But since McCloskey emphasizes, to a much greater extent than Feinberg, the independence and completeness of an entitlement or claim-to, he is willing to recognize as full-fledged rights some of the alleged human rights that Feinberg downgraded by classifying them as mere "manifesto" rights (e.g., the right to an education or to medical care; see McCloskey, 1976b, p. 106, and Feinberg, 1966, pp. 142–43). Feinberg, on the other hand, denies the adequacy and completeness of a mere claim-to and criticizes McCloskey for thinking that one can dispense with the claim-against element and still have a full-fledged right (see Feinberg, 1970, p. 256).

McCloskey's key notion—"entitlement"—is merely a verbal synonym of "right," and as such the notion is not particulary illuminating or informative.[10] Thus, there seems to be a certain vagueness at the heart of his theory. Furthermore, McCloskey never tells us how an entitlement generates (or even relates to) other normative categories, such as duties or immunities or powers. Insofar as the notion of entitlement is intelligible, it seems to amount to nothing more than the normative grounds sufficient to establish a person's eligibility to some good—and this is what we meant by our suggestion that McCloskey's entitlements are very similar to Feinberg's valid claims-to. But the equation of an entitlement in this sense with a full-fledged right seems subject to Bentham's critical dictum that hunger is not bread.

RIGHTS AS CONSTELLATIONS OF HOHFELD ELEMENTS

Both Feinberg and McCloskey characterize rights by focusing on the kind of normative element—a valid claim or an entitlement, respectively—that all rights allegedly contain. These are "essential element" theories of rights. An alternative to this approach has been emerging in the essays of Carl Wellman. His theory develops the idea that rights are constituted by groups of elements, specifically the normative elements or "fundamental legal conceptions" identified by Hohfeld. But Wellman does not think that an apt characterization of these elements and their order is sufficient. Rather he explicitly appeals, as we shall see, to an alleged *function* of rights to explain what it is that makes *rights* out of these various constellations of elements.

As we saw earlier, Hohfeld believed that a legal right could be constituted by any one of four elements: a claim, a liberty, a power, or an immunity. But he regarded one of the types, the claim right, as the preeminent kind of legal right and, accordingly, as that which is "most properly called a right" (Hohfeld, 1964, pp. 36, 39). Wellman follows Hohfeld in believing that any of these four kinds of elements may be fundamental to a given right. He does not, however, follow Hohfeld in thinking that each right is best viewed as consisting of just the one element. Instead he follows Alf Ross (1958) in holding that every right is a complex normative structure that typically involves *several* of these elements. In order to keep these complex entities within manageable bounds, Wellman distinguishes between the *defining core* of a right—which consists in that Hohfeld element (or pair of elements) fundamental to the existence of the right—and the *associated elements* (i.e., other of the Hohfeld elements) that contribute to the satisfaction of the core. Thus a given right, say the creditor's right to repayment, will include not only a core, the *claim* against the debtor for repayment, but also a *liberty* (to call or not call for repayment after the due date) and a *power* (to waive the due date or even the repayment or, in the event of nonpayment, to seek remedy or redress) and an *immunity*—to be protected from arbitrary or willful cancellation of the indebtedness (see Wellman, 1975b, pp. 52–53, for this example).[11] "When we classify rights as liberty-, claim-, power-, or immunity-rights, it is to their defining cores that we refer. Whatever other legal elements may be contained in any right, they belong to this right because of their relation to its core" (Wellman, 1978b, p. 53; see also 1978a, pp. 218–20, and 1975b, p. 59). The core serves to give stability to a right, maintaining its unity over time even when its associated elements are changing.

But if the core gives unity to a particular legal right, constituting it the right that it is, what gives unity, in the face of the evident diversity of core elements, to rights as a class? How can these all be rights in the same sense? In dealing with this question Wellman draws on an idea of Hart's and suggests that structures that constitute rights can be distinguished from other complex normative structures in terms of *function*. Hart (1973, pp. 196–97) had said that what was common to many, but not all, legal rights is that they confer on the rightholder the ability to choose what shall occur within some limited domain. Thus these rights involve, on Hart's view, a legally respected individual choice. Wellman broadens and generalizes Hart's idea in order to indicate what is common to *all* rights: "The function of a legal right is to resolve . . . conflicts by giving legal priority to the desires and decisions of one party over those of the other. A legal right is the allocation of a sphere of freedom and control to the possessor of the right in order that it may be up to him which decisions are effective within that defined sphere" (Wellman, 1975b, p. 52). The associated elements are tied to the core in virtue of their contribution to this freedom and control (Wellman, 1978a, p. 219).

This characterization of a right as a structure conferring autonomy to the holder gives unity, Wellman believes, to the concept of a right.[12] Although rights can take elements of any one of the four kinds as their core, with attendant variation in the constituency of associated elements, all rights are put to the same use. It is this functional unity that gathers rights into a well-defined family, not the presence of some single normative relation, such as the right-duty nexus. (See Wellman, 1978a, pp. 220–21.)

Wellman applies this analysis to moral and human rights. Here, instead of having *legal* liberties, claims, powers, and immunities, one will have *ethical* analogues of these elements (see Wellman, 1978b, p. 55). A human right is a species of ethical right; it is a "cluster" of ethical liberties, etc., that together constitute "a system of ethical autonomy possessed by an individual as a human being vis-à-vis the state" (Wellman, 1978b, p. 56).

One difficulty with Wellman's analysis is that he is insufficiently cautious in using words such as "freedom," "control," and "autonomy" without qualifying phrases. The right of a creditor to repayment doesn't give him total control over the return of his funds: that, after all, can be made impossible by a fire that destroys all the debtor's assets, or by the actions of other creditors in seizing all the debtor's assets. In any case the control provided by a right will attach only to the wills of those parties whose acts and decisions are governed by the right. And such control will be contingent on compliance with the norms that constitute the right. Thus, the kind of control offered by the possession of a right is much more limited, and thus much weaker, than Wellman's vocabulary suggests.

A second objection to an analysis in terms of autonomy is that if one defines a right as a system of autonomy, then only beings capable of the exercise of autonomy can have rights, and this makes it impossible for infants, the terminally unconscious, and the senile to have rights. Wellman seems inclined to accept this conclusion (1979) and probably would deny that it is an objection; but this is extraordinarily unpersuasive (see MacCormick, 1976, for background).

Another objection bears on the widely held view that there are two basic, competing theories as to the function of rights: the "will" theory, in which the role of rights is said to be the conferring of autonomy, and the "interest" theory, in which it is said to be the protecting of important interests. (See MacCormick, 1976, p. 305; Kleinig, 1978, pp. 40-43; and Arnold, 1978, p. 80.) But it is clearly possible to have both these functions as functions of rights, often of a single right. Thus it seems to us arbitrary, where both functions are normally served by almost all rights, to single out one of the functions and to give it definitional weight (as Wellman has done).

RIGHTS AS TRUMPS OVER COLLECTIVE GOALS

While Wellman's theory of rights mixes a characterization in terms of distinctive normative elements with a characterization in terms of function, Ronald Dworkin (1977) provides a functional account that is concerned largely with the role rights play in relation to other normative considerations, and which is therefore more closely related to issues of the justification of rights. Dworkin holds that the important thing about rights is that they give the rightholder an especially strong justification for acting in a certain way or for demanding a certain benefit, a justification which is independent of and which will generally triumph in competition with collective goals such as welfare, prosperity, or security. In short, rights function as trumps over collective goals, and this is what is distinctive about them (Dworkin, 1977, pp. 91-92).

For a principle to provide a guarantee of a benefit that is independent of and stronger than appeals to collective goals, it must have two characteristics. First, it must be individuated. This means that the principle must define a class such that every member of the class is assigned the benefit. In contrast, policies designed to attain collective goals — such as promoting the general welfare or maximizing the GNP — are concerned with aggregate benefit rather than with the benefits (or disbenefits) that accrue to particular individuals. A claim based on such policies will not amount to a right, even if the policy considerations invoked are very powerful, since it will lack the necessary individuated character (Dworkin, 1977, pp. 90-91). Second, the principle must be a strong or high-priority moral or legal consideration. It must have sufficient weight that its dictates yield to those of collective goals only in clear and present emergencies (Dworkin, 1977, pp. 92, 191f, 195) — or at least are not such as to be generally outweighed by them in normal circumstances. The kind of justification peculiar to rights doesn't depend on whether a particular assignment of a good maximizes attainment of some collective goal; the principle invoked, rather, provides an independent guarantee of the benefit.

Dworkin believes that for a moral principle to have these two characteristics it cannot itself be based on some collective goal, such as general utility, but must rather be based on considerations of individual dignity or equality of respect (Dworkin, 1977, pp. 180, 182, 227, 273). Thus, Dworkin contends that his account of rights as trumps is heavily dependent on a nonutilitarian theory of justification. This particular linkage between his characterization of rights and the kind of justification they presumably require could make Dworkin's theory unattractive to many philosophers.[13] It may, however, despite Dworkin's view, be possible to describe the function of rights as trumps in such a way as to make rule utilitarian accounts of moral rights compatible with this function.

TOWARD A SYNTHESIS

Some interesting accounts of the concept of a right have been developed in the period under discussion. Their emergence has coincided with a general rejection of the traditional view that rights can be adequately explicated entirely in terms of duties. Each of the theories surveyed has some philosophical advantages, and it appears that many of these features could be combined in a single theory.

A valuable feature of Feinberg's theory is his account of the evolution of new rights out of independent claim-to elements. As he and McCloskey suggest, it is often possible to recognize the desirability of assigning a legal or moral advantage to someone prior to knowing who should bear the corresponding burdens. And as these writers emphasize, such assignments may actually require separate justificatory procedures. There does not appear to be any reason why these points could not be incorporated into other theories, such as those of Wellman and Dworkin.

There are some important advantages in theories such as Wellman's that emphasize that rights are complex normative structures. One is that such theories explicitly recognize that more than two parties are typically involved in the normative relations that constitute a right. In addition to the rightholder and the primary addressee of the right, public officials and other persons are often assigned normative positions by rights. Wellman has provided a number of examples of the role of such parties in upholding rights (Wellman, 1975b, pp. 49–53). A second advantage is that a theory such as Wellman's allows for a variety of groups of normative elements to constitute a right. Within such a theory it is easy to accommodate Lyons's point that some of our constitutional rights are constituted by governmental disabilities rather than duties and McCloskey's point that a single entitlement may have a variety of implications in different situations.

Finally, an analysis incorporating an account of the function of rights seems to offer a vantage point for explaining how various constellations of elements can, in spite of their diversity, all be rights. What is needed now, we have suggested, is critical interaction between those who emphasize the conferring of autonomy and those who emphasize the protecting of basic interests in their accounts of the role of rights.

Perhaps Dworkin's functionalist account of rights can provide a suitably broad framework for such critical interaction to occur with some result. It might prove useful then to follow Dworkin in building the notion of substantial weight in competition with other considerations into one's general characterization of what rights are. For this would appear to be ground held in common by competing theories.

II. The Defeasibility of Rights

We now turn to a survey of attempts to understand conflicts beween rights and between a right and other considerations. Philosophers regard few, if any, rights as absolute in the sense that such rights can never be justifiably overridden in any circumstance.[14] And although Dworkin may be correct in saying that an essential feature of rights is that they are powerful enough as moral or legal considerations to prevail generally in competition with such collective goals as welfare, security, or prosperity, we are for the most part unable to give full and precise specifications of the scope and weight of particular legal or moral rights. As Hart (1961, p. 124) argues, the nature of our world, the limits of our knowledge, the indeterminacy of our aims, and the "open texture" of our language make such full specification a virtual impossibility.

In order to recognize and describe the incompleteness and indeterminacy of rights, especially as regards their weight in competition with other considerations, a number of vocabularies have been introduced. Hart speaks of rights that are *defeasible* (1948–49, p. 175). Dworkin speaks of indeterminate rights as *abstract* (1977, p. 93). And McCloskey has introduced a whole set of concepts: real rights, conditional rights, etc. (1976b, pp. 105-11). But the most widely used vocabulary in this area is that of *prima facie rights*.

The vocabulary of prima facie rights was adapted from the distinction drawn by W. D. Ross between prima facie duties and duties *sans phrase*. When this distinction is applied to rights, a right *sans phrase* is one that has always dictated the result that ought to be followed in cases to which it applies, whereas a prima facie right is merely one that should so dictate unless stronger considerations intervene. As A. I. Melden points out, a prima facie right is not just an apparent right; rather it is a right that "qualified as it is, is real enough and not merely apparent and presumptive, in short, a [right] that further investigation cannot dispel as unreal or unfounded" (Melden, 1972, pp. 483, 491). Describing a right as prima facie serves to indicate that it is not absolute and that we are unable to give a full specification of its weight.[15] Nowadays, philosophers are likely to assume that almost all rights are prima facie in this sense.

The notion of prima facie rights has been subject to considerable criticism in recent years, on the grounds that it falsely suggests that a right that is overridden by stronger considerations ceases to be a right at all in such a situation. As Herbert Morris puts it, "It is seriously misleading to turn all justifiable infringements into noninfringements by saying that the right is only prima facie, as if we have, in concluding that we should not accord a man his rights, made out a case that he had none" (Morris, 1968, p. 499; see also Melden, 1972, p. 491). It has also been emphasized that some cases of justifiable infringement may give rise to a duty to compensate the injured person; this suggests that the right even though justifiably overridden had not disappeared altogether, for otherwise the infringement would not have generated or triggered the subsequent duty to provide compensation (Melden, 1972; McCloskey, 1976b; Thomson, 1977). Those who make this point generally distinguish between violating a right and infringing it — the latter occurring only in cases where the right is justifiably overridden.

There is, however, no difficulty in squaring the notion of a prima facie right with the fact that a right does not just vanish in cases where it is applicable but where its dictates are justifiably not followed. To do this one needs to distinguish between *conditions of possession*, which specify who has or can have the right (and whether it can be waived, forfeited, nullified, given up, or transferred), the *scope* of a right, which specifies what the right is to and in what situations, and the *weight* of a right, which involves a partial or full specification of what should be done in cases of conflict between the right and other considerations.[16] To describe a right as prima facie is to say something about its weight but not about its scope or conditions of possession.

When a right (say, the right to freedom of speech or assembly) is overridden in a particular case (for example, to avoid a riot), this does not imply that the rightholder ceases to possess the right. Moreover, rather than viewing this case as being covered by an exception built into the scope of the right — which would require us to say that a person had the right to freedom of speech or assembly but that it did not cover cases where it was likely to trigger a riot — we can view it as being covered by a specification of the right's weight. Here we would say that a person had the right to freedom of speech and that it applied even where it was likely to trigger a riot, but that it was subordinate to some stronger considerations, such as public safety, in those cases. Thus we can deal with situations in which a right is overridden without having to say that in such cases people don't have the right at all. Whether one or the other of these ways of conceiving how a right handles, or should be developed to handle, conflicts with other considerations depends on the kind of situation, e.g., whether it occurs frequently or very rarely or whether it permits one to draw administrable boundaries, and on the normative considerations involved, e.g., whether the case of conflict is central to the values that the right serves to protect or whether it is a marginal case and thus can be excepted in all cases without great loss to those values.

Describing a right as prima facie does not prevent us from beginning to specify its weight. For the vocabulary of prima facie rights will be needed as long as there are rights in which a tolerably full specification has not been accomplished (see Feinberg, 1973, chapter 5). It is important to note that the indeterminacy contemplated here is an indeterminacy of result in cases of conflict with other normative considerations. If we could specify the weight of a given right in conflicts with all of its possible competitors, we could then dispense with the notion of a prima facie right, although other sorts of indeterminacy and hence defeasibility – e.g., in regard to the general conditions for having or for applying the right or in regard to its scope – might remain.

It is also useful to distinguish between the primary and secondary guidance provided by a right. The primary guidance provided by the right to a fair trial pertains to the procedures that are to be used in determining a person's guilt or innocence in a criminal case. But if this primary guidance is justifiably or unjustifiably not complied with in a particular case, the right may yet provide secondary guidance by requiring that any infringement be done in a certain way or that the rightholder be compensated in a certain way. Thus a right might yield to stronger considerations in a case and yet still operate in that case by providing secondary guidance. The inclusion of a wide range of guidance as part of a right is clearly envisioned by Wellman (1975b, pp. 49-53). It would seem equally reasonable to treat some general principles of compensation and other matters of secondary guidance as a background feature of a whole system of rights rather than view them as part of the content of most individual rights.

III. Human Rights

The development of measures for the international promotion of human rights since World War II has brought the concept of human rights into use around the world. The *Universal Declaration of Human Rights* of the United Nations (1948) gave fairly definite content to the category of human rights, and the *European Convention on Human Rights* (1950, effective 1954) and the two United Nations *Covenants* (1966, entered into force 1976)[17] have made human rights part of international law. A number of philosophers, including Cranston (1973), Feinberg (1973), Mayo (1967), and Raphael (1967a,c), have attempted to provide philosophical analyses of the idea of human rights, and in this section we survey and evaluate these analyses.

Philosophical analyses of concepts are often partially prescriptive, and this is certainly true of analyses of the concept of human rights. Although philosophers who attempt to analyze this concept usually mention the *Universal Declaration,* they do not generally take it, or the extensive list of rights that it contains, to be very important. They tend to spend more time talking about Locke than about contemporary developments. Although international organizations have taken the view that there are *many* human rights, philosophers have generally preferred a shorter list. Cranston, for example, largely follows the older natural rights tradition and takes rights to "life, liberty, and a fair trial" as paradigms of human rights (Cranston, 1973, p. 65). Feinberg accepts a wider range of rights as examples of human rights, but he too is doubtful that economic and social rights are full-fledged human rights. Since they cannot now be implemented in many countries, they remain mere claims-to and thus mere "manifesto rights."[18]

Feinberg defines human rights as "generically moral rights of a fundamentally important kind held equally by all human beings, unconditionally and unalterably" (Feinberg, 1973, p. 85). Cranston characterizes human rights as moral rights that are of paramount importance, that are of all people against all people in all situations, and that are possessed by people simply as people rather than as occupants of some station or role (Cranston, 1973, pp. 6-7, 21, 67, 69). There are many issues raised by these definitions, but we will restrict ourselves to four: (1) human rights as moral rights; (2) human rights as universal rights; (3) human rights as unconditional rights; and (4) the addressees of human rights. The sense in which human rights are rights has already been discussed in connection with particular analyses of the concept of a right.

HUMAN RIGHTS AS MORAL RIGHTS

One finds general agreement among philosophers that human rights are moral rights, but the implications of this characterization are not always clear. Feinberg says that "the term 'moral rights' can be applied to all rights that are held to exist prior to, or independently of, any legal or institutional rules" (Feinberg, 1973, p. 84). Cranston contrasts moral rights with positive rights; the former, unlike the latter, are not necessarily enforceable, and their existence cannot be established by appeal to some authority (Cranston, 1973, pp. 5–6).

The word "moral" seems to be doing much of the same work in this context that the word "natural" used to do.[19] Describing rights as natural implied that they were not conventional or artificial in the sense that legal rights are, and the same is implied by describing human rights as moral rights. The vocabulary of "moral rights" has the advantage over the vocabulary of "natural rights" of not committing one to the view that human rights norms are somehow built into human nature or the universe. (See Feinberg, 1973, p. 85.)

But describing human rights as moral rights implies that the norms that constitute human rights are moral norms, and thus human rights can exist only if in some sense moral norms exist. Now, it is possible for moral, and hence human, rights to exist even if moral norms are conventional or are relative to culture; but if human rights are to serve their role as international standards of political criticism, then such a conventional morality would have to include some norms that are accepted worldwide.

In classifying human rights as moral rights one may wish to distinguish between actual and critical moralities. A utilitarian like Mill might allow that there is little agreement worldwide in actual moralities about basic rights but nevertheless claim that human rights exist in the most defensible critical morality, namely utilitarianism (see Lyons, 1977). The *Universal Declaration,* after all, was not designed to codify those rights that everyone already accepted; it was intended as "a common standard of achievement for all peoples and all nations" to be promoted by "teaching and education" (1948, Preamble).

Another peculiarly elusive feature of human rights, in their role as moral norms, is that the procedure for deciding whether something is a human right is not wholly settled. For we find that the vocabulary of human rights may be used upon the completion of any of several steps; the presence of these stages has introduced a degree of ambiguity into assertions that a human right exists. Accordingly, a person who has been persuaded that there is a moral entitlement to something may assert that there is a human right to that thing. A more standard use of the human rights vocabulary occurs at the completion of the next stage. Here the assertion that there is a human right to something would mean not simply that there is an entitlement to that thing but also that the means are now available for the implementation of this right in most countries and that within a justified critical morality there now exist obligations that support the right. And at the completion of a third step (should such occur), one might assert that there is a human right to something with the meaning that all people now possess an effective social or legal right in this area. A similar usage might occur when one was speaking not of all people but only of a particular country or region (see Martin, 1980). Thus one might say that the human right to freedom from racial discrimination now exists in Western Europe.

Institutionalization at the latter, regional or international, level has already occurred — most clearly in the *European Convention on Human Rights* (where effective enforcement procedures are available) and arguably in the United Nations *Covenants* of 1966. It should be noted, however, that where such international mechanisms exist some intergovernmentally created institutional rights may be called human rights as a matter of course. It is unlikely that all of these will prove to have adequate moral title. Thus it may be necessary to distinguish between those human rights that have normative standing and those that are merely institutional.

UNIVERSALITY

The first article of the *Universal Declaration* asserts that "All human beings are born . . . equal in dignity and rights" (1948). This egalitarian thrust of the human rights movement, with its accompanying attacks on privilege, discrimination, and caste, has been one of its most salient features. And the widespread acceptance of the view that all people should have the same basic rights shows the extent to which an egalitarian philosophy has triumphed. (See Nielsen, 1968, and Young, 1978, for criticism of the egalitarian viewpoint.) The view that human rights are, in Feinberg's words, "held equally by all human beings" (1973, p. 85) goes together with the view — to be discussed next — that human rights are held by people unconditionally simply as human beings.[20]

An assertion of universality in this context admits of weak and strong interpretations. One issue here pertains to whether the scope of "all persons" means all persons living now or all persons at all times, including the remotest cave dweller. If the latter, strong, interpretation is taken, one must formulate human rights so that they do not presuppose institutions (e.g., trials, lawyers, higher education, social security) that have developed rather late in human history. This is not, in fact, the kind of formulation one finds in human rights documents. Both eighteenth- and twentieth-century documents make essential reference to contemporary institutions. This matter has not been adequately addressed by philosophers. (But Nelson, 1974, has raised the important issue that many human rights are actually special rights, and not general ones at all; both Edel, 1971, and Wainwright, 1967, have provided interesting discussions of aspects of the topic of universality.)

A second issue about universality pertains to the kinds of situations to which human rights can apply. Cranston argues that a right to holidays with pay cannot be a human right because this is a right that, at best, belongs only to employees and, hence, not to all people (Cranston, 1973, p. 67). Although we do not wish to deny his conclusion about this alleged human right, it is important to distinguish between, say, a right that arises from being an employee and a right that arises from being a human being but that applies in all circumstances where people are employees. This is a distinction between the conditions for having a right and the conditions in which one can enjoy or actualize a right (see Benn, 1978, pp. 59–60). If people have human rights to a fair trial and to compensation for property taken by the state, these rights do not arise from being accused of a crime or from owning property: they arise simply from being a person, but they only apply and can only be enjoyed under these circumstances. It is also helpful here to distinguish between rights that prohibit doing something altogether (e.g., a prohibition of torture) and rights that prohibit doing something unless it is done in a certain way (e.g., taking property unless this is accompanied by fair compensation). In the case of rights generated by all-out prohibitions, the conditions under which one has the right are the same as the conditions under which one is in a position to enjoy or actualize it. Perhaps Cranston meant, in criticizing the view that economic and social rights are human rights, to restrict human rights to rights that prohibit something altogether and not just circumstantially; but if he did, then the right to a fair trial cannot be a human right.

UNCONDITIONALITY

Cranston says that "human rights are not rights which derive from a particular situation; they are rights which belong to a man simply because he is a man" (Cranston, 1973, p. 7; see also Hart, 1955, pp. 175–76). Feinberg views human rights as rights that people have "unconditionally and unalterably" (1973, p. 85; see also 1978, p. 97). Although many problems are raised by the idea that all people have some basic rights independent of their station in life, independent of which rights are recognized by their governments, and independent of their race, sex, or religion, this idea gives to human rights much of their political appeal by strengthening the sense in which they are universal and by allowing people to claim rights not recognized by governments.

As should be clear from our earlier discussions of defeasibility and universality, it will not do to assert that human rights are unconditional in every respect. There are many ways in which a right can be conditional. Defining a right, after all, involves setting out a variety of conditions. Further, a universal right may be conditional in regard to an explicit exception built into its scope, or in regard to the possibility of being outweighed in a particular case by stronger considerations. But these types of conditionality do not contradict the claim at issue. The thesis of unconditionality is intended to exclude only those conditions that make possession of the right contingent on the holder's having a certain social position, or on the right's recognition by government, or on the holder's race, sex, or religion.

Feinberg's claim that human rights are possessed "unalterably" presents more serious difficulties. This claim seems to be a successor to the eighteenth-century idea that natural rights are "inalienable." Although the word "inalienable" has sometimes been used — misleadingly — as a synonym for "unconditional" or "indefeasible," it is important to distinguish these notions.[21] "Unconditionality," as we have seen, rules out some but not all restrictions on scope. Defeasibility, at least as the term is currently used by philosophers, pertains to whether a right can be challenged and overridden. Neither of these matters bears on whether one can cease to have (either in general or in a particular case) a right that one formerly had, yet this is what inalienability is about. B. A. Richards, although he does not distinguish adequately between issues of possession, scope, and weight, has argued persuasively that eighteenth-century writers who asserted the inalienability of rights principally meant "that no man can waive or voluntarily relinquish any of these rights" (Richards, 1969, pp. 393–98). Although this weak interpretation of inalienability may be historically correct, inalienability in this sense is of limited political importance.[22] The greater worry today is about governments taking people's rights away, not about people giving them up voluntarily. In any event the precise issue posed is whether a human right can be (either generally or in a particular case) waived, given up, transferred, forfeited, or annulled.

The easiest way to deal with this issue, it seems to us, is to set aside the ambiguous and misleading notion of inalienability. Thus, when the UN's *Universal Declaration* asserts that human rights are inalienable (as in the first sentence, where it speaks of the "equal and inalienable rights of all members of the human family"), we should not expect or interpret this to mean that such rights are possessed literally unalterably. For some of the rights asserted to be human rights (e.g., the right to take part in the government of one's country or the right to freedom of movement and residence) are ones that can justifiably be withdrawn — temporarily or even permanently — from those who commit serious crimes. But it is also important to be able to assert that some human rights (e.g., the right not to be tortured) cannot be forfeited by bad conduct or otherwise become nonbinding on governments. This can be done directly and in precise terms; it does not require misleading and too general claims about "inalienability" or "unalterability."

THE ADDRESSEES OF HUMAN RIGHTS

All the great human rights manifestos were intended to impose restraints upon states. Individuals were involved as beneficiaries of these restraints but not as the parties to whom the manifestos were addressed. In spite of this historical connection between human rights and governments, there is a wide spectrum of opinion about who the addressees of human rights are. Cranston does not mention governments at all in his characterization of human rights. On his view, human rights are rights of all individuals *against all individuals*. "[T]o say that all men have a right to life is to impose on all men the duty of respecting human life" (Cranston, 1973, pp. 68–69).

A similar position is taken by Raphael, who distinguishes two senses of "universal moral right." "In the stronger sense it means a right of all men against all men; in the weaker sense it means simply a right of all men, but not necessarily against all men" (Raphael, 1967a, p. 65). The latter rights involve the responsibilities of states and are viewed as "rights of the citizen." Universal moral rights in the stronger sense are viewed as genuine "rights of man" (Raphael, 1967a, p. 66), although Raphael thinks it appropriate to include rights of the citizen in international declarations of rights.

Although Feinberg does not assert this about all human rights, he holds that the right to life is a "*double-barreled* claim" addressed both to the world at large as a demand that individuals respect life and to the state as a demand for legal enforcement of protections for life (Feinberg, 1978, p. 96). Mayo defines a human right as "a claim on behalf of all men . . . to action by a state government" and says that "the reasons for this qualification are historical rather than conceptual" (Mayo, 1967, p. 77, italics removed). And Wellman—to conclude this survey—proposes a narrow definition in which a human right is viewed "as an ethical right of the individual as human being vis-à-vis the state" (Wellman, 1978b, p. 55).

The diversity of opinion and the lack of substantial arguments on this issue suggest that it has not been carefully attended to by most of these authors. Cranston's view completely ignores history. It also has the implausible consequence that the right to a fair trial, which Cranston gives as an example of a human right, is a right which one has against all people rather than against one's government. On the other side, the views of Mayo and of Wellman (at least as far as his definition goes) seem to leave out the individual completely as an addressee of human rights. Even if states are the primary addressees of most human rights norms, individuals may still have duties as secondary addressees to promote human rights in cases where they are in a position to do so. This kind of approach has practical as well as philosophical significance because of the contemporary recognition of the interrelations between the social and political spheres. A human right such as the right to freedom from racial discrimination (see *Universal Declaration* article 2; also articles 7, 16, and 23) is likely to require social as well as political changes for its realization. Thus Feinberg's approach seems to come closest to being adequate, but different accounts may have to be given of different human rights. This, too, is an area where additional work is needed.

IV. Conclusion

Happily, our survey indicates that solid work has been done and progress made in a number of areas. Part of this progress involves the emergence of a useful analytical framework for rights. It is now far from being the case that "we don't really know what a right is." And in that most vexed of areas, natural or human rights, clear and defensible—although weakened—interpretations of many earlier assertions about such rights have become available. In our survey we did not deal with work on the justification of rights or on the important related issue of who or what can be said to have rights (but see Martin, 1983). We hope, however, that a clearer view of analytical approaches to the concept of rights will be helpful to the large number of philosphers who are now trying to deal with such normative issues about rights.

Acknowledgments

We appreciate the suggestions provided by several of the principals whose views were discussed in this paper. In addition, for comments and criticism we are especially indebted to Alan Fuchs, Louis Henkin, G. C. MacCallum, Jr., Stephen Munzer, David Schmidt, and Janet Sisson. We also want to acknowledge with thanks the help of Aurora Ripley, Constance Ducey, and Karen Reeder Bell.

Work on this chapter was done during tenure of a grant, in Martin's case, from the University of Kansas General Research Fund (number 3566-20-0038) and of fellowships, in Nickel's case, at the Aspen Institute for Humanistic Studies (Colorado) and at the National Humanities Center (North Carolina). We are grateful for this support.

Notes

1. A more comprehensive listing of such work is found in our "Bibliography on the Nature and Foundations of Rights, 1947–1977," *Political Theory* 6, no. 3 (August 1978): 395–413.

2. Thus, we would interpret the view that rights are to be characterized by linking them to interests as pertaining, principally, either to the justification of rights (e.g., MacCormick, 1977; Feinberg, 1978) or to their proper distribution (e.g., Feinberg, 1974). Similarly, the idea that rights are essentially connected with needs—an idea advocated by Kaufman (1971) and Tranøy (1975) and criticized cogently by McCloskey (1976a)—is best understood, we believe, as indicating a justificatory ground for some rights. It is worth noting that almost all theorists regard rights as justified, in some sense, but not all of them have advanced explicit theories of justification, or clearly identified the justificatory strand in their characterization of rights.

3. Closely associated historically with this notion of the correlativity of rights and duties are accounts that equate having a right with being the beneficiary of an obligation. Bentham, for example, said that "to assure to individuals the possession of a certain good, is to confer a *right* upon them" (*Works* III, ed. Bowring, 1843, p. 159). Hart (1955, 1962, 1973) has criticized Bentham's view, and David Lyons (1969) has attempted to restate the "beneficiary theory" so as to preserve it from these criticisms. Hart's criticisms have been cogently described and amplified in Kearns (1975). It now seems unlikely that the beneficiary theory can be reconstructed in such a way as to make it tenable as an account of what it is to have a right. In particular, if there are good objections to the thesis that every right must involve a second-party duty, and we shall see shortly that there are, then these are also good objections to the beneficiary theory as a definition of what a right is.

4. This thesis has deep roots in the philosophical literature on rights and has been advocated, without commitment to the parallel thesis that duties logically entail rights, by MacDonald (1946–47), Hart (1955), and Mayo (1967). Although Hart advocated the idea that rights entail duties, his critique (1961) of sanctionist theories of law removes one of the motivations for adhering to it. These theories, deriving from Austin, view the legal sanction as creating the duty and the duty as creating the right. In our period of survey, the Benthamite view that every right implies the existence of a remedy or sanction has seldom been defended. But a weaker view, which connects the existence of a right with the appropriateness of using sanctions to uphold the right, whether or not they are actually available, is advocated by Kleinig (1978, p. 44).

5. Thus, Hohfeld (1964 edition of 1919 original) identified four basic types of rights, each type having a unique second-party correlative. For a legal *claim right,* the correlative element is a legal duty of some second party. Analogously, the legal *liberty* to do X—which consists in the absence of any duty on the agent's part to refrain from X—is matched with other people's lack of a claim that X not be done by the agent. A legal *power* to do X consists in a person's legal competence to perform an act which will create, or at least bring to bear, certain legal consequences for a second party—and the situation of the second party constitutes his liability (or susceptibility) to that particular power. Finally, a person's *immunity* from X is necessarily correlated with a lack of power on the part of others to do X, and thus the correlative of an immunity is a disability. The four italicized elements were thought by Hohfeld to give legal "advantage" (1964, p. 71)

and their correlates legal "disadvantage." Thus, Hohfeld conceived rights as devices for the parceling out of legal advantage and disadvantage to individuals in four distinct patterns. (See Perry, 1977, p. 42n for a helpful chart, adapted from Hohfeld, 1964, p. 36.) Hohfeld's work has occasioned a substantial amount of philosophical discussion. Here one should note Brady (1972), Fitch (1967), Kanger (1966, 1972), Lindahl (1977), Moritz (1960), Mullock (1970), Perry (1977), and Pörn (1970).

6. Hohfeld treated "X's claim to A against Y" as the same relation, seen from X's perspective, as "Y's duty to X in regard to A." On this account the vocabularies of claims and duties are interchangeable, and Feinberg's theory would become a variant of the theories just discussed that explicate rights in terms of duties. But it is not clear that Feinberg is using "claim" in precisely this Hohfeldian sense.

7. Bernard Mayo (1967) offers an account of rights in terms of claims that is somewhat less complex than Feinberg's. According to Mayo, "a right is just a claim" (p. 75). By "claim" Mayo seems to mean not a set of normative considerations or some normative element, but rather an instance of the action of claiming. Thus Mayo seems to have succumbed to the temptation that Feinberg resisted, namely, the equation of the normative considerations which justify claims with the act of claiming. But the implausibility of so treating rights is slightly reduced by Mayo's willingness to allow that rights are justifiable claims, although he thinks that this qualification is "otiose" (p. 76).

8. Although Feinberg does not himself do this, we hyphenate these phrases for purposes of clarity.

9. The view that rights are entitlements, in roughly the sense intended by McCloskey, is also found in Wasserstrom (1964, p. 630) and in Nozick (1974). Wasserstrom defends the view that statements about rights cannot be fully replaced by statements about duties because rights involve an entitlement to make claims on others, because a claim based on a right is not a mere request for charity, and because failures to comply with rights involve injuries or wrongs. But as Arnold (1978, p. 82) points out, there is no reason that high-priority duties of identifiable persons to treat specific people in specific ways cannot have these same characteristics and thus perform the same function as a right.

10. McCloskey admits both these points (see 1975, p. 403, and 1976b, p. 105). Indeed, the most he is willing to say, using the language of entitlements, is that "what is common to all rights [is] an entitlement" of some sort (McCloskey, 1976b, p. 104; see also p. 102).

11. For Wellman, the core of a right could be a pair of elements (of the same basic kind). Thus, for example, a given claim right might have two distinct claims as its core. (See, e.g., Wellman, 1978b, p. 56.)

12. An analytical framework for rights very similar to Wellman's is developed in some detail by Flathman (1976).

13. For fuller discussions of Dworkin's views on rights, see Nickel (1977) and Richards (1977).

14. See Feinberg's discussion of absolute rights (1973, pp. 79-83). His view is criticized by James (1976). The relative weights of rights has been established to some extent within U.S. constitutional law through the idea of "preferred freedoms." Fourteenth Amendment criteria such as "fundamental rights" and "suspect classifications" have also served to give priority to some considerations over others.

15. Through their general use of this vocabulary, contemporary philosophers have attempted to disarm critiques of natural or human rights that are premised on the implausibility of saying that these rights can never be overridden in any circumstances. Furthermore, the notion of a prima facie right allows philosophers to give plausible interpretations of the universality and unconditionality of human rights. Everyone can be said to have a prima facie right unconditionally, because the presumptive and indeterminate character of a prima facie right allows one to deal with trade-offs without having to deny the continued possession of the right (see Feinberg, 1978, pp. 98ff).

16. Other aspects of rights that need to be distinguished include the *conditions of engagement,* which specify whether the right is continuously in force or only comes into play when invoked by the holder, *whom the right is against,* the *normative elements* the right contains, and the *system of norms* that generates the right (e.g., a legal system or a morality). It is obvious that different kinds of rights can be distinguished in terms of differences that occur at these locations. A variety of useful distinctions about rights is found in Feinberg (1973, pp. 55-73).

17. See Brownlie (1980) for the texts of these documents.

18. Defenses of the view that economic and social rights are genuine human rights are found in Nickel (1978-79) and in the essays by Raphael (1967b), with criticisms by Cranston.

19. Some philosophers, e.g., Hart (1955) and Rawls (1971, esp. note 30 on pp. 505–6), continue to talk of *natural* rights, but probably do so in the restricted sense indicated.

20. The difference that is often noted in arguments about abortion between *humans* as members of the species and *persons* as those human beings who are not fetuses, not severely retarded, not permanently comatose, etc., is one that is not, unfortunately, reflected in most of the human rights literature. We suspect that some human rights are rights of all human beings (e.g., the right not to be tortured) and that others are rights of all persons (e.g., the right to participate in government).

21. One example of such confusion, using "indefeasible" and "inalienable" interchangeably, is found in Nielsen (1968, p. 573). Another, this one involving "unconditional" and "inalienable," is in Brown (1955, pp. 208–9).

22. Both Feinberg (1978) and Schiller (1969) similarly restrict "inalienability," both for historical reasons. Feinberg's essay, however, offers an important variety of supplementary terms.

Bibliography

Arnold, Christopher. 1978. "Analyses of Right." In Kamenka and Tay, eds., *Human Rights.* Pages 74–86.

Becker, Lawrence C. 1977. *Property Rights: Philosophic Foundations.* London: Routledge & Kegan Paul.

Benditt, Theodore M. 1978. *Law as Rule and Principle: Problems of Legal Philosophy.* Stanford, Calif.: Stanford University Press. Pages 158–76.

Benn, S. I. 1967. "Rights." In Paul Edwards, ed., *Encyclopedia of Philosophy,* vol. 7. New York: Macmillan and Free Press. Pages 191–95.

––––––. 1978. "Human Rights—For Whom and For What?" In Kamenka and Tay, eds., *Human Rights.* Pages 59–73.

Benn, S. I., and Peters, R. S. 1965. *The Principles of Political Thought.* New York: Free Press. Originally published 1959 as *Social Principles and the Democratic State.* London: Allen & Unwin.

Bradley, F. H. 1927. *Ethical Studies.* 2nd ed. London: Oxford University Press. First published 1876. The section on rights appears as an appendix to Essay V, "My Station and Its Duties," under the title "Note to Essay V: Rights and Duties." Pages 207–13.

Brady, James B. 1972. "Law, Language and Logic: The Legal Philosophy of Wesley Newcomb Hohfeld." *Transactions of the Charles S. Peirce Society* 8: 246–63.

Brandt, Richard B. 1959. *Ethical Theory.* Englewood Cliffs, N.J.: Prentice-Hall.

Braybrooke, David. 1972. "The Firm but Untidy Correlativity of Rights and Obligations." *Canadian Journal of Philosophy* 1: 351–63.

Brown, Peter G., and MacLean, Douglas, eds. 1979. *Human Rights and U.S. Foreign Policy.* Lexington, Mass.: Lexington Books.

Brown, Stuart M. 1955. "Inalienable Rights." *Philosophical Review* 64: 192–211.

Brownlie, Ian, ed. 1980. *Basic Documents on Human Rights.* 2nd ed. London: Oxford University Press.

Cranston, Maurice. 1967. "Human Rights, Real and Supposed." In D. D. Raphael, ed., *Political Theory and the Rights of Man.*

––––––. 1973. *What Are Human Rights?* 2nd ed. London: Bodley Head.

Dworkin, Ronald. 1977. *Taking Rights Seriously.* Cambridge, Mass.: Harvard University Press. Appendix added 1978, pp. 291–368.

Edel, Abraham. 1971. "Some Reflections on the Concept of Human Rights." In E. H. Pollack, ed., *Human Rights.* Buffalo, N.Y.: Jay Stewart for AMINTAPHIL. Pages 1–23.

Feinberg, Joel. 1964. "Wasserstrom on Human Rights." *Journal of Philosophy* 61: 641–45.

––––––. 1966. "Duties, Rights and Claims." *American Philosophical Quarterly* 3: 137–44.

––––––. 1970. "The Nature and Value of Rights." *Journal of Value Inquiry* 4: 243–57.

––––––. 1973. *Social Philosophy.* Foundations of Philosophy Series. Englewood Cliffs, N.J.: Prentice-Hall.

––––––. 1974. "The Rights of Animals and Unborn Generations." In William T. Blackstone, ed., *Philosophy and Environmental Crisis.* Athens: University of Georgia Press. Pages 43–68.

––––––. 1978. "Voluntary Euthanasia and the Inalienable Right to Life." *Philosophy and*

Public Affairs 7: 92–123.

———. 1980. *Rights, Justice, and the Bounds of Liberty: Essays in Social Philosophy*. Princeton, N.J.: Princeton University Press. Contains reprints of Feinberg 1966, 1970 (together with "A Postscript to the Nature and Value of Rights," pp. 156–58), 1974, and 1978.

Fitch, Frederic B. 1967. "A Revision of Hohfeld's Theory of Legal Concepts." *Logique and Analyse* 10: 269–76.

Flathman, Richard. 1976. *The Practice of Rights*. Cambridge: Cambridge University Press.

Fried, Charles. 1978. *Right and Wrong*. Cambridge, Mass.: Harvard University Press.

Golding, Martin P. 1968. "Towards a Theory of Human Rights." *Monist* 52: 521–49.

———. 1978. "The Concept of Rights: A Historical Sketch." In E. and B. Bandman, eds., *Bioethics and Human Rights*. Boston: Little, Brown. Pages 44–50.

Hart, Herbert L. A. 1948–1949. "The Ascription of Responsibility and Rights." *Proceedings of the Aristotelian Society* 49: 171–94.

———. 1955. "Are There Any Natural Rights?" *Philosophical Review* 64: 175–91.

———. 1961. *The Concept of Law*. Oxford: Clarendon Press.

———. 1962. "Bentham." Lecture on a Mastermind series. *Proceedings of the British Academy* 48: 297–320. See especially pages 313–17.

———. 1973. "Bentham on Legal Rights." In A.W.B. Simpson, ed., *Oxford Essays in Jurisprudence*. 2nd series. Oxford: Clarendon Press. Pages 171–201.

———. 1979. "Utilitarianism and Natural Rights." *Tulane Law Review* 53: 663–80.

Hohfeld, Wesley N. 1964. *Fundamental Legal Conceptions*. New Haven, Conn.: Yale University Press. The two papers printed under the above title first appeared as articles in the *Yale Law Journal* 23 (1913): 16–59 and 26 (1917): 710–70. Subsequent to Hohfeld's death in 1918, the articles were reprinted, with manuscript changes by the author, in a single book by Yale University Press, 1919, edited and with an introduction by Walter W. Cook. Reprinted 1923 and 1964, the latter with an additional foreword by Arthur L. Corbin.

James, Gene G. 1976. "Feinberg on Absolute Legal Rights." *Journal of Thought* 11: 16–23

Kamenka, E., and Tay, A.E.S., eds. 1978. *Human Rights*. London: Edward Arnold; New York: St. Martin's Press.

Kanger, Stig. 1972. "Law and Logic." *Theoria* 38: 105–29.

Kanger, Stig, and Kanger, Helle. 1966. "Rights and Parliamentarism." *Theoria* 32: 85–115.

Kaufman, Arnold S. 1971. "Wants, Needs, and Liberalism." *Inquiry* 14: 191–206.

Kearns, Thomas R. 1975. "Rights, Benefits and Normative Systems." *Archiv für Rechts- und Sozialphilosophie* 61: 465–83.

Kleinig, John. 1978. "Human Rights, Legal Rights and Social Change." In Kamenka and Tay, eds., *Human Rights*. Pages 36–47.

Lindahl, Lars. 1977. *Position and Change: A Study in Law and Logic*. Synthese Library 112. Dordrecht: Reidel.

Lyons, David. 1969. "Rights, Claimants, and Beneficiaries." *American Philosophical Quarterly* 6: 173–85.

———. 1970. "The Correlativity of Rights and Duties." *Nous* 4: 45–55.

———. 1977. "Human Rights and the General Welfare." *Philosophy and Public Affairs* 6: 113–29.

———. 1979. "Introduction." In David Lyons, ed., *Rights*. Belmont, Calif.: Wadsworth.

McCloskey, H. J. 1965. "Rights." *Philosophical Quarterly* 15: 115–27.

———. 1975. "The Right to Life." *Mind* 84: 403–25.

———. 1976a. "Human Needs, Rights and Political Values." *American Philosophical Quarterly* 13: 1–11.

———. 1976b. "Rights—Some Conceptual Issues." *Australasian Journal of Philosophy* 54: 99–115.

MacCormick, Neil. 1976. "Children's Rights: A Test-Case for Theories of Rights." *Archiv für Rechts- und Sozialphilosophie* 62: 305–17.

———. 1977. "Rights in Legislation." In P.M.S. Hacker and J. Raz, eds., *Law, Morality, and Society: Essays in Honour of H.L.A. Hart*. Oxford: Clarendon Press. Pages 189–209.

MacDonald, Margaret. 1946–1947. "Natural Rights." *Proceedings of the Aristotelian Society* 47: 225–50.

Machan, Tibor. 1980. "Some Recent Work in Human Rights Theory." *American Philosophical Quarterly* 17: 103–15.

Markovits, Inga. 1978. "Socialist vs. Bourgeois Rights—An East-West Comparison." *University of Chicago Law Review* 45: 612–36.

Martin, Rex. 1980. "Human Rights and Civil Rights." *Philosophical Studies* 17: 391–403.
_____. 1983. "On the Justification of Rights." In G. Fløistad, ed., *Philosophy of Action,* forthcoming. *Chronicles,* vol. 3. International Institute of Philosophy, Paris.
Mayo, B. 1967. "What Are Human Rights?" In D. D. Raphael, ed., *Political Theory and The Rights of Man.* Reprinted, abbreviated, *Aristotelian Society* Suppl. Vol. 39 (1965): 219–36.
Melden, A. I. 1972. "The Play of Rights." *Monist* 56: 479–502.
_____. 1977. *Rights and Persons.* Oxford: Basil Blackwell; Berkeley: University of California Press. Chapter 1, with revisions, incorporates Melden, 1972.
Milne, A.J.M. 1968. *Freedom and Rights.* New York: Humanities Press.
Montague, Phillip. 1980. "Two Concepts of Rights." *Philosophy and Public Affairs* 9: 372–84.
Moritz, Manfred. 1960. *Ueber Hohfelds System der Juridischen Grundbegriffe.* Library of Theoria 7. Lund, Sweden: G.W.K. Gleerup.
Morris, Herbert. 1968. "Persons and Punishment." *Monist* 52: 475–501.
Mullock, Philip. 1970. "The Hohfeldian No-Right: A Logical Analysis." *Archiv für Rechts- und Sozialphilosophie* 56: 265–72.
Nelson, William N. 1974. "Special Rights, General Rights, and Social Justice." *Philosophy and Public Affairs* 3: 410–30.
Nickel, James W. 1977. "Dworkin on the Nature and Consequences of Rights." *Georgia Law Review* 11: 1115–42.
_____. 1978–1979. "Is There a Human Right to Employment?" *Philosophical Forum* (Boston) 10: 149–70.
Nielsen, Kai. 1968. "Scepticism and Human Rights." *Monist* 52: 573–94.
Nozick, Robert. 1974. *Anarchy, State, and Utopia.* New York: Basic Books.
Perry, Thomas D. 1977. "A Paradigm of Philosophy: Hohfeld on Legal Rights." *American Philosophical Quarterly* 14: 41–50.
Pörn, I. 1970. *The Logic of Power.* Oxford: Basil Blackwell.
Raphael, David Daiches. 1967a. "Human Rights, Old and New." In Raphael, *Political Theory and the Rights of Man.* Pages 54–67. Reprinted from *Aristotelian Society* Suppl. Vol. 39 (1965): 205–18.
_____, ed. 1967b. *Political Theory and the Rights of Man.* Bloomington: Indiana University Press.
_____. 1967c. "The Rights of Man and the Rights of the Citizen." In Raphael, ed., *Political Theory and the Rights of Man.*
Rawls, John. 1971. *A Theory of Justice.* Cambridge, Mass.: Harvard University Press.
_____. 1980. "A Kantian Conception of Equality." In V. Held, ed., *Property, Profits, and Economic Justice.* Belmont, Calif.: Wadsworth. Reprinted from *Cambridge Review* (February 1975): 94–99.
Regan, Donald H. 1978. "Glosses on Dworkin: Rights, Principles, and Policies." *Michigan Law Review* 76: 1213–64.
Richards, B. A. 1969. "Inalienable Rights, Recent Criticism and Old Doctrine." *Philosophy and Phenomenological Research* 29: 391–404.
Richards, David A. J. 1977. "Taking *Taking Rights Seriously* Seriously: Reflections on Dworkin and the American Revival of Natural Law." *New York University Law Review* 52: 1265–1340.
Roshwald, Mordecai. 1958–1959. "The Concept of Human Rights." *Philosophy and Phenomenological Research* 19: 354–79.
Ross, Alf. 1958. *On Law and Justice.* London: Stevens; Berkeley: University of California Press, 1959.
Ross, W. D. 1930. *The Right and the Good.* Oxford: Clarendon Press. The section on rights appears as an appendix to Chapter 2 under the title "Appendix I. Rights." Pages 48–56. See also pages 59–62.
Scanlon, T. M. 1977. "Rights, Goals, and Fairness." *Erkenntnis* 11: 81–95. Reprinted, revised, in S. Hampshire, ed., *Public and Private Morality.* Cambridge: Cambridge University Press. Pages 93–111.
_____. 1979. "Freedom of Expression and Categories of Expression." *University of Pittsburgh Law Review* 40: 519–50.
Schiller, Marvin. 1969. "Are There Any Inalienable Rights?" *Ethics* 79: 309–15.
Shue, Henry. 1980. *Basic Rights.* Princeton, N.J.: Princeton University Press. See especially chapter 1.
Singer, Marcus G. 1972. "The Basis of Rights and Duties." *Philosophical Studies* 23: 48–57.

Thomson, Judith J. 1977. *Self-Defense and Rights.* The Lindley Lecture, 1976. Lawrence: University of Kansas.

Tranøy, Knut Erik. 1975. "'Ought' Implies 'Can': A Bridge from Fact to Norm?" Part 1: *Ratio* 14 (1972): 116–30. Part 2: "From Human Needs to Human Rights." *Ratio* 17 (1975): 147–75.

Villey, Michel. 1969. *Seize essais de philosophie du droit.* Paris: Dalloz.

Wainwright, William J. 1967. "Natural Rights." *American Philosophical Quarterly* 4: 79–84.

Wasserstrom, Richard. 1964. "Rights, Human Rights, and Racial Discrimination." *Journal of Philosophy* 61: 628–41.

Wellman, Carl. 1975a. *Morals and Ethics.* Glenview, Ill.: Scott, Foresman.

———. 1975b. "Upholding Legal Rights." *Ethics* 86: 49–60.

———. 1978a. "Legal Rights." In *Uppsalaskolan—Och Efteråt.* Stockholm: Almqvist and Wiksell. Pages 213–21.

———. 1978b. "A New Conception of Human Rights." In Kamenka and Tay, eds., *Human Rights.* Pages 48–58.

———. 1979. "Consent to Medical Research on Children." *Archiv für Rechts- und Sozialphilosophie* 12 (n.s.): 85–105.

Young, Robert. 1978. "Dispensing with Moral Rights." *Political Theory* 6: 63–74.

chapter 8

Some Recent Work in Human Rights Theory

TIBOR R. MACHAN

Every man has a property in his own person, this nobody has any right to but himself.

John Locke, The Second Treatise of Civil Government

The right of man to freedom is not based on the union of man with man, but on the separation of man from man.

Karl Marx, "On the Jewish Question"

Through the shift of emphasis from natural duties or obligations to natural rights, the individual, the ego, had become the center and origin of the moral world, since man—as distinguished from man's end—had become that center or origin.

Leo Strauss, Natural Right and History

Introduction

As has been noted frequently, professional philosophers are once again attending to political philosophy. From its post–World War II revival to the present, Anglo-American political philosophy has been punctuated with references to human rights, moral rights, natural rights, and related topics. As a way of advancing the argument and assisting the various inquiries related to it, I want to take stock of the recent literature on human rights. I will include works that aim to identify, analyze, elaborate, criticize, and otherwise take into consideration rights or rights-oriented principles that purport to be fundamental guidelines to political life and organization.

My plan is to begin with the work of noncognitivist human rights theorists, who constitute a distinctive group.[1] (The discussion will appear to be chronological, simply because those whose views I will present did write in something like a sequence.) I will follow this with a presentation of cognitivist human or natural rights theories (again only giving the impression of chronological progress). In general, I will make it evident throughout why we can divide the relevant philosophers into two distinct groups. There are, first, those who treat human rights as part of ordinary normative discourse, merely in need of and subject to clarification and elaboration; then we meet those who find it necessary to show the concept of human or natural rights to be sound and applicable to human political life, whatever may be supportive of or contrary to this within ordinary normative discourse.

Although there may have been pre-Hobbesian utterances of nascent natural rights theories,[2] I will assume both that Hobbes was the first to develop the idea of rights as it is presently used and that Locke made palatable and popularized Hobbes's idea.[3] As is well known, the ridicule to which Hume and Bentham subjected the Hobbesian-Lockean state of nature and natural rights thesis considerably diminished its potency in philosophical circles. To be sure, Rousseau, Kant, Hegel, Mill, and Spencer—to mention a few—all adapted the natural rights idea to their own purposes; but their episodic and idiosyncratic invocation of the idea hardly rehabilitated it to its Lockean vigor. And, between Spencer's time and the end of World War II, few tried to defend rights theories or the type of polity usually associated with it, namely, a constitutional republic based on the rights mentioned in the Declaration of Independence. During the period of positivism, logical atomism, and logical empiricism, not only talk of human or natural rights, but talk of any sort of purportedly meaningful, let alone possibly true, normative position had been all but completely abandoned, especially within the mainly secular Anglo-American philosophical community.

Perhaps it was the popular acceptance of some version of human or natural rights theory (which influenced the constitutions of several new nations and the United Nations Charter) that prompted, eventually, some attention to the idea of human rights from academic philosophers. Or perhaps the currency of rights talk in the speech of our times has prompted language-oriented philosophers to take up the subject of rights. It is evident that having the right to do something or to have something is an ordinary notion today and has been for decades. Also, in times of political and legal turmoil, the idea is used abundantly. Philosophers, as persons and citizens, might themselves find rights talk useful in our politically volatile times.

Noncognitivist Rights Theories

With hindsight, it makes good sense to start this survey with a discussion of the work of Margaret Macdonald, the first participant in the revival of rights discussions, with her widely reprinted paper "Natural Rights."

MACDONALD ON TAKING A STAND

Working in the tradition of accepting three distinct types of propositions—"tautological or analytic," "empirical or contingent," and "expressions of value"—Macdonald (1967, p. 37) placed "A human being has a right to be free" within the last category. She explained why it may have been thought to belong in the first but argued that only as a "barren tautology," namely, "*x* is human entails *x* has natural rights," could this be so. But, Macdonald observed, this cannot be, because "it is hard to believe that a barren tautology generated the ardours of that time in which it was [according to Wordsworth in *The French Revolution*] good to be alive and to be young was 'very heaven'" (Macdonald, p. 42).

Nor can natural rights talk be placed in the "empirical or contingent" category: the proposition "A human being has a right to be free" or "*A*, a human being, has a natural right to be free" clearly does not belong in the second category, since no "deduction from observation of bodies in sense perception" (Macdonald, p. 39) leads to knowledge of either natural law or natural rights. The sensible alternative is that such a proposition belongs in the third category.

> In short, "natural rights" are the conditions of a good society. But what those conditions are is not given by nature or mystically bound up with the essence of man and his inevitable goal, but is determined by human decision [Macdonald, 1967 p. 48].

Putting it differently, "To assert that 'Freedom is better than slavery' or 'All men are of equal worth' is not to state a fact but to *choose a side*. It announces, *This is where I stand"* (Macdonald, p. 49). Macdonald's noncognitivist position, familiar to most contemporary philosophers in the larger context of metaethics, is well summarized as follows:

> There are no certainties in the field of values. For there are no true or false beliefs about values, but only better or worse decisions and choices. And to encourage the better decision we need to employ devices which are artistic rather than scientific. For our aim is not intellectual assent, but practical effects. These are not, of course, absolutely separate, for intellectual assent to a proposition or theory is followed by using it. But values, I think, concern only behavior. They are not known, but accepted and acted upon [Macdonald, 1967, pp. 54–55].

MELDEN'S PERFORMATIVE RIGHTS

A more sophisticated noncognitivist theory of human rights is found in A. I. Melden's several contributions to the discussion. His 1952 paper in the symposium "The Concept of Universal Human Rights" presented a theory expounded in greater detail in numerous works, including chapter 6 of his *Rights and Persons* (1977). The earlier work, however, was argued more in the phraseology of ordinary language analysis and thus provides us with a distinctive outlook, whereas in *Rights and Persons* Melden's theory is expressed as an informal version of Alan Gewirth's neo-Kantian deductive derivation of human rights from certain essential facts about persons as moral agents.

Melden claimed that "A man has the right to life" is neither a description nor a conclusion from a logical argument (1977, p. 180). Instead, such an utterance "is a complicated performance"; any reasons we offer to support our moral utterances are of "relevance to the significance conditions of such utterances" (ibid.). Violations of human rights, in turn, "are wrong, not because the factual statements describing such actions entail statements that such actions are wrong, but because such factual statements are incompatible with factual statements that describe the significance conditions of our ordinary moral discourse" (ibid.).

Melden anticipated a form of argument applied to rights theory by H.L.A. Hart; but whereas Hart's position was essentially hypothetical, Melden's showed itself to be categorical, in the last analysis:

> human rights are fundamental to special moral rights. For (a) unless the sorts of action were performed that would satisfy the appeal to human rights there would be no sense in the given context in speaking of special moral rights since the significance conditions of such discourse would not be present, and (b) it does make sense to think of human rights as taking precedence over all the other rights moral or otherwise, since there can be no valid moral exception to the establishment of a moral community—the sort of community in which alone moral discourse has any use—and the claim is that the variety of things listed as human rights are essential to such a community [1977, p. 186]

Since this moral community, where promising and related moral speech are undertaken, exists, the significant conditions for moral speech are required. "The function of the adjective 'human' is then to direct our attention to these *de facto* qualities which form part of the significance conditions of the appeal to human rights and indirectly of all moral discourse" (Melden, 1977, p. 186).

The noncognitivism in Melden's view involves the argument's reliance on linguistic considerations, on the implications drawn from what is being said in human communities—instead of the facts of human nature, regardless of the discourse accepted in various communities. Yet Melden did not maintain dogmatic loyalty to the linguistic mode of philosophizing, as we see from his defense of the universalizability of human rights (given official expression in the United Nations Universal Declaration of Human Rights): "human beings, notwithstanding vast differences of all sorts, are sufficiently alike to permit the establishment of relations of trust even between those of radically different cultures" (pp. 186–88). And Melden, unlike Macdonald, did not seem to insist on giving normative utterances an emotive interpretation. For him, moral principles seem to be on the order of general rules by which certain conventions can be performed.

BLACKSTONE'S DESIRED IDEALS

Another noncognitivist view was offered by William T. Blackstone. His initial discussions of human rights in "Equality and Human Rights," fit within this category neatly enough, although later his metaethical position no longer appeared so clear-cut.

Blackstone held that "human rights talk is generally metaethically neutral [and] must be evaluated on normative grounds" (1968, p. 627). He rejected the view that "to say a person has a human right is not to assert a proposition" and believed that there can be "rational grounds for the adoption of norms" (1968, p. 632). Nevertheless, since norms, and specifically human rights, rest in the last analysis on a "decision . . . based . . . on some *desired ideal,* some concept of a desirable human existence or society [that is] arbitrary in the sense of being ultimate" (1968, p. 638), Blackstone's position was noncognitivist:

> not only must we *decide* which rights (like the right to education, working opportunities, medical care, the franchise, and a minimum income) are to be included under the rubric of human rights. But in any given circumstance, we must also decide on a set of criteria requisite for the fulfillment of any particular right so included. In this sense both the concept of human rights and any particular human rights are open concepts, continually subject to challenge and debate. These decisions, it seems to me, must be based not only on the *factual knowledge* of the conditions (economic, educational, and so on) of life at a given time and place but also upon some *desired ideal . . .* which . . . provides rational grounds for the adoption of norms for behavior (which might include human rights) conceived as instruments in effecting that desired ideal [Blackstone, 1968, p. 638].

Before his untimely death in the fall of 1977, Blackstone produced numerous analyses on human rights, legal rights, the controversy over the rights of animals, etc. Generally, just as Melden and Gregory Vlastos (whom I'll discuss later), Blackstone defended human rights reflecting both the ideals of liberty and well-being. Since rights are instruments to achieving desired ideals, whatever a social and political philosopher identifies as the desired ideal will dictate for such a philosopher the content of human rights. It would appear that Blackstone and many other American political philosophers accepted as their starting point what seemed to be the desired ideal within the culture in which they did their work, and then proceeded to identify the general principles or conditions that would make the attainment of that ideal possible.

SOVIET HUMAN RIGHTS THEORY

Vladimir Kudryavtsev's "The Truth about Human Rights" appeared in 1974 and was translated into English in 1976.[4] The following somewhat lengthy quotation indicates the relevance of his position to the present discussion.

> In criticizing the bourgeois view of democracy and human freedoms and rights, it should be borne in mind that the anti-communist position on these questions is often based on an idealistic understanding of rights. It is claimed that human rights are allegedly inbuilt into "human nature." The social character of rights and duties is denied. The bourgeois ideologues would make it appear as if human rights have nothing to do with the social and political nature of the given social system and state, and that the citizens' duties are something alien to the individual and imposed

upon him by society. This is the source, on the one hand, of anarchistic discourses on "universal human rights," and, on the other, of exhortations to refuse to perform important civic duties, to refuse to observe the laws of the country.

As can be seen from the foregoing, human rights are a social and class concept. There are no human rights in the abstract, in isolation from society. A right is an opportunity guaranteed by the state to enjoy the social benefits and values existing in the given society. For this reason the one and the same right (for instance, the right to education) has an entirely different content in different historical and social circumstances [Kudryavtsev, 1976, p. 199].

In view of the Marxist stress on the historical changes of human societies, and in view of the reasonable assumption that Kudryavtsev is arguing from within that framework, the above is a good illustration of the more concrete application of Blackstone's view that the character of human rights is tied to the desired ideal of a society.

VLASTOS'S PRIMA FACIE RIGHTS

The balancing of various human rights as "instruments in effecting [some] desired ideal" became a prominent task confronted by human rights theorists with views similar to Blackstone's. As a means for achieving this balance, *prima facie* rights theories have been proposed. Since taking freedom and welfare rights, for example, as absolute would lead to problems, inasmuch as sometimes those rights conflict—the welfare provider's freedom with the welfare recipient's welfare—some nonabsolute characterization of rights appeared to be warranted. Among the several prima facie rights theories, Gregory Vlastos's seems to have been most thorough.

In his "Justice and Equality," Vlastos agreed with those who subscribed to "the talk of prima facie duties and of rights as moral claims upon our attention and action that may, however, be forfeited" (Vlastos, 1970, p. 83). He developed this position into a prominent contender among human rights theories. For Vlastos, human rights are prima facie in "that the claims of any of them may be over-ruled in special circumstances" (Vlastos, 1970, p. 82). He accepted that human rights have "a fundamental place . . . in our scheme of justice" but rejected that they are absolute (as maintained by some natural rights theorists) because there are cases which call for our violating them (Vlastos, 1970, p. 84). There are circumstances, Vlastos argued, when "the claims of right R are 'over-ruled' by those of right S," namely, when "the obligation to comply with demands associated with S is a stronger one (or 'takes precedence over,' 'outweighs') than the obligation to comply with demands associated with R" (Vlastos, 1970, p. 82). Since Vlastos thought one right may overrule another right—indeed, any right may at some time overrule any other right—his is a bone fide prima facie rights theory.

Vlastos's characterization of human rights as prima facie allowed him to propose a system of such rights in which "freedom rights" (e.g., to speak or publish, to participate in political activities) are placed in balance with "welfare rights" (e.g., to obtain an education, to receive health care), with cases of apparent conflict worked out individually, by weighing the strength of the moral obligations and rights (Vlastos, 1970, p. 94). John Rawls was later to advance a view with similar, concrete, political policy conclusions, but without making much use of rights theory. Addressing an imagined total stranger who holds a meritocratic moral position, Vlastos says:

> no matter how *A* and *B* might differ in taste and style of life, they would both crave relief from acute physical pain. In that case we would put the same value on giving this to either of them, regardless of the fact that *A* might be a talented, brilliantly successful person, *B* "a mere nobody". . . . In just this sense we hold that (1) *one man's well-being is as valuable as any other's.* And there is a parallel difference in

our feeling for freedom. . . . We feel that choosing for oneself what one will do, believe, approve, say, see, read, worship, has its own intrinsic value, the same for all persons, and quite independently of the value of the things they happen to choose. . . . For us (2) *one man's freedom is as valuable as any other's* [Vlastos, 1970, pp. 93–94].

Because the right to freedom and the right to well-being can often conflict — as when a doctor's right to take a vacation conflicts with a patient's right to care — as absolute rights they could not coexist. Prima facie rights, on the other hand, do not pose the problem that if they conflict we must conclude that one of them does not exist. It is understood about prima facie rights that respecting them is conditional upon there being no more severe moral considerations which may require violating them. In the case of prima facie, as opposed to absolute rights, this would not involve a violation at all, merely an implementation of the result of having weighed the rights and found one or some as having prior significance in some situation.

The doctrine of prima facie rights has been criticized often. For now it is important to see that any rights theorist who advances the view that there are inherently conflicting, yet basic, human rights will have to rely on something like the prima facie rights position.

FEINBERG — FROM HUMAN TO ANIMAL RIGHTS

Feinberg's position is distinctive thus far in that, as in his 1974 paper, he defends rights as claims.

To have a right is to have a claim *to* something and *against* someone the recognition of which is called for by legal (or other institutional) rules, or in the case of moral rights, by the principles of an enlightened conscience [Feinberg, 1974, p. 190].

The view is noncognitivist in that it emerges from a consideration of linguistic usage — to a large extent, the actual language of positive or legal rights. In this respect, Feinberg's linguistic methodology departs from Melden's, for example, by focusing on an area of specialized human discourse, not on ordinary language. Feinberg is also distinctive among rights theorists in holding that rights as claims emerge in the context of having interests, a view related to his reliance upon analysis of legal discourse.

Yet the most interesting feature of Feinberg's position is that it makes possible the derivation of rights of animals. Since he has offered an analysis of human or basic rights based on analysis of legal discourse, it is not very surprising that Feinberg finds it possible to do the same for animals. "Statutes making cruelty to animals a crime are now very common, and those, of course, impose legal duties on people not to mistreat animals" (Feinberg, 1974, p. 191). He asks, "Is it natural to speak of the animal's right to his inheritance in cases [where a proxy makes a claim on behalf of an animal]? If a trustee embezzles money from the animal's account, and a proxy speaking in the dumb brute's behalf presses the animal's claim, can he not be described as asserting the animal's rights?" Feinberg further maintains that we can conclude that "the animal itself claims its rights through the vicarious actions of a human proxy speaking in its name and in its behalf" (Feinberg, 1974, p. 193).

Others have derived animal rights based on traditional utilitarianism. Thus, Peter Singer relies on Bentham's argument that the ascription of rights is based on the recognition of some entity as capable of experiencing suffering. In contrast to Singer's utilitarian view, Robert Nozick suggests that his natural rights-based "moral side constraints" may be applicable to animals. But Nozick himself does not develop this idea and asks more questions than he answers about the topic.[5]

Feinberg's method of extending the language of legal rights to animals illustrates, I think, one possible consequence of employing linguistic analysis in coming to grips with certain normative issues. It will be instructive now to bring to a conclusion the survey of noncognitivist contributions to the consideration of human rights by presenting Martin P. Golding's discussion in "Towards a Theory of Human Rights." This paper may be viewed as a transitional development because its language suggests a bridging of the gap between noncognitivist and cognitivist rights theories.

GOLDING'S CONCERN WITH CRITERIA

Golding is less concerned with the language of norms than with what there is about human existence as such that can give rise to considerations of human rights. He observes of human beings and their mode of existence (1968, pp. 522–28) the following characteristics:
1. A capacity to engage in voluntary activity.
2. Desires and interests.
3. A capacity consciously to engage in purposive activity.
4. A capacity to communicate demands.
5. A capacity for conscious response to demands.
6. The possibility of clash between demands.
7. Community.

Golding expands on these characteristics and then answers the question of "what is involved in conceding something that someone claims as his human right."

> For someone to ask me to concede something to him as a human right is implicitly to ask whether I admit the notion of a human community at large, which transcends the various special communities of which I am a member; whether I admit him as a member of this larger community; and whether I admit a conception of a good life for this community. . . . The question, then, of whether human rights exist, or, better, whether any individual has a right as a human being, now shifts to (i) the defensibility of the notion of the human community and to (ii) the defensibility of any fairly concrete conception of the good life for mankind [Golding, 1968, pp. 548–49].

Golding's challenge is one that suggests the course of theoretical development charted by traditional natural rights theorists. While the noncognitivist approach had been prominent, only a few individuals — usually somewhat removed from academic philosophy (e.g., Jacques Maritain, Ayn Rand) — had tried to travel that course. The ideal of knowing what is right and just and good, by means that are available to any serious and capable inquirer, seems to have held out a promise for those thinkers that was, for the noncognitivists, a hopeless if not irresponsible expectation.

Golding's call for an approach to human rights theory that really asked for philosophers interested in human rights to try and see whether the naturalist or cognitivist program might not be carried out after all, was issued just when several individuals were beginning to take up this very challenge.

Back to Natural Human Rights

It is unlikely that the various branches of philosophy move along independent lines of inquiry. Developments in one branch have an impact on what can and will be contemplated in another. However objective and self-critical professional philosophers might wish to be, some ideas must be accepted as relatively stable because of time and related constraints. Within these ideas, work can ensue; and if one presupposes different ideas, one faces difficulties vis-à-vis the community of professional philosophers. Until appropriate developments have occurred in other areas, it is necessary to explicate and defend at length one's presuppositions.

The concept of nature in "the nature of X" did not fare well in the period of the prominence of noncognitivism. Definitions had been thought of, under nominalist influences, as stipulative, extremely volatile, or even arbitrary. And a nominalist conception of human nature does not easily yield universal political principles.

In the last few decades important developments have occurred; talk of the nature of man, human nature, or the essence of being a human being or person became once again philosophically palatable, so that rights theories based on such concepts became more visible. In some cases, the changed approaches emanated outside academic philosophy. One such case with subsequent influence on academic philosophical scholarship, including natural rights theory, is the philosophical work of the novelist and essayist, Ayn Rand.

RAND'S OBJECTIVISM

Rand, whose essays contain a mixture of analysis, argument, and polemic, placed herself in diametrical opposition to what she considered the metaethically subjectivist, ethically altruist, and politically collectivist trends of our time.[6] Even those who do not agree with Rand's work may admit that she perceived the issues in question accurately, if somewhat dramatically. It is not entirely unexpected, moreover, that one who rejects subjectivism, altruism, and collectivism would embark upon the development of a natural rights theory within the province of political philosophy.

Rand wrote about human rights first in her novels but later presented her position in her paper "Man's Rights." Several professional philosophers have discussed her views (e.g., Nozick, George Mavrodes, John Hospers, and Fred Miller), and several have built on her position (e.g., Eric Mack and I).

Rand developed an entire philosophical system, Objectivism, of which her normative ethics and politics are integral parts. She defends a contextualist theory of knowledge in which essences are said to be both epistemological and capable of being proven objectively sound.[7] The latter is especially important for her natural rights theory. Holding that "Every political system is based on some code of ethics," Rand says

> A 'right' is a moral principle defining and sanctioning a man's freedom of action in a social context. There is only *one* fundamental right (all others are its consequences or corollaries): a man's right to his own life. Life is a process of self-sustaining and self-generated action; the right to life means the right to engage in self-sustaining and self-generated action — which means, the freedom to take all the actions required by the nature of a rational being for the support, the furtherance, the fulfillment and the enjoyment of his own life. (Such is the meaning of the right to life, liberty, and the pursuit of happiness.) [Rand, 1967, p. 322]

If it were not true that a rational being *should* take the actions required for the support, etc., of his own life, Rand's support for the existence of human rights would not exist. This is because

> "Rights" are a moral concept — the concept that provides a logical transition from the principles guiding an individual's actions to the principles guiding his relationship with others. . . . *Individual rights are the means of subordinating society to moral law* [Rand, 1967, p. 320].

A right, for Rand, "pertains only to action — specifically, to freedom of action. It means freedom from physical compulsion, coercion or interference by other men" (1967, p. 322). In this respect Rand's view differs from the substantive normative politics of many who are concerned with human rights. For her, no one has any general right to have something done to him or provided for him. Thus the right to property, for example, "is not the right *to an object,* but to the action and the consequences of producing or earning that object" (ibid.).

A summary statement of Rand's view appears in her novel *Atlas Shrugged*, and it shows the line of argument she holds leads to her view on rights:

> *Rights* are conditions of existence required by man's nature for his proper survival. If man is to live on earth, it is *right* for him to use his mind, it is *right* to act on his own free judgment, it is *right* to work for his values and to keep the product of his work. If life on earth is his purpose, he has a right to live as a rational being [Rand, 1957, p. 322].

We find here a central element of Rand's value theory, in general, and a clue to how she tried to solve (or dispose of) the "is/ought" problem, something every cognitivist needs to confront. She rejected ancient natural teleology, according to which human life has a purpose set by nature or God, which each person is morally obligated to fulfill.[8] Rand's ethics, as expounded in her "Causality versus Duty," spelled out a hypothetical moral imperative, so that only if one chooses a life qua human being will the required moral principles be binding. Since, however, the basic alternative to choosing human life for any human being is not choosing such a life, and since there is only a human life that a human being can choose other than death (consistently), the ethics and politics Rand developed retain their categorical status as standards for guiding human conduct.

As to the substantive politics Rand claimed to have derived from her ethics and basic principles of natural rights, this would amount, by her own account, to a laissez-faire constitutional government similar to the Lockean system.

MACK'S EGOISM AND RIGHTS

Among philosophers close to Rand's view, Eric Mack and I have concentrated on human rights theory.[9] Mack, in "Egoism and Rights," elaborated upon and developed the rights we found defended by Rand, and he not only showed their more detailed application to social, economic, and political issues, but focused specifically on the hard cases. (He argued his case for ethical egoism in "How to Derive Ethical Egoism," prior to the attempt to work out the case for natural rights.) His rights theory, moreover, stresses both the deontological and teleological aspects of normative structures, something other egoists have not worked out clearly.

Mack noted that his primary concern was "to refute the claim that egoism on the one hand, and rights and obligations on the other, are incompatible" (Mack, 1973, p. 5), a claim made by James Rachels, among others, in his "Two Arguments Against Egoism." Mack explained that, since

> the rights that I shall discuss are . . . possessed by a person in virtue of the fact that each person ought to act in his own self-interest and the obligation which this fact places upon other persons, and these rights are not possessed in virtue of any special relationship in which the right-holder stands to other persons, it is appropriate to refer to those rights as "natural rights" [Mack, 1973, p.5].

Although Mack derived natural rights from egoism, he was not urging that a simple personal ethical egoism will yield the results. He believed that others—including Nathaniel Branden, who elaborated Rand's position—had failed to develop the case for human rights carefully enough to differentiate between personal and impersonal ethical egoism, as well as between obligations derived from self-interest alone and those derived from a consideration of the nature of moral agency.

At this point, with our concern being to introduce some notion of rights and obligations based upon impersonal egoism, there is a great temptation to argue in a way that employs an intrinsic conception of moral values. That is, one is inclined to find some subtle way of saying, "since each person's acting in his own interest has moral value, each person should act in such a way that each other person may act in his own interest. No party should prevent another party from acting in that other party's interest—as long as such actions themselves do not prevent some third party from acting in his respective interest." But it is obvious that from Smith's commitment to impersonal ethical egoism nothing follows about the value to Smith of Jones' acting self-interestedly [Mack, 1973, p. 17].

In short, Mack rejected the idea that there need be utility for A in the self-interested action of B, thus securing some ground for A's abstaining from violating the freedom of B to take this action. Mack's position emerged as follows in the end:

There is something about persons in virtue of which some actions with respect to them are unjustified. . . . This something is that, (a) given ethical egoism, whenever one person (say Smith) acts with respect to another (say Jones), the first party acts in the face of the fact that the second ought to act in his own interest, and (b) given that this is a fact (a moral fact, if one likes) the first party's actions may literally constitute acting as if it is not the case that the second ought to act in his own interest, and (c) the justification of such action requires a denial of impersonal ethical egoism [Mack, 1973, p. 31].

Mack's concern with the compatibility of egoism and natural rights is but one of the phases of the ongoing discussion about the relationship between individualism and the moral foundation of the liberal or libertarian political order. While attempting to avoid giving his theory of rights a quasi-utilitarian defense, Mack has also made room in this theory for the teleological features of human action, thus combining elements of normative theories generally held to be antagonistic.

As to the substantive aspects of Mack's position, he is one among several political theorists today who is closer to anarchism than others among natural rights theorists, as shown by his recent criticism of Nozick.[10]

NOZICK'S TRANSCENDENTAL RIGHTS THEORY

In his *Anarchy, State, and Utopia* Nozick did not set out to prove that human beings have certain Lockean rights. He proceeded, instead, by positing these rights and examining whether the kind of social and political system that flows from such rights (if implemented) accords with our moral intuitions better than would alternative systems (e.g., Marx's, Rawls's). Despite Nozick's apparent rejection of the requirement to deal with the foundational problems, there is a kind of metaethical thesis underlying this approach. It may be that Nozick does not find it satisfactory—he said there is a "gap" in his theory (Nozick, 1974, p. 9). Nevertheless, it is one method by which some might think it is possible to establish that certain moral or political principles are indeed universally binding on us.

By using the "argument from best explanation" approach, Nozick seemed to rely on a kind of transcendental deduction. He could be answering the question, what makes our moral and political intuitions meaningful and possible? If these intuitions have cognitive significance—if we treat them as evidence for or witness to moral truths—and if they are best accounted for and integrated by reference to certain Lockean natural rights, then we may, the argument could run, agree that these Lockean natural rights exist. This feature of Nozick's theory has not received much attention. Some have noted, however, that since we have conflicting intuitions, some of which are unaccounted for by Nozick's Lockean rights assumption, something is missing from Nozick's position. My concern here is merely to mention Nozick's metaethical approach, since it is not worked out in his early works on ethics and politics. I wish to focus more on the substance of his rights theory.

In *Anarchy, State, and Utopia*, Nozick began with a reply to the challenge of natural rights anarchists—e.g., Murray N. Rothbard—who claim that no government or state can be established without the violation of the nature rights of some individuals. Nozick saw that it is indeed problematic when governments claim a monopoly on the protection and preservation of rights: they risk violation of the rights of those who might also engage in such activities by subjecting all to their exclusive administration of justice and their idea of due process.

Nozick maintained, however, that the fear of arbitrariness (from haphazard responses to rights violations) justifies establishing a monopolistic authority. He argued that people should subject those in their vicinity (even when they are unwilling) to a single authority, because otherwise constant fear would reign in the area. These and related considerations led Nozick to advocate a minimal state. But he felt he had overcome the anarchist obstacles and showed that, in the last analysis, his minimal state would involve less of a risk of rights violation than would leaving the protection and preservation of rights in the hands of people at large.

The central point for our purposes is that Nozick thought the result of his explorations, namely, the minimal state, accorded with our intuitions about personhood and what we may ask of people to do for themselves and for others. In view of this, the basic principles that led to such a system would have to be admitted as correct or suitable. This is the manner in which Nozick defended the substance of Locke's natural rights theory. While in his view liberty is the greatest political value, to be protected and preserved by constant attention to the natural rights of individuals, Nozick agrees with Rand, Mack and others, but unlike many of them he does not offer a direct argument for natural rights.

GEWIRTH'S DEDUCTIVISM

A distinctive approach to human rights is taken by Alan Gewirth. In *Reason and Morality* (1978b), which brings together the various strands of his argument (elaborated upon in various journals during the last decades), Gewirth placed scare quotes around "natural" when he mentioned H.L.A. Hart's views (p. 130). Yet immediately thereafter he said, "The argument in this section supports the view that rights are necessarily rather than contingently connected with being human" (ibid.), a claim not easily distinguished from those usually subscribed to by natural rights theorists. The distinctive character of this position is brought out more, however, in the following discussion, where Gewirth engaged in what is usually called conceptual analysis:

> the basis of rights must be sought in the conviction necessarily held by every human agent that he has rights to the necessary conditions of action by virtue of his having purposes and pursuing goods [Gewirth, 1978b, p. 103].

Gewirth argued for bridging the "is/ought" gap by deriving from "the beliefs each human agent necessarily has about his own rights of action" the fact that each agent "has inherent rights" (ibid.). In this way he established "the Principle of Generic Consistency [which] satisfies the conditions for being the supreme principle of morality" (Gewirth, 1978b, p. 199).

> Every agent, by the fact of engaging in action, is logically committed to the acceptance of certain evaluative and deontic judgments and ultimately of a moral principle which requires that he respect in his recipients the same generic features of action, freedom and well being, that as rational he necessarily claims as rights for himself. By virtue of this logical necessity, the PGC is rationally justified as a categorically obligatory moral principle [Gewirth, 1978b, p. 198].

In *Reason and Morality* Gewirth took care to dispose of certain doubts and difficulties related to the form and content of his theory. He treated numerous philosophical issues, including a central problem for his conception of action (as involving voluntariness), namely, the problem of determinism. In these areas he relied on Kantian and neo-Kantian (self-referential) reductio arguments. His effort to dispel worries concerning the relationship between the formal and the material (or substantive) aspects of his moral and political theory is very probably original and philosophically challenging. He explained that

> The PGC . . . combines the axiological substantive content of moral duties with a formal consideration of consistency or mutuality. It is not only that the agent must act in accord with his recipient's rights to freedom and well-being; what gives this its justificatory basis is that the agent also, and necessarily, acts in accord with his own rights to freedom and well-being [Gewirth, 1978b, p. 203].

As to the substance of his moral theory, Gewirth is far from an egoist of any sort. Nor can we classify Gewirth's ethical position as distinct from his political stance; the two appear to be indistinguishable. It is not that the latter is derived from the former, but that the two are conjoined in Gewirth's theory from start of finish. His rights theory begins with the "necessary conditions of actions . . . within the whole sphere of practice, over all other practical goods, since, by definition, without these conditions no other such goods can be attained by action" (Gewirth, 1978b, p. 205). This accounts, also, for Gewirth's view that we not only have freedom rights but welfare rights as well, something not usually defended by those in the Lockean tradition. (But see Melden, who in *Rights and Persons* (1977, p. 248) claims to follow Locke and argues that times have changed and we need to adjust our idea of human rights accordingly.)

Gewirth's basic rights to freedom and well-being are derived from the two necessary conditions for purposive action, namely, choice and capability. He argued that "action, in the strict sense that is relevant to moral and other practical precepts, has two interrelated generic features: voluntariness or freedom and purposiveness or intentionality." And he held that "the basic capabilities of action, whereby the agent has basic goods, are the most necessary of all, since without these he would be able to act either not at all or only in certain very restricted ways." Therefore, Gewirth concluded, each person has rights both to freedom and to well-being (Gewirth, pp. 27, 63).

Although Gewirth is a cognitivist and explicitly argued for the derivability of "ought" judgments from "is" judgments, he differs from most other cognitivist human rights theorists in his substantive politics. Here his views are closer to Vlastos's, Blackstone's, Melden's, and others than to those of Nozick. And he is not alone among cognitivists of whom this can be said.

DWORKIN'S DUE PROCESS RIGHTS

At first, Ronald Dworkin's position appears to fit well within a Lockean natural rights tradition.

> Individual rights are political trumps held by individuals. Individuals have rights when, for some reason, a collective goal is not a sufficient justification for denying them what they wish, as individuals, to have or to do, or not sufficient justification for imposing some loss or injury upon them [Dworkin, 1977, p. xi].

But whereas Lockean rights are principles governing the relationship among individuals, Dworkin's rights theory pertains to the principles governing the relationship between individuals and their government.

Dworkin said that his theory "will be embedded in a more general political and moral philosophy which may in turn depend upon philosophical theories about human nature or the objectivity of morality" (Dworkin, 1977, p. vii), but this broader framework was not developed by him. In *Taking Rights Seriously* he discussed mainly the implications of his rights theory and his general antipositivist stance for purposes of understanding the judicial process, of conceptualizing the function of the judge in the legal process, and of criticizing legal theorists with different views. In general, Dworkin was concerned with identifying the limits of governmental authority by reference to a view of human rights.

In line with this stress on rights as principles of (substantive) due process, Dworkin denied that human beings have a general right to liberty.

> I have in mind the traditional definition of liberty as the absence of constraints placed by a government upon what a man might do if he wants to. . . . This conception of liberty as license is neutral amongst the various activities a man might pursue, the various roads he might wish to walk. It diminishes a man's liberty when we prevent him from talking or making love as he wishes, but it also diminishes his liberty when we prevent him from murdering or defaming others [Dworkin, 1977, p. 267].

Dworkin agreed that "If someone has a right to something, then it is wrong for the government to deny it to him even though it would be in the general interest to do so." He believes this is the sense of "a right" which is "principally used in political and legal writing and argument in recent years" (Dworkin, 1977, p. 269). So he concluded:

> I do not think that the right to liberty would come to very much, or have much power in political argument, if it relied on any sense of the right any weaker than that. If we settle on this concept of a right, however, then it seems plain that there exists no general right to liberty as such. I have no political right to drive up Lexington Avenue [a one-way street]. . . . The vast bulk of the laws which diminish my liberty are justified on utilitarian grounds, as being in the general interest or for the general welfare; if, as Bentham supposes, each of these laws diminishes my liberty, they nevertheless do not take away from me anything that I have a right to have [Dworkin, 1977, p. 269].

What does Dworkin believe we have a right to as such? It is "the right to treatment as an equal . . . the right to equal concern and respect in the political decision about how . . . goods and opportunities are to be distributed" (Dworkin, 1977, p. 273).

Dworkin believes his theory and the principle he advocates have objective foundation, but in *Taking Rights Seriously* we find that he relied mainly on conventional ideas to support his analysis. Thus he appealed to common views about the proper powers of the state. Dworkin seems to accept the distributionist functions of the state and to view individual rights as those principles that should preserve the system and govern the process of distribution. He illustrated the implications of his theory by numerous cases familiar to most people who have an awareness of contemporary political life. He argued that from his view it follows that discrimination against Marco DeFunis by the University of Washington School of Law, on grounds that this will lead to a socially desirable goal (e.g., upgrading the quality of life for blacks in the United States), was justified, as are busing programs and other exercises of the government's police powers opposed by many on grounds that these limit individual liberty. Since no right to liberty exists, this opposition, Dworkin holds, is unjustified.

SHUE'S SUBSISTENCE RIGHTS

In his *Basic Rights,* Henry Shue argues for a theory of rights that includes both so-called *security* and *subsistence* rights as basic rights all persons possess.

> The substance of a basic right is something the deprivation of which is one standard threat to rights generally. The fulfillment of a basic right is a successful defense against a standard threat to rights generally. This is precisely why basic rights are basic. That to which they are rights is needed for the fulfillment of all other rights. If the substance of a basic right is not socially guaranteed, attempts actually to en-

joy the substance of other rights remain open to a standard threat like the deprivation of security or subsistence [Shue, 1980, p. 34].

In some respects Shue's position is not different, in substance, from Vlastos's,
Gewirth's, and others who have wanted to identify as human rights both rights to
liberty and rights to welfare or happiness. The standard welfare statist characterization of rights is clearly evident in Shue's work, as in James W. Nickel's, who also
argues for the right to employment as a basic right. What is noteworthy in Shue's
presentation of his case is that he attempts to overcome a standard objection to the inclusion of subsistence rights as basic human rights, namely, the point that whereas
security rights are negative, subsistence rights are positive. As Shue frames the objection,

> Since subsistence rights are positive and require other people to do more than
> negative rights require—perhaps more than people can actually do—negative
> rights, such as those to security, should be fully guaranteed first [Shue, 1980,
> p. 37].

Shue's reply is that "neither rights to physical security nor rights to subsistence fit
neatly into their assigned sides of the simplistic positive/negative dichotomy. . . . In an
organized society . . . no one would have much interest in the bare rights to physical
security," that is, the only rights that require no positive effort for their respect by
others. Instead, what one is really interested in are what "might be called rights-to-be-
protected-against-assault-upon-physical-security," that is, rights against government
to be provided with protection against assault, something the fulfillment of which
clearly requires positive performance. Shue puts the point clearly when he says that
"In any imperfect society enjoyment of a right will depend to some extent upon protection against those who do not choose not to violate it" (p. 39). Accordingly, the
positive/negative dichotomy is practically irrelevant, and the argument that aims to
show the priority of negative rights falls to pieces. Shue goes on to spell out the vast
redistributionist consequences of this argument, chronicling the undesirable and tragic
results of neglecting subsistence rights in the conduct, for example, of American
foreign policy. While there is little that is novel from the point of view of method of
argumentation of Shue's work (whose approach is somewhat like that of Rawls and
clearly distinguishable from the natural rights theorists I have been dealing with in the
last section of my discussion), the substance of the rights doctrine Shue develops is important and worth mentioning in this survey.

Criticism—Particular and General

This chapter has offered a fairly complete survey of recent philosophical discussions
of human rights and has identified some general similarities and differences that have
surfaced within the various theories discussed. My task here will be aided if, instead of
trying desperately to include all theorists, reference is made in the last section to some
difficulties facing those whose views have been considered.

The central problem with Macdonald's view appears to be that there is no way it can
be made rationally convincing—something that the very idea of human or natural
rights would appear to require. The point is not that crooks and moral imbeciles will
stubbornly reject such views as that freedom is better than slavery. It is rather that by
Macdonald's own admission one's position on human rights will amount to no more
than one's opinion on opera or on the quality of Eliot's poetry. It is not a great problem in these areas that no certainties exist. Here, differences of opinion rarely entail
actions that infringe on others' choices concerning their lives and conduct. The issue
with human rights, however, is intimately wedded to the task of settling disputes in
ways that reasonable human beings will find persuasive. Generally, this problem
besets all noncognitivist approaches to identifying political principles.

Melden's reliance on the language of morals appears to be more capable of yielding a universalizable principle. Yet vis-à-vis his views the following criticism could be telling: the language of morality could well change as moral convictions and practices change. It may be difficult for most of us to conceive of a moral position in which voluntariness is denied, since choice and virtue have been connected in much of Western moral philosophy, at least since Aristotle. But there have always been those who advocated a morality that is supposed to be related to a "higher freedom" than the freedom of the individual to choose his or her own conduct. A morality of subjugation and self-abasement can yield the conclusion that human rights are tools of selfishness and must be renounced in favor of reliance on leadership, collective choice, etc. It is doubtful that a language completely infused with these ideas would yield anything like the human rights that Melden believes follow from a consideration of the moral community and the moral discourse of that community.

It is even more difficult to imagine that Blackstone's instrumentalist approach can yield universal human rights. The desired ideals of societies differ. If these ideals are the justicatory court of last resort, the resulting human rights will vary greatly from community to community. Blackstone's theory permits virtually any country today to claim that its polity accords with human rights. In most communities there exists no meaningful procedure for identifying the desired ideal, and this itself puts difficulties before Blackstone's view. We may note, in this connection, the example provided in Kudryavtsev's discussion of "human" rights, which can hardly help us in our need for universalizable standards of human social life. The historicism of Marxism, of course, from which this view derives, is probably responsible for the relativism we find in Kudryavtsev's position.

Vlastos's theory is limited in scope, and we should ask only whether Vlastos's idea of prima facie rights avoids the problem of conflict among human rights. If we accept, as Vlastos does, that these rights are the fundamental principles of justice, and if they must be weighed against each other, we do not solve the problem of finding a standard for weighing the mutually exclusive prima facie rights. We are left with arbitrariness.

Feinberg's linguistic approach faces problems similar to those Melden's approach faces, especially because Feinberg unhesitatingly relies on the language and conventions of positive law. Thus while *he* wished to exclude plants from the rights-bearing entities, certain legal commentators have recently argued for legal standing for trees and even mountains.[11] Generally, ordinary and even specialized language analysis can yield intolerable looseness in normative areas, so that, e.g., if "human" and "rights" cannot be shown to mean something definite, human rights will be hopelessly variable and flexible, useless as standards for social and legal justice. The current proliferation of human rights in the realm of realpolitik may already show this result of a certain approach to human rights within professional philosophy.

Rand's position is more extensive and tries to be more rigorous than the noncognitivist views, and thus faces more problems. Essentialism, for one, has to be treated here more extensively. Can Rand ultimately distinguish between human life as self-sustaining and self-generated versus the similar phenomena in relation to computerlike beings? The egoism on which Rand's rights theory rests gives great emphasis to the value of individual lives; whereas there are those who maintain that persons are in fact parts of a greater organism, e.g., humanity, and the egoistic stress on the right to liberty and property would not be warranted if this were so.[12]

Mack's position must also face up to problems that confront Rand. Mack has not dealt with some issues Rand has taken time to handle; for example, whether talk of the *nature* of something is really defensible against nominalist (e.g., Quinean) criticisms. It is also questionable whether Mack's handling of lifeboat cases is adequate since by his view the individuals involved in such circumstances ought to try to kill one another, a position very difficult to reconcile with ordinary moral convictions.

Nozick's transcendental argument establishes only that, from the premise that people value liberty, it follows that the assumption of their having Lockean rights is reasonable. But people value the absence of liberty as well, even if only for others and perhaps only under extreme conditions. But then assumptions in conflict with Lockean rights may also be reasonable, in which case the question arises whether some other principles not yielding this conflict might not have to be found.

Gewirth's merging of morality and politics encounters serious problems for his rights theory. The element of choice in human life depends for its culpable suppression upon others, so it makes sense to defend the right to freedom. But one would have to worry about capability or capacity even (especially) if one were all alone. But this would imply that one has a right to capability apart from human community life (i.e., others who should respect it), which is a curious result. Gewirth may be correct to hold that children have rights against parents concerning enablement, since parents have produced the children and have thus assumed responsibilities, but this may not be true of the society at large. So whereas choice and social life do present us with political problems, the fact that we need capabilities in order to carry out our purposes presents us with moral problems, that is, considerations of what ought to be done and by whom apart from how a general human community would have to be organized.

Dworkin's acceptance of the utilitarian functions of the state or government needs to be given support against the objection that such an extensively empowered state is acting without authority derived from either consent or sound moral principles. Dworkin said in *Taking Rights Seriously* that he is working within a liberal framework, yet he fails to answer this kind of challenge anywhere and relies on accepted practice in his support of the wide-scale coercive powers of contemporary states.

Moreover, Dworkin's concern with administrative justice omits consideration of the purposes of such administration. Can one identify principles of just administration without knowing its purpose?

Some objections can be raised against Henry Shue's defense of the equal status of security and subsistence rights. For one, the tradition against which Shue argues, in which negative rights are given priority if not exclusive attention, does not speak about security rights. For that tradition, starting from Locke, human beings by nature have a right to liberty, i.e., to decide on and carry out their actions without other persons' interference. But security is a much broader concept than liberty, for it can be threatened by nonhuman agents. One's physical security is vulnerable not only to those who would violate one's rights not to be murdered or assaulted or stolen from, but also by hurricanes, disease, and other forces of nature.

More important, Shue may be making a serious mistake in thinking that we have a natural right to have our security protected. If we did, why should we pay for government protection? The respect of a right by another need not be compensated, yet government's protection of our rights must be. In the Lockean tradition, for example, governments are established to provide protection against rights violators, and the justification for establishing government includes the fact that human beings have the right to liberty. In Shue's scheme, as in Dworkin's and Nickel's, the legitimacy of government is assumed without argument, and indeed we are said to have a right to governmental activities. Yet, unless governmental activities can be justified, the anarchist's objections stand against this institution. Notwithstanding Shue's efforts to repel the objection that he has confused the right to liberty with some alleged right to be protected from those who would violate this right, that objection is on solid grounds.

Some more general questions about the idea of human rights should be added to these few considerations concerning the specific human rights theories. First there is the Marxist criticism that human rights are premature, since what will be the human species is presently still divided into classes with necessarily conflicting interests.

From a very different source we find human natural rights rejected as unjustifiably egalitarian, too accepting of the initial moral equality of human beings. Here comes to mind the kind of criticism Leo Strauss and his students have been leveling at classical liberals. Following Plato, these critics assert that Locke and the Declaration of Independence of the United States were wrong because the different circumstances of human beings place them in different moral positions from the outset. The egalitarian strain in Locke's argument for natural human rights, involving toleration for any competing idea and conduct, suggests a subtle logical problem: the theory's inability to account for its superiority to other, competing theories of justice.

Others argued, interestingly, that talk of human rights is anti-individualistic because it presupposes that the essence of man is more important than each person's individuality. Shirley Robin Letwin has said that individualism and naturalism are incompatible. The very idea of objectively founded universal moral standards flies in the face of the view that each of us is a unique individual with his or her own chosen destiny in life.

Finally, it seems that cultural relativism still remains one of the most powerful problems vis-à-vis universalistic theories, such as those advancing various ideas about human rights. There really seem to be too many different ideas of what is socially good. Whether this undermines all conceptions of human rights or only those tied to one specific moral theory is unclear. Yet any human rights theory must come to grips with the challenge posed by the enormous cultural differences, with definite impact on social and political structures, found throughout the world.

Undoubtedly, several theorists have answered some or perhaps even all the relevant questions, at least for the time being, so that these criticisms or challenges may be outdated. Most of those whose views are outlined in this essay have tried to attend to the various tasks implicit in the questions raised above.[13] Still, it is worth reminding those concerned with discussions of human rights — and in some sense everyone has a stake in the outcome — of what general and particular difficulties face anyone interested in a reasonably complete and adequate theory on the topic.

Notes

1. By noncognitivism I mean any metaethical position that amounts to the denial of the possibility of proving, demonstrating, or otherwise establishing — in ways available for general human understanding (not by revelation or intuition) and communication (not ineffably) — that something is morally good and right, or evil and wrong; or that human beings should, morally, act in certain ways or refrain from acting in certain ways; or that certain moral responsibilities, obligations or duties are binding on human beings as such; or that some virtues apply to each human being such that one should cultivate them; and so forth. The noncognitivist idea is that nothing along these lines can be made the object of human knowledge. (Some who would admit to the possibility of moral knowledge are nonetheless noncognitivists in virtue of their view that this kind of knowledge is drastically different from the kind we may be expected to achieve in such areas as physics, biology, law, or mechanical engineering.)

2. For a brief historical recapitulation, see Martin P. Golding, "The Concept of Rights: A Historical Sketch." See also Fred D. Miller, Jr., "The State and the Community in Aristotle's *Politics*," *Reason Papers* vol. 1 (1974): 61–69, where we are told that "Aristotle associates [a] theory with the sophist, Lykophrom, whom he quotes as calling the law 'a guarantee (or guarantor) of mutual rights *(dikaion)'* (1280bi0–ii)." For a controversial and very provocative analysis of the development of the concept of natural rights (from the concept of natural *right*), see Leo Strauss, *Natural Right and History*.

3. See my *Human Rights and Human Liberties* for a discussion of the difference between Hobbes's and Locke's ideas of rights. For additional discussions, see Strauss, chapter 5, and several papers in D. D. Raphael.

4. For further discussion of human rights from a Marxist or neo-Marxist perspective, see the entire issue of *Soviet Studies in Philosophy* 16, no. 3 (1977–78).

5. For a development of Nozick's position toward a comprehensive account of animal rights, see Robert W. Hanula and Peter Waverly Hill, "Using Metaright Theory to Ascribe Kantian Rights to Animals Within Nozick's Minimal State," *Arizona Law Review* 19 (1977): 242–83.

6. I take the terms "subjectivist," "altruist," and "collectivist" to be well enough understood so as to require no explanation here. It should be noted, however, that Rand's idea of altruism is closer to August Comte's (in *Politique Positive,* 1851–54) than to Thomas Nagel's (in *The Possibility of Altruism,* 1970).

7. See Ayn Rand, *Introduction to Objectivist Epistemology* (New York, 1967). Rand says that she escapes the troubles of early essentialists because they were either extreme or moderate realists, whereas "objectivism regards [essence] as *epistemological . . .* in the sense that the classification of 'essential characteristic' is a device of man's method of cognition—a means of classifying, condensing and integrating an ever-growing body of knowledge" (p. 50).

8. See Strauss, *Natural Right and History,* who claims that "From the point of view of Aristotle . . . the issue between the mechanical and the teleological conception of the universe is decided by the manner in which the problem of the heavens, the heavenly bodies, and their motion is solved" (p. 8), citing *Physics* 196a25 ff, 199a3–5 in support. But see also Allan Gotthelf, "Aristotle's Conception of Final Causality," *The Review of Metaphysics* 30 (1976): 253, who maintains that "for Aristotle organic development is actually *directive,* without implying (as the 'immaterial agency' interpretation does) that it is direct*ed.*" In general, contemporary value theory, including accounts of human rights, requires the solution of numerous problems, not the least of which is whether a secular conception of the universe makes teleological accounts of human action possible.

9. My own efforts in this area have focused on synthesizing the varied and distinct issues in philosophy that contribute to a sufficiently complete theory of human community life, including human rights theory. I have tried to do what has been spelled out by Samuel Scheffler:

> Given the metaphysical association of the [natural rights] tradition, such philosophers must explain what they mean by assigning rights to people. They must, further, say something about the source of these rights, and they must deal with a variety of epistemic questions [Scheffler, 1976, p. 62].

10. See Mack's "Nozick's Anarchism," in *Anarchism,* edited by J. Roland Pennock and John W. Chapman (New York, 1978), pp. 43–62. Other natural rights anarchists include Murray N. Rothbard and Peter Danielson. See also *The Journal of Libertarian Studies* 1, no. 1 (1977). Mack doubts that governments can justify monopolizing many so-called police powers—e.g., being the exclusive law enforcer, administrator of punishment, etc.

11. Christopher Stone, *Should Trees Have Standing?* (Palo Alto, 1975).

12. Lewis Thomas, *Lives of a Cell* (New York, 1976).

13. Human rights theory is very much a live topic today within both the professional philosophical and the larger (international legal and lay) communities. By the time this book is published, several scheduled publications and conferences will have added to the discussion within philosophy itself. The present chapter may be regarded, therefore, as a taking stock of developments in mid-stream.

Bibliography

Becker, L. C. 1979. "Three Types of Rights." *Georgia Law Review* 13 (Summer): 1197–1220.

Blackstone, W. T. 1968. "Equality and Human Rights." *The Monist* 52: 616–39.

_____ . 1971a. "The Justification of Human Rights." In E. H. Pollack, ed., *Human Rights.* Buffalo, N.Y.

_____ . 1971b. "Human Rights and Human Dignity." *The Philosophical Forum* 3: 3–37.

_____ . 1972. "The Concept of Political Freedom." *Social Theory and Practice* 2: 421–38.

Branden, Nathaniel. 1969. *The Psychology of Self-Esteem.* New York.

Danielson, Peter. 1978. "Taking Anarchism Seriously." *Philosophy of the Social Sciences,* vol. 8. Pp. 137–52.

Dworkin, Ronald. 1977. *Taking Rights Seriously.* Cambridge, Mass.: Harvard University Press.

Feinberg, Joel. 1970. "The Nature and Value of Rights." *Journal of Value Inquiry* 4: 243–57.

_____ . 1974. "The Rights of Animals and Unborn Generations." In W. T. Blackstone, ed., *Philosophy and Environmental Crisis.* Athens, Georgia. Pp. 43–68.

Finnis, John. 1980. *Natural Law and Natural Rights.* Oxford.

Fishkin, J. S. 1979. *Tyranny and Legitimacy.* Baltimore.

Flew, Antony. 1979. "What Is a Right?" *Georgia Law Review* 13 (Summer): 1117–41.

Fletcher, G. P. 1979. "The Right to Life." *Georgia Law Review* 13 (Summer) 1371–94.

Gewirth, Alan. 1967. "Categorical Consistency in Ethics." *Philosophical Quarterly* 17: 289–99.

———. 1971. "The Normative Structure of Action." *The Review of Metaphysics* 25: 238–61.

———. 1978a. "The Golden Rule Rationalized." *Midwestern Studies in Philosophy* 3: 133–47.

———. 1978b. *Reason and Morality.* Chicago.

———. 1979. "The Basis and Content of Human Rights." *Georgia Law Review* 13 (Summer): 1143–69.

Golding, M. P. 1968. "Towards a Theory of Human Rights." *The Monist* 52: 521–49.

———. 1971. "Private Right and the Limits of Law." *Philosophy East and West* 21: 375–88.

———. 1978. "The Concept of Rights: A Historical Sketch." In E. B. Bandman, ed., *Bioethics and Human Rights.* Boston. Pp. 44–50.

Goodrum, G. R. 1977. "'Acting as if': A Criticism of Eric Mack's 'Egoism and Rights.'" *The Personalist* 58: 277–81.

Hart, H.L.A. 1948–1949. "The Ascription of Responsibility and Rights." *Proceedings of the Aristotelian Society* 49: 171–94.

———. 1955. "Are There Any Natural Rights?" *Philosophical Review* 64: 175–91.

Hospers, John. 1972. *Human Conduct.* New York.

Kudryavtsev, Vladimir. 1976. "The Truth About Human Rights." *Human Rights* 5: 193–99.

Lyons, David, ed. 1979. *Rights.* Belmont, Calif.

Macdonald, Margaret. 1967. "Natural Rights." In Peter Laslett, ed., *Philosophy, Politics and Society.* Oxford. Pp. 33–55.

Machan, T. R. 1971. "A Rationale for Human Rights." *The Personalist* 52: 216–35.

———. 1973. "Human Rights: Some Points of Clarification." *Journal of Critical Analysis* 5: 30–39.

———. 1975a. *Human Rights and Human Liberties.* Chicago.

———. 1975b. "Law, Justice, and Natural Rights." *Western Ontario Law Review* 14: 119–30.

———. 1976. "Prima Facie versus Natural (Human) Rights." *Journal of Value Inquiry* 10: 119–31.

———. 1978. "Are There Any Human Rights?" *The Personalist* 59: 165–70.

———. 1980. "On Human Rights, Feudalism, and Political Change." In A Rosenbaum, ed., *Philosophy of Human Rights.* Westport, Conn.

———. 1981. "Wronging Rights." *Policy Review* 17: 37–58.

———. 1982. "A Reconsideration of Natural Rights Theory." *American Philosophical Quarterly* 19: 61–72.

Mack, Eric. 1971. "How to Derive Ethical Egoism." *The Personalist* 52: 735–43.

———. 1973. "Egoism and Rights." *The Personalist* 54: 5–33.

———. 1974. "Individualism, Rights, and the Open Society." In T. R. Machan, ed., *The Libertarian Alternative.* Chicago.

———. 1976. "Hart and Natural and Contractual Rights." *Philosophical Studies* 29: 283–85.

———. 1977. "Natural and Contractual Rights." *Ethics* 87: 145–53.

Martin, Rex, and Nickel, James W. 1978. "A Bibliography on the Nature and Foundation of Rights, 1947–1977." *Political Theory* 6: 395–413.

Mavrodes, George. 1972. "Property." *The Personalist* 53: 245–62.

Melden, A. I. 1952. "The Concept of Universal Human Rights." In *Science, Language and Human Rights.* Philadelphia.

———. 1959. *Rights and Right Conduct.* Oxford.

———. ed. 1970. *Human Rights.* Belmont, Calif.

———. 1977. *Rights and Persons.* Berkeley.

Miller, R. W. 1981. "Rights and Reality." *Philosophical Review* 90: 358–407.

Montefiore, A. C. 1961. "Goodness and Choice." *Aristotelian Society* Suppl. Vol. 35: 45–80.

Nickel, J. W. 1978–1979. "Is There a Human Right to Employment?" *The Philosophical Forum* 10 (Winter-Summer): 149–70.

Nozick, Robert. 1971. "On the Randian Argument." *The Personalist* 52: 282–230.

———. 1974. *Anarchy, State, and Utopia.* New York.

Paul, Ellen Frankel, ed. 1984 (forthcoming). *Human Rights, Social Philosophy & Policy* 1 #2.

Pennock, J. R., and Chapman, J. W., eds. 1981. *Human Rights.* Nomos 23. New York.

Pilon, Roger. 1979. "Ordering Rights Consistently: Or What We Do and Do Not Have Rights To." *Georgia Law Review* 13: 1171–96.

———. "Corporations and Rights: On Treating Corporate People Justly." *Georgia Law Review* 1245–1370.

Rachels, James. 1974. "Two Arguments Against Egoism." *Philosophia* 4: 297–314.

Rand, Ayn. 1957. *Atlas Shrugged*. New York.

_____. 1967. "Man's Rights." In Ayn Rand, *Capitalism: The Unknown Ideal*. New York. Pp. 320–28. Reprinted 1968 in John Hospers, ed., *Readings in Introductory Philosophical Analysis*. Englewood Cliffs, N.J.: Prentice-Hall.

_____. 1970. "Causality versus Duty." *The Objectivist* 9: 1–6.

Raphael, D. D., ed. 1967. *Political Theory and the Rights of Man*. Bloomington, Illinois.

Richards, D.A.J. 1979. "Human Rights and the Moral Foundations of the Substantive Criminal Law." *Georgia Law Review* 13: 1395–1446.

Rothbard, M. N. 1978. *For a New Liberty*. New York.

Schauer, Frederick. 1981. "Can Rights Be Abused?" *Philosophical Quarterly* 31: 225–230.

Scheffler, Samuel. 1976. "Natural Rights, Equality and the Minimal State." *Canadian Journal of Philosophy* 6: 59–76.

Shue, Henry. 1980. *Basic Rights*. Princeton, N.J.: Princeton University Press.

Singer, Peter. 1975. *Animal Liberation*. New York.

Strauss, Leo. 1952. "On Locke's Doctrine of Natural Rights." *The Philosophical Review* 61: 475–502.

_____. 1970. *Natural Right and History*. 2nd ed. Chicago.

Tuck, Richard. 1979. *Natural Rights Theories*. Cambridge: Cambridge University Press.

Vieira, Edwin, Jr. "Rights and the United States Constitution: The Declension from Natural Law to Legal Positivism." *Georgia Law Review:* 1447–1500.

Vlastos, Gregory. 1970 "Justice and Equality." In A. I. Melden, ed., *Human Rights*. Belmont, Calif. Pp. 76–95.

chapter 9

Recent Work on the Concept of Liberty

WILLIAM A. PARENT

Geoffrey Marshall recently claimed that "in a properly ordered world of concepts liberty would be adjudged an item in the vocabulary of politics so damaged in use as to deserve recall for radical readjustment and repair."[1] My principal aims in this essay are to show why Marshall is right and to work toward a conception of liberty that can play an important role in any respectable moral-political theory. I began this task several years ago (Parent, 1974). This chapter includes many of the arguments found there, as well as analyses of other work on liberty published since 1973.

There is a basic methodological assumption underlying my approach. I do not believe that the concept of liberty admits of only one correct meaning or definition. People committed to different ideals and values are likely to construe "liberty" in different ways, and no proof or argument can settle once and for all where usage is right. W. B. Gallie called concepts like these "essentially contested," and he persuasively affirmed that anyone who sets out to establish what such a concept really means is bound to fail.[2]

This is not to say that reasons are unavailable for preferring one conception of liberty to others; I am about to argue that we ought to conceive of liberty in a certain way. My arguments do not result in the conclusion that liberty must be understood in this way. They do, however, constitute a persuasive case for choosing one definition of liberty over its competitors.

What kinds of reasons are relevant in making a choice among divergent concepts of liberty? I hold that the following considerations should be given some weight (they are, as it were, desiderata of conceptual analysis): substantial consistency with ordinary language; richness of conceptualization; theoretical elegance; explanatory power. To elaborate briefly, ordinary usage will be our starting point, but departures therefrom can sometimes be justified. Strict adherence to common ways of speaking would be warranted only if everyday talk were completely free of contradiction, imprecision, and ambiguity. Unhappily it is not, hence the need to revise and refine – but not to the point where the revisions themselves become the source of conceptual muddles and paradox.

Conceptual richness is attained by scrupulous respect for the many, valid distinctions embedded in our language. These distinctions comprise a veritable treasure-chest of fundamental insights and intuitions. To ignore or dismiss them is often easy and tempting, but the gain in expediency comes at the expense of intellectual integrity. Conceptual discrimination is also indispensable for securing theoretical elegance. A conceptual schematism that obscures basic differences between related but distinct concepts is both sloppy and superficial. Finally, any adequate definition of liberty should fit into a vocabulary of politics (to use Marshall's term) that will enable us to explain all that we think needs explaining or justifying without relegating any well-established moral-political concept to disuse or redundancy.

I. *Berlin's* Two Concepts of Liberty

Since the publication more than twenty years ago of *Two Concepts of Liberty,* Sir Isaiah Berlin's inaugural address to Oxford University, some books and many articles have been written with the purpose of elucidating the nature of social freedom or liberty. Because Berlin's ideas have generated so much contemporary interest and have had such an impact on the approach and thinking of other philosophers concerned with the problem, I begin my essay with their detailed evaluation.

In his inaugral lecture Berlin discusses the two concepts of liberty that, in his opinion, stand out as centrally important among the more than two hundred different senses of the term recorded by historians of thought. He calls these the negative and positive concepts. I shall first summarize Berlin's discussion, beginning with the former, and then will present my objections to his principal contentions.

Negative freedom is involved in defining the area within which persons should be left to do what they want without interference by others. To be negatively free essentially means not to be interfered with in the pursuit of one's desires. In Berlin's words: "I am normally said to be free to the degree to which no human being interferes with my activity. Liberty in this sense is simply the area within which a man can do what he wants" (Berlin, 1958, p. 7).[3] Hence, anyone who deliberately prevents me from satisfying my desires, attaining my goals (p. 7), fulfilling my wishes (p. 8), or making choices (p. 16) — Berlin uses these phrases interchangeably — infringes upon my freedom.

That such interference must be deliberate is implied, Berlin thinks, by the concepts of coercion and enslavement contained in the meaning of unfreedom. Thus, if I accidentally lock A in his room and thereby make it impossible for him to do what he wants, no one would accuse me of rendering him unfree to leave. But we would, on the other hand, describe a man whose government deliberately makes it impossible for him to buy food as unfree to do so, for he is, while A was not, a victim of an insidious form of coercion (Berlin, 1958, p. 8).

Berlin also emphasizes that the mere incapacity to perform some action does not imply unfreedom to perform it. We would not, nor should we, regard the physically handicapped as unfree to engage in strenuous exercise or the mentally retarded as unfree to succeed in college unless it could be shown that their inability to do these things resulted from the deliberate actions of other persons or groups. Berlin's point is well taken, but I shall shortly show that he is wrong in thinking that an inability to act caused by the deliberate activity of others is sufficient for unfreedom.

The second, or positive, concept of freedom Berlin discusses is involved in answering the question what, or who, is or should be the source of control or interference that can determine someone to do or be one thing rather than another. Freedom in this sense consists essentially of rational self-determination or self-mastery. It derives from man's desire to be in control of his own destiny. A proponent of positive liberty wants his life and decisions to depend on himself, not on external forces. He wants to be an instrument of his own will rather than of others; to be a subjec., not an object; to be moved by purposes that originate with him, not with someone else.

The concept of self-mastery seems at first glance straightforward and innocuous; we think we understand what it means. We can, for example, point out the kind of people who are obviously not masters of themselves — e.g., drug addicts, alcoholics, and compulsive gamblers. But, as Berlin points out, the concept naturally suggests (and many philosophers have interpreted it to imply) a peculiar dualistic theory of the person; according to this theory, each of us is composed, on the one hand, of a "real" self, the transcendent, dominant controller, and on the other of a bundle of feelings and passions to be disciplined and brought to heel. Philosophers subscribing to this metaphysical interpretation of rational self-mastery usually identify the "real" self with reason, with man's "higher" or autonomous nature; and they contrast it with his "lower" animal nature, which on their view is made up entirely of irrational impulses and uncontrollable desires. Moreover, they are inclined to argue that rational self-mastery, understood to imply this kind of "dualism," constitutes the only genuine purpose of man and therefore should take precedence over and be pursued at the expense of other goals that he might mistakenly think are equally important. Indeed, man can and should be forced to be free in this positive sense, however violently his poor, unreflecting, desire-ridden self may cry out against this process. In Berlin's words: "Freedom is not freedom to do what is irrational, or stupid, or bad. To force empirical selves into the right pattern is no tyranny, but liberation" (Berlin, 1958, pp. 32–33).

To this theory of positive freedom Berlin raises two major objections. First, rational self-mastery is not the sole nor even necessarily the most important goal in life. Instead it is just one among several possible goals not all of which are commensurable (Berlin, 1958, p. 56). Second, the contention that force to achieve rational self-mastery can be justified, that anyone who does not realize what is truly good for him should be made to realize it, is morally bankrupt. To oppress, torture, or coerce men in the name of their freedom in fact betrays the most dangerous kind of moral despotism. For Berlin, power can never rightfully be exercised over any mentally sane adult except to prevent him from harming others (Berlin, 1958, p. 35).

There are, I believe, a number of serious difficulties with Berlin's account of negative and positive freedom, as summarized above, which have gone largely unnoticed by his students and critics and which unhappily reappear in many post-1958 writings. They deserve careful consideration here.

First, Berlin's various characterizations of negative unfreedom (the deliberate interference with any kind of human activity, of a person's doing what he wants or wishes, of the attainment of his goals, or of his making choices) are not all equal. Obviously, an activity in which a person is engaged need not be one he wants or chooses to pursue, nor need it result in the attainment of his goals. Moreover, making choices is not always identical with achieving one's goals (it would only be so for someone whose aim was to be able to choose his own course of action), nor is it something we would necessarily choose to do. So as it stands, one cannot always be certain precisely what Berlin means when he refers to *the* concept of negative liberty.

To confuse matters even more, Berlin occasionally identifies negative liberty not with any kind of non-interference, but with what results from non-interference, namely an area of personal life entirely immune from outside intrusion. So we have yet another concept of freedom to ponder, a concept that comes very close to expressing the basic idea of privacy. Indeed, Berlin often uses the term "privacy" while discussing negative liberty; e.g., he continually emphasizes the need for private life and equates the feeling we derive from being free with the sense of privacy (Berlin, 1958, pp. 10–11). Clearly, however, liberty and privacy ought not to be equated. Persons who lack the social freedom to undertake everyday activities, for instance prisoners in solitary confinement, nevertheless may have plenty of privacy. Berlin's failure to differentiate between these two values is especially puzzling in view of his admonition against confounding related but conceptually distinct political ideals (Berlin, 1958, p. 39).

In the address Berlin claims, as if this were a reason for accepting the definition, that all the great English political philosophers conceive of negative liberty as non-interference with a person's desires (Berlin, 1958, p. 8). But plainly they do not. Hobbes, for example, equates liberty with the absence of external impediments to motion. This definition is different from Berlin's in at least two respects: it specifies that only a certain class of impediments can jeopardize freedom; and it does not incorporate any reference to a person's doing what he wants — to Hobbes, someone might very well be rendered unfree to do what he dislikes.

I believe there are at least two good reasons why we should reject Berlin's definition of liberty. A prisoner is socially unfree to assume the responsibilities of an executive, whether or not he desires to assume them. Similarly, a man who locks his wife in their home deprives her of the liberty to leave, even though it is conceivable she does not want to leave. Interfering with a person's desires, though sometimes sufficient to curtail his freedom, is not necessary for such curtailment. And Berlin's definition carries the absurd implication that anyone's freedom can be enlarged merely by decreasing the number of his desires. There are, of course, different ways to restore a man's freedom to act, but the extirpation of his desires is not one of them. Conditioning a slave to want only what he has does not make him a free man.

Two final comments respecting Berlin's account of negative liberty: first, it is simply not true that a man can be rendered unfree to act only through the deliberate activity of someone else. If X closes up his shop, forgetting that Y is still inside, and later is asked for an explanation, he can say, "I temporarily deprived Y of his freedom, but I didn't do it deliberately." Second, Berlin is mistaken in believing that anyone who deliberately deprives another of the ability to perform an activity curtails his liberty to do so. X might deliberately deprive Y of the ability to walk by shooting him in the back, but he does not render Y socially unfree to walk; rather he deprives him of the physical capacity to do so. The terms "deliberate deprivation of ability" and "interference with freedom" have different designata. It is important to remember, however, that a person's liberty to do Z will prove of little value to him if someone deliberately destroys his ability to exercise it.

Without question, the real object of Berlin's treatment of positive liberty is not the ordinary, metaphysically naïve sense of "rational self-mastery," but the philosophical interpretation of this concept with its bifurcation of the person into an autonomous self, on the one hand, and an empirical self, on the other. We may agree with Berlin that this interpretation is consistent with and has in the past been used to justify injustice and oppression. But cannot the methods of illogic and spurious metaphysics just as easily be employed to distort Berlin's concept of negative liberty and produce justifications of tyranny? All we have to do is argue for the existence of a "real" self whose "true" desires are quite different from and basic conflict with those arising from our animal nature. No concept is entirely immune from this kind of distortion; since the villain of the piece is metaphysical extravagance, why does Berlin insist on obscuring this fact and attacking the concept of rational self-mastery instead?[4]

Moreover, nothing in the ordinary meaning of rational self-mastery precludes the recognition of other equally important ends. Positive liberals who steadfastly refuse to read any sort of metaphysical dualism into their theory need not and probably would not regard freedom as the only genuine human ideal; instead they would ascribe at least as much value to goods like justice, peace, and equality of opportunity, since without them the worth of rational self-mastery would be significantly impaired. So Berlin's contention that positive liberalism is inhumane because it denies a pluralism of values is relevant only when the concept of freedom is subjected to philosophical disfigurement.

The point emerging from all this is that Berlin's essay does not provide any reasons why alcoholics, drug addicts, compulsive gamblers, and other persons in bondage to powerful, often irrational impulses should not be called unfree to pursue most of the activities which men displaying rational self-mastery in the ordinary sense are able to perform. The idea that freedom consists essentially of exercising discipline and control over one's impulses, in just the way alcoholics and addicts might, does not survive Berlin's criticisms unmarked.

Berlin could have followed another route in criticizing the positive concept of freedom. Instead of attempting to show that the philosophical explication of rational self-mastery leads to tyranny and is inconsistent with a pluralism of values, he might simply have asked: Does rational self-mastery, under any interpretation, reflect what we ordinarily mean by liberty? I believe it does not. Consider, for example, the situation of an addict who is driven to steal in order to support his habit: the addict exhibits little or no rational self-mastery, yet he still has the social freedom to engage in illegal activities. Indeed, this is precisely the problem confronting law enforcement officials, who must attempt to render him at least temporarily unfree to do so. The loss of rational self-mastery, then, may well lead to, but is not constitutive of, unfreedom as we ordinarily conceive of it. Conversely, some prisoners might somehow manage to acquire an understanding of and control over their base criminal impulses through rehabilitation. These considerations indicate that liberty cannot be adequately elucidated as rational self-mastery.

II. Berlin's Latest Thoughts on Liberty

We have now to examine Berlin's most recent ideas on liberty set forth in the introduction to his *Four Essays on Liberty* (1969). For our purposes the most significant thing about this introduction is Berlin's realization that liberty cannot adequately be defined as the non-interference with a person's doing what he wants. He comes to reject his old definition because it implies that one way to render a man free consists of extinguishing all his desires, and this is clearly absurd; and it encourages the use of repressive techniques for controlling behavior. Curiously enough, Berlin fails to notice an even more obvious defect of this definition, which I mentioned above — its implication that a person's freedom cannot be abridged as long as he is doing something he dislikes.

Berlin now maintains that freedom properly conceived is the absence of obstacles, resulting from alterable human practices, to possible choices and activities (Berlin, 1969, p. xxxix). If these obstructions are the intentional result of alterable human practices, then in Berlin's judgment it is appropriate to speak of oppression; but not all instances of unfreedom need be oppressive in this sense. So Berlin abandons, and wisely so, his earlier insistence that unfreedom must involve the deliberate interference with human activity. With respect to the kinds of social practices posing the most immediate and dangerous threats to negative freedom, Berlin emphasizes those discriminatory economic and educational policies that promote a situation wherein entire groups are shut off from benefits that are then allowed to accumulate exclusively in the hands of the more advantaged citizens. This sort of discrimination builds walls around classes of men and effectively shuts the door to their future development (Berlin, 1969, pp. xlvii–xlviii).

Difficulties with Berlin's new definition become evident when we consider the following facts: illness, ignorance, bias, and hatred often constitute obstacles to a person's acting in various ways. And they often result from alterable human practices — e.g., unsanitary working conditions have been known to cause illness; racist institutions and customs are responsible for much hatred and bias. Yet we do not and need not say that a person who is prevented from pursuing a given activity by illness, ignorance, bias, or hatred that results from alterable human practices has been rendered unfree in the social sense to do so. Instead, we can say that persons often can be deprived of the physical ability, the skill or intelligence, the fair-mindedness, and the compassion necessary for them to undertake different tasks. This conceptualization is much more precise and perspicuous than Berlin's.

Discriminatory economic and educational policies, which according to Berlin portend serious consequences for human freedom, in fact do not render their victims unfree to advance materially, but rather deny them the fair opportunity to do so. A person who is refused a job because of his race and who is prevented from attending decent schools because he comes from the "wrong neighborhood" normally would and should express his moral outrage in the language of opportunity, not freedom. He is being denied the *chance* to work and to acquire a satisfactory education. (Of course, persons who are not given the opportunity to fulfill their goals will probably find any freedom they have to do so of little value.)

Interestingly enough, Berlin on at least two occasions identifies the concepts of liberty and opportunity, first maintaining that liberty is opportunity for action (Berlin, 1969, p. xlii), then arguing that the problem of how an overall increase in liberty in particular circumstances is to be secured and distributed reduces to the question how the maximization of opportunities is in any concrete case to be achieved (xlviii). It seems evident, though, that someone's having the social freedom to do something is not sufficient to warrant the statement that he has the opportunity to do it. It makes perfect sense to say, for example, that a young man, although socially free to attend a concert, nonetheless lacks the opportunity to do so and therefore cannot go either because he is too busy or has not been given any tickets. Depriving someone of the liberty to act is not the same thing as refusing him the opportunity to do so, and the problem of increasing and distributing freedom cannot be reduced to a question about the maximization of opportunities.

In sum, our final judgment must be that Berlin's decade-long endeavor to elucidate the nature of liberty fails. His belief, yet unexamined, that there are two distinct concepts of liberty that can be isolated from one another and analyzed separately, each on its own merits, has also come under attack in recent writings. Among these, Gerald MacCallum's essay is perhaps the most widely discussed and influential, so I will now turn to an evaluation of it.

III. MacCallum's "Negative and Positive Freedom"

MacCallum challenges the view that it is possible and useful to distinguish between two kinds or concepts of social freedom, negative and positive. He argues that this distinction has never been made sufficiently clear and at any rate can serve only to obfuscate the really critical issues to be examined if the differences dividing philosophers concerned with freedom are to be understood. MacCallum's own view is that the social freedom of some agent or agents is always freedom from some constraint or compulsion on, interference with, or barrier to doing, not doing, becoming, or not becoming something. Social freedom is thus always *of* something (an agent or agents), *from* something, *to* do, not do, become, or not become something (MacCallum, 1967, p. 314). It refers to a triadic relation whose form can be schematized as follows: X is (is not) free from y to do (not do, become, not become) z.

In MacCallum's judgment, instead of concentrating on kinds of freedom and asking which concept is the correct or most humane, à la Berlin, we should interpret all controversies about freedom as disagreements over the appropriate ranges of one or more of the x, y, and z variables. The fundamental questions in political philosophy center around these disagreements; to present them as involving the meaning of "freedom" defeats any attempt at rewarding, fruitful argument. In MacCallum's words: "It would be far better to insist that the same (triadic) concept of freedom is operating throughout (disputes over freedom), and that the differences, rather than being about what freedom is, are, for example, about what persons are, and about what can count as an obstacle to or interference with the freedom of persons so conceived" (MacCallum, 1967, p. 320—the parentheses are mine). We should, for example, look upon the disagreements between, say, Hobbes's theory of freedom and Rousseau's, or Marx's and Mill's, as essentially differences concerning, among other things, what the nature of a person is, and not as disputes over what it means to be free.

But is it possible to translate all genuine statements about the freedom of agents into the xyz schema? MacCallum answers that a statement is not intelligible as a statement about the freedom of agents until one is in a position to fill in the elements of this schema. In the end, he argues, discussions concerning the freedom of agents can be meaningful and rationally assessed only after each term of the triadic relation is specified or at least understood. In support of this argument MacCallum considers a number of familiar idioms that do not contain any explicit reference to two of the three variables and shows that each can be understood to be about the freedom of agents because each can be translated into the triadic schema. Thus, (a) "free beer" is thought to be intelligible as an expression about human freedom because it is understood to refer to beer that people are free from the ordinary restrictions of the market place to drink without paying for it (MacCallum, 1967, p. 316); (b) property is free from encumbrance" makes sense as a statement about the freedom of agents because it can be interpreted to mean that owners of land are free from certain well-known restrictions to use, enjoy, and dispose of the land as they wish (p. 316); and (c) "freedom from hunger" can also be regarded as an expression about the freedom of agents, for we can understand it to signify a state of affairs where people are free from barriers constituted by various specifiable agricultural, economic, and political conditions to get enough food to prevent hunger (p. 318).

MacCallum's thesis can be formulated even more precisely as follows: if a statement is really about the social freedom of agents, then it can be translated into the xyz schema; conversely, if a statement can be translated into this schema, then it is intelligible as or can be understood to be about the social freedom of agents. MacCallum emphasizes that he is interested only in the conditions under which the talk about human freedom is intelligible. (This restriction excludes from consideration uses of "free of" and "free from" in statements like "the sky is free of clouds," where "free" simply means "without" or "rid of" [MacCallum, 1967, p. 315].)

The most serious difficulty with MacCallum's analysis is that there are meaningful statements of the form "X is (is not) free from y to do z" that do not imply any assertions about the social freedom (unfreedom) of agents. MacCallum's thesis (that if a statement can be translated into this triadic schema it can be understood to be about social freedom) should, therefore, be rejected. Consider, for example, the following statements, where "X" ranges over persons:

a. X is free from time-consuming duties to take a vacation.
b. X is free of prejudice to judge the case.
c. X is finally free of guilt feelings to resume a normal life.

None of these ought to be construed as a statement about liberty. The first implies only that X has the opportunity to take a vacation; (b) should be understood as a claim about X's attitude, so it can be true even when X has been deprived of the liberty to judge the case — e.g., someone has kidnapped him; (c) says simply that X possesses the peace of mind necessary to begin living again, a statement that is consistent with his being rendered unfree to do so.

An important point to emerge from the above analysis is that "freedom" in the social sense is not a substantive corresponding to the adjectives "free from" and "free of" as redness corresponds to the adjective "red."[5] Whenever you describe something as red it is always possible to use "redness" also, but "free of" and "free from" are applicable in many cases where "liberty" is not. Whether a statement of the form "X is free from y to do z" is intelligible as a statement about X's social freedom depends upon the referent of the y variable, for only certain kinds of preventing conditions are commonly regarded as threats to a person's liberty. MacCallum should have carefully discriminated among different kinds of preventing conditions and should have maintained that "freedom" is applicable only when those belonging to a certain class or classes — e.g., physical restraints imposed upon a person from without — are present.

MacCallum's essay is nevertheless significant because it does emphasize a much overlooked truth: translatability into the xyz schema is a necessary condition of the intelligibility of any claim about social freedom. Whenever we use "freedom" in the social sense we ought to specify, or at least be able to specify, who is free from what conditions to perform what activity.

MacCallum mentions the political scientist Felix Oppenheim as one of the few writers who does adopt this rule, but he says that Oppenheim limits far too sharply the ranges of the xyz variables. Since I have just recommended such a limitation myself, now would be an appropriate time to consider Oppenheim's work in some detail.

IV. *Oppenheim's* Dimensions of Freedom

Oppenheim wants to provide adequate explicative definitions of some of the basic terms employed in political theory, including "influence," "control," "power," and, of course, "social freedom" and "social unfreedom." He wants, that is, to provide definitions that will enhance the clarity and precision of the definienda, thereby reducing the ambiguities and inconsistencies of ordinary usage. Oppenheim's final objective, and what he takes to be the most pressing task confronting political theorists today, is the construction of a conceptual apparatus free of imprecision, obscurity, and contradiction. In what follows I shall argue that his analyses of social freedom and unfreedom do not contribute to this objective but instead have rather obvious counterintuitive implications and beget serious logical muddles and paradoxes.

The central contention of Oppenheim's chapter on social unfreedom is that there are two ways to render an actor X ("actor" ranges over individuals and groups) unfree to do x: one can prevent him from doing it, or one can make it punishable for him to do it. I shall first examine the contention that preventing someone from acting constitutes a deprivation of his freedom to act.

Oppenheim begins his analysis by equating "Y prevents X from doing x" with "X cannot do x as a result of some action y of Y," and then advances the following two definitions:

(a) Where the probability that X would bring about x if he chose is extremely small, or where X theoretically can do x, but only at the risk of severe deprivation, it is impossible for him to do it, or to say the same thing, he cannot do it.

(b) Y prevents X from doing x, if and only if, were X to attempt x he would with practical certainty fail to bring it about or suffer extreme deprivation, as a result of some action y of Y [Oppenheim, 1961, p. 63].

With regard to (a), Oppenheim acknowledges that he is extending the meaning of impossibility but defends this extension on the grounds that it makes the concept more readily applicable to real-life situations. But his avowed objective is to provide adequate explicative definitions of terms like "prevention," not to inflate their meanings almost beyond recognition just so they might enjoy a wider application. That Y prevents X from doing x implies that X did not do x, but this is not implied by (b): men sometimes manage to defy great odds and accomplish what the polls indicated could not be done, and they also occasionally act despite the risk of severe deprivation.

Using (b) and the belief that preventing a person from acting is one way to render him unfree as premises, Oppenheim derives the following two theses concerning social unfreedom:

T1. If, upon attempting x, X would with practical certainty fail to bring it about as a result of some action y of Y, then X is with respect to Y unfree to do x.

T2. If, upon attempting x, X would with practical certainty suffer extreme deprivation as the result of some action y of Y, then X is with respect to Y unfree to do x.

Serious problems beset both theses. Looking first at T1, it is rather obvious that the practical certainty of failure to act does not always imply unfreedom to act. Let "x" stand for "getting to the church on time" and "y" for "stealing X's car." And let us suppose that the only way X can get to church on time is by taking his car. Then X will almost certainly fail to bring about x as the result of y, but we should infer from this not that X lacks the social freedom to do x with respect to Y, but rather that Y has deprived X of the means (of transportation) necessary to do it. Or let "x" stand for "competing in the track meet" and "y" for "feeding X an anaesthetic just prior to the meet." Under these conditions X will with practical certainty fail to compete in the meet, but we should infer from this not that he lacks the freedom to do so with respect to Y, but that Y has impeded his ability to do so. These inferences are to be preferred because they are more-accurate descriptions of what has happened to X.

In T2, if X is unaware of the probable severe deprivation in store for him, there seems to be no reason why he should be called unfree in any sense to do x, inasmuch as the prospect of imminent suffering would have no causal bearing on his decision whether or not to do it. What Oppenheim must have meant can be expressed by amending T2 as follows:

T2ª. If, upon attempting x, X would with practical certainty suffer extreme deprivation as the result of some action y of Y, and X knows this, then X is with respect to Y unfree to do x.

There are at least two problems with T2ª. First, it is consistent with the possibility of X's doing something he is unfree to do, and this is, I believe, entirely acceptable. Consider the many individuals who have performed actions, started movements, and initiated reforms while knowing full well that their so doing would cause others to inflict severe, sometimes unjustified punishment on them. Should we, do we in fact, say that such individuals were deprived of their liberty to behave as they did? Of course not. When we say that someone has been deprived of his social freedom to do x at t, part of what we mean is that he *cannot* do x at t. Second, even in those cases where X does not do x because he knows Y will punish him as a result, it is more accurate and precise to say either that Y has infringed upon his freedom of choice or has undermined his will to do x. Oppenheim himself emphasizes (in his final chapter) that social freedom and freedom of choice have different meanings and should not be confounded with one another. The former is a political, the latter a metaphysical, concept.

Oppenheim has some more things to say about the relation between prevention and unfreedom when discussing degrees of power and freedom in Chapter 8. His basic thesis reads thus:

T3. If Y prevents X from doing x, the degree of X's unfreedom to do x is a function of the utility of doing x and the disutility of being prevented from doing x [Oppenheim, 1961, p. 190].

Utility, in turn, is measured by how much or strongly X wants to do x. If he is prevented from doing x, then the greater his desire to do it the greater the limitation upon his freedom. Oppenheim illustrates this point with the example of a majority voting down a bill which the minority strongly favors: the majority's action infringes upon the minority's freedom to a greater degree than if the issue had been less important to them (Oppenheim, 1961, p. 190). But here Oppenheim confuses the degree of unfreedom with the degree to which a person or group feels unfree, or feels aggravated and frustrated because he or it is unfree. If Y physically restrains two persons from doing x he renders both unfree to do it, although if one of them really wanted to do x while the other did not care we might very well conclude that Y's action made the former feel more unfree (frustrated, upset) than the latter. Perhaps feelings can be measured in degrees, but it is extremely doubtful whether unfreedom can be. T3 needs to be modified along the following lines:

T3ª. If Y prevents X from doing x, and thereby renders him unfree to do x, the degree to which X feels unfree, or feels aggravated and frustrated because he has been rendered unfree, is a function of the utility of doing x and of the disutility of being prevented from doing x.

We now have to consider the second way in which, according to Oppenheim, a person can be rendered unfree to act, namely by making it punishable for him to do so. Oppenheim correctly points out that the expression "Y makes it punishable for X to do x" can mean one of two things: Y actually penalizes X for having done x, or Y has a general disposition to punish X whenever he does x. Given Oppenheim's contention that punishability constitutes a sufficient condition of social unfreedom, we can attribute the following two theses to him:

T4. If Y actually penalizes X for having done x, then X was with respect to Y unfree to do x.

T5. If Y makes it punishable in the dispositional sense for X to do x, then X is to that extent unfree to do x with respect to Y.

With regard to T4, Oppenheim first clarifies precisely what actual penalization is involved. If Y holds that X did x and therefore performs some action y which deprives X, then Y is said to penalize X for having done x. Y deprives X provided the situation in which Y finds himself as a result of y is less valuable to him than it would have been without Y's intervention.

But T4 so interpreted leads to absurd conclusions. For instance, it implies that a person can be socially unfree to do something he has already done. Of course, if a thief, say, is apprehended and imprisoned, he is for the period of his incarceration unfree to steal again; but this is not the same as saying that he was unfree before his capture to break the law. And T4 requires us to hold that if X wants badly to be imprisoned, then Y's placing him in jail for violating the law does not infringe upon his freedom: in Oppenheim's words, "If Y's action does not actually deprive X, Y does not penalize him in the behavioral sense and hence does not make him unfree in any respect" (Oppenheim, 1961, p. 73). This is nonsense. Anyone in jail has suffered a loss of freedom, his state of mind notwithstanding.

Turning now to T5, Oppenheim explicates punishability in the dispositional sense thus: Y makes it punishable for X to do x to the extent that, were X to do x, he would be penalized for having done so as the result of some action y of Y's (Oppenheim, 1961, p. 72). Oppenheim's explication, it should be noted, is not in accord with the ordinary meaning of punishability, according to which Y's making it punishable for X to do x implies that X would be liable to punishment from Y were he to do x. At any rate, according to T5, as Oppenheim understands it we should say, for example, that drivers are "officially unfree" to exceed the speed limit to the extent they are actually being fined for doing so (p. 77), and that drivers in the United States are officially more free to violate traffic regulations than those in France, inasmuch as in France there are fewer patrol cars and it is much easier to argue one's way out of a summons.

But, once again, do we need to say these things? Is it really necessary to speak in such cumbersome, unwieldly and confusing language? All one has to say, after all, is that, other things being equal, drivers are less likely to speed to the extent they are punished for doing so, and that because it is considerably easier for drivers in France to speed with impunity than for drivers in America, the former are, on the whole, and other things being equal, less reluctant about doing so. Under most circumstances we have the social freedom to violate traffic regulations; the question is whether we are willing to exercise this freedom in view of, among other things, the likelihood of our being apprehended and punished. So it seems that T5 fails to advance the cause of conceptual perspicuity espoused by Oppenheim and therefore, by his own criterion of adequacy for explicative definitions, should not be included in any scientific reinterpretation of the vocabulary of political science.

In sum, then, each of Oppenheim's major theses concerning the nature of social unfreedom proves upon close examination to be inadequate. I will now show that his explication of social freedom is also unacceptable.

Like MacCallum, Oppenheim rejects the two-concepts view of Berlin. Social freedom is a relation between actors, so any genuine statement about it must be translatable into a statement of the form "X is free to do x with respect to Y." It is by definition both "freedom from" (being constrained or restrained by somebody) and "freedom to" (do something) (Oppenheim, 1961, p. 112).

To clarify the nature of liberty, Oppenheim introduces the concept of a person's not being free to act. The government makes it neither impossible nor punishable to pay income taxes. Hence we are not unfree to pay them. But the government does make it necessary for us to pay them and therefore we are not, Oppenheim maintains, officially free in this regard. Similarly, voters in Belgium, while not unfree to vote, are nonetheless not free to do so either because it is officially mandatory to participate in elections there (Oppenheim, 1961, p. 111). In light of this distinction Oppenheim advances the following thesis:

T6. with respect to Y, X is not free to do x to the extent that X is, with respect to Y, either unfree to do x or unfree to abstain from doing x (111).

That is, being unfree to do x entails not being free to do it, and being unfree not to do x entails not being free to do it. Unpacking T6 we can derive the following four propositions:

 a. If Y prevents X from doing x, then X is to that extent not free to do x.
 b. If Y makes it punishable for X to do x, then X is to that extent not free to do x.
 c. If Y makes it mandatory or necessary for X to do x — i.e., if he prevents X from not doing x — then X is to that extent not free to do x.
 d. If Y makes it punishable for X not to do x, then X is to that extent not free to do x.

Social freedom, according to Oppenheim, is the contradictory, not of unfreedom, but of not being free to act. So X is free to do x with respect to Y to the extent that X is neither unfree to do x nor unfree to abstain from doing x (Oppenheim, 1961, p. 111). Or

T7. If Y does not prevent X from doing x and does not make it punishable for him to do it and does not make it necessary for him to do it and does not make it punishable for him not to do it, then X is to that extent free to do x with respect to Y (Oppeheim, 1961, p. 111).

Reflecting on these two theses, it becomes plain that (a) and (b) of T6 should both be rejected for the same reasons that prevention and punishability are not sufficient conditions of social unfreedom. As for propositions (c) and (d), they rest on confusion. While someone who makes it necessary for X to do x or punishable for him not to do so may properly be said to deprive him of any freedom of choice, this is not the same thing as depriving him of the liberty to do x.[6] Indeed, X's doing x, whether involuntarily or not, bespeaks of his social freedom to do so. Oppenheim should have said the following:

c[1a]. If Y makes it necessary for X to do x, then to that extent X has no free choice in the matter; and if he does x against his will, then his behavior is involuntary.

d[1a]. If Y makes it punishable for X not to do x,[7] then X is to that extent without any free choice in the matter; and if he does x against his will, then his behavior is involuntary.

Regarding T7, the claim that if Y doesn't prevent X from doing x then X is with respect to Y free to do x is true; a person's not being prevented from engaging in a certain activity constitutes *by itself* a sufficient condition of his liberty to do so. According to T7, however, to determine whether X has the liberty to do x with respect to Y we must know not only that Y doesn't prevent X from doing x, but also that Y doesn't make it necessary for X to do it, punishable for him to do it, or punishable for him not to do it. If Y does any one of these things, we cannot, in Oppenheim's judgment, call

X free to do x with respect to Y. But as I have just argued, Y's making it either necessary for X to do x or punishable for him not to do it is relevant only to the question whether X has any freedom of choice in the matter. And even if Y makes it punishable for X to do x, this does not imply that X is without the liberty to do x. We must, then, judge Oppenheim's overall effort to provide empirical, scientifically valid interpretations of social freedom and unfreedom a failure. I next examine the works of one of the most important political philosophers writing today, H. J. McCloskey.

V. H. J. McCloskey

McCloskey specifically addresses the question "What is liberty?" in two of the many essays he has written on liberalism over the past twenty years. In the first, entitled "A Critique of the Ideals of Liberty," two concepts of negative liberty and four of positive liberty are distinguished and evaluated as follows:

i. Negative liberty$_1$ = non-interference. McCloskey questions the legitimacy of this ideal on the grounds that not all interferences with a person are normally regarded as abridging liberty—e.g., one individual's hitting another.

ii. Negative liberty$_2$ = non-interference with one's rights. McCloskey correctly points out that this is not a genuine concept of liberty, since not every interference with a person's rights must or should be condemned as a deprivation of liberty—e.g., the unwarranted invasion of privacy.

iii. Positive liberty$_1$ = self-determination. McCloskey contends that this is an obvious and incontestable sense of "liberty." Hence, if A interferes with B for the purpose of restoring B's autonomy, and if A is successful, then the action does not properly constitute a denial of B's liberty (McCloskey, 1965, p. 490).

Here McCloskey's position is open to criticism. As I argued earlier when discussing Berlin's positive concept of liberty, having the capacity to be self-directing is neither necessary nor sufficient for a person to be (socially) free. And whether interferences that restore self-determination should be called infringements of liberty depends entirely on the form they take. Suppose A has B involuntarily committed to a state institution, where after years of therapy B finally becomes autonomous. In cases like this we should say that B suffered a temporary denial of liberty but for a good cause. So (iii) should not be accepted as a bona fide concept of liberty.

iv. Positive liberty$_2$ = reasonable self-determination. McCloskey argues that this too is a genuine concept of liberty. He writes: "A person is not free if he does not know what he is doing. Hence stupid, unreasonable behavior can, with some point, be said not to be fully free" (McCloskey, 1965, p. 502). But as I have maintained all along, if a person actually performs an action, whether he knows what he is doing or not, it is logically most cumbersome to call him unfree to do so. Moreover, a person's exhibiting reasonable self-determination is one, doubtless very desirable, way of exercising freedom, but we have to recognize the fact that many individuals are not disposed to act reasonably, and this may make their freedom subject to limitations for the good of everyone else.

v. Positive liberty$_3$ = opportunity to enjoy one's rights. McCloskey gives two reasons on behalf of (v) as a legitimate concept of liberty. First, it has been so regarded in the literature of liberalism. Second, people do complain that they are not free if they cannot enjoy their rights but do not complain in the same way about coercion that does not impinge upon the enjoyment of their rights (McCloskey, 1965, pp. 503, 504).

But the question that needs to be asked is whether (v) should have figured prominently in past liberal writings. I have already argued (Sections II and III) that liberty and opportunity represent two distinct moral-political ideals. Of course the deprivation of liberty is often accompanied by a loss of opportunity, and vice versa, but this is no reason for compounding the two values.

With regard to McCloskey's second reason supporting (v), whether the inability to enjoy rights justifies the issuance of a liberty-grievance will depend upon the source of the inability. Sick and poor people might not be able to enjoy their rights to life, but they should not describe their plight in terms of social freedom — unless of course they were sick and poor as a result of having been enslaved or imprisoned in some way. Similarly, that people fail to express a liberty grievance when subject to coercion that does not violate their rights admits of several different explanations — e.g., perhaps they realize that the coercion was totally warranted. Such failure, then, does not support (v).

vi. Positive liberty$_4$ = opportunity to be self-perfecting. McCloskey attempts to defend this concept by claiming, among other things, that (a) the element of free decision and self-determination is an essential component of this account; (b) to be self-frustrating or self-destructive is to be unfree in a significant sense; (c) if the opportunity to be self-perfecting is treated as a distinct, non-liberty ideal, self-perfection is in danger of being confused with the very different ideal of perfection of self (McCloskey, 1965, pp. 505, 506).

But a person who has the opportunity to be self-perfecting may not make free decisions and be self-determining. Furthermore, neither self-determination nor free decision is an essential component of social freedom. With regard to (b), a person who lacks the opportunity to be self-perfecting is not necessarily self-frustrating or self-destructive. And even if self-frustration or self-destruction does result from denying a person this opportunity, it does not follow that he is socially unfree in any respect. Finally, McCloskey never explains or defends (c). Why could not one just as easily argue that law and order ought to be equated with justice, since otherwise it is in danger of being confused with racism?

In his piece "Liberalism," McCloskey again levels a broadside against the negative concept of liberty, which he identifies with the state of being let alone, or non-interference. In his mind "There is something paradoxical and unsatisfactory about any attempt to explain a political value or any good as an absence of some kind" (McCloskey, 1974, p. 14). More specifically,

> The victim of a stroke or an accident who is paralyzed so that he can neither speak nor move but who is conscious, and who with treatment and care could regain some of his powers, if let alone to die enjoys complete negative liberty, I find it hard to see why this state should be called one of liberty [McCloskey, 1974, p. 15].

But the proponent of negative liberty will surely respond to these criticisms by pointing out that (a) many political ideals are properly explicated as absences — e.g., peace is the absence of war, justice is (at least in part) the absence of arbitrary discriminations; and (b) there is an important distinction between liberty and the value of liberty, so we shouldn't infer unfreedom from the fact that a person cannot enjoy the state he is in.

Relevant to this last point, we must take note of an important ambiguity in the expression "should not be called" (that figures prominently in McCloskey's analysis of the stroke victim's situation). Claiming that a certain state should not be called one of liberty can mean simply that it would be inappropriate under the circumstances to say this; i.e., it would serve no purpose and could even be regarded as perverse. Or it can mean that to describe the state in terms of liberty would be conceptually unwarranted or incorrect; i.e., it would betray a misunderstanding of the concept. McCloskey's argument trades on this ambiguity. Granted the stroke victim should not be called free, in that this would serve no purpose, it doesn't follow, and McCloskey offers us no independent argument for believing, that the person should not be called free because this would involve a conceptual blunder.

McCloskey continues his rebuttal of negative liberty by affirming that not all interferences with a person are infringements upon his liberty. If A assaults and injures

B, B's complaint will not be that A has deprived him of his freedom. True enough, but this criticism only shows that if the concept of negative liberty is to be viable it will have to be identified with something other than the absence of interference simpliciter. And there are such alternative explications (as we shall see).

McCloskey thinks, as he did nine years earlier, that liberty should be conceived as a form of self-determination. His main argument in support of this positive conception is clearly stated:

> Consider the provision of hearing aids to deaf people to enable them to enjoy music, receive instruction in various arts, engage in work they wish to engage in, and the like, where the aid is given both to one rendered deaf by an explosion, and to one born deaf. In each case, their freedom to enjoy music, television, to receive oral education, to engage in many avenues of work, is the result of the provision of this facility [McCloskey, 1974, p. 16].

Why? Because they are able to do more things. In McCloskey's words: "The person who is deaf, dumb, blind, or crippled may need to be helped by coercively taxing others to provide aid and facilities, or by coercively educating the individual himself; in each case his liberty is enlarged in the sense that he has a wider range of action and of effective choice" (McCloskey, 1974, p. 16).

The advocate of negative liberty has a persuasive reply to this argument, however. There are many different ways of increasing an individual's options. Providing liberty is one of them to be sure, but it needs to be clearly distinguished from others, like the provision of opportunity, means, knowledge, desire, etc. McCloskey's argument collapses these important distinctions. Liberty becomes, in his account, a huge grab-bag of diverse concepts. Such an inflationary definition robs liberty of its distinctive function, which can only be identified by isolating the particular way in which it (as opposed to the concepts of opportunity, means) relates to choice and action. In short, McCloskey's advocacy of positive freedom suffers from the serious problem of conceptual inelegance. One might go one step further and ascribe to it the equally unforgivable sin of conceptual evisceration.

There is another difficulty with McCloskey's position. How is a state dedicated to freedom supposed to ensure a wide range of action and effective choice to all its citizens, given the incontrovertible fact that persons have many different aims and goals in terms of which they conceive their true self-actualization? McCloskey is cognizant of this problem. It leads him to affirm that the state's goal is not positive liberty per se, but positive liberty defined by reference to rights. Furthermore, this reference to rights must be included in any adequate conception of positive liberty (McCloskey, 1974, p. 14). Hence the pursuit of capricious or harmful goals cannot be defended, nor should it be supported on liberty grounds.

McCloskey's maneuver still does not remedy the problem of conceptual obfuscation, however. There are any number of ways to enhance the morally legitimate exercise of self-development, and it isn't at all obvious why each of them should be conceptualized in the language of liberty—especially when this strategy begets a terribly cumbersome and largely functionless concept. In addition, and this is a criticism applicable to every positive theory of liberty, to equate freedom with the morally legitimate pursuit of goals departs radically from ordinary usage, according to which liberty is a condition of human action and not an element or dimension thereof. I do not mean, of course, to denigrate the ideals of self-mastery and self-fulfillment. I only mean to question whether they must or should be regarded as ideals of liberty. Can't we say, explain and justify all that needs saying, explaining, and justifying without destroying or compromising valid conceptual distinctions?

S. I. Benn and W. L. Weinstein, whose views I consider next, at one time agreed with me that positive conceptions of liberty ought to be put aside. But in later writings they have moved toward the position of those positive liberals who define liberty in terms of the ability to choose. My principal objective in the next section is to examine the reasons behind their major and, I think, most unfortunate conversion.

VI. Benn and Weinstein

THEIR EARLY VIEWS

In the tenth chapter of the Benn and Peters *The Principles of Political Thought* [9] S. I. Benn attacks political figures who try to reconcile the spread of state regulation with liberty by defining the latter in terms of opportunity or ability. The main trouble with such positive interpretations of liberty, according to Benn, is that they drain the concept of all descriptive meaning. In his words: "If we want freedom to remain significant as a moral demand, we must be prepared to see it rub shoulders with less exalted ideals, like personal security, full employment, and so on, without wanting it to swallow the lot" (Benn and Peters, 1958, p. 249).[10] Benn recommends that liberty be identified with the absence of restraints imposed by the power of other men. This definition enables us to distinguish liberty from other related but distinct values, thereby providing the conceptual framework within which we can intelligently assess the impact of social legislation concerning education, health care, taxation, etc., on human well-being.

While Benn's objective is certainly commendable, his proposed definition of liberty is problematic. An expensive education, job discrimination, physical disability, and personal qualities such as shyness or laziness may on occasion serve as restraints to human behavior, but they are not usually regarded as interferences with social freedom. I have argued all along that only certain kinds of restraints or obstacles are properly thought to render a man socially unfree to act. The important point to note here, however, is that Benn's conception can be amended to meet this objection. This is precisely what I shall do in the next section.

In his 1965 essay "The Concept of Liberty in Nineteenth Century English Political Thought" W. L. Weinstein contends that our everyday language is sufficiently varied and precise to eliminate the need to change the basic, negative meaning of "being free" or to equate it with other things (Weinstein, p. 160). What is its basic meaning? According to Weinstein liberty is the absence of interference or coercion by other human beings (Weinstein, p. 146). Contrasting this definition with other theories of freedom that have been advanced by positive liberals, Weinstein makes the following points: (a) It is a mistake to equate liberty with any kind of power or capacity to act; when we ask whether a man is free to do something, our concern is not with whether he has the power to do it. (b) Nor does the concept of self-development throw any light on what "liberty" means; rather it constitutes one possible goal or purpose of being free (Weinstein, p. 151). (c) Social benefits such as low-cost housing and welfare are means to self-development and therefore will undoubtedly render man's freedom more valuable, but they are not constitutive of his freedom (Weinstein, p. 153). (d) Finally, liberty should not be confused with self-knowledge. A prisoner, after all, might come to know himself well in jail, but this does not entail that he thereby becomes more free (Weinstein, p. 159). Self-knowledge is valuable, not because it increases a man's freedom, but because it enables him to make wiser, more rational choices. Weinstein is surely wise in drawing these distinctions.

At the close of his essay Weinstein briefly discusses a couple of cases where it is, in his mind, difficult to determine whether his definition is applicable. If an oligarchy sets out deliberately to keep the rest of society illiterate by not providing schools, the similarity between this policy and direct legal prohibition goes beyond their achieving the same results. So a good case can be made for accusing the oligarchy of violating men's freedom to attend school. And if X is deliberately weakened or "conditioned" (as in brainwashing) by Y, the resemblance to coercion is so close that we may be justified in calling X less free and not merely less capable of using his freedom (Weinstein, p. 162).

But while there may be doubt whether these cases involve deprivations of freedom as Weinstein defines it, it is clear they do not entail threats to freedom properly conceived. The oligarchy is attempting to deny to the rest of society not the freedom, but the opportunity to receive an education; Y deprives X only of the ability to think for himself. Weinstein's definition needs to be amended in such a way that only certain kinds of interferences and coercion are classified as dangers to freedom. Not all interferences curtail freedom (see the discussion of McCloskey's essay in the last section). Nor does the use of coercion always result in a loss of freedom; persons sometimes pursue activities in spite of warnings or threats not to do so; and even when coercion does work, the expressions "deprivation of will (resolve, determination)" and "deprivation of desire (inclination)" often provide a more accurate description of what it effects.

BENN AND WEINSTEIN'S TURNABOUT

Mass persuasive techniques such as commercial advertising and political propaganda, which aim to manipulate opinion and shape preferences, provide the subject matter of Benn's 1967 article, "Freedom and Persuasion." While admitting that these influences are less successful than many early alarmists of the 1950s suggested, Benn contends they nevertheless do constitute a definite threat to freedom, their subtle, often inconspicuous techniques notwithstanding. But freedom conceived as the absence of interference or restraints by other men is insufficient to account for this threat and for the uneasiness contemporary liberals experience when confronted with it. Advertisers and propagandists do not, after all, restrain or interfere with the consumer; on the contrary, they seek to create a willing accord between the buying public and themselves. Consequently a reexamination of concepts such as liberty and interference is in order. Benn's objective is "to extend the application of the classical concepts of liberalism so that they can function coherently in the discussion of persuasive 'techniques'" (Benn, 1967, p. 260).

The concept of freedom the liberal needs to form his objections to certain of these persuasive techniques is none other than rational self-mastery (Benn, 1967, p. 262), for in many cases commercial advertising and political propaganda make it extremely difficult for the exposed person to make up his own mind concerning different products, issues, and life-styles. Of course not all persuasive techniques jeopardize freedom in this sense. Persuasion by arguments that invite and respond to criticism, for example, is perfectly consistent with a person's determining his own mode of existence in his own way. But there are nonrational persuasive techniques that are not consistent with this value, and Benn devotes much of "Freedom and Persuasion" to suggesting criteria for identifying them.

The basic difficulty underlying Benn's conversion pertains to his belief that the classical concepts of liberalism *must* be reexamined and extended with a view to making them applicable to opinion manipulation. Why is it necessary for the liberal or anyone else bothered by mass persuasive techniques to express his criticisms in terms of liberty—especially when there are other concepts available that more accurately describe the threat posed by these techniques? Surely all we need say is that the widespread use of commercial advertising and political propaganda threatens man's ability to think for himself and consequently makes it difficult for him to realize the full worth of his liberty. The persuasion industry imperils human rationality, not social freedom. Stating the problem in this manner reflects a commitment to conceptual clarity; it preserves the subtleties of political discourse without betraying any liberal principles.

In "Being Free to Act, and Being a Free Man," published in 1971, Benn and Weinstein reject the negative definition of liberty as the absence of coercion or restraints for the following reason. Consider the cases of two men: X cannot purchase eggs because he hasn't enough money; Y does the only thing permitted by law, but it is something he would have done anyway. According to the negative definition, X, having been impeded or restrained from purchasing eggs, must be called unfree to do so, while Y, who is not impeded or restrained, must be considered free to disobey the law. But it is odd to call X unfree to buy eggs, inasmuch as the option of having free eggs was never open to him in the first place (Benn and Weinstein, p. 202). And it is also odd to call Y free to disobey the law, since this option is not really available to him (Benn and Weinstein, p. 197).

These cases suggest to Benn and Weinstein that deciding between available alternatives, not the absence of impediments or restraints, lies at the heart of freedom. Thus they contend that to be free means "to be able to choose among available courses bearing in mind their expected consequences both good and ill" (Benn and Weinstein, p. 198). Freedom should be identified with the nonrestriction of available options (p. 201). This definition enables us to avoid calling X unfree to purchase eggs; charging a price for eggs, although it impedes or restrains X from buying them, does not close any option that once was available. And it enables us to call Y unfree, since the law in question does limit otherwise available courses of action; whether Y would have chosen them or not makes no difference.

The first and most obvious problem with the Benn and Weinstein position is that the two formulations they give of their proposed definition of freedom are not equivalent. It is one thing to say that X has the general ability to choose from available options, and quite another to say that there are no restrictions on these options. The first statement refers to a specific property belonging to X, the second does not. Furthermore neither formulation adequately explains what liberty is. To be *free* in the social sense does not entail having the capacity to choose, nor does this capacity entail social freedom. And there are a number of ways to restrict a man's available options without invading his liberty — e.g., by knocking him unconscious or depriving him of the necessary means to act.

Benn and Weinstein clearly would have been better off had they attempted to amend the standard negative definition of liberty in such a way that the lack of financial resources, for example, would be excluded from the class of impediments or restraints substitutable for the y term in the triadic schema "X is free from y to do z." I will now propose such an amendment, one that will yield, finally, a "proper" account of liberty — of its meaning and its place in the family of basic moral-political concepts.

VII. Liberty Defined

Following Joel Feinberg (1980), we can usefully distinguish four kinds of constraints: (1) negative, which are essentially absences — e.g., the lack of money; (2) positive, which are existing objects, rules, events; (3) internal, which exist within the person; and (4) external, which exist outside the person. "Constraint" denotes, of course, anything that prevents an individual from pursuing a course of action. My suggestion is that we define "liberty" by restricting the scope of the "y" variable to positive, external constraints. To say that X is (socially) unfree to do y means, then, that X is prevented from doing y by the presence or imposition of positive, external constraints. These constraints, by their very presence, close off or eliminate y as an option for X. Finally, we should construe the z variable as ranging over both physical actions, such as walking, and mental activities, such as thinking, imagining, etc.

It seems to me that there are three and only three basic categories of positive external constraints. In the first category are those of a physical, material nature. These include, most obviously, walls, chains, shackles, etc., as well overpowering physical force. In the second category we find constraints of a formal nature. These include rules and regulations of the civil law which, for example, make it impossible for people to get divorces, make out wills, or enter into certain contractual relationships without following stipulated procedures. The third class of positive external constraints includes those uses of moral coercion that preempt X's ability to choose whether or not to do z. Admittedly this kind of extremely effective coercion is rare; in the vast majority of cases a person threatened or intimidated can still choose not to cooperate. But there are occasions (for instance, when X is given no time to think about compliance — he is told to do z immediately or else) that do, I believe, justify claims of unfreedom.

My analysis has some notable implications. For one thing, it implies that the criminal law in and of itself — i.e., considered apart from the question of enforcement — does not curtail individual liberty. What we should say instead, in my view, is that the criminal law aims to deprive individuals of the desire (will, resolve, motivation) to perform the prohibited actions. Lawmakers must hope that the existence of rules with attached sanctions forbidding murder, rape, robbery, etc., will work to reduce crime by producing *internal constraints* to lawless behavior, the most prominent being conscience and fear. Deterrence is a mode of prevention, of course, but it is far less effective than the deprivation of liberty.

Why have so many philosophers and lawyers been disposed to affirm that the criminal law does infringe upon liberty? I believe there are several explanations for this. First, that there is a law against murder, say, does mean that we are not at liberty to kill innocent people just for the fun of it. But "at liberty" here means nothing more than "permission." We should not confuse this concept with that of social freedom. Second, if the criminal law is effectively enforced, then most individuals who do commit offenses will be apprehended and incarcerated. But this shows only that those who exercise their social freedom to break the law will probably suffer a loss of this freedom later on. Finally, some persons bent on violating the law will be caught in the process. Their liberty is curtailed, to be sure, but not by the written law itself.

Construing liberty as the absence of positive external constraints enables us to make a number of useful distinctions among different modes of prevention. Here is a very brief account of the most important among them.

1. The deprivation of *liberty*.
2. The denial or deprivation of *ability*. This most often involves the withholding of knowledge (either practical or theoretical) or the impairment or destruction of an individual faculty.
3. The denial or deprivation of *authority*, where "authority" denotes some form of official permission to act.
4. The denial or deprivation of *power*, where "power" denotes some form of official or unofficial control over persons.
5. The denial or deprivation of *will* (desire, resolve, determination). This mode of prevention is plainly psychological. It occurs through brainwashing, preaching, psychological conditioning, threats, intimidation, and so on.
6. The denial or deprivation of *means*, where "means" designates the financial wherewithal or other material possessions necessary to perform an action.
7. The denial or deprivation of *opportunity*. This can happen in many ways, including 1, 2, and 6. Most frequently, however, it involves a person's not being given the time to do z, not being told about z, not being given adequate consideration for z (where several people have applied to do it), or having to do something else instead. The important point to notice here is that while 1 entails 7, 7 does not entail 1. It is possible to deprive X of the opportunity to do 2 without infringing upon his liberty.

Let us apply this conceptual schematism to a concrete example. Consider how Z might stop B from dating C. He can:

lock B in his room (liberty);
severely injure B (ability);
deny B permission to go out (authority);
convince B that C is a cad (will);
refuse to give B money for gas or the theater (means);
refuse to tell B that C had called (opportunity).

The advantages of this schematism are significant. It promotes or forces an awareness of the fact that there are social values beside liberty that merit our attention and respect. Liberty is not the only thing that matters for human beings. In other words, we ought to realize that the ideal of human flourishing is multifaceted. Furthermore, the schematism is rich, elegant, neat, and substantially congruent with ordinary language, thus satisfying the main desiderata of conceptual analysis (see the introduction). It is the product of a careful, disciplined inquiry and as a result does not suffer the problems of superficiality and oversimplification. Finally my position should facilitate clarity of thought on a number of important issues. For example, it underscores the fact that while every deprivation of liberty limits (but does not altogether destroy) choice, not every limitation or choice constitutes a deprivation of liberty.

The definition defended here is meant only to clarify our understanding of liberty. It cannot serve as a norm for adjudicating conflicting claims to liberty. There are those who would regard this as a real deficiency of my account. But it seems to me that questions concerning the conditions under which social freedom should and should not be interfered with belong to substantive political philosophy and can only be answered by a theory of justice, such as has recently been proposed by John Rawls.

Indeed, in my judgment many of the positive conceptions of liberty defended by philosophers in the past should be construed not as definitions, but as principles constituting criteria for assessing claims to liberty. Consider, for example, the conception of liberty as rational self-mastery. Only confusion results from *identifying* liberty with this value. But it is possible, even credible, to equate rational self-mastery with a goal or end of liberty. Thus we have the principle of justice, that everyone has a prima facie right to achieve rational direction over his life; and this principle can be used, along with others, in resolving disputes concerning the legitimate distribution of liberty. Conceptions of liberty in terms of opportunity should be treated similarly. And, of course, we need to ensure that persons are not subject to arbitrary or purposeless restraints; but again the best way to do this consists not of defining liberty in such a way that only rational restraints can be said to abridge it, but of embodying in principles of justice prohibitions against unfair or pointless infringements upon liberty.

In Section VIII I examine some of the more important analyses of liberty that have appeared since 1971; in Section IX I briefly evaluate the connection between liberty and social-economic policy, a subject of increasing interest among philosophers; and finally I comment on the views of Rawls and Dworkin in Section X.

VIII. Analyses of Liberty in the 1970s

JOEL FEINBERG

Feinberg identifies liberty with the absence of coercion (1973, p. 7). He then distinguishes two forms of coercion: direct force or prevention, such as imprisonment, and the threat of harm backed by enforcement power. I shall henceforth refer to these as physical and moral coercion. In Feinberg's opinion, most uses of moral coercion leave their victims with a choice. They put a price tag on noncompliance and leave it up to the threatened person to decide whether the price is worth paying (Feinberg, 1973, p. 8). But there are cases of overwhelmingly coercive threats, where the alternative to compliance is some unthinkable disaster such as the death of a child. In these cases, Feinberg argues, the victims really have no choice but to comply (1973, p. 7).

How does this distinction bear on the nature of liberty? Is Feinberg saying that liberty ought to be conceived not as the absence of coercion per se, but as the absence of coercion that preempts choice? He never makes this clear to readers of *Social Philosophy*. But in a later piece, "The Interest in Liberty on the Scales," he resolves the uncertainty by claiming that "the interest in liberty as such—as opposed to the various interests we have in doing the things we may be free or unfree to do—in an interest in having as many open options as possible with respect to various kinds of action, coercion, and possession" (Feinberg, 1980, p. 36). Here Feinberg clearly defends what he calls the open option theory of liberty (p. 38), a theory that removes most forms of moral coercion from the class of liberty-limiting restraints.

There are two basic difficulties with Feinberg's account. First, even overwhelmingly coercive threats leave their victims with a choice; we aren't transformed into helplessness by them. They do not make noncompliance impossible for us. And if they do work, it is through the deprivation of will or resolve. Second, the open option theory is open to criticism. It implies that every increase in X's options constitutes an increase in his liberty, but as I have argued there are a good many ways to open up options for X that do not impact on his liberty. Of course we should value having as many choices as possible, but we should also realize that choice and liberty are not interchangeable ideals. What Feinberg should have said is that the interest in liberty is an interest in ensuring that choices are not closed off by positive external constraints. The interest in having as many open options as possible is an interest in human agency itself, or an interest in human flourishing, one (and only one) dimension of which is liberty.

VAN DEN HAAG

Ernest Van den Haag also equates liberty with the absence of coercion, and he defines "coercion" as force or the threat of force or of some deprivation deliberately used to control persons (Van den Haag, 1978, p. 63). This conception, like Feinberg's, suffers from being insufficiently discriminatory. I have argued that most forms of moral coercion, to be successful, must aim to weaken or undermine desire—i.e., they must be the source of internal constraints.

But despite Van den Haag's failure to capture the distinctive idea of liberty, his essay contains many illuminating and useful observations. Here are some of them:

i. It is not a lack of social freedom not to be able to do what nature does not permit anyway (here we should speak of the lack of ability).

ii. Liberty must not be confused with making good use of it—e.g., "Rationality is a prerequisite for making good use of one's freedom, but though helpful in making good use of it, rationality is not freedom" (Van den Haag, 1978, p. 64).

iii. Coercion used in an effort to make people better off should not be defended in the name of liberty. Thus, "parental or governmental restrictions of freedom may be justifiable in terms of the welfare of the purported beneficiary—but we should not describe them as increases in or as implementations of the freedom of the persons restricted" (Van den Haag, 1978, p. 67).

iv. Liberty ought not to be confused with either desirelessness or the fulfillment of desire, for these are psychological states, whereas "liberty" refers to an external matter (or as I would prefer to say, condition) granted or withheld by others (Van den Haag, 1978, p. 68).

v. Poverty does not cause the poor to be less free than the rich. Rather, the poor have less ability (here I would add that they lack the means and consequently many of the opportunities) to enjoy their liberty (Van den Haag, 1978, p. 81).

These perceptive comments clearly reflect Van den Haag's conviction that an exclusive preoccupation with liberty, and the accompanying neglect or disparagement of other social values, invites trouble on many fronts. I share this conviction and applaud Van den Haag's largely successful effort to elaborate upon it.

BERT AND CULVER

The essay "Paternalistic Behavior" by Bert and Culver is another useful contribution to the literature on liberty. The authors utilize distinctions I have urged between liberty and the concepts of ability, means, and opportunity in order to clarify the notion of paternalistic interference. Most of the well-known analyses of paternalism[12] define it in terms of liberty-infringement, but Bert and Culver very persuasively argue that many instances of paternalistic intervention do not curtail liberty. Consider, for example, the following two cases: A knows that B is very depressed, and in order to ensure that B does not take his own life A removes all of the sleeping pills from their home; and A stops B from undertaking some very dangerous action by crippling him. In the first case we have a paternalistic action involving the denial of means and therewith of opportunity, in the second a paternalistic action involving disablement. Through their careful analysis Burt and Culver provide the best argument possible for the principle they themselves invoke, that we must distinguish between the different ways in which behavior can be controlled (Bert and Culver, p. 47).

BERGMANN

Frithjof's Bergmann's *On Being Free* is a stimulating and provocative work that, like Van den Haag's, contains much useful advice for the student of liberty. He maintains, for example, that it is extremely important to proffer a relatively narrow definition of "liberty," one that captures the concept's distinctive function and value (Bergmann, 1977, p. 135). He also argues against comparing a life that is by and large unfree but dreadful in many other ways to one that is by and large free but at the same time advantaged in a number of other ways. Thus the difference between, say, Hitler's Germany and Sweden is not *just* that there is less freedom under the former. Other fundamental differences exist as well, and these ought not to be forgotton (Bergmann, p. 8). Bergmann is here expressing the need for conceptual discrimination. Finally, Bergmann usefully emphasizes the ubiquity of choice even under coercive circumstances: "nothing at all that those who try to coerce us have in their arsenal, nothing in their array of instruments from the deprecating puzzled look to prison and the threat of torture, can ever constitute itself as a final barrier, a wall of sheer impossibility" (Bergmann, p. 70). Even abject slaves and prisoners have some opportunity for choice.

How does Bergmann understand freedom? He considers and then rejects the negative concept of liberty as the absence of obstacles to action, principally on the grounds it cannot be reconciled with the hard fact about choice stated above. Obstacles, in his view, only make actions easier or harder; they do not destroy altogether a person's options (Bergmann, p. 75).

Unfortunately Bergmann fails to differentiate among different kinds of obstacles. Threats, warnings, and other forms of moral coercion do not take away the choice of noncompliance, but the imposition of positive external constraints on X *does* make his performance of certain actions impossible. These are the actions he has been rendered unfree to undertake, notwithstanding the fact that he still has other choices to make. A prisoner has been deprived of the freedom to attend city council meetings — he cannot choose to do this. But of course he can choose whether to eat his meal or not. Bergmann's attempt to repudiate negative liberty is not persuasive, then, since it rests upon the unwarranted premise that all obstacles can be assimilated in their impact on choice to those which make actions easier or harder to perform.

In place of the negative conception of liberty Bergmann proffers an analysis that makes the idea of personal identification with one's self crucial. An action is free, according to him, if the agent identifies with (or sees himself in) the elements from which it flows (Bergmann, p. 37). Freedom is the acting out of one's identity, a kind of self-expression. The unfree person, in turn, is essentially at odds with himself. He suffers a kind of psychic alienation. Bergmann sums up his position nicely in the following passage:

> We have turned away from the envisioning of freedom as an absence, as the smoothing out of obstacles, as the removal of hindrances till the air becomes too thin to breathe, in favor of pursuing a very different goal: that of reaching, making contact with, and even of submitting to the forces of the self, so that they may be expressed and released [Bergmann, p. 90].

To be attuned with oneself is doubtless a worthwhile ideal, but why should we identify it with being free? One very good reason for not doing so is that it flagrantly contravenes common usage, according to which liberty is a condition of agency and not a personal characteristic or property. Another good reason for refusing Bergmann's invitation is that it has some very odd implications. Do we really want to say, for instance, that a person who is being physically compelled to do z is still free as long as he identifies with his being treated in this way (perhaps he has a very poor self-image and therefore considers himself to be a proper object of physical coercion)?

Bergmann has, in my view, confused liberty with several distinct values, including personal integration or integrity, authenticity, individuality, and self-knowledge. Each of these states is important for the intelligent, successful exercise of one's freedom, but they should not be construed as constitutive elements of freedom itself. We can explain and justify the ideal of an integrated, whole personality without appropriating the term "free" to describe it.

STEINER

Like Bergmann, Hillel Steiner correctly maintains that threats do not curtail liberty, since they do not make noncompliance impossible for the threatened person (Steiner, 1975, p. 43). For this same reason offers, however tempting, do not curtail liberty. Steiner also argues, again most persuasively, that liberty should not be equated with the absence of constraints to the fulfillment of desires nor with the absence of constraints to the satisfaction of one's "real" desires (for a criticism of these conceptions see Section I).

The most intriguing and creative part of Steiner's essay consists of his attempt to fashion a new definition of negative liberty in terms of the idea of possession. His argument proceeds as follows. Consider the difference between individual A, who is incarcerated in a cell that happens to contain a mummy case, and individual B, also incarcerated in a cell, but whose plight is worse than A's because he is locked inside the mummy case. We should say that the extent of prevention is greater with respect to B because he can make use of less physical space and fewer material objects than A can. More generally, then, the greater the amount of physical space and/or material objects the use of which is blocked to one person by another, the greater is the extent of the prevention experienced (Steiner, 1975, p. 47).

Steiner next affirms that to act is to occupy portions of physical space and to dispose of material objects. These are the physical components of action. Therefore, my freedom to do z implies that all of the physical components of doing z are simultaneously unoccupied and/or undisposed of by others. Steiner relates this to the concept of possession by defining the latter as the relation between an agent and the portion of physical space he occupies and between an agent and the material objects of which he disposes. So an individual possesses an object when he enjoys exclusive physical control over it—when what happens to it is not subject to someone else's choice (Steiner, p. 47).

Given these premises about prevention, action, and possession Steiner believes we are justified in believing that statements about liberty are reducible to statements about possession. Indeed, liberty *is* the personal possession of physical objects (Steiner, p. 48).

We may want to praise the inventiveness Steiner displays in arriving at this theorem. And we may very well be pleased to see a philosopher attempting to articulate the meaning of liberty in language that is startlingly fresh and unusual compared to past statements of liberalism. But is his position credible? Should we conceive of social freedom as the personal possession of physical objects? Certainly, ordinary language does not support this conception. Nor does common sense, for we ordinarily associate what a person possesses with his means and power (influence) to act, not with his freedom to act. The former are significant factors in determining how valuable someone's freedom is, but they are not commonly thought to be constitutive of that freedom. Poor and powerless people may have unbounded liberty. This fact is difficult to reconcile with Steiner's view.

Where does Steiner go wrong? Very early in the essay he affirms that "an individual is unfree if, and only if, his doing of any action is rendered impossible by the action of another individual" (Steiner, p. 33). Steiner believes that this definition is obviously correct; his possession theorem clearly presupposes it. And this is precisely the problem, for as I have argued all along we ought not to think that every time B makes it impossible for A to do z he has thereby infringed upon A's liberty. There are innumerable ways to prevent A from doing z, and nothing of theoretical or practical significance is gained by collapsing them all together under "deprivation of liberty." On the contrary, such a maneuver is conceptually irresponsible and will inevitably perpetuate careless, slipshod reasoning.

DAY

J. P. Day avers that while offers do not curtail liberty, threats do. His argument is ingenious but not very convincing. Suppose B says to A, "Your money or your life." According to Day, B has deprived A of his liberty in the sense that he has made it impossible for A to do the conjunctive action of keeping his money and staying alive (Day, 1977, p. 259). The difficulty with Day's argument has to do with the notion of a conjunctive action. It seems plain to me that keeping his money and staying alive is not something A does. Rather it constitutes a state of affairs or a condition in which A would like to find himself. Day has not established that threats make their victims unfree to do certain things. He has only shown that threats make certain states of affairs more or less likely to occur. (And they do this by affecting our will or resolve to act.)

Day goes on to investigate the relation between the statements "A is unfree to do z" and "B makes A unable to do z." He asks us to consider three ways in which B can make A unable to walk from L to Y: (1) by imprisoning A; (2) by cutting off his legs; and (3) by breaking his left ankle. We do not hesitate to say, according to Day, that in (1) A has been deprived of his freedom. With respect to (2) we are disposed to say that B deprived A of the ability, not the freedom, to walk from L to Y. But in case (3) we are prepared to allow that A has been deprived of his freedom (Day, p. 264). Day asks why this is so. His answer is that A's inability in (3) (and in [1]) is retrievable, whereas in (2) it is not. We do not think or talk of A's being unfree to do z, unless B has made A unable to do it in such a way that A will once again be able to do it. Hence, Day arrives at the conclusion: A is unfree to do z if, and only if, B makes A retrievably unable to do z (Day, pp. 264–65).

This definition is no more convincing than Steiner's. In fact it is patently unacceptable. It implies, for example, that a prisoner who has absolutely no chance of ever being released cannot be described as unfree. This is the kind of paradox that inevitably results from ignoring the important distinctions among modes of prevention outlined in Section VII. What Day should have said is that cases (2) and (3) both involve a deprivation of ability. The difference between them is the difference between a retrievable and an irretrievable loss of ability. Neither should be conceptualized in terms of liberty.

STERBA

James Sterba offers the following account of what it means to restrict a person's liberty: "Any intentional or unintentional act of commission for which others are morally responsible interferes with a person's life and thereby restricts his liberty, if that act prevents him from doing something he could otherwise do" (Sterba, 1978, p. 119). According to Sterba, then, if A robs B and thereby prevents B from attending a concert he must be described as having restricted B's liberty. Likewise, if A prevents B from attending the concert by assigning him extra chores to do that evening, or by temporarily blinding him, we must say that A has restricted B's liberty. Obviously, this account suffers from needless inflation. It forces us to speak in terms of freedom when concepts like means, opportunity, and ability much more accurately and precisely explain why B cannot attend the concert.

DRAUGHON

W. E. Draughon's principal concern is with judgments of relative freedom. He explicitly acknowledges at the outset that his analyses rely on the subjective standard of how people are likely to feel when placed in different situations. Here are three of his conclusions:

  1. "People who can see either of two films that they want to see but are not allowed to see a third film that they want to see are less free than people who can attend either of two concerts that they want to attend" (Draughon, p. 32).
  2. A person is more free with one acceptable option than if all of his options are unacceptable, and more free still as the utility of that option increases (Draughon, p. 33).
  3. "Although people who do not know that they have unreliable information may feel as free as someone who has reliable information, it seems reasonable to say that they are not as free" (Draughon, p. 36).

Should we accept Draughon's judgments? With respect to 1, the people in the first group might feel more free than those in the second. Perhaps this is all that Draughon means to say, in which case he should have said it! The claim that A (or a group of individuals {A}) is less free than B (or {B}) can only be meaningful if translated to read: A (or {A}) is free to do fewer things than B (or {B}). Finally, the fact that A is not allowed to see a film does not necessarily mean that he is unfree to do so.

With regard to 2, some people might very well feel more free or regard their freedom as being more valuable if they have one acceptable option than if all of their options are ineligible. And as that option becomes more attractive these people might feel even freer. Perhaps this is all that Draughon means to say, but, then, why didn't he? I can see no reason at all for accepting 2 as it stands.

As for 3, the reliability of a person's information will almost certainly determine how wisely or efficiently he will exercise his freedom. Why should we go further, however, and assert some sort of a logical relation between reliability of information and liberty? Common usage does not support such a move, and the principle of conceptual discrimination strongly condemns it.

Draughon concludes his piece by asserting: "one has liberty to the extent that one is able to do, be, become, or think whatever or however one wants to whenever one wants to . . . and to the extent that one is able to carry out one's decision" (Draughon, p. 41). This account of liberty, like most of the other definitions we have discussed, is far too broad. Draughon offers no compelling reason why we ought to accept it, and I have already given several reasons why we should not.

IX. Liberty and Social-Economic Policy

As I mentioned earlier, an increasing number of philosophers are exploring the connection between a commitment to liberty (or the right to liberty) and the justification of various social-economic policies. I now will take a brief look at what some of them say on this important subject.

H. J. McCloskey (1974, p. 25) thinks that "real" freedom requires a great deal of positive social legislation, providing citizens with whatever aids and services they need for moral self-development. Richard Taylor, beginning with the assumption that freedom cannot consist of mere helplessness, argues for a positive conception of liberty as enablement. He then attempts to justify welfare programs on the ground they contribute to this positive freedom (Taylor, 1973, p. 120). Sandra Farganis maintains that the concept of positive freedom allows us to see the women's movement in a new perspective. It forces us to ask, What is it to be a woman? And it concentrates our attention on the steps that women must take, sometimes with the assistance of government, if they are to realize their true selves (Farganis, 1977, p. 66).

The basic difficulty with these and similar accounts of the relation between liberty and government policy is that they all rely on a spurious concept of liberty. I have no quarrel with the values of self-development and self-knowledge. Nor do I wish to denigrate or underestimate the importance of money, health, knowledge, and opportunity to everyone's achieving his distinctively human potential. What I do question, for reasons stated above, is the need for a conceptualization of these "moral truths" that focuses exclusively on liberty. We can make out a much more precise, accurate, and therefore effective argument on behalf of social welfarism by recognizing and respecting differences among fundamental human values. Let us recognize liberty for what it is, not confuse it with other distinct states or conditions.

Proponents of negative liberty usually manage to escape this difficulty, or at least it isn't such a major problem for them. But they do not always set forth a convincing view of the relation between liberty and social-economic policy. William Donnelly, for example, contends that an affluent society's irresponsible failure to ameliorate poverty, illness, and other human evils should be condemned in the language of liberty (Donnelly, 1978, p. 168). Similarly, Joel Feinberg claims that governments which try to reduce the poverty, illness, and other internal constraints that are the products of deliberately imposed but modifiable social arrangements should be praised in the name of freedom (Feinberg, 1973, p. 9).

These conceptualizations are misleading and unnecessary. We can criticize inexcusable government inaction much more perspicuously and therefore much more forcefully by isolating the different human values at stake and by explaining how each is being destroyed or jeopardized by the failure to act. We need to see that liberty, while an extremely important good, is no more important than health, opportunity, income, or knowledge. The state, in its pursuit of the common good, must not unjustly neglect any of these goods. Nor should theorists conceive of them all as different aspects of liberty.

Perhaps the most explicit effort to defend the inclusion of economic factors among liberty-defining constraints is made by Norman Daniels. If I cannot afford to send my children to school, Daniels argues, then I am unfree to do so, because if I do send them they will be sent home by external forces (1977, p. 201).

One of Daniels's aims is to show that welfare legislation can be defended in terms of liberty. Unfortunately his reasoning is blatantly slipshod. If I cannot afford to send my children to school, then what we should say is that I lack the *means* for doing so. A person without the means for doing x will ordinarily not try to do it. If he should try, however, and is forcibly turned back, *then* we should say that his being prevented from doing x by the use of force (not in this instance by the lack of money) constitutes a deprivation of liberty. Daniels confounds these two situations. It is one thing for a person to be prevented from attending school by poverty, quite another for him to be prevented by physical expulsion.

James Sterba is another contemporary philosopher who joins the ranks of Mc-Closkey, Daniels, Taylor, et al., in holding that liberty per se demands much more governmental activity in the form of positive (assistance) legislation than past liberals have realized. Sterba equates an acceptable minimum of liberty with the liberty that is necessary for satisfying the basic needs of all citizens for food, shelter, medical care, and self-development. Sterba tries to clarify this rather opaque assertion by affirming that an acceptable minimum of liberty would provide each citizen with the same liberties, and some of these would in turn enable a person to acquire the goods and services necessary for satisfying his basic needs (Sterba, 1978, p. 120).

This line of reasoning is very obscure indeed: we need to know exactly how Sterba perceives the connection between liberty and the satisfaction of basic needs. Of course liberty itself is a basic need (as are all the primary goods). And of course in order to obtain food, shelter, clothing, etc., persons must have some freedom. But Sterba clearly has something more than these truths in mind, for he immediately begins to talk about liberties to obtain basic needs. Unaccountably he does not explain how we get from liberty to liberties. If we are supposed to understand liberties as positive rights, and this is the most plausible interpretation of Sterba's agrument, then the question still remains how we are supposed to deduce these from an acceptable minimum of liberty. It seems the only way to do this would be to introduce a mediating premise about the value of liberty and the government's duty to guarantee *that*. Needless to say, a much simpler and more direct strategy would be to accept the fundamental principle that governments are obligated to meet the basic needs of all their subjects and deduce from this premise a system of particular rights, including the right to liberty. Whichever of these two routes we take to positive entitlements, the point remains that liberty per se isn't capable of generating them.

Another essay, and the final one I will discuss, that illustrates the futility of trying to squeeze too much from the concept of liberty is E. Loevinsohn's article, "Liberty and the Redistribution of Property." Loevinsohn's argument can be broken down into the following stages:

1. Redistribution schemes of taxation infringe upon the liberty of citizens to decide how to use the products of their labor.

2. Nonredistributive policies also curtail liberty, however, since under them the producers of goods keep the goods for themselves and others are prevented from using or consuming them by the threat of legal penalties.

3. When force or the threat of penalties is used to prevent someone from pursuing some possible course of action, the degree to which his liberty is thereby curtailed depends (other things being equal) on how important the course of action in question is to him" (Loevinsohn, p. 232). So if action x is closed off to you by the use of force, and if x means little to you, then you lose less liberty than would have been the case had x meant a great deal to you.

4. The recipients of goods under the nonredistributive scheme have a greater desire to use or consume them than do the producers.

5. Therefore, to coercively prevent the recipients from using or consuming these goods constitutes a greater curtailment of liberty than is involved in coercively preventing the producers from doing so.

6. Therefore, the redistributive alternative is better, judged by the standard of liberty.

Loevinsohn's argument turns essentially on premise (3). Should we accept it? I think the answer is clearly no, for it confuses the extent to which a person's liberty is curtailed with the very different question of how important a curtailment of liberty is to that person — how much it matters to him. The former is a conceptual-logical issue, the latter a psychological one. One of Loevinsohn's own examples illustrates my point. Suppose Y is prevented from drinking at his favorite spring, while X is also prevented from drinking at a spring but it really does not matter to him which spring he drinks from. Loevinsohn asserts that Y's liberty is more significantly curtailed than X's, but this is a nonsequitur. All that follows from the example is that Y *suffered more* from the interference and, therefore, had to endure a greater *emotional loss* than X did.

It should by now be obvious that arguments for any kind of welfare state will have to go well beyond the requirements of liberty itself. Indeed, such arguments might well have to include an attempt at justifying the loss of liberty that results from compulsory redistribution.

X. Rawls and Dworkin

John Rawls's *A Theory of Justice* and Ronald Dworkin's *Taking Rights Seriously* are two highly influential works that aim (in part) to strengthen the philosophy of liberalism. Rawls develops and defends a liberal theory of justice, Dworkin a liberal theory of law.

Rawls correctly observes that (a) the general description of liberty must always specify who is free (or not free) from this or that constraint (or set of constraints) to do (or not to do) so and so (Rawls, 1971, p. 202); (b) things like poverty, ignorance, and lack of means diminish the worth of liberty, not liberty itself (p. 204); (c) disagreements relating to the values of different liberties can only be settled by a theory of justice (p. 202). But Rawls mistakenly believes that legal duties and prohibitions as well as coercive influences arising from public opinion and social pressure deserve to be counted among the constraints which do limit one's liberty (Rawls, p. 202). As I have argued, only certain kinds of laws are properly deemed infringements upon social freedom, while public opinion and social pressure can undermine a person's will or resolve, but not his liberty, to act. Rawls's conception of liberty needs to be qualified in much the same way as did Benn and Weinstein's early definitions.[13]

Dworkin distinguishes two concepts of liberty. There is liberty as license, which he (unhappily in my view) equates with the degree to which a person is free from legal or social constraints to do what he wants; and there is liberty as independence, which he identifies with the status of a person as an independent and equal being, not subservient to others (Dworkin, 1977, p. 262). Dworkin does not explicitly criticize the former concept, but he does make it clear that he prefers the latter. Indeed, he argues that the right to independence or equality is *the* single most fundamental right we possess, while the longstanding belief in a right to liberty as license is ludicrous (Chapter 12).

The trouble with Dworkin's position is, of course, that independence or equality ought not to be seen as a concept of liberty at all. This is not to say that independence and equality are frivolous or insignificant values. It is to say, however, that we can best formulate criticism of laws that jeopardize them by calling them what they are, not confusing them with other, distinct goods. Dworkin should have spent more time constructing a viable conception of negative freedom. Then he would have seen that there is most definitely a right to liberty.

Dworkin believes that Mill's *On Liberty* promotes liberty as independence (Dworkin, p. 263). I have no doubt that Mill does argue for human individuality and equality, but he also argues for negative liberty. *On Liberty* is full of talk about constraints, impediments, compulsion, etc. One of Mill's great strengths is that, unlike Dworkin, he does not confuse liberty with other basic values.

Notes

1. Geoffrey Marshall. "Viewpoint," *Times Literary Supplement,* May 23, 1980, p. 580.
2. W. B. Gallie, "Essentially Contested Concepts," *Proceedings of the Aristotelian Society* 56 (1956): 167–98.
3. See Berlin's introduction to his *Four Essays on Liberty* (Oxford, 1969).
4. On this point I am in agreement with Marshall Cohen's criticism of Berlin. See his "Berlin and the Liberal Tradition," *The Philosophical Quarterly* 10 (1961): 216–28.
5. Here I follow the argument of D. P. Dryer, "Freedom," *The Canadian Journal of Economics and Political Science* 30 (1964): 444–48.
6. Strictly speaking, Y's making it punishable for X not to do x deprives X of the freedom of choice to do x only if (a) X knows of the punishment Y has planned for him in case he does not do x; (b) X knows or believes he will fall victim to this punishment if he fails to do x; or (c) this punishment is so severe for X that he can no longer regard the alternatives to not doing x as viable.
7. Here again I would explicate punishability in the manner of note 6.
8. In my 1973 piece I devoted Section V to a critical analysis of D. P. Dryer's essay, "Freedom," and Section VI to a study of C. W. Cassinelli's work *Free Activities and Interpersonal Relations.* Considerations of space have forced me to eliminate these discussions from the present work.
9. In the preface the authors, S. I. Benn and R. S. Peters, state that the political ideas advanced in their work are Benn's and the moral ideas, Peters's. They also make it clear there is no substantial disagreement between them over any of these ideas.
10. The emphasis on the importance of conceptual discrimination in political theory, so marked here, also finds expression in Benn's 1964 "Some Reflections on Political Theory and Behavioral Science," *Political Studies* 12: 237–42. In this later essay Benn writes that the work of clarification that has to be done in the language of politics "should aim to show how confusions result from the failure to make distinctions" (pp. 241–42). And making the proper distinctions between freedom and other related but distinct values requires that one preserve the subtleties of political discourse. It is regrettable that in his more recent writings Benn comes to defend a conception of freedom that does not preserve these subtleties.
11. Of course these modes do overlap. For example, by depriving X of the means necessary to do z I may also destroy his desire to do it. But this fact does not lessen the importance of recognizing the genuine differences between 1 through 7.
12. The classic contemporary essay is of course Gerald Dworkin's "Paternalism" in R. Wasserstrom, ed., *Morality and the Law* (Belmont, Calif.: Wadsworth, 1971), pp. 107–26.
13. As regards Rawls's thesis that liberty can only be restricted for the sake of liberty, H.L.A. Hart has persuasively argued that it is only credible if "liberty" is construed in an unacceptably broad way to include the imposition of harm and suffering on persons. Otherwise the thesis has the absurd implication that I may not be physically constrained from assaulting my neighbor. See Hart's essay "Rawls on Liberty and its Priority," in the Daniels volume.

Bibliography

Benn, S. I. 1964. "Some Reflections on Political Theory and Behavioral Science." *Political Studies* 12: 237–42.
_____ . 1967. "Freedom and Persuasion." *Australasian Journal of Philosophy* 45: 259–75.
Benn, S. I., and Peters, R. S. 1958. *The Principles of Political Thought.* New York: Free Press.
Benn, S. I., and Weinstein, W. L. 1971. "Being Free to Act, and Being a Free Man." *Mind* 80: 194–211.
Bergmann, Frithjof. 1977. *On Being Free.* Notre Dame, Ind.: University of Notre Dame Press.
Berlin, Isaiah. 1958. *Two Concepts of Liberty.* Oxford: Oxford University Press.
_____ . 1969. *Four Essays on Liberty,* Oxford: Oxford University Press.
Bert, B., and Culver, C. 1976. "Paternalistic Behavior." *Philosophy and Public Affairs* 6: 45–67.
Bowie, N., and Simon, R. 1977. *The Individual and the Political Order.* Englewood Cliffs, N.J.: Prentice-Hall.
Cassinelli, C. W. 1966. *Free Activities and Interpersonal Relations.* The Hague: Martinus Nijhoff.
Cohen, Marshall. 1960. "Berlin and the Liberal Tradition." *Philosophical Quarterly* 10: 216–28.

Daniels, Norman. 1977. "Equal Liberty and Unequal Worth of Liberty." In N. Daniels, ed., *Reading Rawls*. New York: Basic Books. Pp. 253–81.

Day, J. P. 1977. "Threats, Offers, Law, Opinion, and Liberty." *American Philosophical Quarterly* 14: 257–72.

Dilman, Ilham. 1961–1962. "The Freedom of Man." *Proceedings of the Aristotelian Society* 62: 39–62.

Donnelly, W. 1974. *The Terms of Political Discourse*. Toronto: D. C. Heath and Co.

Donnelly, W. E. 1978. "Liberty: A Proposed Analysis." *Social Theory and Practice* 5: 29–44.

Dryer, D. P. 1964. "Freedom." *The Canadian Journal of Economics and Political Science* 30: 444–48.

Dworkin, Ronald. 1977. *Taking Rights Seriously*. Cambridge: Harvard University Press.

Farganis, Sandra. 1977. "Liberty: Two Perspectives on the Women's Movement." *Ethics* 88: 62–73.

Feinberg, Joel. 1973. *Social Philosophy*. Englewood Cliffs, N.J.: Prentice-Hall.

_____ . 1980. *Rights, Justice, and the Bounds of Liberty*. Princeton: Princeton University Press.

Gill, John. 1971. "The Definition of Freedom." *Ethics* 82: 1–20.

Kaufman, A. S. 1962. "Professor Berlin on 'Negative Freedom.'" *Mind* 71: 241–43.

Loevinsohn, E. 1977. "Liberty and the Redistribution of Property." *Philosophy and Public Affairs* 6: 226–39.

MacCallum, G. 1967. "Negative and Positive Freedom." *The Philosophical Review* 76: 312–34.

McCloskey, H. J. 1965. "A Critique of the Ideals of Liberty." *Mind* 74: 483–508.

_____ . 1974. "Liberalism." *Philosophy* 49: 13–32.

Oppenheim, Felix. 1961. *Dimensions of Freedom*. New York: St. Martin's Press.

Parent, W. A. 1974. "Some Recent Work on the Concept of Liberty." *American Philosophical Quarterly* 11: 149–67.

Pennock, J. R., and Chapman, John. 1972. *Coercion*. New York: Atherton Press.

Rawls, John. 1971. *A Theory of Justice*. Cambridge: Harvard University Press.

Spitz, David. 1961. "The Nature and Limits of Freedom." *Dissent* 8: 78–83.

Steiner, Hillel. 1975. "Individual Liberty." *Proceedings of the Aristotelian Society* 75: 33–50.

Sterba, James. 1978. "Neo-Libertarianism." *American Philosophical Quarterly* 15: 115–21.

Stigler, George. 1978. "Wealth, and Possibly Liberty." *Journal of Legal Studies* 7: 213–17.

Taylor, Richard. 1973. *Freedom, Anarchy, and the Law*. Englewood Cliffs, N.J.: Prentice-Hall.

Van den Haag, E. 1978. "Liberty: Negative or Positive." *Harvard Journal of Law and Public Policy* 1: 63–87.

Weinstein, W. L. 1965. "The Concept of Liberty in Nineteenth Century English Political Thought." *Political Studies* 13: 145–62.

White, D. M. 1970. "Negative Liberty." *Ethics* 81: 185–204.

PART VI

Art and Imagination

———————◆———————

chapter 10

Some Recent Work on Imagination

LILLY-MARLENE RUSSOW

The topic of imagination is one of the odd subjects which almost seems to disappear for long periods of time. It has attracted the attention of scattered historical figures from Aristotle to Kant; but since Ryle addressed himself to the problem of mental images, the contemporary literature on imagination has revolved mainly around a few narrowly defined issues. Recently, however, there has been a surge of interest in imagination, a development that is welcome for several reasons.

First, imagination is part of the mental life of most people and, as such, deserves to be considered a legitimate topic in philosophy of mind. Thus, one reason for investigating imagination might be a desire to show how it could fit into the broader context of debates about the general nature of mind and mental states. Ryle's attempts to do this are familiar by now; more recently, D. M. Armstrong* and D. C. Dennett (in *Content and Consciousness*) have also discussed imagination within the framework of specific theories of mind. This sort of project seems especially worthwhile in light of the fact that imagination seems to be a paradigm of a mental event in its most troublesome form. There is an apparent lack of publicly observable phenomena or behavior that might be reliably associated with imagining. In addition, the description of the object of imagination — what we are aware of — raises many difficult questions, especially for materialist theories of mind. Finally, imagination embodies in a clear way all the most important features of an intentional act of consciousness: when we imagine, we always imagine *something,* but the object imagined is usually not present, and may not really exist at all. For all these reasons, imagination ought to be recognized as an important topic in philosophy of mind, and deserves the attention it is once again beginning to attract.

In addition to the interest that imagination generates for its own sake, many of the specific problems that are associated with imagination also lead to a renewed demand for a coherent analysis of imagination. The issue of mental images may be the first such topic to come to mind, but the problem of separating and connecting the many different senses of the world "imagine," as well as questions about how reference to the object which is imagined is determined, also supply good reasons for wanting to investigate the topic of imagination. Although it is not possible to discuss all the major issues related to imagination in this paper, there are many such important questions covered in the works included in the concluding bibliography.

---

*When discussing general positions or concerns rather than specific claims, I shall restrict the reference to the name of the relevant philosopher; full references can be found in the bibliography. When specific claims are attributed to a writer, page numbers to the appropriate work will be found in the text.

I. Mental Images

Of all the doctrines to have come under fire from modern philosophy of mind, the idea that we see mental pictures seems to be one of the hardest to get rid of. Despite numerous attacks by philosophers from Ryle to Dennett, there are still many arguments to be found in defense of mental images; the issue has by no means been decided.

The arguments in support of mental images can be classified roughly into two groups. The first sort of approach tries to present images in a theory-neutral sort of way; thus, one can find claims about mental images that are supposed to be independent of any particular theory about what imagination (or mental events in general) is. For example, Arthur Danto tries to argue, in "Concerning Mental Pictures," on the basis of "facts" about imagination—his introspective reports—that there must be mental images, and that any theory of imagination must account for these images. He claims that this description is neutral with respect to theories of mind or imagination, and that it is more generally a "non-philosophical" and "non-theoretical" claim (Danto, 1958, p. 19). One problem with this sort of position is that it is not at all clear that these claims really are theory-neutral. Descriptions of imagination that involve reference to mental images, or idioms that imply the existence of mental images, may be unduly influenced by the vocabulary and accepted phrases of the language we speak or by the accepted "common-sense" view of imagination.

A more sophisticated version of this sort of argument also tries to show that any adequate theory of imagination must accept mental images, but does so without assuming that introspection provides direct evidence of the existence of mental images. Instead, this sort of argument points to objectively established facts about imagination, and argues that the only way to account for such facts is to admit mental images into one's analysis of imagination. The facts cited in such an argument may vary: Lawrie, for example, is one of several who use psychological data about eidetic imagery to support his conclusion that imagination must involve seeing mental images. In a slightly different context, Fodor draws on a wide variety of psychological experiments to argue that certain kinds of thinking must involve "iconic" inner representations, i.e., images. Others, like M. J. Baker, base their arguments on the similarity of imagination to perception.

There are, of course, attempts to counter this last tactic by showing how the similarity between imagination and perception might be preserved, admitted, or even explained, without admitting the existence of mental images. In response to these arguments in favor of mental images, Gareth Matthews has offered a clever argument to the effect that a similarity between two activities does not entail a similarity between the objects of the activity. Indeed, the similarity between an act of imagining and one of perceiving does not even allow us to infer the need for an object of imagination at all. Following the same sort of line, Lowell Kleiman has argued that even though imagining is a kind of seeing, we are not thereby committed to positing some odd sort of image in the mind's eye to explain how this is possible. The sense of "seeing" involved in this latter claim is a bit obscure; in order to avoid this problem, a more recent article (Russow, "Towards a Theory of Imagination") argues that the "perceptual feel" of imagination can be accounted for without mental images, and without collapsing imagination and perception into one activity.

The major objection to the strategy employed by this first general type of argument for mental images is that the status of mental images is at best established only as long as no theory of imagination succeeds in explaining the facts cited without recourse to mental images. Thus, if one develops a theory that can adequately account for the relevant psychological data, the similarity of imagination to perception, and all of the other facts about imagination usually associated with mental images, the arguments in favor of mental images no longer carry any weight. For that reason, some supporters of mental images prefer a different approach to this issue.

This second way of defending mental images is more complex. It involves the construction of a theory of imagination that accepts mental images. Thus, Hannay (*Mental Images: A Defence* and "To See a Mental Image") is but one example of a philosopher who defends mental images by trying to show that his analysis of imagination as seeing mental images is the best possible account of that phenomenon. On a less ambitious scale, Ishiguro and Dilman, among others, use a less reified form of mental images as part of an analysis of imagination.

Several philosophers have directly attacked the view of mental images presented in these theories. For example, O. Hanfling casts serious doubt on Ishiguro's attempt to provide a less mysterious and objectionable account of mental images. Ishiguro has suggested that mental images might function representationally—that is, they might be images *of* something—without having any real properties of their own. Hanfling labels this the "drop-out" theory of images, and correctly argues that there is no way, given Ishiguro's analysis, of explaining how images come to be images of one particular thing rather than another (Hanfling, 1969, p. 168).

One might extend this criticism of Hanfling's by pointing out more general problems that affect image-theories of imagination. It has often been noted that such theories seem notably unsuccessful at explaining exactly what images are supposed to be, what sort of properties they are supposed to have, how we are aware of them, and how they function. All of this often prevents an image-theorist from offering an adequate account of the activity of imagining; the details are too vague. Image-theories, at least the ones mentioned here, may not be able to explain these things simply because even the best-developed theories often fail to specify what we are aware of when we are aware of an image. To mention just one specific result of this general vagueness: unless we know more about the properties of an image, we will be unable to explain why an awareness of such an image should be like *seeing* a physical object, rather than like thinking about it in some more abstract way.

Hannay is one of the few defenders of mental images who avoids this particular objection, but he does so at the cost of pushing the whole problem one step back. In his theory, images are purported to have properties like colors and shapes, but it is still left unclear how images in the mind could be the sort of thing that can be colored. Until this is clarified, we may have a definition of "mental image," but we do not yet have an adequate theory of imagination, or even a particularly clear idea of what sort of thing could satisfy the proposed definition.

Another line of attack has been proposed. D. C. Dennett, in "Two Approaches to Mental Images," has argued that many philosophical discussions of mental images are the result of a conflation of two different, legitimate approaches, the result being an illegitimate account that rests on an equivocation on "image." The first legitimate approach is a scientific one, which treats images as the possible causes of the beliefs we form when we imagine. The second alternative is the phenomenological approach, which treats the image merely as an intentional object—hence makes no claims at all about its ontological status—and tries to piece together a description of the object of our beliefs and reports, taking our beliefs as definitive of *that,* but with no special status as to the actual mechanism of imagination. Any theory that is concerned with the objects of our beliefs, that takes the beliefs as indicative of what an image must be, and that also makes ontological claims about the real existence of such images on the basis of those beliefs, confuses the two approaches. This "spurious *third* approach to mental images . . . tries to treat mental images as both incorrigibly known and causally efficacious" (Dennett, 1978, p. 186).

One might well object to Dennett's implication that anything which does not match one of the two sanctioned approaches must therefore result from a conflation of the two and must be "spurious." He has not, for example, made room for a conceptual analysis of imagination, which may or may not discover that images form an integral part of the activity of imagintion. But this, like the previous difficulties with mental images, points to the need for a theory of imagination, without which a proper analysis of mental images, or an argument for or against mental images, is hopelessly incomplete.

A promising line of argument that has not yet been mentioned is the one generally known as the "adverbial theory of images": the view that having a vivid image, for example, is nothing over and above imagining *vividly*. This sort of interpretation has been defended by J. Douglas Rabb and Robert Audi, but, as Rabb points out, this position seems compatible with, if not implicit in, anti-imagist accounts such as the one advanced by Squires. One interesting version of this analysis of image-reports is offered by Jonathan Bennett; in the course of a discussion of Berkeley's and Locke's theories of ideas, he devotes a few pages to the problem of images. There, he suggests that "I have an image of a man," ought to be analyzed as "I am significantly like the way I am when I see a man and recognize him as a man." Although Bennett's analysis does not employ the same terminology as Rabb's or Audi's, it would seem that it is still a variation of the adverbial approach, one that emphasizes how far removed from the traditional image-theory this approach really is.

The adverbial theory is carried even further in the last group of arguments about images to be considered in this section. In phenomenological analyses of imagination, such as those developed by Ehman and Casey (and others mentioned in Section IV), the image is seen primarily as a *way* of grasping an object. As Sartre indicates, on this view it would be misleading to think of an image as a "thing" at all. These theories seem to use the phrase "mental image" while eschewing any tendency to reify parts of the act of imagining. For that reason, despite references to images, it seems misleading to classify these theories of imagination as image-theories at all.

II. *Mental Images and Theories of Cognition*

In addition to investigations of mental images in the context of the activity of imagining, there are other frameworks within which mental images have recently become an important issue. Specifically, serious questions have been raised about whether or not thinking, storing and processing information, drawing inferences, and other mental activities show signs of involving mental images. While such questions often do not directly consider the activity of imagining, the resulting perspective on mental images will clearly have some effect on considerations about imagination.

Arguments about images in cognitive activity often straddle the line between philosophy and cognitive psychology; even those that are clearly philosophical occasionally draw on psychological data. Thus, Sober is basically concerned with how a person might represent information to himself, what sorts of representations seem to be used, and whether image-representations might be reduced to some linguistic form of encoding. Most of his arguments are concerned with strictly philosophical issues, but he also draws on certain psychological experiments to support his conclusion that some representations are images and cannot be reduced to linguistic formats.

Many more psychological experiments, often having to do with problem-solving and information-processing, are cited by Jerry Fodor in order to justify the claim that certain kinds of cognitive activity involve mental images, or iconic, nondiscursive representations of information. His discussion is unusually complete, in that he not only draws a conclusion on the basis of certain experimental data, but, like Sober and Howell, also considers some of the standard philosophical puzzles about the nature of images; in addition, he draws on these resources to critique the analyses offered by psychologists of the relevant data. His conclusion is that images *simpliciter* cannot function as representations in the required way, but that some sorts of thinking do require iconic or nondiscursive representations; hence, he suggests that the image is always accompanied by a description that determines what the image is an image of, what it represents, and other factors about the information conveyed by the image (Fodor, 1975, pp. 190-91). In sum, Fodor argues that "images under a description are often the vehicle of internal representation" (p. 192).

Other works in this area are more unambiguously psychological. Some, like Simon's article, are based on fairly detailed analyses of specific experiments, and provide a great deal of information that is also relevant to any philosophical discussion of imagination. Others, like Neisser's article, are more abstract and theoretical, yielding some insight into how a psychologist approaches the issues of mental images and imagining. Finally, some attention has been paid to information processing in computer models; some important Artificial Intelligence work on mental images is discussed by Pylyshyn. All these studies provide useful background for more strictly philosophical discussions of mental images.

III. Reference in Imagination

The problem of reference in imagination—what it is that makes something an act of imagining x rather than y—is often associated with the question of what it is that makes something an image of x. In general, two factors seem relevant to both these concerns: resemblance or similarity, and intentions.

E. J. Furlong, for example, argues that the similarity of imagining x to seeing x determines that we are imagining x rather than y; otherwise, our act would have resembled the act of perceiving y. This response to questions about reference raises many new questions about how the two acts are similar, and what accounts for that similarity.

In addition to the vagueness about the exact nature of the similarity, one can reasonably expect that such an analysis will have difficulty dealing with certain cases of imagining objects that resemble something else. For example, this analysis of reference would not allow one to claim that one is imagining John rather than his identical twin brother, Jack. More importantly, it may run into the familiar empiricist problem of distinguishing an act of imagining any triangle, or no specific triangle, from that of imagining *this* equilateral triangle, which is green on a white background, small, and balanced on its point.

In order to avoid some of these problems, Hanfling and Williams propose more complex solutions, both of which hinge on distinctions between imagining and visualizing. For Hanfling, the object which is *visualized* is identified in terms of its resemblance to a perceived object, but both agree that the object of an act of *imagining* is determined by the imaginer's intentions, what he sets out to imagine.

In a similar vein, Fodor has—as noted in Section II—argued that some cognitive activities contain an image under a description. The image itself is iconic or pictorial, but it is the description that determines what the image represents (Fodor, 1975, pp. 184-91). With all these accounts, it is instructive to consider how far the description or intention might take over the work of the image—how far removed the resulting analysis is from merely having an image—before the image itself begins to fulfil no discernable useful function and the whole account begins to look more like a descriptive analysis of imagination.

Two other approaches to the problem of reference should also be mentioned. D. R. Cousin, in "On the Ownership of Images," suggests that a causal account of our beliefs might be relevant to questions of what we imagine. Norvin Richards offers a multifaceted analysis of reference based on an extended analogy between the way an act of imagination refers to its object and the way in which a picture can be said to represent something—a relation that involves considerably more than resemblance. Both accounts seem to have the consequence that an imaginer might be unable to tell at all what he is imagining, or might be mistaken about what he takes to be the object of his imagination.

In actuality, the correct solution to the problem of explaining how an act of imagination is directed toward its object will probably depend in part on an adequate analysis of what the whole act of imagining is like, and how to explicate what we do when we imagine. Given the dubious status of mental images, any analysis of reference that depends on resemblance must be prepared to specify precisely in what respect imagination is similar to perception. Similarly, questions need to be answered about the exact nature of an intention to imagine x, and what that involves. An adequate general theory of imagination seems like the proper first step toward answering such questions in a way that would provide a foundation for dealing with the issue of reference in imagination.

IV. Theories of Imagination

Many specific problems associated with imagination, such as the ones discussed here, eventually lead to broader questions about the nature of imagination and the possibility of formulating a more comprehensive theory or analysis of imagination. Conversely, an adequate theory of imagination should be able to explain puzzles such as the link between imagination and perception, or how an act of imagination refers to its object; and, in general, must be prepared to deal with the specific issues that arise in the context of imagination.

It is not surprising, then, to find that some theories of imagination arise directly out of a desire to address a specific problem. One such example is found in Dennett's *Content and Consciousness,* in which a desire to eliminate mental images seems to be at least part of the motive for developing a theory of imagination. On the other hand, a general theory of imagination can spark renewed interest in a more specific issue: Hannay's theory of imagination has inspired new debates about the status of mental images.

Although many theories might be discussed here, I shall, somewhat arbitrarily, restrict the discussion to four examples. First, I shall examine Dennett's attempt to explain imagining in a way that will allow him to accommodate it without strain in his general analysis of mental states. From there, I shall move on to a brief consideration of Hannay's theory of imagination; although it has already been mentioned in Section I, in the context of mental images, I wish now to consider its merits more generally as a theory of imagination. Finally, I will also offer a few comments about Roger Scruton's analysis of imagination as presented in *Art and Imagination,* and Mary Warnock's treatment of a similar approach to imagination in *Imagination.* Although these four theories have been selected because they represent widely divergent views on key issues, they all share a concern for the overriding question "What is going on when we imagine something?" rather than a more-limited focus on one specific aspect of imagination.

D. C. DENNETT

Dennett's theory of imagination, as put forward in Chapter VII of *Content and Consciousness,* is acknowledged to be an adaptation of J. M. Shorter's position. Dennett moves beyond Shorter's analysis, however, and focuses on the fact that imagination presents a challenge to materialist theories of mind, including his own.

The brief comments on imagination seen from what Dennett calls "the sub-personal level" seem neither helpful nor particularly relevant; an attack on the view that neurons form little pictures at the back of the brain strikes one as a straw man argument. It is only on "the personal level" that we are given an interesting account of what

Dennett thinks we do when we imagine something. In order to avoid accepting mental images, Dennett advocates Shorter's contention that imagining ought to be understood along the lines of depicting or describing rather than an observing of mental pictures. Actually, Dennett's position here is even more radical than Shorter's. Shorter finally concludes that the "logic" of imagining is halfway between that of depicting and seeing a picture; by contrast, Dennett discusses only depicting and describing, with emphasis on the latter.

The analysis of imagination that Dennett wishes to defend, then, is that "imagining is depictional or descriptional, not pictorial" (Dennett, 1969, p. 135). Such a view has a number of advantages: no mental images need be posited, and one can easily account for the incompleteness or vagueness of some of the things we imagine without resorting to an appeal to "fuzzy pictures." Some descriptions simply contain more information than others, so some instances of imagining will be more detailed than others. Nevertheless, some objections to this theory must be considered.

The first, and perhaps most important, objection to Dennett's theory is that this analysis sidesteps some of the central questions about imagination. Dennett takes note of the link between imagination and perception when he adds to Shorter's account the stipulation that imagination is describing *limited to a certain point of view* (Dennett, 1969, pp. 135-36) but this does not explain the link. We can understand why perception is limited to a certain point of view (why, to use Dennett's example, we don't usually see both the inside and the outside of a barn at the same time), and can explain these limitations in terms of the location of our eyes, orientation of the head, paths of light rays, etc. Likewise, we can explain why pictures present things from a certain perspective or point of view. If imagination does not involve anything like seeing or seeing a picture, Dennett has not yet explained why the same limitations should affect imagination. Pointing out this similarity was perceptive, but only makes it harder for Dennett to give a convincing account of imagination simply in terms of descriptions, which have no such limitations inherent in them. Since the perspectival quality of imagination, and more generally the similarity of imagination to perception, seem to support image theories of imagination, and since Dennett has little to offer in place of such a conclusion, his analysis ultimately fails to convince us that we can dispense with mental images.

Another criticism of Dennett's analysis is based on the common sense observation that I can describe some things better than I can imagine them, and vice versa. I can describe in detail the inner workings of my car's engine, but my image of a running engine is considerably poorer and less detailed than my descriptions. On the other hand, I can imagine a favorite bit of music, or the smell of baking bread, much better than I can describe them. Neither of these should be the case if imagining is describing.

ALASTAIR HANNAY

In contrast to Dennett's attempt to explain imagination without admitting mental images, we have already seen that Hannay's whole theory is predicated on an acceptance of the claim that we do see mental images. Thus, he begins the development of his theory by stating that images have "pictorial properties" which are "seen materially, not intentionally" (*Mental Images,* p. 163). We are also told that "to be a pictorial property is at least to be seen as part of a picture, as having certain representational value" (ibid.). This much seems clear: Hannay is claiming (a) that mental images have certain properties in their own right, (b) that we are directly aware of those properties — we materially see them in much the same sense that we see the properties of the paper in front of us — although the image may also have properties that we are not aware of, and (c) that pictorial properties are those properties in virtue of which x can be an image of, can represent, y.

In addition to these points, Hannay further clarifies the idea of a pictorial property, and hence his conception of images which have such properties, by noting that

> it seems reasonable to suppose that pictorial properties must be composed of elements that are not pictorial—for example particles of color pigment in the case of physical representations—and that pictorial properties therefore also stand in the non-pictorial relation of 'being composed of' to these elements [Hannay, 1971, p. 164].

Many theories agree with Hannay's on this point; i.e., they accept the idea that images have properties of their own—as distinct from properties which they are said to have merely in virtue of their being images of something with those properties—in virtue of which they represent the object being imagined. Or, to use Hannay's terminology, the image "has determinate properties of its own," and "in virtue of some of those properties, [the image] presents the appearance of that thing [the object which is imagined]" (Hannay, 1971, p. 172).

We are faced with two alternatives at this point. We can either admit, as Hannay seems to do, that images have colors and shapes just as physical objects do, or we might argue that words like "red" or "round" are used analogously when applied to images. In either case, awareness of the properties of an image is assumed to be similar in "phenomenological feel" to the perception of the same or corresponding properties of physical objects. Both of these alternatives encounter serious difficulties.

The ascription of a property such as "round" to something usually entails more than the claim that the thing looks round, and it seems impossible to preserve the distinction between *being* round and *looking* round if we take the position that mental images really are round in the same sense that pennies are round. If, on the other hand, we rest our case on the position that properties of images are merely analogous to properties of physical objects, we run the real risk of trying to defend a view that is overly sketchy—a view that is not complete enough to answer our questions about imagination in general.

ROGER SCRUTON

The third theory to be considered is the one defended by Roger Scruton in *Art and Imagination*. In a fashion, his theory can be seen as an attempted compromise between a theory such as Dennett's and an image theory of the sort defended by Hannay. Here, imagining is again analyzed as a descriptional form of thought, but it is also distinguished from "having an image," which is treated as another legitimate phenomenon to be investigated.

According to Scruton, imagining something is to be analyzed as entertaining an unasserted thought about that thing; usually the thought is a description appropriate to, but not believed true of, the object of imagination (Scruton, 1974, p. 98). Although he does think that imagination and having an image are closely related activities, Scruton goes beyond the characterization of imagination just summarized when he attempts to explain what "having an image," "picturing," or "imaging" involves. Noticing that an image shares many of the characteristics of sensations, e.g., intensity and exact duration, Scruton concludes that "these features . . . seem to show that imagery, like sensory-experience, lies across the boundary between thought and sensation." (p. 101). However, the similarity between imagination and sensation is taken to be "irreducible" (p. 104) and presumably also unanalyzable.

Scruton must maintain this sort of distinction between imagining and imaging in order to avoid the sort of difficulties that beset most other descriptional theories of imagination (e.g., Shorter's or Dennett's): the observation that we can describe some things better than we can imagine them, and vice versa. Scruton suggests that the relevant point here is analogous to Bertrand Russell's distinction between knowledge by acquaintance and knowledge by description (pp. 105-6). Although he is somewhat vague, it seems, on the basis of the examples Scruton gives, that imagining without having an image is like mere knowledge by description, whereas having an image or imagining by means of an image becomes more like knowledge by acquaintance.

Given this sort of approach to the problem of explaining the difference between imagining and describing, one might expect Scruton to rely on the same sort of distinction between imagining with and without the aid of images to explain other similarities between some instances of imagining and perception, the differences between imagination and more abstract forms of thought, and the "perceptual feel" of imagination. That is, one would expect the cases of imagining with images to be connected to perception via the already noted similarity between images and sensations. And, as has been noted, Scruton takes this similarity to be irreducible.

Since the relation of imagination to perception is achieved, apparently, through the mediation of a sensationlike image, Scruton seems to have avoided the objection that a descriptional analysis of imagination will fail to preserve the essentially perceptual characteristics of imagination. In order to elaborate on this theme, Scruton turns his attention to seeing and "seeing as" — for example, seeing a figure as a duck or as a rabbit. "Seeing as," then, serves as a link between imagination and perception by showing how much of our ordinary perception involves "seeing as."

This emphasis illustrates an important trait of Scruton's theory: he is often interested in the function or context of imagining and images, sometimes to the exclusion of direct investigation of the nature of the phenomenon. Of course, Scruton is presenting his account of imagination in the context of a discussion of aesthetics and, given his purposes, it would be unfair to demand a detailed analysis of perception, imagination, and mental images. If a complete theory of imagination is wanted, more work is needed in these and other areas, but the account offered by Scrutton is, nonetheless, illuminating and provocative, as well as an important factor in his overall treatment of aesthetic experience.

MARY WARNOCK

The last discussion of imagination to be dealt with here is Warnock's, presented in *Imagination*. Her treatment of the subject is in some respects quite similar to Scruton's: both accept mental images, both take Wittgenstein's analysis of "seeing as" as a significant point of departure, and both are interested in the role of imagination in aesthetic experience. Nonetheless, the differences between Warnock's views and Scruton's are perhaps as important as the similarities. Whereas Scruton emphasizes the similarity of the image to sensation, Warnock wishes to focus on the more-intellectual side of the image. Moreover, she warns against trying to separate images, and image-forming, from imagining: "We cannot speak of imagining without speaking of images. . . . But the image cannot be treated as an independent object which must be examined on its own" (Warnock, 1976, p. 172).

Warnock's basic theme, developed via a survey of both philosophical discussions of imagination (primarily Hume's, Kant's, and Sartre's) and the views of artists on imagination (Coleridge and Wordsworth) is threefold. She argues that (a) there is a unified sense of imagination that underlies the very diverse uses of the term "imagination"; (b) imagination is basically a way of understanding, interpreting, and giving meaning to our experiences of the world; and (c) this process must involve the creation of images. To defend the first of these three propositions, Warnock attempts to show, in considerable detail, how the diverse discussions of imagination that she surveys all have a common thread involving an intellectual process of understanding. The second point is again established via a critical analysis of the views she discusses; attention to areas of agreement and difference allow her to delineate her own thesis in more precise detail. The third claim is taken to be, in some sense, self-evident: "Obviously, whichever kind of experiences we are talking about, it is absolutely essential to the description of them that we use such terms as 'image'" (Warnock, 1976, p. 167).

Just as there are similarities with respect to scope, approach, and aims to be discerned when Warnock's theory is compared with Scruton's, so, too, there are similarities in the problems that are encountered. Like Scruton, Warnock does not try to defend mental images in any well-developed way against the standard criticisms of image-theories; indeed, Warnock manages to interpret Ryle (1976, pp. 152-56) in a way that makes it sound as if he accepts mental images. The acceptance of mental images is simply not fully justified or defended. In much the same way, one wonders what arguments might be given for Warnock's general view of imagination, if one were to survey a different portion of the literature on the subject, e.g., Aristotle, or painters rather than poets. In short, Warnock's discussion, like Scruton's, is suggestive and far-ranging in some respects, but does not address some of the central questions one might expect to find in a theory of imagination.

V. The Phenomenological Tradition

Little has been said so far about imagination in the phenomenological tradition; this omission is mainly due to the fact that it is often difficult to isolate discussions of imagination in the work of Husserl and others from the broader context within which they occur (although a good introductory survey of the views of Brentano, Husserl, Merleau-Ponty, and Sartre—in more detail than can be given here—can be found in Part IV of Warnock's *Imagination*). Within the past few years, new work has been done—notably by Ed Casey—on phenomenological approaches to imagination, but until recently the only well-known works specifically focusing on imagination are two books by Jean-Paul Sartre: *Imagination: A Psychological Critique* (Forrest Williams, translator; Ann Arbor, 1962) and *The Psychology of The Imagination* (Bernard Frechtman, translator; New York, 1966).

For the most part, however, discussions of imagination are to be found only within much broader treatments of consciousness. Husserl, for example, discusses imagination both in the *Logical Investigations* (J. N. Findlay, translator; New York, 1970) and in *Ideas* (W. Royce Gibson, translator; London, 1962), but does so primarily in the context of perception and appearances. His ideas on this subject had a profound effect on Sartre, who saw his own work on imagination as, in part, a rejection of Husserl's close association of imagination with perception.

Merleau-Ponty follows Husserl in treating imagination as a phenomenon closely connected with perception. In *The Phenomenology of Perception* (Colin Smith, translator; New York, 1962) he sometimes discusses imagination and hallucination as a way of clarifying or further developing some aspect of his analysis of perception.

References to imagination can also be found embedded in phenomenological discussions of intentionality; imagination is sometimes cited as a paradigm example of an intentional act whose object—that which is being imagined—need not really exist. Although such discussions may shed light on the intentional aspect of imagination, usually little attention is paid to the specific characteristics of imagination that separate it from any other act of consciousness.

More recently, several philosophers have offered new insight into phenomenological investigations of imagination, often concentrating on both the similarities and the differences between imagination and perception, or between imagination and other, similar mental acts. The most extensive account of this sort has been done by Edward Casey; other analyses (often in response to Casey) can be found—among other places—in articles by Silverman, Harper, Todes, and Sallis.

The preceding overview of imagination in the phenomenological tradition has been exceedingly sketchy, but serves to indicate the sort of insight that might be gained by a closer look at analyses which focus on the experience itself, rather than the language with which we express the final results of imagining.

VI. Related Areas of Interest

Although it is obvious that a philosophical analysis of imagination should not duplicate the work of psychological studies, there are nevertheless some important facets of psychological research in this area which a philosophical investigation cannot afford to ignore. In addition to the work in cognitive psychology discussed in Section II, two topics of vital concern to philosophical treatments of imagination are eidetic imagery, a phenomenon often cited in support of the claim that we see mental images, and studies on the many similarities between standard cases of imagining on the one hand, and hallucinations, after-images, and hypnagogic images on the other. These and other areas relevant to philosophical theories of imagination (e.g., the confusion between imagining and perceiving first studied in the experiments by C. W. Perky) are discussed in three works that provide surveys of recent psychological findings about imagination. These three books, by Paivo, Richardson, and Segal, have been included in the bibliography, which is otherwise restricted to more philosophical discussions.

Many of the other important issues related to imagination have not been covered in the preceding discussion, although relevant articles are cited in the bibliography. One such issue that has attracted much interest lately is the relation of imaginability to possibility. A better understanding of what imagining involves might put us in a better position to see the relation between an ability to imagine an event or state of affairs and questions about whether or not such a state is possible.

In pursuing this sort of epistemological question about imagination, another natural question that arises is whether a person might learn something new about a thing — something he might not discover by thinking about it in some other way — by imagining it. This sort of concern is often connected with a historical perspective on imagination, since the faculty of imagination has occupied a central role in the epistemological theories of many important figures in the history of philosophy. Thus, the bibliography that follows includes articles on imagination in Aristotle, Spinoza, and Kant, to mention but a few important figures in the historical development of treatments of imagination.

Finally, we have already noted that some philosophers (Scruton, Warnock, Dilman) have pointed out the apparent connection between "seeing as" and imagination. Pursued in depth, this observation can lead to an investigation of imagination as a creative activity, and the role of imagination in aesthetics.

Acknowledgments

I wish to thank the American Association of University Women for their support; much of the background research for the original version of this chapter (*American Philosophical Quarterly,* 1978) was completed while I was on a fellowship from them.

Bibliography

In general, the following bibliography is limited to philosophical works published between 1957 and 1980. A few earlier articles of major importance, however, and a few psychological studies have been included.

Alexander, H. G. 1963. "Suggestions Concerning Empirical Foundations of Imagination." *Philosophy and Phenomenological Research* 23: 427–31.
Anscombe, G.E.M. 1958. "Pretending." *Proceedings of the Aristotelian Society* Suppl. Vol. 32: 279–94.
Armstrong, David M. 1968. "Mental Images." In D. Armstrong, *A Materialist Theory of Mind.* London: Routledge & Kegan Paul.
Attfield, R. 1970. "Berkeley and Imagination." *Philosophy* 45: 237–43.
Audi, Robert. 1978. "The Ontological Status of Mental Images." *Inquiry* 21: 348–61.

Austin, J. L. 1958. "Pretending." *Proceedings of the Aristotelian Society* Suppl. Vol. 32: 261–78.

Ayffre, A. 1959. "A World of Images." *Philosophy Today,* vol. 3: 128–35.

Baker, M. J. 1954. "Perceiving, Imagining and Being Mistaken." *Philosophy and Phenomenological Research* 14: 520–35.

Beardsmore, R. W. 1980. "The Limits of Imagination." *British Journal of Aesthetics* 20: 99–114.

Bennett, Jonathan. 1971. "Ideas and Meaning: Berkeley." In *Locke, Berkeley, Hume: Central Themes.* Oxford: Oxford University Press.

Blair, R. G. 1970. "Imagination and Freedom in Spinoza and Sartre." *Journal of the British Society for Phenomenology* 1: 13–16.

Block, Ned. ed. 1981a. *Imagery.* Cambridge: MIT Press.

———. ed. 1981b. *Readings in Philosophy of Psychology,* vol. 2. Cambridge: MIT Press.

Blocker, H. Gene. 1972. "Another Look at Aesthetic Imagination." *Journal of Aesthetics and Art Criticism* 30: 529–36.

Bossart, W. H. 1980. "Sartre's Theory of the Imagination." *Journal of the British Society for Phenomenology* 11: 37–53.

Brook, J. A. 1975. "Imagination, Possibility, and Personal Identity." *American Philosophical Quarterly* 12: 185–98.

Bunting, I. A. 1970. "Sartre on Imagination." *Philosophical Studies* (Ireland) 19: 236–53.

Cameron, J. M. 1961–1962. "Poetic Imagination." *Proceedings of the Aristotelian Society* 62: 219–40.

Candlish, Stewart, 1975. "Mental Images and Pictorial Properties." *Mind* 48: 260–62.

———. 1976. "The Incompatibility of Perception: A Contemporary Orthodoxy." *American Philosophical Quarterly* 13: 63–68.

Carrier, David. 1973. "Three Kinds of Imagination." *Journal of Philosophy* 70: 819–31.

———. 1978. "Imagination and Our Image of the Mind." *Philosophical Forum,* vol. 9 (1978) pp. 393–99.

Casey, Edward. 1970–1971. "Imagination: Imagining and the Image." *Philosophy and Phenomenological Research* 31: 475–90.

———. 1974. "Towards a Phenomenology of Imagination." *Journal of the British Society for Phenomenology* 5: 3–19.

———. 1976a. "Comparative Phenomenology of Mental Activity: Memory, Hallucination, and Fantasy Contrasted with Imagination." *Research in Phenomenology* 6: 1–25.

———. 1976b. *Imagining: A Phenomenological Study.* Bloomington: Indiana University Press.

———. 1977. "Imagining and Remembering." *Review of Metaphysics* 31: 187–209.

———. 1978. "Imagining, Perceiving, and Thinking." *Humanitas* 14: 173–96.

Chappell, Vere. 1963. "The Concept of Dreaming." *Philosophical Quarterly* 13: 193–213.

Cohen, J. 1974. "Reflections on the Structure of Mind." *Scientia* 109: 403–25.

Collins, Arthur W. 1967. "Philosophical Imagination." *American Philosophical Quarterly* 4: 49–56.

Courtney, Richard. 1971. "Imagination and the Dramatic Act: Comments on Sartre, Ryle, and Furlong." *Journal of Aesthetics and Art Criticism* 30: 163–70.

Cousin, D. R. 1970. "On the Ownership of Images." *Analysis* 30: 206–8.

Danto, Arthur. 1958. "Concerning Mental Pictures." *Journal of Philosophy* 55: 12–20.

Deitsch, Martin. 1972. "Visualizing." *Mind* 81: 113–15.

Dennett, D. C. 1969. "Mental Imagery." In *Content and Consciousness.* London: Routledge & Kegan Paul. Chapter 6.

———. 1978. "Two Approaches to Mental Images." In *Brainstorms.* Montgomery, Vt.: Bradford Books, 1978. Chapter 10.

Desmond, William. 1976. "Collingwood, Imagination, and Epistemology." *Philosophical Studies* (Ireland) 24: 82–103.

Dilman, Ilham. 1967. "Imagination." *Proceedings of the Aristotelian Society* Suppl. Vol. 41: 19–36.

———. 1968. "Imagination." *Analysis* 23: 90–97.

Ehman, Robert R. 1965. "Imagination, Dream, and the World of Perception." *Journal of Existentialism* 5: 389–402.

Engmann, Joyce. 1976. "Imagination and Truth in Aristotle." *Journal of the History of Philosophy* 14: 259–65.

Flew, Annis. 1953. "Images, Supposing, and Imagination.' *Philosophy* 28: 246-54.

Flew, Anthony. 1956. "Facts and 'Imagination.'" *Mind* 65: 392-99.

Flynn, Thomas R. 1975. "The Role of the Image in Sartre's Aesthetics." *Journal of Aesthetics and Art Criticism* 33: 431-42.

Fodor, Jerry. 1975. *Language of Thought*. New York: Thomas Y. Crowell Co. Pp. 173-94.

Foster, Steven. 1969. "Eidetic Imagery and Imagiste Perception." *Journal of Aesthetics and Art Criticism* 28: 133-45.

Franklin, R. L. 1978. "The Trouble with Images." *Canadian Journal of Philosophy* 8: 113-15.

Furlong, E. J. 1961. *Imagination*. London: George Allen and Unwin, Ltd.

_____. 1969. "Mental Images and Mr. O. Hanfling." *Analysis* 30: 62-64.

_____. 1970. "Mr. Urmson on Memory and Imagination." *Mind* 79: 137-38.

Gary, Ann. 1977. "Mental Images." *The Personalist* 58: 28-38.

Greenway, A. P. 1974. "Imaginal Knowing." *Journal of the British Society for Phenomenology* 5: 41-45.

Grimsley, Ronald. 1972. "Sartre and the Phenomenology of the Imagination." *Journal of the British Society for Phenomenology* 3: 58-62.

Gross, Barry R. 1973. "Professor Furlong, Imagining, and Imaging." *Studi Internazionali di Filosofia* 5: 199-208.

Hanfling, O. 1969. "Mental Images." *Analysis* 29: 166-73.

Hannay, Alastair. 1970. "Wollheim and Seeing Black and White as a Picture." *British Journal of Aesthetics* 10: 107-18.

_____. 1971. *Mental Images: A Defence*. London: George Allen and Unwin, Ltd.

_____. 1973. "To See a Mental Image." *Mind* 82: 161-83.

Hanson, Bernard. 1962-1963. "Meaning and Mental Images." *Proceedings of the Aristotelian Society* 63: 86-92.

Harper, Ralph. 1978. "The Range and the Role of the Imagination." *Humanitas* 14: 145-60.

Haynes, Peter F. R. 1976. "Mental Imagery." *Canadian Journal of Philosophy* 6: 705-20.

Howell, Robert. 1976. "Ordinary Pictures, Mental Representations, and Logical Forms." *Synthese* 33: 149-74.

Hume, Robert D. 1970. "Kant and Coleridge on Imagination." *Journal of Aesthetics and Art Criticism* 28: 485-96.

Ihde, Don. 1970. "Auditory Imagination." In F. I. Smith, ed., *Phenomenology in Perspective*. The Hague: Martinus Nijhoff. Pp. 208-16.

Ingram-Pearson, Clive W. 1961. "Ideas and Images." *Review of Metaphysics* 14: 452-62.

Ishiguro, Hide. 1966. "Imagination." In B. Williams and A. Montefiore, eds., *British Analytic Philosophy*. New York: Humanities Press. Pp. 153-78.

_____. 1967. "Imagination." *Proceedings of the Aristotelian Society* Suppl. Vol. 41: 37-56.

Kaplan, Edward K. 1972. "Gaston Bachelard's Philosophy of Imagination: An Introduction." *Philosophy and Phenomenological Research* 33: 1-24.

Jackson, Frank. 1976. "The Existence of Mental Objects." *American Philosophical Quarterly* 13: 33-40.

Khatchadourian, Haig. 1966. "About Imaginary Objects." *Ratio* 8: 77-89.

Kielkopf, Charles F. 1968. "The Pictures in the Head of a Man Born Blind." *Philosophy and Phenomenological Research* 28: 501-13.

King-Farlow, J. 1969. "'Mine' and the Family of Human Imaginings." *Inquiry* 12: 225-35.

Kleiman, Lowell. 1971. "Imagining." *Journal of Value Inquiry* 5: 267-75.

Kleiman, Lowell. 1978. "Mental Images: Another Look." *Philosophical Studies* 34: 169-76.

Kuehl, James. 1970. "Perceiving and Imagining." *Philosophy and Phenomenological Research* 31: 219-24.

Lawrie, Reynold. 1970. "The Existence of Mental Images." *Philosophical Quarterly* 20: 253-57.

Lemos, R. M. 1963. "Ideas, Images, and Sensations." *Theoria* 29: 56-69.

Levi, Albert William. 1964. "The Two Imaginations." *Philosophy and Phenomenological Research* 25: 188-201.

Lisska, Anthony J. 1976. "Aquinas on *Phantasia*." *Thomist* 40: 294-302.

Lycos, K. 1965. "Images and the Imaginary." *Australasian Journal of Philosophy* 43: 321-38.

Machan, Tibor. 1969. "A Note on Conceivability and Logical Possibility." *Kinesis* 2: 39-42.

Malcolm, Norman. 1970. "Memory and Representation." *Nous* 4: 59-71.

Mannison, D. S. 1975. "Dreaming an Impossible Dream." *Canadian Journal of Philosophy* 4: 663-75.

Margolis, Joseph. 1966. "After Images and Pains." *Philosophy* 41: 333-40

Matthews, Gareth. 1974. "Review of *Mental Images: A Defence,* by Alastair Hannay." *Philosophical Review* 83: 252–54.

———. 1979. "Mental Copies." *Philosophical Review* 78: 53–73.

Maund, J. B. 1977. "On the Distinction between Perceptual and Ordinary Beliefs." *Philosophy and Phenomenological Research* 38: 209–19.

McKenna, Ross. 1974. "The Imagination: A Central Sartrean Theme." *Journal of the British Society for Phenomenology* 5: 63–70.

Mischel, Theodore. 1961. "Collingwood on Art as Imaginative Expression." *Australasian Journal of Philosophy* 39: 241–50.

Morgan, Kathryn Pauly. 1974. "A Critical Analysis of Sartre's Theory of Imagination." *Journal of the British Society for Phenomenology* 5: 20–33.

Murdoch, Iris. 1961. "Against Dryness." *Encounter* 16: 16–20.

Neisser, Ulric. "Perceiving, Anticipating, and Imagining." Unpublished manuscript. Pp. 89–105.

Neuman, Mathias. 1978. "Towards an Integrated Theory of Imagination." *International Philosophical Quarterly* 18: 251–75.

Nimmo, W. 1974. "The Notion of Unconscious Phantasy." *Journal of the British Society for Phenomenology* 5: 55–58.

Novitz, David. 1980. "Of Fact and Fancy." *American Philosophical Quarterly* 17: 143–49.

Odegard, Douglas. 1971. "Images." *Mind* 80: 262–65.

Oosthuizen, D.C.S. 1968. "The Role of Imagination in Judgments of Facts." *Philosophy and Phenomenological Research* 29: 34–58.

Paivo, Allan. 1971. *Imagery and Verbal Processes.* New York: Holt, Rinehart and Winston.

Perkins, Moreland. 1970. "The Picturing in Seeing." *Journal of Philosophy* 67: 324–25.

Phillipe, M. E. 1971. "*Phentasia* in the Philosophy of Aristotle." *Thomist* 35: 1–42.

Pleydell-Pearce, A. G. 1974. "Imagination and Perception." *Journal of the British Society for Phenomenology* 5: 37–40.

Pole, David. 1976. "Art, Imagination, and Mr. Scruton." *British Journal of Aesthetics* 16: 195–209.

Preuss, Peter. 1976. "Mannison's Impossible Dream." *Canadian Journal of Philosophy* 6: 535–42.

Price, H. H. 1964. "Appearing and Appearances." *American Philosophical Quarterly* 1: 3–19.

Pylyshyn, Zenon W. 1981. "Imagery and Artificial Intelligence." In Ned Block, ed., *Readings in Philosophy of Psychology,* vol. 2. Cambridge: Harvard University Press.

Rabb, J. Douglas. 1973. "Review of *Mental Images: A Defence,* by Alastair Hannay." *Dialogue* 12:164–66.

———. 1975a. "Imagining: An Adverbial Analysis." *Dialogue* 14: 312–18.

———. 1975b. "Prolegomenon to a Phenomenology of Imagination." *Philosophy and Phenomenological Research* 36: 74–81.

Rader, Melvin. 1974. "The Imaginative Mode of Awareness." *Journal of Aesthetics and Art Criticism* 33: 131–37.

Rankin, K. W. 1967. "The Role of Imagination, Rule Operations, and Atmosphere in Wittgenstein's Language Games." *Inquiry* 10: 279–91.

Richards, Norvin. 1973. "Depicting and Visualizing." *Mind* 82: 218–25.

Richardson, Alan. 1969. *Mental Imagery.* New York: Springer Publishing Company.

Russell, Bertrand. 1958. "What is Mind?" *Journal of Philosophy* 55: 5–11.

Russow, Lilly-Marlene. 1980. "Audi on Mental Images." *Inquiry* 10: 353–56.

———. 1980. "Towards a Theory of Imagination." *Southern Journal of Philosophy* 18: 353–69.

Sallis, John. 1975. "Image and Phenomenon." *Research in Phenomenology* 5: 61–75.

Scholar, Michael. 1971. "Aristotle: *Metaphysics* 101N1–3." *Mind* 80: 266–68.

Scruton, Roger. 1974. *Art and Imagination: A Study in the Philosophy of Mind.* London: Methuen.

Segal, Sidney, 1971. *Imagery: Current Cognitive Approaches.* New York: Academic Press.

Sharpe, R. A. 1975. "Hearing As." *British Journal of Aesthetics* 15: 217–25.

Shorter, J. M. 1952. "Imagination." *Mind* 41: 528–42.

Silverman, Hugh J. 1978. "Imagining, Perceiving, and Remembering." *Humanitas* 14: 197–207.

Simon, Herbert A. "On the Forms of Mental Representation." Unpublished manuscript. Pp. 3–18.

Smith, Brian. 1965. "Dreaming." *Australasian Journal of Philosophy* 43: 48–57.

Smith, Quentin. 1977. "Sartre and the Matter of Mental Images." *Journal of the British Society for Phenomenology* 8: 69–78.

Smythies, J. R. 1958. "On Some Properties and Relations of Images." *Philosophical Review* 67: 389–94.

Snoeyenbos, Milton H., and Elsa A. Sibley. 1978. "Sartre on Imagination." *Southern Journal of Philosophy* 16: 373–89.

Sober, Elliot. 1976. "Mental Representations." *Synthese* 33: 101–48.

Sokolowski, Robert. 1977. "Picturing." *Review of Metaphysics* 31: 3–28.

Squires, J.E.R. 1968. "Visualizing." *Mind* 77: 58–67.

Strawson, P. F. 1970. "Imagination and Perception." In L. Foster and J. W. Swanson, eds., *Experience and Theory*. Amherst: University of Massachusetts Press. Pp. 31–54.

Tannenbaum, Jerrold. 1971. "In Defense of the Brain Process Theory." *Philosophy and Phenomenological Research* 31: 552–63.

Theobald, David. 1967. "The Imagination and What Philosophers Have to Say." *Diogenes* 57: 47–63.

Todes, Samuel. 1966. "Comparative Phenomenology of Perception and Imagination." *Journal of Existentialism* 7: 3–20.

Urmson, J. O. 1970. "Memory and Imagination." *Mind* 79: 137–38.

Von Morstein, Petra. 1974. "Imagine." *Mind* 83: 228–48.

Walton, Gilbert. 1969. "Imagination and Confirmation." *Mind* 78: 580–87.

Warnock, Mary. 1970. "The Concrete Imagination." *Journal of the British Society for Phenomenology* 1: 6–12.

_____. 1970. "Imagination in Sartre." *British Journal of Aesthetics* 10: 323–36.

_____. 1976. *Imagination*. Berkeley: University of California Press.

Wetherick, N. E. 1974. "On Pure Phenomenological Psychology and the Imagination." *Journal of the British Society for Phenomenology* 5: 51–54.

White, Alan R. 1969–1970. "Seeing What is not There." *Proceedings of the Aristotelian Society* 70: 61–74.

Williams, Bernard. 1968. "Imagination and the Self." In P. F. Strawson, ed., *Philosophy of Thought and Action*. London: Oxford University Press. Pp. 192–213.

Wollheim, Richard. 1965. *On Drawing an Object*. London: H. C. Lewsi.

_____. 1974. "Identification and Imagination." In R. Wollheim, ed., *Collection of Critical Essays*. Garden City, N.Y.: Doubleday Anchor Books. Pp. 172–95.

chapter 11

———————◆———————

Recent Work on Aesthetics

JOSEPH MARGOLIS

If we canvass Anglo-American analytic aesthetics from approximately the 1950s to the beginning of the eighties, the principal contributions fall fairly clearly into three movements: (a) reaction, in the fifties, to the idealist theories chiefly of Croce (1922) and Collingwood (1938); (b) the development, in the late fifties and early sixties, of a relatively strict and comprehensive empiricism; (c) reaction, in the sixties and seventies, to empiricist theories, prominently those of Beardsley (1958) and Sibley (1959), and an increasing emphasis on the aesthetic relevance of nonperceptual factors. These trends are somewhat complicated in that, as we approach the present moment, contributions are more and more characteristically inclined to explore conceptual relations holding between aesthetics and other philosophical domains and to accommodate specialized and interdisciplinary studies of the arts themselves. But perhaps most significantly, the insularity of analytic philosophy begins to show signs of being breached by the discovery and rediscovery of a rich Continental tradition in aesthetics — in particular, recent work in phenomenology, hermeneutics, structuralism, existentialism, deconstructivism, Marxism, and semiotics.

Until very recently, contributions appeared chiefly, though not exclusively, in the journals; aesthetics itself has been concerned with a very wide range of rather loosely related issues; and a good many of the best-known papers have been both eclectic and somewhat desultory in the search for a comprehensive ontology of art and methodology of the various forms of criticism and history of the arts. There is now a distinct resurgence of systematic accounts. It will prove convenient, therefore, in canvassing the field, to select certain clusters of papers in order to identify the salient quarrels of the three periods identified, and then to survey more broadly the emphasis of the most recent literature.

The characteristic contributions of Anglo-American aesthetics within the period canvassed are fairly sampled, first, in Elton's anthology (1954) and then, successively, in Margolis's two anthologies (1962, 1978). The first exhibits the earlier vogue of opposing idealism and exploiting in a very general manner the new analytic currents informed principally by the inquiries of Wittgenstein. Since that time, idealism has distinctly declined as the inevitable opponent, and analytic contributions have become more detailed in their inquiries into critical language, somewhat fragmentary, decidedly eclectic, and even inchoate in their preference of philosophical models. The first of Margolis's collections provides a reasonable sample of the most discussed of the earliest analytic papers as the trend settled in the early sixties. Since that time, Anglo-American aesthetics has become predominantly analytic. Margolis's second collection samples the salient quarrels of the relatively mature phase of analytic aesthetics, chiefly centered on the renewed interest in the ontology of artworks and the methodology of criticism: the emphasis rests with the transition from a strongly empiricist orientation to the variety of views that stress the importance of nonperceptual factors—the history and circumstances of production, intentionality, conceptual considerations (as in conceptual art and forgery) that resist perceptual specification, cultural influences, interpretive possibilities, and the like. Other larger anthologies that converge to some extent include Dickie and Sclafani's (1977) and Kennick's (1979).

Of all the questions that fall within the range of aesthetics, those that concern the nature of criticism lend themselves to the most systematic ordering. Here, the principal topics bear on the description, interpretation, appreciation, and evaluation of works of art, the analysis of the characteristic predicates employed in critical remarks either by professionals or amateurs, and the very variety of functions that critical exchange is designed to serve—including, for instance, instruction and the exhibition of taste, the analysis and comparison of artworks. We may also include here questions regarding the relevance or lack of relevance of comments about perceivable properties of a work of art, or about the conditions of production of a given work, or biographical information about the artist, or about the sorts of responses of an aesthetic percipient.

Theories about such issues have become increasingly prominent and have challenged the adequacy of the empiricist orientation. There is no way to organize the relevant discussion simply, but the issues are clearly interrelated.

From the time of the appearance of Elton's collection, one may fairly say, the Anglo-American analysis of the language of criticism has been pointedly pursued against the background of Margaret Macdonald's (1954) and Arnold Isenberg's (1949) accounts. Each of these authors, in his own way, has been intent on insisting that supporting evidence for a critical "verdict" about some work of art could not, in principle, be supplied so as to oblige another to accept that verdict. Neither wished to deny the relevance of supporting reasons for a judgment rendered, but Isenberg was inclined to argue that a critical judgment is at bottom a matter of taste or feeling, and Macdonald argued that reasons supplied are rather more like the detailing or "presenting" of what it is one appreciates in a given work than the provision of decisive evidence. Both rather misleadingly speak of "verdicts," although it is clear that their accounts do not intend the term in its usual sense. The common tendency of their discussion is relatively widespread. For example, it has been reinforced, particularly where emotional or expressive qualities of artworks are in question, by John Hospers (1960) and Henry Aiken (1945), so that it appears to infect their descriptions. And to the extent that the interpretation of artworks is construed in terms of preferences of taste, as in C. L. Stevenson's discussion (Margolis, 1962), critical judgments not overtly valuational in nature have been construed as not confirmable in the usual way in which matters of fact are (following, in Stevenson's case, the well-known account of value judgments as inherently persuasive, 1944, 1950).

More recently, there has been a tendency to qualify the nature of aesthetic judgments or mute the sense in which they are straightforward judgments: evidentially supporting reasons that may confirm or disconfirm a given judgment may be thought not to be required, or even to be strictly relevant or eligible, although some sort of congruently supporting "considerations" of what is aesthetically or perceptually "presented" may still be pertinent or even required. Here, there is some inclination to blend the views of Macdonald and R. M. Hare (1952), in the sense in which an aesthetic "judgment" may be said to have a certain action-guiding or taste-orienting (though not a moral) function, may be said not to take the logical form of an assertion or statement, and may be said to be open to appreciative divergences. Perhaps the most representative accounts of this sort appear in Roger Scruton (1974) and Alan Tormey (1973). The alleged advantages, however, are neither entirely clear nor compelling. For example, supporting "reasons" are often thought to be peculiarly restricted in relevance to the perception and appreciation of each individual work — therefore, to resist generalizability. But where generalization is thought indefensible, it is still necessary — as Frank Sibley's account shows — to construe aesthetic judgments as genuine judgments or claims; and, particularly on Hare's view, which Scruton professes to follow, generalizability with respect to prescriptives is not only possible but required. Again, it is often claimed (as in both Scruton's and Tormey's accounts) that the condition for "accepting" an apparent judgment (description or interpretation) rests less on adopting or accepting argumentatively pertinent propositions as in sharing a certain "affective" response. But it is hard to see that such a response can fail to be cognitively qualified; and the point of insisting that it is affective or experiential has more to do with ensuring some sort of "direct" encounter with an actual work than it has to do with construing an apparent judgment simply as a kind of reaction. The proof lies with the fact that it is still required, in order that appreciation obtain with respect to a given work, that one see or appreciate correctly what has been "presented." Third, the adjusting maneuver is often intended to accommodate a variety of nonconverging, possibly even formally incompatible, "responses" to what is taken to be presented in a particular artwork; here, it may be thought that, to preserve such a variety of appreciative responses, one must give up the model of argumentatively ordered propositions. But this is not so: one has only to provide for truth-values weaker than those of truth and falsity — for instance, for plausibility, aptness, reasonableness — and for the defense of relativism (Margolis, 1980).

The tendency of discussions of this sort (and they are by no means in agreement with one another) falls very nicely in accord with that first wave of reaction to G. E. Moore's account of good as a nonnatural property, in the sense that valuationally significant predicates in the aesthetic setting may be admitted to designate the properties of an artwork. The Naturalistic Fallacy has gradually lost its fearsome aspect, and theorists in aesthetics (as well as in ethics and allied fields) have found it possible to reconsider the ascription of such attributes as objectively confirmable. The traditional view regarding public canons for the evaluation of objectively discriminable properties — that is, of perceptually discernible value-laden properties — is upheld in its naturalistic form in Monroe Beardsley's *Aesthetics* (1958), where it is maintained that criteria corresponding to such broad-gauged judgments as of "unity," "harmony," and "balance" may be explicitly formulated and employed. Even J. A. Passmore's critical paper (1951) shows that that author is prepared to support, contrary to the reader's first impression, objective valuational criteria, though not perhaps of the same gauge that Beardsley is confident may be provided. The analysis of relevant valuational usage in P. H. Nowell-Smith's *Ethics* (1954) marks more definitely the beginning of the recovery of objectively attributable predications both in ethics and aesthetics, with a fuller appreciation of the variety of conditions on which these may be appropriately used.

The most sustained and distinctive account of narrowly aesthetic concepts has been supplied by Sibley (1959) — in a way that is explicitly opposed to intuitionism (nonnaturalism) but not fully defended in that regard. Sibley maintains that characteristically aesthetic concepts, such as "garish," "dainty," and the like, cannot be segregated into descriptive and valuational components and are in fact not condition-governed at all, as are, in a variety of ways which he details, other characterizing predicates. His account is original and challenging and has generated a considerable literature. In fact, Sibley's paper may well be the single most-discussed paper in Anglo-American aesthetics. The puzzle remains that aesthetic qualities are taken to be objective and perceivable, to be complex in the sense in which they depend on nonaesthetic qualities, but simple in the sense in which criteria for their occurrence cannot be specified. In this respect, Isabel Hungerland (1963) has relevantly argued that Sibley's principal specimen terms do not allow for a contrast between what only seems to be so and what is really so. The upshot is that we cannot tell whether (and in what sense) one may perceive an object to be relevantly characterizable, as opposed to merely being entitled to impute a quality on the basis of one's own taste. Also, the question may be raised as to whether so-called aesthetic concepts do show a common (and this particular) logical pattern; Sibley himself concedes that there may be exceptions, and the analysis of important categories such as the baroque and the tragic do not seem to be readily analyzable along the lines suggested. It is difficult to see how, if categories of period style are aesthetically relevant, it can be denied that aesthetic predicates are sometimes condition-governed (in a sense opposed by Sibley) or that aesthetic predicates cannot be logically uniform; or how, if they are not aesthetic concepts (because they are condition-governed), the original claim could be more than self-serving. The most sustained criticism of Sibley's thesis along these lines appears in Peter Kivy (1973) — in particular, regarding the use of "unity" in music — and in Ted Cohen (1973). In cognitive terms, Sibley has not yet shown how to support the thesis against an intuitionist interpretation or how to keep it from being construed in terms of the intrusion of personal and variable taste.

Since Moore, the discussion of value judgments has increasingly turned away from an almost exclusive concern with the use of "good" to predicates that have significant descriptive force. That valuational terms are used in other than descriptive ways, for instance for commending purposes, is part of the permanent contribution of analysts like Nowell-Smith and Hare. But, more pointedly for aesthetics, the early confidence of Helen Knight (1936), who holds that there are formulable sets of criteria for all the characteristic uses of "good" in such phrases as "good show-dog," "good novel," "good tennis racquet," "good landscape," does not seem to be supported. The objectivity of relevant judgments need not be jeopardized in challenging Knight's view. Criticism characteristically does not and, as William Kennick (1958) argues in summarizing the accumulating evidence, need not work by applying rules to cases. A variety of analysts, chiefly in the ethical and legal spheres (for instance, Kurt Baier, 1958; Philippa Foot, 1958–1959; H.L.A. Hart, 1948–1949), have tried to recover the objectivity of particular valuational predicates applied in context-sensitive ways. The issue rests in part on the easy confusion of two senses of "objective" values: one (shared by so-called naturalists and non-naturalists: cognitivists), that values are actual discernible properties inhering in things — even if they depend on complex relations between humans and independent objects); the other, that public procedures are available for confirming and disconfirming claims about the presence of values (taken, as by noncognitivists, to correspond to whatever shifting and evolving human interests obtain).

It is clear, of course, that aesthetic judgments characteristically (though not exclusively) depend on (one's) taste. The Kantian division of aesthetic and moral values, however, revived in an ingenious form by Stuart Hampshire (1954), may be shown to be untenable. Aesthetic and moral judgments exhibit common logical properties (including dependence on personal taste) and, within each domain, there appear to be logically diverse types of judgment. The most general account showing that the aesthetic and the moral cannot be viewed as separate genera of judgment may be found in J. O. Urmson (1957–1958). And Margolis (1980) has shown that value judgments are of at least two types (ranging across both domains) — "findings," which logically behave as factual judgments do, except that the predicates employed are valuationally significant; and "appreciative judgments," which depend on our particular tastes. Both are evidentially supportable; appreciative judgments, though logically weaker than findings, are not, for that reason, less objective (in the procedural sense). Furthermore, the admission of relatively formal procedures for confirming and disconfirming judgments and claims is entirely neutral regarding the ontic status of values themselves. In a word, both cognitivist and noncognitivist accounts of values have been developed in response to Moore's early challenge.

Special attention has been paid to so-called expressive qualities. Traditionally, with the idealists, these have been linked to an account of artistic creativity; alternatively, following the example of Santayana, they have been construed as a projection of the response of the aesthetic percipient. Varieties of these views may be found, for example, in Stephen Pepper (1938) and L. A. Reid (1931). Fairly recently, expressive qualities have been construed as confirmable in a public way. The view has been somewhat opposed by Hospers and Aiken, both of whom are inclined to view relevant comments as personal and subjective; also by Beardsley, but (as in "The Affective Fallacy" (Wimsatt and Beardsley, 1954a) for the altogether different reason that aesthetic considerations are thought to preclude attention to affective responses. Beardsley's account is constrained by his well-known adherence to a strongly empiricist view of aesthetic experience.

At the present time, the principal alternatives are probably best represented in the views of Guy Sircello (1972) and Alan Tormey (1971). Tormey insists on treating expressive properties as the perceptually discriminable properties of artworks (that "also [may] designate intentional states of persons"), which (he holds) do not entail any prior act of expression (on the part of the artist). Sircello (as well as Lyas, 1973) introduces a wide range of expressive predicates that cannot be understood—whose designata cannot be "discerned"—independently of reference to the expressive state of the originating artist. Tormey's view is somewhat exclusive; Sircello's, not. Tormey is quite right, of course, in holding that if, say, a face is expressive of impatience, no one (having a face exhibiting such an expression) need be expressing impatience. On the other hand, Sircello is quite right in supposing that to construe Eliot's *Prufrock* as expressing a certain attitude toward life may be taken to be an alternative way of construing Eliot as having expressed that attitude; that (in any case) the analysis and confirmation of the property require attention jointly (inseparably) to the poem and the poetic effort of the originating artist.

Clearly, the issue depends on more fundamental matters, namely, on what a reasonable account of the boundaries of the aesthetic may be, and on how (in accord with such an account) we ought to construe the nature and limits of an artwork. Curiously, neither Sircello nor Tormey has pursued the issue. Thus, if, resisting the empiricist tradition (which has almost completely failed to provide a theory of art), we construe artworks as "utterances," "gestures," or what may be taken to be (internally) produced by the distinctive activity of artists, it would be impossible to resist Sircello's account—without precluding Tormey's. It is difficult, therefore, to fathom Tormey's resistance, unless it is motivated by an implicit commitment to empiricistlike constraints. We may note, here, that the Continental tradition, particularly the hermeneutic (most fully developed in the work of Hans-Georg Gadamer [1975]), construes artists' intentions and expression in an historical and cultural sense rather than a narrowly psychological; correspondingly, it provides for the aesthetic relevance of nonperceptually accessible factors that inform the interpretation of what particular artworks may be supposed to "present." The analytic orientation characteristically fails to accommodate the ontological peculiarities of human history and culture and fails to provide an account of intentions and intentionality wider than the psychologically explicit. In the hermeneutic setting—whether in agreement with or in opposition to the Romantic tendencies of Schleiermacher and Dilthey—the expressive cannot but be a special and limiting case of what is historically emergent. Here, the influence of Heidegger (and, of course, of Marx and Hegel) and the relative absence of that influence within the analytic tradition are particularly telling and noticeable.

Another cluster of issues centers on the interpretive efforts of critics. Stevenson, as already noted, conflates interpretive efforts with the expression of personal taste and preference and causal influences on preference. He concerns himself not at all with the question of professional criteria nor with the distinction between evaluating a work of art and evaluating an interpretation of a work of art. The argument, to this extent, is unconvincing. A number of commentators have explored the issue in ways reasonably free of Stevenson's reductive view; and Stevenson himself is obliged, notably in *Ethics and Language* (1944), to face a corresponding difficulty in construing technical criteria of truth and validity as somehow not "normative." Granting relatively clear-cut professional canons (admittedly somewhat informal), the discussion has moved along two distinct lines. Some theorists, notably Beardsley and Pepper (1955), have held that defensible interpretations of a given work must all be ideally convergent, even if (as Beardsley would insist) the ideal interpretation cannot be supplied. Margolis has argued, to the contrary, that, given a work of art whose describable properties are noted or conceded without dispute, it is in principle possible to provide defensible, plural, nonconverging, even incompatible interpretations (cf. Matthews, 1977). Suggestions along this line may be found also in Macdonald (1952–1953, 1954), though qualified in the manner already discussed.

The issue is a complex one. Apart from the strongly persuasionlike model that Stevenson favors, Beardsley's and Margolis's views probably represent the polar extremes regarding interpretation, within the analytic tradition. Beardsley (1970) maintains that artworks are autonomous objects whose properties it is the business of critics to disclose; that interpretation constitutes a particularly difficult subeffort within critical description, in which professional skill and virtuosity must be called into play; and that critical judgments are always capable of being assessed as true or false. Margolis holds a view opposed on all counts: first, that it is impossible to specify the boundaries of artworks in such a way as to be able to say, in a manner comparable with whatever precision obtains in demarcating physical objects, what is "in" or only "imputed" to an artwork—for all pertinently disputed attributes; second, that interpretation presupposes, but is conceptually or logically distinct from, description; and third that, given the nature of artworks and the methodological peculiarities of interpretation, critical judgments may (and must) take truth-values other and weaker than those of truth and falsity—in particular, the values of plausibility, aptness, and the like. On closer inspection, Beardsley concedes that one cannot always draw the requisite demarcation between what is "in" and not "in" a given work—particularly regarding literary texts, as in response to an argument of Frank Cioffi's (1963–1964); and he does not actually demonstrate that critical judgments (particularly interpretive judgments) must be capable of supporting assessments of truth and falsity (or, at any rate, given the asymmetry of a more than two-valued system, assessments of truth). In fact, Beardsley noticeably ignores the problem of the "boundaries" of artworks; hence, although his thesis is internally coherent and eligible, he does not actually provide a full-fledged defense of his own thesis or a demonstration that the opposed view is mistaken or avoidable. Once concede that interpretive judgments may take truth-values weaker than truth and falsity, a moderate or "robust" relativism becomes clearly tenable; judgments that, on a model of truth and falsity, are contradictories or contraries need no longer be thus construed. Conceding that much, we need not hold that all judgments are relativizable in the same respect (radical relativism)—a matter quite distinct from that of skepticism or indeterminacy regarding what "there is."

The question obviously obliges us to review the issue of the ontology of art. We shall put it aside for the time being. But it may be useful to note that the question of the boundaries of artworks—in particular, literary texts, which Beardsley tends to emphasize—has always been viewed as remarkably puzzling by the Continental authors. This is central, for instance, in the somewhat confused but extremely perceptive and influential account offered by Roman Ingarden (1973a,b), explored most recently in terms of reader-response theory by Wolfgang Iser (1978). But it also appears, prominently, in the Marxist tradition, for example in the work of Terry Eagleton (1976) and even of the somewhat unorthodox and partial disciple of Georg Lukács, Lucien Goldmann (1980). It is also central to the development of the structuralist and poststructuralist ("deconstructive") tradition, notably in the work of Roland Barthes

(1974) and Jacques Derrida (1974). Ingarden's ontology is probably the most influential of the Continental theories; but it is noticeably unconvincing in its insistence on the merely schematic nature of an actual artwork—confusing the schematic aspects of what an actual work "intends" and its determinate (necessarily nonschematic) properties as an actual object.

In all these accounts and in others favored in the Continental tradition, the implicit emphasis is upon the inadequacy of an empiricist or purely perceptually grounded conception of an artwork. Interestingly, Beardsley (1970) has engaged in a sustained dispute with E. D. Hirsch (1967), who himself represents a kind of Romantic reaction both to the post-Heideggerian forms of hermeneutics (threatened with relativism) and the extreme empiricist doctrine (Beardsley's) that precludes the relevance of artists' intentions *ab initio*. The remarkable thing is that both Beardsley and Hirsch treat the artwork (the literary work) as a well-demarcated, autonomous, and relatively stable object: Hirsch holds (along hermeneutic lines) that its nature is such that the intent of the original artist may be reliably recovered and that *that* provides the only norm for admissible interpretations of it; Beardsley holds that its nature is such that the artist's intention is not relevant to a specification of its actual properties, which are directly perceivable. But neither explains what an artwork or text is in virtue of which their respective claims could be vindicated. Hirsch's account has the advantage, however, that in spite of its implausibility—and even internal inconsistency—it signals the inadequacy of the empiricist orientation. An even more extreme commitment to the availability and exclusive authority of the author's intention has recently been advanced by P. D. Juhl (1980).

There is, to consider a second run of issues, a cluster of classic questions about the literary arts, which, although they do not have any clear unity, are readily collected. The principal topics concern at least fiction and metaphor. Two symposia in the *Proceedings of the Aristotelian Society* (1933, 1954) have been particularly instructive about fiction. There, we may see that an earlier concern had been the elimination of fictional entities from the real world, what may fairly be regarded as an extension of the attack on idealism launched by Moore and Bertrand Russell. The pivotal issue had been reference to characters in fiction; under the influence of linguistic analysis, discussion gradually settled on the fictional use of sentences. Discussants, therefore, all subscribe to the view emphatically put by R. B. Braithwaite (1933) that the required distinction must be detailed within "one world"; but there is considerable divergence about the logical properties of fictional sentences. Gilbert Ryle (1933) had been strenuously criticized by Moore for thinking that fictional sentences might, by a fluke of chance, turn out to be true. But Ryle himself had held that fictional characterizations employ only "pseudo-predicates," and Moore's correction was itself decidedly ambiguous and even, in a way, a repetition of Ryle's mistake. For Moore (1933) uses locutions that cannot escape being construed as referring to fictional entities, and he holds that what is given in the story is "false." Furthermore, Moore finds it necessary to cast the concept of a story as a set of statements that the author makes, and this leads him to speculate about authors' biographies in an altogether unnecessary way.

What we may say is this: first, *if* we refer to fictional entities, then, contrary to Moore, what we say may be true; similarly, *if* we refer to fictional entities, then, contrary to Ryle, fictional characterizations need not be pseudo-characterizations. Both Moore and Ryle, therefore, were (in rather different ways) persuaded by Russell's account of denotation (construed in terms of reference). The assumption here involved has come to be called the Axiom of Existence, although both John Searle (1969), who thus dubs it, and Strawson, whom he professes to follow, rather uneasily concede that characters (such as Sherlock Holmes) somehow "exist-in-fiction" (seemingly in violation of Braithwaite's constraint). Margolis (1977) has shown that the Axiom leads to intolerable paradox, particularly given the uncertainty of ontology, and that, contrary to the usual view, W. V. Quine does not actually subscribe to it but only to a much weaker thesis (in accord with which successful reference must be construed intentionally and may obtain even when referents do not exist). Margolis's suggestion, then, is that reference be construed grammatically, not ontologically. More recently, Nicholas Wolterstorff (1980) has supported the Axiom, advancing two principles: the principle of Exemplification ("Everything x is such that for every property P and every time t, x has P at t only if x exists at t") and the Principle of Completeness ("For everything x and every property P, x either has P or lacks P"). His argument depends largely on claiming that the property of reference must be had or possessed by fictional entities; hence, such entities must, on the two principles, exist. But this is simply a non sequitur and fails to demonstrate that reference has any ontological import at all (which the paradoxes of the Axiom cannot but encourage us to avoid). For, if reference has only grammatical, linguistic, or intentional force, then the relevance of the principles for fiction is doubtful. Fictional worlds have no reality at all; they are only imagined or imagined to exist; hence, in imagining fictional creatures, we imagine—relative to Wolterstorff's principles—that we are referring to them. Alternatively put, in referring to them, we are referring to what we imagine to exist but which utterly lacks reality. So, if we do not conflate the question of reference with the question of (really) possessing attributes, Wolterstorff's conclusions can be avoided. (For example, if, in *Mrs. Dalloway,* Richard Dalloway and Hugh Whitbread look into a shop window, *what* determinate proportions must the window have or lack?)

The best account in these symposia is undoubtedly that of Macdonald (1954), who carefully distinguishes fiction from lies and falsehoods, construing it as an implicit conspiracy between reader and author in terms of which questions of truth and falsity about the actual world are (qua fiction—not narrative) waived. A position very much like that of Ryle's, but stated even more positively, is advanced by Beardsley (1958), who believes that a story may actually turn out to be true. But his account fails to distinguish, for instance, between the logical function of sentences used to tell a story and the reasons for which a court of law may choose to treat an account as a libel rather than a fiction. The puzzles of reference in fiction may be resolved by distinguishing that use of sentences (which Macdonald discusses) by which we are to imagine a certain world to exist (that does not exist and that, qua fiction, cannot exist) from those uses (given the imaginary world) that correspond with those eligible in the real world; the problem of reference is thereby reconciled with current discussions of the referring use of language. To concede that we can imagine a fictional world to exist is necessarily to concede that we can refer to what we can thus imagine. Anything less threatens coherence.

But the problem of truth in fiction, and in literature in general—and even in art in general—remains interesting. The most promising adjustment has involved an application of Moore's well-known account of a certain sort of implication. The concept has been most systematically explored, in a nonaesthetic context, by Isabel Hungerland (1960). And, in the aesthetic context, it has been applied to fiction notably by Morris Weitz (1950) and Hospers (1960). Difficulties are of two sorts. For one, it is necessary to distinguish verisimilitude in a novel or fiction from the (so-called "contextually implied") truth of a fiction. Weitz's discussion shows the ease with which one may slide from a comparison of a fictional character or scene with elements of the real world (verisimilitude) to a detailing of propositions about the actual world allegedly "implied" by the fiction itself. And for another, one must distinguish the view that a work of art is a clue to the artist's convictions from that which holds that the work of art somehow presents or "implies" statements that might otherwise have been asserted. Hospers's discussion shows the difficulty of distinguishing between our making inferences about the author's views to discriminating propositions that are "contextually implied" by the fiction itself. The real problem remains that of the informality of the type of implication identified. But, also, the issue shows once again the inadequacy of a strictly empiricist orientation. For, on the empiricist view, we have no clear sense of how, restricting ourselves to the art object, we *can* draw consequences bearing on the intentional life of artists and authors. An earlier argument, T. M. Greene's (1940), maintained that works of art were straightforwardly propositions—whether paraphraseable or not; but Greene never explained the sense in which they were propositions or could, as such, be true. A more promising thesis regarding fictional truth—though one which does not dispose of the implication problem—holds that fiction may be true "to" the world rather than true "of" it, in the sense that human life comes to be compellingly interpreted in terms of the "life" of a Hamlet or a Quixote, as opposed to the sense in which the validity of a fictional character is confirmed by some induction over actual careers (cf. Margolis, 1966).

The principal questions regarding poetry concern metaphor and symbol, but symbol lends itself to a larger discussion involving all the arts. The single most influential paper on metaphor is undoubtedly that of Max Black (1954–1955). Paraphraseability is generally regarded as the central issue. Beardsley (1958), for instance, treats metaphor as a "significant attribution" that, apart from its ornamental features, may be paraphrased by singling out the appropriate connotation and supplying attributions truly or falsely ascribed to the relevant object. Beardsley, therefore, is inclined to associate metaphor with assertion and statement; hence, it becomes more or less a puzzle to be solved with ingenuity. Paul Henle (1958) develops an iconic theory of metaphor, which concerns both paraphraseability and the question of the basis for a metaphoric invention. He is unable to distinguish metaphor satisfactorily from catachresis (which at least Gustaf Stern, in his well-known account [1931], had warned about). Also, although he employs C. S. Peirce's category of the iconic, Henle considerably strains Peirce's view of the limits of iconic similarity. I. A. Richards (1936) had already considered grounds other than similarity as a basis for metaphor, and the ubiquity of resemblances of all sorts suggests that mere resemblance can hardly explain metaphor. But Richards, departing from Aristotle, had held metaphor to be an essential feature of language. He has been followed in this by a number of writers, but most discussants treat metaphor correctly as logically dependent on nonfigurative uses of language, without necessarily supposing that the figurative and the nonfigurative form well-defined linguistic strata.

In fact, the entire enterprise of paraphrase requires the distinction. Black adopts a moderate position, allowing for paraphraseability for certain metaphors but holding, in his most characteristic view—in what he terms "the interaction view of metaphor"—that paraphrase would involve a loss of "cognitive" content, that metaphor provides a new insight into things. He views metaphor as a sort of "filter" through which the world may be seen in a fresh light but which antecedent language has not yet reached; "successful" metaphors will then decay in the manner of catachresis. Margolis (1980) has argued that paraphrase is not so much inadequate as irrelevant to metaphor; that metaphor is primarily a deliberate "game" involving the semantic features of language, by which we deliberately deform things and the use of characterizing terms so that we play with them as if they were the same or similar, while knowing or believing that they are not. In pursuing a metaphor, we then elaborate such implicit identities and attributions for the sake of the game; but metaphor is not, syntactically, an identity or attribution. The purpose of metaphor and paraphrase, therefore, are at odds with one another.

On this view, metaphor is not correctly described syntactically (Beardsley, 1958, 1962), although it is true that the semantic deformations involved do exploit relevant sets of predications. In fact, as Christine Brooks-Rose (1958) observes, metaphor may obtain in the absence of any explicit attributive structures. On the other hand, as Cohen (1975) neatly shows, certain sentences may be construed as making both literal and metaphoric sense ("No man is an island"); hence, if syntax is favored over semantic considerations, one may have to admit as well the relevance of pragmatic considerations, namely, in the speech-act context in which sentences are uttered. What

must be made clear, however, is that, although language functions in speech-act contexts and by the use of sentences, nothing follows from that regarding the specific
analysis of metaphor. It is also important to realize that the theory of metaphor cannot be restricted (any more than a theory of meaning in general) to linguistic considerations merely (cf. Putnam, 1975); attention must inevitably be drawn to the
beliefs, associations, and accumulating information of a society. Similarly, there cannot be any fixed or essential conceptual linkages involving classificatory and
predicative notions in virtue of which the metaphoric can be clearly demarcated as
such (for instance, contra Jerrold Katz [1972] and Samuel Levin [1977]). Finally,
language cannot be taken to be stratified as literal and figurative; one must, on any
reasonable theory, variously construct what may be contextually viewed as the pertinent literal sense of given expressions, relative to which the metaphoric constitutes a
semantic deformation. This way of putting matters also improves on Black's formulation (cf. Hesse, 1963) since, for one thing, metaphor need not involve any cognitive innovation and, for another, if it did, it would eventually have to decay by way of some
form of catachresis (as cognitively absorbed). Also, the idea that metaphor constitutes
some form of semantic game not primarily concerned with the truth conditions of
sentential utterances strongly suggests (for instance, contra Davidson [1978]) the inadequacy of a purely extensionalist theory of language. Davidson's thesis treats
metaphor in terms of the use rather than the meaning of expressions; his intention is to
obviate the need for distinguishing between literal and figurative sense. But the
paradoxes of treating metaphor in terms of literal sense (for instance, the possibility
that metaphors may make no literal sense) and the difficulty of treating natural
languages in a detailed way in terms of literal sense alone (for instance, as supporting
Davidson's attempt [1967] to apply Tarski's conception of truth) to natural languages
betray the weakness of the intended economy. About poetry in general, it may at least
be said that I. A. Richards's attempt (1936) to assign a distinctive logical or linguistic
function has been largely abandoned. It seems inappropriate to speak of poetry as
contrasted with or functionally similar to fiction, if for no other reason than that fictional tales and science may be presented poetically.

Recently, poetry has been construed in terms of a speech-act model (in a sense
drawn from the work of John Austin, John Searle, and William Alston). The
straightforward difficulty confronting this view, however, is just the one Richards
fails to resolve: that there are no obvious logical, semantic, syntactic, pragmatic, the-
matic, ideological, or ontological constraints on poetry. This also counts against the
theories of the Russian Formalists (cf. Erlich, 1981) and the Prague Circle (Travaux,
1929), whose work directly and indirectly has influenced the speech-act thesis. The
most explicit claims are those of Beardsley (1970) and Richard Ohmann (1971), who
hold that poetic utterances are imitations of speech acts. Unfortunately, these authors
do not explain what an imitation of a speech act is as distinguished from a speech act
assigned in a fictional context (in imagining Hamlet to speak, do we imagine him to
perform speech acts?); and they cannot but admit (Beardsley, explicitly) that, as in *De
rerum natura,* even in the lyric utterances of a poet, *if* a speech-act model is pertinent
to the analysis of nonpoetic discourse, it must (without entailing derivative, second-
order, imitative, or similar status) be literally applicable to poetry as well. But if so,
then the distinction of poetry cannot be made out by the imitative thesis. John Searle
(1974) has recently attempted to formulate a speech-act theory of fiction; but the
logical puzzles of fictional reference are quite independent of the speech-act issue, and
fictions obtain in contexts more ample than that of literary narrative.

Another application of the speech-act model has relied heavily on the notion of
"conversational implicatures" developed by H. P. Grice (1975, 1978). Perhaps the
most sustained application appears in an account by Mary Louise Pratt (1977) (cf.
Hanscher, 1977). Grice's reasonable thesis is that, in context, particular utterances
have distinct "implicatures" (by implicatures, Grice means to collect formal en-

tailments and a range of logically loose connections that cannot be formally reduced). The trouble is that Grice does not actually tie his account to the consequences of particular kinds of independently identifiable speech acts, does not provide criteria for detecting which acts or which implicatures obtain in context, and does not provide clear grounds for determining how to characterize in a non-question-begging way what, regarding context, serves to specify relevant implicatures. In short, there is all the appearance of rigor and precision in Grice's account, but it is utterly incapable of providing the advantage promised. The only way of telling which implicatures are relevant is to understand the significance of a given text: the alleged implicatures are really internal to any reasonably coherent grasp of a literary work; there *are* no reliable criteria regarding context or utterance, accessible independently, that could serve in a determinate way to facilitate our reading of a particular text. It is entirely fair to say that Grice's maxims of implicature are vacuous and trivial ("Be relevant." "Make your contribution as informative as is required" [for the current purposes of the exchange]. "Do not make your contribution more informative than is required"). On the other hand, in applying his apparatus, Pratt inadvertently provides a *reductio* of the entire undertaking; for she herself quite plausibly concedes that there may be a variety of speech-act moves in literature that are intended to violate the very type of "cooperation" that Grice supposes always applies "in context" and that actually informs his own sanguine view about implicatures and their detection. This means, of course, that one cannot tell what is implicated without understanding what is intended in any literary work; and understanding what is relevantly intended (which Grice cannot help us with) trivially entails whatever the theory of implicatures was originally supposed to make methodologically accessible. The appreciation of this sort of difficulty is characteristic of recent structuralist and poststructuralist accounts of narrative, which have come to influence analytic aesthetics considerably—for instance, in Barthes (1974), Genette (1980), and Derrida (1974).

There have also appeared, in recent aesthetics, two quite strenuously debated but rather special issues. One concerns the so-called Intentional Fallacy; the other, the question of the definition of art. The first was prompted by the appearance of William Wimsatt and Monroe Beardsley's well-known paper (1954b); the second, by the appearance of Morris Weitz's discussion of the problem of definition (1956). Regarding the first, Wimsatt and Beardsley held that the artist's intentions were neither available nor aesthetically relevant (nor desirable) in the critical appreciation of literature (or the other arts). Their discussion is spoiled somewhat by an altogether too mentalistic view of intentions. They are criticized in this regard by Theodore Redpath (1957): Redpath suggests quite reasonably that an artist's intention may sometimes be discovered without going outside the work itself, which if admitted would be a *reductio* of Beardsley's view. The aesthetic relevance of an artist's intentions has been defended, on independent grounds, by, among others, Hungerland (1955) and Eliseo Vivas (1955). Furthermore, a careful reading of the original article will show that the artist's intentions are actually not taken to be necessarily unavailable or even irrelevant; what the authors insist on is that the artist's intention cannot be a privileged criterion by which to decide what a work means. The controversy is additionally complicated by the fact that Beardsley has since construed the problem as one of being actually able to fix the artist's intention and of determining the extent to which a work produced falls short of such intention. But this very nearly undermines the original thesis. At the present time, the question of the aesthetic relevance of the artist's intention is seen to be inseparable from (a) the fate of empiricist aesthetics; (b) the ontology of artworks; and (c) the evolving tradition of hermeneutics and hermeneutically influenced theories of interpretation and response. The rejection of empiricist aesthetics provides for the relevance of historical, biographical, causal, and other factors that cannot be sensorily restricted; the elaboration of the ontology of artworks obliges us to consider the distinction of art and other cultural phenomena as opposed to purely physical objects;

and the hermeneutic tradition confirms the sense in which the intentional nature of artworks entails the relevance of the creative — the historical and psychological — conditions under which particular works are interpreted to be the works they are. The most sustained account of the hermeneutic sort is undoubtedly Hans-Georg Gadamer's *Truth and Method* (1975). But while it affords a strong sense in which the "fusion of horizons" (the sense in which, as readers of literature, say, we share with earlier poets and novelists an evolving historical existence that enables our interpretive responses to be relevant to the appreciation of their texts), Gadamer has noticeable difficulty in repudiating or tempering the extreme possibilities of relativism — which he distinctly opposes — at the same time, as a consequence of his view, he also opposes the adequacy of a trans- or ahistorical method of valid criticism and cultural truth.

Weitz's discussion depends on his attempted application of Wittgenstein's well-known account of "family resemblances" to the concept of art. He argues that it is in principle not possible to define any "empirical" concept in terms of necessary and sufficient conditions. But he also holds (1977) that definitions are essentialist in nature. There are considerable difficulties with his view, which has undergone a number of revisions. For one thing, Wittgenstein in the passage in question does not preclude definition, but only shows that concepts resting on "family resemblances" are readily usable. For another, Weitz finds (in the original paper) that Aristotle's definition is false, although not inappropriately formulated. And finally and most important, Weitz does not satisfactorily distinguish between the logical job of defining a concept and that of extending its use: he appears to foreclose on the possibility of the first by appealing to the implications of the second. His recent revisions do reinforce the important Wittgensteinian thesis that concepts that are not fixed in an essentialist way or in terms of necessary and sufficient conditions are indeed serviceable. But he actually offers no theory of definition or of why definition must be essentialist in nature (cf. Mandelbaum, 1965), and he does not explain how he recognizes bona fide and inadmissible specimens of given concepts (he complains, for instance, against "the insanity of modern art," that is, the insanity of treating modern art as art). More to the point, he fails to consider that it is quite possible both to admit definitions in terms of necessary and sufficient conditions and to deny essentialism (*and* to accommodate the open-textured function of the term "art") — a general position regarding meaning most fully developed by Hilary Putnam (1975).

A number of once-prominent quarrels have now receded somewhat in importance. For one, there is the matter of Susanne Langer's theory of symbolic forms. First formulated in *Philosophy in a New Key* (1942), it was decisively criticized by Ernest Nagel (1943), who showed quite clearly how difficult it was to construe the nonverbal structures of music and the other arts in terms analogous to the syntactic and semantic dimensions of language — "symbolic forms." Langer had expanded her theory without satisfactorily meeting Nagel's objection; and in her later collection of essays (1962) she has more or less abandoned the designation "symbolic" for the distinction she had in mind. The formal properties of symbol systems have been explored most fully by Nelson Goodman (1969), although his account imposes strictures (in terms of what he calls "notationality") that are not, and probably cannot be, exhibited by any natural language or cultural code. For that reason, his well-known distinction between autographic and allographic arts (the distinction regarding arts, like painting, that are individuated in terms of the history of production, and arts, like music, that are individuated in terms of compliance with a notation) founders. For one thing, no natural notation — linguistic, musical, choreographic — fixes or can fix strict compliance in the way Goodman requires. Pitch and tempo, for instance, are inseparable in music; yet Goodman admits that tempo cannot be allographically fixed. Second, no such compliance is actually necessary since, in any case, numerical identity can always be determined relative to conditions of production. And third, no arts, contrary to Goodman's claim, lack autographically pertinent features: intentional considerations are always relevant, and strict allographic requirements are impossible to satisfy. Again, reference to the symbolic, the representational, the intentional, the expressive, the semiotic essentially threatens the empiricist orientation and has been so construed in recent theories (for instance, in Goodman, Danto [1981], Margolis [1980], and Schapiro [1973]). But it also recovers the importance of the problem of interpretation (where the symbolic plays an entirely different role) and the possibility of defending a form of relativism. The concept of representation itself has become the focus of a variety of puzzles, largely centered on the distinction (provided by Goodman) between monadic and dyadic representation (that is, where what is represented does not or does exist independently) and on comparison and resemblance, particularly where portraiture and naturalistic scenes are involved (cf. Hermerén, 1969; Novitz, 1975; and Walton, 1970, 1971).

Interest has also centered on the nature of aesthetic experience (Beardsley, 1958; Sparshott, 1963; Vivas, 1955; Stolnitz, 1960). Earlier accounts had tended to draw attention to distinctive discriminations made possible by aesthetic orientation itself. L. A. Reid (1935), for instance, had argued that the expressive qualities of a work of art are simply projections of the response of an aesthetic percipient. Similar though not entirely unequivocal views have been put forward by Pepper (1938), who was inclined to hold that there are properties of a work of art not discriminable unless one takes an aesthetic attitude to it. Ducasse (1929) also held that there are distinctive qualities that can only be "ecpathized," that is, discriminated if one adopts the aesthetic attitude; but, revealingly, he excludes meanings from aesthetic discrimination. All such doctrines are somewhat akin to the views of such theorists as Edward Bullough (1912-1913) and the empathists (Langfeld [1920] and Lee [1913]): Bullough's thesis has been recently revived, but the original difficulties of his doctrine have not been resolved—in particular, that the negative and positive scales of "distancing" have nothing in common, which upsets the "antinomy of distance," and that the doctrine is merely designed to favor certain special aesthetic values (as with the empathists). Tomas (1959) has claimed that aesthetic discrimination attends only to "appearances"—in order to assign a distinctive object to the aesthetic concern. In this, he has been criticized by Sibley (1959), who points to the resultant anomalies. Beardsley (1958) has committed himself to a view similar to Tomas's. Possibly the most ambitious effort to distinguish aesthetic perception from the sort that obtains in science is offered by Virgil Aldrich (1963), who contrasts "basic imagination" with "observation," which he takes to be fundamentally different aspects of perception. It is difficult to see, however, why aesthetically relevant discriminations require a distinct "mode" of perception. Aldrich's illustrations (1958) do not seem to force us to that conclusion. Margolis (1960) has argued that there is no distinctive perceptual "mode" corresponding to aesthetic interest, although perception, imagination, memory, association, and the like play a number of distinct roles in the appreciation of a work of art. A similar view is advanced by George Dickie (1964), specifically against Beardsley. The concept of the "perception" or "experience" of a work of art is misleadingly unified, and a whole host of special problems arises regarding all the conceivable "ingredients" of such perception. For instance, special questions arise even for visual perception, as in representational art—which had been discussed briefly by Isenberg (1944), Ziff (1951), and Stevenson (1958).

The matter of visual perception and representation has, quite recently, become extremely important, centering primarily on the sense in which resemblance must be construed in terms of interpretive conventions or natural similarities. Goodman has favored an extreme conventionalist view; and Ernst Gombrich (1960) has attempted to combine elements of natural similarity with convention (as in his account of Constable's art). Certainly, the conventional cannot be ignored, which goes entirely against the "ecological optics" of J. J. Gibson (1966, 1978). But also, contra Goodman—and quite independent of the issue of *trompe l'oeil*—perceived similarities (as between Wellington and a portrait of Wellington) cannot be entirely accounted for in terms of representational codes. The relevant literature is now considerable (cf. Maynard, 1972; Wartofsky, 1972). Again, the question of the appropriate sense in which one may be said to "perceive" literature had already been broached by David Prall (1936) and Sidney Zink (1945). Clearly, the empiricist orientation (cf. Bell, 1914) cannot but be profoundly strained by the admission of literature. And in general, the search for distinctive values, perceptions, experiences in the aesthetic setting – instructively, for instance, in such different writers as Dewey (1934) and Vivas (1955) – may, not unreasonably, be regarded as vestigial remains of the original Kantian division between the aesthetic and the moral.

Currently, philosophical aesthetics appears to be focused increasingly on the ontology of artworks and the recovery of the irreducibly cultural nature of art. A number of discussants have employed the type/token distinction in various ways, which was perhaps first used in aesthetics by Richard Rudner (1958) and C. L. Stevenson (1957). Richard Wollheim (1968), for example, treats the plastic arts in a radically different way from music and literature, identifying paintings and sculptures as physical objects and literary and musical works (chiefly) as abstract type-entities. But, for one thing, he fails to explain how the characteristically intentional properties of the first can be directly ascribed in the plastic arts (without falling back to mere associations or imputations on our part). And, for another, he seriously confuses the type/token idiom, insisting that types and tokens can and must share relevant properties: how, for instance, could a musical performance and "the" music (the allegedly abstract type) share properties of tempo and pitch? Wolterstorff (1975) modifies the account ingeniously by holding that types and tokens share predicates, not properties. But his proposal faces corresponding difficulties. For one thing, the thesis entails a form of essentialism not independently defended: the shared predicates designate properties that all "properly formed" tokens must exhibit (which is certainly contestable: think, for instance, of omitting scenes from dramatic performances, changing dance steps in established ballets, performing musical compositions with a variety of instruments, and the like). Either anomalously, artworks like music utterly lack perceptual properties (being abstract entities or universals) or they "possess" them in the Pickwickian sense that their (token) performances possess them (tokens and types being different entities and entities of entirely different kinds). Again, one may well ask how, in terms of the tradition of universals, types (construed as universals) can be said to be created and destroyed (rather than, say, "discovered"). Third, the "shared predicate" thesis is both otiose and parasitic on whatever we may say about treating particular tokens as, say tokens of the same sonata or play.

Margolis (1980) has defended the view that types and tokens are heuristic or heuristically introduced particulars (that types are not universals but abstract particulars) and that particular artworks may, for all the arts (but in accord with different criteria), be treated indissolubly as tokens-of-types. Hence, for purposes of individuating an artist's production, we may count abstract particulars (types) like sonatas, plays, and dances. (Obviously, we must be able to refer to what does not exist – which links the ontology of art to the puzzle of fictional reference.) But artworks (sonatas, plays) exist only as tokens-of-types, even if (for contingent reasons) certain paintings, sculptures, buildings are unique particulars. Furthermore, on Margolis's view, artworks are culturally emergent and physically embodied, that is, entities (rather like Strawson's persons [1959], though for reasons different from Strawson's) to which both physical and psychological or intentional or cultural properties may be ascribed. In fact, all and only cultural entities are tokens-of-types and embodied. The notion of embodiment is intended to avoid Cartesian dualism while, at the same time, admitting the irreducibility of intentional ascriptions *and* the irreducibility of embodied entities that (like persons) cannot exist independently of some appropriate embodiment. In short, both the type/token and the embodiment relationship are construed as relations between particulars: the first, a heterodox form of instantiation of one particular by another, assigned to heuristically introduced entities (for purposes of individuation); the second, based on a novel interpretation of "is" distinct from identity and composition, actually exhibited by emergent phenomena (persons, words and sentences, artworks) that exist only in the intensionally specified space of human culture, emergently linked to physical particulars.

In an early paper, Danto (1964) had introduced the "'is' of artistic identification," which he explicitly contrasted with the "is" of identity and used to mark the ontological complexity of the cultural or institutional nature of artworks. The notion has remained undeveloped (cf. Danto, 1981), although Danto clearly intended it in a sense entirely different from Dickie's curious thesis (1974), that artifacts have the very status of art conferred upon them institutionally by some determinate and appropriate act. Danto's thesis is ingenious and ontologically important, in that he demonstrates the impossibility of detecting the difference between artworks and other artifacts that are not artworks solely on perceptual grounds — for instance, the difference (apart from size) between Erle Loran's diagram of one of Cézanne's paintings of his wife and Roy Lichtenstein's *Portrait of Madame Cézanne*. All those who have turned recently to the ontology of art — Wollheim, Wolterstorff, Goodman, Danto, Margolis — have, one way or another, disclosed the inadequacies of the empiricist orientation. On the whole, however, these explorations have made only minimal contact with Continental movements — in particular, with phenomenology, structuralism, hermeneutics, Marxism, and semiotics. But the convergent themes of both these currents distinctly favor an emphasis on historicity, both the intentional and intensional complexities of cultural phenomena, and a tolerance for relativizing the critical and appreciative grasp of individual works of art. Also, liberating the philosophy of art from the peculiar restrictions of empiricism enables the theory of criticism and appreciation to range well beyond traditionally aesthetic constraints, so that moral, political, religious, and other culturally relevant aspects of art may be deemed pertinent in principle to its production and appreciation.

Bibliography

Aiken, Henry. 1945. "Art as Expression and Surface." *Journal of Aesthetics and Art Criticism* 4.

Aldrich, Virgil C. 1958. "Picture Space." *Philosophical Review* 67.

_____ . 1963. *Philosophy of Art*. Englewood Cliffs, N.J.: Prentice-Hall.

Baier, Kurt. 1958. *The Moral Point of View*. Ithaca, N.Y.: Cornell University Press.

Barthes, Roland. 1974. *S/Z*, trans. by Richard Miller. New York: Farrar, Strauss and Giroux.

Beardsley, Monroe C. 1958. *Aesthetics*. New York: Harcourt, Brace.

_____ . 1962. "The Metaphorical Twist." *Philosophy and Phenomenological Research* 22.

_____ . 1970. *The Possibility of Criticism*. Detroit: Wayne State University Press.

Bell, Clive. 1914. *Art*. London: Chatto and Windus.

Black, Max, ed. 1950. *Philosophical Analysis*. Ithaca, N.Y.: Cornell University Press.

_____ . 1954–1955. "Metaphor." *Proceedings of the Aristotelian Society* 55.

Braithwaite, R. B. 1933. "Imaginary Objects." *Proceedings of the Aristotelian Society* 12.

Brooks-Rose, Christine. 1958. *A Grammar of Metaphor*. London: Secker and Warburg.

Bullough, Edward. 1912-1913. "Psychical Distance as a Factor in Art and an Aesthetic Principle." *British Journal of Psychology* 5.

Cioffi, Frank. 1963-1964. "Intention and Interpretation in Criticism." *Proceedings of the Aristotelian Society* 64.

Cohen, Ted. 1973. "Aesthetic/Non-aesthetic and the Concept of Taste: A Critique of Sibley's Position." *Theoria* 29.

_____ . 1975. "Figurative Speech and Figurative Acts." *Journal of Philosophy* 71.

Collingwood, R. G. 1938. *The Principles of Art*. London: Oxford University Press.

Croce, Benedetto. 1922. *Aesthetics*. 2nd ed. Translated by Douglas Ainslee. London: Macmillan & Co.

Danto, Arthur C. 1964. "The Artworld." *Journal of Philosophy* 61.

————. 1981. *The Transfiguration of the Commonplace.* Cambridge: Harvard University Press.

Davidson, Donald. 1967. "Truth and Meaning." *Synthese* 17.

————. 1978. "What Metaphors Mean." *Critical Inquiry* 5.

Derrida, Jacques. 1974. *Of Grammatology.* Translated by Gayatri Chakravorty Spivak. Baltimore: Johns Hopkins University Press.

Dewey, John. 1934. *Art as Experience.* New York: Minton, Balch.

Dickie, George. 1964. "The Myth of the Aesthetic Attitude." *American Philosophical Quarterly* 1.

————. 1974. *Art and the Aesthetic.* Ithaca, N.Y.: Cornell University Press.

Dickie, George, and Richard J. Sclafani, eds. 1977. *Aesthetics.* New York: St. Martin's Press.

Ducasse, C. J. 1929. *The Philosophy of Art.* New York: Dial Press.

Eagleton, Terry. 1976. *Criticism and Ideology.* London: NLB.

Elton, William, ed. 1954. *Aesthetics and Language.* Oxford: Basil Blackwell.

Erlich, Victor. 1981. *Russian Formalism.* 3rd ed. New Haven, Conn.: Yale University Press.

Foot, Philippa. 1958–1959. "Moral Beliefs." *Proceedings of the Aristotelian Society* 59.

Gadamer, Hans-Georg. 1975. *Truth and Method.* Translated from 2nd ed. Edited by Garrett Barden and John Cumming. New York: Seabury Press.

Genette, Girard. 1980. *Narrative Discourse.* Translated by Jane E. Lewin. Ithaca, N.Y.: Cornell University Press.

Gibson, J. J. 1966. *The Senses Considered as Perceptual Systems.* Boston: Houghton Mifflin.

————. 1978. "The Ecological Approach to the Visual Perception of Pictures." *Leonardo* 12.

Goldmann, Lucien. 1980. *Essays on Method in the Sociology of Literature.* Translated by William Q. Boelhower. St. Louis: Telos Press.

Gombrich, E. H. 1960. *Art and Illusion.* New York: Pantheon.

Goodman, Nelson. 1969. *Languages of Art.* Indianapolis, Ind.: Bobbs Merrill.

Greene, T. M. 1940. *The Arts and the Art of Criticism.* Princeton, N.J.: Princeton University Press.

Grice, H. P. 1975. "Logic and Conversation." In Peter Cole and Jerry L. Morgan, eds., *Syntax and Semantics.* Vol. 3. New York: Academic Press.

————. 1978. "Further Notes on Logic and Conversation." In Peter Cole, ed., *Syntax and Semantics.* Vol. 9. New York: Academic Press.

Hampshire, Stuart. 1954. "Logic and Appreciation." In William Elton, ed., *Aesthetics and Language.* Oxford: Basil Blackwell.

Hanscher, Michael. 1977. "Beyond a Speech-Act Theory of Literary Discourse. *Modern Language Notes* 92.

Hare, R. M. 1952. *The Language of Morals.* Oxford: Clarendon Press.

Hart, H.L.A. 1948–1949. "The Ascription of Responsibility and Rights." *Proceedings of the Aristotelian Society* 49.

Henle, Paul. 1958. "Metaphor." In Paul Henle, ed., *Language, Thought and Culture.* Ann Arbor: University of Michigan Press.

Hermerén, Göran. 1969. *Representation and Meaning in the Visual Arts.* Lund: Scandinavian University Books.

Hesse, Mary B. 1963. "The Explanatory Function of Metaphor." *Models and Analogies in Science.* London: Sheed and Ward.

Hirsch, E. D., Jr. 1967. *Validity in Interpretation.* New Haven: Yale University Press.

Hook, Sidney, ed. 1966. *Art and Philosophy.* New York: New York University Press.

Hospers, John. 1960. "Implied Truths in Literature." *Journal of Aesthetics and Art Criticism* 19.

Hungerland, Isabel C. 1955. "The Concept of Intention in Art Criticism." *Journal of Philosophy* 52.

————. 1960. "Contextual Implication." *Inquiry* 4.

————. 1963. "The Logic of Aesthetic Concepts." *Proceedings of the American Philosophical Association* 36.

Ingarden, Roman. 1973a. *The Literary Work of Art.* Translated by George G. Grabowicz. Evanston, Ill.: Northwestern University Press.

————. 1973b. *The Cognition of the Literary Work of Art.* Translated by Ruth Crowley and Kenneth R. Olson. Evanston, Ill.: Northwestern University Press.

Isenberg, Arnold. 1944. "Perception, Meaning, and the Subject-matter of Art." *Journal of Philosophy* 41.

————. 1949. "Critical Communication." *Philosophical Review* 58.

Iser, Wolfgang. 1978. *The Act of Reading.* Baltimore: Johns Hopkins University Press.

Juhl, P. D. 1980. *Interpretation.* Princeton: Princeton University Press.

Katz, Jerrold J. 1972. *Semantic Theory*. New York: Harper & Row.

Kennick, William E. 1958. "Does Traditional Aesthetics Rest on a Mistake?" *Mind* 57.

_____ , ed. 1979. *Art and Philosophy*. 2nd ed. New York: St. Martin's Press.

Kivy, Peter. 1973. *Speaking of Art*. The Hague: Martinus Nijhoff.

Knight, Helen. 1936. "The Use of 'Good' in Aesthetic Judgments." *Proceedings of the Aristotelian Society* 36.

Langer, Susanne K. 1942. *Philosophy in a New Key*. Cambridge: Harvard University Press.

_____ . 1962. *Philosophical Sketches*. Baltimore: Johns Hopkins University Press.

Langfeld, H. S. 1920. *The Aesthetic Attitude*. New York: Harcourt, Brace.

Lee, Vernon. 1913. *The Beautiful*. Cambridge: Cambridge University Press.

Levin, Samuel R. 1977. *The Semantics of Metaphor*. Baltimore: Johns Hopkins University Press.

Lyas, Colin. 1973. "Personal Qualities and the Intentional Fallacy." In *Philosophy and the Arts*. Royal Institute Lectures in Philosophy, vol. 6, 1971–1972. New York: St. Martin's Press.

Macdonald, Margaret. 1952–1953. "Art and Imagination." *Proceedings of the Aristotelian Society* 53.

_____ . 1954a. "Some Distinctive Features of Arguments Used in Criticism in the Arts." In William Elton, ed., *Aesthetics and Language*. Oxford: Basil Blackwell.

_____ . 1954b. "The Language of Fiction." *Proceedings of the Aristotelian Society* 27.

Mandelbaum, Maurice. 1965. "Family Resemblances and Generalization Concerning the Arts." *American Philosophical Quarterly* 2.

Margolis, Joseph. 1960. "Aesthetic Perception." *Journal of Aesthetics and Art Criticism* 19.

_____ , ed. 1962. *Philosophy Looks at the Arts*. New York: Charles Scribner's Sons.

_____ . 1966. "Three Problems in Aesthetics." In Sidney Hood, ed., *Art and Philosophy*. New York: New York University Press.

_____ . 1977. "The Axiom of Existence: Reductio ad Absurdum." *Southern Journal of Philosophy* 15.

_____ , ed. 1978. *Philosophy Looks at the Arts*. 2nd ed. Philadelphia: Temple University Press.

_____ . 1980. *Art and Philosophy*. Atlantic Highlands, N.J.: Humanities Press.

Matthews, Robert J. 1977. "Describing and Interpreting Works of Art." *Journal of Aesthetics and Art Criticism* 36.

Maynard, Patrick. 1972. "Depiction, Vision, and Convention." *American Philosophical Quarterly* 9.

Moore, G. E. 1933. "Imaginary Objects." *Proceedings of the Aristotelian Society* 12.

Nowell-Smith, P. H. 1954. *Ethics*. Harmondsworth: Penguin Books.

Novitz, David. 1975. "Black Horse Pictures: Exposing the Picturing Relation." *Journal of Aesthetics and Art Criticism* 34.

Ohmann, Richard. 1971. "Speech Acts and the Definition of Literature." *Philosophy and Rhetoric* 4.

Passmore, J. A. 1951. "The Dreariness of Aesthetics." *Mind* 60.

Pepper, Stephen. 1938. *Aesthetic Quality*. New York: Charles Scribner's Sons.

_____ . 1955. *The Work of Art*. Bloomington: Indiana University Press.

Prall, David. 1936. *Aesthetic Analysis*. New York: Thomas Y. Crowell.

Pratt, Mary Louise. 1977. *Toward a Speech Act Theory of Literary Discourse*. Bloomington: Indiana University Press.

Putnam, Hilary. 1975. *Philosophical Papers*. Vol. 2. Cambridge: Cambridge University Press.

Redpath, Theodore. 1957. "Some Problems of Modern Aesthetics." In C. A. Mace, ed., *British Philosophy in the Mid-Century*. London: George Allen and Unwin.

Reid, L. A. 1931. *A Study in Aesthetics*. London: George Allen and Unwin.

Richards, I. A. 1935. *Science and Poetry*. Rev. ed. London: K. Paul, Trench, Trubner.

_____ . 1936. *The Philosophy of Rhetoric*. London: Oxford University Press.

Rudner, Richard. 1958. "The Ontological Status of the Esthetic Object." *Philosophy and Phenomenological Research* 10.

Ryle, Gilbert. 1933. "Imaginary Objects." *Proceedings of the Aristotelian Society* 12:

Schapiro, Meyer. 1973. *Words and Pictures*. The Hague: Martinus Nijhoff.

Scriven, Michael. 1954. "The Language of Fiction." *Proceedings of the Aristotelian Society* 27.

Scruton, Roger. 1974. *Art and Imagination*. London: Hutchinson.

Searle, John. 1969. *Speech Acts*. Cambridge: Cambridge University Press.

_____ . 1974. "The Logical Status of Fictional Discourse." *New Literary History* 6.

Sibley, Frank (F.N.). 1959. "Aesthetics and the Looks of Things." *Journal of Philosophy* 56.

_____ . (F.N.). 1963. "Aesthetic Concepts." *Philosophical Review* 68.

Sircello, Guy. 1972. *Mind & Art.* Princeton: Princeton University Press.

Sparshott, F. E. 1964. *The Structure of Aesthetics.* Toronto: University of Toronto Press.

Stern, Gustaf. 1931. "Meaning and Change of Meaning." In *Götesborgs Högskolas Årsskrift,* Vol. 38: 1. Göteborg: Weltergren and Kerbers Förlag.

Stevenson, C. L. 1944. *Ethics and Language.* New Haven: Yale University Press.

————. 1950. "Interpretation and Evaluation in Aesthetics." In Max Black, ed., *Philosophical Analysis.* Ithaca, N.Y.: Cornell University Press.

————. 1957. "On 'What is a Poem?'" *Philosophical Review* 66.

————. 1958. "Symbolism in the Non-representative Arts." In Paul Henle, ed., *Language, Thought, and Culture.* Ann Arbor: University of Michigan Press.

————. 1962. "On the Reasons That Can Be Given for the Interpretation of a Poem." In Joseph Margolis, ed., *Philosophy Looks at the Arts.* New York: Charles Scribner's Sons.

Stolnitz, Jerome. 1960. *Aesthetics and Philosophy of Art Criticism.* Boston: Houghton Mifflin.

Strawson, P. F. 1959. *Individuals.* London: Methuen.

Tomas, Vincent. 1959. "Aesthetic Vision." *Philosophical Review* 68.

Tormey, Alan. 1971. *The Concept of Expression.* Princeton: Princeton University Press.

————. 1973. "Critical Judgments." *Theoria* 39.

Travaux du Cercle Linguistique de Prague. 1929. I.

Urmson, J. O. 1957–1958. "What Makes a Situation Aesthetic?" *Proceedings of the Aristotelian Society* 31.

Vivas, Eliseo. 1955. *Creation and Discovery.* New York: Noonday Press.

Walton, Kendall L. 1970. "Categories of Art." *Philosophical Review* 79.

————. 1971. "Pictures and Make-Believe." *Philosophical Review* 80.

Wartofsky, Marx. 1972. "Pictures, Representation, and the Understanding." In Richard Rudner and Israel Scheffler, eds., *Logic and Art.* Indianapolis, Ind.: Bobbs-Merrill.

Weitz, Morris. 1950. *Philosophy of the Arts.* Cambridge: Harvard University Press.

————. 1956. "The Role of Theory in Aesthetics." *Journal of Aesthetics and Art Criticism* 15.

————. 1977. *The Opening Mind.* Chicago: University of Chicago Press.

Wimsatt, William K., Jr., (and Monroe C. Beardsley). 1954a. "The Affective Fallacy." In W. K. Wimsatt, Jr., *The Verbal Icon.* Lexington: University of Kentucky Press.

————. 1954b. "The Intentional Fallacy." In W. K. Wimsatt, Jr., *The Verbal Icon.* Lexington: University of Kentucky Press.

Wollheim, Richard. 1968. *Art and Its Objects.* New York: Harper and Row.

Wolterstorff, Nicholas. 1975. "Worlds of Works of Art." *Journal of Aesthetics and Art Criticism* 35.

————. 1980. *Works and Worlds of Art.* Oxford: Clarendon Press.

Ziff, Paul. 1951. "Art and the 'Object of Art.'" *Mind* 60.

Zink, Sidney. 1945. "The Poetic Organism." *Journal of Philosophy* 42.

Index